Routledge Revivals

The Growing Economy

First published in 1968, this is the second part of Professor Meade's *Principles of Political Economy*, which presents a systematic treatment of the whole field of economic analysis in the form of a series of simplified models which are specifically designed to show the interconnections between the various specialist fields of economic theory.

In this volume, Professor Meade is concerned with the theory of economic growth and the rates at which various economic quantities are growing. In order to do this, he introduces capital goods into the system and allows for growth through capital accumulation, population expansion and technical progress. His analysis is divided into two models: a one product model and a many-product model.

T0271687

The Growing Economy

Principles of Political Economy Volume II

J. E. Meade

Routledge
Taylor & Francis Group

First published in 1968
by George Allen & Unwin Ltd

This edition first published in 2012 by Routledge
2 Park Square, Milton Park, Abingdon, Oxon, OX14 4RN

Simultaneously published in the USA and Canada
by Routledge
711 Third Avenue, New York, NY 10017

Routledge is an imprint of the Taylor & Francis Group, an informa business

© 1968 George Allen & Unwin Ltd

Publisher's Note
The publisher has gone to great lengths to ensure the quality of this reprint but
points out that some imperfections in the original copies may be apparent.

Disclaimer
The publisher has made every effort to trace copyright holders and welcomes
correspondence from those they have been unable to contact.

A Library of Congress record exists under ISBN: 76219458

ISBN 13: 978-0-415-52648-7 (hbk)
ISBN 13: 978-0-203-10659-4 (ebk)
ISBN 13: 978-0-415-62175-5 (pbk)

THE GROWING ECONOMY

BY

J. E. MEADE

C.B., F.B.A.

Being Volume Two of A

PRINCIPLES OF POLITICAL ECONOMY

London

GEORGE ALLEN & UNWIN LTD

RUSKIN HOUSE · MUSEUM STREET

FIRST PUBLISHED IN 1968

PRINTED IN GREAT BRITAIN
in 10 *on* 11 *point Times type*
UNWIN BROTHERS LIMITED
WOKING AND LONDON

PREFACE

This volume is a sequel to *The Stationary Economy*, which was much criticized by the reviewers for the narrowness of its scope and the clumsiness of its expression but which—I am glad to say—seems to have been found useful by students and decorative by librarians. The present volume relies heavily on, and makes frequent references to, the analysis in the earlier volume, which should be regarded simply as a book of exercises in some of the basic tools of economic theory which are necessary for the subsequent analysis of more realistic models.

But while the subject matter of the present volume is more realistic than that of the earlier volume in that it introduces capital goods into the system and allows for growth through capital accumulation, population expansion, and technical progress, nevertheless it still remains very unrealistic.

(1) In the first place it deals almost exclusively with equilibrium growth. In passing from the harmonious quiet of the abstract model to the untidy bustle of the real world one moves from (*a*) positions of static equilibrium such as those discussed in *The Stationary Economy*, through (*b*) states of steady growth in which the initial proportions and relationships in the economy are such that all the relevant variables can grow at the same constant growth rate, through (*c*) states of equilibrium growth in which the variables cannot all grow at the same constant rate, but in which all citizens correctly guess what the future holds in store for them so that no citizen ever regrets any decision which he has taken, to (*d*) states of growth through time in which expectations are often disappointed and are revised in the light of events, so that the economic system may lurch along in a disequilibrated and often fluctuating manner through time. The analysis in the present volume stops well short of any proper discussion of (*d*).

(2) The present volume still assumes conditions in which perfect competition is possible. In particular it assumes (i) the absence of indivisibilities so that there are constant returns to scale in the productive system and (ii) a given set of consistent and independent preferences for each consumer. As a result the volume avoids all problems of monopoly and imperfect competition.

(3) The present volume still assumes that there are no external economies or diseconomies, that there are no goods which cannot be consumed individually but must be bought and used socially, and that there are no choices between goods which cannot be determined by a market mechanism as opposed to a political decision. For this reason the functions of government discussed in the present volume are very restricted.

(4) The present volume is still restricted in its scope to a closed economy. There is no discussion of the international repercussions between a number of separate economies each with its own national government in control.

(5) Just because *The Stationary Economy* and *The Growing Economy* even in combination are thus so restricted in their scope, they can contain no rounded assessment of that balance between free market transactions and governmental interventions and between private and public ownership of property which may be most appropriate—when all relevant reactions are taken into account—for the attainment of the social and economic objectives of society.

When I first embarked on the present ambitious project I had no conception of the scale of the task of an up-to-date 'specialist in generalization' in economic analysis and policy. Whether I shall ever complete the task becomes increasingly problematical. The first two volumes in this series have taken some eight years to write. I am now a reasonably healthy sixty-year-old; and I leave it to the reader in consultation with an actuary to calculate, if he so wishes, the probability of these further five subjects being adequately covered.[1]

There is now an immense literature on the theory of economic growth and it is impossible for me to acknowledge the sources of all the ideas contained in the present volume. Like all who work in this field I owe a very great debt to the admirable survey of the subject made by Professors R. C. O. Matthews and F. H. Hahn. Sir John Hicks' *Capital and Growth* appeared after the main structure of the present work was completed; but I am relieved to find that his work is complementary to, rather than competitive with, mine. I have been immensely stimulated by my colleagues in Cambridge who have made such notable contributions to the subject—Professor Joan Robinson, Professor Kaldor, Professor Lord Kahn, Mr D. G. Champernowne,

---

[1] If each of these five subjects were covered by a separate volume, I would entitle them:—
1. The Fluctuating Economy.
2. The   ?   Economy.
3. The Public Economy.
   or
   The Social Economy.
4. The International Economy.
5. The Mixed Economy.

I am offering a prize of $1 (subject to exchange-control regulations) for suitable titles for 2 and 3 above. For 3 Professor Harry Johnson has competed with 'The Public Economy' and Professor Robert Mundell with 'The Social Economy'. I am inclined to reject the entries of 'The Lumpy Economy' and of 'The Imperfect Economy' for 2, though I search for an adjective which puts the stress on indivisibilities in the economy which makes imperfections of competition inevitable.

Dr Pasinetti. At an early stage of this work Professor R. M. Solow read what I had written and purged it of much nonsense. Chapter XVII of this volume owes much to the work of Mr P. Sraffa. Chapter VIII describes the 'golden rule' associated with the work of Professor E. S. Phelps. In Chapter XXI I have made extensive use of Professor W. J. Fellner's *Probability and Profit* and the footnote at the end of my chapter is directly plagiarized from his book. Professor K. J. Arrow's 'learning by doing' suggested to me many of the distinctions drawn in Chapter IX. For Chapters XII and XIII I am particularly indebted to Mr M. J. Farrell for a paper on life-cycle savings and to Dr J. A. Mirrlees who has made such notable contributions to this part of the subject and who gave me much help on the analysis—and in particular on the mathematics—in the Note to Chapter XIII and the Note to Chapter XXIII.

The Note to Chapter XIII is a slightly revised version of an article by myself published in *The Review of Economic Studies*, Vol. XXXII, No. 1 and reproduced here with the kind permission of the editors of the Review.

Finally, I would like to express my special thanks to my colleague Dr C. J. Bliss who read the whole of my typescript in its last stages and made a number of most important comments which have led me to recast some of the basic analysis in the book. He has certainly removed many muddles in my argument. He must not, however, be held responsible for the blemishes which I have chosen to retain or for the new blemishes which I have inadvertently introduced in my attempts to meet his criticisms.

J. E. MEADE

Christ's College
Cambridge
May 1967

CONTENTS

PART 2. THE MANY-PRODUCT MODEL

In this volume an attempt is made to discuss the theory of economic growth with a minimum of mathematical analysis. In the main text no differential or integral calculus is employed; such mathematical techniques are used (and even so very sparingly) only in footnotes and appendices which the general reader may avoid. Nevertheless there remain certain measurements and manipulations of rates of growth which must be employed in the main text. These processes could be most readily and easily expressed in terms of the differential calculus; but it is the purpose of this introductory note to explain them without any explicit use of the differential calculus, so that the non-mathematical reader will be in a position to read the text of this work without undue difficulty.

In this volume we shall be concerned with the rates at which various economic quantities are growing. In order to measure such rates of growth we shall take a 'day' as our basic atom of time; and purely for simplicity of our arithmetical examples we shall assume that there are 100 days in a year. Consider some quantity such as L, the total working population. Suppose, for example, that L were 1,000,000 men at the beginning of day 1 and 1,000,200 at the beginning of day 2. We will write ΔL as representing the absolute increase in L from one day to the next day, so that in our example ΔL in the course of day 1 is 200 men.

ΔL is simply the increase in the number of men between one day and the next; but it is, of course, also numerically equal to the absolute rate of increase of L on day 1, measured in terms of men per day. Thus in our example, since $\Delta L = 200$, it follows that the working population is rising between day 1 and day 2 at a rate of 200 men per day. Purely for convenience we shall often in our numerical examples speak of such rates in terms not of men per day, but of men per year. Thus if L is rising at a rate of 200 men per day, we shall often express this by saying that L is rising at a *daily* rate of 20,000 men per 100 days, i.e., at a *daily* rate of 20,000 men a year. But when we say that L is rising today at a daily rate of 20,000 men a year, we do not mean that L will necessarily be 20,000 men greater this time next year, i.e. in 100 days' time; we mean only that it will be 200 men greater tomorrow. Of course, if L not only rises today at this rate but also continues on each of the following 99 days to rise at the same daily rate of 20,000 men a year (i.e. at the rate of 200 men a day), then L will in fact be 20,000 greater in a year's time. But this implies not only that the rate of increase today is at the rate of 20,000 a year but also that this daily rate remains constant for the rest of the year.

When we mean that the working population will in fact be 20,000 greater this time next year, we shall say that it is rising at an *annual* rate of 20,000 a year. When we mean only that it will be 200 greater this time tomorrow, we shall say that it is rising at a *daily* rate of 20,000 a year. When the context makes the meaning clear or where the difference is irrelevant for the particular case under discussion, we shall speak simply of a rise at a rate of 20,000 a year.

But there is another and for our purposes a much more convenient way of expressing this same change in L. If L rises from 1,000,000 to 1,000,200 between day 1 and day 2, we can say that L rises by a proportion $\dfrac{200}{1,000,000}$ in the course of the day. Now $\dfrac{200}{1,000,000} = \dfrac{2}{100} \times \dfrac{1}{100} = \dfrac{2}{100}$ of 1 per cent. We can say that L has risen by $\dfrac{2}{100}$ of 1 per cent in the day. This measure is expressed by $\dfrac{\Delta L}{L}$, the absolute increment of L as a proportion of the absolute size of L.

$\dfrac{\Delta L}{L}$ is simply the proportional increase in the number of men between one day and the next; but it is, of course, also a numerical measure of the proportional rate of increase of L on day 1, measured in terms of percentages per day. Thus in our example since $\dfrac{\Delta L}{L} = \dfrac{2}{100}$ of 1 per cent, it follows that between day 1 and day 2 the working population is growing at a proportional rate of $\dfrac{2}{100}$ of 1 per cent per day. Purely for convenience we shall often in our numerical examples speak of such rates in terms of percentages per annum. Thus if L is rising at a proportional rate of $\dfrac{2}{100}$ of 1 per cent per day, we shall often express this by saying that L is rising at a daily proportional rate of 2 per cent per 100 days or 2 per cent per annum. But when we say that L is rising today at a daily proportional rate of 2 per cent per annum, we do not mean that this time next year it will be 2 per cent greater than it is now; we mean simply that tomorrow it will be $\dfrac{2}{100}$ of 1 per cent greater than it is today.

In the case of such a daily proportional growth rate it is not even true that if it remained constant at 2 per cent per annum over the full 100 days of a year, the proportional change over the year would be 2 per cent. On the contrary, because of a phenomenon similar to that of compound as opposed to simple interest, the increase over the year would be somewhat greater than 2 per cent. If L is increasing today at a daily rate of 2 per cent per annum, we mean that it will increase by $\frac{2}{100}$ of 1 per cent or by $0\cdot0002$ of itself in the course of the day. If today it is 1,000,000, tomorrow it will be $1,000,000 \times 1\cdot0002$. But if the proportional rate of growth remains unchanged, the day after tomorrow, it will be $1\cdot0002$ times what it is tomorrow, i.e. $1,000,000 \times (1\cdot0002)^2$. Thus in 100 days' time it will be $1,000,000 \times (1\cdot0002)^{100}$ or 1,020,210. L will have risen by 20,210 and not by 20,000 (which is 2 per cent of its present value) over the year.

The distinction which we have just made corresponds to the distinction between simple and compound interest; and in this volume we shall be frequently concerned with the rate of interest. Thus suppose that the rate of interest at which money can be borrowed is $\frac{2}{100}$ of 1 per cent per day. Then if \$100 is borrowed today, the borrower will owe $\$100 \times 1\cdot0002$ tomorrow; if this is re-borrowed at the same rate of interest of $\frac{2}{100}$ of 1 per cent per day, then the day after tomorrow the borrower will owe $\$100 \times (1\cdot0002)^2$; and so on, until at the end of a year of 100 days he will owe $\$100 \times (1\cdot0002)^{100} = \$102\cdot021$. As it is easier to speak of the rate of interest in terms of percentages per annum rather than percentages per day, we shall speak of the above situation as one in which the borrower borrows money at a *daily* rate of interest of 2 per cent per annum. If he borrows money for a year at the simple rate of 2 per cent per annum (so that, borrowing \$100 today, he will owe \$102 at the end of the year) we shall call this borrowing money at an *annual* rate of interest of 2 per cent per annum. In many cases it will be sufficiently clear from the context or it will be immaterial to the argument which situation we have in mind. In that case we shall simply speak of borrowing money at a rate of interest of 2 per cent per annum.

This is exactly the same convention which we use in speaking of proportional growth rates of other variables. To revert to our previous example, suppose that a population of 1,000,000 is growing by $\frac{2}{100}$ of 1 per cent of itself each day, so that by the end of a year of 100 days it would be $1,000,000 \times (1\cdot0002)^{100} = 1,020,210$. Then we shall say that this population is growing at a *daily* growth rate of 2 per cent per annum. If, however, we are talking of a population which is growing simply by 2 per cent of itself each year, so that by the end of a year of 100 days it would be equal to $1,000,000 \times 1\cdot02 = 1,020,000$

we shall talk of it growing at an *annual* growth rate of 2 per cent per annum. Once again where the difference is immaterial for the argument or where the context itself makes the meaning clear, we shall talk simply of a growth rate of 2 per cent per annum.

In this volume we shall be much more frequently concerned with proportional than with absolute rates of growth. In the main text of this work then, whenever we speak of growth rates without further qualification, we shall mean proportional and not absolute rates of growth. We shall use a small letter to represent the daily proportional growth rate in any variable whose absolute value is expressed by the corresponding capital letter. Let us summarize this notation with our previous example:—

L = the size of the working population at the beginning of any day (e.g. 1,000,000 men);

ΔL = the increase in the working population in the course of the day (e.g. 200 additional men); and

l = the daily proportional growth rate of the population (i.e. in our example $\frac{200}{1,000,000}$ per day $= \frac{2}{100}$ of 1 per cent per day = 2 per cent per annum).

Certain relationships between these variables should be noted.

(1) While l measures the proportional growth rate, Ll measures the absolute growth rate. In our example, $Ll = 1,000,000 \times \frac{200}{1,000,000}$ per day, i.e. a daily absolute growth rate of 200 per day or 20,000 per annum.

(2) If l is expressed in terms of the daily proportional growth rate per day (and not per annum), then Ll (i.e. 200 men per day) is numerically equal to ΔL (i.e. an increase of 200 men in the course of the day).

(3) If l is expressed in terms of the daily proportional growth rate per day (and not per year), then l (i.e. $\frac{2}{100}$ of 1 per cent per day) is numerically equal to $\frac{\Delta L}{L}$ (i.e. $\frac{200}{1,000,000} = \frac{2}{100}$ of 1 per cent).

So far we have only been defining the terms which we shall use to express rates of growth. But we must now turn to some manipulations of these rates of growth which involve more than mere definition.

Suppose that we are dealing with some variable which is the product of two other variables. Suppose, for example, that we are concerned with the total wage bill (LW_l) which is made up of the total number of workers (L) multiplied by the wage per worker (W_l). If L today is 1,000,000 and W_l today is a wage rate of $1,500 a year, then we have a total wage bill running today at the daily rate of

$1,500,000,000 a year. Now suppose that l (the growth rate of L) is a daily rate of 2 per cent per annum and w_l (the growth rate of W_l) is a daily rate of 6 per cent per annum. By our definitions this means that L rises by $\frac{2}{100}$ of 1 per cent of itself and W_l by $\frac{6}{100}$ of 1 per cent of itself between today and tomorrow. Thus LW_l will have gone up from $1,000,000 \times \$1,500 = \$1,500,000,000$ today to $1,000,200 \times \$1,500 \cdot 9 = \$1,501,200,180$ tomorrow. This is a daily growth rate of $\frac{1,200,180}{1,500,000,000} \times 100$ per cent per day or of $\frac{1,200,180}{1,500,000,000} \times 100 \times$ 100 per cent per annum $= 8\frac{12}{10,000}$ per cent per annum. Thus the daily proportional growth of LW_l (namely $8\frac{12}{10,000}$ per cent per annum) is approximately equal to the sum of the daily growth rates of L and of W_l (namely $l + w_l = 2$ per cent per annum $+ 6$ per cent per annum $= 8$ per cent per annum). The discrepancy is negligible. The wage bill is growing at 2 per cent per annum because of the growth of the number of workers and at 6 per cent per annum because of the growth of the wage rate per man; and the total wage bill will be growing at approximately the sum of these two rates.

From this example we can also see that the expression $LW_l(l + w_l)$ is a good approximate measure of the absolute rate of increase of LW_l. In our numerical example $LW_l(l + w_l) = \$1,500,000,000 \times \frac{8}{100}$ per annum $= \$1,500,000,000 \times \frac{8}{10,000}$ per day $= \$1,200,000$ per day, whereas the true increase of LW_l in the day is $\$1,200,180$.[1] Once again the discrepancy is negligible.

These discrepancies would not be negligible if the growth rates were much higher. Suppose, to take an extreme case, that $l = 20$ per cent per day (i.e. a daily growth rate of 2000 per cent per annum) and $w_l = 60$ per cent per day (i.e. a daily growth rate of 6000 per cent per annum). Then between today and tomorrow LW_l would rise from $1,000,000 \times \$1,500 = \$1,500,000,000$ to $1,200,000 \times \$2,400 = \$2,880,000,000$. This is an increase of $\frac{1380}{1500} \times 100$ per cent or 92 per cent per day (i.e. a daily growth rate of 9200 per cent per annum). But $l + w_l$ is only 80 per cent per day (i.e. a daily growth rate of 8000 per cent per annum). Such a discrepancy could not well be neglected.

[1] It follows also from this example that, if l and w_l are expressed as growth rates per day, $LW_l(l + w_l)$ is a good approximate measure of $\Delta(LW_l)$, the absolute increase of LW_l in the course of a day.

We shall in fact be assuming throughout the volume that the day is a sufficiently short period of time for the proportional changes in our variables between one day and the next to be sufficiently small for discrepancies due to calculations of this kind to be neglected.

The same kind of approximate calculation can be applied to ratios between two variables as well as to the product of two variables. Consider the ratio $\frac{Y}{L}$ where Y is total income in the economy, so that $\frac{Y}{L}$ is income per head of the working population. Suppose that Y is growing today at a daily growth rate of 4 per cent per annum and L at a daily growth rate of 1 per cent per annum (i.e. $y =$ a daily growth rate of 4 per cent per annum or $\frac{4}{100}$ of 1 per cent per day and $l =$ a daily growth rate of 1 per cent per annum or $\frac{1}{100}$ of 1 per cent per day). Then tomorrow $\frac{Y}{L}$ will be $\frac{1 \cdot 0004 \, Y}{1 \cdot 0001 \, L} = \frac{Y}{L} \times 1 \cdot 0003000099$.

Between today and tomorrow $\frac{Y}{L}$ will have risen by an amount equal to $\frac{Y}{L} \times 0 \cdot 0003000099$. Now $0 \cdot 0003000099$ does not differ significantly from $0 \cdot 0003$. Thus the standard of living will for all practical purposes have risen by $0 \cdot 0003$ of itself in the day i.e. at a rate of $\frac{3}{100}$ of 1 per cent per day or a daily growth rate of 3 per cent per annum.

Income is rising today at a rate of 4 per cent per annum and tending to raise the standard of living by 4 per cent per annum; the number of mouths to be fed is rising today at a rate of 1 per cent per annum and therefore tending to reduce standard of living by 1 per cent per annum. As a result the standard of living is rising at a daily growth rate of approximately 3 per cent per annum. Thus the daily proportional growth rate in the standard of living $\left(\frac{Y}{L}\right)$ can be measured for all practical purposes by $y - l$. Similarly the absolute rate of rise in the standard of living from one day to the next can be approximately measured by $\frac{Y}{L}(y - l)$. Thus in our example with $y - l$ equal to a daily rate of 3 per cent per annum, $\frac{Y}{L}(y - l)$ is equal to an absolute rate of increase of $\dfrac{Y}{L} \times 0\cdot03$ per annum, whereas the true

absolute daily rate of increase is $\dfrac{Y}{L} \times 0\cdot0003000099$ per day or

$\dfrac{Y}{L} \times 0\cdot0300099$ per annum. It follows also that if we express y and l

as rates per day, $\dfrac{Y}{L}(y - l)$ is a good numerical measure of $\Delta\left(\dfrac{Y}{L}\right)$, the

absolute increase in $\dfrac{Y}{L}$ in the course of the day.

The same type of approximate calculation can be applied to a ratio between products. If LW_l is the wage bill and NW_n is the total of rents (the number of acres of land N multiplied by the rent per acre W_n), then the ratio of wages to rents is $\dfrac{LW_l}{NW_n}$. As we have seen, we can for all practical purposes measure the proportional rates of increase in LW_l by $l + w_l$ and in NW_n by $n + w_n$. We can, as we have seen for all practical purposes, measure the proportional rate of increase in a ratio between two variables by the difference between the proportional rates of increase of the two variables concerned, so that the

proportional rate of growth in $\dfrac{LW_l}{NW_n}$ is measured approximately by

$l + w_l - n - w_n$ and the absolute rate of growth of $\dfrac{LW_l}{NW_n}$ by

$\dfrac{LW_l}{NW_n}(l + w_l - n - w_n)$. To take an example, suppose that between today and tomorrow there are the following rises in L, W_l, N, W_n:—
in L from 1,000,000 to 1,000,200, i.e. at a daily growth rate of 2 per cent per annum; in W_l from \$1500 to \$1500·9, i.e. at a daily growth rate of 6 per cent per annum; in N from 100,000 to 100,010, i.e. at a daily growth rate of 1 per cent per annum; in W_n from \$100 to \$100·1, i.e. at a daily growth rate of 10 per cent per annum. Then $\dfrac{LW_l}{NW_n}$ will have changed from

$$\frac{1{,}000{,}000 \times \$1500}{100{,}000 \times \$100} \quad \text{to} \quad \frac{1{,}000{,}200 \times \$1500\cdot9}{100{,}010 \times \$100\cdot1}$$

i.e. from 150 to 149·955052, a fall of 0·044948 (i.e. a fall at a daily absolute rate of 4·4948 per annum). Now $l + w_l - n - w_n = 2 + 6 - 1 - 10$ per cent per annum $= -3$ per cent per annum or $-\dfrac{3}{100}$ of 1 per cent per day, so that $\dfrac{LW_l}{NW_n}\left(l + w_l - n - w_n\right) =$

$150 \times (-0 \cdot 0003)$ per day $= -0 \cdot 045$ per day, i.e. a fall of $0 \cdot 045$ a day or at a daily absolute rate of $4 \cdot 5$ per annum. But $4 \cdot 5$ is a good approximate measure of $4 \cdot 4948$. Thus $l + w_l - n - w_n$ is a good approximate measure of the proportional growth rate of $\dfrac{LW_l}{NW_n}$; $\dfrac{LW_l}{NW_n}\left(l + w_l - n - w_n\right)$ is a good approximate measure of the absolute rate of growth of $\dfrac{LW_l}{NW_n}$; and if l, w_l, n, w_n are expressed as rates per day, $\dfrac{LW_l}{NW_n}\left(l + w_l - n - w_n\right)$ is a good approximate measure of $\Delta\left(\dfrac{LW_l}{NW_n}\right)$ the absolute increase in $\dfrac{LW_l}{NW_n}$ in the course of the day.

The inaccuracies of statements such as these we shall in the main text of this volume assume to be quite negligible, so long as we reckon in terms of a basic unit of time so short as a single day. Thus, to summarize, we shall use the following measures of proportional and absolute rates of growth of a quantity at any one point of time (i.e. between one day and the next):—

Quantity Concerned	Daily Proportional Growth Rate	Daily Absolute Rate of Growth
A	a	Aa
AB	$a + b$	$AB(a + b)$
$\dfrac{A}{C}$	$a - c$	$\dfrac{A}{C}(a - c)$
$\dfrac{AB}{CD}$	$a + b - c - d$	$\dfrac{AB}{CD}(a + b - c - d)$

PART I

THE ONE-PRODUCT MODEL

CHAPTER I

SIX ASSUMPTIONS

In Chapter I of *The Stationary Economy* we enumerated ten
assumptions upon which the static analysis of that volume was
constructed. In this and the following volume we intend to alter
those assumptions to the extent necessary to investigate the dynamic
properties of the static system of that volume. For this purpose at
least four of those ten assumptions must be abandoned.

In the first place, to investigate the dynamic properties of our
economic system we must allow it to grow; and economic growth
may be the result of any of three main causes: (i) continuous improvement of technical knowledge so that more can be produced by any
given amount of the factors of production, (ii) growth in the size of
the working population, and (iii) growth in the size of the accumulated stock of man-made instruments of production, i.e. of capital
goods of all kinds. This means the abandonment of three of the basic
assumptions of *The Stationary Economy*,[1] since we must now
introduce into our system the factor 'capital' and its accumulation by
'saving' and must allow both for a continuous change in the size of
the working population and also for a continuous improvement of
technical knowledge.

In the second place, we shall no longer retain the simple monetary
assumption which we made in *The Stationary Economy*, namely that
the spending habits of the population were such as to keep the money
national income constant at $100 million a day.[2] For, as we shall see
later in this volume, it will be convenient for the purposes of
exposition to assume that there are certain financial authorities in
charge of monetary affairs; and we shall vary our assumptions about
the behaviour of these authorities in ways which are convenient for
exposition and which we will specify from time to time.

Of the remaining six assumptions of *The Stationary State*, five will
be maintained in the same form in this volume and the sixth will be
maintained in a somewhat modified form. To be precise, unless we
expressly state the contrary at some stage in the analysis, we shall
throughout this volume make the following six assumptions.

[1] Namely assumptions (4), (5), and (6) on pp. 26 and 27 of *The Stationary
Economy*.
[2] Assumption (10) on page 28 of *The Stationary Economy*.

(1) We assume that we are dealing with a closed economy.[1]

(2) We assume that conditions are such as to make possible perfect competition or perfect potential competition in all markets.[2]

(3) We assume that there are no indivisibilities and that there are in consequence constant returns to scale in the economy.[3]

(4) We assume that there are no external economies or diseconomies in the community.[4]

(5) We assume that each individual citizen has a given, independent, and consistent set of preferences.[5]

(6) In *The Stationary Economy* we assumed[6] that there was no Government expenditure and no Government taxation. We shall continue to assume that there is no Government expenditure on goods and services. There are no communal real needs (of which defence, police, justice, etc., are the classical examples) which have to be met by State action. But in the modern economy this public finance of communal needs is only one of the three main functions of the Government's Budget. Budgetary policy can also be designed (i) so as to affect the distribution of the total national expenditure as between current consumption, on the one hand, and savings for the finance of additions to the stock of real capital equipment on the other hand and (ii) so as to affect the distribution of personal incomes and personal wealth as between various classes of citizens.

(i) If the State raises a high level of taxation from its citizens or receives interest, profits, or rents on any property owned by it, and if it spends none or only a part of this on current communal needs, then there is a surplus of revenue over current expenditure in the budget. This Budget Surplus represents public savings. Suppose, for example, that the State raises $100 m. a year from the income tax, spends nothing on current purposes, and directly or indirectly lends the whole of the Budget surplus of $100 m. a year to private entrepreneurs for investment by them in extensions of their capital plant and equipment.[7] Those private citizens who pay the tax have their

---

[1] Assumption (1) on page 26 of *The Stationary Economy*.

[2] Assumption (3) on page 26 as developed on pages 29–32 of *The Stationary Economy*.

[3] Assumption (7), page 27 of *The Stationary Economy*.

[4] Assumption (8), page 27 of *The Stationary Economy*.

[5] Assumption (9), page 28 of *The Stationary Economy*.

[6] Assumption (2), page 26 of *The Stationary Economy*.

[7] This 'lending' by the State to private enterprise would quite probably take the very indirect form of a redemption of an outstanding National Debt. The State buys up $100 m. worth of its outstanding debt; and this debt is sold to it by private businessmen who use the capital so raised to finance expenditure of $100 m. on the purchase of new plant and equipment.

freely disposable incomes reduced by $100 m. a year. Suppose that as a result they spend $60 m. less on consumption and reduce their private savings by $40 m. As a net result expenditure on current consumption has gone down by $60 m. a year and total savings have gone up by $60 m. a year (public savings being up by $100 m. a year and private savings down by $40 m. a year).

Conversely the Government might run a Budget Deficit of $100 m. a year, borrowing this sum from private savers and using the funds either for the finance of current communal consumption (which we are ruling out by assumption in this volume) or else for distribution as direct payments to individuals to supplement their incomes. Such 'transfer payments' as we shall call them might take the form of payments of interest on outstanding debts of the State to private citizens (the National Debt), of old age pensions or family allowances or, conceivably, of straightforward subsidies to all personal incomes. If as a result of receiving these transfer payments of $100 m. a year the recipients spent $60 m. a year more on consumption goods and services and saved $40 m. more a year, then total consumption would be up by $60 m. and total savings down by $60 m. (public savings down by $100 m. and private savings up by $40 m.).

(ii) Taxes and transfer payments can be combined. Some citizens (e.g. the rich) may be taxed and the proceeds used to make transfer payments to other citizens (e.g. the poor).

Our sixth assumption throughout this volume will be that there is no State expenditure on real goods and services, but that there may be taxation raised from the citizens and/or transfer payments made by the State to the citizens. This set of assumptions allows us to consider the use of budgetary policy for the two purposes of affecting (i) the levels of total consumption and of total savings in the community and (ii) the distribution between persons of freely disposable private incomes (i.e. of incomes after the payment of tax and/or after the receipt of transfer payments).

It is a very important consequence of these budgetary assumptions that the State may at any one time be indebted to private citizens. If, starting with a clean slate, it has been running a Budget Deficit of $100 m. a year for 10 years, then at the end of that period it will owe $1000 m. to private citizens. There will at that point of time be a National Debt of $1000 m. outstanding. Conversely, if, starting with a clean slate, the State had been running a Budget Surplus of $100 m. a year for 10 years, it would at the end of that period own $1000 m. of property—which might take the form of a debt to it by private individuals. There would be a 'National Asset' of $1000 m. outstanding.

In *The Stationary Economy* we were dealing with only two

categories of factors of production—labour (which covered the services of men and women of various grades of ability, etc.) and land (which covered the services of natural resources of various grades of fertility, etc.). The introduction into this volume of another category of factors of production—namely, capital goods or man-made instruments of production of all kinds—marks a basic change in the whole system; it is not simply that we have three instead of two factors of production; the system is qualitatively different. Why is this so? What is the fundamental nature of 'capital'?

At first sight it might appear that we could treat capital in much the same way as we treated land. Both represent instruments of production. A farmer employs labour and uses it with some land, some ploughs, some harrows, etc., to produce his output. Each of these is a factor of production; each will contribute to the production; each will thus command a price in the market; and so on. But there are two fundamental differences between lands of various kinds as we have conceived them in *The Stationary Economy* and capital goods. We assumed that natural resources were given in amount by nature and were indestructible; on the other hand, capital goods are man-made and are perishable. Raw materials and machines must be produced by man before they can be used as instruments of production and they perish either because (like raw materials) they are embodied in the final product or (like machines) they are gradually worn out with age and use. For these reasons the introduction of such man-made instruments of production or capital goods as factors of production complicates the analysis in at least four essential respects.

(1) First, in *The Stationary Economy* in the absence of capital goods we were able to neglect the role played by time in the economic system. We were able to assume that the original factors of production (land and labour) produced 'an immediate output' of goods and services for final consumption which were 'almost instantaneously' sold to the final consumers. In other words on any one day the available land and labour produced outputs of perishable goods and services which must satisfy consumers' needs that same day or else be wasted.

With the introduction of man-made instruments of production this is no longer the case. The tools which are used today with today's land and labour must have been produced yesterday or the day before. Or, to put the same thing the other way round, land and labour may be used today to produce, not consumption goods, but tools which will be used to produce consumption goods tomorrow or the next day. In other words we are no longer faced with the choice between using today's resources to add to today's consumption or else wasting them in unemployment and idleness. We can use today's resources to maintain or improve our stock of capital goods so that more consumption goods can be produced in the future. The introduction of man-made instruments of production necessarily involves us in problems of the programming of consumption over time. Shall we have less today in order to have more tomorrow?

(2) As a second result of this same phenomenon, it is no longer possible to neglect problems connected with expectations and uncertainty. Man-made instruments of production take time to construct and, in many cases, take time to wear out. Today resources are used to lay down the keel of a ship, tomorrow resources will be used to build upon the keel, and so on until the ship is launched. The ship itself will then be used the next day, the day after, the day after that, and so on, until it is scrapped. The entrepreneur has to decide today whether to lay down the keel. Whether or not this will turn out to have been a wise decision will depend upon the future course of the costs of building on this keel (for the total cost of the ship will be thus affected) and also upon the future course both of the costs of operating the ship and also of the freight rates at which the services of the ship can be sold over its useful life when it has been built (for the total return on the cost will be so decided). The entrepreneur must make some forecast of the probable course of events far into the future; and we must therefore consider what determines his expectations and how he does—and how he should—behave when, as is in fact inevitable, he is uncertain about the future. We could neglect these problems in *The Stationary Economy* when today's output was sold in today's market regardless of what the future held in store.

(3) In the case of labour or of land or of any original factor which is given in amount the market price which will be paid for it will, in our competitive conditions, depend solely upon the demand for it. These demand conditions for factors of production were examined at length in *The Stationary Economy*. But in the case of man-made instruments of production what is the input in one industry (the tool-using industry) is the output of another industry (the tool-making industry). The market price of a tool will depend not only upon the demand conditions for it (the value of its marginal product in the tool-using industry) but also upon its supply conditions (its marginal cost in the tool-making industry). Consumption goods are outputs but not inputs; labour and land are inputs but not outputs; capital goods are outputs as well as inputs.

(4) This input–output relationship of capital goods can become very complicated. Steel is used in machinery to produce coal which

is used to produce steel which is used to produce motor vehicles which are used to carry steel which is used to produce coal which is sold to the final consumer. Of the hundreds of thousands of different sorts of capital goods each one could theoretically be an input in the production of every other one as well as an input in the production of every final consumption good. How then are the costs of these capital goods determined? The cost of coal depends upon the cost of steel but the cost of steel depends upon the cost of coal.

The four considerations which we have just explained make the treatment of capital in economic analysis particularly important and, alas, particularly difficult to expound simply. We shall for this reason proceed by making at first one extreme simplifying assumption—namely that there is literally only one product in our economy which serves the role both of a consumption good and of a capital good. To take a simple example, the economy consists solely and entirely of farms producing corn. The inputs into the farm are land, labour, and an amount of corn used as seed; the output of the economy is corn which in turn can either be bought for consumption or can be used as a capital good to be sown again for the next harvest.

We will elaborate on this model in the following chapters. But it is already clear that this model of the economy preserves two of the special features of capitalistic production—those numbered (1) and (3) on pages 26 and 27 above. The element of time must now play an essential role since by consuming less corn today and ploughing more of today's output of corn back as an input into the farm one can increase tomorrow's harvest of corn and so raise tomorrow's standard of consumption. Moreover, the basic input–output relation is present in this model, since the price of the use of corn as a factor of production will depend both upon the marginal productivity of corn sown as seed in the farm and also upon the cost at which corn can be produced by the farm for use as seed. But our one-product model does enable us to a large extent to neglect the other two special features of capitalistic production—those numbered (2) and (4) on page 27 above. Uncertainty in entrepreneurial planning would virtually disappear except for any uncertainty about the money price of corn; and we shall in our one-product model be able to make a simple monetary assumption about the price of corn which will enable us virtually to neglect the problems of expectations and uncertainty. Moreover, when there is only one product the complicated criss-cross input–output relationships which we noted under (4) above simply cannot arise.

This one-product model of capitalistic production which we shall maintain throughout Chapters II to XIV is, of course, extremely unrealistic. The reader may regard it simply as a necessary exercise in certain basic relationships before we turn to the many-product model of capitalist production in Chapters XV to XXIII. But it is suggested that it may have a further use. The reader may regard the one product as being simply an index number of all real goods produced by the economy; 'real goods' have a double aspect—there is the stock of 'real goods' which measures the real capital equipment of the community and there is the output of 'real goods' upon which depends the level of real consumption and the rate at which addition can be made to the capital stock of 'real goods'. In this index-number way our one-product model will in fact tell us something of essential importance about what goes on in the actual world. But it is very incomplete. It hides nearly all problems of expectations and uncertainty; and it neglects the criss-cross input–output relationships between different industries. Such problems will be taken up only when we come to Chapter XV.

CHAPTER II

MONEY, PRICES, AND INTEREST IN THE ONE-PRODUCT MODEL

Economic growth depends upon the interplay of productive potential and of effective demand. Real income cannot continue to rise unless an increase in the supply of the productive factors, labour and capital, and/or an improvement in technical knowledge enables more goods and services to be produced. But real income will not in fact grow unless the producers can find markets in which to sell the increased output; if not, productive potential will be wasted in unemployment and idleness. In this volume we shall be concerned with productive potential rather than with effective demand; we are engaged in asking what are the effects in a fully competitive economy of population growth, capital accumulation, and technical progress on the output that will be produced, provided always that a market can be found for the products. Only in a later volume will we be concerned with a proper investigation of the problems of defining and maintaining the most appropriate level of money demand to achieve the fullest use of the real opportunities of growth. Nevertheless, the problems of productive potential and of monetary demand are so closely linked that it is impossible to divorce them completely. In this volume we shall at each stage make the simplest possible set of assumptions about monetary and financial institutions to enable us to proceed on the basis that full employment of all resources is maintained and that a market is found for everything that is produced.

The central feature of the simple financial model which we shall employ in Part 1 of this volume is that the money selling price (P_y) of our single product (Y) is constant and expected to be constant. That is to say, every producer of Y has for long found that he can always sell his output of Y at a given market price and for this reason expects (and, as it turns out, rightly expects) that he will be able to sell his output in the future at the same price. By what institutions this remarkable result can be achieved will be discussed later in this chapter. Let us for the moment concentrate on what the nature of the entrepreneur's task will be if the selling price of his product is constant and is known to be constant.

We assume[1] that there are a number of citizens (Messrs A B C D, etc.) who own a certain amount of factors of production of three kinds: their own labour (L), amounts of land (N), and a stock of our single product (K—e.g. a certain amount of seed corn). Each day these citizens hire out these factors in competitive factor markets to the entrepreneurs running the firms and farms. Each day with these

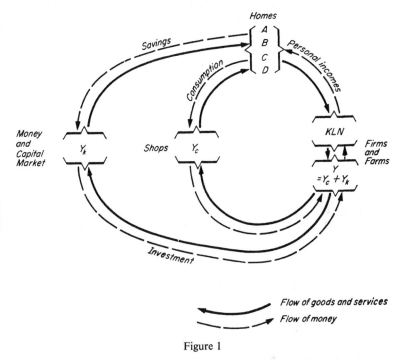

Homes

Savings

Consumption

Personal incomes

Money
and
Capital
Market

Y_k

Shops

Y_c

KLN

Firms
and
Farms

Y
$= Y_c + Y_k$

Investment

→ Flow of goods and services

→ Flow of money

Figure 1

factors the entrepreneurs produce a certain output (Y—i.e. a certain output of corn) which is either used for sale in the shops as consumption goods (Y_c) to the housewives (Mrs A B C D, etc.) or else is sold through the capital market (which we will describe later) to the owners of the factors (Messrs A B C D, etc.) as an addition to the capital stock (Y_k) which they own and which they can then in turn hire out on a daily basis to the entrepreneurs for further productive operations.

There are three important points to be noted in this schema.

First, the daily output Y is only the daily net output of the firms

---

[1] Figure 1 (which may be compared with the corresponding Figure 1 on page 29 of *The Stationary Economy*) may help the reader to visualize the model described in this chapter.

and farms, that is to say, the total day's output of 'corn' less that amount of corn which is necessary for the repayment by the entrepreneurs to the citizens of that capital stock of corn (K) which the citizens hired out to the entrepreneurs at the beginning of the day.

Second, just as the labour (L) and the land (N) are owned by the ordinary citizens (Messrs A B C D, etc.) who hire out to the entrepreneurs by the day the services of the labour at a wage rate (W_l) and the services of the land at a rate of rent (W_n), so the stock of real equipment belongs to the ordinary citizens who hire out its use by the day to the entrepreneurs at a rate of 'rental' (W_k). Thus in our corn economy W_k measures the amount of money which an entrepreneur pays to the owner of a bag of corn to hire that amount of corn for a day; at the end of the day the entrepreneur must give back to the owner a bag of corn plus W_k units of money.

A clear distinction must thus be drawn between the rates of hire of services of a factor (W_l W_n W_k) and the prices which would have to be paid for the outright purchase of a factor (P_l P_n P_k). P_l would be the price of buying a slave; W_l is the wage to be paid for the use of a man's labour for one day. P_n is the price which would have to be paid to buy outright an acre of land; W_n is the rent which must be paid to hire an acre of land for one day. P_k is the price which must be paid to purchase outright a unit of the man-made instrument of production K (e.g. a bag of corn); W_k is the rental which must be paid to hire the use of a unit of K for one day (i.e. the obligation being to return that unit of K plus a rental of W_k at the end of the day).[1] Since there is only one product corn which comprises both the output of the firms and farms (Y) and also the stock of real capital (K), in our present one-product model we have by definition $P_k \equiv P_y$, i.e. the price of a bag of corn.

Third, in the case of capitalistic production which we are now examining great care must be taken to be precise about the timing of all operations. We assume that at 8.0 a.m. on each working day (e.g. Wednesday) the owners of the factors of production (Messrs A B C D, etc.) come into the firms and farms and hire out the services of these factors (K L N) for the coming day to the entrepreneurs running the firms and farms at rates of daily hire (W_k W_l W_n) determined competitively between the owners and the entrepreneurs. The entrepreneurs use these factors for the day and at 4.0 p.m. at the

[1] As we shall not be dealing with a slave economy the term P_l will not be used in this volume. The above notation represents a necessary, but unfortunate change from the notation used in *The Stationary Economy*; in that volume P_l, P_n, etc., were used where we now use W_l, W_n, etc. When *The Stationary Economy* was first written, the necessity in the case of capital which would arise in *The Growing Economy* of distinguishing between the W's and P's in the case of inputs was unfortunately overlooked.

close of the same day (Wednesday) the output appears. This output is sold at 8.0 a.m. next morning (Thursday). Also at 8.0 a.m. next morning (Thursday) the factors are paid for the work done on the previous day (Wednesday) and the terms (W_k W_l W_n) are fixed on which the coming day's (Thursday's) work shall be done.

The entrepreneur, we will assume, knows on Wednesday morning what technical possibilities will be available for him to use during Wednesday's productive operations. He does not, of course, know on Wednesday morning what techniques may be available for Thursday's operations. But this ignorance will not disturb his decisions on Wednesday morning. He then knows (i) at what prices he can hire the services of the factors for Wednesday and (ii) how much output he can produce on Wednesday. If—and this is to be the central feature of our monetary assumptions—he knows on Wednesday morning the price at which Wednesday's output will sell on Thursday morning, he has no uncertainty to complicate his Wednesday morning decisions.

In this model full employment is maintained simply by the fact that the owners of the factors and the entrepreneurs, through the forces of competition or of potential competition, settle on Wednesday morning on factor prices which, given the supplies of the factors available for productive use on Wednesday and given the technical knowledge available on Wednesday, are equal to the marginal products of the factors valued at the constant money selling price of the product. The whole of the apparatus of analysis of competition and marginal productivity discussed at length in *The Stationary Economy* can be applied to the present model. Thursday's supplies of the factors may differ from Wednesday's and Thursday's technical knowledge may differ from Wednesday's; Thursday's factor prices may, therefore, differ from Wednesday's; but if the selling price of the product is the same and known to be the same, on each successive day competition will fix factor rentals (W_k W_l W_n) which are equal to the value of that day's marginal product for each factor. If the price fixed for the factor's services were higher than the value of its marginal product, there would be unemployed factors; and competition among the owners of the factors would bring the price down. If the price were lower than the value of the marginal product of the factor, there would be an excess demand for the factor and competition among employers would drive the price up.

It will be observed that in our model the terms on which the factors will be paid for Wednesday's operations were fixed at the beginning of the day's operations but that the actual payments of wages, rents, and rentals to the factors were made only after the day's work was done at the same time as the resulting output was sold on Thursday

B

morning. This means that the entrepreneur receives the revenue from the sale of his product at exactly the same time as he pays the factors which have produced that product (Thursday morning at 8.0 a.m.). This assumption, combined with the assumptions of perfect actual or potential competition and complete certainty for productive operations, which we have just described, mean that we can assume that the entrepreneurs make no profits or losses. They compete with each other to pay rewards to the factors equal to the known values of their marginal products; with constant returns to scale this accounts for the whole of the product, neither more nor less; and the payments to the factors are made at the same moment of time as the sales proceeds of the product are received.

But these results depend essentially upon our assumption that the money price at which the potential daily output of the economy's productive system can be sold, remains constant and is fully expected to remain constant at a given level P_y. How could such a situation in the market for the product be achieved? It depends, of course, upon the demand conditions for the product being such that, at the given price P_y, purchasers will purchase on Thursday morning just that quantity of Y which is available on Thursday morning from Wednesday's productive operations. This demand for Y will proceed from two sources—consumption demand and investment demand.

When the housewives (Mrs A B C D, etc.) go into the shops at 8.0 a.m. on Thursday morning they will know what incomes their husbands will be receiving at the same time on Thursday morning in payment for the services rendered on Wednesday. They will know what incomes they received the day before (on Wednesday morning), the day before that (on Tuesday morning), and so on. They will also know the amount and value of the property which they have accumulated out of their past savings and which they already own when they go into the shops on Thursday morning. They will not, however, yet know what incomes their husbands are going to earn on Thursday, Friday, Saturday and so on. They will, however, probably have formed some expectations about their future prospects of income in view of their past experience of increases or decreases in the rates of pay (W_k W_l W_n) which they have been able to receive from the factors which they own. In the light of these considerations (the level of their real incomes, their expectations about future real incomes, and the amount of property which they already own) they must decide how much they wish to spend on consumption goods for current enjoyment—the alternative being, of course, to cut down on current consumption in order to save their current income and thus add still more to their properties.

Later in this volume (Chapters XII to XIV) we shall have to devote considerable attention to the factors which are likely to affect this choice between current consumption and savings. At the moment we will simply note the fact that the choice must be made. There is, however, no reason to believe that the housewives at 8.0 a.m. on Thursday morning will decide to spend for consumption in the shops on Wednesday's output exactly the same amount as the already known sum which their husbands will be receiving at the same moment (8.0 a.m. on Thursday) in respect of the production of Wednesday's output. If they spend less than this, they are saving that amount out of their current incomes. But this means that on Thursday morning the demand for Wednesday's output will be deficient (and its selling price will therefore fall) unless there is some supplementary demand for the product to fill the gap.

This supplementary demand must take the form of the demand for the product for investment purposes, i.e. the demand by Messrs A B C D, etc., for part of Wednesday's output to add to the stocks of capital equipment which they own and which they hire out on subsequent days as a productive factor to the entrepreneurs running the firms and farms. How is this investment demand determined?

It is at this point that we must introduce monetary and financial institutions into our model. We will assume as we did in Chapter I of *The Stationary Economy* (p. 28) that there is a unit of money which we call the $1 note. All transactions are fixed in terms of $1 notes and all obligations can be legally settled in terms of $1 notes. But money income now (unlike the conditions in *The Stationary Economy*) can be saved instead of being spent on current consumption, and personal properties are thus accumulated. We shall accordingly allow for lending and borrowing in our economy. We shall make no special restrictive assumptions about the forms which such borrowing and lending may take. Any citizen can lend money to, or borrow money from, any other citizen on any terms on which they agree. Some loans will be for long periods, some for short periods; and the rates of interest at which the various forms of loan are made will be determined by competition between borrowers (who seek lenders offering loans at low interest) and lenders (who seek borrowers offering to borrow at high interest). We may envisage all sorts of firms and institutions growing up in what we may call the Money and Capital Market.

We do, however, make one very special positive set of assumptions about one special institution in the Money and Capital Market— namely, about the official governmental institution which we will call the Central Bank which is responsible for issuing the $1 notes in terms of which all legal liabilities are ultimately expressed. We assume in Part 1 of this volume simply that the Central Bank deals only in daily loans of $1 notes. At 8.0 a.m. every morning it fixes the Bank Rate for the day, i.e. the rate of interest at which it is equally willing either to borrow $1 notes for the day from any citizens or to lend $1 notes for the day to any citizen—the Central Bank having the right to print as many $1 notes as may be necessary to fulfil the latter task. We assume that loans, like other payments, are made at 8.0 a.m. each morning and that when a day's loan is made, the interest on it is paid when the loan is repaid. Thus a Bank loan of $100 made at 8.0 a.m. Wednesday morning is repaid with the interest on it at 8.0 a.m. on Thursday morning.

The result of these assumptions is that in the Money and Capital Market the rate of interest charged by one citizen to another for the loan of money for one day can never be above that day's Bank Rate (since the borrower could always borrow from the Central Bank). Rates of interest charged for loans for longer periods may, of course, differ from this; and later in Part 2 of this volume (see pp. 314–318 below) we will say something about the way in which they may differ. But the structure of interest rates will always be based upon the rate of interest for money loans for one day as set by the current Bank Rate.

We suppose now that the Central Bank sets the Bank Rate each morning with the intention of influencing the selling price of a unit of the product so that it remains stable at, for example, $100 per unit of the product. Each morning there will in fact be a level of Bank Rate which will cause the market price of the product to stand at $100 that morning. That this is so becomes apparent when one considers the factors which, in our model, will determine the demand by Messrs A B C D, etc., for the product for investment purposes, i.e. for the purpose of adding to the stock of real capital which they own and hire out to the entrepreneurs.

Consider the following numerical example in which the Central Bank is seeking to stabilize the price of a unit of the product at $100 ($P_k = P_y = \$100$). Suppose that on Thursday morning the producers are offering a rental (W_k) of $0·03 for the use for one day of a unit of the product as a piece of capital equipment. Consider a citizen who expects that on Friday morning the selling price of a unit of the product will be $100·02.[1] Suppose now that the Central Bank sets a Bank Rate for the day equal to a daily rate of 5 per cent per annum which is equivalent—assuming always a year of 100 days

[1] We have expressly taken a case of a citizen who is not convinced that the price stabilization policy will succeed but expects some degree of unplanned price inflation. We shall argue that even if inflation is expected, the Central Bank can stabilize the price, and that the price stabilization policy will be still easier if inflation is not expected.

—to a daily rate of $\frac{5}{100}$ or $0 \cdot 05$ per cent per day. In this case our citizen can hope to make a profit on buying the product for capital investment if its price on Thursday morning is below \$100, but will expect loss from such investment if its price is above \$100.

For suppose the current price of the product on Thursday morning were \$100. Then he can borrow \$100 from the Central Bank at $0 \cdot 05$ per cent for the day; and on Friday morning will have to repay to the Central Bank \$100 $+ \frac{0 \cdot 05}{100} \times$ \$100 (i.e. principal and interest on his loan). With the \$100 on Thursday morning he can purchase a unit of the product and on this can earn $\$0 \cdot 03$ in rental; and he can resell (so he expects) the product at $\$100 \cdot 02$ on Friday morning. He will receive (so he expects) $\$100 \cdot 02 + \$0 \cdot 03$ ($= \$100 \cdot 05$) and will have to repay \$100 $+ \frac{0 \cdot 05}{100} \times$ \$100 ($= \$100 \cdot 05$) to the Central Bank. If, however, the current price of the product were less than \$100, he would expect a profit from investment in the product; if, for example, the product cost \$99, he could borrow \$99 from the Central Bank which would involve him in the repayment of \$99 $\left(1 + \frac{0 \cdot 05}{100} \right)$ in principal and interest next morning; but he would still expect to receive $\$100 \cdot 02 + \$0 \cdot 03$ or \$100 $\left(1 + \frac{0 \cdot 05}{100} \right)$ for the hire of the product today and its resale tomorrow.

In brief, we can put the point this way. By borrowing money to invest in a capital good a citizen can expect to receive next morning (i) a rental or 'profit' on the day's use of the instrument and (ii) tomorrow's selling value of the instrument. He will have to pay tomorrow (iii) the principal sum which he borrows to cover today's price of the instrument which he buys and (iv) the day's interest on the borrowing. If (i) + (ii) is greater than (iii) + (iv), the investment is expected to be profitable. But (iv) can always be reduced by lowering Bank Rate. The incentive to invest in any given state of the market and of expectations can thus be increased by lowering Bank Rate. The Bank Rate can thus be set at a level which will stimulate investment demand to the extent necessary to raise the selling price of today's output to the desired target level.[1]

---

[1] This is subject to the assumption that tomorrow's price of the capital good is not expected to be so much *below* today's price that the loss in the expected value of the capital good is greater than the day's hire which can be earned on it. In this case today's Bank Rate would have to fall below zero in order to maintain today's investment demand for the product. We shall neglect this possibility.

In order to be precise about the timing of the different variables, it is perhaps worth while expressing the relationship discussed in the last paragraph in a more precise form. Let

W_{k0} be the rental for the use of a unit of K during day 0, this rental being fixed at 8 a.m. on day 0 but paid at 8 a.m. on day 1,

P_{k0} be the price paid for a unit of K at 8 a.m. on day 0,

$_0P_{k1}$ be the price at which, at 8 a.m. on day 0, it is expected that a unit of K will be sold at 8 a.m. on day 1,[1]

$_0p_{k0} \left(= \dfrac{_0P_{k1} - P_{k0}}{P_{k0}} \right)$ be the proportional rate of rise in the price of K expected at 8 a.m. on day 0 to occur in the course of day 0,

i_0 be the rate of interest fixed by the Central Bank at 8 a.m. on day 0 for a loan for day 0, the interest and principal being payable at 8 a.m. on day 1, and

$_0i'_0$ be the rate of profit expected to be earned in the course of day 0 on investment in a unit of K made at 8 a.m. on day 0.

If then we consider an investment in a unit of K made at 8 a.m. on day 0, items (i), (ii), (iii), and (iv) of the penultimate paragraph can be expressed as follows.

(i) The rental is W_{k0}. (ii) The expected value of the capital good tomorrow is $_0P_{k1}$. (iii) The principal needed to invest in the instrument is P_{k0}. (iv) The amount payable in interest tomorrow is $i_0 P_{k0}$. The investment will be profitable if

$$(1 + i_0) P_{k0} < W_{k0} + {_0P_{k1}}$$

$$\text{i.e. if } i_0 < \frac{W_{k0}}{P_{k0}} + \frac{_0P_{k1} - P_{k0}}{P_{k0}} \tag{2.1}$$

Now $\dfrac{_0P_{k1} - P_{k0}}{P_{k0}}$ is the expected proportional rate of rise of the price of the capital good, i.e. the expected rise $(_0P_{k1} - P_{k0})$ expressed as a proportion of the current price (P_{k0}). We write this as $_0p_{k0}$ and call it the 'expected rate of capital gain'. $\dfrac{W_{k0}}{P_{k0}}$ is the current rental for a unit of the capital good expressed as a ratio of its current price and we

---

[1] A full discussion of expectations needs a more complicated notation. Citizen's A expectations may not be the same as those of citizen B. Thus we should write $_{a0}P_{k1}$, $_{b0}P_{k1}$, etc., for the prices of K which citizens A, B, etc., expect at 8 a.m. on day 0 to rule at 8 a.m. on day 1. Moreover, citizen A may not be at all certain about the future course of prices. He may expect the price K to be $_{a0}P'_{k1}$ with probability π', $_{a0}P''_{k1}$ with probability π'', and so on. When we come to deal with uncertainty in more detail (Chapters XXI and XXII below) we shall introduce these complications. At the moment we assume simply that at any point of time all citizens have the same single expectation about the future course of the price of any product.

will call this the 'current rate of return'. The sum of the current rate of return and of the expected rate of capital gain is the rate of profit which the investor in fact expects to get on his investment in current yield and capital appreciation in the course of day 0. This we call $_0i'_0$ (the rate of profit expected at 8 a.m. on day 0 to be gained during day 0). Then $_0i'_0 = \dfrac{W_{k0}}{P_{k0}} + p_{k0}$ and the investment will be made if $i_0 < _0i'_0$.

Thus investment is profitable if the current rate of interest is less than the rate of return on the capital good plus the expected rate of capital gain, i.e. is less than the expected rate of profit. By setting i at a lower level on Thursday morning the Central Bank can increase the profitability for citizens to borrow money on Thursday morning to invest in the purchase of the product on Thursday morning for investment purposes; by setting i at a higher level the Central Bank can make such investment less profitable. But an increase on Thursday morning in the total amount spent on the product for investment purposes will tend to raise the price (P_y) offered for the given output of the product (i.e. Wednesday's output) available for sale on Thursday morning; a decrease in the total amount spent on the product on Thursday morning will lower the price of the product ruling on Thursday morning. An omniscient Central Bank (we will return to the problems of a Central Bank which lacks omniscience in a later volume) could set i each morning at the level which would induce just so much investment expenditure on the product as, together with the housewives' demand for the product, would cause total demand for the product to equal the total available supply of the product at the desired level for the stabilized price.

We shall consider in a later volume the dynamic processes which are involved in applying stabilization policies. At this point let us merely note that in the solution of this problem nothing succeeds like success. Suppose, to take an example, that prices had been rising for some time at a daily rate of 10 per cent per annum and that they were expected to do so in the future. In this case there is an expected rate of capital gain at a daily rate of 10 per cent per annum. Suppose that the Central Bank wanted to stop this price inflation and to stabilize the price level at its current level. Suppose further that the current rate of return on capital were at a daily rate of 5 per cent per annum. Then the expected rate of profit is at a daily rate of 15 per cent per annum (10 per cent + 5 per cent). The Bank Rate must be set in the region of a daily rate of 15 per cent per annum to contain the inflation. But suppose that it is so set that prices are successfully stabilized. The rate of capital gain falls from a daily rate of 10 per cent per annum to nil. Sooner or later the expected rate of capital gain will fall from 10 per cent per annum; but how soon and how far? If this morning the expected rate of capital gain has fallen from 10 per cent to 4 per cent per annum, then the expected rate of profit will have fallen from 15 per cent (10 + 5 per cent) to 9 per cent (4 + 5 per cent). The Central Bank will clearly have the most difficult job in adjusting the actual Bank Rate to keep in line with the changing expected rate of capital gain. But suppose that the Central Bank has been successful in stabilizing the price for a considerable period and has announced its intention to continue to do so. The expected rate of capital gains is likely to have fallen to zero and to remain at zero; citizens will expect no change in price. On any day, t, the Central Bank will now have the task of adjusting Bank Rate (i_t) to the current

rate of return $\left(\dfrac{W_{kt}}{P_{kt}}\right)$ which will be a much less volatile quantity; and

the expected rate of capital gain $({_t}p_{kt})$ can be ignored. A firm expectation that prices will remain stable is a great help to the policy of keeping them stable.

This banking policy for the control of investment demand in such a way as to stabilize the selling price of the product can be supplemented by a budgetary policy designed for the same purpose. Thus the Government, in line with the assumptions made in Chapter I (pp. 24–25 above), can tax citizens' incomes and by reducing their free spendable incomes can reduce the housewives' demands on the product for current consumption. Or the Government can supplement housewives' incomes with transfer payments and thus induce them to spend more on current consumption than would otherwise be the case. In the former case the budget surplus would provide a flow of public savings on to the money and capital market to supplement private savings; in the latter case the budget deficit would be financed by governmental borrowing (at the current rate of interest) which would drain off part of the private savings of individual citizens. It is the combination of Bank Rate and Budgetary Surplus or Deficit which will control the situation. A high Budget Surplus (with correspondingly low private consumption) plus a low Bank Rate (with a correspondingly high incentive to invest) will maintain total demand $(P_y \, Y)$ with a relatively high proportion spent on investment $(P_y \, Y_k)$ and a relatively low proportion on current consumption $(P_y \, Y_c)$; a high Budget Deficit (with correspondingly high private consumption) plus a high Bank Rate (with a correspondingly low incentive to invest) could maintain total demand at the same level $(P_y \, Y)$ but with a larger proportion spent on current consumption $(P_y \, Y_c)$ and a smaller proportion devoted to investment in new capital equipment $(P_y \, Y_k)$.

In Part 2 of this volume when we come to deal with the many-product economy we shall rely to a large extent on budgetary policy to maintain monetary stability. In this Part, in which we assume a one-product economy, this is not necessary, and for the time being we will assume that stability is ensured solely by a monetary policy which controls i so as to affect the incentive to invest in such a way as to maintain $P_y \equiv P_k$ at a constant level.

We proceed then on the assumption that the Central Bank attains perfect success in its task of stabilizing the selling price of the product. We have already seen that, with the other assumptions of our model, this means that the entrepreneurs have no uncertainties to face and that, as in the static competitive conditions of *The Stationary Economy*, every factor will receive for its services a reward equal to the value of its current marginal product. But while our assumptions successfully remove all problems of uncertainties and expectations from the planning of productive operations, they do not remove all problems of uncertainty and expectations from other sectors of the economy. It may be useful to close this chapter by mentioning the uncertainties which will still remain in our economy.

In the first place, the future levels of the rates of pay for the services of the factors $(W_k \ W_l \ W_n)$ are all uncertain. They will depend upon the future of technical progress and the future supplies of the factors. This means that the future incomes of the citizens are uncertain. This will have considerable importance in the decisions which are made about how much to save and how much to spend on consumption out of current incomes. If future incomes obtainable from existing factors are expected to rise rapidly, the incentive to save now (i.e. to cut down still further today's relatively low standard of consumption in order to raise still further tomorrow's relatively high standard of consumption) will be much reduced.

Secondly, while the stabilization of the price of the product will eliminate the possibility of capital gains or losses on investment in capital equipment, it will not remove the possibility of capital gains or losses on the ownership of land. The future price of land (P_n) may rise or fall above or below the current level, even though the price of the capital good (P_k) is stable. If we imagine conditions in which population is growing rapidly, capital is being accumulated rapidly, and technical inventions are of a sort to make land more and more important in productive processes, then the rent of an acre of land (W_n) will be rising relatively to the rental for a unit of capital equipment. Land will be becoming more valuable relatively to capital equipment; P_n will be rising relatively to P_k; if P_k is stabilized, P_n will be rising absolutely. This possibility of capital gains or losses on land has two important influences in our model.

(1) If a citizen is rational in his attitude towards income and expenditure, he should treat capital gains (or losses) as part of his income. He starts with, say, $1000 of property; during a given period he receives, say, $100 from the hire of the factors he owns (i.e. from wages, rent of land, and rentals on capital equipment) plus (or minus) any interest which he receives (or must pay) on loans which he has lent to (or borrowed from) others; and during the same period the property which he already owns goes up in value by, say, $20. Now if during this period he spends nothing on consumption, he will end up with property worth $1120 ($1000 original property + $100 income from wages, rents, profits, and interest + $20 capital gains). The $120 from income including capital gains is the true income which he has received and which he has available to spend on consumption or to save and to add to his property during the period in question. In brief, in our model capital gains or losses from land are possible; and their influence on the decisions to save or spend must not be forgotten.

(2) The possibility of capital gains on land will affect the present price which a citizen will pay for an acre of land (P_n). In the production process land (N) and capital equipment (K) are very different in their technical features; but to the individual citizen investing money which he has saved or borrowed they are merely two alternative forms of property on which income can be earned—in the case of capital equipment (if its price is successfully stabilized) in the form of the rental (W_k) received on the hiring out of its services and in the case of land from rent (W_n) plus possible capital gain or minus possible capital loss ($_0P_{n1} - P_{n0}$).

From page 39 above we know that when the price of K is not expected to rise or fall, the expected rate of profit on a unit of K will be $_0i'_0 = \dfrac{W_{k0}}{P_{k0}}$, the current rate of return on K. But with complete certainty that the price of capital will not rise or fall, this rate of profit will be expected with complete certainty. In perfect competition, therefore, there will always be an incentive to expand investment in K if the actual rate of interest is less than this current rate of return on K and to invest less in K if the actual rate of interest is greater than this current rate of return. It follows that in competitive equilibrium with a stable price of K the rate of interest must be set by the Central Bank at a level precisely equal to this current rate of return so that

$$i_0 = \frac{W_{k0}}{P_{k0}} \quad \text{or} \quad P_{k0} = \frac{W_{k0}}{i_0}$$

In other words, in such circumstances the price of a unit of K on any day will be equal to the capitalized value of that day's rental.

But in the case of land the price of a unit of land on any day will exceed or fall short of the capitalized value of the day's rent $\left(\dfrac{W_{n0}}{i_0}\right)$ according as, in addition to the rent, a capital gain or loss is expected from a rise or fall in the price of the land itself.

How much the price of land will exceed or fall short of this capitalized value of a day's rent will depend upon the magnitude of the capital gains or losses which different citizens expect, the extent to which they are certain or uncertain about these capital gains, and their attitudes to risk and uncertainty.

We shall postpone a discussion of all these problems of uncertainty until we come to Part 2 of this volume (cf. Chapters XXI and XXII). In a many-product economy we shall be obliged to pay much attention to risk and uncertainty, since they are central features of the productive system itself, whereas in our present one-product model they are of very much less importance. In our present model, if we assume that the Central Bank successfully stabilizes the selling price of the single product, there is no entrepreneurical uncertainty in the productive process itself; and we shall for the present simply neglect the effect which citizens' uncertainties about the future of their incomes and about the future price of land may have upon their decisions about how much to save and about their choice between holding property in the form of land or in the form of real capital.

For the rest of Part 1 of this volume (Chapters III to XIV) we shall assume that the product price (namely, $P_y \equiv P_k$) is stabilized by monetary policy at \$1. It follows that the wage rate of labour, the rental of capital, and the rent of land (namely, W_l, W_k, and W_n) can all represent either the money or the real rewards of the factors. If $W_l = \$100$, then the real wage rate is 100 units of corn; and similarly for W_k and W_n. A unit of corn is in effect not only our unit of measurement of output (Y) and of the capital stock (K); it is in effect our monetary unit of account as well.

CHAPTER III

OF PROPDEMS, PLANTCAPS, AND OTHER STATES OF SOCIETY

Before we turn to an examination of the production system in our one-product perfect-competition capitalist economy there is one more set of institutional arrangements which must be discussed. We have already considered in *The Stationary Economy* (pp. 189–91) the importance of the distinction between the effects of price changes upon the distribution of income and their effects upon the efficiency of the economic system. Thus to give employment to a large amount of labour in a competitive economy endowed with little land and capital may involve a very low real wage rate, particularly if the elasticity of substitution between labour on the one hand and land-cum-capital on the other hand is very low. This will result in a very small proportion of the national output accruing in wages to the workers and in a very large proportion of the national income accruing to the owners of property in the form of rents, interest, and dividends on land and capital.

Whether or not this distribution of income between wage-incomes and property-incomes leads to an unequal distribution of income between individual citizens will depend upon two things: (1) the distribution of earning power between individuals and (2) the distribution of the ownership of property between individuals. As we shall see, these two distributions can play an exceptionally important role in the analysis of a growing economy.

In what follows, until we reach Chapter XIV, we shall illustrate the importance of these two distributions by building our models upon either one or the other of two possible extreme assumptions about the distribution of earning power and of the ownership of property between individuals.

At one extreme we shall assume a perfectly equal distribution of earning power between all individual citizens and a perfectly equal distribution of the ownership of property between them. This we shall call the case of a Property-Owning Democracy or, for brevity, a *Propdem*. In a Propdem every citizen is like every other citizen in that all earn the same wage rate and all own the same amount of property. Every citizen is a representative citizen in that he receives his *pro rata* share of wages and his *pro rata* share of income from property. A change in the distribution of national output between wage incomes and property incomes has no effect upon the distribution of income between individuals.

If we start on day 0 in a Propdem, we shall stay in a Propdem only if all citizens save the same proportion of their incomes. If, however, Mr A saves more than Mr B then, though both started on day 0 with the same property and the same income, on day 1 Mr A will own more property than Mr B. We would no longer be in a true Propdem. We must, therefore, assume for a continuing Propdem (i) that all citizens have the same earning power, (ii) that all citizens start with the same amount of property on day 0, and (iii) that all citizens have the same savings function, i.e. that faced with the same personal income, the same rate of interest, etc., each citizen saves the same amount of income.

It is not in fact an essential feature of assumption (iii) that the proportion (S) of income saved by each citizen should be constant over time, but only that in the circumstances ruling at any one time this proportion S should be the same for every citizen. The savings proportion may in fact rise or fall as income per head rises or falls or as the rate of interest goes up or down. At a later stage of our analysis (Chapters XII and XIII) we shall have to consider these possibilities in more detail. But for the time being we shall in fact assume (though it is not a necessary feature of a true Propdem) that the savings proportion S is not only the same at any given time for all citizens, but also that it is fixed and constant over time regardless of what may be happening to income per head or the rate of interest or any other variable in the economic system.

Moreover we have in one other way also overstated the conditions necessary for a true Propdem. It is not strictly necessary that at any one moment of time every citizen should earn the same amount of wages, own the same amount of property, and save the same amount of incomes as every other citizen, but only that every citizen of any given age at any given point of time should earn, own, and save the same as every other citizen of that same age at the same point of time. We shall at a later stage in our enquiry (see Chapters XII and XIII) allow for the fact that each citizen may have a life-cycle of earnings, property-ownership, and savings—earning nothing in childhood and in retirement but much during working life, saving much during working life and dissaving during retirement, owning property on retirement all or part of which he may consume during retirement. The essential feature of a Propdem is that all citizens born at any point of time go through the same life-cycle so that at any point of time all citizens of a given age are earning, saving, and owning the same amounts.

The Growing Economy

Solely for simplicity of exposition we shall for the time being neglect the life-cycle of earnings, savings, and ownership and refer to a Propdem as a society in which at any given point of time every citizen is like every other citizen in these respects. We will correct this over-simplification in Chapters XII and XIII.

So much for a Propdem. At the other extreme we shall assume that there are two quite distinct types of citizen—a two-nation economy. There are workers who do all the work and who own no property and there are capitalists who own all the property and who do no work. We will call this a case of Plantation Capitalism or, for short, a *Plantcap*. In a pure Plantcap at any given time every worker of a given age earns the same wage as every other worker of that same age and every capitalist of a given age owns the same amount of property as every other capitalist of that same age. But the distribution of the national output between individuals is now vitally affected by the distribution of income between wage-income and property-income. A shift from wages to property-incomes is a shift from those individuals who are workers to those individuals who are capitalists.

If we start now on day 0 in a Plantcap, we shall remain in a Plantcap only if all savings are made by capitalists and no savings by workers. For a true continuing Plantcap we must, therefore, assume (i) that all workers have the same earning power, (ii) that all workers start on day 0 with zero property and save nothing, (iii) that all capitalists do no work, and (iv) that all capitalists start on day 0 with the same amount of property and have the same savings function.

It is not an essential feature of assumption (iv) that the proportion (S_p) of his property income which each property owner saves should be constant over time, but only that, given the level of the relevant variables at any one time, this proportion should be the same for each capitalist so that property should remain equally distributed between the capitalists. But for the time being we shall assume that in a Plantcap the proportion of property-incomes saved (S_p) does in fact remain constant over time.

These two cases of Propdems and Plantcaps, are, of course, extremes which are never fully realized in practice. In the real world a private-enterprise economy is likely to be of an intermediate kind— some citizens being mainly workers but owning some property and others owning much property but receiving also an earned income. Such a mixed state of Society we will call a *Propcap* (i.e. a Property-Owning Capitalism). At a later stage (Chapter XIV) we shall consider some of the factors which will decide whether a Propcap is likely to approximate towards a Propdem or towards a Plantcap.

Propdems, Plantcaps, and Propcaps are not the only possible forms of Society. Governmental measures may be taken to make a Propcap function more nearly as a Propdem and less as a Plantcap. It is possible by a system of progressive income tax (falling mainly on rich property owners) the proceeds of which were used to pay social benefits to the poor (mainly the workers) largely to equalize personal incomes in what would otherwise be essentially a Plantcap. Suppose that in such an economy there were a structural change which caused a smaller proportion of the national income to represent wage costs and a larger proportion to represent rents and profits. With a progressive tax-subsidy system such a shift of income from pre-subsidy wages to pre-tax property-incomes would not in fact cause an equivalent shift from workers to property owners, because much of the shifted income would be levied in tax on rich capitalists and paid back in benefits to poor workers.[1] A state of Society in which progressive taxes and subsidies were introduced into a Plantcap or a Propcap in order virtually to divorce the personal distribution of income from the distribution of income between wages and property incomes we may call a *Welstat* (i.e. a Welfare State).

At a later stage in this volume (Chapter XIX) we shall turn to a consideration of these same issues in a planned socialist economy—what for short we may call a *Plansoc*. In such an economy all property is owned by the State and all savings for the finance of additions to the real capital of the community are made through the State which distributes in incomes to the individual citizens for expenditure on their personal consumption less than the value of the total output of the community—the difference being used by the State to acquire capital equipment for capital development. In such a system a set of 'shadow' or 'accounting' prices for the factors of production ('shadow' wage rates for various types of labour, 'shadow' rents for various types of natural resource, 'shadow' prices for various types of man-made instruments of production, a 'shadow' rate of interest, and so on) can be used to guide the managers of the socialized plants to make the most efficient use of resources by maximizing the excess of the 'shadow' value of their output over the 'shadow' costs of their inputs. But the actual personal incomes of the citizens can to a large extent be divorced from the 'shadow' values of their services by various means such as the adjustment through taxation or subsidization by the State of the 'shadow' earnings of the workers. (See *The Stationary Economy*, Chapters XIV and XV.)

Prices or rentals of factors of production have in fact a double role to play: first, as guides to efficient production, marking scarce factors as expensive and plentiful factors as cheap; and, second, as

---

[1] Such a policy raises, of course, very important issues concerning the effects of such fiscal arrangements upon incentives to work, enterprise, and save. But these issues will not be discussed in this volume.

mechanisms for the personal distribution of income and wealth, paying much to those who own a great amount of scarce factors and little to those who own but a small amount of plentiful factors. Propdems, Welstats, and Plansocs have one basic feature in common; in each case the two roles played by factor prices are divorced from each other in the sense that, while variations in the prices of factors are used as guides to the efficient use of resources, nevertheless they do not imply variations in the distribution of incomes between individuals.

There remains yet one more basic form of Society which for the sake of completeness we will mention, although we shall not discuss it in this volume. This is the state of Society in which factor prices are consciously used as a means for varying the distribution of income among individuals without countering the effect which such a policy may have in inducing an inefficient use of resources. We will call this the Trade Union Community or, for short, the *Tradcom*. For example, by trade union action or by State regulation minimum wage rates may be fixed for certain groups of workers who would otherwise receive low personal incomes or maximum rents may be set for certain natural resources whose owners might otherwise receive unreasonably high incomes. Such action may well cause an inefficient excess supply (i.e. unemployment) of the labour in question and an inefficient excess demand for the natural resource whose employment may no longer be confined by a high cost to the uses in which it is most productive. Plantcaps and Tradcoms have this in common; in both cases the two roles of factor prices (as guides to the use of resources and as mechanisms for the personal distribution of incomes) are not divorced from each other. But while in a Plantcap factor prices are used to obtain an efficient use of resources (at the expense of a just distribution of income) in a Tradcom they are used to obtain a just distribution of income (at the expense of an efficient use of resources).

In the immediately following chapters (Chapters IV to XIII) we shall analyse economic growth in a fully competitive society which takes the extreme form either of a Propdem or of a Plantcap. Propcaps, Plansocs, and Welstats will make their appearance at later stages in this volume. Tradcoms will not reappear.

Having now, in the preceding chapter, set up a model for a competitive economy of a financial policy which will maintain monetary demand so as to preserve full employment and having, in this chapter, outlined two simple institutional models relating to the distribution of earning power and of the ownership of property in such a competitive economy, we are at last in a position to consider the factors determining the growth of the productive potential in such an economy.

CHAPTER IV

THE ONE-PRODUCT MODEL OF CAPITALISTIC PRODUCTION

We build our model of the productive system in the following way. We assume that there is one product (Y) whose daily output is either consumed (Y_c) or used to put back as an instrument of production or capital good into the productive system (Y_k). We assume that there are three factors of production: the capital good (K), labour (L), and land (N). We can express this basic production system in the following way:

$$Y = Y_c + Y_k = F(K\, L\, N\, t) \qquad (4.1)$$

where t stands for time and thus dates the day's production with which we are concerned. The expression states that the day's output (Y) which is used either for consumption (Y_c) or for investment in the productive system (Y_k) depends upon, or is a function of, ($F[\ldots\ldots]$) the amounts of the factors (K, L, and N) used for the day's production and upon the actual date (t) of the day's operations, since this will determine whether modern advanced knowledge or only old-fashioned techniques of production are available. Let us comment on the meaning of this expression in more detail.

In the above production function Y measures the day's *net* output of the product and K measures the size of the capital stock of the product whose services were available for use on the day in question. In terms of our simple example of corn-farming, suppose 1000 units of corn seed were sown on the morning of day t and that at the end of the day as a result of the day's farming operations 1100 units of corn were available in one form or another on the farm. Then $K = 1000$ and $Y = 1100 - 1000 = 100$. The net output of the farm on day t is only 100 units because, out of the gross output of 1100, 1000 units are required to replace the capital stock of corn for the next day's farming operations.

If of this net output of 100 units of corn, 60 move into the shops and are consumed at 8 a.m. on day $t + 1$, then $Y_c = 60$ and Y_k, therefore, $= 40$. Y_k thus measures the increase in the capital stock of corn available for the next day's operations. At the beginning of day t $K = 1000$; at the beginning of day $t + 1$ $K = 1000 + 40$.

This is the process of postponement of consumption for the purpose of capital accumulation.

We are saying that the net output of the product available at the end of any day (Y) depends upon, or is a function of, the inputs at the beginning of that day of capital stock (K), labour (L), and land (N). But this production function may change from day to day as a result of improved technical knowledge. Tomorrow given amounts of K, L, and N may be able to produce more Y than they could today. This we express by saying that Y depends not only upon the size of the factor inputs (K, L, and N) but also upon the actual date of the operations (t), since as time passes technical progress may raise the productivity of the factors of production.

Each of the three factors K, L, and N will contribute to the output Y and each, therefore, will have a marginal product.[1] That is to say, there will be a specific increase in the day's net output of Y which would result from an increase of one unit in the amount of K available for use, with L and N constant; this would measure the marginal product of the capital stock K. And similarly for the marginal products of labour (L) and land (N). We will express the marginal products of K, L, and N at any one time as $\dfrac{\partial Y}{\partial K}$, $\dfrac{\partial Y}{\partial L}$, and $\dfrac{\partial Y}{\partial N}$ respectively.[2] The marginal products of labour $\left(\dfrac{\partial Y}{\partial L}\right)$ and of land $\left(\dfrac{\partial Y}{\partial N}\right)$ present no difficulties which have not already been explored in Chapters VII and VIII of *The Stationary Economy*. They are simply

---

[1] The analysis is exactly comparable to that used in Chapters VII and VIII of *The Stationary Economy*.

[2] The reader who is unfamiliar with the differential calculus need not abandon hope at this point. Consider the expression $\dfrac{\partial Y}{\partial L}$ for the marginal product of labour. Suppose that 3 extra workers are added to a very large working force (so that 3 workers are a very small addition to the total labour force), that there is no change in the amount of capital equipment (K) or land (N), and that as a result of the small increase in the labour force the day's output of corn goes up by 60 grains. This we express by saying that there is an increase of ∂L (3 men) in the labour force which causes a rise of ∂Y (60 grains of corn) in the output. The marginal product of labour is then 60 grains of corn per 3 men or 20 grains of corn per man, i.e. $\dfrac{60 \text{ grains of corn}}{3 \text{ men}}$ or $\dfrac{\partial Y}{\partial L}$. $\dfrac{\partial Y}{\partial L}$ means, therefore, the small increment of output (∂Y) which would result from an increment of 1 unit in the input of labour ($\partial L = 1$) on the assumption that all other inputs are constant. Thus $\dfrac{\partial Y}{\partial L}$ simply means the marginal product of labour; and similarly for $\dfrac{\partial Y}{\partial K}$ and $\dfrac{\partial Y}{\partial N}$.

the additions to output brought about by the use of a unit increase of labour or a unit increase of land respectively. In essence the marginal product of the capital good $\left(\frac{\partial Y}{\partial K}\right)$ is the same; it is the increase in the net daily output of corn which would be caused by having a unit increase in the stock of corn seed in use in the farm. But it has one special feature in our one-product model; because the output (Y) is measured in the same units as the input (K)—e.g. both in terms of corn—it can be expressed as a rate of return, a rate of interest, or a rate of profit. The marginal product of labour must be measured in terms such as 60 units of daily corn output per 3 additional men employed on the farm or 20 units of daily corn output per man (see footnote 2 on page 50). The marginal product of the capital good, however, will be measured in terms such as 10 grains of daily corn output per 10,000 additional grains of seed corn maintained on the farm or a rate of return of $0 \cdot 1$ per cent per day on an increment in the stock of the capital good. On our assumption that there are 100 days in a year, this would represent a marginal rate of return on the capital stock (K) at a daily rate of 10 per cent per annum. We shall have to return to this measurement of the marginal productivity of capital in due course. For the time being we can treat it in exactly the same way as the marginal productivity of any other factor. $\frac{\partial Y}{\partial K}$ thus measures the increase in the daily output of corn which would be caused by having one more unit of corn in the capital stock of corn, the other factors remaining unchanged in amount.

Let us consider then how we can express economic growth in terms of this very simple one-product capitalistic production function. In fact between day 1 and day 2 there are four conceivable reasons why net output (Y) may rise: the capital stock (K) may be greater because more real capital has been accumulated, the amount of work done (L) may be greater because of an increase in the size of the population, the amount of land available for use (N) may for some reason or another be greater,[1] and finally technical progress may be occurring which enables more to be produced with any given amounts of the factors. We can express this by saying that the increase in net output between day 1 and day 2 will be equal to the increase in the supply of capital times the marginal product of capital *plus* the increase in the supply of labour times the marginal product of labour *plus* the

---

[1] We shall in due course revert to the assumption that the amount of land is fixed and unalterable. But let us for the moment assume that we are in the Netherlands in order to be able to examine certain characteristics of our production function which are brought out best if the inputs of all three factors are changing.

increase in the supply of land times the marginal product of land *plus* the remaining increase in the output due simply to technical progress or

$$\Delta Y = \frac{\partial Y}{\partial K} \Delta K + \frac{\partial Y}{\partial L} \Delta L + \frac{\partial Y}{\partial N} \Delta N + \Delta Y'$$

where ΔY is the increase in output between day 1 and day 2, ΔK, ΔL, and ΔN are the increases in the amounts of K, L, and N respectively, and $\Delta Y'$ is the increase in output due solely to technical progress. This expression can be written as

$$\frac{\Delta Y}{Y} = \frac{K}{Y}\frac{\partial Y}{\partial K}\frac{\Delta K}{K} + \frac{L}{Y}\frac{\partial Y}{\partial L}\frac{\Delta L}{L} + \frac{N}{Y}\frac{\partial Y}{\partial N}\frac{\Delta N}{N} + \frac{\Delta Y'}{Y}$$

or

$$y = Uk + Ql + Zn + r \qquad (4.2)$$

where $y = \dfrac{\Delta Y}{Y}$, $k = \dfrac{\Delta K}{K}$, $l = \dfrac{\Delta L}{L}$, $n = \dfrac{\Delta N}{N}$, $r = \dfrac{\Delta Y'}{Y}$, $U = \dfrac{K}{Y}\dfrac{\partial Y}{\partial K}$,

$Q = \dfrac{L}{Y}\dfrac{\partial Y}{\partial L}$, and $Z = \dfrac{N}{Y}\dfrac{\partial Y}{\partial N}$.

Let us consider this final form of our expression in some detail. Since ΔY is the increase in output between one day and the next and Y is the existing level of output, $\dfrac{\Delta Y}{Y}$ or y measures the proportional rate of growth of output. Thus if $\Delta Y = 10$ and $Y = 10,000$, output is growing by 10 units a day on an initial level of 10,000 or at a rate of $\dfrac{10}{10,000}$ or $0\cdot1$ per cent per day. With a year of 100 days, we could say that between these two days output was growing at a daily rate of $100 \times 0\cdot1$ or 10 per cent per annum. Thus $y\left(\equiv \dfrac{\Delta Y}{Y}\right)$ measures the proportional rate of growth (or what for short we will call the growth rate) of the national income. Similarly k, l, and n represent the growth rates of the factors K, L, and N. In exactly the same way $r\left(\equiv \dfrac{\Delta Y'}{Y}\right)$ measures the growth rate in output which would have occurred as a result of technical progress if there had been no increase in the factor supplies (i.e. if $k = l = n = 0$); and this we will call the rate of technical progress.

Our expression $y = Uk + Ql + Zn + r$ thus represents the relationship between the growth rate of output and the growth rates of the inputs and the rate of technical progress, which cause the growth of output. U, Q, and Z clearly measure the contributions which the growth rates in the various factor supplies make to the growth of output. We must examine their meaning with some care.

Consider Q which determines the contribution of the growth rate of the labour supply (l) to the growth rate of output (y). Now $Q = \frac{L}{Y}\frac{\partial Y}{\partial L}$. This can be regarded in any one of three ways: (i) either as the proportional marginal product of labour or (ii) as the proportion of the total net output Y which would be paid in wages if labour were paid a wage equal to the value of its marginal product or (iii) as the ratio between the marginal and the average product of labour.

$$\frac{L}{Y}\frac{\partial Y}{\partial L} = \frac{\partial Y}{Y} \div \frac{\partial L}{L}$$ or the percentage increase in net output $\left(\frac{\partial Y}{Y}\right)$

which would be caused by a given percentage increase in the amount of labour $\left(\frac{\partial L}{L}\right)$ if the supply of capital goods and technical knowledge were unchanged. For example, if a 1 per cent increase in L would cause a $\frac{1}{2}$ of 1 per cent increase in Y, then $\frac{\partial Y}{Y} \div \frac{\partial L}{L} = \frac{1}{2}$. Regarded in this light we can consider $\frac{L}{Y}\frac{\partial Y}{\partial L}$ as being the proportional marginal product of L.

But $\frac{L}{Y}\frac{\partial Y}{\partial L} = \frac{L\frac{\partial Y}{\partial L}}{Y}$. Since $\frac{\partial Y}{\partial L}$ is the marginal product of L, $L\frac{\partial Y}{\partial L}$ is the total income which would be paid to L if L were paid a reward equal to its marginal product. It follows that $\frac{L\frac{\partial L}{\partial Y}}{Y}$ is the proportion of the total net output (Y) which would go in wages $\left(L\frac{\partial Y}{\partial L}\right)$ if labour (L) were paid a reward equal to its marginal product $\left(\frac{\partial Y}{\partial L}\right)$. Regarded in this way $\frac{L}{Y}\frac{\partial Y}{\partial L}$ is the proportion of the national output which will be paid in wages if labour is paid a reward equal to its marginal product.

But $\frac{L}{Y}\frac{\partial Y}{\partial L}$ also $= \frac{\partial Y}{\partial L} \div \frac{Y}{L}$. But $\frac{\partial Y}{\partial L}$ is the marginal product of labour and $\frac{Y}{L}$ is output per head or the average product of labour, so that, regarded in this way, $\frac{L}{Y}\frac{\partial Y}{\partial L}$ measures the ratio of the marginal to the average product of labour.

The similar proportional marginal net product of land Z or $\frac{N}{Y}\frac{\partial Y}{\partial N}$ measures the percentage increase in his output which any entrepreneur could achieve by using 1 per cent more land; this will also measure the proportion of the national output going to rents in our perfectly competitive economy; and it will also measure the ratio of the marginal to the average product of land.

Similarly, U or $\frac{K}{Y}\frac{\partial Y}{\partial K}$ can be regarded either as the proportional net marginal product of the capital stock K (i.e. the percentage increase in net output which would occur if the capital stock increased by 1 per cent without any change in the amount of labour or land employed or in technical knowledge) or as the proportion of the national income that would be paid out as interest on the capital stock if capital were paid a 'reward' equal to its net marginal product or as the ratio between the marginal and the average product of capital.

In the case of U, the proportional marginal product of capital, there is an important special relationship to be noted. We can rewrite $U = \frac{K}{Y}\frac{\partial Y}{\partial K}$ as $\frac{\partial Y}{\partial K} = \frac{UY}{K}$. We have already seen that the marginal product of capital $\left(\frac{\partial Y}{\partial K}\right)$ in our one-product model can be expressed as a rate of profit, e.g. as 10 per cent per annum. This is clearly true of the expression $\frac{UY}{K}$; since in a competitive economy U is the proportion of the national income going to profits, UY is total profits and $UY \div K$ is profit per unit of capital. When the money price of K is constant we know that the rate of profit will be equal to $\frac{W_k}{P_k}$ (see page 39 above); and if the money price of our single product $(P_k \equiv P_y)$ is stabilized at unity (see page 43 above), then the rate of profit $\left(\frac{W_k}{P_k}\right)$ is numerically equal to the money rental (W_k). Moreover in a competitive economy (see page 42 above) the rate of interest (i) must be equal to the rate of profit (i') so that we have

$$i = i' = \frac{UY}{K} = \frac{W_k}{P_k} = W_k \qquad (4.3)$$

We shall make frequent use of these relationships in what follows.

There is also an important relationship between U, Q, and Z to be noted. Constant returns to scale mean that if all three factors were increased by 1 per cent (without any change in technical knowledge) then total output would also increase by 1 per cent. This means that the sum of the three proportional marginal products $(U + Q + Z)$ of K, L, and N would be equal to one. If, for example, U and Q both $= \frac{1}{4}$, this would mean that Z must $= \frac{1}{2}$; for if a 1 per cent increase in K causes Y to rise by $\frac{1}{4}$ per cent and a 1 per cent increase in L causes Y to rise by another $\frac{1}{4}$ per cent, a 1 per cent rise in N must cause Y to rise by the remaining $\frac{1}{2}$ per cent in order that a 1 per cent rise in all three factors should in combination cause Y to increase by a full 1 per cent. It follows that if the proportional marginal product of land (Z) is positive, $U + Q$ must be less than unity.

Another way of seeing this relationship is as follows. We have already shown in Chapter VIII (pp. 107–9) of *The Stationary Economy* that if there are constant returns to scale the payment to each factor of a reward equal to its marginal product will account for the whole of the net output produced, neither more nor less. It follows that where there are three factors, K, L, and N, the proportion of the national output going to K when K is paid its marginal product *plus* the proportion going to L when L is paid its marginal product *plus* the proportion going to N when N is paid its net marginal product will just add up to the whole of the national output. In other words, $U + Q + Z = 1$.

We can now leave the Netherlands and revert to the assumption that the amount of land is fixed so that $n = 0$. We can then write equation (4.2) as

$$y = Uk + Ql + r \qquad (4.4)$$

where y, k, and l are the proportional rates of growth of Y, K, and L respectively, where r is the rate of technical progress, where U is the proportional marginal product of K, or the proportion of the national income paid out in profit on capital, and where Q is the proportional marginal product of L or the proportion of the national product paid out in wages. When necessary we will write $Z (= 1 - U - Q)$ as the proportion of the national output going to rent of land. This is the simple basic formula for the rates of equilibrium growth in our simple one-product model of competitive capitalistic production.[1]

---

[1] The simple-minded reader, like the author, may find it illuminating to consider a simple numerical example at this stage. Suppose that the rate of technical progress (r) were 2 per cent per annum, that the balance of births and deaths gave a rate of growth of the working population (l) of 1 per cent per annum, that the savings habits of the community were causing the capital stock of the man-made instrument of production to accumulate at a rate of growth (k) of 3 per cent per annum, that the proportional marginal product of capital (U) were $\frac{1}{4}$, and that the proportional marginal product of labour (Q) were $\frac{1}{2}$. Then total net output would be growing at a rate (y) of $\frac{1}{4} \times 3$ per cent $+ \frac{1}{2} \times 1$ per cent $+ 2$

We must now say something further about the term r in equations (4.2) and (4.4). This term is simply a measure of the extent of technical progress in the sense that it measures the proportional rate at which output could be raised simply by improved technical knowledge and without any change in the amounts of the factors themselves. But this says nothing about the nature of the improvement in technical knowledge. If $r = 2$ per cent, then, with the given amounts of K, L, and N, 2 per cent more can be produced than before. But this does not imply any answer to the question whether the technical progress is of a kind which makes L much more (or much less) valuable at the margin relatively to K and N. Is the invention one which in some sense saves K and N relatively to L or saves L relatively to K and N? Moreover, perhaps at the moment the economy is working with much L relatively to K and N; it is using labour-intensive methods of production; if $r = 2$ per cent, we know that with these methods of production 2 per cent more could be produced with the same factors; but suppose that the economy had in the past accumulated more capital and was now working with more capital-intensive methods of production; would the same improvement in technical knowledge still enable 2 per cent more to be produced than could have been produced in its absence?

For some very limited purposes it is sufficient to know the value of r, i.e. the extent to which output can be increased with the existing equipment of resources of capital, labour, and land. But for the great majority of questions of economic interest it is necessary to know much more about the nature of technical progress: e.g. does it tend to save one factor rather than another? is it more helpful to labour-intensive than to capital-intensive economic systems? and so on.

Technical improvements can, of course, be of any kind and have any sort of effect upon inputs of factors and outputs of products, provided only that they enable some inputs to be reduced without a reduction of output or output to be increased without an increase in inputs. But in order to be able to build models of the economic system which can be handled with relative ease, we shall confine ourselves to the examination of the effects of technical improvements all of which fall within a limited, though very broad, class of improvements. We shall confine our attention to technical progress which takes the form of some combination of what we shall call labour-expanding, capital-expanding, land-expanding, or output-expanding technical progress. Let us explain what we mean by these terms.

per cent p.a. or $3\frac{1}{4}$ per cent p.a. of which $\frac{1}{4} \times 3$ per cent would be due to capital accumulation $\frac{1}{4} \times 1$ per cent to population growth and 2 per cent to technical progress.

Suppose some technical wizard were to visit the economy each year and, waving his effective magic wand over the whole economy, were to say: 'Let there be a need for 100 units of labour wherever there would have been a need for 102, had I not waved this wand.' Then we would say that there was technical progress taking the form of a 2-per-cent-per-annum labour-expansion. Whatever techniques of production were being used, whether labour-intensive or capital-intensive, 100 men would next year do the effective work which 102 men would otherwise have been needed to do.

Similarly there would be capital-expanding technical progress of 3 per cent per annum if our technical wizard were to say: 'Let there be a need for 100 units of capital wherever there would otherwise have been a need for 103'; and there would be land-expanding technical progress of 1 per cent per annum if he were to say: 'Let there be a need for 100 units of land wherever there would otherwise have been a need for 101.'

Our technical wizard might, however, have said: 'Let there be 104 units of output wherever there would have been 100, had I not waved this wand.' This change we may define as being due to output-expanding technical progress at a rate of 4 per cent per annum. But it would, of course, be output-expanding technical progress only if the 4 per cent improvement in output would occur without any change in the inputs of K, L, or N, whatever those inputs might be, regardless, that is to say, of whether labour-intensive, capital-intensive, or land-intensive techniques were being used.

In the case of factor-expanding technical progress we need to distinguish between a factor of production measured in 'natural units' and the same factor of production measured in 'efficiency units'. If, for example, the number of workers is going up by 2 per cent per annum but technical progress is expanding the effectiveness of each worker by 3 per cent per annum, then the labour force in natural units is rising by 2 per cent per annum but in efficiency units it is rising by $2 + 3 = 5$ per cent per annum; and the effect upon output and, indeed, upon the whole of the productive system is exactly as if the labour force had risen by 5 per cent without any technical progress.

Let us write $L^* = LL'$ where L^* measures the amount of labour in efficiency units and L the amount of labour in natural units. $L' \left(= \dfrac{L^*}{L} \right)$ then measures the effectiveness of labour, i.e. the amount of effective work done by each natural man. We can then write $l^* = l + l'$ where l^* is the growth rate of labour in efficiency units, l the growth rate of the working population, and l' the rate of labour-expanding technical progress. We can have similar relationships between the efficiency and the natural units for the other factors, so that

$$
\left.
\begin{array}{ll}
L^* = L L' & \text{and} \quad l^* = l + l' \\
K^* = K K' & \text{and} \quad k^* = k + k' \\
N^* = N N' & \text{and} \quad n^* = n + n'
\end{array}
\right\} \tag{4.5}
$$

We will also write y' for the rate of output-expanding technical progress.

There is one further similar set of relationships which we must consider. Suppose W_l is the money wage per man hour of labour and that L' is the amount of effective work achieved by a man hour of labour. Then we may write $W_l^* = \dfrac{W_l}{L'}$ where W_l^* is the money wage cost per effective unit of work achieved. Thus if the money wage rate (W_l) remains constant, but the effectiveness of each unit of labour (L') is doubled, the money cost per unit of effective work achieved W_l^*) is halved. We may call W_l^* the wage rate of labour measured in effective units and W_l the wage rate of labour measured in natural units. For small changes (see page 18 above) we may write $w_l^* = w_l - l'$ or $w_l = w_l^* + l'$, i.e. the growth rate of the wage per head is equal to the growth rate of the wage cost per effective unit of labour *plus* the growth rate in the effectiveness of labour. Similar relationships hold for the other factors so that we have

$$
\left.
\begin{array}{ll}
W_l^* = \dfrac{W_l}{L'} & \text{and} \quad w_l = w_l^* + l' \\[2ex]
W_k^* = \dfrac{W_k}{K'} & \text{and} \quad w_k = w_k^* + k' \\[2ex]
W_n^* = \dfrac{W_n}{N'} & \text{and} \quad w_n = w_n^* + n'
\end{array}
\right\} \tag{4.6}
$$

In what follows we will suppose that year by year there are constant rates of labour-expanding, capital-expanding, land-expanding, and output-expanding technical progress (i.e. constant values of l', k', n', and y'). We can now proceed to express r, the combined rate of technical progress in any one year, in terms of a combination of l', k', n', and y' which in our models will be the underlying components of r.

Suppose that technical progress had been solely labour-expanding ($k' = n' = y' = 0$). Then we could rewrite equation (4.2) in the form

$$
\begin{aligned}
y &= Uk + Q(l + l') + Zn \\
&= Uk + Ql + Zn + Ql'
\end{aligned} \tag{4.7}
$$

The meaning of labour-expanding technical progress at a rate l' is simply that it is as if the labour force had grown by $l + l'$ instead of by l and there had been no other change in technical knowledge. We can, therefore, transform equation (4.2) by omitting r from equation (4.2) and instead of r replacing l with $l + l'$ in the equation; and thus we get equation (4.7).

In a similar manner capital-expanding (or land-expanding) technical progress could be shown by replacing k with $k + k'$ (or n with $n + n'$) i.e. equation (4.2) and omitting r from the equation. In order to express output-expanding technical progress one would need simply to replace r in equation (4.2) with y'. For with output-expanding technical progress alone no distinction is to be drawn between natural and efficiency units for the factors, but—whatever may happen to the growth of the factors in natural units—output is higher than it would have been in the absence of technical progress in a proportion equal to y'. Thus with output-expanding technical progress equation (4.2) can be rewritten in the form

$$y = Uk + Ql + Zn + y' \qquad (4.8)$$

Now we can allow for any combination of factor-expanding or of output-expanding forms of technical progress, so that from equations (4.7) and (4.8) we can rewrite equation (4.2) as:

$$\begin{aligned} y &= U(k + k') + Q(l + l') + Z(n + n') + y' \\ &= Uk + Ql + Zn + y' + Uk' + Ql' + Zn' \qquad (4.9) \end{aligned}$$

This is exactly the same as equation (4.2) with

$$r = y' + Uk' + Ql' + Zn' \qquad (4.10)$$

In fact the rate of technical progress r is simply the sum of the rates of output-expanding technical progress and of factor-expanding technical progress, the latter weighted by the proportional marginal products of the relevant factors (U, Q, and Z).

With constant returns to scale $U + Q + Z = 1$ (cf. p. 55 above). It follows that $y' = Uy' + Qy' + Zy'$. In other words there is in this case no relevant economic distinction between output-expanding technical progress of y' and a combination of capital-expanding technical progress of y' *plus* labour-expanding technical progress of y' *plus* land-expanding technical progress of y'. The economic common-sense of this is clear. If $y' = 2$ per cent, then this means that one can produce 2 per cent more with the same amount of the factors. But if one then reduced all the factors by 2 per cent, one would— because of constant returns to scale—reduce output by 2 per cent back to its original level. Thus to say that one could always produce

2 per cent more with the same amount of the factors is the same thing as saying that one could always produce an unchanged amount with 2 per cent less of each of the factors.

With $y' = Uy' + Qy' + Zy'$

one can rewrite (4.10) as

$$r = U(k' + y') + Q(l' + y') + Z(n' + y')$$

We can, therefore, if we so wish cease altogether to consider output-expanding technical progress. For suppose that there were capital-expanding technical progress of 1 per cent, labour-expanding technical progress of 2 per cent, land-expanding technical progress of 3 per cent, and output-expanding technical progress of 4 per cent, this would be economically (in conditions of constant returns to scale) exactly the same thing as saying that there was capital-expanding technical progress of 5 per cent, labour-expanding technical progress of 6 per cent, and land-expanding technical progress of 7 per cent. Accordingly we shall in what follows speak only in terms of factor-expanding technical progress, having incorporated all output-expanding technical progress into the measures of factor-expanding technical progress. We can accordingly rewrite (4.9) and (4.10) as

$$\left.\begin{array}{l} y = Uk + Ql + Zn + r \text{ where } r = Uk' + Ql' + Zn' \\ \text{or, if we suppose that } N \text{ is constant (i.e. } n = 0\text{), as} \\ y = Uk + Ql + r \text{ where } r = Uk' + Ql' + Zn' \end{array}\right\} \quad (4.11)$$

The rate of technical progress, r, in (4.11) will not necessarily be constant even though k', l', and n' are all constant. But there are two very relevant conditions in either of which r will in fact be constant.

In the first place, if $k' = l' = n'$ we have (since $U + Q + Z = 1$) $r = k' = l' = n'$. r will then be constant at this value. This is, of course, the case of pure output-expanding technical progress at a rate y'. As we have seen, $y' = Uy' + Qy' + Zy'$, so that if k', l', and n' are all constant at the same level y', we have simply $r = y'$.

In the second place, even if k', l', and n' are not equal to each other, r in equation (4.11) will be constant if U, Q, and Z are constant; and U, Q, and Z will remain constant if the elasticities of substitution between the factors capital, labour, and land are all numerically equal to unity. This can be seen in the following way. Now that we are confining our attention solely to factor-expanding technical progress we are dealing, as it were, with an unchanged relationship or production function expressing output as the result of given inputs of capital, labour, and land measured in efficiency units. Let us then confine our attention to output and to the amounts of factors measured in efficiency units required to produce that output. We have already shown in *The Stationary Economy*[1] that if all elasticities of substitution are numerically equal to unity changes in factor proportions will have no effect upon the distribution of income. If, for example, labour rises relatively to capital and to land, the increased amount of labour earning wages relatively to the amounts of capital and land earning profits and rents (which will tend to raise the share of wages) will be just offset by the fall in the marginal product and so in the wage per unit of labour relatively to the rent or rental per unit of land and capital (which will tend to lower the share of wages). Thus with elasticities of substitution between the factors all numerically equal to unity, the proportional marginal products of the factors (and so the shares of the total output going to the factors) —namely U, Q, and Z—will remain constant. Thus in this case from equation (4.11) with constant k', l', and n', r will also be constant.

We are now in a position to consider how various types of technical progress may in themselves tend to raise or to lower the demand for one factor relatively to another. In order to simplify the exposition let us consider a two-factor economy; we assume, that is to say, that labour and capital, but no land, are required for production. Output is the result of certain inputs of capital and of labour, both measured in efficiency units. In order to isolate the effects of technical progress let us assume that there is no capital accumulation in natural units (i.e. no saving) and no population growth. Output grows solely because capital becomes more effective at a rate k' and labour more effective at a rate l'. We will consider the three cases $k' < l'$, $k' = l'$, and $k' > l'$, i.e. the three cases in which technical progress is predominantly labour-expanding, predominantly output-expanding, or predominantly capital-expanding. We wish to know whether these various types of technical progress will shift demand relatively from labour to capital or *vice versa*. We will say that the invention is biassed against wages (or against profits) if it tends to lower (or to raise) Q (the proportional marginal product of labour) and to raise (or to lower) U (the proportional marginal product of capital).

It can readily be seen that the effect of the improvement in technical knowledge depends not only upon the form of the technical progress but also upon the size of the elasticity of substitution between the factors. This is shown in Table I where μ stands for the numerical value of the elasticity of substitution between the two factors capital and labour, measured in efficiency units. The entries in Table I, namely $+$, 0, and $-$, depict the situations in which Q, the proportion of the national income going to labour, will rise, remain

[1] See *The Stationary Economy*, pp. 114–15 and 47–50.

unchanged, or fall. All the entries in the cases in which $k' = l'$ are 0, because if both factors, measured in efficiency units, increase by the same proportion, there will be no change in the proportions in which they are employed and so no change in their relative marginal productivities.[1] Also all the entries in the cases in which $\mu = 1$ are zero; for when the elasticity of substitution between the two factors measured in efficiency units is numerically equal to unity, a change in factor proportions will, as we have just seen, leave the distribution of income between them unchanged.

Table I

	$k' < l'$	$k' = l'$	$k' > l''$
$\mu > 1$	+	0	−
$\mu = 1$	0	0	0
$\mu < 1$	−	0	+

But consider the case in which $k' < l'$ and $\mu > 1$. Now, measured in efficiency units, labour is rising relatively to capital; if the elasticity of substitution between the two factors is high ($\mu > 1$), then the proportional change in the relative prices of the factors will be less than the proportional change in their relative quantities; labour will gain more by being larger in amount relatively to capital than it will lose by having a lower reward per unit relatively to that of capital; the proportion of the national income going to labour will rise. But if labour had gone up relatively to capital ($k' < l'$) but the elasticity of substitution between them were low ($\mu < 1$), labour would lose more on a fall in relative reward per unit than it would gain on the rise in relative amounts and Q would fall. Similarly, with $k' > l'$ and $\mu > 1$ labour would lose more on relative quantity than it would gain on relative price and Q would fall; but with $k' > l'$ and $\mu < 1$ labour would lose less on relative quantity than it would gain on relative price and Q would rise.

It can thus be seen that the bias of technical improvements in shifting demand relatively from one factor to another will depend both upon the type of technical improvement (which factor does it most expand?) and upon the ease of substitution between the various factors measured in efficiency units.[2]

---

[1] The marginal product of each factor measured in efficiency units will remain unchanged, and the marginal product of each factor measured in natural units will rise by the same proportion, namely $k' = l'$.

[2] Table I describes only the situation with two factors of production. The more general situation with three factors of production is given below in Table II (p. 73).

CHAPTER V

CHANGES IN STANDARDS OF LIVING IN PROPDEMS AND PLANTCAPS

We can now consider what it is which determines whether the standard of living will be rising or falling at any point of time.

Let us first consider the case of a Propdem, in which property and earning power are equally distributed among the citizens. In this case we are simply concerned with movements in income per head $\left(\dfrac{Y}{L}\right)$.

The distribution of income between wages and property incomes is of no importance, since each citizen possesses the same share of both types of income. A shift from wages to property incomes means simply that each citizen gains on the swings of property incomes what he loses on the roundabouts of wages.

The proportional rate of growth of income per head $\left(\dfrac{Y}{L}\right)$ is measured by $y - l$, where y is the proportional rate of growth of Y and l is the proportional rate of growth of L. From the expression (4.4) for y on page 55 above we can see that

$$\left. \begin{aligned} y - l &= Uk - (1 - Q)\,l + r \\ &= Uk - (U + Z)\,l + r \\ &= U(k - l) - Zl + r \end{aligned} \right\} \qquad (5.1)$$

From this it is clear that the standard of living will be rising the more quickly (i) the greater is the rate of technical progress (r), (ii) the greater is the rate of capital accumulation (k), (iii) the lower is the rate of population growth (l), and (iv) the smaller is the importance (Z) of the fixed factor land in the productive process. A high importance of capital in the productive process (U) will be favourable (or unfavourable) to a rising standard of living according as the rate of capital accumulation (k) is greater (or less) than the rate of population growth (l).

In brief, capital accumulation and technical progress will be raising real income per head, while an increasing pressure of population on the available resources of land and capital will be reducing output per head. The standard of living will be rising (or falling) according as $Uk - (U + Z)l + r \gtrless 0$, i.e. according as the rate of population growth (l) is less (or greater) than $\dfrac{Uk + r}{U + Z}$.

In a Plantcap the problem is a little more complicated. We must now distinguish between two standards of living—that of the workers who own no property and that of the owners of property who do no work.

The worker's standard of living will depend solely upon the wage rate and will thus be rising or falling according as the marginal product of labour is rising or falling. Thus while $y - l$ measures the rate of change in real output per head or in the average product of labour, w_l measures the rate of change in the wage rate or in the marginal product of labour. When will these two measures differ and when will they coincide?

The answer depends simply upon what is happening to Q, the proportion of income which goes to wages. As we have seen above (p. 53), Q can be expressed as the ratio between the marginal and the average product of labour i.e. as $\dfrac{\partial Y}{\partial L} \div \dfrac{Y}{L}$. In our perfectly competitive system the marginal product of labour is equal to the wage rate, so that $Q = \dfrac{W_l}{Y/L}$. If $w_l > y - l$, i.e. if the growth rate of marginal product of labour (and so the wage of labour) is greater than the growth rate of the average product of labour (and so of output per head), then Q is rising; and *vice versa*.[1] If the proportion of income going to wages is rising (or falling), this is simply another way of saying that the wage per man is going up more (or less) quickly than total output per man.

As we have just seen (p. 62 above), with our assumption that all technical progress is of the factor—and/or output—expanding kind, Q will remain constant if the elasticities of substitution between the factors of production, measured in efficiency units, are numerically equal to unity. In this case then there will be no difference between the growth rate of total income per head ($y - l$) and the growth rate of the wage rate (w_l).

We must, however, turn our attention to the cases in which the relevant elasticities of substitution are not numerically equal to unity, in which cases Q may not be constant and w_l may therefore differ from $y - l$. We must therefore examine what it is which will

---

[1] Since $Q = \dfrac{W_l L}{Y}$, $q = w_l - (y - l)$. In other words the excess of the growth rate of the wage rate over the growth rate of output per head is a measure of the growth rate in the proportion of income going to wages.

determine the value of w_l in conditions in which the elasticities of substitution between the factors are not numerically equal to unity. This is a complicated matter and in this volume in which we are eschewing the use of much mathematics we shall make some very strict limiting assumptions. By confining our attention to factor-expanding types of technical progress we have already made by implication one simplifying assumption, namely that technical progress does not itself alter the ease of substitution between factors of production (measured in efficiency units); it merely affects the number of efficiency units provided by any given number of national units of a factor. Producers are interested in the number of efficiency units of the factors (K^*, L^*, and N^*) which they can employ, and in the ease of substituting one of these for another; technical progress of a factor-expanding character merely alters the amounts of K^*, L^*, and N^* available for employment from given supplies of K, L, and N; it does not affect the ease of substitution between K^*, L^*, and N^*.

But we shall make two additional simplifying assumptions about the ease of substitutability between K^*, L^*, and N^* solely in order to be able to cope with the problem of what determines the growth rate of the wage per natural man (w_l) without excessive complication.

First, we shall assume that the elasticity of substitution between any one factor and any other factor is constant and is unaffected not only by technical progress (the point which we have already noticed), but also by changes in factor proportions. The elasticity of substitution between labour and capital, for example, is assumed to be the same whether there is much or little labour available per unit of capital (i.e. whether labour-intensive or capital-intensive techniques are being used) and whether there is much or little land for the labour and capital to work with.

Second, we shall assume that the elasticity of substitution between any one pair of factors is the same as between any other pair of factors. In an economy with three factors—land, labour and capital—there are three elasticities of substitution with which we are concerned—the substitutability between land and labour, that between land and capital, and that between labour and capital. These may well have different values. A particular factor may be a good substitute for one factor and a bad substitute for another. The final effect upon the wage rate of changes in factor supplies would now depend in a rather complicated manner upon the relationship between these three elasticities of substitution.[1] In this volume we will deal only with the more limited case in which the degree of ease or difficulty of substitution between any one factor and any other is the same.

[1] The relevant formulae are given on pp. 93–100 of the second edition of my *A Neo-Classical Theory of Economic Growth*.

With these strict assumptions we can write

$$\frac{k^* - l^*}{w_l^* - w_k^*} = \frac{n^* - l^*}{w_l^* - w_n^*} = \frac{n^* - k^*}{w_k^* - w_n^*} = \mu \qquad (5.2)$$

where μ is the numerical value of the elasticity of substitution between each pair of factors measured in efficiency units. For example, $\dfrac{k^* - l^*}{w_l^* - w_n^*}$ measures the proportional increase in the ratio of capital to labour measured in efficiency units $\left(\dfrac{K^*}{L^*}\right)$ divided by the proportional decrease in the price of the services of K^* to the price of the services of L^* $\left(\dfrac{W_k^*}{W_l^*}\right)$ which is needed to give the inducement to employ the higher ratio of K^* to L^*. If the elasticity of substitution between K^* and L^* is unaffected by whatever may be happening at the same time to N^*, then the proportional increase in $\dfrac{K^*}{L^*}$ divided by the proportional fall in $\dfrac{W_k^*}{W_l^*}$ must measure the elasticity of substitution between K^* and L^*.[1] Similarly $\dfrac{n^* - l^*}{w_l^* - w_n^*}$ measures the numerical value of the elasticity of substitution between N^* and L^* and $\dfrac{n^* - k^*}{w_k^* - w_n^*}$ the elasticity of substitution between N^* and K^*.

The expressions in (5.2) for the elasticity of substitution between the factors can now be used in the following way in order to determine the effect of changes in the supplies of the factors measured in efficiency units (namely L^*, K^*, and N^*) on the rates of wage, rental, or rent per unit of the factors measured in natural units (namely, W_l, W_k, and W_n). In other words we wish to employ the expression in (5.2) in order to express the growth rates w_l, w_k, and w_n in terms of the growth rates l, l', k, k', n, and n'.

The national output is all paid out in rentals of capital, wages of labour, and rents of land, so that

$$Y = W_k^* K^* + W_l^* L^* + W_n^* N^*$$

From this we can derive the following expression for the relationship between the changes, from one day to the next, in the national income and in its distribution among the various factors:[2]

i.e. $\quad \Delta Y = \Delta(W_k^* K^*) + \Delta(W_l^* L^*) + \Delta(W_n^* N^*)$

$\quad \Delta Y = W_k^* K^* (w_k^* + k^*) + W_l^* L^* (w_l^* + l^*) + W_n^* N^* (w_n^* + n^*)$

---

[1] See *The Stationary Economy*, p. 47. [2] See page 17 above.

so that $\dfrac{\Delta Y}{Y} = \dfrac{W^* K^*}{Y} (w_k^* + k) + \dfrac{W_l^* L^*}{Y} (w_l^* + l^*)$

$\qquad\qquad + \dfrac{W_n^* N^*}{Y} (w_n^* + n^*)$

or $\qquad y = U(w_k^* + k^*) + Q(w_l^* + l^*) + Z(w_n^* + n^*)$ \hfill (5.3)

where U, Q, and Z measure the proportions of the national income paid out in rentals on capital, wages of labour, and rents of land respectively.

But we know also that in an economy with perfect competition, constant returns to scale, and labour-expanding technical progress (see equation (4.11))

$$y = Uk^* + Ql^* + Zn^* \hfill (5.4)$$

If we subtract (5.4) from (5.3) we obtain

$$0 = Uw_k^* + Qw_l^* + Zw_n^* \hfill (5.5)$$

This equation (5.5) expresses a basic relationship in the type of economy which we are examining. Given an unchanged production function with the factors measured in efficiency units and with constant returns to scale, the prices of the factors' services (W_k^*, W_l^*, and W_n^*) depend solely upon the proportions, and not the absolute scale, on which the factors are being employed.[1] If these factor proportions remain constant, then the prices of the factors' services will all remain unchanged ($w_k^* = w_l^* = w_n^* = 0$ in equation (5.5)). But suppose one factor (e.g. N^*) increases in amount so that it must be employed in a greater ratio with the other factors (K^* and L^*), then the marginal product and the price of the services of the more abundant factor will fall ($w_n^* < 0$) and the marginal product and the price of the services of at least one of the other factors must rise (either w_k^* or w_l^* or both must be > 0).[2] There will in fact be a connection between the prices of the different factors' services such that the reductions in some prices will always be associated with rises in others. Equation (5.5) expresses the precise form of this relationship.

The form of this relationship conforms with common sense. With

[1] See *The Stationary Economy*, pp. 106–7.

[2] If N^* were a peculiarly close substitute for L^*, the increased supply of N^* and the consequential fall in its price W_n^* might lead to a reduction in the demand for the close substitute L^*. The increase in N^* would then lead to a fall in W_n^* and a fall in W_l^*; this would be accompanied by a marked rise in W_k^*, the price of the factor with which N^* and L^* could not be so readily substituted. In fact, with our present assumption that the ease of substitution between all factors is the same, N^* could not be more easily substituted for L^* than for K^*. The increased amount of N^* would cause both W^* and W_k^* to rise.

constant returns to scale when factors are paid rewards equal to the value of their marginal products this accounts for the total value of the product. Thus the selling price of the product (which we are assuming to be constant in money terms) is just covered by the wage cost *plus* the interest cost *plus* the rent cost of production; and this remains true whatever happens to factor proportions or to productivity. Suppose then that the wage cost is $0 \cdot 5$ of the total cost, the interest cost $0 \cdot 3$ of the total cost, and the rent cost is $0 \cdot 2$ of the total cost (i.e. $Q = 0 \cdot 5$, $U = 0 \cdot 3$, and $Z = 0 \cdot 2$). In such circumstances if the money rental per efficiency unit of capital rose by 2 per cent, this would represent a rise of $0 \cdot 3 \times 2 = 0 \cdot 6$ per cent in total money cost; and if the money rent per efficiency unit of land rose by 1 per cent, this would represent a rise of $0 \cdot 2 \times 1 = 0 \cdot 2$ per cent in total money cost. But we are assuming that the money price and so the money cost of the product is stabilized, so that if total costs go up by $0 \cdot 6 + 0 \cdot 2 = 0 \cdot 8$ per cent due to rises in capital and land costs, the money wage per efficiency unit of labour must at the same time have fallen by an amount sufficient to cause a $0 \cdot 8$ per cent fall in the total cost per unit of output; with wages making up $0 \cdot 5$ of total costs, the fall in the wage rate per efficiency unit of labour must be $1 \cdot 6$ per cent. In other words the proportional changes in the rates of pay per efficiency unit of the factors (namely, w_l^*, w_k^*, and w_n^*) weighted by the relative importance of the various factors in the make-up of total costs (namely, Q, U, and Z) must sum to zero, to keep the money cost of the product constant. In our numerical example

$$0 = U w_k^* + Q w_l^* + Z w_n^*$$
$$= 0 \cdot 3 \times 2\% - 0 \cdot 5 \times 1 \cdot 6\% + 0 \cdot 2 \times 1\%$$

From (5.5) we have

$$0 = U w_k^* + (1 - U - Z) w_l^* + Z w_n^*$$

i.e. $$w_l^* = U(w_l^* - w_k^*) + Z(w_l^* - w_n^*)$$

But from (5.2) we have

$$w_l^* - w_k^* = \frac{k^* - l^*}{\mu} \quad \text{and} \quad w_l^* - w_n^* = \frac{n^* - l^*}{\mu}$$

so that

$$w_l^* = \frac{U}{\mu}(k^* - l^*) + \frac{Z}{\mu}(n^* - l^*)$$

$$= \frac{U}{\mu} k^* - \frac{(1 - Q)}{\mu} l^* + \frac{Z}{\mu} n^* \qquad (5.6)[1]$$

[1] Since $y - l^* = U k^* - (1 - Q) l^* + Z n^*$, it follows that $\dfrac{y - l^*}{w_l^*} = \mu$.

With the assumptions which we are making we can in fact use the ratio of the

If we write $w_l - l'$ for w_l^*, $k + k'$ for k^*, $l + l'$ for l^*, and n' for n^* in equation (5.6) we obtain

$$w_l = \frac{U}{\mu}(k + k') - \frac{1 - Q}{\mu}l + \frac{\mu + Q - 1}{\mu}l' + \frac{Z}{\mu}n'$$

And similarly we can find that

$$
\left.
\begin{aligned}
w_k &= -\frac{1 - U}{\mu}k + \frac{\mu + U - 1}{\mu}k' + \frac{Q}{\mu}(l + l') + \frac{Z}{\mu}n' \\
w_n &= \frac{U}{\mu}(k + k') + \frac{Q}{\mu}(l + l') + \frac{\mu + Z - 1}{\mu}n'
\end{aligned}
\right\} \quad (5.7)
$$

The expressions in (5.7) describe the influences which will be affecting the reward paid to a natural unit of any one of the factors. Consider the expression for the growth rate of the wage rate (w_l) in (5.7). It states (i) that the wage rate will be raised as a result of the growth ($k + k'$ and n') in efficiency units of either of the co-operating factors K^* or N^* and that this development will be the more important in raising the wage rate of labour the smaller is μ, i.e. the more difficult it is to employ increased amounts of K^* and N^* without an accompanying increase in L^*, (ii) that the growth of population (l) will in itself cause a fall in the wage rate as labour presses on other factors and that this factor depressing the wage rate will also be the more important, the more difficult it is to substitute labour for the other factors and (iii) that labour-expanding technical progress will help to raise the wage rate if $\mu > 1 - Q$, but that if $\mu < 1 - Q$ the pressure of L^* on K^* and N^* caused by

proportional change in the average product per unit of effective work to the proportional change in the marginal product per unit of effective work—namely $\dfrac{y - l^*}{w_l^*}$—as a good measure of the ease of substitution between L^* and the other factors. Suppose that L^* were a very good substitute for the other factors and that L^* was rising in amount relatively to the other factors. Because of diminishing returns to the single factor, the average output per unit of L^* would fall ($y - l^* < 0$). The marginal product of L^* would also fall ($w_l^* < 0$); but if L^* were a very good substitute for the other factors, the fall in W_l^* which was necessary to give an incentive to employ more L^* relatively to the other factors would be very small; and it would in this case be less than the fall in the average output per unit of L^*. In other words $\dfrac{y - l^*}{w_l^*}$ would be very large when the ease of substitution was great. On the other hand if a very large fall in W_l^* was necessary to give an incentive to employ the increased ratio of L^* to other factors, W_l^* would have to fall much more than $\dfrac{Y}{L}$, so that $\dfrac{y - l^*}{w_l^*}$ would be very small. In fact $\dfrac{y - l^*}{w_l^*}$ is a measure of the elasticity of substitution in the cases which we are examining.

labour expansion might so depress W_l^* that, in spite of the rise in L', W_l itself would be reduced. This would mean that the demand for L^* had a price elasticity numerically less than unity so that when L^* was increased by labour expansion the total receipt of wages would thereby be reduced.

We can now compare the movement of the wage rate (w_l) with the movement of income per head ($y - l$). From (5.1) we have $y - l = Uk - (1 - Q)l + r$ so that with the value of r given in (4.11) we have

$$y - l = U(k + k') - (1 - Q)l + Ql' + Zn' \qquad (5.8)$$

From (5.7) and (5.8) we can obtain

$$y - l - w_l = \frac{\mu - 1}{\mu}\{U(k + k') - (1 - Q)(l + l') + Zn'\} \qquad (5.9)$$

The expression in (5.9) enables us to see whether total income per head will be growing more or less quickly than the wage rate (i.e. whether $y - l > w_l$). If $\mu > 1$, income per head will be growing more or less quickly than the wage rate according as

$$(1 - Q)(l + l') \lessgtr U(k + k') + Zn'$$

i.e. as
$$l + l' \lessgtr \frac{U(k + k') + Zn'}{1 - Q} \qquad (5.10)$$

On the other hand if $\mu < 1$, the condition given in (5.10) is reversed.

Thus if the elasticity of substitution between the factors is numerically greater than unity, a sufficiently high combination of population growth and of labour expansion will cause a shift of income to wages; but if the elasticity of substitution is numerically less than unity, the combination of population growth and labour expansion must be sufficiently low to cause this shift to wages.

So much for the standard of living of the workers in a Plantcap. We turn now to a consideration of the standard of living of the owners of property in a Plantcap. The standard of living of the property owners can be expressed as $\frac{Y_p}{L_p}$ where $Y_p = Y - W_lL$ is total income accruing to property and L_p is the number of property owners (L being, of course, the number of workers). The proportional rate of change in $\frac{Y_p}{L_p}$ is $y_p - l_p$ where y_p and l_p are the growth rates of total property incomes and of total property owners respectively.

Now it can be shown that[1]

$$y_p - l_p = \frac{y - Q(w_l + l)}{1 - Q} - l_p \tag{5.11}$$

Substituting in (5.11) for y and w_l from (4.11) and (5.7) we have

$$
\left.
\begin{aligned}
y_p - l_p &= \frac{U}{\mu}\frac{\mu - Q}{1 - Q}(k + k') + \frac{Q}{\mu}(l + l') \\
&\qquad\qquad + \frac{Z}{\mu}\frac{\mu - Q}{1 - Q}n' - l_p
\end{aligned}
\right\} \tag{5.12}
$$

while from (5.7)

$$
w_l = \frac{U}{\mu}(k + k') - \frac{1 - Q}{\mu}l + \frac{\mu + Q - 1}{\mu}l' + \frac{Z}{\mu}n,
$$

It is clear from (5.12) that conditions could arise in which growth caused such a divergence of interest in a Plantcap that income per head actually moved down for one class, while it moved up for the other. Take as an extreme example the following conditions which would lead to the absolute impoverishment of the working classes, while it led to ever increasing income per head for the owners. Suppose that $k + k'$, n', and l_p are all small, that l and l' are both large, and that $\mu < 1 - Q$. Then we could have $y_p - l_p > 0$ and $w_l < 0$. The standard of living of the property owners would be rising at the same time that the standard of living of the workers was falling. These would be conditions in which there was a rapidly increasing pressure of working population upon a fixed stock of natural resources and upon a slowly rising stock of capital equipment; in which the elasticities of substitution between labour on the one hand and capital and land on the other were small so that this rise in population caused a sharp fall in wages and a sharp rise in profits and rents; in which a high rate of labour-expanding technical progress was raising total output, but a strong bias of such progress against wages was directing this increased product to property incomes and away from wages; and in which the number of property owners was growing very slowly so that property incomes did not need to be spread over a rapidly increasing number of owners.

---

[1] $y_p = \dfrac{\Delta(Y - W_l L)}{Y - W_l L}$ where $\Delta(Y - W_l L)$ is the increase in $Y - W_l L$ between today and tomorrow. Now $\Delta(Y - W_l L) = \Delta Y - \Delta(W_l L) = Y_y - W_l L(w_l + l)$; (see pp. 16–17, above). Thus y_p can be written as $\dfrac{1}{Y - W_l L}\{Y_y - W_l L(w_l + l)\}$. But $W_l L = QY$ so that $y_p = \dfrac{y - Q(w_l + l)}{1 - Q}$.

If, however, in (5.12) $\mu = 1$ (unitary elasticities of substitution), and $l_p = l$ (same rates of growth of both classes in the population), then

$$y_p - l_p = w_l = U(k + k') - (1 - Q)l + Ql' + Zn'$$
$$= Uk - (1 - Q)l + r$$

which from (5.1) can be seen to be also equal to $y - l$. In other words, in such circumstances neither high or low substitutabilities, nor divergent rates of population growth would be affecting the distribution of income. In these circumstances, if technical progress were entirely factor- or output-expanding, property incomes per head of property owners and the wage rate would both be growing at the same rate as output per head.

Note to Chapter V

BIASSES IN TECHNICAL PROGRESS

We are now in a position to give in more general terms the conditions in which technical progress of a purely factor-expanding character can be biassed for (or against) wages or any other factor income. We gave an account of this in Table I at the end of Chapter IV in the case of an economy with two factors. We can now extend this to an economy with three factors.

We say that technical progress is biassed for (or against) wages, if, with constant amounts of the factors in natural units ($l = k = n = 0$), the technical improvement would raise (or lower) Q, i.e. would cause the marginal product of labour to go up in a greater (or a smaller) proportion than the average product of labour. We may also say that the technical change is ultra-biassed against wages if the bias was so marked that, with unchanged amounts of K, L, and N, the marginal product of labour not merely failed to rise in as great a proportion as the average product of labour, but actually fell in absolute terms. With a bias against wages the *proportion* of the national income going in wages will fall; with an ultra-bias against wages the *absolute amount* of income going in wages will fall.

With $l = 0$, the growth rate in the average product of labour (namely, $y - l$) is the same as the growth rate in the total national product (namely, y). From (4.11) and (5.7), with $l = k = n = 0$, we have

$$y = Uk' + Ql' + Zn'$$
$$\text{and} \qquad w_l = \frac{U}{\mu}k' + \frac{\mu + Q - 1}{\mu}l' + \frac{Z}{\mu}n' \qquad (5.13)$$

so that $\quad y - w_l = \dfrac{\mu - 1}{\mu} \{Uk' - (1 - Q)\, l' + Zn'\}$ $\qquad$ (5.14)

The marginal product of labour will go up more (or less) quickly than the average product of labour, i.e. Q will rise (or will fall), according as $y \lessgtr w_l$, i.e. (from 5.14) according as

$$\dfrac{\mu - 1}{\mu} \{Uk' - (1 - Q)\, l' + Zn'\} \lessgtr 0 \qquad (5.15)$$

From this expression we can rewrite Table I on page 62 in the form of Table II, where the signs $+$, 0, and $-$ once more denote a rise, no change, or a fall in Q. The expression (5.15) will be zero if either $\mu = 1$ or $(1 - Q)l' = Uk' + Zn'$, so that in both these cases Q will remain unchanged. But the expression in (5.15) will be < 0 if $\mu > 1$ and $(1 - Q)l' > Uk' + Zn'$, so that in this case Q will rise. And similarly for the other entries in Table II.

Table II

	$\dfrac{Uk' + Zn'}{1 - Q} < l'$	$\dfrac{Uk' + Zn'}{1 - Q} = l'$	$\dfrac{Uk' + Zn'}{1 - Q} > l'$
$\mu > 1$	$+$	0	$-$
$\mu = 1$	0	0	0
$\mu < 1$	$-$	0	$+$

From the expression for w_l in (5.13) it can be seen that, since k' and n' cannot be negative, w_l can be negative only if $\mu + Q - 1 < 0$, i.e. only if $\mu < 1 - Q$. But if $\mu < 1 - Q$, then w_l would be negative if

$$Uk' + Zn' < \{(1 - Q) - \mu\}l'$$

i.e. if $\qquad\qquad\qquad l' > \dfrac{Uk' + Zn'}{1 - Q - \mu}$

The technical change would thus be ultra-biassed against wages if (i) $\mu < 1 - Q$ and (ii) $l' > \dfrac{Uk' + Zn'}{1 - Q - \mu}$.

Similar expressions could be found in the same way to measure any bias for, or any bias or ultra-bias against, the other factor incomes.

Such biasses in inventions can be very important in the real world, particularly in conditions resembling those of a Plantcap. It is of the utmost importance, for example, to consider whether certain types of invention may not be so biassed against labour that, while they raise output per head significantly, they raise the marginal product of labour and so the wage rate in a much smaller proportion—or, indeed, possibly even reduce it. But the formulae in this note are themselves very academic. They analyse this question on the assumptions (i) that the elasticities of substitution between each pair of factors are the same—e.g. that capital is as good a substitute for labour as it is for land—(ii) that these elasticities of substitution are not affected by changes in factor proportions—e.g. that labour and capital remain equally good or bad substitutes for each other whatever may happen to the ratio of capital to labour in employment—and (iii) that these elasticities of substitution are unaffected by technical progress since this takes the form solely of factor-expansion—e.g. that no invention will make labour and capital better or worse substitutes for each other. None of these assumptions is likely to be true in the real world. However, the expressions derived in this note do serve to show that even with all these strict simplifying assumptions we have not ruled out the possibilities of inventions of a kind which do have a bias, or even an ultra-bias, for or against particular factor incomes.

CHAPTER VI

THE STATE OF STEADY GROWTH: (1) TWO FACTORS AND NO TECHNICAL PROGRESS

In the last two chapters we have been concerned with the rate of change at any one point of time in three measures of the standard of living namely (i) income per head, (ii) the wage rate, and (iii) property incomes per property owner. We have considered these rates of growth in terms of three basic causes of growth:—(i) the rate of capital accumulation, (ii) the rate of growth of population, and (iii) the rate and nature of technical progress. We intend in this chapter to pass from a consideration of what determines the rates of change in standards of living at any one point of time to a consideration of the question whether these rates of change in standards of living will themselves be rising or falling or will remain at a steady level. We shall examine this question on the assumption that the basic forces behind the three causes of growth (namely the forces of capital accumulation, population growth, and technical progress) themselves remain constant.

As far as the meaning of constancy in the forces behind population growth and technical progress is concerned, no very special problems arise. In the case of technical progress we shall simply assume that the various rates of factor expansion (namely, k', l', and n') continue unchanged day after day; and we will return to a fuller discussion of this matter in Chapter VII. In the case of population growth we shall simply assume that the underlying conditions of mortality and fertility are such that the rates of growth of the working population (l) and—in the case of a Plantcap—of the number of property owners (l_p) remains constant; and we will discuss this assumption in detail in Chapters X and XI.

But the case of capital accumulation is rather different. We cannot well proceed on the simple assumption that the rate of capital accumulation (k) remains unchanged for the following reasons. We have already (Chapter III, pp. 45–46 above) as a first approximation to the definition of constancy in the factors lying behind capital accumulation assumed that this means that in a Propdem a constant proportion (S) of total income is saved and that in a Plantcap a constant proportion of property incomes (S_p) is saved. But constancy in these savings proportions (S or S_p) does not necessarily mean constancy in the rate of capital accumulation. Total savings and so the absolute addition to the capital stock per annum will be SY, where S is the proportion of total income which is saved. In a Plantcap we shall have $S = S_p(1 - Q)$, since $(1 - Q)$ is the proportion of income which is property income and S_p is the proportion of this income which is saved. The rate of annual capital accumulation (k) is the addition to the capital stock in a year expressed as a proportion of the existing capital stock, which can be expressed

$$\left. \begin{array}{l} \text{as} \quad k = \dfrac{SY}{K} \quad \text{in both Propdem and Plantcap} \\[2mm] \text{but with} \quad S = S_p(1 - Q) \quad \text{in a Plantcap.}^1 \end{array} \right\} \quad (6.1)$$

Clearly then, while S (or S_p) remain constant, k may change because of changes in $\dfrac{Y}{K}$ (or in Q).

There may nevertheless be powerful forces at work which tend to make the growth rate of capital approach a constant level, so long as S (or S_p) remain constant. In order to illustrate these forces we will in the present chapter assume that there are only two factors, capital and labour, and that there is no technical progress. We are concerned simply with an economy in which output is growing as a result of population growth and capital accumulation, without a fixed factor land or technical progress affecting the output. In these conditions we can understand the forces leading to a constant rate of capital accumulation in the following way.

At any one moment of time for historical reasons the total stock of

---

[1] In the case in which there are three factors of production, these formulae are true only on the assumption that property owners do not alter their consumption expenditures as a result of capital gains. We are assuming that the price of the product (P_y) and so in our one product economy the price of the capital good itself (P_k) is constant. But the price of an acre of land (P_n) is not necessarily constant. Property owners will therefore make capital gains equal to the proportional rate of growth of the price of an acre of land times the value of all landed property, i.e., capital gains of $NP_n \, p_n$ where p_n is the proportional growth rate in the price of an acre of land. (For example suppose that land values were rising at 3 per cent per annum—$p_n = 3$ per cent per annum—and that total land values were \$1,000,000—$NP_n = \$1,000,000$. Then land owners would be making capital gains at a rate of \$30,000 a year.) If property owners spent on consumption in a Propdem $1 - S$, or in a Plantcap $1 - S_p$, of their incomes including capital gains, then in a Propdem the total output available for additions to the capital stock would be only $Y - (1 - S)(Y + NP_n p_n) = SY - (1 - S)NP_n p_n$; and in a Plantcap it would be only $Y - W_l L - (1 - S_p)(W_k K + W_n N + NP_n p_n) = S_p(W_k K + W_n N) - (1 - S_p)NP_n p_n$. We make the assumption that capital gains do not affect consumption frankly for the purpose of simplifying the argument.

capital may be exceptionally great or exceptionally small. Suppose, by way of example, that the economy has just suffered an earthquake which has destroyed a large amount of capital equipment without killing any of the population. There will be a small amount of capital applied to the given amount of labour in the given state of technical knowledge. The average and the marginal products of capital $\left(\text{namely}, \dfrac{Y}{K} \text{ and } \dfrac{[1 - Q]Y^{1}}{K}\right)$ will be exceptionally high. Given S it follows that $\dfrac{SY}{K}$ will be exceptionally high, so that in a Propdem the rate of capital accumulation $\left(k = \dfrac{SY}{K}\right)$ will be exceptionally high; and given S_{p} it follows that $\dfrac{S_{p}(1 - Q)Y}{K}$ will be exceptionally high, so that in a Plantcap the rate of capital accumulation $\left(k = \dfrac{S_{p}[1 - Q]Y}{K}\right)$ will also be exceptionally high. But this exceptionally high rate of capital accumulation will help to raise the rate of capital accumulation relatively to the rate of growth of population. A more normal supply of capital relatively to labour will begin to restore itself. But this will tend to reduce the average and the marginal products of capital $\left(\dfrac{Y}{K} \text{ and } \dfrac{[1 - Q]Y}{K}\right)$, so that the rate of capital accumulation in a Propdem or in a Plantcap will tend to fall. There are, therefore, basic forces at work which, given constant savings proportions (S or S_{p}), will tend to reduce the rate of capital accumulation (k) if that rate should start at any exceptionally high levels. By the same sort of story, starting for some historical reason with an exceptionally large capital stock, one could show that one would start with an exceptionally low value of k (since $\dfrac{Y}{K}$ and $\dfrac{[1 - Q]Y}{K}$ would be exceptionally low) but that in this case k would tend to rise $\Big($since the exceptionally low rate of capital accumulation would tend to raise $\dfrac{Y}{K}$ and $\dfrac{[1 - Q]Y}{K}\Big)$. We shall proceed by examining the conditions in which this basic set of forces will lead to the result

---

[1] The marginal product of capital is equal to the rate of profit in our competitive system. But total profits are UY, where U is the proportion of income going to profits, so that the rate of profit income is $\dfrac{UY}{K}$. But with no land ($Z = 0$), $U = 1 - Q$, so that the rate of profit is $\dfrac{(1 - Q)Y}{K}$.

that, given the savings proportion S or S_p and given the rate of population growth l, the rate of capital accumulation, though it may start at an exceptionally high or low level, will always tend towards a final steady level.

With our present assumptions of no land and no technical progress, the rate of capital accumulation (k) will normally move to a final steady level at which it is equal to the rate of population growth (l). The reason for this is clear. Consider first the case of a Propdem. If both factors (K and L) were increasing at the same proportional rate, then, because of constant returns to scale, output (Y) would also be growing at the same rate. If, however, K were growing more rapidly than L, then Y would be growing more rapidly than L (because the more rapid growth of K would make some additional contribution to the growth of Y) but less rapidly than K (because L would have to be growing as rapidly as K for Y also to grow as rapidly as K). Thus the rate of growth of Y will be intermediate between that of K and that of L. We shall start with

$$\textit{either} \quad \text{(i)} \quad k > y > l$$
$$\textit{or} \quad \text{(ii)} \quad k < y < l$$

In case (i) with $k > l$ we have $k > y$ so that $\dfrac{SY}{K}$ or k is falling.[1] In case (ii) with $k < l$ we have $k < y$ so that $\dfrac{SY}{K} = k$ is rising. We end up with $k = y = l$.[2] The growth rates of output and of the capital stock both settle down at the same level as the rate of population growth. The standard of living in the Propdem will then be constant; for since $y = l$, $\dfrac{Y}{L}$ is constant; that is to say income per head remains constant because total income rises at the same proportional rate as total population.

This conclusion may at first sight appear very paradoxical. Is

---

[1] If K is growing proportionally more rapidly than Y, $\dfrac{Y}{K}$ will be falling. Thus, with S constant, $\dfrac{SY}{K}$ (which is equal to k) will be falling.

[2] This argument rests on the assumptions (i) that there is not a technically fixed upper limit to output per unit of capital $\left(\dfrac{Y}{K}\right)$ which prevents $\dfrac{SY}{K}$ from ever rising up to equality with l, however small the ratio of capital to labour may become and (ii) that there is not a technically fixed lower limit to $\dfrac{Y}{K}$ which prevents $\dfrac{SY}{K}$ from falling as low as l, however large the ratio of capital to labour may become.

it really true that in a world with two factors and no technical progress the standard of living will remain constant however low the rate of population growth (l) and however high the savings ratio (S) may be? Surely, it may be argued, if the rate of population growth were reduced and the rate of savings raised capital would grow more rapidly than population and income per head would rise. This last assertion is, of course, correct. Suppose we start with a given capital stock (K) and a given working population (L). Then this will be producing a given output (Y). If it so happens that S and l are such that, with these initial values of Y and K, $\frac{SY}{K} = l$, then $k = l$ and there is no change in $\frac{Y}{L}$. If S were greater than this or l smaller than this, then we would have $k = \frac{SY}{K} > l$, so that $k > y > l$, and $\frac{Y}{L}$ would be rising. But $\frac{Y}{L}$ would not rise above a certain level. As long as $\frac{SY}{K}$ remained $> l$, then—as we have seen—$\frac{Y}{K}$ would fall and $\frac{Y}{L}$ rise (because $k > y > l$). But if $\frac{Y}{K}$ had so fallen that $\frac{SY}{Y} = l$, then $\frac{Y}{K}$ would cease to fall and $\frac{Y}{L}$ would cease to rise (because $k = y = l$). In other words if we started in a steady state with $\frac{SY}{K} = l$ and $\frac{Y}{L}$ constant and if there was then a once-for-all rise in S or fall in l, $\frac{Y}{L}$ would start to rise; but it would rise up towards a limited new level; and as soon as it had for all practical purposes reached that new level, it would then stay constant at that new higher level in a new state of steady growth. In the case which we are examining in the long run it is the *absolute level* of the standard of living and not its *rate of growth* which is raised by a rise in S or by a fall in l.

With our present simple assumptions of only two factors and no technical progress the mechanism at work in the case of a Plantcap is very similar. In the absence of rents from land ($Z = 0$) $\frac{(1-Q)Y}{K} = \frac{UY}{K}$, which is the rate of profit i'. (See equation (4.3) above.) We can, therefore, write the rate of capital accumulation as $k = S_p i'$. In this case then k will rise (or fall) according as i' rises (or falls). But in our one-product model (see page 54 above) i' measures the marginal product of K, and with only two factors the marginal product of K will rise (or fall) according as the ratio of K to L falls (or rises). Thus i'

rises (or falls) as $\dfrac{K}{L}$ falls (or rises) i.e., as $k \lessgtr l$. If initially capital is growing less quickly than labour ($k < l$) the marginal product of capital (i') will be rising, so that $S_p i'$ or k will itself be rising; and *vice versa*. We tend once more to move towards a state of steady growth with $k = y = l$ and with $\dfrac{Y}{L}$ constant.[1] Since the wage rate or the marginal product of labour will in this case depend also only on the ratio of K to L, we shall also have a constant real wage rate, i.e., a constant standard of living for the wage earner, in our Plantcap when it has reached its state of steady growth. Since in this state $S_p i' = l$, the rate of profit i' will be lower, the lower is l and the higher is S_p. A low l or a high S_p will, in other words, imply a high ratio K to L, and so a low rate of profit but a high wage rate, in the state of steady growth; but in the long run the wage rate will remain constant at this high level. The outcome in a Plantcap is in this case essentially the same as the outcome in a Propdem.

It will have been observed that the mechanism which we have described whereby, with our present assumptions of two factors without technical progress, a Propdem or a Plantcap reaches a position of steady growth depends upon the substitution of labour for capital or *vice versa*. If capital is growing more quickly than labour ($k > l$), then the average $\left(\dfrac{Y}{K}\right)$ and the marginal (i') product of capital will be falling; the rate of capital accumulation $\left(\dfrac{SY}{K} \text{ in a Propdem and } S_p i' \text{ in a Plantcap}\right)$ will thus fall; and this process will go on until $k = l$. Remembering that $i' = \dfrac{UY}{K}$, we end up in a Propdem with $\dfrac{SY}{K} = l \left(\text{i.e. with } \dfrac{Y}{K} = \dfrac{l}{S}\right)$ and in a Plantcap with $S_p i' = \dfrac{S_p UY}{K} = l \left(\text{i.e. with } \dfrac{Y}{K} = \dfrac{l}{S_p U}\right)$.

This mechanism may well break down if there is in fact little technical possibility for substitution between labour and capital in the productive process. Let us first consider the situation which might arise in a Propdem. Suppose that there are strict upper and lower limits to the amount of labour which can be employed per unit of

---

[1] This solution depends upon the assumption that there is no technologically fixed upper (or lower) limit to the marginal product of capital (i') which prevents $S_p i'$ from rising up to (or declining down to) an equality with l. cf. Footnote (2) on page 78, above.

capital $\left(\frac{L}{K}\right)$. This would imply that there were strict upper and lower limits to output per unit of capital $\left(\frac{Y}{K}\right)$. When labour per unit of capital is at its technically fixed upper limit, output per unit of capital will be at an upper limit; when labour employed per unit of capital is at its minimum, output per unit of capital will be at a minimum. As we have seen, in a Propdem the state of steady growth involves substitution between K and L until $\frac{L}{K}$ is such that $\frac{Y}{K}$ is such that $\frac{SY}{K} = l$ or $\frac{Y}{K} = \frac{l}{S}$. But if $\frac{l}{S}$ is above a technically fixed upper, or below a technically fixed lower, limit of $\frac{Y}{K}$ clearly this mechanism will break down.

What then will happen? To simplify the exposition let us make the extreme assumption that no substitution between K and L is possible so that $\frac{L}{K}$ and $\frac{Y}{K}$ are fixed (where L and K are the amounts of the factors actually used and Y is the amount of the output actually produced).[1] The upper and lower limits of $\frac{Y}{K}$ coincide at some single, technically fixed level. Then $\frac{SY}{K}$ which measures the rate at which the capital stock would be growing if all capital were employed will also be rigidly fixed. It will then be a pure fluke if $\frac{SY}{K} = l$. If $\frac{SY}{K} > l$, then the capital stock will accumulate more rapidly than the working population; and whether we start with a scarcity or a superfluity of capital relatively to labour, sooner or later capital will be superfluous. Capital will become a free good; some of it will be unemployed; the rate of profit will fall to zero; the whole of the output will go to labour; output and labour will grow at the same rate l and the capital stock, already superfluous, will become more and more superfluous. Output per head will remain constant at the technologically fixed level of output per person employed $\left(\frac{Y}{L}\right)$. If $\frac{SY}{K} < l$, then capital will tend to grow more slowly than labour; sooner or later labour will become superfluous; there will be technological unemployment; the wage rate will fall to zero; the rate of profit will rise until the whole of the output is paid out in incomes on property; output and capital

---

[1] As we shall see, there may in this model be unemployed quantities of labour and capital. $\frac{L}{K}$ is the ratio of *employed* labour to *employed* capital.

stock will grow at the rate $\dfrac{SY}{K}$ and the working population—already superfluous—will grow at the faster rate l. Output per man employed will remain constant at the technologically given level $\left(\dfrac{Y}{L}\right)$, but output per head of the community—i.e., the standard of living—will continuously fall as labour grows more rapidly than capital and the ratio of the technologically unemployed to the total population rises.

In a Propdem the mere fact that all income will go to profits if $\dfrac{l}{S}$ is greater than the technically fixed upper limit of $\dfrac{Y}{K}$ or that all income will go to wages if $\dfrac{l}{S}$ is less than the technically fixed lower limit of $\dfrac{Y}{K}$ will itself have no effect upon the working of the system. It will simply mean that the ordinary citizen, who is a representative property-owner as well as a representative worker, will receive his real income and so enjoy the average standard of living in one form rather than another. But in a Plantcap the distribution of income between wages and property-incomes will make a very great difference in two ways. In the first place, it will have the obvious effect of changing the standard of living of workers relatively to that of property owners. But, in the second place, it may have the result of keeping the rate of capital accumulation in line with the rate of population growth $(k = l)$ even though there are no technical possibilities of substitution between the factors of production. We must now examine this new mechanism of adjustment.

Let us consider the case of a Plantcap in which $\dfrac{Y}{K}$ is technically fixed. Since $i' = \dfrac{UY}{K}$, $\dfrac{S_p UY}{K}$ measures the rate at which capital would be accumulated if it were fully employed. Suppose that we start with $\dfrac{S_p UY}{K} > l$, so that the rate of capital accumulation is greater than the rate of population growth. Sooner or later the stock of capital will outgrow the supply of labour; $\dfrac{L}{K}$ will fall below its technically fixed level. The rate of profit will fall and the wage rate will rise. The proportion of income going to profits (U) will fall; and thus $\dfrac{S_p UY}{K}$ will fall. This process can go on until U is zero. In this way, however high the technically fixed ratio of $\dfrac{Y}{K}$ may be, the rate of capital accumulation can always be adjusted downwards through a fall in U (i.e., through a shift of income from property owners who save to wage earners who do not save) until $\frac{S_p U Y}{K}$ or k is adjusted downwards to equal l.

A similar upward adjustment can be made in k though in this case there is a strict upper limit to k. Suppose we start with $\frac{S_p U Y}{K}$ less than l. Then sooner or later labour will tend to become redundant; the technically fixed ratio $\frac{L}{K}$ will mean that sooner or later technological unemployment will threaten to appear. The wage rate will fall and the rate of profit rise; the proportion of income going to profits (U) will rise. $\frac{S_p U Y}{K}$ or k itself will thus rise towards l. But U cannot rise above unity. When all income accrues to the savers (the property owners) k will reach an upper limit of $\frac{S_p Y}{K}$. If l is greater than this, then in the Plantcap there will develop a situation in which an ever increasing ratio of the total employable population will be technologically unemployed; the wage rate will fall to zero; and the workers will have to live on thin air.[1]

In a Plantcap then, provided that $\frac{S_p Y}{K} > l$, the rate of capital accumulation $k = \frac{S_p U Y}{K}$ will adjust itself to the rate of population growth through the distribution of income between wages which are not saved and profits which are at least partially saved. As long as the ratio in which capital and labour are available in the economy differs from the technically fixed ratio $\left(\frac{L}{K}\right)$ in which they are needed for production, either the wage rate or the rate of profit will fall to zero, according to which factor is in excess supply. Thus k will fall to zero if K is in excess supply or rise to $\frac{S_p Y}{K}$ (which is assumed to be $> l$) if L is in excess supply. When the available supplies have been thus adjusted to the technically desired ratio, then they will be kept in balance ($k = l$) by the distribution of income between wages and profits (U) being so fixed as to make $\frac{S_p U Y}{K} = l$. If U began to rise

---

[1] A problem which we will face at a later stage of the analysis (see Chapter XI, below). In fact, of course, in such an extreme Malthusian situation l would fall because of starvation.

above this we would have $k > l$ and there would be a threat of excess supply of K which would cause i' to fall and W_l to rise until U was brought back to its equilibrium level $\left(U = \dfrac{lK}{S_p Y} \right)$. And conversely, if U began to fall below this equilibrium level.

In a Plantcap then there is this additional adjustment mechanism. We do not have to rely solely on the substitutability between labour and capital to keep the system in balance. If the elasticity of substitution between labour and capital is less than unity, then any tendency for the supply of capital to outrun the supply of labour $(k > l)$ will lower the proportion of income paid out in profits and raise the proportion paid out in wages. If some profits but no wages are saved, this will reduce the proportion of total income which is saved and thus tend to reduce the rate of capital accumulation and bring it in line with the rate of population growth.

In our notation if initially $\dfrac{S_p U Y}{K} > l$ and if the elasticity of substitution between L and K is less than unity (though not necessarily zero) we shall have two forces at work adjusting k to l. In the first place, in so far as there is any substitutability between K and L the fall in $\dfrac{L}{K}$ will tend to reduce $\dfrac{Y}{K}$ and so to reduce $\dfrac{S_p U Y}{K}$. In the second place, the fall in $\dfrac{L}{K}$ will, with an elasticity of substitution between L and K numerically less than one, cause U to fall; and this also will tend to reduce $\dfrac{S_p U Y}{K}$ towards l. And conversely, of course, if initially $\dfrac{S_p U Y}{K} < l$.

It may be helpful to some readers to give a geometrical account of the analysis developed in this chapter. This is done in Figure 2. Since we are assuming constant returns to scale and no indivisibilities, it makes no difference to output whether the individual firms are large or small.[1] Let us, solely for the purpose of exposition, suppose that all firms are one-man firms, so that as the working population grows the number of firms grow in the same proportion. We can then represent a firm's production function by the curve O B D F in Figure 2 (i) where $\hat{K} = \dfrac{K}{L}$ represents the amount of K per head (and thus the amount of K employed in any one firm) and $\hat{Y} = \dfrac{Y}{L}$ measures output per head (and thus the output of any one firm).

[1] See *The Stationary Economy*, pp. 31–2 and 106.

When $\hat{K}$ is zero, $\hat{Y}$ will be zero; if there is no capital at all, there will be no output. As capital per head increases (e.g. from OA to OC), output per head will increase (from AB to CD). But since there are diminishing returns to one factor taken alone, the higher is the ratio of capital to labour $\left(\dfrac{K}{L}\right)$, the lower will be the output per unit of capital $\left(\dfrac{Y}{K}\right)$. When $\dfrac{K}{L} = \hat{K} = \text{OA}$, $\dfrac{Y}{L} = \hat{Y} = \text{AB}$. It follows that $\dfrac{\text{AB}}{\text{OA}} = \dfrac{Y}{K}$. In other words output per unit of capital for the one-man firm and for the economy as a whole is measured by the slope of the line OB, when $\hat{K} = \text{OA}$, and by the slope of the line OD, when $\hat{K} = \text{OC}$.

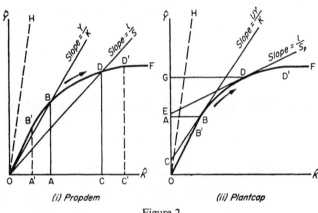

(i) Propdem   (ii) Plantcap

Figure 2

Let us suppose then that we are in a Propdem. Draw on Figure 2 (i) the line OD with a slope equal to $\dfrac{l}{S}$ $\left(\text{i.e. } \dfrac{\text{CD}}{\text{OC}} = \dfrac{l}{S}\right)$. Suppose that for historical reasons we start with a ratio of capital to labour equal to OA. Then, as we have seen, $\dfrac{\text{AB}}{\text{OA}}$ measures the level of output per unit of capital $\left(\dfrac{Y}{K}\right)$. But $\dfrac{\text{AB}}{\text{OA}}$ is $> \dfrac{\text{CD}}{\text{OC}}$. In other words, $\dfrac{Y}{K} > \dfrac{l}{S}$ or $\dfrac{SY}{K} > l$. But $\dfrac{SY}{K} = k$, so that $k > l$. But with $k > l$, $\dfrac{K}{L} = \hat{K}$ will be rising, so that the point A will approach the point C and the point B will approach the point D. When, however, the line BA coincides with the line CD, we shall have $\dfrac{Y}{K} = \dfrac{l}{S}$ so that $k = l$, so that $\dfrac{K}{L} = \hat{K}$

remains constant at the level OC. The economy is now in a state of steady growth at which $k = l$, and, therefore, $y = k = l$. Both output and capital settle down to a constant rate of growth equal to the rate of population growth.

Figure 2 (ii) represents the same argument in the case of a Plantcap. The production function, showing output per head as dependent upon capital per head, is once more shown by the curve O B D F which is the same in Figure 2 (ii) as in Figure 2 (i). The slope of this curve at any point—for example, the slope $\dfrac{AC}{AB}$ at the point B in Figure 2 (ii)—measures the marginal product of K in the one-man firm depicted in Figure 2.[1] In equilibrium this marginal product of capital will be the same in all firms and will thus measure the marginal product of capital in the economy as a whole.

We can now use Figure 2 (ii) to show how the state of steady growth may be reached in a Plantcap. Find on the curve O B D F the point D at which the slope of the curve is equal to $\dfrac{l}{S_p}$ (i.e. $\dfrac{EG}{DG} = \dfrac{l}{S_p}$). Suppose now that we start historically with a ratio of $\dfrac{K}{L}$ equal to AB (i.e. less than GD). Then the slope of the curve at the starting point B (namely $\dfrac{AC}{AB}$) will be greater than the slope of the curve at the point D (namely $\dfrac{EG}{GD}$). But the slope of the curve at the point B measures the marginal product of capital or the rate of profit $\left(\dfrac{UY}{K}\right)$ at the start of our story. But $\dfrac{UY}{K} > \dfrac{l}{S_p}$ so that $\dfrac{S_p UY}{K} = k > l$. Since $k > l$, $\dfrac{K}{L} = \hat{K}$ will be rising from AB towards GD. When $\dfrac{K}{L}$ has grown to GD, the rate of profit $\left(\dfrac{UY}{K}\right)$ will have so fallen that the ratio of savings to the capital stock $\left(\dfrac{S_p UY}{K}\right)$ has so fallen that it is now equal to l. At this point $k = l$ and there is no further change in $\dfrac{K}{L}$ or $\hat{K}$. $\dfrac{Y}{L}$ or $\hat{Y}$ is now constant at the level GO and we have a state of steady growth with $k = y = l$, $\dfrac{Y}{L} = GO$, $\dfrac{K}{L} = GD$, and the rate of profit $= \dfrac{EG}{GD}$.

[1] See *The Stationary Economy*, pp. 116–18.

Let us next consider the cases in which there are rigidly fixed upper or lower limits to the ratio $\frac{K}{L} = \hat{K}$. Suppose that in Figure 2 (i) OC′ represents the maximum level of $\frac{K}{L}$ in the sense that if the supply of K rises above this critical level without any increase in L it will be impossible to find the labour to man up all the available capital equipment for productive use. If $\hat{K}$ increases beyond OC′ there will be no further increase in $\hat{Y}$; all that will happen is that some capital will remain unused. To the right of the point D′ the production function is a horizontal straight line and the marginal product of K is zero.

Suppose that at the other extreme OA′ represents the technologic-ally fixed minimum level of $\frac{K}{L} = \hat{K}$ at which full employment of L can be maintained. If now the supply of labour were to increase without any increase in the supply of capital, there would be no increase in total output, since there is no increase in the capital to equip the additional workers. The additional workers would simply be unemployed. If the number of workers were doubled while the amount of capital remained unchanged, both capital per available worker and output per available worker would be halved, since half the workers would be unemployed.[1] Between O and A′, then, in Figure 2 (i) the production function corresponds to a straight line OB′. With a given supply of labour and with no capital (i.e. at the point O) both $\frac{K}{L}$ and $\frac{Y}{L}$ will be zero. From this point as K increases with a fixed amount of L, so $\frac{K}{L}$ increases and $\frac{Y}{L}$ increases. But until all the L is employed (i.e. until $\frac{K}{L}$ has risen to OA′) output per unit of capital is fixed at the slope $\frac{A'B'}{OA'}$, so that from O to B′ as $\hat{K}$ $\left(\text{and there-fore } \frac{K}{L}\right)$ increases so $\hat{Y}$ $\left(\text{and therefore } \frac{Y}{L}\right)$ increases at the fixed ratio $\frac{Y}{K}$ represented by the slope of the straight line OB′.

We can now use Figure 2 (i) to show how things would work in a Propdem with the fixed upper and lower limits to $\frac{K}{L}$. Suppose that $\frac{1}{S}$

---

[1] In a one-man firm, half a man would be unemployed. It must be remembered that we are assuming there to be no indivisibilities.

is so low that it is less than $\dfrac{C'D'}{OC'}$. Then the point D will lie to the right of the point D'. Suppose, however, that the economy started with full employment of both factors at some such point as B with the ratio of $\dfrac{K}{L}$ equal to OA. Then $\dfrac{Y}{K} = \dfrac{AB}{OA}$. But since $\dfrac{AB}{OA} > \dfrac{l}{S}, \dfrac{Y}{K} > \dfrac{l}{S}$ so that $\dfrac{SY}{K} > l$. But $\dfrac{SY}{K} = k$, so that $k > l$. Therefore, $\dfrac{K}{L}$ will be growing and the economy will move to the point D on the production function. But since in this case D is to the right of D', there will be unemployed capital.[1]

On the other hand suppose that l were much greater or S much smaller, so that $\dfrac{l}{S}$ was equal to the slope of the line OH. Then, starting once more from full employment of both factors with $\dfrac{K}{L} = OA$, we would have $\dfrac{Y}{K} = \dfrac{AB}{OA}$ which is less than the slope of OH. In this case then $\dfrac{Y}{K} < \dfrac{l}{S}$ so that $\dfrac{SY}{K} < l$ or $k < l$. Labour would now be growing more rapidly than capital. We would move down the production function from B towards O. When the point B' was reached, unemployment of labour would appear. $\dfrac{Y}{K}$ would now be at its technologically fixed maximum, but would still be less than $\dfrac{l}{S}$. Thus K would continue to grow less rapidly than L; and this process would go on indefinitely. The maximum technologically possible value of $\dfrac{Y}{K}$ is fixed by the slope of the line OB' and as long as the slope of $\dfrac{l}{S}$ remains steeper than this labour will grow more rapidly than capital; and, since employment will now grow only proportionally to the capital stock with which it has to work, employment will grow at a smaller

---

[1] The economy would inevitably be moving into a position of what may be called complete 'capital glut'. In fact in such a situation mass unemployment of all factors might develop due to a general deficiency of demand. Owing to the relative shortage and high cost of labour, there would be no further productive use available for additional capital equipment. The citizens, if they were earning incomes in full employment, might still wish to save and to refrain from spending the whole of these incomes on consumption goods; but entrepreneurs would have little incentive to borrow these funds to spend on the purchase of new capital goods. Cf. *The Stationary Economy*, pp. 18–19.

proportional rate than the labour supply and the ratio of unemployed to employed labour will rise without limit.[1]

We can use Figure 2 (ii) to show how in these same technical-production conditions a Plantcap may nevertheless manage to adjust the rate of growth of capital to the rate of growth of labour so as to maintain full employment. In Figure 2 (ii) the production function O B D F is exactly the same as in Figure 2 (i). If l and S_p are both positive the slope $\dfrac{l}{S_p}$ must be positive. The point D at which the slope of the curve O B D F is equal to $\dfrac{l}{S_p}$ cannot, therefore, lie to the right of D', since to the right of D' the slope of O B D F is zero. If by some historical mishap we did start with $\dfrac{K}{L} = \hat{K}$ greater than the technological maximum (i.e. at a point on O B D F to the right of D'), some K would be unemployed. In this case the rental of capital (W_k) and the rate of profit will be zero, so that k will be zero. K will cease to grow and with the continued growth of L, $\hat{K}$ will fall. The fall in $\hat{K}$ will continue until the marginal product of capital has risen to $\dfrac{l}{S_p}$. Thus in a Plantcap the extreme form of capital glut is impossible.

But even in a Plantcap it is not always possible to avoid a continuing condition of technological unemployment. Suppose that $\dfrac{l}{S_p}$ is so great that it is equal to the slope of the line OH, i.e. is greater than the slope of the line OB'. Then wherever we may start on the production function O B D F we will have the slope of the curve $\left(\text{measuring the rate of profit } \dfrac{UY}{K}\right)$ less than $\dfrac{l}{S_p}$. In this case with $\dfrac{S_p UY}{K} = k < l$, $\hat{K}$ will be continually falling. When the point B' is reached technological unemployment will appear; with the appearance of unemployment the wage rate will fall to zero; the whole of income will go to profits; U will be equal to 1. But even so $\dfrac{S_p UY}{K}$ will remain less than l, because the technologically maximum possible level of $\dfrac{Y}{K}$ is less than $\dfrac{l}{S_p}$. Population will be growing at a greater rate than the upper limit to the rate of capital accumulation which will be

---

[1] In such cases the economy would inevitably move into a situation of technological unemployment or underemployment typical of some under-developed countries, where there is not enough real capital equipment to give full employment to all the available labour. Cf. *The Stationary Economy*, pp. 18–19.

reached when the whole of the national income goes to profits out of which savings are financed. The volume of technological unemployment will grow without limit. In fact, of course, in a Plantcap a zero wage would imply starvation for the workers and the rate of growth of the working population would itself fall. We shall take up these repercussions of the standard of living upon the growth rate of the population in Chapter XI below.

CHAPTER VII

THE STATE OF STEADY GROWTH: (2) A THIRD FACTOR AND TECHNICAL PROGRESS

In the last chapter we considered at some length how with some exceptions capital accumulation and population growth in a Propdem or a Plantcap might be expected to lead to a state of steady growth if there were no fixed factor, land, and if there were no technical progress. In this chapter we shall introduce both a fixed factor, land, and technical progress; and we shall find that with these complications we cannot always expect the economy to tend towards a state of steady growth.

(1) TWO FACTORS WITH TECHNICAL PROGRESS

Let us start by assuming still that there is no third factor, land, (so that $Z = 0$ and $U = 1 - Q$), but let us now allow for technical progress (so that we no longer assume $k' = l' = 0$). In these conditions we have from (4.11)

$$y = (1 - Q)(k + k') + Q(l + l')$$

and from (5.7)

$$w_k = -\frac{Q}{\mu}k + \frac{\mu - Q}{\mu}k' + \frac{Q}{\mu}(l + l')$$

Now in a Propdem $k = \dfrac{SY}{K}$ so that k will be rising or falling according as $\dfrac{Y}{K}$ is rising or falling, i.e. according as $k \lessgtr y$. So that in the present conditions in a Propdem we know that k will be rising or falling according as

$$k \lessgtr (1 - Q)(k + k') + Q(l + l')$$

i.e.

$$k \lessgtr l + l' + \frac{1 - Q}{Q}k' \tag{7.1}$$

On the other hand in a Plantcap $k = \dfrac{S_p(1-Q)Y}{K}$, which in our present conditions can be seen from (4.3) to imply $k = \dfrac{S_p U Y}{K} = S_p W_k$. With S_p constant we shall, therefore, have k rising or falling according as W_k is rising or falling, i.e. according as

$$w_k \gtrless 0$$

or, in other words, according as

$$-\frac{Q}{\mu} k + \frac{\mu - Q}{\mu} k' + \frac{Q}{\mu} (l + l') \gtrless 0$$

i.e. as $k \lessgtr l + l' + \dfrac{\mu - Q}{Q} k'$ \hfill (7.2)

Let us first consider a Propdem in these conditions. We may call $l + l' + \dfrac{1-Q}{Q} k'$ the 'target' value of k, because k will always be falling if k is greater than the target value and will be rising if it is below this target level. Nevertheless k may no longer tend to a steady constant value because the target itself may be continually changing. Even if l' and k' are constant, we cannot assume that Q is constant unless the elasticity of substitution between K^* and L^* is numerically equal to unity.

Suppose, for example, that $\dfrac{K^*}{L^*}$ is rising and the elasticity of substitution between K^* and L^* is numerically greater than unity, then (see pages 69–70 above) Q will be falling. On the other hand if $\dfrac{K^*}{L^*}$ is rising and the elasticity of substitution is numerically less than unity, then Q will be rising. Now suppose that k happened to be at the target level of $l + l' + \dfrac{1-Q}{Q} k'$. k would for the moment be neither rising nor falling. But with $k = l + l' + \dfrac{1-Q}{Q} k'$ we have $k + k' = l + l' + \dfrac{k'}{Q}$, so that if $k' < 0$ we would have $k + k' > l + l'$. In other words, $\dfrac{K^*}{L^*}$ would be rising. So if the elasticity of substitution between K^* and L^* were numerically greater (or less) than unity Q would be falling (or rising) so that $\dfrac{1-Q}{Q} k'$ would be rising (or falling). The target level of k would thus itself be rising (or falling), so that k itself would start to rise (or to fall).

There is in this case a lower limit to the value of k. Q cannot rise above unity, however much numerically smaller than unity may be the elasticity of substitution between K^* and L^*. The target level of k can, therefore, never fall below $l + l'$. But in the opposite case, i.e. if the elasticity of substitution between K^* and L^* remains always numerically much greater than unity, there is no finite upper limit to the value of k. Since Q may fall indefinitely towards zero, $\dfrac{1-Q}{Q} k'$ may rise indefinitely towards infinity. In this case the rate of growth would become continuously higher and higher with no upper limit.

The behaviour of a Plantcap in the present case is very similar. From (7.2) we now have k falling (or rising) according as k is above (or below) a target level of $l + l' + \dfrac{\mu - Q}{Q} k'$. Once again if k were at this target level we would have $k + k' = l + l' + \dfrac{\mu}{Q} k'$ so that, if $k' > 0$, $\dfrac{K^*}{L^*}$ would be rising. Even if l, l', and k' were constant Q would now be falling if the elasticity of substitution between K^* and L^* were numerically greater than unity. In the opposite conditions Q would be rising. The target level of k might thus itself continually change as k got near to the target level. k would not necessarily ever reach a constant steady level.

Of course, if the elasticity of substitution between K^* and L^* were numerically equal to unity, then we would have $\mu = 1$, and Q would be constant. In both a Propdem and a Plantcap the target level of k would be constant at $l + l' + \dfrac{1-Q}{Q} k'$, and k would reach a steady constant value at this level.

If we substitute this value of k in equations (4.11) and (5.7) writing $Z = 0$ and $U = 1 - Q$, we obtain

$$\left.\begin{aligned} y - l &= l' + \frac{1-Q}{Q} k' \\[2mm] w_l &= l' + \frac{1-Q}{Q} k' \\[2mm] w_k &= 0 \end{aligned}\right\} \qquad (7.3)$$

We can conclude that in the two-factor case with factor-expanding technical progress the economy will move towards a state of steady growth, if the elasticity of substitution between the factors is numerically equal to unity. In this state of steady growth the growth rate of income per head and the growth rate of the wage rate will both be equal to $l' + \dfrac{1-Q}{Q} k'$ and the rate of profit (W_k) will be constant.

Even if the elasticity of substitution is not numerically equal to unity, a state of steady growth will also be approached if technical progress is solely labour-expanding. From (7.1) and (7.2) one can see that if $k' = 0$, k will be rising or falling both in a Propdem and in a Plantcap according as $k \lessgtr l + l'$. The target value of k is now a constant one, namely $l + l'$. If we substitute this value of k in equations (4.11) and (5.7), writing $Z = 0$ and $U = 1 - Q$, we obtain:

$$\left. \begin{array}{l} y - l = l' \\ w_l = l' \\ w_k = 0 \end{array} \right\} \qquad (7.4)$$

A state of steady growth will now be reached in which the growth rate of income per head and of the wage rate are both equal to the rate of labour-expansion and in which the rate of profit is constant. The fact that the wage rate is rising at the same proportional rate as income per head means that the ratio of wages to total income, Q, will be constant in this state of steady growth even though it is not assumed that the elasticity of substitution between labour and capital is numerically equal to unity.

The reason for this result is easy to understand. If there is no capital-expanding technical progress, the growth rate of the capital stock will be the same whether capital be measured in efficiency units (K^*) or in natural units (K). In the state of steady growth k will have reached its target of $l + l'$ or, in other words, $k = k^* = l + l' = l^*$. Capital and labour measured in efficiency units will be growing at the same rate ($k^* = l^*$). $\dfrac{K^*}{L^*}$ will, therefore, be constant. W_l^* and W_k^* will, therefore, both be constant, since there is no change in the factor proportions. $\dfrac{W_k^* K^*}{W_l^* L^*}$ will, therefore, be constant or, in other words, the ratio of profits to wages, $\dfrac{1-Q}{Q}$, will be constant. Moreover, since $K = K^*$, $W_k = W_k^*$ so that a constant W_k^* implies a constant W_k; that is to say, the rate of profit will be constant. Since the wage per unit of efficiency labour (W_l^*) is constant, the wage rate per man will be rising at the rate of labour expansion (i.e. $w_l = l'$). Income per unit of efficiency labour and the wage per unit of efficiency labour will both be constant, which means that income per head and the wage rate per man will be rising at the rate of labour-expansion.[1]

(2) THREE FACTORS WITHOUT TECHNICAL PROGRESS

Let us next consider the case where there are three factors of production, K, L, and N, but there is no technical progress. In this case we have from (4.4) and (5.7)

$$y = Uk + Ql \qquad (7.5)$$

$$\left.\begin{array}{l} w_l = \dfrac{U}{\mu}k - \dfrac{1-Q}{\mu}l \\[2mm] w_k = -\dfrac{1-U}{\mu}k + \dfrac{Q}{\mu}l \\[2mm] w_n = \dfrac{U}{\mu}k + \dfrac{Q}{\mu}l \end{array}\right\} \qquad (7.6)$$

and

In the case of a Propdem $k = \dfrac{SY}{K}$ so that k is rising or falling according as

$$k \lessgtr y$$

i.e. from (7.5),

as $\quad k \lessgtr Uk + Ql$

i.e. as $\quad k \lessgtr \dfrac{Ql}{1-Q}$

i.e. as $\quad k \lessgtr \dfrac{Q}{Q+Z}l \qquad (7.7)$

Thus k will chase the target $\dfrac{Q}{Q+Z}l$. If the elasticities of substitution are numerically equal to unity, then Q and Z will be constant; k will then rise or fall until it is equal to $\dfrac{Q}{Q+Z}l$; and in this state of steady growth we should have from (7.5)

$$y = \dfrac{UQ}{Q+Z}l + Ql = \dfrac{Q}{Q+Z}l.$$

It follows that

$$y - l = \dfrac{Q}{Q+Z}l - l = -\dfrac{Z}{Q+Z}l.$$

---

[1] The whole of this analysis of pure labour-expanding technical progress can be carried out in terms of the geometry on pages 84–90 above if one replaces L with L^* and l with $l + l'$ throughout those pages and in Figure 2.

In other words in this case we shall reach a state of steady growth in which $y = k$ so that $\dfrac{SY}{K}$ is constant; but in this state y and k will be only a fraction $\left(\dfrac{Q}{Q+Z}\right)$ of l, so that $\dfrac{Y}{L}$ will be falling at a proportional rate equal to $-\dfrac{Z}{Q+Z}l$. This will measure the adverse effect of the growing pressure of numbers on the fixed amount of land.

But the attainment of a state of steady growth in these conditions rests upon the assumption that elasticities of substitution between the factors are numerically equal to unity. Suppose, however, that this is not the case and that these elasticities of substitution are all numerically less than unity. Suppose, however, that for the moment we start with $k = \dfrac{Q}{Q+Z}l$ so that, in accordance with (7.7), k will for the moment be constant. Then k is only a fraction $\left(\dfrac{Q}{Q+Z}\right)$ of l and n is zero, so that we have $l > k > n$. Both the ratios $\dfrac{L}{K}$ and $\dfrac{L}{N}$ will be rising so that, with the elasticities of substitution between L and the other factors numerically less than unity, the proportion (Q) of the national income going to wages will fall. At the same time $\dfrac{N}{L}$ and $\dfrac{N}{K}$ will be falling so that, with low elasticities of substitution, Z will be rising. But with Q falling and Z rising, the fraction $\dfrac{Q}{Q+Z}$ will be falling. Therefore, if we started with k at its 'target' level of $\dfrac{Q}{Q+Z}l$, the target level itself would fall and k would in consequence also start to fall. No steady state would in these conditions be possible and $\dfrac{Q}{Q+Z}$ and so the 'target' level of k might fall continuously towards zero.

We can treat a Plantcap in this case of three factors without technical progress in the following way. Let us write $A = S_p(W_kK + W_nN)$ as representing the total of savings in the economy (i.e. S_p times the property incomes of profits—W_kK—*plus* rents—W_nN). Let ΔA represent the increase in savings from one day to the next. Then

$$\Delta A = S_p\{W_kK(k + w_k) + W_nNw_n\}[1]$$

[1] See pages 16–17 above.

If we write a for $\dfrac{\Delta A}{A}$, the growth rate of total savings, we have

$$a = \frac{S_p\{W_k K(k + w_k) + W_n N w_n\}}{S_p\{W_k K + W_n N\}}$$

$$= \frac{U}{U + Z}(k + w_k) + \frac{Z}{U + Z}w_n \qquad (7.8)$$

since $W_k K = U Y$ and $W_n N = Z Y$.

But $k = \dfrac{A}{K}$ so that k will be rising or falling according as

$$k \lessgtr a$$

If we use (7.6) to substitute for w_k and w_n into (7.8), we can see that k will be rising or falling according as

$$(U + Z)\,k \lessgtr Uk - \frac{U(1 - U)}{\mu}k + \frac{UQ}{\mu}l + \frac{ZU}{\mu}k + \frac{ZQ}{\mu}l$$

i.e. according as

$$k \lessgtr \frac{QZ + QU}{\mu Z + QU}l \qquad (7.9)$$

If $\mu = 1$, so that Q, U, and Z are constant, this condition becomes

$$k \lessgtr \frac{Q(Z + U)}{1 - U - Q + UQ}l$$

i.e. as

$$k \lessgtr \frac{Q(1 - Q)}{(1 - U)(1 - Q)}l$$

i.e. as

$$k \lessgtr \frac{Q}{Q + Z}l \qquad (7.10)$$

In this case with Q and Z constant, k would move on to its constant 'target' level of $\dfrac{Q}{Q + Z}l$ and we would have the same result as in the case of a Propdem on page 96 above.

But if μ were not equal to unity, then k would always move in the direction of its 'target' level $\dfrac{QZ + QU}{\mu Z + QU}l$; but, since Q, Z, and U would no longer be constant, this 'target' might itself be moving. Thus k might never reach a constant level in which case no state of steady growth could be attained.

D

(3) THREE FACTORS AND TECHNICAL PROGRESS

Let us now consider the general case in which there are three factors and technical progress.

In a Propdem $k = \dfrac{SY}{K}$ and k will, therefore, be rising or falling according as $k \lessgtr y$. Using the value of y from equation (4.11) this means that k will be rising or falling according as

$$k \lessgtr U(k + k') + Q(l + l') + Zn'$$

i.e. as
$$k \lessgtr \frac{Uk' + Q(l + l') + Zn'}{1 - U} \qquad (7.11)$$

With k', l, l', and n' constant this target for k will itself be constant
(i) if U, Q, and Z are also constant or
(ii) if $k' = 0$ and $n' = l + l'$, in which case the target becomes $\dfrac{Q + Z}{1 - U}(l + l') = l + l'$.

Case (i) implies that the elasticities of substitution between the factors are all numerically equal to unity. Case (ii) would involve a most extreme fluke in the nature of technical progress, since there would have to be no element of capital-expanding technical progress but at the same time the rate of land-expanding technical progress would have to happen to be equal to the sum of the rate of population growth and of labour-expanding technical progress. Case (ii) is so special and peculiar that we shall pay no further attention to it.

The position in a Plantcap is very similar. In this case $k = S_p W_k$ and will therefore be rising or falling according as $w_k \gtrless 0$. Using the value of w_k given in equation (5.7) this means that k will be rising or falling according as

$$\frac{1 - U}{\mu}k \lessgtr \frac{\mu + U - 1}{\mu}k' + \frac{Q}{\mu}(l + l') + \frac{Z}{\mu}n'$$

i.e. as
$$k \lessgtr \frac{(\mu + U - 1)k' + Q(l + l') + Zn'}{1 - U} \qquad (7.12)$$

Once again this target for k will be constant if either (i) $\mu = 1$ so that U, Q, and Z are constant or (ii) $k' = 0$ and $n' = l + l'$ in which case the target is constant at $l + l'$. Once again we shall pay no attention to the second of these two cases.

We will accordingly confine our attention to the possibility of a state of steady growth being reached with three factors and with factor expanding technical progress because the elasticities of substitution are numerically equal to unity so that U, Q, and Z are constant.

With U, Q, Z, k', l', and n' constant the rate of technical progress r which (see equation (4.11)) is equal to $Uk' + Ql' + Zn'$ will itself be constant. We can, therefore, rewrite expressions (7.11) and (7.12) above in the form that both in a Propdem and in a Plantcap with $\mu = 1$ k will be rising or falling according as

$$k \lessgtr \frac{Ql + r}{1 - U} \tag{7.13}$$

where Q, U, l, and r are all constant. We shall move towards a state of steady growth with $k = \dfrac{Ql + r}{1 - U} = \dfrac{Ql + r}{Q + Z}$. Since $y = Uk + Ql + r$ we will then have $y = (Ql + r)\left(\dfrac{U}{Q + Z} + 1\right) = \dfrac{Ql + r}{Q + Z}$,

so that in this state of steady growth we will have:—

$$y = k = \frac{Ql + r}{Q + Z} \tag{7.14}$$

It follows that $y - l = \dfrac{Ql + r}{Q + Z} - l$

i.e. that

$$y - l = \frac{r - Zl}{Q + Z} \tag{7.15}$$

In this case the standard of living $\dfrac{Y}{L}$ will in the state of steady growth be continuously rising or falling according as $r \gtrless Zl$. The outcome depends upon the conflict between technical progress (r) on the one hand and the pressure of population (l) on the fixed resources of the land (Z) on the other.

From (5.7) with $\mu = 1$ and $r = Uk' + Ql' + Zn'$

$$w_l = Uk - (1 - Q)l + r$$
$$= Uk + Ql + r - l$$
$$= y - l.$$

In other words, when the proportion of the national income going to wages is constant, the wage rate will be changing at the same rate as income per head, so that w_l and $y - l$ will have the same value and will in this case be positive or negative according as $r \gtrless Zl$.

It is also of interest to note what will be happening to the rate of profit in the state of steady growth in our present model. The rate of profit is measured by $\frac{UY}{K}$ (see equation (4.3) above); and $\frac{UY}{K}$ can be written as $\frac{U}{S}\frac{SY}{K} = \frac{U}{S}k$. Now we know that in our model k, the growth rate in the capital stock will tend towards the steady value $k = \frac{Ql+r}{Q+Z}$. It follows that the rate of profit in our model will tend towards the steady level of

$$\frac{UY}{K} = \frac{U}{S}\frac{Ql+r}{Q+Z} \qquad (7.16)$$

The rate of profit will, therefore, neither have to fall nor to rise indefinitely in our present model. Once the economy has reached its path of steady growth, the rate of profit can be maintained constant at the above level. This rate will be at a relatively high level if (i) l and r are high, which are both forces keeping up the productivity of capital, (ii) if U, the proportional marginal product of capital, is itself high, (iii) if S, the proportion of income saved, is low which as we have seen is a factor keeping down the supply of the capital stock, and (iv) if Z is low, which will reduce the depressing effect of land scarcity upon the productivity of capital.

To summarize the position reached up to this point in this and the preceding chapter, we shall have models of economic growth which will lead to states of steady growth if

    either (i) there are only two factors and there is no technical progress (Chapter VI);

    and/or (ii) there are two factors and labour-expanding technical progress (Chapter VII, pp. 93–94);

    and/or (iii) there are two or three factors and unitary elasticities of substitution between the factors with or without any combinations of output-expanding labour-expanding, capital-expanding, and land-expanding technical progress (Chapter VII, pp. 95–100).

All these three cases are, of course, special cases. Cases (i) and (ii) allow us to examine the effects of different degrees of substitutability between factors but rely upon the absence of a fixed factor and are very restrictive and special in their assumptions about technical progress. Case (iii) allows for a fixed factor and for a much wider range of assumption about technical progress, but is applicable only to cases of unitary elasticities of substitution between the factors and thus prevents any examination of the effects of exceptionally high or low substitutability. In spite of this to the present author case (iii) seems perhaps the least unnatural set of assumptions and where it is desired in the rest of this volume to choose any single model to illustrate a state of steady growth it will be case (iii) which will normally be used.

It may, therefore, be useful to some readers to give a geometric demonstration of the fact that in the present case (with output- or factor-expanding technical progress and unitary elasticities of substitution) the economy will reach a steady state whether it be a Propdem or a Plantcap. We have already explained (pp. 60–61 above) that in these conditions the proportions (U, Q, and Z) of the national income going to profits, wages, and rents will remain constant. From this we have already drawn two conclusions:

(i) In a Plantcap as well as in a Propdem the proportion of total income saved will remain constant. Since the proportion of income going to property incomes will remain constant at $U + Z$ and since in a Plantcap a constant proportion of property incomes (S_p) is saved, it follows that in a Plantcap a constant proportion of total income—namely, $S_p(U + Z)$—will be saved. So far, therefore, as the savings proportion is concerned we need not in this case distinguish between the analysis of a Propdem or a Plantcap; the proportion of total income saved will in both cases be constant, at S in a Propdem and at $S_p(U + Z)$ in a Plantcap.

(ii) The wage rate and income per head will both rise or fall at the same proportional rate in a Plantcap or a Propdem. We have $\dfrac{W_l L}{Y} = Q$ or $W_l = Q\dfrac{Y}{L}$. The wage rate is, therefore, always a constant proportion of total income per head.

For these two reasons we need only analyse a Propdem. If there is a state of steady growth in a Propdem, there will be a state of steady growth in a Plantcap. If income per head is rising (or falling) in the state of steady growth in a Propdem, the wage rate will be rising (or falling) at the same rate in a Plantcap.

Let us then consider a Propdem with our present conditions in which U, Q, and Z are constant. We wish to show geometrically the conclusion which we have already reached analytically, namely that the economy will always reach a state of steady growth in which $k = y =$ the constant $\dfrac{Ql + r}{Q + Z}$ given in (7.14).

This is shown by means of Figure 3. From our basic formula for the rate of economic growth of total output Y, namely

$$y = Uk + Ql + r$$

we can see that with U, Q, l, and r constant, the rate of growth of net output (y) varies only with variations in the rate of capital accumulation (k). We measure the rate of capital accumulation (k) along the horizontal axis and the consequential rate of growth of output (y) up the vertical axis of Figure 3.

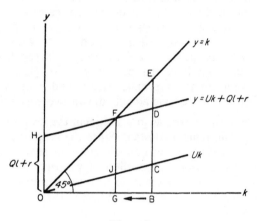

Figure 3

Draw a line OC through the origin O with a slope equal to U (i.e. $\dfrac{CB}{OB} = U$) so that the height of this line above the k-axis measures Uk, which is the contribution of the rate of capital accumulation to the rate of growth of output. For example, if $U = \frac{1}{4}$ and OB = 3 per cent per annum, then CB $= U \times$ OB $= \frac{3}{4}$ per cent per annum, which is the rate of growth of output which is due to capital accumulation. Since U is less than one, the line OC will slope upwards at an angle less than 45°.

But the rate of growth of output (y) also has a constant component equal to $Ql + r$, which represents the contributions of population growth and of technical progress to growth. This can be shown by measuring up the vertical axis a distance OH equal to $Ql + r$ and drawing through H the line HFD parallel to the line OC. The height of the line HFD above the k-axis will measure the total rate of growth of output, y. Thus if $k =$ OB, $y =$ BD, since BC measures the contribution of capital accumulation to y and CD measures the contributions of population growth and technical progress to y.

Finally, through the origin O draw the line OE at 45° to the k-axis. The height of this line above the k-axis measures k itself, since, for example, at the point B EB $=$ OB $= k$. Let the line OE cut HD at F.

Then to the right of F we have OE above HD (i.e. $k > y$) and to the left of F we have OE below HD (i.e. $k < y$).

Let us suppose that we are dealing with an economic system which has accumulated in the past rather a small stock of capital but which has a very high savings ratio, S or $S_p(U + Z)$. The rate of capital accumulation will be exceptionally high because large additions are being made to a small capital stock. Suppose this high rate of capital accumulation is measured by OB in Figure 3. In this case the rate of capital accumulation (k) is greater than the rate of growth of income (y). It follows that $\dfrac{SY}{K}$ will be falling because Y is growing less quickly than K and S is constant. But $\dfrac{SY}{K}$ is the rate of capital accumulation k. It follows that so long as $k > y$, k will be falling. If k starts at the level OB at which $k > y$, then k will move in the direction of the arrow in Figure 3 towards the value OG at which $k = y$ so that $\dfrac{SY}{K}$ is constant so that k is neither rising nor falling.

It could similarly be shown that if k started at a low value—to the left of G, then k would be $< y$, so that $\dfrac{SY}{K}$ would be rising, so that k would be rising towards the value OG.

We can conclude from this that the economy will always move towards a state of steady growth at which $y = k =$ a constant measured by the length FG in Figure 3. Now JF = FG − JG. But JG = $Uk = U \times$ FG. Therefore JF = $(1-U)$ FG or FG $= \dfrac{\text{JF}}{1 - U}$ $= \dfrac{\text{HO}}{1 - U} = \dfrac{Ql + r}{1 - U}$. Since $1 - U = Q + Z$ this is the value for $y = k$ in the state of steady growth already expressed in (7.14).

What is the common sense of all this? Does this particular model have any relevance to the real world or is it a peculiar phenomenon due solely to the extreme simplifying assumption which we are making for our present model?

There is, I think, a general conclusion which one can draw. Economic growth is basically due to three components: capital accumulation, population growth, and technical progress. If over a considerable period of years population growth and technical progress make contributions which are not readily changed by economic considerations, then the relationship between capital accumulation and growth of output will tend to bring the rate of economic growth to a steady level which depends upon the rate of population growth and the rate of technical progress and is *independent of the proportion of income saved.*

At first sight it appears very paradoxical to suggest that whether S be high or low, the rate of growth of output will tend to the same level. But on consideration for the reasons already discussed on page 79 for the simple case of two factors and no technical progress this does not appear so unreasonable a conclusion. Suppose, for example, that there were a sudden but permanent increase in S, the proportion of income saved. Given the current levels of employment (L), stock of capital goods (K), and net output (Y), there would, of course, be a sudden increase in the rate of growth of output. This rise in S will raise $\dfrac{SY}{K}$, the rate of capital accumulation; and the higher rate of capital accumulation will raise the rate of economic growth.

But there will now be forces bringing the rate of capital accumulation and so the rate of economic growth back towards their previous lower levels. Because of diminishing returns to one factor alone[1] (in our simple model because U is < 1) the higher rate of capital accumulation will raise the rate of economic growth by a smaller figure. Thus if the rate of capital accumulation goes up by 1 per cent per annum (e.g. from 3 per cent per annum to 4 per cent per annum), the rate of growth of output will rise by less than 1 per cent per annum (e.g. from 3 per cent per annum to $3\frac{1}{4}$ per cent per annum).

There will thus be a tendency immediately after the sharp rise in S for the capital stock to grow more rapidly than the national income. But if savings vary with the national income rather than with the capital stock, this will, as we have seen, cause the rate of capital accumulation to fall. The result is that the increase in the rate of economic growth which is caused by a sudden rise in the proportion of income saved will not be permanent. It will fall back towards its previous level.

But there will result a permanent rise in the capital stock itself. The rate of capital accumulation will fall back towards its previous level only as and when the capital stock will have grown through greater savings to become permanently larger relatively to the supply of labour and land than it would otherwise have been at every future date. At any date in the future there will be (i) a higher absolute

---

[1] In this volume we are simply assuming constant returns to scale (i.e. constant returns to all factors taken together) and diminishing returns to one factor taken alone. But in the real world there may well be increasing returns to scale. This does not, however, imply that there are increasing returns to one factor taken alone (i.e. that a 1 per cent increase in the capital stock alone would cause a more than 1 per cent increase in total output). Fixed factors like land, as well as labour, would act as restraining elements. Increasing returns to scale would have to be very powerful to lead to increasing returns to the capital stock alone. If, however, such were the case, the analysis in the text would not apply.

capital stock than there would otherwise have been and therefore (ii) a higher ratio of K to L and N than there would otherwise have been and therefore (iii), on the one hand, because of diminishing returns to capital alone, a lower ratio of income to capital than there would otherwise have been, but (iv) on the other hand, a higher real income per head than there would otherwise have been. But the rate of growth of this higher real income per head will not necessarily be greater. In a growing economy a higher proportion of income saved and invested will lead temporarily to a higher rate of growth of income per head and will permanently maintain a higher level of income per head; but it will not necessarily lead to a permanently higher rate of growth of income per head.

CHAPTER VIII

THE LEVEL OF CONSUMPTION IN A
STATE OF STEADY GROWTH

There remains one relationship in a state of steady growth which is of very great importance and which we will discuss in the present chapter. We have shown that in a state of steady growth the *growth rate* of income is unaffected by the proportion of income saved but that the *level* of income is affected by the savings proportion. But how does the savings proportion affect the level of consumption, as contrasted with the level of income, in a state of steady growth? Here there are two opposing tendencies at work. On the one hand, a high savings proportion will, as we have argued, lead to a high level of income. But, on the other hand, a high savings proportion will, of course, mean that there is less available for consumption out of any given level of income. Which influence will prevail? Will a higher savings proportion lead to a higher or to a lower level of consumption in a state of steady growth?

We can examine this question best by considering a Propdem with a constant proportion (S) of the total national income saved and in one of the sets of conditions examined in the two preceding chapters in which a constant S leads to a state of steady growth. In all such cases, as we have seen, the economy would ultimately settle down in a state of steady growth in which the rate of capital accumulation, k, was at some constant level which we will call k_s.[1] Thus we have in all cases of the steady state in a Propdem

$$\frac{SY}{K} = k_s = \text{constant}$$

The problem which we wish to examine is as follows. Suppose that we are in such a state of steady growth and that there is a once-for-all small increase in S, the proportion of income saved. S goes up once-for-all by a small increment ∂S, i.e. by a small proportion equal to $\frac{\partial S}{S}$. The economy will now be out of a state of steady growth.

[1] $k_s = l$ in the conditions described on pp. 75–84; $k_s = l + l'$ in the conditions described on p. 94; and $k_s = \frac{Ql + r}{Q + Z}$ in the conditions described on p. 99.

$\dfrac{SY}{K}$ will have been raised above k_s. But as we have seen (p. 79 and p. 104 above) this exceptionally high rate of capital accumulation will cause diminishing returns to K; $\dfrac{Y}{K}$ will fall, and this will go on until we reach a new state of steady growth with $\dfrac{SY}{K}$ once more restored to its old level of k_s through a fall in $\dfrac{Y}{K}$ which offsets the rise in S.

Consider then some point of time in the distant future and compare the state of affairs which would then be ruling if S had not risen to $S + \partial S$ (which we will call Situation I) with the state of affairs which will be ruling if S has risen to $S + \partial S$ (which we will call Situation II). The question which we wish to raise is whether the level of consumption will be higher or lower in Situation II than in Situation I. It is not obvious which will happen, because of the two conflicting influences at work. On the one hand a higher savings proportion will as we have seen (p. 79 and p. 104 above) cause the capital stock (K) and so the level of total income (Y) to be larger in Situation II than I. But on the other hand the higher savings proportion will reduce the level of total consumption (C) relatively to the level of income (Y), since a smaller proportion $(1 - S)$ of income will be left over from savings and available for consumption. What we intend now to show is that according as the proportional marginal product of capital (U) is greater (or less) than the proportion of income saved (S), so the level of consumption will be greater (or less) in Situation II with the higher proportion of income saved than in Situation I with the lower proportion of income saved.

We can demonstrate this proposition in the following way. In both Situations I and II we shall have $\dfrac{SY}{K} = k_s$ where k_s is the same in both cases, but S, Y, and K are all slightly larger by ∂S, ∂Y, and ∂K respectively in Situation II. Now since

$$\frac{SY}{K} = \text{constant}$$

we have

$$\frac{\partial S}{S} + \frac{\partial Y}{Y} = \frac{\partial K}{K} \text{[1]} \tag{8.1}$$

---

[1] For the ratio $SY \div K$ to be constant SY must rise in the same ratio as K. The proportional rise in K is $\dfrac{\partial K}{K}$ and for small changes in S and Y the pro-

We can see this in an alternative way. This rise in S will cause K and so Y both to rise, as we have already seen (pp. 79 and 104 above). But, because of diminishing returns to K, Y will rise in a smaller proportion than K. The rise in K and in Y will go on until $\frac{Y}{K}$ has fallen to offset the rise in S, i.e. until $\frac{\partial S}{S} = \frac{\partial K}{K} - \frac{\partial Y}{Y}$.

But the production function sets a relationship between $\frac{\partial K}{K}$ and $\frac{\partial Y}{Y}$. Indeed, by definition the proportional marginal product of K is

$$U = \frac{K}{Y} \frac{\partial Y}{\partial K} \text{ (see page 54 above)}$$

$$\text{or} \quad \frac{\partial K}{K} = \frac{1}{U} \frac{\partial Y}{Y} \tag{8.2}$$

Thus if U is $\frac{1}{4}$, K must rise by 4 per cent in order to cause a 1 per cent rise in Y. Thus from (8.1) and (8.2) we can eliminate $\frac{\partial K}{K}$ and get

$$\frac{\partial S}{S} = \frac{\partial Y}{Y}\left(\frac{1}{U} - 1\right)$$

$$\text{or} \quad \frac{\partial Y}{Y} = \frac{U}{1 - U} \frac{\partial S}{S} \tag{8.3}$$

The expression (8.3) simply tells us that if S is 1 per cent greater in Situation II than in Situation I, then with $U = \frac{1}{4}$ Y will be $\frac{1}{3}$ of 1 per cent greater in Situation II than in Situation I.[1]

We know then that the favourable effect on Y of a 1 per cent rise in S will be to cause Y to rise by $\frac{U}{1 - U}$ of 1 per cent. A rise of Y of any given percentage would raise consumption by the same percentage if the same proportion of income were spent on consumption as before. But, of course, a 1 per cent rise in the proportion of income saved will cause some fall in the proportion of income spent on consump-

portional rise in SY is for all practical purposes equal to the sum of the proportional rises in S and Y, i.e. to $\frac{\partial S}{S} + \frac{\partial Y}{Y}$. (See page 17 above.)

[1] If the proportional marginal product of K is $\frac{1}{4}$, K will have to go up by $\frac{4}{3}$ of 1 per cent to make Y go up by $\frac{1}{3}$ of 1 per cent. If K goes up by $\frac{4}{3}$ of 1 per cent and Y by $\frac{1}{3}$ of 1 per cent, $\frac{K}{Y}$ will go up by approximately $\frac{4}{3} - \frac{1}{3}$ of 1 per cent = 1 per cent. This will offset a rise in S of 1 per cent. $\frac{SY}{K}$ will once more be at its original steady-state level, k_s.

tion. What we have then to ask is whether this direct effect of a 1 per cent rise in the proportion of income saved will be to cause the level of consumption out of any given income to fall by more or by less than $\frac{U}{1-U}$ of 1 per cent.

The proportion of income spent is $1 - S$. When S goes up by ∂S, $1 - S$ goes down by ∂S. The proportional fall in the amount of consumption out of any given income is therefore $\frac{\partial S}{1-S}$ or $\frac{S}{1-S} \frac{\partial S}{S}$, so that when S goes up by 1 per cent the direct effect on consumption out of any given income will be to reduce C by $\frac{S}{1-S}$ of 1 per cent.

We can thus compare the two conflicting effects of a 1 per cent increase in S on the level of C:

(i) By adding to the capital stock it will cause the level of income to be $\frac{U}{1-U}$ of 1 per cent higher in Situation II than in Situation I.

(ii) By reducing the proportion of any given income which is spent on consumption it will cause the level of consumption out of any given income to be $\frac{S}{1-S}$ of 1 per cent lower in Situation II than in Situation I.

Thus the favourable effect (i) will be greater or less than the unfavourable effect (ii) according as $U \gtrless S$.

If the proportional marginal product of K, namely U, is large, a small increase in S will by causing an increase in K cause a large increase in Y. This will help to raise the standard of living. But if S is high, a small proportional increase in S will cause a large proportional fall in the proportion of income left over for consumption[1] and so tend to depress the standard of living. Our argument shows a very simple relationship between these two influences. A rise in S will cause consumption to be higher or lower in Situation II than in Situation I simply according as to whether the proportional marginal product of capital or in perfect competition the proportion of the national income going to profits is larger or smaller than the proportion of the national income saved. If in a state of steady growth savings are less than profits, a rise in the savings ratio will cause the level of consumption at any future point of time when a new state of

---

[1] To take an extreme example, if S were 90 per cent, a 1 per cent rise in S would raise S from $0 \cdot 9$ to $0 \cdot 909$ and thus lower $1 - S$ from $0 \cdot 1$ to $0 \cdot 091$. A rise of 1 per cent in S would cause a fall of 9 per cent in $1 - S$ and so a fall of 9 per cent in the level of consumption associated with any given level of income.

steady growth has been attained to be higher than it would otherwise have been. If in a state of steady growth savings are more than profits, a rise in the savings proportion will cause the level of consumption at any future point of time when a new state of steady growth has been reached to be lower than it would otherwise have been.

One implication of this is obvious. It is possible that in a *laissez-faire* competitive growing economy there will be too high a level of private savings. Suppose that the conditions are such in the economy that a constant S does lead to a state of steady growth. Suppose that in this state individuals choose to save a proportion (S) of their incomes which is in excess of the proportional marginal product of capital (U). Then if they reduced their savings ratio, consumption could obviously be immediately raised, since they would be spending more and investing less out of the current national income. But with $S > U$, this rise in the level of consumption could last for ever, even when the new state of steady growth were attained, since in this case—as we have just shown—the permanent percentage fall in income at every future date could be more than compensated by the permanent rise in the proportion of income that was devoted to consumption at every future date.

This does not, of course, imply that *laissez-faire* may not lead to the opposite error of too low a savings ratio. Still less does it imply that *laissez-faire* will always lead to too high a savings ratio. But it does direct our attention to a set of questions to which we shall have to return later. To what extent is it desirable in a growing economy that the State should intervene to influence the proportion of the national income which is devoted to savings as opposed to consumption?

CHAPTER IX

THE DETERMINANTS OF
TECHNICAL PROGRESS

We have so far discussed models of a one-product competitive growing economy on the assumptions that the rate and nature of technical progress, the growth rates of the population, and the savings ratios were all given and constant. But this is, of course, not so. Each of these quantities may itself be much affected by economic developments; and accordingly in this and the following chapters (Chapters X to XIV) we shall consider the way in which economic changes may themselves affect these three basic determinants of economic growth.

We start then in this chapter with a consideration of what it is which determines the rate and nature of technical progress. In fact this question raises issues which are probably as important as—possibly more important than—any others concerning the promotion of economic growth. But we are not in fact going to consider them at all profoundly in this volume. As we shall show in this chapter, the problems connected with the promotion of technical progress in fact are intimately bound up with economic 'indivisibilities' and 'externalities' which it is our intention to assume away in the present volume (see assumptions 3 and 4 on page 24 above). For this reason we shall confine ourselves in this chapter to the briefest statement of the issues involved, hoping that if the author and the reader both persevere we may return to a proper discussion of them in a later volume.

So far in this volume we have in effect tacitly assumed that technical progress occurred by a process of costless inspiration which occurred to all competing producers simultaneously. We may perhaps call this the process of 'learning by inspiration'. On Wednesday each producer has the same knowledge of alternative techniques of production; on Thursday each producer has the same knowledge as on Wednesday plus some additional knowledge which enables certain savings in inputs to be made to produce a given output; and this same additional knowledge has been learned overnight by each producer by inspiration and without any effort on his part.

As soon as we try to make this model of technical progress more realistic we become involved either in economic indivisibilities or in economic external effects.

Consider first the fact that to some extent at least technical progress is the result of the devotion of real factors of production (capital, labour, and land) to research effort which is designed purposely to seek for a certain sort of improvement in techniques of production. We will call this the process of 'learning by research'. Much technical progress in fact takes this form in the modern world. At first sight it might appear very easy to incorporate such activity into the assumptions of this volume simply by calling such a phenomenon not technical progress but capital investment. One can increase the real stock of physical capital by purchasing the product of industry not for consumption but for addition to the capital stock; similarly we can purchase the products of the 'research industry' to increase one's stock of knowledge. An increase in the stock of knowledge just as an increase in the stock of physical capital will enable more to be produced with a given amount of the other factors; thus capital invested in knowledge would have a marginal product. Why should one not forget about technical progress as a separate influence on output and simply include knowledge—which like machinery can be acquired at a certain cost—among the factors of production?

If we proceeded in this way, we would of course have to drop the assumption of a one-product economy. Knowledge is not the same product as corn. We would need to concern ourselves with at least two industries, that producing physical products and that producing knowledge, and with four factors of production—labour, land, the stock of physical capital, and the stock of knowledge. And if the factor intensities in the two industries producing knowledge and the physical product were different we would have to concern ourselves with the determination of the relative prices of these two products[1] and the effect of such price changes on growth. This would, however, merely mean that we would have to postpone a proper discussion of technical progress to the later chapters of this volume where we shall in any case be considering a many-product economy with many forms of physical capital equipment. At that stage we could in principle easily add 'knowledge' as the output of the research industry and as a product used as a capital stock for production in other industries.

But the problems connected with knowledge as the output of an organized and costly research activity are much more far-reaching than this. The nature of a new idea is that, while it may be costly to produce, yet once it is produced it can be used on an indefinitely large scale without adding any more to the cost. Mr A spends a very large

1 Cf. *The Stationary Economy*, Chapter IX.

amount of money and produces, let us say, the idea of a wheel in an economy which previously had no wheels. Once the idea of a wheel is invented the fact that Mr A is using it to produce one wheelbarrow does not mean that he or someone else cannot simultaneously use it to produce another wheelbarrow or simultaneously to produce a motor car or a host of other things. This is not true of investment in any ordinary piece of capital equipment. If Mr A spends resources on constructing a factory building, he can use it, say, to produce its capacity output of 1 wheelbarrow a day. But if he uses it to produce this particular wheelbarrow today neither he nor anyone else can simultaneously use it to produce a second wheelbarrow today or to produce a motor car today.

Thus designed investment in research to produce knowledge necessarily introduces an indivisibility into the economic system. A certain lump-sum must be spent to obtain a new idea; but once that idea has been produced at that cost, the use of the idea as a 'capital factor of production' to produce other products can be spread over an indefinitely large number of units of output of those other products without any additional cost.

We must now distinguish between two cases: first, the case where the idea produced by organized research is useful only to the firm which has organized the research (which we may call 'learning by one's own research') and, second, the case where the idea produced by organized research is useful to each firm regardless of whether that firm organized the research or not (which we may call 'learning by another's research'). In the first case we could no longer maintain the assumption of perfect competition or of perfect potential competition.[1] Consider, for example, the case in which only one giant firm exists in any industry. On the assumption of perfect potential competition we argued that it could not in fact restrict output and raise the price of the product above its cost because if it did so a small competitor would come in and take advantage of the high rate of profit now available in the industry. But this rested on the assumption that the small firm would have as low a cost per unit as the large firm. But if it costs each firm, large or small, exactly the same lump-sum investment in research to get the idea of the wheel, it will not necessarily pay a new small firm to compete away the excess profit margin of a large firm since to reduce its costs to as low a level as that of the large firm the small firm must spread the same total research costs over as large an output as the large firm. But a new firm will not come in if its choice is either to come in on a small scale and ruin itself because its research costs per unit of output will be much higher than that of the large firm or else to come in on a large

[1] Cf. *The Stationary Economy*, pp. 30–1.

scale and ruin both itself and the existing large firm by swamping the market for the product by doubling the total output of the product.

In the second and perhaps more realistic case of learning by another's research, the idea proceeding from one firm's investment in research can equally well be used by all firms. In this case there could still be perfect potential competition. In the example used in the previous paragraph the small firm could come in on a small scale and compete with the large firm, using any ideas which the large firm was using, even though these ideas had all been produced at the expense of the large firm. But in this case we have a straightforward case of an external economy.[1] If one producer by spending money on research can produce ideas at considerable cost to himself which can then be used without cost by anyone else, including his competitors, we are faced with a dilemma. If the institutional arrangements are such that anyone is free to use any ideas, then not many ideas will be produced and technical progress will be slowed down. For it will not pay an individual to spend a great deal on research to reduce his own costs if he knows that all his actual or potential competitors will then reduce their costs without sharing any of the expense of the research. Unless the State intervenes, less than the most efficient amount will be spent on research, since the people who gain will be others than those who bear the cost.

Now the State may intervene through patent laws which enable those who have produced the idea to have the sole use of the idea for a period of time, so that they can obtain the exclusive benefit of the reduction in cost. This may encourage the expenditure of resources on the search for new ideas, but it does so only at the expense of an economically inefficient restriction of the use of the idea when it has been produced. For if the idea of a wheel has been produced and if the fact that Mr A is using the idea of a wheel to produce a wheelbarrow in no real way makes it more difficult for Mr B simultaneously to use the idea to produce a competitive wheelbarrow or a motor car it is wasteful of the idea to say that Mr A may use it but Mr B may not.

Escape from this dilemma may be sought through the State promotion and subsidization of research, the fruits of which can be used freely by all. But in this way we are led on to an anticipation of the whole problem of dealing with external economies and diseconomies which we do not intend to undertake in this volume.

A similar set of problems arises if we allow for the fact that technical progress may occur not only through the process of organized costly research for new methods of production but through the process which has been called 'learning by doing'. Practice may make

1 See *The Stationary Economy*, pp. 27–8.

perfect—or rather less imperfect—in big things as in smaller. The technical efficiency with which one can use a given amount of real resources to produce an output of a given product may well depend upon the amount of the product which one has already produced. It is not merely a question of the worker learning his skill; at the higher technical-scientific level too gaining experience of a problem and practising daily the use of given resources to produce an output will itself suggest new ideas to be tried out on future occasions.

We have once again two possible cases: either a firm will learn only by what it produces itself (which we may call 'learning by doing it oneself') or else a firm will learn by the experience of its rivals as well as by its own experience (which we may call 'learning by the doings of others'). The first possibility is a really important one. Firms may be able to learn much more from their own experience than they can from that of others. In this case, however, we must abandon the assumption of perfect potential competition. The large firm which had been large for a long time would have a great advantage in the amount which it has learned over the small new firm. The new small firm could no longer compete away any excess profit from the old experienced large firm.

The second possibility—namely that the small new firm could have learned just as much as the large old firm from the experience of the large old firm—would enable us to restore the assumption of perfect potential competition. But we would now once more have to admit external economies into our system. Some activities may be better instruments of learning than others; investment in more capital equipment may enable one to learn more about new technical possibilities than employing more labour. As a result a producer may invest in what from the community's point of view is too little new capital equipment if the advantages of his experience with that equipment will accrue to others who will not share the cost of purchase of the new equipment.

In order, therefore, to maintain the assumptions of no indivisibilities and of no externalities we shall in the rest of this volume assume that all learning is by inspiration, that is to say that technical progress just occurs out of the blue by the simultaneous costless inspiration of all producers. We shall have to come back to the topic in a later volume.

But before we avert our gaze from these difficult but important problems, it may be useful to note three implications of learning by research and learning by doing.

(1) It becomes very difficult to maintain a clear distinction between increased output due to technical knowledge on the one hand and increased output due to increased employment of factors of produc-

tion on the other hand. Is the increased output due to learning by research to be ascribed to the capital invested in the research or to the existence of a new idea, the use of which is costless once it exists? Is the increased output due to past experience of doing to be ascribed to the factors used in the past or to the existence of a better set of ideas in the present? We are clearly in a realm of ideas where a complete differentiation between technical progress on the one hand and the use of factors on the other is no longer relevant. Technical knowledge is in part at least a product of other factors; but nevertheless once it exists it differs essentially from other products in that its use by one 'consumer' does not impede its simultaneous use by other 'consumers'.

(2) It is particularly difficult to distinguish in the cases of learning by research and learning by doing between, on the one hand, the possibility of substituting one factor for another in a given state of technical knowledge and, on the other hand, a bias in technical progress which saves or uses a particular factor. Let us consider a particular example. Suppose that because of rapid growth of population the wage rate falls relatively to the rent of land. Producers choose less land-intensive and more labour-intensive methods of production. But in so far as costly research is organized, since land is more expensive and labour is less expensive it will pay to divert research from those projects which would have cut costs but would have involved replacing men with land to projects which would have cut costs but would have involved replacing land with men. It is difficult in such a case to say in the outcome of any rise in the ratio of men to land how much is due to substituting the cheap for the expensive factor in the pre-existing state of technical knowledge and how much is due to a labour-using and land-saving bias introduced into technical progress through the rise in the rent of land relatively to the wage of labour.

An exactly similar point arises in the case of 'learning by doing'. The wage of labour falls relatively to the rent of land. Producers use their present technical knowledge to employ more labour-intensive methods. But then the experience gained by doing things in this way improves their knowledge about labour-saving methods. Is this substitution due to a high elasticity of substitution between labour and land or to a labour-using bias introduced into technical progress? In such a case such a question has very little real meaning.

But we can put the matter this way. Both learning by research and learning by doing, as contrasted to learning by inspiration, will tend to make the economy behave as it would with higher numerical elasticities of substitution between the factors. If the wage rate goes up relatively to the rent of land, learning by research will tend to concentrate research projects more on labour-using land-saving devices and learning by doing will give greater experience in labour-using and land-saving methods. Both tendencies will make it easier as time passes to raise the ratio of labour to land.

(3) These considerations suggest that in the cases of learning by research and learning by doing there are some very important implications involved in 'technical assistance' or the organized transfer of technical knowledge from one economy to another, implications which are not involved in the case of 'learning by inspiration'. Let us suppose that there are two economies, A and B. For historical reasons A is both an economy with more advanced technical knowledge and an economy with a higher ratio of capital to labour than B. The scarcity of capital relatively to labour in A will have made the cost of using labour high relatively to the cost of using capital in A. For many years learning by research and learning by doing in A will have steered the up-to-date technical processes into forms which save labour and use capital. In B, however, capital is very scarce and expensive and labour very plentiful and cheap. What is required is a set of techniques which obtain the maximum output from much labour and little capital. Organized research and conscious learning by doing needs to be directed in the opposite direction in B than in A—to save capital and use labour instead of using capital and saving labour. The direct export of a given technique from A to B may miss many a golden opportunity.[1] It is even possible that by a process which we may call 'forgetting by not doing' techniques which A used to use when capital was still scarce in A will no longer be available although it is an up-to-date version of such techniques which may be most appropriate for B.

[1] This mal-direction of technical effort may in fact be greatly intensified if economy B is also a Tradcom (see p. 48 above). In that case the wage rate may be maintained by government or trade union action or by custom at a level designed to give employed workers a decent living *vis-a-vis* the owners of capital. This wage rate which is too high from the efficiency point of view (though desirable from a distributional point of view) may not only cause unemployment by reducing the number employed per unit of capital and land; it may also blunt the extent to which learning by research and learning by doing would otherwise direct technical progress in the direction of labour-using and land- and capital-saving.

CHAPTER X

DEMOGRAPHIC ADJUSTMENT

So far we have taken the growth rates of a population (both l, the growth rate of the working population, and l_p, the growth rate of the property-owning population) as a constant unaffected by economic changes, but in this and the following chapter we shall turn our attention to the possibility that changes in the standard of living may themselves affect the growth rate of a population. A change in the standard of living might affect the growth rate of a population either through its effect upon mortality or through its effect upon fertility or through both influences. Suppose that a low standard of living led to malnutrition and that this caused (i) a higher incidence of disease and death and (ii) a lower biological fecundity among women. Then a fall in the standard of living would tend to raise death rates and lower birth rates and this in turn would tend to lower the rate of growth of population.

In such a case there could be a set of forces at work mitigating a fall in the real standard of living. Let us take as an example the growth rate of the working population in a Plantcap. Suppose that we start with (i) the working population growing more rapidly than capital equipment ($l > k > n = 0$), (ii) low elasticities of substitution between labour and capital and between labour and land, and (iii) inventions which are strongly biassed against wages. These, as we saw in Chapter V, are the conditions which will cause the pressure of population on resources to lead to a reduction in the real wage rate. In a Plantcap this lowering of the real wage rate represents a fall in the worker's real income; if this in turn causes the growth rate of the working population to fall, then the labour force will grow less rapidly relatively to resources and the fall in the real wage rate will be mitigated.

It is, however, not certain that a fall in the real income per head of a population will reduce the growth rate of that population and *vice versa*. It is conceivable that the opposite will be the case—namely that a rise in real income per head will reduce the growth rate of a population, and *vice versa*. It is in fact often maintained that a rise in the standard of living leads to a greater degree of birth control and to a smaller family pattern of life. In this case the demographic factor, instead of mitigating, could intensify the changes in the movements of labour's income. For suppose that a too rapid rate of growth of labour was causing the workers' income per head to fall. If then the fall in the workers' income caused the working population to grow more rapidly, the growth of labour relatively to other resources would be intensified.

In fact in the real world we do often see high fertility and consequentially high rates of growth of population associated with poverty. But we must be careful not to conclude from this that poverty is necessarily the direct cause of high fertility and wealth the direct cause of low fertility. There are two other possible—and perhaps more probable—explanations of the phenomenon.

In the first place, owing to the more advanced state of medicine in the wealthier communities the great reduction in mortality rates which is such a marked feature of recent times came earlier in the richer communities. With the reduction in mortality rates many more children survive their early years and thus fewer births are needed to obtain a family of a given size. The result is that eventually parents may wish to have less children than before because less births are necessary to provide the desired family size. But the changes in habits needed for this result may take time; and birth rates in the richer communities may be lower because the richer communities have had longer to adjust their ways of life to the sharp reductions which have taken place in infant mortality.

In the second place, poverty may not itself cause high fertility; but both poverty and high fertility may have common causes. Thus poor medical services for the family, a low level of motivation to get on economically in the world, outdated social and religious institutions and customs—factors such as these may both cause people to have large families and also cause the standard of living to be low.

In brief, although poverty and large families may be found together in the real world, this does not necessarily mean that a fall in the standard of living will itself cause people to have larger families. The causal relationship may be simply the other way round —the large families and the pressure of population growth keeping the standard of living low; or both may be due to common causes— poor medical services and unsuitable attitudes and institutions causing both poverty and high fertility; or the association may indicate a time lag in the adjustment of fertility to reduced mortality.

Before we proceed further to discuss the possible influences of the workers' standard of living upon the growth rate of the working population we must consider more carefully what is meant by the 'workers' standard of living'. At first sight it might appear that by the workers' standard of living we mean simply the total income per head of the population in a Propdem in which each working citizen

receives his *pro rata* share of property incomes or the real wage rate
in a Plantcap in which workers rely solely on their wage incomes.
But this is not in fact the whole of the story. A worker may have few
or many dependants to support; a worker with aged parents, wife,
and many children to support will have a lower standard of living
than a bachelor worker without dependants who enjoys the same real
wage rate.

For a working population the ratio of dependants to workers,
which we will call 'the dependency ratio', depends primarily upon the
age and sex composition of the working population. Young children
and old persons do not work, and married women with children find
it more difficult than their husbands to go out to work. We will
discuss later in this chapter the very important demographic factors
which determine the age and sex composition of a population. But
the dependency ratio is affected not only by the age and sex composition of the population, but also by what one may perhaps call
the 'specific work rates'. What proportion of persons of various age–
sex groups go out to work? No infants or very old persons go out to
work. But for older children and less aged adults the proportions who
work in any age group depend upon such things as the customary
school-leaving ages, the normal age of retirement, the proportions
of married and of unmarried women who work, and so on. Moreover, if we are considering the standard of living which can be enjoyed
by a given total population from a given hourly wage rate, we must
consider not only whether a citizen of a given age and sex goes out to
work or not, but also the number of hours' work which he or she does
per week.

These specific work rates (the number of hours' work per day
performed by a citizen of a given age and sex) are partly a matter of
social custom and habit. In some communities it may be thought
inappropriate and in others appropriate that married women
should go out to work. But the specific work rates are also themselves
affected by the standard of living. Increased leisure is one way of
enjoying a higher standard of living. Where real income is high,
children will stay at school longer instead of going out to work to
earn, the normal age of retirement will be lower, the number of
hours work in the normal working day will be reduced. Earnings will
be forgone in order to enjoy more leisure. Now leisure is in fact
simply a very labour-intensive product; one uses one's hours of
potential work not to produce in conjunction with the other factors,
land and capital, the material products bread, shirts, etc., but simply,
without the co-operation of other factors, to produce 'leisure'. One
could, therefore, well treat such variations in specific work rates as a
way of spending one's potential income on the product 'leisure'.

However, for the time being we wish to deal with a one-product model. We have no place for this second very labour-intensive product 'leisure'. We will, therefore, proceed on the assumption that the specific work-rates are rigidly fixed by social custom. The amount of work done, and so the real wage earned, per head of the *total* population depends in this case solely on the age and sex composition of the total population.

When we talk of a standard of living affecting mortality and fertility, we must consider the family and not the individual citizen as a unit. By a family's standard of living we must mean the total real income (including the wages earned at the given specific work rates by all the members of the family) divided by the total number of consumers in the family (including dependent children or aged retired parents among the consumers). But just as there are different 'specific work rates' to be applied to the different members of the family (according to their age and sex) in order to reckon up the 'working force' available in the family, so 'specific need rates' must be applied to the different members of the family (according to their age and sex) in order to reckon up the 'consuming force' represented by the family. A child may need less to consume than an adult. In considering the standard of living of a family those who are in charge of the family and are thus concerned with the distribution of the real income within the family must allot weights which represent the relative needs as consumers of the various members of the family. As a consuming unit a young child may, for example, be reckoned as the equivalent of, say, one half an adult consumer.

Thus we will define the dependency ratio (D) for any population as

$$\frac{\text{the population measured in consuming units}}{\text{the population measured in working units}}$$

where the population measured in consuming units is the sum of the numbers in the different age and sex groups in the population, each weighted by its relevant 'specific need rate', and the population measured in working units is the sum of the numbers in the different age and sex groups in the population, each weighted by its relevant 'specific work rate'. If we assume that the specific need rates and the specific work rates are fixed regardless of the level of the standard of living, the dependency ratio (which will play an important role in the subsequent analysis in the next chapter) will depend solely upon the age and sex composition of the population.

Let us take once more as an example the case of Plantcap, where the working class income is made up solely of wage income. The standard of living depends not only upon the real wage rate per unit of work done, but also upon the dependency ratio. If the working-class family includes a high proportion of persons (adult male workers) whose specific work rates are high relatively to their specific need rates and a low proportion of persons (small children and aged retired persons) whose specific work rates are low relatively to their specific need rates, then the dependency ratio will be low and, for any given real wage rate, the standard of living will be *pro tanto* higher. But this dependency ratio depends upon the age and sex composition of the population.

With this introduction we can turn to our basic demographic questions. How do changes in the standard of living affect fertility and mortality? How do these changes in fertility and mortality in turn affect the age and sex composition of the population and the rate of growth of population and so, in their turn, the standard of living?

In order to answer these questions it is necessary to define mortality and fertility more precisely. For this purpose we must distinguish between crude death rates and crude birth rates on the one hand and specific mortality rates and specific fertility rates on the other hand. By the crude death rate (or crude birth rate) in any community we mean the ratio between total deaths (or total births) during, say, a year and the total population of that country at that time (say, in the middle of that year). Thus if the total population of the community at any one time were 1,000,000, and if total deaths in the course of the year were 30,000, the crude death rate would be $\dfrac{30,000 \text{ a year}}{1,000,000}$, i.e. 30 per thousand, or 3 per cent per annum. Similarly, if total births were 40,000, the crude birth rate would be 40 per thousand, or 4 per cent, per annum. The crude rate of natural increase is the crude birth rate minus the crude death rate or, in our numerical example, 10 per thousand, or 1 per cent, per annum.

But these crude death rates and crude birth rates do not in themselves afford true measures of the underlying forces of mortality and fertility, because they may be greatly affected by the age composition of the population. The risk of death is greatest for the very young and the very old; the risk of child-bearing is high only for those of the child-bearing age and sex. A population which for some reason contained many very young and very old persons but very few women of child-bearing age would show a high crude death rate and a low crude birth rate even though in fact it was a peculiarly healthy community and even though its women were exceptionally fertile. Because of its peculiar age structure such a population might actually be falling; but in due course, as the age structure became more normal, it would start to grow rapidly.

The true incidence of mortality and fertility can be considered only by referring to the schedules of specific mortality and of specific fertility rates in the community. By a specific mortality rate one means the proportion of persons of a given age and sex who die in the community in any one given year. Thus if of every 1000 boys between 0 and 1 year old, 50 die in the course of the year, the specific mortality rate for boys aged between 0 and 1 year is 50 per thousand, or 5 per cent, per annum. Similarly, if to every 1000 women aged between 20 and 21 years there are born 100 babies in the course of a year, then specific fertility rate for women aged between 20 and 21 is 100 per thousand, or 10 per cent, per annum.[1] We can best consider the true underlying forces of mortality and fertility in any community by considering the list of specific mortality rates for each sex and age group and by considering the list of specific fertility rates for each sex and age group. There is an unequivocal reduction in mortality if some specific mortality rates are reduced without any others being raised; and there is an unequivocal reduction in fertility if some specific fertility rates are reduced without any others being raised.

The basic demographic relationship on which we shall found a great deal of our subsequent analysis is as follows. We assume that a woman's child-bearing period covers a number of years and that we start with a population that has some females in every age group up to the end of the child-bearing age. In these conditions if there are given schedules of specific mortality and specific fertility rates and if these rates continue unchanged,[2] then the population will always settle down to a constant age composition and to a constant rate of growth. If the specific mortality rates and/or the specific fertility rates then change, the age composition and the rate of growth will change; but after certain transitional fluctuations in the age composition and the rate of growth, the population will settle down to a new stable age composition and to a new steady rate of growth. We shall now examine these propositions and shall consider the way in which a once-for-all change in specific mortality rates and/or in specific fertility rates will affect the stable age composition and the steady rate of growth.

Let us start by considering the age and sex composition of the population which would result from (i) a constant absolute number of births each year (say, 1000 births each year), (ii) a constant distribution of these births between baby boys and baby girls, and (iii) a given and constant schedule of specific mortality rates. The resulting age and sex composition can be understood by reference to

---

[1] Specific fertility rates will, of course, be zero for all age and sex classes except for women of child-bearing age.

[2] If we rule out parthenogenesis, the constancy of the females' specific fertility rates implies that we start with a population with a male component suitable to provide the mates which maintain the specific fertility rates.

Figure 4. By the height of the column marked 1 we measure the 1000 children born in any given year, the height of the column above the horizontal line measuring the number of boy babies and the depth of the column below the horizontal line measuring the number of girl babies. Given the specific mortality rate for boys aged between 0 and 1, we then know how many will reach the age group 1 to 2. This number is shown by the height above the horizontal line of the solid-line column marked 2. Given then the specific mortality rate for boys in the age group 1 to 2 we know how many will reach the age group 2 to 3 and this number is shown by the height of the solid-line column marked 3. And so on for all the age groups in which any men

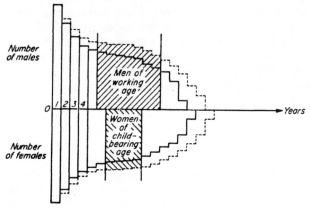

Figure 4

survive. Each column is shorter than its predecessor owing to the mortality in that group. As we have drawn the diagram specific mortality rates, as in real life, are high for the very young and the very old and are low for the intermediate ages.

We can then carry out a similar process for the girl babies and will get a series of columns of ever diminishing depth below the horizontal line, each column indicating the number of women surviving to the corresponding age group.

If specific mortality rates had all been lower, we should have obtained for the men and for the women a series of columns which diminished in a smaller proportion as between one age group and another. Such a series of columns is shown by the broken lines in Figure 4.

Now if (i) the specific mortality rates remain constant over time and if (ii) 1000 babies are born (in the same ratio of boys to girls) every year, we can interpret Figure 4 in another way. So far we have regarded the figure in the following way. Column 1 represents the babies born in 1901; column 2 represents the children aged 1 to 2 who will be alive in 1902; column 3 the children who will be alive aged 2 to 3 in 1903; and so on. But in the conditions stated we could just as well interpret the figure in the following way. Column 1 once more represents the babies born in 1901; but column 2 now represents the babies born in 1900 who have survived to the age group 1 to 2 in 1901; column 3 now represents the babies born in 1899 who have survived to the age group 2 to 3 in 1901; and so on. Thus the height of the columns can in these conditions represent the numbers of persons of given age and sex who are alive in the population at any one given time. The figure is in fact a picture of the age and sex composition of the population at any one time, given (i) constant specific mortality rates, (ii) a constant absolute number of births each year, and (iii) a constant division of these births between baby boys and baby girls. The population will in these conditions remain constant in total size and in age and sex distribution as depicted in the figure.

One can immediately see from the so-called population pyramid in Figure 4 what the dependency ratio will be in the stable population which we are now considering. Suppose, purely for example, that all adult men between certain ages work a full day, that no other citizens in the community work, and that all citizens have the same needs as consumers regardless of age and sex. Then the number of workers will be as shown, for example, in the cross-hatched area above the horizontal line in Figure 4. All the other columns will represent dependants—children, women, or old-aged. Now suppose that specific mortality rates fall and that we move to the new population pyramid as shown by the broken-line columns in Figure 4. What will have happened to the dependency ratio?

Before we answer this question let us note once more that we are assuming that the fall in specific mortality rates is accompanied by a corresponding fall in specific fertility rates so that the total number of births remains 1000 a year in spite of the fact that the fall in mortality means that more potential mothers of child-bearing age survive from their childhood. This fall in fertility is indicated in Figure 4 by the facts that with the broken-line population pyramid there is now a larger number of women of child-bearing age (indicated by the cross-hatched area below the horizontal line) but that nevertheless this larger number of potential mothers is producing the same number of babies per annum as was the smaller number of potential mothers before the fall in mortality.

To return to our question, will the ratio of men of working age to the rest of the population be greater or smaller in the broken-line population pyramid than in the old solid-line pyramid? The answer will depend upon which specific mortality rates have in fact declined most. Let us take three extreme examples.

(1) Suppose first that the declines in mortality rates were concentrated solely on (a) females and (b) males over working age. Then in Figure 4 the broken-line population pyramid would coincide with the previous solid-line pyramid for all males up to the end of working age. The number of working men in the population would be unchanged, since no boy babies had any great chance of survival up to the end of their working lives. But the number of women and of old men would have increased. The dependency ratio would certainly be higher.

(2) But suppose, secondly, that the whole fall in specific mortality rates was among boys of the age just before reaching working age. Then the number of old men relatively to the number of working men would be unchanged (since there was no greater chance of survival from working manhood to old age). The number of working men relatively to the number of boys would have risen (since there is an increase in the proportion of boys who survive to working manhood). The number of working men relatively to dependent females would have risen, since the absolute number of working men would be higher while the absolute number of females would be unchanged. There would thus certainly be a fall in the dependency ratio.

(3) Suppose that there were a fall in the specific mortality rate for babies of one year but that all other specific mortality rates remained unchanged. Then in Figure 4 the columns numbered 1 would remain unchanged; the columns numbered 2 would rise because of the fall in infant mortality; and the subsequent columns would all continue to fall in the same ratio to each other as before. In other words, all the columns in the figure (except the columns numbered 1 which would remain unchanged) would rise in the same proportion. Apart, therefore, from a fall in the ratio of infants in the population the age and sex composition would be completely unchanged, though the numbers in each age and sex group would be greater. Since the number of women of child-bearing age would be greater, fertility rates would, of course, have to be lower in order to produce the same constant number of 1000 births per annum from the greater number of potential mothers. In this case the fall in mortality would cause practically no change in the dependency ratio.[1]

[1] In other words a change in infant mortality is demographically more or less exactly equivalent to an equal and opposite change in fertility. Whether a baby is never conceived or whether it dies shortly after birth (while this certainly has

What we have managed to show with Figure 4 is how the pattern of specific mortality rates determines the age composition of a stable population and how a change in the pattern of specific mortality rates will change the age composition of a stable population—which implies, of course, that specific fertility rates always change by whatever amount is necessary to make possible the maintenance of a stable population with the new mortality rates. But this is merely a preliminary step towards a demonstration of the propositions that, given the conditions stated on page 123 above, with constant schedules of specific mortality rates and fertility rates the population will always settle down to a constant rate of growth (which may, of course, be zero as in the case of a stable population) with a constant age distribution. It is impossible to prove these propositions strictly without use of mathematical analysis which we are avoiding in this volume. We must content ourselves with giving some general indications of the process by which this steady rate of growth and stable age composition is in fact achieved.

We start with the extremely simple demographic model depicted in the top half of Figure 5. Let us suppose that women's child-bearing is confined to one single year of their life; and since we are not being realistic, let us for numerical convenience suppose that all mothers are aged 10 years when their children are born. Then in the top half of Figure 5 we measure actual years along the horizontal axis and the ages of females down the vertical axis. The diagonal line sloping down to the right from the year 1910 then indicates the ages of the female babies born in 1910. In 1911 they are 1 year old, in 1912 2 years old; and so on until in 1920 they are 10 years old and produce their own babies. The vertical arrowed line at the year 1920 in the top half of Figure 5 thus indicates the fact that female babies are born in 1920 to mothers born in 1910. These girl babies of 1920 then grow into mothers by 1930 and have babies; and so on in a ten-year cycle.

But will the girl babies born in 1920 be greater or less than those born in 1910? This clearly depends upon (i) the specific mortality rates of the girl babies in the first ten years of their lives—i.e. how many of the girl babies born in 1910 are alive to be mothers in 1920—and (ii) the specific fertility rate of these mothers aged 10—i.e. how many babies these surviving mothers in 1920 produce. Suppose 1000 girl babies were born in 1910, that 50 per cent of these survive till the age of 10, and that every woman aged 10 has quadruplets of which half are girls—i.e. that there is a specific fertility rate of 400 per cent per annum for women aged 10. Then of the 1000 girl babies of 1910, 500 will survive to be mothers in 1920, and these will produce 1000

great implications for human happiness or distress) makes no appreciable difference to the size, age and sex composition, or growth rate of a population.

girl babies. The population will be just replacing itself. Moreover in 1920, 1930, 1940, and each succeeding tenth year the ratio of infants to mothers will be 2000 to 500 (1000 girls and 1000 boys infants to 500 women aged 10). This element in the age distribution will be fixed.

Suppose now that everything else remains the same except that the mortality among girls is reduced so that of 1000 girl babies born in

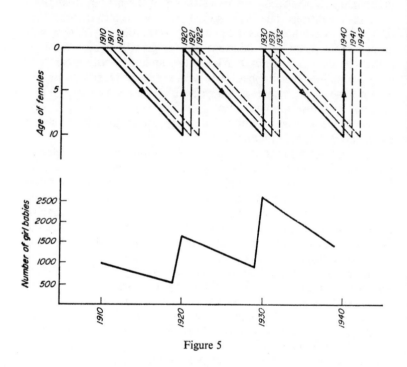

Figure 5

any year not 500 but 800 reach the age of 10. Then from 1000 girl babies in 1910 the number of surviving mothers in 1920 will be 800. These at unchanged fertility rates will have $800 \times 2 = 1600$ girl babies in 1920. Of these 1600 girl babies $1600 \times \dfrac{800}{1000}$ or 1280 will survive to be mothers in 1940, and these mothers will produce 1280×2 or 2560 girl babies in 1940. The number of girl babies will be growing by 60 per cent per decade. But because the specific fertility rate is unchanged the ratio of young infants to mothers will remain 4 to 1. The mothers all have quads; and this fact alone determines this particular element in the age composition.

This very simple demographic model may serve as an introduction to the way in which specific mortality rates between birth and the end of the child-bearing period combined with specific fertility rates determine the underlying rate of growth of the population. But the model completely fails in one respect. Suppose that, as in the numerical example of the last paragraph, the mortality and fertility rates gave an underlying growth rate of 60 per cent *per decade*. There would in our present model be no force at work translating this into a smooth rate of growth of a corresponding percentage *per annum*. This is illustrated in the bottom half of Figure 5.

Suppose that for some historical reason the number of girl babies born in 1910 were 1000, but those born in 1911 were only 950, in 1912 only 900, and so on up to 1919 when only 550 girl babies were born. Then the graph showing the number of girl babies in each subsequent year will be as shown in the bottom half of Figure 5. The number of girl babies born in 1920 will be 60 per cent above those in 1910 and in 1930 will be 60 per cent above those in 1920 (moving along the solid arrowed line at the top of Figure 5). Similarly the number of girl babies born in 1921 will be 60 per cent above those born in 1911 and the number of those born in 1931 will be 60 per cent above those born in 1921 (moving along the broken line at the top of Figure 5). But the broken line for the decades 1911, 1921, 1931, is quite independent of the solid line for the decades 1910, 1920, 1930. The zig-zags in the growth of the number of babies shown at the bottom of Figure 5 would never be smoothed out.

But when we allow for the fact that women pass through not one, but a large number of child-bearing years, there is a smoothing process at work which will in the end bring a steady annual rate of growth of the baby population, given constant specific mortality and fertility rates. The process is illustrated in Figure 6. We measure once more the years along the horizontal axis and the age groups of the population down the vertical axis. We suppose now that childhood lasts till 5 years old, that child-bearing lasts from 5 till 15 years of age, and that old age and retirement starts at the age of 15 and ends with death for all survivors at age 23. The diagonal lines from the top sloping down to the right show the passage of citizens through time and the years of their age. Thus all points on the line numbered 5 show the citizens born in 1905—in 1910 as 5-year-olds, in 1911 as 6-year-olds, and so on. We will call these lines 'vintage lines'. Every point on the line numbered 5 shows 'citizens of the 1905 vintage' at various stages of their maturity.

Consider now the number of potential parents in 1920. These are to be found along the line AB in Figure 6. They stretch from the 5-year-old parents of the 1915 vintage at point A up to the 15-year-old

E

parent of the 1905 vintage at B. The number of parents at A will depend upon the number of babies born in 1915 and upon the specific mortality rates over the first 5 years of life; the number of parents at B will depend upon the number of babies born in 1905 and upon the specific mortality rates over the whole of the first 15 years of life. The 5-year-old parents at A will have a certain specific fertility rate; and the 15-year-old parents at B will have another specific fertility rate. And similarly for the parents of vintages 1906 to 1914 between points B and A. Thus the number of babies born in 1920 will depend

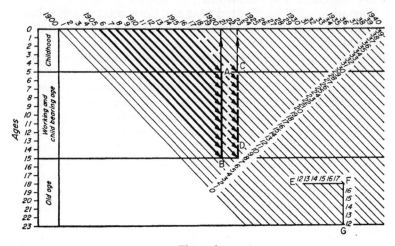

Figure 6

upon the number of babies born in each of the years 1905 to 1915, on all the specific mortality rates between birth and the end of the child-bearing period at age 15, and upon the specific fertility rates of each age of child bearing.

Suppose that these mortality rates and fertility rates were such as to give an underlying constancy to the total population (i.e. were related to each other in the way assumed for the constant population pyramids of Figure 4). Then if the number of babies born were the same in each of the years 1905 to 1915, the number born in 1920 would also be the same. But there might well have been fluctuations in the numbers born in the years 1905 to 1920. In this case it can be seen that these fluctuations will be partially smoothed out in the decade 1920 to 1930. Thus the number of babies born in 1920 is a weighted sum[1] of those born in the years 1905 to 1915; the number of babies

[1] The weights are the survival rates to the relevant year of child-bearing multiplied by the specific fertility rate of that year of child-bearing.

born in 1921 is a weighted sum of those born in the years 1906 to 1916; the number of babies born in 1922 is a weighted sum of those born in the years 1907 to 1917 (as shown in Figure 6 by the vintages of their parents on the line CD); and so on. Clearly then the variations in the number of births in the decade 1920 to 1930 will be less marked than those in the numbers born in the decade 1910 to 1920. For example, a bulge of births in 1915 would cause a bulge of citizens of vintage 15. This would cause a bulge, but much reduced bulge, of mothers during the succession of years 1920 to 1930. There could, therefore, as the result of a bulge of babies in 1915 be an echoing bulge spread over the ten years 1920 to 1930. The echo of this echo would be spread still more thinly over the years 1925 to 1945 (during which some of the babies of 1920 to 1930 would be mothers). And so on until the bulge is wholly smoothed away.

An exactly similar type of smoothing would take place if the underlying forces of fertility and mortality led to a process of growth. Suppose that the number of births in each of the years 1905 to 1915 were the same (say, 1000) but that the specific mortality and fertility rates were such that the number of births in 1920 were larger than this (say, 1600). Then there would be an underlying tendency for the number of babies to grow. But even though there were initial irregularities in the number of births in, say, the decade 1910 to 1920, these irregularities could not persist (as in the case of the zig-zag in the bottom half of Figure 5). The births in 1920 would once more be a weighted sum of those in the years 1905 to 1915, those in 1921 a weighted sum of those in the years 1906 to 1916; and so on. Any initial irregularities would be gradually ironed out.[1]

If then constant specific rates of mortality and fertility have persisted for a long period of time, we shall end up in a situation in which the number of babies born grows each year at a constant rate. Let us suppose, for illustration, that this rate of growth is 2 per cent per annum. It is now easy to show from Figure 6 that the numbers in any other age group in the population will also be growing at this same steady rate of 2 per cent per annum. Consider the line EF in Figure 6. This shows the persons aged 18 in the succession of years 1930, 1931, 1932, 1933, 1934, and 1935. They are respectively citizens

---

[1] The process of smoothing could not, of course, be immediate. A change in specific mortality or fertility rates will lead to a transitional period of adjustment before the new underlying constant rate of growth displays itself. In the note to this chapter a simple numerical example is worked out which shows the sort of variations which may occur during the process of adjustment to changed underlying forces of mortality and fertility.

of vintages 12, 13, 14, 15, 16, and 17. Now if the number of babies born was growing at the constant rate of 2 per cent per annum between 1912 and 1917 and if specific mortality rates are constant, then the citizens of vintage 13 will be 2 per cent more in number than the citizens of vintage 12 on the line EF. In other words the population in the age group 18 will be growing also at 2 per cent per annum.

This argument is true for every age group. We can, therefore, conclude that if the specific mortality and fertility rates remain constant the population will ultimately reach a state in which the numbers in each age group are growing at the same steady rate, say 2 per cent per annum. This means, of course, that the age composition of the population will be constant and unchanging.

The forces determining this constant age distribution can be examined by considering the line FG in Figure 6. Points on this line indicate the persons aged 18, 19, 20, 21, 22, and 23 respectively in the year 1935. They show the age composition of this section of the population in that year. Suppose now that there were no underlying growth in the population. The number of citizens of vintages 12 to 17 would be the same in each vintage on the horizontal line EF. The differences between the number of citizens of vintages 12 to 17 on the vertical line GF would be due solely to the specific mortality rates between the ages of 18 and 23. The age distribution would be determined solely by the mortality rates as in the constant population pyramids of Figure 4. But suppose now that there were an underlying growth rate of 2 per cent per annum. Then as one moved along the horizontal line EF the numbers would rise by 2 per cent between each vintage. Therefore, as one moved up the vertical line GF the numbers would increase for two reasons: first, because the babies in vintage 13 were 2 per cent greater than the babies in vintage 12; and, second, because in the year 1935 citizens of vintage 13 would have been subject to one year's less mortality than citizens of vintage 12. In a population which has reached a state of steady growth and of a constant age distribution, because specific mortality and fertility rates have for long been constant, we can best consider the age composition as being determined in the following way. The basic structure is that given (as in the constant-population pyramids of Figure 4) by the specific mortality rates, but this is modified by the rate of growth. The higher the growth rate, the younger the population age structure in the sense that, with a high growth rate, the numbers in any one age group will be greater than those in the next succeeding age group not only because they have been subject to a year's less mortality but also because they belong to a considerably larger vintage.

These relationships between mortality rates, age structure, and the steady-state rate of growth of a population are illustrated in Figure 7. Let us start with a stable population, i.e. one in which the given specific mortality and fertility rates are such as to lead to a stable population. The solid lines TW and SRZ in Figure 7 are then

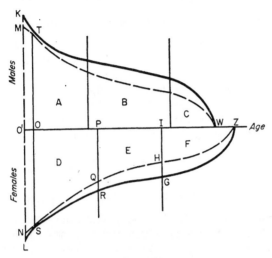

Figure 7

merely a smoothing of the columns shown in Figure 4. Every year OT male babies and OS female babies are born; specific mortality rates are such that, for example, PR out of the OS female babies survive to the age OP; and specific fertility rates are such that the women in the child-bearing ages (i.e. in the area marked E) do in fact produce each year OT male and OS female babies.

Suppose now that the specific mortality rates are the same but that specific fertility rates are, and have for long been, higher. Suppose further that this higher fertility is such as to lead to a steady rate of growth of the population of 2 per cent per annum. Then if OS female babies are born this year, only $\frac{OS}{(1 \cdot 02)^{20}}$ will have been born twenty years ago. The number of women aged 20 this year will, therefore, amount not to OS reduced by the losses due to death between ages 0 and 20, but to only $\frac{OS}{(1 \cdot 02)^{20}}$ reduced by these forces of mortality. In Figure 7 if OP measures 20 years, then the number of women aged 20 years will be $\frac{PR}{(1 \cdot 02)^{20}}$, which we show by the height of the column

PQ. In other words at the ruling mortality rates PR would now survive if OS had been born 20 years ago. But since only $\dfrac{OS}{(1\cdot02)^{20}}$ were born 20 years ago, only $\dfrac{PR}{(1\cdot02)^{20}} = PQ$ will now survive at the same mortality rates. Thus PQ = PR reduced by the 'compound-interest' factor $\dfrac{1}{(1\cdot02)^{20}}$ because, jobbing backwards, the number born in any one year was 2 per cent less than in the following year. Thus we can draw the broken lines TW and SQHZ to measure the numbers in each age and sex group this year, when OT male and OS female babies are born, by discounting the heights of the continuous lines by a compound-interest factor at 2 per cent per annum; as we move to the right in the Figure 7, the height of the dotted line becomes a smaller and smaller proportion of the solid line. Thus if OP is 20 years and OI is 40 years, the ratio $\dfrac{PQ}{PR}$ is $\dfrac{1}{(1\cdot02)^{20}}$; but the ratio $\dfrac{HI}{GI}$ is much lower than this, namely only $\dfrac{1}{(1\cdot02)^{40}}$.

The rise in specific fertility rates which has been necessary to produce this 2-per-cent-per-annum rate of growth can be seen from Figure 7. The area E is reduced by the difference between the continuous and broken lines. This smaller number of women in the child-bearing age (due to the fact that the absolute number of females born in past years was lower) must produce the given number of babies ST.

Thus the ratio of the column ST to the smaller, instead of to the larger, area E shows in some sense the average rise in fertility that must have occurred to cause the 2-per-cent-per-annum growth rate for the population. But this can have been brought about by many different patterns of increased fertility. In particular increased fertility rates in the earlier years of child bearing will make a bigger contribution to this result than equal increases in fertility rates in the later years of child bearing. This is so for two reasons.

(i) The first reason is due to the mortality of women between the earlier and the later years of child bearing. Consider in Figure 7 the line RG which indicates the number of women of various child-bearing ages in the stable stationary population where fertility exactly offsets mortality for the population as a whole. Now IG < PR because of mortality among women of child-bearing age. Simply because there are more potential mothers aged OP years than there are potential mothers aged OI years, a given fertility rate among the younger mothers will produce a larger absolute number of babies than will the same fertility rate among the older mothers. Thus if we start with a stable stationary population a rise in fertility rates among younger mothers will cause a greater rate of population growth than would the same rise in fertility rates among the older mothers.

(ii) But there is a second factor at work. Suppose there were no mortality among women of child-bearing age. In Figure 7 the line RG would be a horizontal straight line, since in the stable stationary population all women aged OP years would live to OI years of age. In this case a fall in fertility rates among older mothers which was offset by an equal rise in fertility rates among younger mothers would have no effect at all on the growth rate or age composition of the population. ST babies would still be born each year; and the fact that their mothers were younger would make no difference. But the situation is quite different if fertility rates are already such as to cause the population to be growing. In Figure 7 even if RG were a straight horizontal line, QH would be rising from left to right (as shown in the Figure). QP, the number of younger mothers, would be greater than IH, the number of older mothers, not because of death between the ages OP and OI but because, with a growing population, women aged OI would be the survivors of an earlier and smaller 'vintage' of girl babies than would the women aged OP. Since QP > HI, a rise in fertility rates among women aged OP would have a larger absolute effect on the number of babies born than would an equal rise in fertility rates among women aged OI. We can conclude that, even in the absence of mortality among women of child-bearing age, in a growing population (though not in a stationary population) a rise in fertility rates among younger women would more than offset the effect on the growth rate of an equal fall in fertility rates among older women.

The common sense of this is clear. The younger are the parents, the shorter is the length of time between the generations. High fertility rates tend to cause a high *rate of growth per generation*. Thus high fertility rates among women aged 20 will tend to produce a high rate of growth per generation of 20 years, whereas high fertility rates among women aged 30 will tend to produce the same high rate of growth per generation of 30 years. Even if there were no mortality among women between 20 years and 30 years of age, the same high fertility rate among the younger women would produce a more rapid *growth rate per annum* than would the same high fertility rate among older women. But if (as would be the case in the stable stationary population) the rate of growth per generation is zero, then the rate of growth per annum will also be zero, whether the generation is one of 20 years or of 30 years.

It is interesting to observe in passing that the growth due to higher fertility (represented by the movement from the solid to the broken curves in Figure 7) could also have taken place as a result of lower infant mortality without any significant effect upon the age or sex distribution of the population. Let us suppose that all specific mortality rates after the first six months of life and all specific fertility rates are the same in both Situations I and II, but that in Situation I (the stable population) infant mortality rates in the first six months are high as compared with Situation II (which is growing at 2 per cent per annum simply because of the lower loss of life in the first six months of babyhood). We can then reinterpret Figure 7 as follows. Let O represent the age of six months. We are considering two populations in both of which OT male babies and OS female babies are six months old this year. To the right of O there is no change in the figure. Since the population in Situation II (shown by the broken line) is growing steadily at 2 per cent per annum while that in Situation I (shown by the solid line) is stable, the number of women aged 20 years 6 months in population II will be only $\dfrac{1}{(1 \cdot 02)^{20}}$ of that shown in population I. But if O′ marks the age zero in the figure, then between O′ and O (i.e. between ages 0 and 6 months) more babies die in population I than in population II. We must therefore start with more births in population I (namely KL) than in population II (namely MN) in order that in both cases we should have the same number (ST) at 6 months of age this year. Fertility is the same: in population I the larger area E of child-bearing women produces a larger number of babies, namely KL, whereas in population II the smaller area E produces the smaller number of babies, MN. But infant mortality is different: KM + NL more babies die in the first six months of life in population I than in population II. The only demographic difference is that there is in population I a slightly larger number of babies between 0 and 6 months (namely KMT and NLS). Demographically—though not, of course, in terms of human welfare and happiness—it makes practically no difference whether family planning reduces births by a given amount or whether infant mortality destroys this same number of babies immediately after birth.

We can now consider the effect on the dependency ratio of an increase in the rate of growth of a population due to higher fertility rates or lower infant mortality, when that population has attained its new steady state with a constant (and higher) growth rate and a constant age and sex distribution. For the sake of simplicity let us assume that the specific need rates are the same for all individuals, regardless of age or sex, and that the specific work rates are zero for all persons other than for men of working age and that they are the same for all men in that age group. Then the dependency ratio would be measured solely by the ratio $\dfrac{\text{total population}}{\text{men of working age}}$ or, in Figure 7, by $\dfrac{A + B + C + D + E + F}{B}$. Has this ratio risen or fallen as a result of the movement from the continuous to the broken boundary lines?

Let us assume that there is little if any change in the ratio $\dfrac{\text{total women}}{\text{total men}}$ i.e. in $\dfrac{A + B + C}{D + E + F}$, as a result of the increased fertility

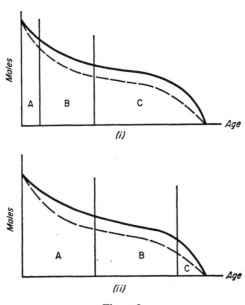

Figure 8

or reduced infant mortality. Then our question becomes: has the ratio $\dfrac{A + C}{B}$ risen or fallen? It is certain that $\dfrac{A}{B}$ has risen; if boyhood lasts from 0 to 15 years and working life from 16 to 60 years, then the various elements in A are reduced by the factors $\dfrac{1}{1 \cdot 02}$, $\dfrac{1}{1 \cdot 02^2}$, $\cdots$ $\dfrac{1}{1 \cdot 02^{15}}$, while the various elements in B are reduced by the factors $\dfrac{1}{1 \cdot 02^{16}}$, $\dfrac{1}{1 \cdot 02^{17}}$, $\cdots$ $\dfrac{1}{1 \cdot 02^{60}}$. Clearly B is reduced in a larger proportion than A. Similarly C is reduced in a larger proportion than B. The higher rate of growth leads to a younger population; and the dependency ratio is raised in so far as there is a higher proportion of young children and it is reduced in so far as there is a lower proportion of old-aged persons in retirement.

Which influence will outweigh the other? This clearly depends upon the relative importance of the two groups. If the number of years of childhood before working life starts is so small and the number of years in retirement so large, that children are very much fewer than persons in retirement, the dependency ratio will fall when the growth rate rises because of increased fertility or reduced infant mortality (see Figure 8 (i)). In the opposite case (see Figure 8 (ii)), the dependency ratio will rise. In fact in the real world children are more important than old-aged in the make-up of dependency. The world is in fact more like Figure 8 (ii) than Figure 8 (i). We may safely assume that a higher rate of population growth due to increased fertility or reduced infant mortality causes a significant rise in the dependency ratio.

Note to Chapter X

NUMERICAL EXAMPLE OF THE PROCESS OF POPULATION GROWTH

The purpose of the numerical example in this note is to give a further insight to the patient reader into the demographic processes whereby given schedules of specific mortality rates and of specific fertility rates will lead to (i) a constant rate of growth of the working population and (ii) a stable age composition and so a stable dependency ratio for the population. Proof of these propositions would require mathematical treatment which is avoided in these volumes. But a numerical example carefully studied may help the reader to an intuitive grasp of the sort of way in which the demographic process works. It will also help to show the sort of fluctuations in age composition and in growth rates that may occur during the transition from one set of fertility and mortality rates to another set of different fertility and mortality rates.

The example worked in this note makes no pretension to realism. It is devised for arithmetical simplicity so as to bring out the basic demographic forces at work. It is for this reason based on the following rather unusual biological assumptions.

(1) Exactly half the babies born are girls and half boys.
(2) Men and women are subject to exactly the same mortality rates.

(3) Men and women die only on their 15th, 30th, 45th, or 60th birthdays.

(4) Women bear children only on their 30th or 45th birthdays.

The result of assumptions (1) and (2) is that in any age group at any time half the population is male and half female, since the same number of male and female babies were born and the same proportion of each sex have survived to the age group in question.

The result of assumptions (3) and (4) is that with constant specific mortality and fertility rates we can accurately depict the demographic development of our population by considering only the four 15-year age groups, 0 to 15, 15 to 30, 30 to 45, and 45 to 60 and by examining the size and age composition of the population only at 15-yearly intervals, say at the dates 1700, 1715, 1730, etc. This is so for the following reasons. We can measure the specific mortality rates simply by the proportion of those who die when they reach their 15th, 30th, 45th, or 60th birthday. Thus if of every 1000 persons who reach their 15th birthday, 500 die on their 15th birthday, we define the specific mortality rate for the age group 0 to 15 as 50 per cent per fifteen years. Similarly we define the specific fertility rate for women aged 15 to 30 as the number of babies which will be born to 1000 women on their 30th birthday. If 1000 women as they pass their 30th birthday produce 2000 babies, then the specific fertility rate for women aged 15–30 is 200 per cent per 15 years.

We can see now why, with these rather peculiar biological assumptions, we can accurately examine the demographic development in our community at 15-year intervals with only four 15-year age groups. Suppose that the number of children aged between 0 and 15 in 1700 were 1000. In 15 years' time, i.e. in 1715, all these children will have passed through their 15th birthday, *regardless of their age distribution within the 15-year age group 0 to 15 in 1700*. If of these children 50 per cent die on their 15th birthday, then in 1715 500 will survive. We can in this way apply the appropriate specific mortality rate to the number in each 15-year age group in 1700 in order to know precisely how many will survive in the next successive 15-year age group in 1715. And similarly with the specific fertility rates. Every woman aged 15 to 30 in 1700 will have passed through her 30th birthday by 1715 and no other woman will have done so; if we know the specific fertility rate for this group of women (i.e. how many babies each will produce as she passes her 30th birthday) we know exactly how many children aged 0 to 15 will exist in 1715 as the offspring of these women. And similarly we shall know how many children aged 0 to 15 will exist in 1715 as the offspring of the women aged 30 to 45 in 1700, if we know (i) the number of women aged 30 to

45 in 1700 and (ii) their specific fertility as they pass their 45th birthday.

This jerky biological process, the hazards of death and birth threatening our citizens only on their 15th, 30th, 45th, or 60th birthdays is, of course, very unrealistic, and is in fact a very poor approximation to the truth. Normally in demographic studies the year rather than the 15-year period is chosen as the unit of time for dates and age groups. For this to give an exactly accurate result we have to make rather similar unreal assumptions—that persons die or give birth only on their birthdays. A period as short as this gives a very good approximation to the truth. Indeed, the shorter the period the more accurate the results. We, for arithmetical convenience, must take a long period like 15 years; and we therefore make our biological forces work in 15-year jerks in order to make the demographic facts fit our arithmetical convenience. The major forces at work can perfectly well be depicted in this unnatural but convenient manner.

Let us turn then to the arithmetical example given in Table III. We start in 1700 with high specific mortality rates; 50 per cent of those who reach the age of 15 die at that age, zero per cent of those who reach 30 die at that age, 50 per cent of those who reach the age of 45 die at that age, and 100 per cent of those who reach the age of 60 die at that age. We start also in 1700 with high specific fertility rates. Every 1000 women on reaching the age of 30 produce 2000 babies and every 1000 women on reaching the age of 45 produce 2000 babies. As we shall see, this pattern of fertility is sufficient to maintain a constant population, given the high mortality pattern.

We can see this by examining the figures given in Table III for the year 1700 in which we assume that there are 1000, 500, 500, and 250 persons respectively in our age groups 0 to 15, 15 to 30, 30 to 45, and 45 to 60. In 1715 there will, therefore, be 500 in the age group 15 to 30 (because 50 per cent of those aged 0–15 in 1700 will survive to 1715); in 1715 there will be 500 in the age group 30 to 45 (because 100 per cent of those aged 15–30 in 1700 will survive to 1715); in 1715 there will be 250 in the age-group 45–60 (because 50 per cent of those aged 30–45 in 1700 will survive to 1715). In 1700 there were 500 persons aged 15–30, of whom half were women. These 250 women will produce 500 babies as they pass their 30th birthday (since their specific fertility rate is 200 per cent), and these babies will all be children between the ages of 0 and 15 in 1715. Similarly, the 500 persons aged 30–45 in 1700 contain 250 women who will produce 500 babies to be numbered among the children aged 0 to 15 in 1715. Thus the total number of children aged 0 to 15 in 1715 will be 1000; and the population in 1715 will exactly repeat in size and in age and sex composition the population of 1700. The total population in each

Table III The Growth of a Population

Stage I. Constant Population. High Mortality. High Fertility.

	Specific Mortality Rates %	Specific Fertility Rates %	Corresponding Stable Age Composition and Growth Rates %	1700	1715	1730	1745	1760
Age Groups 0–15	50	0	44·5	1000	1000	1000	1000	1000
15–30	0	200	22·2	500	500	500	500	500
30–45	50	200	22·2	500	500	500	500	500
45–60	100	0	11·1	250	250	250	250	250
All Ages			100	2250	2250	2250	2250	2250
$l(\%)$			0	—	0	0	0	0
$r(\%)$			0	—	0	0	0	0

Stage II. Population Explosion. Low Mortality. High Fertility.

	Specific Mortality Rates %	Specific Fertility Rates %	Corresponding Stable Age Composition and Growth Rates %	1760	1775	1790	1805	1820	1835	1850	1865	1880	1895	1910
Age Groups 0–15	20	0	41·1	1000	1000	1300	1600	1840	2320	2752	3328	4058	4864	5908
15–30	0	200	27·1	500	800	800	1040	1280	1472	1856	2202	2662	3246	3891
30–45	50	200	22·5	500	500	800	800	1040	1280	1472	1856	2202	2662	3246
45–60	100	0	9·3	250	250	250	400	400	520	640	736	928	1101	1331
All Ages			100	2250	2550	3150	3840	4560	5592	6720	8122	9550	11,873	14,376
$l(\%)$			21	—	30·0	23·0	15·0	26·1	18·6	20·0	21·8	19·9	21·5	21·0
$r(\%)$			21	—	13·4	13·5	22·0	18·5	22·5	20·0	20·8	21·0	20·5	21·0

Stage III. Transition to Constant Population. Low Mortality. Low Fertility.

	Specific Mortality Rates %	Specific Fertility Rates %	Corresponding Stable Age Composition and Growth Rates %	1910	1925	1940	1955	1985	2000	2015	2030	2045	2060	2075	2090	3005	3020	3035	3050	3065	3080	3095
Age Groups 0–15	20	0	33·3	5908	4455	5380	5180	5280	5040	5092	5155	5065	5120	5105	5090	5110	5095	5100	5100	5100	5100	5100
15–30	0	125	26·7	3891	4726	3564	4304	3931	4224	4032	4074	4124	4052	4096	4084	4072	4088	4076	4080	4080	4080	4080
30–45	50	125	26·7	3246	3891	4726	3564	4144	3931	4224	4032	4074	4124	4052	4096	4084	4072	4088	4076	4080	4080	4080
45–60	100	0	13·3	1331	1623	1945	2363	2152	2072	1965	2112	2016	2037	2062	2026	2048	2042	2036	2044	2038	2040	2040
All Ages			100	14,376	14,695	15,615	15,411	15,507	15,267	15,313	15,373	15,279	15,333	15,315	15,296	15,314	15,297	15,300	15,300	15,298	15,300	15,300
$l(\%)$			0	21·0	21·0	-3·7	-5·0	-4·4	1·0	1·3	-1·8	1·1	-0·2	-0·4	0·5	-0·2	0·1	0·1	-0·2	0·1	0	0
$r(\%)$			0	21·0	2·2	6·2	-1·3	2·4	-1·6	0·4	0·4	-0·5	0·4	-0·1	-0·1	0·2	-0·2	0	0	0	0	0

year will be 2250 and its distribution between the age groups will be 44·5 per cent in the age group 0 to 15, 22·2 per cent in each of the age groups 15 to 30 and 30 to 45, and 11·1 per cent in the age group 45–60. If we regard the age group 0–15 as children and the age group 45–60 as the elderly retired, we have 44·4 per cent of the population of working age (of whom half are women) and 55·6 per cent of the population in the dependent groups.

We suppose that this constant population reproduces itself until in 1760 mortality falls. From this year on only 20 instead of 50 per cent of those reaching the age of 15 die at that age. The other specific mortality rates remain unchanged. In Table III Stage II we now observe how this fall in mortality, the specific fertility rates remaining unchanged, causes the population to grow. These new specific mortality and fertility rates will ultimately lead to a situation in which the population grows at a constant rate of 21 per cent per 15 years and maintains a constant age distribution—41·1 per cent of the population in the age group 0 to 15, 27.1 per cent in the age group 15 to 30, 22·5 per cent in the age group 30 to 45, and 9·3 per cent in the age group 45 to 60.

Throughout Stage II of Table III the numbers in the age group 0–15 in any one year are $\frac{1}{2} \times \frac{200}{100}$ times the persons in the age group 15–30 15 years before *plus* $\frac{1}{2} \times \frac{200}{100}$ times the persons in the age group 30–45 15 years before. This represents the specific fertility rates (namely, 200 per cent) of the women (i.e. $\frac{1}{2}$ of the number of persons) in the child-bearing ages 15 years before. The numbers in the age group 15–30 in any one year are $\frac{80}{100}$ of the numbers in the age group 0–15 15 years before; the number in the age group 30–45 in any one year are $\frac{100}{100}$ of the numbers in the age group 15–30 15 years before; the number in the age group 45–60 in any one year are $\frac{50}{100}$ of the number in the age group 30–45 15 years earlier. Thus the population in any one year automatically develops, given the specific fertility and mortality rates, from the population 15 years earlier.

Ultimately, as we have already remarked, the population will attain a state of steady growth with a stable age distribution. But this state is not reached at once. The immediate result of the fall in child mortality in 1760 is simply and solely that in 1775 there are 800 instead of only 500 persons in the age group 15–30. This is a very large percentage increase in the population of working age (namely,

30 per cent) but only a small percentage increase in the total population (13·4 per cent).[1] The immediate effect in 1775 is thus a sharp rise in the proportion of the population in the working age groups. This and the subsequent changes in the age composition are depicted in Figure 9.

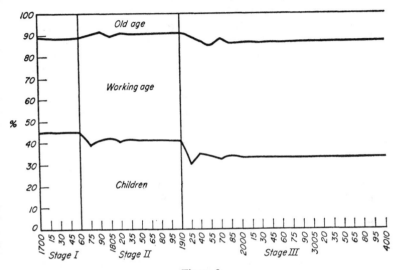

Figure 9

Between 1775 and 1790 the most marked change is the rise in the number of children due to the increased number of parents in 1775 due to the fall in the children's mortality rate in 1760. Between 1790 and 1805 the most marked change is a rise in the number of old persons as the first batch of children subject to lower mortality have grown up to be old men and women. Between 1805 and 1820 there is another sharp rise in the working population; for 1820 is the first year in which both the working age groups contain grandchildren of the first batch of children in 1760 to be subject to the lower mortality rate. These jerky movements in the various age groups are gradually smoothed out as the children in any one year come from parents in the two child-bearing groups of 15 years ago who come, therefore, partly from the children born 30 years ago and partly from those born 45 years ago. Thus the jerks are smoothed out. Or to put the same thing the other way round the children of the children of any one year will appear some in the statistics of 30 years hence and some in

[1] The growth rate in the population of working age is shown by the figures for l and the growth rate in the total population by those for l_t in Table III.

the statistics 45 years hence. Thus any special 'bulge' in the number of children in any one year will be evened out in their repercussions in future years as the 'bulge' parents pass through their two 15-year periods of child-bearing. After 1835 there will in fact in our example be hardly any noticeable jerks left in the development. All age groups will be growing at about 21 per cent per 15 years.

We suppose that this steady growth goes on until 1910 when there is a fall in both specific fertility rates from 200 to 125 children per 1000 women reaching their 30th and 45th birthdays. Now it so happens that given the same reduced mortality rates as ruled during Stage II these reduced fertility rates will ultimately lead to a constant total population with an age distribution of 33·3 per cent of the population in the age group 0 to 15, 26·7 per cent in each of the age groups 15 to 30 and 30 to 45, and 13·3 per cent in the age group 45 to 60. That these mortality and fertility rates are compatible with a constant population can be seen from the following figures:

		Number	Percentage
Age	0–15	1000	33·3
Group	15–30	800	26·7
	30–45	800	26·7
	45–60	400	13·3
All ages		3000	100·0

If we suppose there to be 1000 children, 800 will survive to 15–30; of these the whole 800 will survive to 30–45; of these 400 will survive to 45–60 at the given mortality rates. There would in such a population be $\frac{1}{2} \times 800 = 400$ women in each of the two child-bearing age groups. Since in each age group the specific fertility rate is $\frac{125}{100}$, each age group will produce $\frac{125}{100} \times 400 = 500$ children. The two age groups of child-bearing women will thus exactly replace the 1000 children in the population.

But this constant population will not, of course, be reached at once upon the decline in fertility. In 1925 there will be a marked reduction in the number of children because of the fall in fertility after 1910; but between 1910 and 1925 the numbers will in the older age groups continue to grow because of the growth of children (from whom these older age groups have come) in the periods before 1910. Between 1925 and 1940 the number of children will rise again because, as we have just seen, the number of parents will have continued to grow between 1910 and 1925. From 1910 up to 1955 the old-aged will continue to grow; but in 1970 there will be a sharp fall in the number of old aged who are the first batch of old aged to represent the fewer children born under the new regime of lower fertility. But gradually as the figures in Table III and the lines in Figure 9 show, these jerky movements will be evened out and the community will end up from about 2000 onwards with a constant total population of about 15,300 with a constant age distribution.

In conclusion it may be of interest to compare the three constant age distributions of Stage I (high mortality and high fertility), Stage II (low mortality and high fertility), and Stage III (low mortality and low fertility). Let us call these distributions I, II, and III. Comparing I with III the outstanding features are the fall in the proportion of the young and the rise in the proportion of the old as fertility and mortality are lower. This is the natural result of a fall in mortality when there is a corresponding fall in fertility so that both populations are constant. For more children live to be adults; both those of working age and the old aged rise relatively to the young. In our example all the reduction in mortality is among the children. There is no reduction of mortality at older ages. For this reason the dependency ratio in III is lower than in I. Because there is no change in mortality between those of working age and the old aged, in a constant population the ratio of the old to those of working age will be constant. In our example in both I and III those in the age group 45–60 are one half those in the age group 30–45. But because of the fall in mortality between childhood and working age the numbers of working age rise relatively to the numbers of children. Each working man has to support less children but the same number of old aged. The situation would, of course, have been reversed if there had been little or no fall in mortality between childhood and working age, but much fall in mortality between working age and old age.

Let us next compare II with III. Both II and III are subject to the same specific mortality rates; but II has higher fertility than III so that in II the population is growing whereas in III it is constant. For this reason the age distribution of II will be that of III distorted by a shift away from the old to the young because of growth. One can look at it this way. The numbers in the age group 0–15 at any one time are the persons born during the last 15 years; but those in the age group 15–30 are the survivors of those born 15 years before that. But since the population is growing those born in the last 15 years will be greater than those born in the period 15 years before that. Thus the numbers at any one time in the age group 15–30 relatively to the numbers at the same time in the age group 0–15 will be lower in II than in III. Similarly those in the age group 30–45 relatively to those in the age group 15–30 will be lower in II than in III. And so on for all age groups.

This discussion shows the great desirability on purely economic grounds of maintaining any given balance between mortality and fertility by achieving (i) low mortality among children with low fertility among women rather than by achieving (ii) high mortality among children with high fertility among women. Situation (i) will give a much lower dependency ratio than situation (ii) for a population of any given size and growth rate, since the ratio of adults of working age to children will be higher with (i) than with (ii). Income per head will be higher in (i) than in (ii) because of the lower number of dependants needing support from a worker's income. Another way of seeing the same thing is to observe that in situation (i) children who need capital investment in feeding, clothing, and schooling will stay alive to earn, whereas in situation (ii) they will die before the investment in them gives any return. Of course, this particular economic argument in favour of a reduction in child mortality is valid only if it is combined with a reduction in fertility. A reduction in child mortality with no reduction in fertility raises the rate of growth of the population which brings with it its own economic problems of which no account is taken in the above argument.[1]

[1] The transition from Stage I to Stage II in Table III on page 141 is due to a fall in mortality at age 15, i.e. exactly at the moment of transition from childhood to working age; for reasons similar to those given in paragraph (2) on page 126, this particular pattern of reduced mortality causes the ultimate dependency ratio to be lower in Stage II than in Stage I. The transition from Stage II to Stage III is due to a fall in fertility; and this again, for the reasons given on pages 136–138 above, causes a yet further fall in the dependency ratio.

CHAPTER XI

POPULATION GROWTH AND THE STANDARD OF LIVING

In earlier chapters of this volume (Chapters IV to VIII) we have discussed simple models of a growing economy in which the growth rate of the working population was assumed to be given and constant and unaffected by economic considerations such as the standard of living—even though in an extreme case (cf. p. 83 above) the workers' standard of living might fall to zero. In these models we considered how the growth rate of the working population might affect the standard of living. In the last chapter (Chapter X) we have explained how, with given specific mortality and fertility rates, the population would tend towards a state in which (i) there was a constant age and sex distribution and thus a constant dependency ratio and (ii) there was a constant growth rate of the total population and of the working population. It is now necessary to close the circle by considering how changes in the standard of living, through their effect upon specific mortality and fertility rates, may affect the dependency ratio and the growth rate of the population and so—by the mechanisms discussed in Chapters IV to VIII—may in turn feed back and affect the standard of living itself.

In so far as mortality is concerned, there are, of course, many influences at work other than the standard of living which determine specific mortality rates. Most important of these is the state of medical knowledge and practice. For example, medical preventive measures can eliminate malaria from a community. This will greatly reduce specific mortality rates at any given level of the standard of living; that is to say, at any given level of nutrition, housing, clothing, etc., the chances of survival at any given age will be greater—and may be much greater—after the medical measures to eliminate malaria have been taken. But the standard of living is undoubtedly itself also a factor affecting mortality. This is certainly so for low levels of the standard of living. When people are on the verge of extreme poverty, a reduction in the standard of living will lead to increased malnutrition and lack of protection against the elements, and specific mortality rates will rise; and at this sort of level a rise in the standard of living may well improve the chances of survival. At higher levels of the standard of living, mortality may be very little decreased (or increased) by a rise (or fall) in the standard of living. Indeed, it is just possible that a higher standard of living might in such cases, by leading to over-indulgence of one form or another, lead to an increase in mortality. But broadly speaking we can conclude in so far as mortality is concerned: (1) that there are most important non-economic conditions such as medical knowledge and practice which affect mortality; (2) that at the lower levels of the standard of living a rise (or fall) in the standard of living is likely to decrease (or increase) mortality substantially; but (3) that at higher levels of the standard of living a rise (or fall) in the standard of living is likely to have little effect upon mortality.

It is more difficult to say with any confidence what effect a change in the standard of living is likely to have on fertility. Once again there are very important non-economic factors affecting fertility. The extent to which reliable, simple, and acceptable contraceptives are known and are readily available in the community will be a decisive factor determining how effectively the citizens in the community can carry out their wishes to have small rather than large families. Social and religious customs and norms will help to determine the age of marriage, the willingness to use contraceptives, the desire for large or small families, and sexual practices on which fertility rates will in part depend. Another most important factor which may affect fertility, in so far as family planning and birth control methods are accepted, is the level of mortality rates among children. In a community where there is very high mortality among children many babies must be born in order to achieve a few survivors. Where surviving children are wanted to carry on the family name or to support the parents in old age, many more births will be planned where infant mortality is high than where it is low. This can in fact be an important factor keeping fertility in line with mortality, though there is likely to be a considerable time-lag between a fall in mortality and the changes in fertility habits which this reduction in mortality may ultimately induce.

But given the social and religious norms, the availability of contraceptives, and the levels of child mortality, in what way is a rise or fall in the standard of living itself likely to affect fertility? It is impossible to be confident in giving any very definite answer to this question. There are certain considerations which may make a rise in the standard of living tend to raise fertility. Thus it is possible that at low standards of living an improvement in nutrition and similar conditions may increase the biological fecundity of women. At the other end of the scale, where the standard of living is already very high and most of the amenities of modern life are already achieved, a still further rise in the standard of living may induce parents to increase the size of their families; they may like to use their greater economic opportunities to have around them a larger number of happy and well-cared-for children.

But there are certainly some important considerations, which may well be most operative in conditions of life between the extremes of poverty and affluence, causing a rise in the standard of living to give inducements for a smaller family. Children will be less needed to go out to work early as a means of supplementing an inadequate family income. Indeed, social norms and legislation may themselves change as a result of a rise in the general standard of living; and the age at which children are permitted to start work may be raised as a result of a rise in the standard of living so that a numerous family of small children becomes more of an economic liability and less of an income-earning asset. Finally, as the standard of living rises people may become more aware of opportunities and activities other than, indeed rival to, the rearing of a large family of children; they may become less ignorant and more rational as a result of a higher standard of living and as a result they may have greater knowledge of, and opportunities for, birth control; they may become less fatalistic in their attitudes to family size and more ambitious about the futures of their children. All these things may induce them to reduce the number of their children.

Changes in the standard of living may thus affect specific mortality and fertility rates and thus both the dependency ratio and the growth rate of the population. Changes in the standard of living may also affect the proportion of income saved in a community, a poor community being unable to save as high a proportion of its income as a richer community. The factors which affect these savings proportions will be considered later (Chapters XII to XIV). But in the models in this chapter we will simply make the mechanistic assumption that savings proportions may be affected by the standard of living of the population making the savings.

We will accordingly proceed to build a large number—no less than a dozen—models of an economy in a state of steady growth in which both the proportion of income saved and the rate of growth of population are affected by the standard of living. We shall assume (i) that when the standard of living is very low indeed, mortality must be very high and the rate of growth of the population must be very low or even negative, (ii) that as the standard rises from these starvation levels mortality falls and the rate of population growth rises, and (iii) that as the standard rises still further the control by contraception of fertility increases so that the rate of growth of population falls off again. We shall also assume that the proportion of income saved rises with the standard of living. These combined assumptions about the effect of the standard of living on population growth and on savings enables one to illustrate forcibly the possible vicious spiral of poverty and virtuous spiral of wealth. If a richer country has a smaller growth of numbers pressing on resources and a larger savings proportion to add to its capital resources, then the rich can easily become rich while the poor may merely stagnate. Our models will consistently illustrate this point.

In the models considered in this chapter we shall confine our attention to states of steady growth (cf. Chapters VI and VII above). That is to say, we shall be considering the questions (i) whether on certain assumptions about the effect of the standard of living on the dependency ratio, on the growth rate of the population, and on the savings proportions a state of steady growth is possible and (ii) what will be the characteristics of such a state of steady growth if it is possible. We shall not be examining the questions whether and, if so, by what path the economy will move into a state of steady growth if it happens for historical reasons to start in conditions (e.g. with a stock of capital relatively to its population) which are inappropriate for a state of steady growth. This is a serious deficiency in the analysis; and our present demographic assumptions underline the importance of the limitation of the analysis to states of steady growth. For the assumption of a state of steady growth includes, it should be remembered, a steady state for the population in the sense that the current specific mortality and fertility rates have been ruling for so long a time that the population has a constant age and sex distribution and a constant growth rate. For this demographic reason, if for no other, any transition from one steady state to another would be a prolonged process. In spite of this it is hoped that the analysis in this chapter is not entirely valueless. It is hoped that the models displayed will help to give an insight into some of the most important possibilities which arise if standards of living do affect fertility and mortality; and in any case they can at least provide useful exercises in this type of economic analysis.

It may be helpful in advance to give some classification of the various demographic models which are to be built. This classification is indicated in Table IV.

It naturally makes a great difference in considering the demographic problem of the pressure of numbers on resources whether labour is or is not a reasonably good substitute for other resources—capital and land. Our first main distinction will, therefore, be between those cases in which some significant substitution is possible and those in which very little substitution is possible. The former set of cases we shall illustrate by the assumption that the elasticities of substitution between all factors is numerically equal to unity (see the model on page 99 above) and we will call these the 'Unity' cases. The second case we will illustrate by the extreme assumption that no substitution at all is possible between the factors of production and these we will call the 'Zero' cases. Each of these technical-production situations may be combined with different economic institutions relating to the ownership of property, and these we will illustrate by the extreme assumptions which we have already explained as typifying a Propdem or a Plantcap. This gives four main technical-institutional combinations: Unity Propdem, Unity Plantcap, Zero Propdem, and Zero Plantcap. Finally, as is indicated in the last column of Table IV

Table IV

Elasticity of substitution between factors of production	Economic institutions	Outcome of models	
Unity	Propdem	One.	All progress
		Two.	All stagnate
	Plantcap	One.	All progress
		Two.	Capitalists progress and workers stagnate
		Three.	Capitalists stagnate and workers progress
		Four.	All stagnate
Zero	Propdem	One.	All progress
		Two.	All stagnate
	Plantcap	One.	All progress
		Two.	Capitalists progress and workers stagnate
		Three.	Capitalists stagnate and workers progress
		Four.	All stagnate

in each of these cases the other relevant conditions, which it is our purpose to examine, may be such that any relevant class of persons in the community may find themselves in a position in which they are enjoying an ever-rising standard of living or in a position in which their standard of living is stagnant at a constant unchanging level. This gives us in all twelve possible situations which we shall name, in accordance with Table IV, Unity Propdem One, Zero Plantcap Three, and so on.

Our procedure will now be: first, to consider how to represent our assumptions about savings and population growth in a Propdem; second, how to represent these things in a Plantcap; third, to apply these representations to cases of Unitary substitution (i.e. to consider the models in the top half of Table IV); and, last, to examine all the Zero models (bottom half of Table IV).

As one last preliminary aid to the exposition it may be useful to state here for easy reference the notation which will be used in this chapter.

L_t, L_p, and L_w stand for the total, the property-owning, and the working-class populations respectively, each measured in consuming units. In a Propdem $L_t = L_p = L_w$.

L_a = total population available for work, measured in working units, and L = total population actually employed, measured also in working units, so that $\dfrac{L_a - L}{L_a}$ = the unemployment percentage. In full employment $L_a = L$.

S = proportion of total income saved in a Propdem and S_p = proportion of property-owners' income saved in a Plantcap.

D (the dependency ratio) $= \dfrac{L_w}{L_a}$ which in a Propdem is the same as $\dfrac{L_t}{L_a}$.

Y = total income. $(1 - Q)Y = Y_p$ = property owners' income. $\hat{Y} = \dfrac{Y}{L}$ and $\hat{Y}_p = \dfrac{(1 - Q)Y}{L_p}$.

K = total capital.

N = total land.

Q = proportion of Y paid in wages.

In the Unity cases r is the rate of output-expanding technical progress and U, Q, and Z are the proportional marginal products of K, L, and N.

In the Zero cases $\dfrac{1}{\alpha}$ is the amount of K needed to produce one unit of Y and $\dfrac{1}{\beta e^{l't}}$ is the amount of L needed to produce one unit of Y, so that l' is the rate of labour-expanding technical progress. For the uninstructed reader the meaning of $\beta e^{l't}$ is described below. (See footnote on page 170.)

Let us begin then by considering the representation in a Propdem of the savings and demographic assumptions mentioned above (pages 149 –150). This is done in Figure 10. In Figure 10 (i) we measure income per head $\left(\dfrac{Y}{L_t}\right)$ up the vertical axis and the proportion of income saved (S) along the horizontal axis. Our assumption is that at very low levels of income per head there will be no saving, but that thereafter as income per head rises the proportion of income saved will rise until it reaches some limiting maximum value (S^{lim}). This is indicated by the curve relating S to $\dfrac{Y}{L_t}$. We draw the distance OA to measure one unit, so that if OB is S, BA is $1 - S$. The rectangle BCEA then measures $\dfrac{(1-S)Y}{L_t}$ or consumption per head, which is the measure of the standard of living. We assume that the curve S is such that as $\dfrac{Y}{L_t}$ increases so the area BCEA increases. In other words, as income per head increases, the standard of living—namely consumption per head—rises also.

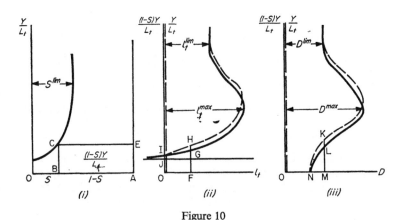

Figure 10

In Figure 10 (ii) the solid-line curve shows the rate of growth of the population (l_t) as a function of the standard of living $\left(\dfrac{[1-S]Y}{L_t}\right)$. We assume that there is some real starvation level (namely OJ) below which no one could live. As consumption fell to this level, mortality rates would rise until the population was declining at an infinitely rapid rate. There is some level of consumption rather greater than OJ (namely OI) at which the population is stationary. As the standard of living then rises, specific mortality rates fall and the rate of population growth increases up to some maximum figure which we shall name l_t^{max}. As the standard of living rises still further, fertility rates decline and l_t falls to some level l_t^{lim}. Beyond this point as the standard of living rises l_t is assumed to remain constant at l_t^{lim}.

It will, however, be convenient for our analysis to express the rate of growth of the population, not as dependent upon consumption per head $\left(\dfrac{[1-S]Y}{L_t}\right)$ but as dependent upon income per head $\left(\dfrac{Y}{L_t}\right)$. This transformation is easily made by means of Figure 10(i). Measure up the broken-line vertical axis of Figure 10(ii) $\dfrac{Y}{L_t}$ instead of $\dfrac{(1-S)Y}{L_t}$; take any value of $\dfrac{(1-S)Y}{L_t}$ such as FG; find from Figure 10(i) the value of $\dfrac{Y}{L_t}$ which corresponds to this value of $\dfrac{(1-S)Y}{L_t}$; draw the line FH equal to this value of $\dfrac{Y}{L_t}$. Then the broken-line l_t curve so derived shows l_t as a function of $\dfrac{Y}{L_t}$. When $\dfrac{(1-S)Y}{L_t}$ is FG, then l_t is OF; but when $\dfrac{(1-S)Y}{L_t}$ is FG, $\dfrac{Y}{L_t}$ is HF; therefore, when $\dfrac{Y}{L_t}$ is HF, l_t is OF. We shall in our analysis use the broken-line l_t-curve in Figure 10(ii) as showing how l_t depends upon $\dfrac{Y}{L_t}$.

In Figure 10(iii) the solid-line curve shows D, the dependency ratio, as dependent upon the standard of living $\left(\dfrac{[1-S]Y}{L_t}\right)$. Since the standard of living is assumed to affect specific fertility and mortality rates, it will determine the steady-state level of the dependency ratio (D) as well as the steady-state level of the rate of growth of the population (l_t). (See pages 131–138 above.) If the standard of living affected mainly the infant mortality rate and the fertility rates, then (see pages 136–138 above) we might assume that the higher is the rate of growth of the population the higher will be the dependency ratio. We have in fact drawn Figure 10(iii) upon some such assumption. D increases for all values of $\dfrac{(1-S)Y}{L_t}$ for which l_t increases, reaches a maximum value $D^{\max}$ for the same value of $\dfrac{(1-S)Y}{L_t}$ as l_t reaches its maximum $l_t^{\max}$ and then falls to its ultimate limiting constant level $D^{\lim}$ at the same value of $\dfrac{(1-S)Y}{L_t}$ at which l_t reaches its ultimately limiting constant level $l_t^{\lim}$. D cannot, however, ever fall below some finite positive level; it could conceivably be infinite, if there were only consumers and no workers in the population; but if workers have themselves consumption needs, then there is some lower limiting positive value below which the ratio of total population in consuming units to total population in working units cannot fall. For this reason we depict D as cutting the horizontal axis at the point N at which D has the positive value, ON.

We can transform the solid-line curve showing D as dependent upon $\dfrac{(1-S)Y}{L_t}$ into the broken-line curve of Figure 10(iii), showing D as dependent on $\dfrac{Y}{L_t}$ in exactly the same way as we transformed the solid-line curve into the broken-line curve in Figure 10(ii). Let LM be any value of $\dfrac{(1-S)Y}{L_t}$; find from Figure 10(i) the corresponding value of $\dfrac{Y}{L_t}$; let KM depict this value of $\dfrac{Y}{L_t}$. Then if a value of $\dfrac{(1-S)Y}{L_t}$ of LM causes D to be equal to OM, a value of $\dfrac{Y}{L_t}$ of KM will have the same effect upon D.

In Figures 10(ii) and (iii) the broken-line vertical axis and the broken-line curves show the growth rate of the population and the dependency ratio as dependent upon income per head of the population *measured in consuming units* $\left(\dfrac{Y}{L_t}\right)$. It will, however, be more convenient to depict the growth rate of the population, the dependency ratio, and the savings proportion as dependent upon income per head of the population *measured in working units* $\left(\dfrac{Y}{L_a}\right)$. This can readily be done by a further transformation which is shown in Figures 11(i), (ii), and (iii). The broken-line curves of Figure 10 now become the solid-line curves of Figure 11, showing D, l_t, and S as dependent upon $\dfrac{Y}{L_t}$. These in turn are transformed into the broken-line curves of Figure 11 $\left(\text{showing } D, l_t, \text{ and } S \text{ as dependent upon } \dfrac{Y}{L_a}\right)$ by the following procedure.

The area OABC in Figure 11(i) equals $\dfrac{Y}{L_t} \times D = \dfrac{Y}{L_t} \times \dfrac{L_w}{L_a}$. But in a Propdem $L_w = L_t$, so that $\dfrac{Y}{L_t} \times D = \dfrac{Y}{L_a}$, i.e. income per unit of available population measured in working units. We can thus from Figure 11(i) obtain a relationship between $\dfrac{Y}{L_t}$ and $\dfrac{Y}{L_a}$. When $\dfrac{Y}{L_t}$ is equal to OA, $\dfrac{Y}{L_a}$ is equal to the area OABC; and so on. We can now transform the solid-line curve in Figure 11(ii) in the following way.

Consider a value of $\frac{Y}{L_t}$ equal to GH; from Figure 11(i) find the corresponding value of $\frac{Y}{L_a}$; let this be represented by FH in Figure 11(ii); then if we measure $\frac{Y}{L_a}$ up the broken-line vertical scale in Figure 11(ii) the broken-line curve so obtained will represent l_t as dependent upon $\frac{Y}{L_a}$. When $\frac{Y}{L_t}$ is GH, l_t will be OH; but when $\frac{Y}{L_a}$ is FH, $\frac{Y}{L_t}$ will be GH; therefore, when $\frac{Y}{L_a}$ is FH, l_t will be OH.

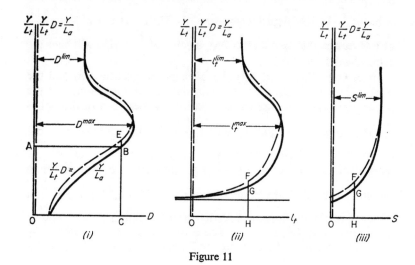

Figure 11

We can also transform the solid-line curve in Figure 11(i) showing D as dependent on $\frac{Y}{L_t}$ by the same means into the broken-line curve of Figure 11(i) showing D as dependent upon $\frac{Y}{L_a}$. Consider the value OA of $\frac{Y}{L_t}$. The value of $\frac{Y}{L_a}$ is then given by the area OABC; let this be represented by CE. Then when $\frac{Y}{L_t}$ is OA, D is equal to OC; but when $\frac{Y}{L_a}$ is CE (i.e. equal to the area OABC), $\frac{Y}{L_t}$ is OA and therefore D is equal to OC.[1]

[1] In this exposition we assume that the area OABC always increases as OA increases. This is not strictly necessary. If the solid-line D-curve is sloped up to the left from D^{max} to D^{lim} with a sufficiently gentle slope, the area OABC might fall as

By an exactly similar process we can transform the solid-line S-curve of Figure 11(iii) $\left(\text{showing } S \text{ as dependent upon } \dfrac{Y}{L_t}\right)$ into the broken-line S-curve $\left(\text{showing } S \text{ as dependent upon } \dfrac{Y}{L_a}\right)$ through the relationship between $\dfrac{Y}{L_t}$ and $\dfrac{Y}{L_a}$ shown in Figure 11(i). When the solid-line S-curve has the height GH, the broken-line S-curve will have the height FH, just as in the case of the two curves in Figure 11(ii).

In our discussion of Propdems in this chapter we shall make use of the broken-line curves of Figure 11 showing D, l_t, and S as dependent upon the level of $\dfrac{Y}{L_a}$. In all those cases in which there is full employment of labour so that $L_a = L$, we shall be showing D, l_t, and S as dependent upon $\dfrac{Y}{L}$ which we will write as $\hat{Y}$.

So much for the depiction in a Propdem of our assumptions about savings, population growth, and the dependency ratio. We must next consider how they are to be represented in a Plantcap. In this case we must consider their representation for property-owners and for workers separately.

For property owners we can confine our attention to figures like Figure 10(i) and (ii). Since property owners do no work, the dependency ratio is in their case meaningless. This means that we can ignore the whole of the transformation shown in Figure 11 and section (iii) of Figure 10. But we do assume that the proportion of income which property owners save depends upon their income per head. For the representation of this we can use a construction like Figure 10(i) if we measure up the vertical axis income per head of property owners $\left(\text{namely } \dfrac{[1 - Q]Y}{L_p}\right)$ instead of income per head of

OA increased. In this case over this range $\dfrac{Y}{L_a}$ would fall as $\dfrac{Y}{L_t}$ increased, and the broken-line D- and l_t-curves in Figure 11 would over this range slope down from right to left instead of up from right to left. What would this mean? Suppose as the standard of living rose contraception was very rapidly introduced so that the ratio of child dependants to workers fell extremely rapidly. Then it would be possible for a *lower* income per worker to be associated with a *higher* standard of living. *If* the standard of living *were* higher than it is, then fertility would be so much lower that the number of children to be kept by each worker would be so much reduced that the higher standard of living could in fact be maintained even if income per worker were reduced. We shall not pursue this *curiosum* further; we will simply assume that D is never so much reduced by a rise in the standard of living that it is possible to obtain a rise in the standard of living without some rise in income per worker.

the total population $\left(\frac{Y}{L_t}\right)$ and if we measure the proportion of their income which capitalists save (namely S_p) instead of the proportion of total income saved (namely S) along the horizontal axis. Any area such as ABCE in Figure 10(i) now represents $\dfrac{(1 - S_p)(1 - Q)Y}{L_p}$, namely the capitalists' consumption per head which corresponds to their income per head $\left(\dfrac{[1 - Q]Y}{L_p}\right)$ measured up the vertical axis. Similarly in Figure 10(ii) we can measure the standard of living of capitalists $\left(\text{namely } \dfrac{[1 - S_p][1 - Q]Y}{L_p}\right)$ upon the vertical axis and the rate of growth of the capitalist population (l_p) along the vertical axis. This will give us a curve corresponding to the solid-line curve in Figure 10(ii) with the same general shape. We can then convert this solid-line curve of Figure 10(ii) showing l_p as dependent upon $\dfrac{(1 - S_p)(1 - Q)Y}{L_p}$ into a broken-line curve showing l_p as dependent upon $\dfrac{(1 - Q)Y}{L_p}$ by the same means as before. If FG is now any given value of consumption per head of capitalists—namely $\dfrac{(1 - S_p)(1 - Q)Y}{L_p}$,—we can from Figure 10(i) see what value of income per head of capitalists in the vertical axis—namely $\dfrac{(1 - Q)Y}{L_p}$ —corresponds to the given value of the area ABCE which now represents $\dfrac{(1 - S_p)(1 - Q)Y}{L_p}$; and we can draw this as HF on Figure 10(ii). Then if capitalists' consumption per head of FG $\left(\text{namely } \dfrac{[1 - S_p][1 - Q]Y}{L_p} = \text{FG}\right)$ gives $l_p = \text{OF}$, then capitalists' income per head of HF $\left(\text{namely } \dfrac{[1 - Q]Y}{L_p} = \text{HF}\right)$ also gives $l_p = \text{OF}$.

As for the representation of workers in a Plantcap we can confine our attention to figures similar to those of Figure 11(i) and (ii). Since workers do not save the whole transformation in Figure 10 and section (iii) of Figure 11 are now irrelevant. Since workers receive only wage incomes and do no savings, the workers' standard of living in a Plantcap is equal to total wage income (QY) per head of the working-class population measured in consuming units (L_w). Measure $\dfrac{QY}{L_w}$ instead of $\dfrac{Y}{L_t}$ up the solid-line vertical axis in Figure 11 and measure l_w instead of l_t along the horizontal axis of Figure 11(ii). We can then draw the solid-line curves showing D and l_w as dependent upon the working-class standard of living $\left(\dfrac{QY}{L_w}\right)$ in Figure 11(i) and (ii). The area OABC in Figure 11(i) will then represent $\dfrac{QY}{L_w}D = \dfrac{QY}{L_a}$ and can thus be used to show the relationship between $\dfrac{QY}{L_w}$ (the working-class standard of living) and $\dfrac{QY}{L_a}$ (wage earnings per worker or—in full employment—the wage rate W_l). By means of this relationship, as in the broken-line curves of Figure 11(i) and (ii), D and l_w can be shown, not as dependent upon $\dfrac{QY}{L_w}$, but as dependent upon $\dfrac{QY}{L_a}$.[1]

We are now at last ready to examine in detail the various cases enumerated in Table IV. We will start with the Unity cases shown in the top half of that table. If we assume that there is a constant rate of output-expanding technical progress, r, then these cases are cases of the model examined on pages 99–103 above, i.e. cases in which, because all elasticities of substitution are numerically equal to unity, the proportional marginal products U, Q, and Z are constant. In these cases, from equations (7.14) and (7.15) we know that in a state of steady growth the following two conditions will be fulfilled:

$$y = \frac{Ql + r}{1 - U} \tag{11.1}$$

$$y - l = \frac{r - Zl}{1 - U} \tag{11.2}$$

But since in a state of steady growth $y = k$ and since $k = \dfrac{SY}{K}$, we have as a third condition:

$$\frac{SY}{K} = \frac{Ql + r}{1 - U} \tag{11.3}$$

In these cases there will also always be full employment of all three factors in any state of steady growth. For if any factor were unemployed, a reduction of its wage rate or rental relatively to that of the other factors would enable more of it to be used with the other factors. We can, therefore, also write $L = L_a$ in all these cases.

---

[1] We assume that the broken-line curves showing D and l_w as dependent upon $\dfrac{QY}{L_a}$ give only one value for D or for l_w for each value of $\dfrac{QY}{L_a}$. In other words, we assume that the area OABC always increases as OA increases. See footnote on page 156 above.

We can now apply these relationships to the broken-line curves of Figure 11 in order to examine the situation in a Unity Propdem. Since $L_a = L$, we can write $\frac{Y}{L}$ or $\hat{Y}$ instead of $\frac{Y}{L_a}$ in Figure 11. Figure 12 reproduces these broken-line curves from Figure 11 and shows that two kinds of states of steady growth are now possible.

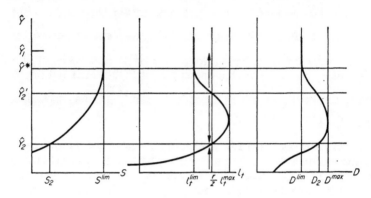

Figure 12

Unity Propdem One. In Figure 12 there is an output per worker, $\hat{Y}^*$, which provides a standard of living sufficiently high to bring S, l_t, and D all to their constant limiting values S^{lim}, l^{lim}, and D^{lim}. If (i) $\hat{Y}$ is in fact equal to or above this level as at $\hat{Y}_1$ and if (ii) $\hat{Y}$ is then rising or at least not falling, S and l_t will remain constant at this level. Since in this case D also will be at its constant level D^{lim}, we have $l = l_t$, i.e. the working population will be growing at the same rate as the total population in terms of consumption-need units. We shall then have a state of steady growth with S constant at S^{lim} and l constant at l_t^{lim}. But to be and remain in this state of steady growth, three conditions must be fulfilled:

(1) In order that S and l should stay at their constant values S^{lim} and l_t^{lim}, $\hat{Y}$ must not be falling. Since $\hat{Y} = \frac{Y}{L}$, we can see from equation (11.2) that this implies $\frac{r}{Z} \geqslant l_t^{lim}$ and we have so depicted the situation in Figure 12.

(2) In order that S and l_t should be at their constant value levels S^{lim} and l_t^{lim}, $\hat{Y}$ must be $\geqslant \hat{Y}^*$.

(3) In order that the economy should be in a state of steady growth we can see from equation (11.3) that it is necessary that
$$\frac{S^{lim} Y}{K} = \frac{Q l_t^{lim} + r}{1 - U}.$$

Condition 2 can be intuitively interpreted as implying that in order to be in a state of steady growth of this kind at any given point of time L must be sufficiently small for the pressure of population on the resources of N and K then available to be so slight that output per worker is above the critical level $\hat{Y}^*$.

Similarly condition 3 can be intuitively regarded as implying that by a process such as that described on pages 102–103 above the amount of capital (K) has been so adjusted relatively to the amounts of the other resources (L and N) that output per unit of capital $\left(\dfrac{Y}{K}\right)$ is such that $k\left(=\dfrac{SY}{K}\right)$ is equal to the steady-state level of $y\left(=\dfrac{Ql+r}{1-U}\right)$.

Thus provided that $l_t^{\lim} < \dfrac{r}{Z}$ and provided that the absolute size of the population at the point of time with which we are concerned is not too large relatively to the then state of technical knowledge and to the supply of natural resources, a state of steady growth is possible in which income per head will continually grow.[1] The essential pre-condition is that the limiting constant rate of growth of population ($l_t^{\lim}$) should not be greater than the critical level $\dfrac{r}{Z}$. If $l_t^{\lim}$ is greater than this, no such state of steady growth is possible, and the economy will be able to reach a state of steady growth only of the stagnant kind described in the next paragraph.

Unity Propdem Two. Suppose that either of the two basic demographic conditions of *Unity Propdem One* were not fulfilled. Suppose, that is to say *either* that $l_t^{\lim} > \dfrac{r}{Z}$ or that we are dealing with an economy in which there is a very heavy pressure of population relatively to the available natural resources and to the state of technical knowledge at the point of time with which we are concerned. Then the economy may find itself in the stagnant state of steady growth depicted by $\hat{Y}_2$ in Figure 12. If $\hat{Y}_2$ is, as depicted in the figure, at that level which causes the rate of population growth l_t to be equal to $\dfrac{r}{Z}$, then $\hat{Y}$ can be constant at this level. For if it is constant at this level, D will be constant at D_2. But if D is constant, $l_t = l$. But if $l = l_t = \dfrac{r}{Z}$, then—from equation (11.2)—$\hat{Y} = \dfrac{Y}{L}$ is constant, and

---

[1] At a rate equal to $\dfrac{r - Zl_t^{\lim}}{1-U}$. See equation (11.2).

F

from (11.1) $y = \dfrac{r}{Z}$. We can then have a state of steady growth in which

(i) $y = k = l = \dfrac{r}{Z}$, (ii) output per worker will be stagnant at $\hat{Y}_2$, and (iii) S will be S_2.

For this state of steady growth to be possible, three conditions must be fulfilled.

(1) $\dfrac{r}{Z} \leqslant l_t^{\max}$. If this were not so, then—whatever the standard of living might be—there could not be a rate of growth of population sufficiently great to cause stagnation.

(2) $\dfrac{Y}{L} = \hat{Y}_2$. The absolute population at any given point of time must be of a size to cause a pressure on resources which brings output per head down to the level $\hat{Y}_2$.

(3) $\dfrac{S_2 Y}{K} = \dfrac{r}{Z}$. As we have seen, in this case the steady-state level of y is $\dfrac{r}{Z}$. In order, therefore, that $k = y$ we must have $\dfrac{S_2 Y}{K} = \dfrac{r}{Z}$. In other words by a process of the kind described on page 103 K must have been adjusted to the other resources L and N so as to give an output per unit of capital $\left(\dfrac{Y}{K}\right)$ which allows k to equal y.

It will be seen from Figure 12 that there is another and higher level of the standard of living—namely, Y_2'—at which $l_t = \dfrac{r}{Z}$. A stagnant state of steady growth would be possible—with the corresponding values of S and D—at this point in an exactly similar way and on exactly similar conditions as those which we have just discussed for Y_2. There is, however, a basic difference between these two cases. In the case of Y_2 the l_t-curve cuts the $\dfrac{r}{Z}$ line upwards from left to right. This can be interpreted in the following way.

Suppose that at any given time the absolute size of the population was so great relatively to the then available resources of land and capital that, in view of the then prevailing state of technical knowledge, output per head and the standard of living were reduced below the critical level $\hat{Y}_2$. This would mean that, if the steady-state rate of population growth were adjusted to this low standard of living, the population would be growing sufficiently slowly relatively to the growth of capital resources[1] and technical knowledge for output per

---

[1] Assuming also that the stock and rate of growth of capital had also been adjusted to its steady-state level. See pp. 163–164 for a discussion of this point.

head to be rising (i.e. $l_t < \dfrac{r}{Z}$) so that $\hat{Y}$ would move towards $\hat{Y}_2$. And conversely if at any time the population were in absolute size rather smaller than was appropriate to this steady-state stagnation level, output per head would be sufficiently high to raise $\hat{Y}$ somewhat above $\hat{Y}_2$. In this case the rate of growth of population would be more rapid relatively to the growth of the capital stock and of technical knowledge than was compatible with the maintenance of the existing output per head, so that $\hat{Y}$ would fall towards $\hat{Y}_2$.

But the case is very different with the stagnation point $\hat{Y}_2'$. In this case if the population is of a size at any one time to cause $\hat{Y}$ to be a little less than $\hat{Y}_2'$, the steady-state value of l_t would be greater than was compatible with the preservation of the existing level of output per head, and $\hat{Y}$ would tend to fall further away from $\hat{Y}_2'$. Conversely, if the absolute size of the population at any one time were sufficiently small to raise $\hat{Y}$ somewhat above $\hat{Y}_2'$ the steady-state value of l_t would be reduced so that with the given rate of growth of capital resources and technical knowledge $\hat{Y}$ would grow still higher.

We cannot from this infer directly that $\hat{Y}_2$ is a stable and $\hat{Y}_2'$ an unstable position. To consider the stability or instability of an economic system one must consider the relationships between all the different rates and modes of adjustment of the various factors involved, a matter which we propose to take up in the next volume in this series. But on the face of it there is a much better chance of remaining in a stagnation steady-state of type $\hat{Y}_2$ than in one of type $\hat{Y}_2'$; and in the rest of this chapter we shall consider stagnation steady-states only of the former kind. But to reach a state of steady growth of this kind we must imagine two processes finding simultaneously their steady-state solution. First, on the general lines discussed in the immediately preceding paragraphs, if the absolute size of the population is inappropriately small (or large) for a steady-state position the consequential rise (or fall) of the standard of living above (or below) the steady-state level must have raised (or reduced) the rate of growth of population relatively to the rate of growth of capital resources and of technical knowledge so as to bring the standard of living to its steady-state level. But, secondly and simultaneously, if the capital stock is inappropriately large (or small) for the steady-state position, the abnormally low (or high) output per unit of capital $\left(\dfrac{Y}{K}\right)$ must have lowered (or raised) the rate of capital accumulation $\left(\dfrac{SY}{K}\right)$ so as to bring the capital stock into its appropriate steady-state relationship with the amount of land, labour, and technical knowledge available, so that by a process similar to that described on pages 102–103 above y is brought into equality with k. We shall reach a stagnation steady-state then only if the interrelationships and time-lags between these two processes of adjustment of population and of capital stock respectively are such that each can simultaneously reach its steady-state solution. It is this assumption which we shall in effect be making without further justification in the rest of this chapter.

We can turn next to the cases in which the elasticities of substitution between the factors are all still numerically equal to unity, but in which the economy is institutionally a Plantcap. We have now to examine the four possible outcomes of the Unity Plantcap family enumerated in Table IV. These cases are illustrated in Figure 13.

We have now two distinct populations to consider, the population of capitalists (L_p) and the population of workers (L_w). The standard of living of the former is measured by $\dfrac{(1-Q)Y}{L_p}$ which we shall call $\hat{Y}_p$ and of the latter by $\dfrac{QY}{L_w} = \dfrac{QY}{L}\dfrac{1}{D} = \dfrac{W_l}{D}$. Either standard may be progressing or may be stagnant, so that we have the four possible outcomes tabulated for the Unity-Plantcap family in Table IV. We can make some general remarks about the conditions in which each standard will progress or be stagnant before we consider each outcome in turn.

Consider first the working-class population at the bottom of Figure 13. To reach a state of steady growth it is a necessary condition that l should be constant; and l can be constant only if l_w and D are constant. There are two cases in which this can be so. First, as exemplified by W_{l13} in Figure 13, the wage rate may be so high that both l_w and D have reached their constant limiting values $l_w^{\lim}$ and $D^{\lim}$. In this case the wage rate and the working-class standard of living can be continuously rising without any change in l_w or, in consequence, in l. Second, as exemplified by W_{l24} in Figure 13, the wage rate may be such as to make $l_w = \dfrac{r}{Z}$. In this case the wage rate can be stagnant at this level. For if it were constant at this level, D would be constant at D_{24}; therefore, $l = l_w = \dfrac{r}{Z}$; but with $l = \dfrac{r}{Z}$, $\dfrac{Y}{L}$ is constant (see equation [11.2]); therefore, if $W_l = W_{l24}$, l can remain constant at $\dfrac{r}{Z}$.

Consider next the capitalist population. To reach a state of steady growth it is necessary that S should be constant. But $S = (1-Q)S_p$. Since Q is constant, we must have S_p constant. But there are two types of situation in which S_p can be constant, as can be seen from the top half of Figure 13. First, as illustrated by $\hat{Y}_{p12}$ in Figure 13, the capitalists' standard of living may be so high that S_p has reached its constant limiting value $S_p^{\lim}$, in which case a rising standard of living for the capitalists is compatible with a constant value of S_p and so of S. Second, as illustrated by $\hat{Y}_{p3}$ and $\hat{Y}_{p4}$ in Figure 13, S_p may be constant because the capitalists' standard of living is stagnant. For this to be so $\hat{Y}_p = \dfrac{(1-Q)Y}{L_p}$ must be constant, i.e. y must equal l_p. But the value of y depends upon whether l is constant at $l_w = l_w^{\lim}$ or at $l_w = \dfrac{r}{Z}$. In the former case—i.e. the case shown by $\hat{Y}_{p3}$—we have $l_p = y = \dfrac{Q l_w^{\lim} + r}{1 - U}$.[1] (See equation [11.1].) In the latter case—i.e. the case shown by $\hat{Y}_{p4}$—we have $l_p = y = l = \dfrac{r}{Z}$.

It will once more be observed from Figure 13 that the l_w-curve cuts the $\dfrac{r}{Z}$ line, sloping upwards from right to left, at a level of W_l higher than W_{l24}. This is a possible steady-state stagnation point, but we shall ignore it on the grounds described on page 163 above. If the wage rate were slightly above (or below) such a point, l_w would be less than (or greater than) $\dfrac{r}{Z}$; and in this case $\dfrac{Y}{L}$, and so the wage rate W, or $\dfrac{QY}{L}$, would move still further away from this alternative stagnation level. Similarly, for the capitalists there are stagnation levels of $\hat{Y}_p$ above $\hat{Y}_{p3}$ and $\hat{Y}_{p4}$ at which the l_p-curve cuts the lines $\dfrac{Q l_w^{\lim} + r}{1 - U}$ and $\dfrac{r}{Z}$ respectively. But in both these cases a small rise (or fall) in the capitalists' standard would cause the steady-state level of l_p to become less (or more) than the given value of y—namely $\dfrac{Q l_w^{\lim} + r}{1 - U}$ or $\dfrac{r}{Z}$ respectively—so that $\hat{Y}_p = \dfrac{(1-Q)Y}{L_p}$ would diverge still further from these alternative stagnation levels.

Let us then briefly consider each of the four possible outcomes in turn.

Unity Plantcap One. This is the combination of $\hat{Y}_{p12}$ with W_{l13} in

[1] $\dfrac{Q l_w^{\lim} + r}{1 - U} = \dfrac{Q}{Q + Z} l_w^{\lim} + \dfrac{Z}{Q + Z}\dfrac{r}{Z}$. In other words it is a weighted average of $l_w^{\lim}$ and $\dfrac{r}{Z}$. It lies, therefore, between $l_w^{\lim}$ and $\dfrac{Z}{r}$ and is so shown in Figure 13.

Figure 13. Both populations can enjoy a rising standard of living. For this to be so, five conditions must be fulfilled.

(1) For the workers' standard of living to be rising we must have $\dfrac{QY}{L_w}$ rising. For this to be so we must have $l = l_w^{\lim} < \dfrac{r}{Z}$. In Figure 13 we have drawn $\dfrac{r}{Z}$ to the right of $l_w^{\lim}$. If, however, $l_w^{\lim}$ were $> \dfrac{r}{Z}$, no state of steady growth with a rising working-class standard of living would be possible.

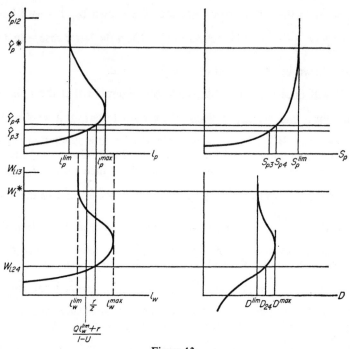

Figure 13

(2) For the capitalists' standard of living to be rising we must have $\dfrac{(1-Q)Y}{L_p} = \hat{Y}_p$ rising. For this to be so we must have $l_p^{\lim} < y$. But with $l = l_w^{\lim}$, $y = \dfrac{Q l_w^{\lim} + r}{1 - U}$. So our condition becomes $l_p^{\lim} < \dfrac{Q l_w^{\lim} + r}{1 - U}$, and we have in Figure 13 so drawn the l_p-curve. If, however, $l_p^{\lim}$ were $> \dfrac{Q l_w^{\lim} + r}{1 - U}$ we could not have a rising standard of living

for the capitalists combined with a rising standard of living for the workers.

(3) For l to be constant at l_w^{lim} we must have $W_l \geqslant W_l^*$. In other words the absolute size of the working population must be sufficiently small relatively to the other factors to attain the critical level for the wage rate, W_l^*.

(4) For S_p to be constant at S_p^{lim} we must have $\hat{Y}_p \geqslant \hat{Y}_p^*$. In other words the absolute number of capitalists must be sufficiently small to raise property incomes per property owner up to this critical level.

(5) The process of adjustment of k to equality with y necessary for the achievement of a state of steady growth (cf. pages 102–103 above) must have resulted in a stock of capital relative to other resources which brings $\dfrac{SY}{K}$ to its steady-state level of $\dfrac{Ql+r}{1-U}$ (see equation [11.3]) which with $S = (1-Q)S_p{}^m$ and $l = l_w^{\text{lim}}$ requires an output per unit of capital $\left(\dfrac{Y}{K}\right)$ such that $(1-Q)S_p^{\text{lim}}\dfrac{Y}{K} = \dfrac{Ql_w^{\text{max}}+r}{1-U}$.

Unity Plantcap Two. In this case we combine $\hat{Y}_{p12}$ with W_{124}. Capitalists can progress, but workers stagnate. For this five conditions must be fulfilled.

(1) $l_w^{\text{max}} > \dfrac{r}{Z}$. For the workers to stagnate $W_l = \dfrac{QY}{L}$ must be at a level at which $l_w = \dfrac{r}{Z}$. For in this case $l_w = l = y$, so that $\dfrac{QY}{L}$ is then constant at this level. This would be impossible if $l_w^{\text{max}} < \dfrac{r}{Z}$. In that case there would be no wage rate which would raise the rate of growth of the working population to a stagnation level.

(2) $l_p^{\text{lim}} < \dfrac{r}{Z}$. The rate of growth of the capitalist population at its constant limiting value must be less than the rate of growth of the national income and so of the capitalists' constant share of that income, if their standard is to rise progressively.

(3) $W_l = W_{124}$. The absolute size of the working population must be sufficiently large, given the other resources, to bring the wage rate into the region of this stagnation level. There will then be forces (cf. p. 165 above) pulling W_l into equality with the stagnation level, W_{124}.

(4) $\hat{Y}_p \geqslant \hat{Y}_p^*$. The absolute size of the capitalist population must be sufficiently small to raise property incomes per head of property owners up to the 'progress' level.

(5) $(1 - Q)S_p^{\lim}\dfrac{Y}{K} = \dfrac{r}{Z}$. In this case with $y = l = \dfrac{r}{Z}$ the steady-state

value of y is $\dfrac{r}{Z}$. The capital stock must have been adjusted to the

other factors so that $\dfrac{Y}{K}$ is at a level which makes $k = \dfrac{SY}{K} = y = \dfrac{r}{Z}$

with $S = (1 - Q)S_p^{\lim}$.

Unity Plantcap Three. This is a combination of $\hat{Y}_{p3}$ with W_{l13}. The five conditions for this are:

(1) $l_w^{\lim} < \dfrac{r}{Z}$. Only on this condition can workers' standards progressively rise.

(2) $l_p^{\max} \geqslant \dfrac{Ql_w^{\lim} + r}{1 - U}$. Since in this case $l = l_w^{\lim}$, $y = \dfrac{Ql_w^{\lim} + r}{1 - U}$.

Capitalists' standards can stagnate only if $\hat{Y}_p = \dfrac{(1 - Q)Y}{L_p}$ is
constant, i.e. only if l_p is equal to this value of y. But this would be
impossible if the maximum value of l_p—namely $l_p^{\max}$—were less than
this.

(3) $W_l \geqslant W_l^*$. The absolute size of the working population must
be small enough to raise the wage rate at least up to the critical level
at which l_w reaches its constant level $l_w^{\lim}$.

(4) $\hat{Y}_p = \hat{Y}_{p3}$. The absolute size of the capitalist population must
be sufficiently great to have reduced property income per property
owner into the vicinity of this stagnation level. There will then be
forces (cf. p. 165 above) pulling $\hat{Y}_p$ into equality with the stagnation
level $\hat{Y}_{p3}$.

(5) $\dfrac{(1 - Q)S_{p3}Y}{K} = \dfrac{Ql_w^{\lim} + r}{1 - U}$. The process of adjustment of the

size of the capital stock must have proceeded until $k = y$, so that the
economy is in a state of steady growth.

Unity Plantcap Four. $\hat{Y}_{p4}$ is combined with W_{l24}. The five conditions now are:

(1) $l_w^{\max} > \dfrac{r}{Z}$, so that there can be a stagnation level of W_l which

equates l_w to $\dfrac{r}{Z}$, so that l equals y so that $\dfrac{Y}{L}$ and so W_l remains

constant.

(2) $l_p^{\max} \geqslant \dfrac{r}{Z}$, so that there can be a stagnation level of $\hat{Y}_p$ which

equates l_p to $\dfrac{r}{Z}$ and so to y, so that $\hat{Y}_p$ remains constant.

(3) $W_l = W_{l24}$. The absolute size of the working population must be such as to have brought the wage rate into the region of the stagnation level.

(4) $\hat{Y}_p = \hat{Y}_{p4}$. The absolute size of the capitalist population must be such as to have brought property income per property owner into the region of the stagnation level.

(5) $\dfrac{(1-Q)S_{p4}Y}{K} = \dfrac{r}{Z}$. The process of adjustment of the capital

stock necessary for making $k = y$ and so for the attainment of a steady state must have been completed.

It will be observed that each of the four possible outcomes of the Unitary Plantcap case which we have just discussed is compatible with the same l_p-curve, l_w-curve, S_p-curve, and D-curve and with the same assumed values of U, Q, Z, and r. All that is necessary to obtain one result rather than another in the conditions depicted in Figure 13 is a difference in the absolute size of the capitalist and working-class initial populations.[1] Result One requires that both populations be small; Result Two that L_p should be small and L_w large; Result Three that L_p should be large and L_w small, and Result Four that both populations be large. This fact relies, however, on the assumptions that both l-curves slope upwards from right to left after a certain standard of living is reached. Thus Results One and Two

require $l_p^{\lim}$ to be less than both $\dfrac{Ql_w^{\lim}+r}{1-U}$ and $\dfrac{r}{Z}$ whereas Results Three

and Four require both $\dfrac{Ql_w^{\lim}+r}{1-U}$ and $\dfrac{r}{Z}$ to be less than $l_p^{\max}$. Similarly,

Results One and Three require $l_w^{\lim} < \dfrac{r}{Z}$ whereas Results Two and Four

require $\dfrac{r}{Z} < l_w^{\max}$. In fact, of course, the l-curves may not satisfy these

conditions. With some l-curves some of these states of steady growth

---

[1] It is the existence of a fixed factor N which makes the absolute size of the population so important. Given at any one time the state of technical knowledge and the amount of land, a large population (with its appropriate steady-state supply of capital) will, in the cases examined in the text, lead to a low income per head and stagnation, while a small population (with its appropriate supply of capital) will lead to a high income per head and to progress. See note at end of this chapter (pp. 186–187 below).

will be impossible. The reader can readily work out for himself the implications of different *l*-curves.

We turn now to the cases enumerated in the bottom half of Table IV; and we shall thereby see what a great difference it makes to the results of demographic pressures if it is impossible to substitute one factor for another. For all these Zero cases we shall assume that the production system is of the following kind. $\frac{1}{\alpha}$ measures the amount of capital required to produce one unit of output, so that αK is the amount of Y that could be produced by a capital stock K, if there were no scarcity of any other factor. $\frac{1}{\beta e^{l't}}$ measures the amount of labour required to produce one unit of output, so that $\beta e^{l't} L_a$ measures the amount of Y that could be produced by a labour force L_a, if there were no scarcity of any other factor.

The assumption that $\beta e^{l't} L_a$ measures the output that could be produced by L_a means that we are assuming labour-expanding technical progress at a rate of l'. Potential output per unit of capital is fixed at α. But potential output per unit of labour is not fixed at β but grows at a constant growth rate l', so that at any point of time t it will have become $\beta e^{l't}$.[1]

We assume that there is no scarcity of land so that Y is in fact equal to the lesser of the two potential outputs αK and $\beta e^{l't} L_a$. If $\alpha K > \beta e^{l't} L_a$, then $Y = \beta e^{l't} L_a$ and there is some capital left unemployed because there is not enough labour to man the machines. If $\alpha K < \beta e^{l't} L_a$, then $Y = \alpha K$ and there is some labour unemployed because there are not enough machines for all the workers to find employment. We are in this chapter interested only in problems of population pressure, and we shall, therefore, confine our attention to the cases in which, while there is no scarcity of land, there is some scarcity of capital.

We can, therefore, always write

$$Y = \alpha K = \beta e^{l't} L \leqslant \beta e^{l't} L_a \qquad (11.4)$$

This expression states that, since K is scarce, output (Y) is equal to the potential output of capital (αK). Since $\frac{1}{\beta e^{l't}}$ is the amount of labour required to produce a unit of output we can decide the actual level of employment of labour by the equation $Y = \beta e^{l't} L$. But there

---

[1] Those ignorant of such matters can follow the rest of the argument if they regard $\beta e^{l't}$ as standing for what potential output per head would be at any time t if it started at a level β at time 0 and increased continuously for t years at a daily growth rate l'.

may now be some unemployment, if L (the demand for labour to man up the K) is $< L_a$ (the available supply of labour), i.e. if $\beta e^{l't}L < \beta e^{l't}L_a$. If, however, $\beta e^{l't}L = \beta e^{l't}L_a$, then there is full employment of labour as well as of capital. One of our purposes in the following exercises is to see in what conditions labour will be fully employed.

In brief, it will be seen that we are assuming that there is no scarcity of land and that technical progress is necessarily of the labour-expanding variety. These rather extreme assumptions turn out to be necessary if one is to build a set of relatively simple models in which a state of steady growth can be reached in an economy in which no substitution is available between the factors, i.e. in which the amounts of capital and of labour required per unit of output are both, at any given time, rigidly fixed.

In the model $\beta e^{l't}$ measures output per worker employed $\left(\dfrac{Y}{L}\right)$, and it sets, therefore, an upper limit to output per worker available for employment $\left(\dfrac{Y}{L_a}\right)$. $\dfrac{Y}{L_a}$ will reach this upper limit only if K is sufficiently large to provide work for all available labour so that there is full employment and $L = L_a$. It follows that throughout our discussion of the Zero cases we must assume the following relationship:

$$\frac{Y}{L_a} \leqslant \beta e^{l't} \tag{11.5}$$

Moreover, so long as capital is a scarce resource, $Y = \alpha K$ so that $k = \dfrac{SY}{K} = \alpha S$. Also, since $Y = \alpha K$ and $Y = \beta e^{l't}L$, we have $y = k = l + l'$. In other words since there are fixed technical coefficients between output and capital (α) and between output and employment as expanded by technical progress (β), the growth rate of output (y) must be equal to the growth rate of the capital stock (k) and the growth rate of the labour which finds employment (l) must equal the growth rate of output less the rate of labour-expanding technical progress ($y - l'$). We can conclude therefore that, so long as capital is a scarce resource, in all Zero cases, whether they are in a state of steady growth or not,

$$y = k = \alpha S = l + l' \tag{11.6}$$

We can now use these relationships to examine the Zero Propdem cases which are illustrated in Figure 14. The solid-line curves of Figure 14 reproduce the broken-line curves of Figure 11 and show the effect of the level of $\dfrac{Y}{L_a}$ (through its influence on the standard of living $\dfrac{(1-S)Y}{L_t}$) upon the steady-state values of the savings ratio (S), the growth rate of the population (l_t), and the dependency ratio (D). For convenience of exposition the S-curve from the left-hand section of the Figure is reproduced, after multiplication by the constant output–capital ratio α, as the broken αS-curve in the central section of the figure.

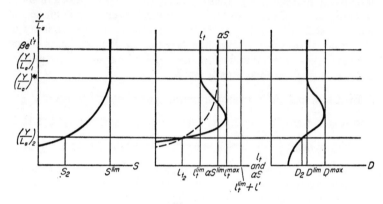

Figure 14

Zero Propdem One. This is the case where the standard of living continuously rises. To have a steady-state solution of this kind we must enjoy an income per available worker $\left(\dfrac{Y}{L_a}\right)$ which is sufficiently high (i.e. at least as high as $\left(\dfrac{Y}{L_a}\right)^*$ in the figure) to make S, l_t, and D reach their constant limiting values S^{lim}, l_t^{lim}, and D^{lim} and $\dfrac{Y}{L_a}$ must be rising so that S, l_t, and D remain constant at S^{lim}, l_t^{lim}, and D^{lim}. We can then have a constant rate of growth for total output Y of $y=\alpha S^{\text{lim}}$ and for the standard of living $\dfrac{Y}{L_t}$ of $y - l_t = \alpha S^{\text{lim}} - l_t^{\text{lim}}$.

For this solution to be possible four conditions must be fulfilled.
(1) $\beta e^{l't} \geqslant \left(\dfrac{Y}{L_a}\right)^*$. At the point of time in which we are interested, namely t, technical knowledge must have advanced to a point which enables output per head to be as high as the critical level $\left(\dfrac{Y}{L_a}\right)^*$ which it is necessary for output per available worker to attain, in order to raise S, l_t, and D to their constant limiting values S^{lim}, l_t^{lim},

and $D^{\lim}$. If this were not so it would be technologically impossible to sustain a state of steady growth with S, l_t, and D at these constant limiting values.

(2) $\dfrac{K}{L_a} > \dfrac{1}{\alpha}\left(\dfrac{Y}{L_a}\right)^*$. There must be sufficient capital stock (K) available relatively to the available working force (L_a) to give sufficient employment to enable output per available worker $\left(\dfrac{Y}{L_a}\right)$ to rise at least up to the critical level $\left(\dfrac{Y}{L_a}\right)^*$. Since $Y = \alpha K$ $\dfrac{Y}{L_a} = \alpha\dfrac{K}{L_a}$. But we must have $\dfrac{Y}{L_a} \geqslant \left(\dfrac{Y}{L_a}\right)^*$, so that we require $\alpha\dfrac{K}{L_a} \geqslant \left(\dfrac{Y}{L_a}\right)^*$.

(3) $\alpha S^{\lim} > l_t^{\lim}$. In order that the standard of living $\left(\dfrac{Y}{L_t}\right)$ should be rising progressively we must have $y > l_t$. But $y = \alpha S^{\lim}$, so that with $l_t = l_t^{\lim}$ we require $\alpha S^{\lim} > l_t$.

(4) $l_t^{\lim} + l' \geqslant \alpha S^{\lim}$. With D constant at $D^{\lim}$, we have $l_a = l_t = l_t^{\lim}$. From (3) it follows that $y - l_a = \alpha S^{\lim} - l_t^{\lim}$. But in order that output per available worker should continuously rise at this steady rate of $\alpha S^{\lim} - l_t^{\lim}$, it is necessary that labour-expanding technical progress should at least fill the gap, namely that $l' \geqslant \alpha S^{\lim} - l_t^{\lim}$. In other words, K will be growing continuously at a rate equal to $\alpha S^{\lim}$, while L_a in a steady-state in which D is constant at $D^{\lim}$ will be growing continuously at a lower rate, namely $l_t^{\lim}$. If capital is to remain a scarce resource, the rate at which labour per unit of output, and so also per unit of capital, can be economized (namely, l') must at least fill the gap. Figure 14 has been so drawn that $l_t^{\lim} < \alpha S^{\lim} < l_t^{\lim} + l'$ so that both conditions 3 and 4 are satisfied.

Zero Propdem Two. Suppose now that the conditions depicted in Figure 14 were unchanged except that at time t the population is very much bigger although the capital resources are unchanged. In consequence output per available worker is much lower, namely at $\left(\dfrac{Y}{L_a}\right)_2$ instead of $\left(\dfrac{Y}{L_a}\right)_1$. We may now well be in a state of steady growth with a stagnant standard of living. For this case to be possible the following four conditions must be fulfilled.

(1) $\beta e^{l't} \geqslant \left(\dfrac{Y}{L_a}\right)_2$. Technology must, of course, be sufficiently advanced to make possible an output per head as high as the stagnation level of $\dfrac{Y}{L_a}$.

(2) $\dfrac{K}{L_a} = \dfrac{1}{\alpha}\left(\dfrac{Y}{L_a}\right)_2$. The size of the working population (L_a) must have adjusted itself to the size of the capital stock (K) in such a way as to make output per available worker $\left(\dfrac{Y}{L_a} = \dfrac{\alpha K}{L_a}\right)$ equal to the stagnation level $\left(\dfrac{Y}{L_a}\right)_2$. As we shall see (p. 175 below), there are forces which will tend to pull L_a into this stagnation relationship with K if it should be moderately out of line. Our requirement is that L_a should be sufficiently great, relatively to the available K, to bring output per available worker into the region of the stagnation level.

(3) The l_t-curve and the αS-curve must intersect. For $\dfrac{Y}{L_t}$ to be stagnant we must have $y = l_t$. But $y = \alpha S$; therefore for stagnation we must have $l_t = \alpha S$. Such an intersection of the two curves is shown in Figure 14 where $\dfrac{Y}{L_a} = \left(\dfrac{Y}{L_a}\right)_2$ and $l_t = l_{t2}$. This determines the corresponding levels of $S = S_2$ and $D = D_2$.

(4) $l' \geqslant 0$. Our fourth condition is that no shortage of labour should appear. In order that a growth rate of output of y should be sustained a growth rate of $l = y - l'$ is needed. But $y = \alpha S_2$ so that we need $l = \alpha S_2 - l'$. But with D constant at D_2 we have $l_a = l_t = l_{t2} = \alpha S_2$. Thus we have $l = l_a - l'$. In this stagnation case the demand for labour will necessarily grow less quickly than the available labour so long as there is any technical progress. No labour shortage can appear so long as $l' \geqslant 0$.

Indeed one marked feature of both Zero Propdem cases is the probability of growing unemployment. In Zero Propdem One there could by a fluke be a continuing condition of full employment of both capital and labour. This would occur if (i) at time t the population were of the exact size to make $\dfrac{Y}{L_a} = \beta_e l't$, since as we have seen this is the condition which makes the total working population match the total available supply of capital equipment, and (ii) $\alpha S^{\lim} = l_t^{\lim} + l'$, since this is the condition which will make $k(=\alpha S^{\lim})$ grow at the rate which matches the growth rate of the labour force ($l_t^{\lim}$) and the rate of labour-expanding technical progress (l'). But this last condition is, of course, a mere fluke. If $\alpha S^{\lim} < l_t^{\lim} + l'$, the standard of living can continue to grow at $\alpha S^{\lim} - l_t^{\lim}$; but the unemployment percentage will be rising since the ratio of total labour available to labour actually employed will grow at a rate of $l_t^{\lim} + l' - \alpha S^{\lim}$. If $\alpha S^{\lim} > l_t^{\lim} + l'$, sooner or later there will be a shortage of labour. In this case there will be full employment of labour; output per available worker will grow at l' instead of $\alpha S^{\text{lim}} - l_t^{\text{lim}}$; and as long as the capital stock continues to grow at an absolute rate equal to αS^{lim} times the amount of capital actually employed, more and more of it will lie idle and unused.

In Zero Propdem Two if there is any labour-saving technical progress unemployment of labour is bound to grow. Capital now grows at αS_2 and the labour force grows at the same rate ($l_a = l_{t2} = \alpha S_2$). But, as we have seen, the demand for labour grows only at the rate $l = y - l' = \alpha S_2 - l'$, since labour per unit of output is economized at the rate l'. Thus $l_a - l = l'$, which means that the ratio of labour available for employment to labour actually employed grows at the rate of labour-expanding technical progress.

It will be observed from the centre part of Figure 14 that as it is drawn the αS-curve cuts the l_t-curve also at a second point higher than $\left(\dfrac{Y}{L_a}\right)_2$. We have not considered this point for the reasons explained on page 163 above. At l_{t2} a small rise (or fall) in $\left(\dfrac{Y}{L_a}\right)_2$ would make the steady-state value of αS fall below (or rise above) that of l_t, and, with a constant D so that $l_t = l_a$, $\dfrac{Y}{L_a}$ would thus tend to move back towards $\left(\dfrac{Y}{L_a}\right)_2$. But at the higher value of $\dfrac{Y}{L_a}$ where the l_t-curve cuts the αS-curve upwards from right to left, the opposite would be the case; a small rise (or fall) in $\dfrac{Y}{L_a}$ would now make the steady-state value of αS rise above (or fall below) that of l_t, and, with $l_a = l_t$, $\dfrac{Y}{L_a}$ would tend to move still further from its stagnant level.

But is there in fact likely to be an intersection of the αS-curve and the l_t-curve of the kind suggested at $\left(\dfrac{Y}{L_a}\right)_2$? Now it is probable that the values of α, S^{lim}, and l_t^{lim} are such that $\alpha S^{\text{lim}} > l_t^{\text{lim}}$. The αS-curve could, of course, lie to the right of the l_t-curve for all values of $\dfrac{Y}{L_a}$. This could be the case if fertility were well controlled at all standards of living. In this case the only type of state of steady growth possible would be of the progressive Zero Propdem One kind.

Another possibility, illustrated in Figure 15, is that, while $\alpha S^{\text{lim}} > l_t^{\text{lim}}$, the value of $\dfrac{Y}{L_a}$ at which $S = 0$ is higher than the value of $\dfrac{Y}{L_a}$ at which $l_t = 0$. As the standard of living is reduced, the point at which people cease to save is reached sooner than the point at which infant mortality rises sufficiently to prevent all growth of numbers. In this case, of course, the αS-curve must cut the l_t-curve; there must be a stagnation solution; but this necessary intersection would be one in which the l_t-curve cut the αS-curve in the 'wrong' way. If this were the case, then at all standards of living still lower than this stagnant intersection, l_t would exceed αS and the standard would tend to fall indefinitely. There might, it is true, as in Figure 15 be another intersection of the

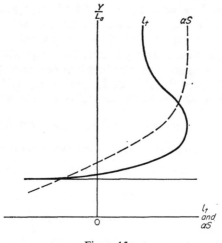

Figure 15

l_t-curve and the αS-curve at negative values of l_t and S. When the standard of living was low enough, the population would be declining because of very high infant mortality; and at the same time the rate at which people would live on any capital already accumulated (i.e. the negative value of S) might cause the capital stock to fall at the same rate as the population was declining. The population and the capital stock would both die out at nicely adjusted constant rates.

The αS-curve and the l_t-curve as drawn in Figure 14 assume that as the standard of living falls, the population ceases to grow before savings fall to zero. In this case, the condition $\alpha S^{\lim} < l_t^{\lim}$ is compatible with the type of double intersection shown in Figure 14.

We can now turn to the Zero Plantcap cases which are illustrated in Figure 16. In all these Plantcap cases there will once more in any state of steady growth be full employment of both factors, labour and capital. If there were unemployed labour, competition would drive down the wage rate, and when the workers' standard of living had fallen sufficiently low the steady-state rate of growth of the working-class population would fall to zero or even change into a steady rate of decline. With a zero elasticity of substitution between labour and capital the proportion of the national output going to wages would fall and that accruing to property owners would rise; and since in a Plantcap no wages, but some property incomes are saved, this shift of income from wages to property incomes would increase the proportion of the national income which was saved and so raise the rate of capital accumulation. By this mechanism, if the economy

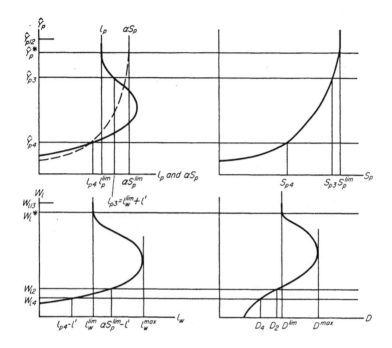

Figure 16

started with too much labour to man the available machines, the rate of growth of the working population would decline and that of the stock of machines would rise. Conversely, if the economy started with too many machines relatively to the number of workers, the rate of profit would be brought down to zero by the forces of competition; savings in a Plantcap would dry up entirely; the capital stock would cease to grow until the working population had once more caught up with it. If these negative feedback forces do lead to a state of steady growth, then that state must be such that the amount of capital matches the amount of labour and there is full employment of both factors. We can once again write L for L_a throughout our analysis.

In any state of steady growth $D \left(= \dfrac{L_w}{L_a} \right)$ will be constant and with $L_a = L$ this implies that $l = l_w$. Moreover, since $1 - Q$ is the proportion of income going to profits and since S_p is the proportion of property incomes saved, $(1 - Q)S_p$ is the proportion of income saved. Now we know from equation (11.6) that in all Zero cases, with a scarcity of K, $y = \alpha S = l + l'$. It follows that in the present case

$$y = \alpha(1 - Q)S_p = l_w + l' \tag{11.7}$$

From this it is clear that

$$\left.\begin{aligned} (1 - Q) &= \frac{l_w + l'}{\alpha S_p} \\[2mm] Q &= \frac{\alpha S_p - l_w - l'}{\alpha S_p} \end{aligned}\right\} \tag{11.8}$$

and

These expressions give the distribution between wages and profits which, on the principles discussed in the last paragraph, is necessary to maintain full employment of both factors.

Moreover, since $\beta e^{l't}$ measures output per worker, at any moment of time t we have $\dfrac{Y}{L} = \beta e^{l't}$, so that $\dfrac{QY}{L}$ (which measures the wage rate W_l) $= Q\beta e^{l't}$. From (11.8) we can express this as

$$W_l = \frac{QY}{L} = \frac{\alpha S_p - l_w - l'}{\alpha S_p} \, \beta e^{l't} \tag{11.9}$$

Armed with expressions (11.7), (11.8), and (11.9), giving the three basic conditions necessary for a state of steady growth in all the Zero Plantcap cases, we can now distinguish between the four possible outcomes in these cases.

This is illustrated in Figure 16, where the solid-line curves are exactly the same as in Figure 13. We will consider each of the four possible outcomes in turn.

Zero Plantcap One. This is the case in which the standard of living of both the workers and the capitalists continuously rises. For this to be the case the populations of both the workers and the capitalists must be small enough relatively to the existing stock of capital that $\hat{Y}_p$ and W_l are sufficiently high to bring l_p, l_w, S_p, and D to their constant limiting values $l_p^{\lim}$, $l_w^{\lim}$, $S_p^{\lim}$, and $D^{\lim}$. The rates of growth of the two populations must also be sufficiently low to ensure that income per head can continuously rise. Finally, technical progress must be sufficiently advanced to enable an output per head to be produced which will make possible a sufficiently high wage rate to enable l_w and D to be at their limiting constant levels, $l_w^{\lim}$ and $D^{\lim}$. We can express these conditions more precisely as follows.

1. In order that there should be a state of steady growth with l_w and S_p at their limiting constant values we have from (11.7) $y = \alpha(1 - Q)S_p^{\lim} = l_w^{\lim} + l'$. Thus from (11.8) we have $Q = \dfrac{\alpha S_p^{\lim} - l_w^{\lim} - l'}{\alpha S_p^{\lim}}$. Since Q cannot be negative, it follows that a necessary condition for this state is that $l_w^{\lim} < \alpha S_p^{\lim} - l'$. If $l_w^{\lim}$ were greater than this, then even if the whole of income went to profits ($Q = 0$), there would not be a sufficient level of savings to make the growth rate of capital ($\alpha[1 - Q]S_p$) high enough to keep in line with the combined growth rate of labour ($l_w^{\lim}$) and the rate of labour-expanding technical progress (l').

2. We have seen in discussing condition (1) that $y = l_w^{\lim} + l'$ and that $1 - Q$ is constant at $\dfrac{l_w^{\lim} + l'}{\alpha S_p^{\lim}}$. In order that the capitalists' standard of living should be rising, $\hat{Y}_p = \dfrac{(1 - Q)Y}{L_p}$ must be rising. With $1 - Q$ fixed, this means that l_p must be $< y$. Therefore, the present case needs as a necessary condition that $l_p^{\lim} < l_w^{\lim} + l'$. If this were not so, the capitalist population would grow too quickly relatively to total profits for any progressive increase in the capitalists' standard of living to be possible.

3. Since $\dfrac{1}{\alpha}$ is the amount of K needed to produce one unit of Y and $\dfrac{1}{\beta e^{l't}}$ is the amount of labour required to produce one unit of Y at the point of time t with which we are concerned, we must have $\dfrac{K}{L_a}$ at time t equal to $\dfrac{\beta e^{l't}}{\alpha}$ in order that there should be full employment of labour. For the economy to be in full employment equilibrium, L_a must have this value at time t in terms of the volume of capital (K) then in existence.

4. For the standard of living of the capitalists at time t to be not less than the critical level $\hat{Y}_p^*$ required to set l_p and S_p at $l_p^{\lim}$ and $S_p^{\lim}$, we have $\hat{Y}_p \equiv \dfrac{(1 - Q)Y}{L_p} \geqslant \hat{Y}_p^*$. But $1 - Q = \dfrac{l_p^{\lim} + l'}{S_p^{\lim}}$ and $Y = \alpha K$. Therefore, we have as a necessary condition that at time t

$$L_p \leqslant \frac{l_p^{\lim} + l'}{S_p^{\lim}} \frac{\alpha}{\hat{Y}_p^*} K.$$

Only if the number of capitalists is thus small enough in relation to the amount of capital available at time t will their standard of living be as high as the necessary critical level.

5. At time t $Q\beta e^{l't}$ measures $\dfrac{QY}{L}$ or W_l, so that $\dfrac{\alpha S_p^{\lim} - l_w^{\lim} - l'}{\alpha S_p^{\lim}} \beta e^{l't}$ measures W_l. For this to be at least as high as the critical level necessary to bring l_w and D to their constant levels $l_w^{\lim}$ and $D^{\lim}$ we have as a necessary condition

$$\beta e^{l't} \geqslant \frac{\alpha S_p^{\lim}}{\alpha S_p^{\lim} - l_w^{\lim} - l'} W_l{}^*$$

Only if technical knowledge is sufficiently advanced at time t to raise $\beta e^{l't}$ to this level, will it be possible to have a wage rate above the critical level $W_l{}^*$.

Zero Plantcap Two. This is the case in which capitalists' standards are progressively rising while the wage rate stagnates, illustrated by $\hat{Y}_{p12}$ and W_{12} in Figure 16. Now in order that the wage rate should stagnate, i.e. in order that $W_l = \dfrac{QY}{L} = Q\beta e^{l't}$ should remain constant, Q must continually fall at the rate of labour-expanding technical progress l'. Such stagnation of the wage rate can occur if the working population, at a constant wage rate, grows as quickly as the capital stock; but it means that all the benefits of labour-expanding technical progress will accrue to the owners of capital. The share of wages Q will become smaller and smaller and will approach zero without ever being quite equal to zero; and the share of profits $1 - Q$ will become larger and larger until it is for all practical purposes equal to one.

For our steady-state from (11.7) we see that we need

$$y = \alpha(1 - Q)S_p^{\lim} = l_w + l'.$$

But as Q approaches zero, for all practical purposes y becomes constant at $\alpha S_p^{\lim}$ and l_w at $\alpha S_p^{\lim} - l'$. Our five conditions now become:

1. W_{12} must be, for all practical purposes, at the level which makes $l_w = \alpha S_p^{\lim} - l'$, as is illustrated in Figure 16. For this to be so, we must have $l_w^{\max} \geqslant \alpha S_p^{\lim} - l'$. If there were no level of l_w as great as $\alpha S_p^{\lim} - l'$, the population pressure could not in any conditions be heavy enough to cause the wage rate to be stagnant.

2. Since $1 - Q$ is for all practical purposes equal to unity, $1 - Q$ may be treated as a constant; and the capitalists' standard of living,

$\hat{Y}_p \equiv \dfrac{(1-Q)Y}{L_p}$, will be rising if $l_p < y$. For this to be so in our present case we need $l_p^{\lim} < \alpha S_p^{\lim}$.

3. At time t we must have $\dfrac{K}{L_a} = \dfrac{\beta e^{l't}}{\alpha}$ in order that there should be full employment of both factors. (See page 179 above.) The number of workers must be of this size in relation to this level of K at time t, if there is to be full employment of both factors in our steady state.

4. For the capitalists' standard of living to be at or above its critical level $\hat{Y}_p^*$, we must have at time t $\hat{Y}_p \equiv \dfrac{(1-Q)Y}{L_p} \geqslant \hat{Y}_p^*$. With $1 - Q$ for practical purposes equal to 1, and with $Y = \alpha K$, this condition becomes

$$ L_p \leqslant \frac{\alpha}{\hat{Y}_p^*} K $$

5. At time t we have $W_l = \dfrac{QL}{Y} = Q\beta e^{l't}$. In our state of steady growth, therefore, at time t $1 - Q = 1 - \dfrac{W_l^*}{\beta e^{l't}}$. In order to be in the state of steady growth which we are now examining $1 - Q$ must be so nearly equal to unity that we can treat $y = \alpha(1-Q)S_p^{\lim}$ as equal to $\alpha S_p^{\lim}$ for the purpose of considering y to be at a steady-state level. The state of technical knowledge must, therefore, be sufficiently advanced at time t to reduce $\dfrac{W_l^*}{\beta e^{l't}}$ to a very small fraction.

In this case as we have already explained the proportion of the national income going to profits will rise without limit until for practical purposes profits absorb the whole income. The wage rate earned by the workers will be kept by the competition of the pressure of their numbers on the available resources of capital at a constant level, just sufficient to keep their numbers growing in line with the accumulation of capital by the capitalists. Moreover, the higher is the rate of labour-expanding technical progress l', the lower need the rate of growth of the numbers of workers be, and the lower, therefore, will be the absolute level of the wage rate. Indeed, if $l' < \alpha S_p^{\lim}$, the wage rate will be so low as to induce such impoverishment that the working-class population actually declines steadily at a rate equal to $l' - \alpha S_p^{\lim}$.

Zero Plantcap Three. In this case capitalists' standards stagnate, while workers' standards continuously rise. If workers' standards are to rise continuously, we must have $l = l_w^{\lim}$, so that $y = l_w^{\lim} + l'$.

Output must rise at a steady rate equal to the sum of the growth rate of the number of workers plus the rate of labour-expanding technical progress. Capitalists' standards, $\hat{Y}_p = \dfrac{(1-Q)Y}{L_p}$, can stagnate if $1 - Q$ is constant and L_p is rising at the same rate as Y, i.e. $y = l_p$. These conditions can be fulfilled if the capitalists' standard of living is, as depicted by $\hat{Y}_{p3}$ in Figure 16, at a level which makes $l_p = l_w^{\lim} + l'$. We can then have $y = l_w^{\lim} + l' = l_{p3}$. But if $\hat{Y}_p$ is at this level S_p will be at the level S_{p3} in Figure 16, so that $y = \alpha(1 - Q)S_{p3} = l_w^{\lim} + l' = l_{p3}$. From this it is clear that

$$Q = \frac{\alpha S_{p3} - l_w^{\lim} - l'}{\alpha S_{p3}}.$$

Only if Q has this value will the rate of growth of the capital stock $\alpha(1 - Q)S_{p3}$ be kept in line with the expansion of the effective labour force $l_w^{\lim}+l'$. We can thus express our five conditions in the following way:

1. In order that Q should not be negative we must have

$$l_w^{\lim} < \alpha S_{p3} - l'.$$

In Figure 16 this is depicted as being the case, since in the top left-hand section of the Figure the αS_p broken-line curve passes to the right of the l_p solid-line curve at the value of $\hat{Y}_p$ which makes $l_p = l_w^{\lim} + l'$. If $l_w^{\lim}$ were greater than this, a continuously progressing standard of living for the workers could not be combined with stagnation for the capitalist.

2. In order that there should be some level of capitalists' standards which would make $l_p = l_w^{\lim} + l'$, we must have

$$l_p^{\max} \geqslant l_w^{\lim} + l'.$$

If this were not so, it would be impossible that the number of capitalists should rise so quickly as to keep their standards stagnant when the workers' standards were rising.

3. As in the case of Zero Plantcap One (see condition 3 on page 179 above), the size of the working population at time t must satisfy the condition

$$\frac{K}{L_a} = \frac{\beta e^{l't}}{\alpha}$$

for there to be full employment of labour in a steady state at time t; given the supply of capital K at that time.

4. In order that the capitalists' standard of living should be at

the stagnation level at time t we must have $\hat{Y}_p \equiv \dfrac{(1-Q)Y}{L_p} = Y_{p3}$.

But, as we have seen $1 - Q = \dfrac{l_w^{\lim} + l'}{\alpha S_{p3}}$, so that, with $Y = \alpha K$, our condition becomes

$$L_p = \frac{l_w^{\lim} + l'}{\alpha S_{p3}} \frac{\alpha}{\hat{Y}_{p3}} K.$$

The capitalist population must be of this size relatively to the existing capital stock for the capitalist standard of living to be at the stagnation level.

5. In order that it shall be technically possible for the workers to have at time t a wage rate as high as the critical level W_l^* needed to keep l_w at $l_w^{\lim}$, the state of technical knowledge at time t must be sufficiently advanced. By the argument used to establish condition 5 for Zero Plantcap One (see page 180), we can see that this condition is

$$\beta e^{l't} \geqslant \frac{\alpha S_{p3}}{\alpha S_{p3} - l_w^{\lim} - l'} W_l^*.$$

Zero Plantcap Four. This is the case where both the capitalists and the workers have a stagnant standard of living. As in Zero Plantcap Two, if the wage rate $\left(W_l = \dfrac{QY}{L} = Q\beta e^{l't}\right)$ is to stagnate Q must fall at a proportional rate equal to l', to offset the rise in output per worker. A state of steady growth may be reached when $1 - Q$ is approximately equal to 1. Since $y = \alpha(1 - Q)S_p$, in the state of steady growth with a stagnant wage rate we shall have for all practical purposes $y = \alpha S_p$. As $1 - Q$ approaches 1, an ever higher proportion of an ever growing national income will accrue to profits; but the capitalists' standard can also be stagnant if the number of capitalists to share in these profits is growing at the same rate. But since $1 - Q$ may be treated as for all practical purposes constant at unity, $\hat{Y}_p \equiv \dfrac{(1-Q)Y}{L_p}$ will be stagnant if $y = l_p$. Therefore from (11.7) we have

$$y = \alpha S_p = l_w + l' = l_p$$

From this we can find the value of $\hat{Y}_{p4}$ as being that which causes l_p to be equal to αS_p. The corresponding values of l_p and S_p are shown in Figure 16 at l_{p4} and S_{p4}. Since $\alpha S_p = l_w + l'$ if capital accumulation and the growth of the effective labour force are to be kept in line, we must in this case have $l_w = \alpha S_{p4} - l'$ and this determines the steady-state value of l_w and so of W_{l4} and D_4 as shown in Figure 16.

Of course, if $l' > \alpha S_{p4}$, l_w might be negative; the stagnation wage rate would be so low as to cause a steady decline in the working-class population.

We can now express our five conditions as follows:

1. In order that there should be a value of l_w equal to $\alpha S_{p4} - l'$ it is necessary that

$$l_w^{\max} \geqslant \alpha S_{p4} - l'$$

If $l_w^{\max}$ were less than this, the workers' population could not grow fast enough to cause stagnation of the wage rate.

2. Since for capitalists' stagnation we have $l_{p4} = y = \alpha S_{p4}$ we must have an intersection between the l_p-curve and the αS_p-curve. If the l_p-curve were for all values of $\hat{Y}_p$ to the left of the αS_p-curve, there could not be a high enough rate of growth of the capitalist population to cause a stagnation in the capitalists' standards.[1] It is to be observed that Figure 16 illustrates two intersections of the l_p-curve and the αS_p-curve. But for the reasons discussed above (pages 162–163), we confine our attention only to the lower of these two points.

3. The size of the working population relatively to the capital stock at time t must satisfy the equation

$$\frac{K}{L_a} = \frac{\beta e^{l't}}{\alpha}.$$

See condition 3 for Zero Plantcap One (p. 179 above).

4. The size of the capitalist population must be such that $\hat{Y}_p \equiv \dfrac{(1-Q)Y}{L_p} = \hat{Y}_{p4}$ so that with $1 - Q$ equal for all practical purposes to unity and with $Y = \alpha K$, we have

$$L_p = \frac{\alpha}{\hat{Y}_{p4}} K$$

as expressing the steady-state size of L_p relatively to K.

It will be observed that each of the four possible outcomes of the Zero Plantcap cases is compatible with the same l_p-curve, l_w-curve, S_p-curve, and D-curve and with the same assumed values of α, β, and l'. (Cf. the similar situation for the four Unity Propdem cases discussed on page 169 above.) All that is necessary to obtain one result

---

[1] If the αS_p-curve were to the left of the l_p-curve for all positive values of l_p, there would nevertheless probably be an intersection of the αS_p-curve and the l_p-curve at a negative value of l_p. Cp. Figure 15 on page 176 above. In this case l_{p4} would be negative and *a fortiori* $l_{w4} = \alpha S_{p4} - l' = l_{p4} - l'$ would be negative. Both classes would have so low a stagnant standard of living that both would be dying out—the working-class population more rapidly than the capitalists.

rather than another from the particular conditions displayed in Figure 16 is that the absolute populations L_w and L_p should be of the appropriate size relatively to the capital stock K and the state of technical knowledge $\beta e^{l't}$ at the point of time t in which we are interested. As the reader can easily verify for himself this possibility rests upon the fact that both the *l*-curves slope upwards from right to left after a certain standard is reached. The reader must work out for himself which of the four results would be possible and which not if the interrelationships between the various curves and constants were other than those depicted in Figure 16, which has been so constructed expressly so as to be able to illustrate all four cases with the same set of curves.

Unity Plantcap Three and Zero Plantcap Three are both cases in which the workers thrive and the capitalists stagnate. This may seem to be a very paradoxical situation. It is not the usual idea of a Plantation Capitalism that the toilers become better and better off, while the capitalist-employers stay at a low level of consumption. There may indeed be an absurdity in our assumptions in these cases. For if the workers' standards were continually rising, would it be sensible to assume that they never saved anything? What makes the assumptions of a Plantcap plausible as a working model is that there should be so low a stagnant wage rate that the workers can really not afford to save anything. They must perforce live from hand to mouth, while the capitalists with a higher and perhaps progressing standard of living can afford to save. For this reason we ought perhaps to rule out both Unity and Zero Plantcap cases One and Three as being situations in which sooner or later the Plantcap assumptions would break down because the thriving workers would start to save.

The reader must now be left to use these models for his own purposes; but it may be useful to indicate briefly a few general observations that can be made from an examination of Figures 12, 13, 14, and 16. Suppose that a public health policy (e.g. the elimination of malaria) or a family-planning policy (e.g. a mass insertion of inter-uterine devices) shifts an *l*-curve appreciably to the right or to the left.

Any population whose standard was progressively rising would as a result of a shift of its *l*-curve to the left experience a still more rapid rate of rise in its standard. As a result of a shift of its *l*-curve to the right it would experience a less rapid rise in its standard, or if the shift were sufficiently great it might move from the category in which a rising standard were possible to one in which the only possible state of steady growth was a stagnant one.

Any population whose standard was stagnant would as a result of a shift of its *l*-curve to the right find a new stagnation state with a still lower standard of living. The decreased mortality due to the elimination of malaria would be replaced by the higher mortality due to the starvation levels of income resulting from the increased pressure of population on resources. On the contrary a shift of the *l*-curve to the left would lead to a new stagnation situation but at a higher standard of living, or if the shift of the *l*-curve to the left was sufficiently great a stagnation steady state would become impossible and would give place to a state of steady growth with a continually progressing standard of living.[1]

Note to Chapter XI

THE PRESSURE OF LABOUR AND CAPITAL ON THE LAND

Let us consider for the purposes of illustration the case examined in Chapter XI (pp. 161–164) under the heading Unity Propdem Two, depicted in Figure 12. In this case we have a Cobb-Douglas production function of the form

$$Y = R\, N^Z\, K^U\, L^Q\, e^{rt} \tag{11.10}$$

where R is a constant.

In the stagnation case of Unity Propdem Two we have

$$y = k = \frac{SY}{K} = \frac{r}{Z} \tag{11.11}$$

Moreover, $\dfrac{Y}{L}$ must have the particular value which makes $l = \dfrac{r}{Z}$; thus

$$\frac{Y}{L} = \hat{Y}_2 \tag{11.12}$$

where $\hat{Y}_2$ is the value of $\dfrac{Y}{L}$ at which in Figure 12 the *l*-curve cuts the vertical line $\dfrac{r}{Z}$

From (11.10) and (11.11) we have

$$\frac{r}{SZ} = R\, N^Z\, K^{U-1}\, L^Q\, e^{rt} \tag{11.13}$$

---

[1] Another exercise which the reader is encouraged to undertake is to ask in each of the twelve cases examined in this chapter what would be the effect upon the standards of living, unemployment, and the division of income between wages and profits of an improvement in the rate of technical progress—i.e. a rise in *r* in the Unity cases and in *l'* in the Zero cases.

and from (11.10) and (11.12) we have

$$\hat{Y}_2 = RN^Z K^U L^{Q-1} e^{rt} \qquad (11.14)$$

At any point of time t equations (11.13) and (11.14) give us two equations in the two unknowns K and L. Their solution gives

$$L = \left\{ RN^Z e^{rt} \left(\frac{1}{\hat{Y}_2}\right)^{1-U} \left(\frac{r}{SZ}\right)^{U} \right\}^{\frac{1}{Z}}$$

and

$$K = \left\{ RN^Z e^{rt} \left(\frac{1}{\hat{Y}_2}\right)^{Q} \left(\frac{r}{SZ}\right)^{1-Q} \right\}^{\frac{1}{Z}}$$

These equations show what the absolute size of L and K must be, given N and t, in order to have (i) a population which reduces income per head to the stagnation level and (ii) a capital stock which is in a steady-state relationship with the other factors L and N.

CHAPTER XII

SAVINGS: (1) PERFECT SELFISHNESS

We turn now from our consideration of the determinants of the rate of technical progress (r) and of the growth rate of the working population (l) to a consideration of the determinants of the proportion of income saved (S). In Chapters VI to VIII we simply assumed that the savings proportion was given and constant and we examined the effects of any such given savings proportion upon growth. In Chapter XI we assumed that the savings proportion might be affected by the standard of living without enquiring further into the reasons why this might be so. We must now examine in more detail the economic considerations which may influence the citizen's choice between saving and spending.

Before we embark upon the economic analysis of these questions, a very strong word of warning is necessary. In no part of the subject matter of economics is it more necessary to supplement economic analysis with sociological and other studies. The motives for capital accumulation are very varied—the miser's desire simply to accumulate, the desire to display great wealth or to leave a vast property on one's death, the automatic putting aside of a customary proportion of income or of all income over and above a customary standard of consumption, and so on. But in the following pages we shall not treat the factors affecting the propensity to save in this manner. We shall in fact be discussing what a citizen *should* save on the basis of a cold economic calculus. This calculus is of the following kind.

We assume that the citizen's only interest in saving is in order to alter the time pattern of consumption. He cuts down his present consumption and saves solely in order that either he or his heirs may have greater resources from which to increase their consumption in the future. The act of saving is the act of denying oneself some consumption now in order that someone may have a higher standard of living in the future. On this basis an examination of the determinants of the propensity to consume will fall into two parts: (i) the citizen is assumed to have a given set of preferences between various combinations of consumption now and of consumption in the future; (ii) the citizen is confronted with a market rate of return on any property which he accumulates and this determines how much consumption he or his heirs can have next year or the year after for every unit of consumption which he forgoes this year in order to increase this year's savings. The citizen is then assumed to plan his savings and so the time pattern of his consumption so as to satisfy his preferences under (i) to the best extent made possible by the market conditions under (ii).

This type of analysis is undoubtedly very incomplete. But it is worth undertaking for two reasons. First, it may well indicate some—though not all—of the motives which do in fact determine most citizens' savings habits. Second, it provides a useful introduction to an important group of problems of economic planning by the State; for an examination of the way in which citizens would behave if they wished to achieve a certain aim is clearly very relevant to an examination of the way in which the government should try to influence behaviour if it wishes this aim to be achieved. The planning of the pattern of consumption through time is often accepted as a major function of governmental policy in the modern world for reasons which we shall examine later.

In order that this model should make sense we must make certain assumptions about the capital market. Our citizens can save and invest their savings on the capital market in such a way as to lend their savings directly or indirectly to other citizens to invest in capital equipment for use in the firms or farms (see pages 35–36 above). Citizens can thus borrow money from other citizens to invest in such capital equipment and can thus have money debt liabilities offset by real capital assets. Private citizens can dissave; they can finance an excess of consumption above their incomes by living on any property which they have previously accumulated or inherited. Moreover, propertyless citizens can also borrow to finance an excess of consumption over income—but not without limit. If they could so borrow without limit, everyone would live all the time like a multi-millionaire. Each citizen each year would borrow whatever was necessary to pay the interest due on his previous borrowing and to finance an infinitely exalted standard of living. Such borrowing is excluded from our model by assuming that each citizen's net borrowing is limited to the amount which he will be able to repay, together with interest on his borrowing, out of his future earnings and his future receipts from gifts over the remainder of his life. He can mortgage his future receipts, but he cannot borrow beyond that.

We assume that all these borrowings and lendings will take place at the same daily rate of interest (i.e. at a rate equal to the Bank Rate discussed on page 36 above) if they take the form of short-term loans of one day's duration. But they may equally well take the form of loans for longer periods of time in which case the structure of the rates of interest payable on them will be based upon the daily Bank

Rates expected to rule over the period of the loan (see page 35 above and pages 314–318 below). We can for the time being conduct our analysis as if all borrowings and lendings were made solely on a daily basis, each loan which remains unpaid for a longer period being renewed from day to day at that day's Bank Rate.

Finally, in order to isolate for examination the pure theory of the choice between present and future consumption, we shall at this stage of our analysis banish all problems of uncertainty. This can be done only by making the assumptions: (i) that every citizen on day 0 has the same firm expectation about the future movement of every relevant price in the economy, i.e. every citizen on day 0 expects firmly that the rate of interest will be precisely i_1 on day 1, i_2 on day 2, and so on, and that the wage rate will be W_{l1} on day 1, W_{l2} on day 2, and so on; and (ii) that in fact these firm expectations happen to turn out to be correct. This assumption of perfect foresight raises very great difficulties to which we shall return in due course (see Chapter XVIII below). For the time being in order to isolate one part of our problem we assume simply that in fact every citizen does expect every price to behave in the future in the way in which it will in fact behave if they all happen to have this expectation.

We are now in a position to consider the general principles on which a citizen can plan the economically most satisfactory pattern of consumption over his life. Children are maintained by their parents during childhood; at the end of childhood they start earning until retirement; during this period they themselves produce and bring up children; on retirement they cease to earn but continue to consume out of their savings or out of what they have received as an inheritance when their parents died or out of support given to them by their children; and on their death they may leave some property to their own children. Consider then a citizen at the moment when he ceases to be a child and goes out to earn as an adult. He has now to plan his consumption pattern over the remainder of his life. Shall he start by consuming very little in his first years of life so that he can consume much when he is old and so that he can when he dies leave much to his own children?

Let us first consider what consumption patterns are open to him. Suppose that he knows that he has five 'days' to live, during the first three of which he will earn $\hat{E}_1$, $\hat{E}_2$, and $\hat{E}_3$ respectively;[1] suppose that he knows that at the end of day 2 he will inherit $\hat{I}_2$ from his father who will die on that day; suppose that he plans when he dies on day 5 to leave $\hat{B}_5$ to his children; and suppose that he knows that the rates

---

[1] $\hat{E}_1$ is the earnings in respect of work done during day 1, the payment for which is made at 8 a.m. on day 2. Similarly the payments $\hat{C}_1$, $\hat{I}_1$, $\hat{B}_1$, etc., are made at 8 a.m. on day 2 (i.e., at the *end* of day 1).

of interest will be i_1, i_2, i_3, i_4, and i_5 in the five remaining days of his life. What patterns of consumption over the five remaining days of his life are open to him?

The answer is that he can choose any combination of consumption levels on the five remaining days of his life—namely, $\hat{C}_1$, $\hat{C}_2$, $\hat{C}_3$, $\hat{C}_4$, and $\hat{C}_5$—provided that the present discounted value of $\hat{C}_1$, $\hat{C}_2$, $\hat{C}_3$, $\hat{C}_4$, and $\hat{C}_5$ is not greater than the present discounted value of $\hat{E}_1$, $\hat{E}_2$, and $\hat{E}_3$ *plus* the present discounted value of $\hat{I}_2$ *minus* the present discounted value of $\hat{B}_5$. This can be seen in the following way. We can imagine our citizen going about his affairs in the following rather indirect manner. He starts at the beginning of day 1 (end of day 0) borrowing the largest possible sum that he can by mortgaging all his future receipts $\hat{E}_1$, $\hat{E}_2$, $\hat{E}_3$, and $\hat{I}_2$. He hands over the rights to $\hat{E}_1$, $\hat{E}_2$, $\hat{E}_3$, and $\hat{I}_2$ to those from whom he has raised this capital sum in return for this capital sum; he invests this capital sum on the capital market; he puts aside a sufficient part of it to have accumulated to $\hat{B}_5$ at compound interest by the time of his death to cover his bequests to his children; and he then plans his own consumptions $\hat{C}_1$, $\hat{C}_2$, $\hat{C}_3$, $\hat{C}_4$, and $\hat{C}_5$ so that as he finances them from the interest and principal of the remaining capital sum the whole of his capital fund will have been used up by the end of his life.

How much then can he borrow at the beginning of day 1 on the expectation of $\hat{E}_1$, $\hat{E}_2$, $\hat{E}_3$, and $\hat{I}_2$? On $\hat{E}_1$ he can raise at the beginning of day 1 a capital of $\dfrac{\hat{E}_1}{1 + i_1}$; for on this capital sum at the beginning of day 2 he will have to repay the capital sum $\left(\dfrac{\hat{E}_1}{1 + i_1} \right)$ *plus* one day's interest on the capital sum $\left(i\, \dfrac{\hat{E}_1}{1 + i_1} \right)$ a total of $\hat{E}_1$, which is what he receives in wages at the beginning of day 2. Similarly, on $\hat{E}_2$ he can raise $\dfrac{\hat{E}_2}{(1 + i_1)(1 + i_2)}$; for at the beginning of day 2 he will owe capital plus one day's interest on this sum, i.e. $(1 + i_1)$ times this sum, and at the beginning of day 3 he will owe $(1 + i_2)$ times the sum owed at the beginning of day 2, so that at the beginning of day 3 he will owe $\dfrac{\hat{E}_2}{(1 + i_1)(1 + i_2)} \times (1 + i_1)(1 + i_2) = \hat{E}_2$ so that his earnings in respect of day 2 will be just sufficient to cover the sum borrowed at the beginning of day 1. Thus he can raise at the beginning of day 1 the present discounted value of $\hat{E}_1$, $\hat{E}_2$, $\hat{E}_3$, and $\hat{I}_2$ or a sum of

$$\frac{\hat{E}_1}{1 + i_1} + \frac{\hat{E}_2 + \hat{I}_2}{(1 + i_1)(1 + i_2)} + \frac{\hat{E}_3}{(1 + i_1)(1 + i_2)(1 + i_3)} \quad (12.1)$$

He must put aside a sum equal to $\dfrac{\hat{B}_5}{(1+i_1)(1+i_2)(1+i_3)(1+i_4)(1+i_5)}$ to cover his bequests to his children, because this sum invested at the beginning of day 1 will have become $(1 + i_1)$ times itself by the beginning of day 2, $(1 + i_1)(1 + i_2)$ times itself by the beginning of day 3, and so on, until it is worth $\hat{B}_5$, just enough to cover his bequests by the beginning of day 6. He has, therefore, at the beginning of day 1, left over to finance his future consumption a capital sum equal to

$$\frac{\hat{E}_1}{(1 + i_1)} + \frac{\hat{E}_2 + \hat{I}_2}{(1 + i_1)(1 + i_2)} + \frac{\hat{E}_3}{(1 + i_1)(1 + i_2)(1 + i_3)}$$

$$- \frac{\hat{B}_5}{(1 + i_1)(1 + i_2)(1 + i_3)(1 + i_4)(1 + i_5)} \qquad (12.2)$$

Suppose now that our citizen plans a stream of consumption $\hat{C}_1$, $\hat{C}_2$, $\hat{C}_3$, $\hat{C}_4$, $\hat{C}_5$ over his life-time. From the capital sum in (12.2) he will have at the beginning of day 1 to set aside $\dfrac{\hat{C}_1}{1 + i_1}$ to finance a consumption of $\hat{C}_1$ at the beginning of day 2, since $\dfrac{\hat{C}_1}{1 + i_1}$ will have accumulated with interest to $\dfrac{\hat{C}_1}{1 + i_1} \times (1 + i_1) = \hat{C}_1$ in a day's time. Similarly he must set aside $\dfrac{\hat{C}_2}{(1 + i_1)(1 + i_2)}$ to finance $\hat{C}_2$, since this is the sum which will have accumulated to $\hat{C}_2$ after two days. And so on. Thus the capital sum needed at the beginning of day 1 to finance the future consumption stream $\hat{C}_1$, $\hat{C}_2$, $\hat{C}_3$, $\hat{C}_4$, $\hat{C}_5$ will be the present discounted value of this stream, namely,

$$\frac{\hat{C}_1}{(1 + i_1)} + \frac{\hat{C}_2}{(1 + i_1)(1 + i_2)} + \frac{\hat{C}_3}{(1 + i_1)(1 + i_2)(1 + i_3)}$$

$$+ \frac{\hat{C}_4}{(1+i_1)(1+i_2)(1+i_3)(1+i_4)} + \frac{\hat{C}_5}{(1+i_1)(1+i_2)(1+i_3)(1+i_4)(1+i_5)}$$
$$(12.3)$$

He can choose any combination of $\hat{C}_1$, $\hat{C}_2$, $\hat{C}_3$, $\hat{C}_4$, and $\hat{C}_5$ which he likes provided that the expression in (12.3) does not exceed the expression in (12.2).

The choice of the best pattern for this stream of consumptions may be regarded as falling into two parts; first, the choice of the time shape of the consumption stream and, second, the choice of the absolute starting level for that stream. For examples of the first part of the choice we ask whether our citizen wants to maintain a constant level of consumption over his life (i.e. $\hat{C}_1 = \hat{C}_2 = \hat{C}_3 = \hat{C}_4 = \hat{C}_5$); or a level of consumption which starts relatively low, rises as his needs for maintaining his own children rise, and falls again as his needs decline in old age; or a level of consumption which progressively improves and raises his standards by, say, 10 per cent from day to day over his life (i.e. $\hat{C}_5 = (1 \cdot 1)\hat{C}_4 = (1 \cdot 1)^2 \hat{C}_3 = (1 \cdot 1)^3 \hat{C}_2 = (1 \cdot 1)^4 \hat{C}_1$). But having decided the shape of the flow $\hat{C}_1 \ \hat{C}_2 \ \hat{C}_3 \ \hat{C}_3 \ \hat{C}_5$, he must then decide the level $\hat{C}_1$ at which he will start this stream. If the time shape of the stream is decided, then the maximum feasible starting point $\hat{C}_1$, is given by the requirement that the present discounted value of these consumption outgoings should not exceed the present discounted value of his net receipts from earnings and inheritance. Having decided the time shape for his consumption stream, the maximum feasible starting point is thus given by the present discounted value of his future revenues.

We will now proceed to consider the factors which are likely to affect the time shape and so the level of a citizen's consumption stream, given the time shape and the level of his stream of receipts (other than interest). In order to simplify this examination we shall in the rest of this chapter ignore all such receipts except earnings. This we shall do by assuming that citizens receive nothing in inheritance from their parents or in support from their children and do not plan to support their own parents or to leave anything in bequests to their children. We shall call this the assumption of 'perfect selfishness'; each citizen in planning the time shape and level of his consumption stream thinks only of himself; he has no concern for the welfare of his children once he has brought them up and launched them into adulthood and he has no concern for the welfare of his aged parents once they have launched him into adulthood.[1] Each citizen plans a consumption stream for himself which has the same present discounted value as the future stream of his earnings. $\hat{I}_2$ and $\hat{B}_5$ in expressions (12.1) and (12.2) are both equal to zero.

There are two main factors which will influence the time shape of the consumption stream which a citizen will plan.

In the first place, it will be much affected by the time shape of his future consumption needs. Immediately upon entering adulthood

---

[1] For the sake of simplicity the assumption of perfect selfishness has been expressed as if the wife and mother in the family does not exist. It is, of course, implied that the husband and wife together form a unit which takes no action to affect the welfare of their aged parents or of their children once their children have been launched into adulthood.

G

these needs are likely to be relatively low. But they will rise as he has more and more children to support; and they will fall as his children one by one reach adulthood and become self-supporting. His needs may then again remain fairly constant; but in so far as an old man is less active, his needs may become somewhat simpler and smaller as he enters into old age. Such a pattern of needs alone would suggest that his consumption stream would be planned to start at a relatively low level, rise rather rapidly to a peak as his children are born, fall again fairly quickly as his children grow up, and then still later decline slowly as his needs decline in old age.

But, in the second place, the time shape of his consumption stream may be greatly affected by the level of the rate of interest. Suppose for the moment (i) that his needs remained constant over his life and (ii) that the rate of interest was zero, so that he could borrow $100 with the obligation to repay only $100 at any future time or could lend $100 with the right to receive back only $100 at any future time. Then one might expect our citizen to plan a constant level of consumption over his life. Since the rate of interest is zero, the capital sum which he can raise at the beginning of day 1 on the security of his future earnings would be simply the sum of his future earnings—i.e. $\hat{E}_1 + \hat{E}_2 + \hat{E}_3$. And, again because the rate of interest is zero, the present value of his future consumptions would be simply the sum of these consumptions—$\hat{C}_1 + \hat{C}_2 + \hat{C}_3 + \hat{C}_4 + \hat{C}_5$. He cannot in this case affect the total sum of his consumption over his life by postponing consumption. If he consumes $100 less at the beginning of day 2 and invests the money, he will only thereby be enabled to consume $100 more at the beginning of, say, day 4; there will be no interest accumulated on this investment. In these circumstances he is likely to spread his consumption evenly over the five days of his life $\left(\text{i.e. so that } \hat{C}_1 = \hat{C}_2 = \hat{C}_3 = \hat{C}_4 = \hat{C}_5 = \dfrac{\hat{E}_1 + \hat{E}_2 + \hat{E}_3}{5}\right)$. For suppose that he did not do so and, let us say, consumed only 50 on day 2 and 150 on day 3. He would probably be better off if he consumed 100 on day 2 and 100 on day 3, since the cut from 150 to 100 on day 3 might be a cut into luxuries while the rise from 50 to 100 on day 2 might be a rise which enabled him to consume in greater quantity goods which were more essential to his welfare. An even spread of a given total of consumption will probable be preferred to an uneven spread of the same given total of consumption.

But if the rate of interest is not zero, the total of consumption is not unaffected by the unevenness of its spread. Thus if the rate of interest is 10 per cent per annum, a reduction of $100 in this year's consumption will enable him to consume $110 more next year, since he will have both the principal ($100) and interest ($10) on his savings available to spend. He loses by greater unevenness—cutting into more essential consumption this year in order to finance less essential consumption next year; but he gains by having a greater total of consumption over the two years together. Clearly the higher is the rate of interest, the more likely is the gain from increased total to outweigh the loss from uneven spread. In other words, the higher is the rate of interest on any day, the greater is the rate at which consumption is likely to be planned to rise between that day and the next. If the rate of interest were 20 per cent per annum, one would expect a much more pronounced upward trend in our citizen's time shape of consumption than if the rate were only 2 per cent per annum.

The starting level of our citizen's consumption stream will be determined by the total capital sum which he can command at the beginning of day 1, which is equal to the present discounted value of his future earnings. This in turn will be determined by three factors. In the first place, it will clearly be greater, the higher is the general level of earnings which our citizen may expect. Second, it will be greater, the lower is the rate of interest. He can borrow a greater capital sum now in return for a given future total payment (to cover interest and repayment of principal), the lower is the rate of interest which he has to pay on the principal sum borrowed. But, in the third place, the time shape of future earnings will be important. Distant earnings are worth less now than earnings in the immediate future, since the former have to be discounted over a longer period of time than the latter. A given total sum of earnings has, therefore, a greater present value if the earnings are spread evenly over the years than if they start low and rise to a greater height in the distant future. On the other hand, a given reduction in the rate of interest (which will raise the present value of future earnings whatever their time shape may be) will have a greater proportional effect in raising the present discounted value of a stream of earnings most of which will accrue only in the far distant future than it will in raising the present discounted value of a stream of earnings most of which are expected to accrue in the immediate future.

These various relationships are illustrated by one possible state of affairs which is shown in Figure 17.[1] We measure the days of our citizen's adult life along GK, and the height of the curve marked EF measures his earnings in each day of his life. He starts at a modest

[1] The reader is expressly warned that this figure illustrates only one possible pattern out of a very large number of possibilities. It is not intended to suggest that this is the only possible, or indeed the most probable, case. It is designed only to serve as one illustration of the principles involved.

salary of GE; and this is assumed to rise slowly at first and then more rapidly to a height of JF at the time of his retirement after GJ days of work. He lives for another JK days in retirement without any earnings.

We can draw another curve CD the height of which represents our citizen's consumption on each day of his adult life. This we have shown as rising from a low level of CG consistently throughout his life till it reaches KD on the day of his death. This consistent upward trend in the curve CD is intended to show the influence of a positive rate of interest; our citizen always finds it worth while facing some restriction on today's consumption because a positive rate of interest enables him to obtain a greater total of consumption by postponing it from today till tomorrow. But we have shown the curve CD as rising rapidly in the first years of his adulthood and less rapidly in the later years. This is intended to illustrate the fact that our citizen's needs may well be greatest in the middle years of his adulthood while he is bringing up his children.

As we have drawn the figure our citizen has two periods in which his earnings exceed his consumption and two periods in which his consumption exceeds his earnings. For the first days of his adulthood (GH) his low needs plus the gain in total consumption obtainable from the postponement of consumption have brought his consumption below even his modest starting salary. For the intermediate period of his life as an earner (HI) his heavy family needs have brought his consumption above his earnings. For the last years of his earning life (IJ) his high earnings and lower needs have brought his earnings above his consumption. In his years of retirement (JK) his earnings are zero and, therefore, necessarily exceeded by his consumption.[1]

For the curve CD to be a feasible pattern of consumption it is necessary that the present discounted values of the two areas (i.e. between G and H and between I and J) by which the earnings curve exceeds the consumption curve should be equal to the present discounted value of the two areas (between H and I and between J and K) by which the consumption curve exceeds the earnings curve. For the curve CD to be the actual optimum curve, it is necessary that

---

[1] In passing it should be noted that an excess of the CD-curve over the EF-curve at any point in our citizen's life does not necessarily mean that the citizen is at that point spending more than his income. He is spending more than his earnings, but not necessarily more than his earnings *plus* the interest on any capital which he has saved on previous days. At G he is certainly saving, since to start with he has no capital and no debts and his consumption is less than his earnings. But between H and I he does not necessarily dissave. The excess of his consumption over his earnings can at least in part be financed by the interest earned on what he has saved between G and H.

our citizen, given the pattern of his needs, should not prefer to transfer a unit of consumption at the current rate of interest from any one day to another.

Suppose now that our citizen were faced at the outset of his adult-hood with a set of higher expected interest rates for each day of his adult life, his earnings (the curve EF) and his needs remaining as before. What difference would there be in his plans for his consumption stream (i.e. in the height and shape of the CD-curve)? Since the discount rates would be higher the present discounted value both

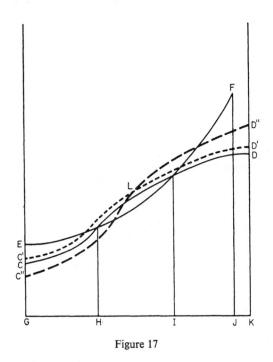

Figure 17

of the earnings stream and also of the consumption stream would be reduced. If—because retirement comes after working and because heavy parental responsibility comes after early manhood—in general consumption is later in time than earnings, then the effect of a rise in interest rates will be to lower the present discounted value of the existing consumption stream more than it lowers the present discounted value of the earnings stream. If this is so—and we have assumed it to be so for the purposes of Figure 17—then our citizen would not exhaust all the present capital value of his earnings, if he maintained his consumption stream unchanged as on the line CD.

He would have something over; and maintaining the same time shape for his CD-line, he could start it at a higher level. This possibility is illustrated by the dotted line C′D′ which has become a feasible consumption stream because of the rise in interest rates. In this case his savings in the first year of his adulthood fall from EC to EC′. He need save less for his old age because he can earn more interest on his early savings and can thus accumulate more easily for his old age.

But the rise in the rates of interest is likely to make him more willing to postpone early consumption for later consumption, because for each extra unit of early consumption which he postpones he can obtain more later consumption than he could do previously with the lower rate of interest. The dotted C′D′-curve is likely to be tilted down to the left and up to the right. How great this extra tilt will be will depend upon how ready our citizen is to give up evenness in consumption in order to gain an extra amount of consumption in total. If he is willing to face much more unevenness for a little more in total, then the extra tilt given by a rise in interest rates will be great. A possible outcome is shown by the broken line C″D″. In this case the extra tilt is great—so great indeed that GC″ is reduced below GC. Our young citizen saves more because, although he need save less in order to finance any given consumption in his old age, he can get so much more for what he saves now that the exchange is worth while.[1]

It is worth while considering in a little more detail the sort of factors which may lie behind a citizen's preference for various time-patterns of consumptions. Consider the six possible patterns of consumption over the five days of life, illustrated in Table V. All the

Table V

Patterns of Consumption	Levels of Consumption at the ends of days:				
	1	2	3	4	5
I	100	100	100	100	100
II(a)	50	75	100	125	150
II(b)	50	75	125	100	150
III	150	125	100	75	50
IV(a)	50	150	100	125	75
IV(b)	50	150	125	100	75

[1] C′D′ and C″D″ are only two out of the infinite number of time streams of consumption which are feasible in the new conditions. He will choose that one out of this infinite family of feasible time paths which fits best with his pattern of needs and with his preference between an even spread and a high total level of

six patterns illustrated in the table give the same total of consumption over the five days, namely 500 in all. The difference between them lies solely in the spread of this pattern over time. The following factors may affect the decision which our citizen at the beginning of day 1 would make if he were offered a choice between the six possible patterns.

1. *The pattern of needs.* As we have already seen, one consideration which is likely to affect a man's choice is to fit the time pattern of his consumption to that of his needs. A man whose needs will be much greater in the middle days than on day 1 or day 5 is likely to prefer IV(b) to the other possibilities. But let us, solely for the purpose of simplification, for the remainder of this analysis assume that his needs are constant.

2. *Lack of foresight and of memory.* The spendthrift type of man who can think only of today is likely to choose pattern III. He starts on day 1 with the highest daily level of consumption which is offered to him; he goes on to the next highest level of consumption only one day ahead; and so on. But this same individual when he is old will on day 5 probably wish that he had chosen pattern II(a) because on day 5 he would then be enjoying the highest daily level of consumption which is open to him; he would only be one day distant from the time (yesterday) when he was enjoying the next highest level of consumption; and so on. Such a man has little foresight and a short memory. At the other extreme is the man who thinks of his life in the same way as a whole pattern, no matter at what point of time in his life he may survey it. He will not regret his choice once it is made. By what considerations will his choice be influenced?

3. *Variability.* There is much reason to believe that such a man will prefer the regular and constant level of consumption in pattern I to the variable level of consumption in the other patterns. All the patterns other than I have one feature in common. They contain one day at 50, one day at 75, one day at 100, one day at 125, and one day at 150, only the order of these days being different. Any one of these patterns can thus be changed into pattern I by shifting 50 units of consumption from the day at 150 to the day at 50, and 25 units of consumption from the day at 125 to the day at 75. But both of these shifts are likely to bring an increase in enjoyment, since both involve a cut from a relatively high level of consumption (i.e. a cut into relative luxuries) in order to raise a relatively low level of consumption (i.e. an addition to relative essentials).

4. *Irregularity.* All patterns other than I have the same variability

consumption. By choosing C″D″ instead of C′D′ he gains in total consumption the excess of the area between the C″D″ and C′D′-curves to the right of L over that area to the left of L.

of consumption in the sense that each pattern has one day each at 50, at 75, at 100, at 125, and at 150. But compare patterns II(*a*) and II(*b*). II(*b*) is less regular than II(*a*) in the sense that in II(*a*) consumption increases regularly by 25 each day, whereas in II(*b*) it goes by steps of +25, +50, −25, +50. It is probable that II(*a*) will be preferred to II(*b*). A steady progression of improvements will enable a man gradually to raise his standards, getting used to each improvement and incorporating it permanently into his pattern of life before he proceeds to the next. With pattern II(*b*) he has a huge improvement between days 2 and 3, but must give up much of it on day 3. Pattern IV(*a*) is the most irregular in the table, whereas—apart from pattern I—patterns II(*a*) and III are the most regular and are equally regular, pattern II(*a*) being a regular upward pattern and pattern III(*a*) a regular downward pattern.

If regularity is a desired feature of a consumption pattern, an important result follows. Compare pattern II(*a*) with II(*b*) and pattern IV(*a*) with IV(*b*). In both cases (*a*) differs from (*b*) only in that in (*a*) we have 100 followed by 125 and in (*b*) 125 followed by 100 as between days 3 and 4. If one asks which of these two orders does a man prefer, there may be no single answer. A man may well prefer II(*a*) to II(*b*) (i.e. 100 followed by 125) but IV(*b*) to IV(*a*) (i.e. 125 followed by 100) because II(*a*) is more regular than II(*b*) while IV(*b*) is more regular than IV(*a*). Thus if regularity is desired, the preference between two orders in which certain consumptions occur may itself be affected by the orders in which other consumptions have occurred or will occur.

5. *Progression or Regression.* Patterns II(*a*) and III are equally variable and equally regular, but the one is a regular progression upwards and the other a regular regression downwards. A man may well prefer II(*a*) to III. It may be much more pleasant to start at a low level and gradually to incorporate improvements into one's standard of living than to start at a high level and gradually to reduce one's standard.

The preceding paragraphs will serve to show how the choice between various time patterns of consumption may depend upon many factors. In order, however, to be in a position to build one or two much simplified models in order to illustrate some factors at work in the economy we shall proceed to make the heroic assumption that variability is the only one of the above five factors which affects the choice of time patterns of consumption, or in other words we shall assume (i) that needs are constant, (ii) that there is no impatience or shortness of memory, and (iii) that the order in which the days' consumptions come is irrelevant, so that regularity or irregularity, progression or regression make no difference to the choice. Our citizen would in fact prefer pattern I on Table V to all the other patterns, but as between all the other patterns he would be indifferent.[1]

We can summarize these assumptions in the following way. The individual citizen has a consistent set of preferences between various combinations of consumption levels at various points of time. Thus he knows whether or not he prefers the combination (I) of 100 units today, 90 units tomorrow, 110 units the day after tomorrow and so on or the combination (II) of 98 units today, 90 units tomorrow, 113 units the day after tomorrow, and so on. His preferences are consistent in the sense that if he prefers combination (I) to combination (II) and combination (II) to some other combination (III), then he also prefers (I) to (III). But we make two further special assumptions about his preferences. (i) We assume that he has no pure time preference. It makes no difference to him whether he has 100 today and 105 tomorrow or 105 today and 100 tomorrow. (ii) We also assume that his preferences between consumption in any one year and any other year are independent of the level of his consumption in other years. For example, if he prefers 100 today plus 105 tomorrow to 101 today plus 102 tomorrow, he will do so whatever has been the pattern of his consumption before this year and whatever may be the expected pattern of his consumption after next year.

The meaning of these special assumptions about the citizen's consumption preferences will become clearer as the argument is developed. But broadly speaking their implication is as follows. The citizen's total welfare over time will depend upon the levels of his standard of living on various days: one day at 100, one day at 105, two days at 106, one day at 110, and so on. But the order will make no difference: 100, 105, 106, 106, 110 is neither better nor worse than 105, 106, 100, 110, 106. But, of course, 50 followed by 150 is not the same as 100 followed by 100, although both combinations give a total of 200 for the two days. To fall from 100 to 50 today may mean cutting into the most indispensable necessities, while rising from 100 to 150 tomorrow may mean enjoying only a few unnecessary additional luxuries. 100 followed by 100 will probably be preferred to 50 followed by 150. But we assume that 50 followed by 150 has the same

[1] These assumptions are not quite so devastating as they may sound. To allow for variations in consumption which match needs would not introduce a great change in principle, though it would seriously complicate the models. Moreover, in fact the models which we shall consider will result in regular upward progressions of consumption, so that if regularity and progression were themselves desired little or no difference would in fact be made to the results of the models. To allow for lack of foresight and lack of memory would introduce by far the most important changes of principle into our analysis. We will say a little more about this at a much later stage. (See Chapter XXIII, pp. 489–492 below.)

value as 150 followed by 50. The citizen does not mind on which day
the stringency and on which day the surfeit comes.

Let us start by considering on these assumptions a citizen's
preference between consumption on any one day and on any other
day—for example between consumption today and consumption
tomorrow. This preference map is shown in Figure 18. We measure

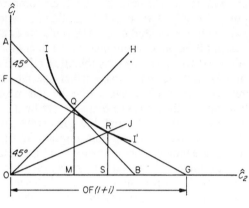

Figure 18

along the vertical axis the amount consumed today ($\hat{C}_1$) and along
the horizontal axis the amount consumed tomorrow ($\hat{C}_2$). Any point
in the figure represents a combination of consumption today and
consumption tomorrow; for example, at R our citizen is depicted as
consuming SR today and OS tomorrow. Through R we can draw our
citizen's indifference curve II′ which shows the locus of all the points
which describe combinations of $\hat{C}_1$ and $\hat{C}_2$ which have the same value
to our citizen as the combination at the point R. Any combination of
$\hat{C}_1$ and $\hat{C}_2$ to the North East of II′ would make our citizen better off
than at R; any combination to the South West of II′ would make him
worse off.

We draw II′ as having all the same characteristics of a consumer's
indifference curve as those assumed in *The Stationary Economy*
(Chapter II, pages 34–6). In particular we assume that II′ slopes
downwards from left to right, since to be equally well off our citizen
must have more tomorrow if he has less today. We also assume that
the slope of II′ becomes gentler and gentler as we move down from
left to right. This means that for one reason or another our citizen
prefers stability to variability in his level of consumption. The more
we move South East from Q (where $\hat{C}_1 = \hat{C}_2$) in the direction of I′,
the greater is $\hat{C}_2$ and the less is $\hat{C}_1$; the greater, therefore, is the

variability from day to day in consumption. Our citizen may simply just prefer sameness to variation. But there is perhaps another and more basic factor at work. The less our citizen has today and the more he has tomorrow, the less willing he is to give up still more of today's consumption (which will now mean cutting into basic necessities) in order to raise tomorrow's consumption (which will now mean adding only a few frivolous luxuries to his standard of living).

But in addition to these general characteristics the indifference map in Figure 18 has some special features due to two special assumptions which we have stated on page 201 above. We are assuming that the map of preferences between $\hat{C}_1$ and $\hat{C}_2$ is independent of what is consumed on other days. In other words we can draw the indifference curve II′ in Figure 18 and it will remain unchanged whatever may have been the level of consumption on past days and whatever may be expected to be the levels of consumption after tomorrow. Moreover, we are assuming that there is no time preference which implies that our citizen would be equally well off with 90 for $\hat{C}_1$ and 110 for $\hat{C}_2$ or with 110 for $\hat{C}_1$ and 90 for $\hat{C}_2$.

Geometrically this second assumption means that in Figure 18 the curve II′ would remain unchanged if we drew $\hat{C}_1$ instead of $\hat{C}_2$ along the horizontal axis and $\hat{C}_2$ instead of $\hat{C}_1$ up the vertical axis. If we draw the line OH at 45° through the origin O, cutting II′ at Q, then the curve QI′ is a mirror image of the curve QI; that is to say, if we folded the page along the line OH, QI would coincide with QI′. It follows from this that at the point Q the curve II′ cuts the line OH at right angles;[1] that is to say, the tangent AB to the curve II′ at Q itself makes angles of 45° into the vertical and the horizontal axes. The common sense of this is easily understood. At the point Q our citizen will consume tomorrow the same amount as today; and at this point he will, therefore, place the same value on an additional unit of tomorrow's consumption as he does on an additional unit of today's consumption. The marginal rate of substitution between $\hat{C}_1$ and $\hat{C}_2$ is unity. In contrast to this at R he would be expecting a higher level of consumption tomorrow than he is enjoying today, and he would therefore value an additional unit of consumption today more highly than an additional unit of consumption tomorrow; the tangent FG at R has a gentler slope than the tangent AB at Q.

We can next introduce the idea of the elasticity of substitution between $\hat{C}_1$ and $\hat{C}_2$. How quickly does the marginal value of an addition to tomorrow's consumption relatively to the marginal value of an addition to today's consumption fall off as tomorrow's

[1] If II′ cut OH at any other angle, then in folding the page along the line OH QI would clearly not coincide with QI′.

consumption grows relatively to today's consumption? This elasticity of substitution can be measured in exactly the same way as the elasticity of substitution was measured in *The Stationary Economy* (cf. Chapter II, pages 47–50). The slopes of the lines such as AB and FG can be taken to represent the price of $\hat{C}_2$ in terms of $\hat{C}_1$. Thus the slope of AB means to our citizen that he can obtain OB more units of consumption tomorrow for every OA of consumption given up today. In this case $\frac{OB}{OA} = 1$, which must mean that the rate of interest is zero; if he saves $100 today he can as a result consume only $100 more tomorrow. The slope of FG is, however, less than this. This must mean that the rate of interest (i) is positive; for every OF given up this year, he obtains OG next year; and $\frac{OG}{OF}$ is greater than unity. For example, if he saves $100 today, he can as a result consume $100·05 more tomorrow, if the rate of interest is $\frac{5}{100}$ of 1 per cent a day (i.e. a daily rate of 5 per cent per annum). $\frac{OG}{OF}$ thus equals $1 + i$ or in our numerical example 100·05 per cent.

Now the numerical value of the elasticity of substitution between $\hat{C}_2$ and $\hat{C}_1$ is the proportional increase in the ratio of $\hat{C}_2$ to $\hat{C}_1$ divided by the proportional decrease in the price of $\hat{C}_2$ in terms of $\hat{C}_1$. Between the points Q and R the price of $\hat{C}_2$ in terms of $\hat{C}_1$ has fallen by a proportion equal to the rate of interest.[1] Between the points Q and R the ratio of $\hat{C}_2$ to $\hat{C}_1$ has changed from OM/QM to OS/RS, so that the proportional change in this ratio is

$$\frac{\dfrac{OS}{RS} - \dfrac{OM}{QM}}{\dfrac{OM}{QM}}$$

But $\frac{OM}{QM} = 1$, so that the above expression becomes

$$\frac{OS - RS}{RS}$$

---

[1] At Q one can get one unit of $\hat{C}_2$ for the price of one unit of $\hat{C}_1$. At R one can get $1 + i$ units of $\hat{C}_2$ for the price of one unit of $\hat{C}_1$; for example, with a daily rate of interest equal to 5 per cent per annum, one can get 1·0005 units of $\hat{C}_2$ for the price of 1 unit of $\hat{C}_1$, and the price of $\hat{C}_2$ relatively to the price of $\hat{C}_1$ has fallen by $\frac{5}{100}$ of 1 per cent.

But OS — RS is the increase in consumption between today and tomorrow and RS is today's consumption. Thus the above expression is equal to the proportional rate of increase in consumption between today and tomorrow which will take place at the rate of interest i. Let us call this growth rate of consumption $\hat{c}$.

Let us use the symbol σ for the (numerical) value of the elasticity of substitution between $\hat{C}_2$ and $\hat{C}_1$. This symbol σ is simply defined as meaning the proportional increase in the ratio of $\hat{C}_2$ to $\hat{C}_1$ divided by the proportional decrease in the ratio of the price of $\hat{C}_2$ relatively to the price of $\hat{C}_1$. But between the points Q and R the proportional increase in the ratio of $\hat{C}_2$ to $\hat{C}_1$ is, as we have just seen, simply the proportional rate of growth of consumption, namely $\hat{c}$, while the proportional fall in the price of $\hat{C}_2$ relatively to the price of $\hat{C}_1$ is simply the rate of interest i. Thus we have

$$\sigma = \frac{\hat{c}}{i} \quad \text{or} \quad \hat{c} = \sigma i.[1]$$

What in the name of common sense does this mean? The problem with which our citizen is trying to cope is to plan the pattern of his consumption over the years. Shall he save little or much for the purpose of raising his future consumption little or much relatively to his present consumption? The rate of interest (i) tells him how much more he can consume if he consumes tomorrow rather than today. The elasticity of substitution (σ) is numerically large (or small) according as the marginal value of tomorrow's consumption falls off slowly (or rapidly) relatively to the marginal value of today's consumption as he raises tomorrow's consumption relatively to today's consumption. There are thus two factors which should make him plan to raise his consumption rapidly from one day to the next: (1) a high rate of interest which will enable him to get much more consumption tomorrow for a given sacrifice of consumption today and (2) a high (numerical) value of the elasticity of substitution, which means that as he raises tomorrow's consumption relatively to today's consumption the valuation of yet more consumption tomorrow does not fall much relatively to the valuation of a given further sacrifice of today's consumption. The formula $\hat{c} = \sigma i$ tells us that the optimum rate of growth of his consumption at any point of time should be equal to i multiplied by σ. If at any given point of time i is a daily rate of 5 per cent per annum and σ is $\frac{1}{2}$, then he should plan his consumption pattern so that his consumption is today rising at a rate of $2\frac{1}{2}$ per cent per annum.

[1] An alternative method for obtaining this result is discussed in the note to this chapter. (See pp. 212–219 below.)

In many of the models which follow we shall treat σ as a constant, i.e. as independent of the absolute levels of $\hat{C}_1$ and $\hat{C}_2$. But this is not necessarily true. Indeed, there is reason to believe that σ may be very small at low levels and at very high levels of $\hat{C}$, while it may be comparatively large at intermediate levels of $\hat{C}$. As we shall see later, this possibility can be of the greatest importance for the analysis of savings.

The reason for believing that the value of σ may vary in this way is indicated in Figure 19. There may well be—indeed certainly is—a

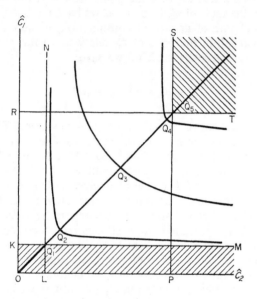

Figure 19

minimum level of consumption on any day which is necessary to keep body and soul together. Let this level be represented by OK. Then any combination of $\hat{C}_1$ and $\hat{C}_2$ which lies in the shaded area below KM is equally nasty, as it involves immediate death on day 1 to him. It follows that the horizontal line Q_1M represents the indifference curve which passes through Q_1. If our citizen is at Q_1, he has just enough on day 1 and day 2 (OL = OK) to keep body and soul together. No matter how high the rate of interest is he will not reduce $\hat{C}_1$ below OK in order to increase $\hat{C}_2$ above OL, as he would die on day 1 and be unable to enjoy day 2. At Q_1 σ is zero.

At the other extreme there may be a level of consumption (OR = OP) beyond which our citizen can imagine no needs. If so, the whole shaded area to the left of PS and above RT is equally, but only equally, attractive to him. It represents full satisfaction of his economic needs on both days. At Q_5 also σ will be zero. If our citizen is at Q_5, then no matter how high the rate of interest may be he will not reduce $\hat{C}_1$ below PQ_5 (since this could entail some loss of satisfaction) in order to raise $\hat{C}_2$ above RQ_5 (since this brings no gain at all).

Between Q_1 and Q_5—for example at Q_3—σ may be quite large. But if σ is zero at Q_1 and at Q_5 and quite large at Q_3, it may well be lower in the neighbourhood of Q_1 and Q_5 (i.e. at Q_2 and Q_4) than it is in the intermediate position at Q_3. If this is so, then σ will be very low at very low values of $\hat{C}$, will grow larger for higher values of $\hat{C}$ but after a while will fall again to a very low level as $\hat{C}$ rises to a great height at which all economic needs are satisfied.

But let us for the time being revert to the assumption that σ is constant, whatever may be the actual level of $\hat{C}$. For this is the simplest case in which we can examine the way in which S is determined. Let us suppose that the conditions of production are such that a state of steady growth is possible; and for this purpose we will take as an example the case where U, Q, and Z are all constant. (See pages 99–103 above.) Let us ask what the level of S will be in such a state of steady growth on our present assumptions that σ is constant and that people save only for the perfectly selfish purpose of financing their own future consumption.

It is in fact very difficult to give a precise answer to this question without some mathematical analysis.[1] In the present text we must confine ourselves to making some rather general intuitive observations.

In a state of steady growth the growth rate of the wage rate will be given independently of the level of S. In the case which we are using as an example, in which U, Q, and Z are constant, the growth rate of the wage rate (see equation (7.15) on page 99 above) will be $w_l = \dfrac{r - Zl}{1 - U}$ which we assume to be positive (i.e. $r > Zl$). We are assuming σ to be a given constant and that the working life of each citizen and the length of his subsequent retirement are also given and constant. Moreover, in a state of steady growth the rate of interest (i) will also be constant, although it is not a given constant, but is part of the solution which we are seeking. Choose any constant value of i.

---

[1] This analysis is examined in the note to Chapter XIII. Assume that $\hat{I} = 0$ in equations (13.23) (p. 254 below). The solution of those equations then gives the value of i in conditions of perfect selfishness. This solution for i is illustrated at the points A, B, and C on Figure 33 (p. 260 below). Given this value of i we can then derive S from equations (13.14) and (13.15) (pp. 248–249 below).

We have now determined the time shape of each citizen's earnings and consumption, which are illustrated in Figure 20. Our citizen's working life is GJ and his retirement JK. The height of the curve EF shows his wage rate throughout his working life and is rising at a growth rate of $w_l = \dfrac{r - Zl}{1 - U}$. If now we know σ and i, we can show the time pattern of our citizen's consumption which (i) throughout his life will grow at the same rate of σi and (ii) must start at a level which makes the present discounted value of the excess of his consumption over his earnings during retirement equal to the present discounted

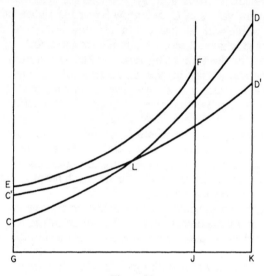

Figure 20

value of the net excess of his earnings over his consumption during his working life. CD represents such a path with a σ and an i so high that $\sigma i > \dfrac{r - Zl}{1 - U}$ so that the CD-curve rises more rapidly than the EF-curve, while C'D' represents the case with so low a σ and an i that $\sigma i < \dfrac{r - Zl}{1 - U}$.[1]

The pattern of the earnings and consumption curves shown in Figure 20, together with the rate of interest, will determine the savings–dissavings pattern for our citizen during his life. As drawn in

[1] If σi were very low, C'G might be greater than GE. But for simplicity of exposition we will assume that the starting point of consumption is always below that of earnings.

Figure 20 he certainly saves throughout his working life since at each stage of his working life his earnings alone, to say nothing of his income from interest on his past savings, exceed his consumption. The dissaving of this capital and the interest on it finance his consumption during retirement.

But to determine the total economy's savings relatively to the total national income we must bear in mind that the population is growing. For this reason at any point of time there will be few old persons in retirement relatively to the number of young persons entering the labour market, because the old will belong to a smaller vintage than the young. (See page 132 above.) In other words there will be few dissavers relatively to savers. Moreover, since the wage rate is going up at a rate equal to $\dfrac{r - Zl}{1 - U}$, the young persons will be entering on a pattern of earnings and consumption of the same shape as that given in Figure 20 but with a high starting point for earnings (GE) and therefore a high starting point for consumption (GC), whereas the old retired dissavers will be dissaving (e.g. KD) at a low level related to long-past and therefore low starting levels for earnings and consumption. With a rising population there will be many savers relatively to dissavers, and with a rising wage rate each saver will be saving much in respect of a high-level pattern of earnings and consumption while each dissaver will be dissaving little in respect of a low-level pattern throughout his life.[1]

It is the complicated interrelationship of all these influences which will determine the ultimate ratio of total savings to total national income (S) in the state of steady growth, given the rate of interest (i). But for each rate of interest (i) there will be a different level of the savings proportion (S). Now if σ is sufficiently large, a rise in i will raise the steady-state level of S. For since $\hat{c} = \sigma i$, a small rise in i will cause a large rise in $\hat{c}$ if σ itself is large. In other words in Figure 20 a rise in i, given the earnings curve and the lengths of working life and of retirement, will cause a large increase in the steepness of the CD-curve. In this case (see page 198 above) GC must fall relatively to EG. The fact that with a higher interest rate our citizen will need to save less to finance a given consumption during old age is more than offset by the fact that he finds it worth while to postpone consumption now in order to enjoy much more consumption in the future. On balance he saves more. Net savings go up relatively to the national income.

---

[1] These two influences are not totally independent. Since $w_l = \dfrac{r - Zl}{1 - U}$, a high rate of growth of population causes a somewhat lower rate of growth of the wage rate. Thus the higher the number of savers relatively to dissavers, the lower somewhat the ratio of each saver's savings to each dissaver's dissavings.

We can thus draw a curve such as AB in Figure 21 which shows at each constant level of i what the corresponding steady-state value would be of the proportion of their incomes which citizens as a whole would want to save. We can draw another curve JK showing the proportion of the national income which at various rates of interest must be devoted to investment in new capital goods instead of to consumption in order to maintain a steady rate of growth (i.e. a rate of growth of the capital stock—k—equal to the rate of growth of total output—y). We know that $\dfrac{SY}{K} = k$ and also $\dfrac{UY}{K} = i$ (see

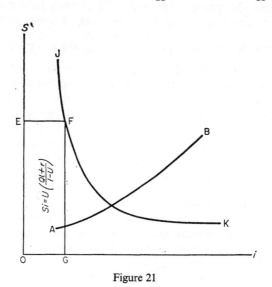

Figure 21

equations (6.1) and (4.3)). It follows that $S = \dfrac{U}{i}k$. But in a state of steady growth $k = y$ and in our example with U, Q, and Z constant $y = \dfrac{Ql + r}{1 - U}$. (See equation (7.14).) Thus we have $S = \dfrac{U}{i}\left(\dfrac{Ql + r}{1 - U}\right)$ or $Si = U\left(\dfrac{Ql + r}{1 - U}\right)$ as expressing the proportion of the national income which must be saved to be devoted to investment to maintain a steady rate of growth at the rate of interest i. The curve JK in Figure 21 is accordingly so drawn that the area EFGO is constant at $U\left(\dfrac{Ql + r}{1 - U}\right)$. Where the JK-curve cuts the AB-curve we have the steady-state values of S and i.

Without reference to the mathematics in the Note to Chapter XIII it is difficult to say anything more precise about the values of S and i on the present assumption of perfect selfishness among savers. It will, however, prove possible to make much more precise statements in the next chapter about the level of S when we turn to the assumption of perfect altruism (which we will there define) among savers. It will turn out there that we are vitally concerned with the question whether the assumption of perfect selfishness results in a growth rate of the consumption curve which is greater or less than that of the earnings curve. As we have seen from the discussion of Figure 20, either outcome is a possibility. The result depends upon the level of i and so upon the complicated relationships discussed in the preceding paragraphs. We can, however, make one simple definite statement about this outcome. If there were no period of retirement and citizens saved simply in order to enjoy more in the later years of earning than in the earlier years of earning, then the steady-state rate of interest would necessarily be such as to make consumption grow at a greater rate than earnings. The reason for this is very straightforward. The steady-state growth rate of earnings is given by $\dfrac{r - Zl}{1 - U}$ and of consumption is given by σi. Suppose that the steady-state value of i were such $\left(\text{namely, } \dfrac{1}{\sigma} \dfrac{r - Zl}{1 - U}\right)$ as to make the two growth rates the same. Then as can be seen in Figure 22 the starting point of consumption would coincide with the starting point of earnings. Any lower starting point (as at C′D′ in Figure 22) would mean that the citizen saved throughout his life and would be left with an unused property at his death, which is incompatible with the assumption of perfect selfishness on his part. Any higher starting point (as at C″D″ in Figure 22) would mean that his consumption throughout his life exceeded his earnings, so that he dissaved throughout his life, which is incompatible with the assumption of perfect selfishness on the part of his parents or of his children, *vis-a-vis* himself. His consumption curve would, therefore, throughout his life coincide with his earnings curve. He and every other citizen would, therefore, save nothing. S would be zero. But if S were zero for every citizen throughout his life, no citizen would ever hold any property. K would be zero. But with a zero stock of capital the rate of interest would be very high;[1] and we could safely assume, therefore, that σi could not

---

[1] With our assumption of constant U, Q, Z we have a Cobb-Douglas production function $Y = R^{N}Z^{L}Q K^{U}e^{rt}$ where R is a constant. This gives $i = \dfrac{UY}{K} = \dfrac{UR^{N}Z^{L}Q e^{rt}}{K^{1-U}}$ which $\rightarrow \infty$ as $K \rightarrow 0$.

be as low as $\dfrac{r - Zl}{1 - U}$. Equilibrium would only be compatible with a

rate of interest higher than $\dfrac{1}{\sigma}\dfrac{r - Zl}{1 - U}$, so that CD was more steeply
sloped than EF, so that citizens had an incentive during their early
years to accumulate some capital which they would consume in
addition to their earnings during their later years.

For there to be a state of steady growth there must be some
savings, and for there to be some savings in the absence of any period
of retirement the rate of interest must be sufficiently high to make
the consumption curve rise more steeply than the earnings curve as
in the case of C'''D''' in Figure 22.

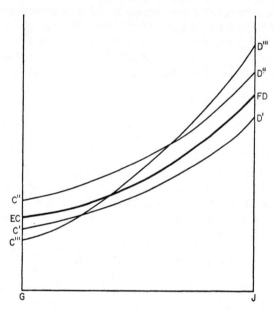

Figure 22

Note to Chapter XII

AN ALTERNATIVE METHOD OF REPRESENTING
A CITIZEN'S PREFERENCE BETWEEN TIME
PATTERNS OF CONSUMPTION

For the purpose of this note we shall make the same basic assumptions about a citizen's choice between various combinations of
consumption on different days as we made on page 201 of the main

text; but instead of starting our analysis from the preference map between levels of consumption in any two days (see Figure 18 on page 202) we shall adopt a more general way of depicting our citizen's preference between different sets of consumption levels. For this purpose we need to take two benchmarks of levels of consumption in order to make comparisons with all other levels of consumption. It is convenient to take as one benchmark-level of consumption a very low level and as the other benchmark-level of consumption a very high level. Let us call these two levels of consumption $0 a year and $100 a year. These two figures are chosen solely for arithmetical convenience. Thousands of dollars might be more realistic—i.e. a range from $0 to $100,000 a year. Moreover, the lowest conceivable level is not in fact zero but something above a basic subsistence level, e.g. $400 a year. So a more realistic range might be $400 to $100,400. The range $0 to $100 may be taken as measuring in thousands of dollars the excess of consumption over some low arbitrary minimum level.

Consider any level of consumption between these two extremes, for example $50 a year. Let us ask our citizen whether he would prefer (I) a year's consumption at $50 a year or (II) the combination of six months of consumption at $0 a year plus six months of consumption at $100 a year. He will probably say that he prefers (I) to (II) although in both cases his average rate of consumption is the same, namely $50 over the whole year. A preference for (I) over (II) expresses simply a preference for a steady over a variable level of consumption. (See page 203 above.)

We could now improve the offer to our citizen under (II) in the last paragraph by giving him the choice of, say, only 5 months at $0 a year and 7 months at $100 a year or only 4 months at $0 and 8 months at $100 a year, and so on. Clearly if we turned (II) into an offer of 0 months at $0 a year plus 12 months at $100 a year he would prefer (II) to (I). At some intermediate point he will be indifferent between (I) and (II). Let us suppose that he is indifferent between (I) 1 year at $50 a year and (II) $0 \cdot 25$ of a year at $0 a year plus $0 \cdot 75$ of a year at $100 a year. We will, for reasons which will become clearer as we proceed, call this fraction $0 \cdot 75$ the 'utility index of consumption' at the rate of $50 a year.

We can similarly discover a utility index for consumption at every level in between $0 and $50. This is depicted in Figure 23 where we measure the level of consumption along the horizontal axis and the utility index of that consumption up the vertical axis. Thus, for example, in Figure 23 we have depicted the utility index of consumption at $50 a year as $0 \cdot 75$ (AC $= 0 \cdot 75$) which means that our citizen would be indifferent between (I) $50 a year for a year and (II) $0 a year for 0·25 of a year plus $100 a year for 0·75 of a year. Similarly we have depicted the utility index of consumption at $20 a year as 0·45 (DF = 0·45) which means that our citizen would be indifferent between (I) $20 a year for a year and (II) $0 a year for 0·55 of a year plus $100 a year for 0·45 of a year. And similarly for the other points on the curve O D G A K Q.

If our citizen prefers a steady to a variable level of consumption, the points on the curve O D G A K Q will all lie above the straight diagonal line O E I B L Q. Consider once more the case of consumption at $50 a year. Our citizen prefers (I) a whole year at $50 to (II) half the year at $0 a year plus half the year at $100 a year. But BC measures one half a year, so that AC must be greater than BC. Similarly for all other levels of consumption. The excess of the height of the utility index curve over the diagonal line measures the preference for a steady over a variable income.

One can go one step further than this. The curve O D G A K Q not only lies above the line O E I B L Q, but also becomes less and less steeply sloped as one moves along it from left to right. Take any two points on the curve such as D and A. Join them together with the straight line D H A. Then one can show that any point on the utility index curve between DA will lie above the straight line D H A; and it is clear that if this is always true, then the slope of the curve O D G A K Q must become gentler and gentler as one moves along it to the right. Our proposition can be demonstrated in the following way. Consider the level of consumption of $35 for a year which is half way between $20 a year and $50 a year. Because of his preference for a steady income our citizen will prefer

    (I) one year at $35 a year
to (II) 0·5 of a year at $20 a year plus 0·5 of a year at $50 a year.

But the utility index of $20 is 0·45, which means that 1 year at $20 is the equivalent of 0·55 of a year at $0 a year plus 0·45 of a year at $100 a year. Therefore 0·5 of a year at $20 a year is the equivalent of 0·5 × 0·55 of a year at $0 a year plus 0·5 × 0·45 of a year at $100 a year. Similarly 0·5 of a year at $50 a year is the equivalent of 0·5 × 0·25 of a year at $0 a year plus 0·5 × 0·75 of a year at $100 a year. It follows that our citizen will prefer

    (I) one year at $35
to (II) (0·5 × 0·55 + 0·5 × 0·25) of a year at $0 a year
      + (0·5 × 0·45 + 0·5 × 0·75) of a year at $100 a year

i.e. to (II) 0·4 of a year at $0 a year
      + 0·6 of a year at $100 a year.

It follows that the utility index for consumption at the level of $35 will be greater than 0·6. But 0·6 is the height of the line HJ whose height is half way between DF (= 0·45) and AC (= 0·75). In other words the point G will lie above the point H.

We have therefore shown that the slope of the curve O D G A K Q will become gentler and gentler as we move along it from left to right. We may call this phenomenon the 'diminishing marginal utility of consumption'. Our index has, it turns out, been constructed in such a way that the larger is the level of consumption the less will the utility index be raised by adding yet one more $1 to the level of consumption.

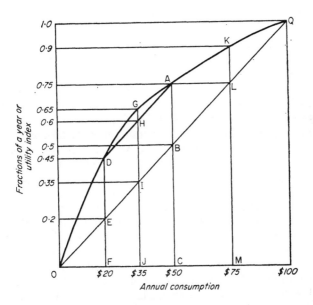

Figure 23

But this utility index is only one particular way of expressing our citizen's preferences between different combinations of levels of consumption in different years. What is the purpose of expressing his preferences in this particular way? The method has the very great merit that our citizen, if he behaves in a consistent way, should always prefer that combination of levels of consumption in different years which will maximize the sum of the utility indices for those various levels of consumption. Consider the following example, which is illustrated in Figure 23. Would our citizen prefer

(I) one year at $35 a year
plus one year at $50 a year

or (II) one year at $20 a year
plus one year at $75 a year?

With (II) he gets more in the second year if he will accept less in the first year. Will he consider the sacrifice worth the gain?

Consider combination (I). Since the utility index for $35 is 0·65, $35 for a year is the equivalent of $0 a year for 0·35 of a year and plus $100 a year for 0·65 of a year. Similarly $50 for a year is the equivalent of $0 a year for 0·25 of a year plus $100 a year for 0·75 of a year. Thus combination (I) is the equivalent of $0 a year for 0·35 + 0·25 (= 0·6) of a year plus $100 a year for 0·65 + 0·75 (= 1·4) of a year. In a similar manner we can see that combination (II) is the equivalent of $0 a year for 0·55 + 0·1 (= 0·65) of a year plus $100 for 0·45 + 0·9 (= 1·35) of a year. Combination (I) will therefore be preferred to combination (II); and this preference is indicated by the fact that the sum of the utility indices for $35 and $50 (0·65 + 0·75 = 1·4) is greater than the sum of the utility indices for $20 and $75 (0·45 + 0·9 = 1·35).

We now have a utility index for consumption at various levels of such a kind that it should be the objective of our citizen to plan his consumption over time so as to maximize the sum of the utility indices of his different annual levels of consumption. In other words the utility which our citizen will derive from two levels of consumption, $\hat{C}_1$ in year one and $\hat{C}_2$ in year two, will be the sum of $U(\hat{C}_1) + U(\hat{C}_2)$ where U is the utility index as depicted in Figure 23. It will be his objective so to arrange his consumption plan $\hat{C}_1$, $\hat{C}_2$ as to maximize $U(\hat{C}_1) + U(\hat{C}_2)$. By giving up a small amount of $\hat{C}_1$ ($d\hat{C}_1$) he can get $(1 + i)d\hat{C}_1$ units of $\hat{C}_2$, where i is the annual rate of interest. His total utility will, therefore, be maximized only if the utility lost through reducing $\hat{C}_1$ by one unit is equal to $(1 + i)$ times the utility gained by raising $\hat{C}_2$ by one unit, i.e. only if $U'(\hat{C}_1)(1 + i) = U'(\hat{C}_2)$. We define the elasticity of substitution between $\hat{C}_1$ and $\hat{C}_2$ as

$$= \frac{\text{proportional increase in } \hat{C}_2/\hat{C}_1}{\text{proportional decrease in } U'(\hat{C}_2)/U'(\hat{C}_1)}.$$

since the marginal utilities of $\hat{C}_2$ and $\hat{C}_1$ measure their prices i.e. the rate at which one would wish to substitute the one for the other. If we wish to measure the value of σ at this point where $\hat{C}_1 = \hat{C}_2$, then a rise of interest from zero to i will decrease $U'(\hat{C}_2)/U'(\hat{C}_1)$ from 1 to $1 + i$ and will raise the proportion between the two years' consumption from 1 to $\hat{C}_2/\hat{C}_1$, so that

$$\sigma = \frac{\dfrac{\hat{C}_2 - \hat{C}_1}{\hat{C}_1}}{-(1 - 1 - i)} = \frac{\hat{c}}{i}.$$

This is the formula obtained in the text on page 205.

If we assume that σ is constant we have to find a formula for relating U to $\hat{C}$ in Figure 23 such as to make constant

$$- \sigma = \frac{d\left(\dfrac{\hat{C}_2}{\hat{C}_1}\right) \bigg/ \dfrac{\hat{C}_2}{\hat{C}_1}}{d\left\{\dfrac{U'(\hat{C}_2)}{U'(\hat{C}_1)}\right\} \bigg/ \dfrac{U'(\hat{C}_2)}{U'(\hat{C}_1)}} \qquad (12.4)$$

The formula which does this is in fact

$$U(\hat{C}) = B - \frac{\alpha}{1 - \alpha} A \, \hat{C}^{-(1-\alpha)/\alpha} \qquad (12.5)$$

where A, B, and α are constants, $\hat{C}$ is the level of consumption in any year and $U(\hat{C})$ is its utility index. Differentiation of (12.5) gives $U'(\hat{C}_1) = A\hat{C}_1^{-1/\alpha}$ and $U'(\hat{C}_2) = A\hat{C}_2^{-1/\alpha}$. Using these expressions in (12.4) and differentiating gives $\sigma = \alpha$, so that the formula in (12.5) expresses a utility index for $\hat{C}$ when the numerical value of the elasticity of substitution between any two $\hat{C}$'s (e.g. $\hat{C}_1$ and $\hat{C}_2$) is constant at α.

If $\alpha < 1$ then the utility function given in (12.5) can be depicted by the solid-line curve in Figure 24. With $\alpha < 1$ we can see from (12.5) that $U \to B$ as $C \to \infty$ so that U has an upper limit equal to B. However rich they may be citizens cannot exceed B in utility. On the other hand as $\hat{C} \to 0$ so $U \to -\infty$. With consumption progressively below the bare subsistence level people tend to become infinitely unhappy. But as $\hat{C}$ falls, U reaches zero when $B = \frac{\alpha}{1 - \alpha} A \hat{C}^{-(1-\alpha)/\alpha}$ or $\hat{C} = \left(\frac{\alpha}{1-\alpha} \frac{A}{B}\right)^{\alpha/(1-\alpha)}$. Let us now compare our earlier utility index of Figure 23 with this utility index of equation (12.5) and of Figure 24. For any given value of $\sigma = \alpha$, we need to find values of the constants A and B in equation (12.5) which correspond with the benchmarks of consumption levels used for the utility indices of 0 and 1 in Figure 23. As we explained on page 213, we can interpret the level of consumption in Figure 23 as the excess of consumption in thousands of dollars over a low arbitrary minimum of \$400. From equation (12.5) we can see that $U = 0$ when $B = \frac{\alpha}{1 - \alpha} A \, \hat{C}^{-(1-\alpha)/\alpha}$, i.e. when $\hat{C} = \left(\frac{\alpha}{1 - \alpha} \frac{A}{B}\right)^{\alpha/(1-\alpha)}$, so that this expression for $\hat{C}$ measures the low arbitrary minimum of $400 in excess of which we are measuring our units of consumption for Figure 23. Thus the point M in Figure 24 corresponds to the point O in Figure 23. Moreover, equation (12.5) tells us that $U = 1$ when $B - 1 = \dfrac{\alpha}{1-\alpha} A\hat{C}^{-(1-\alpha)/\alpha}$, i.e. when $\hat{C} = \left(\dfrac{\alpha}{1-\alpha}\dfrac{A}{B-1}\right)^{\alpha/(1-\alpha)}$, so that this expression for $\hat{C}$ measures the high arbitrary value of $100,400 which we are taking as the benchmark for a utility index of 1. Thus for any given value of $\sigma = \alpha$, the two

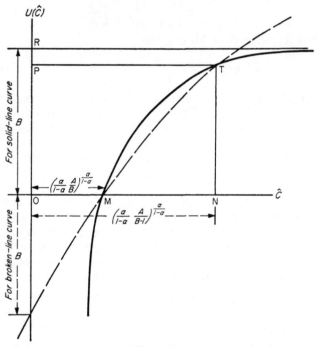

Figure 24

equations $\left(\dfrac{\alpha}{1-\alpha}\dfrac{A}{B}\right)^{-\alpha/(1-\alpha)} = \$400$ and $\left(\dfrac{\alpha}{1-\alpha}\dfrac{A}{B-1}\right)^{\alpha/(1-\alpha)} = \$100,400$ give the values of A and B which correspond to the two benchmark values of consumption $400 and $100,400. With these values of A and B the curve OQ in Figure 23 corresponds to the section MT of the curve in Figure 24 where OM measures the lower and ON the upper benchmark level of consumption. We have in fact chosen benchmarks such that with consumption less than OM the utility index becomes negative ('pleasure' gives place to 'pain') and such that, however great consumption may become, we cannot ever attain more 'utility' than the value of B given by the solution of our two benchmark equations.

If, however, $\alpha = \sigma$ were greater than unity there would be no upper limit to the index U, and (as can be seen from equation (12.5)) B would now measure the level of U when $\hat{C}$ was zero. To make the expression in equation (12.5) correspond with the benchmarks used for Figure 23 we would use the same two benchmark equations—in the forms $\left(\dfrac{\alpha-1}{\alpha}\dfrac{-B}{A}\right)^{\alpha/(\alpha-1)} = \$400$ and $\left(\dfrac{\alpha-1}{\alpha}\dfrac{-B+1}{A}\right)^{\alpha/(\alpha-1)} = \$100,400$—but B would in this case have to be a negative figure. The curve would now be of the kind shown by the broken line on Figure 24.

CHAPTER XIII

SAVINGS: (2) PERFECT ALTRUISM

The analysis in the preceding chapter was written on the assumption of perfect selfishness, that is to say, on the assumption that each citizen planned his savings simply in order to alter the time shape of his own consumption. He did not expect to receive any inheritance from his parents or any support from his children in his old age; nor did he intend to support his own parents in their old age or to leave any wealth to be inherited by his children. This assumption makes it possible to conceive of two quite distinct types of inequality in the distribution of income and wealth which we may call 'inter-class inequality' and 'inter-generation inequality'.

By inter-class inequalities we mean inequalities between rich and poor citizens of the same generation. Some citizens who own much property and/or have an especially high earning power will be much better off than those who own little or no property and/or have very limited earning power. In order to isolate for examination what we have called inter-generation inequality let us assume away the problems of inter-class inequality by confining our attention to a Propdem in which every citizen of a given age at any one point of time owns the same amount of property, has the same earning power, and is influenced by the same conditions and motives to save as every other citizen of that same age at that same point of time. Inter-class inequality in such circumstances will not exist.

But there may well exist what we will call inter-generation inequality. At any one point of time the elderly parent may be enjoying a different standard of consumption than that being enjoyed at the same calendar date by a young man just entering upon his adulthood. If there were perfect selfishness in the sense in which we have used that term in the last chapter, fathers in retirement at any given date may be enjoying a standard of living much in excess of the meagre standards enjoyed at that time by their sons or, on the other hand, sons at work may at any one time be enjoying a standard of living much in excess of that enjoyed at the same time by their fathers in retirement. Inter-generation inequality can work in either direction.

Inter-generation inequality could be removed if fathers considered the welfare of their sons as much as their own welfare, while sons considered the welfare of their fathers as much as their own. In this case inter-generation inequalities would be removed. If perfect selfishness resulted in such a rise in a citizen's consumption level over his life that in his old age he would be enjoying a much higher standard of living than his son would be enjoying at the same date, this inequality between the son's and father's standard could be corrected by the father planning to bequeath some inheritance to his children. If the father had had this in mind earlier on when he first entered his adulthood, he might well have planned the same time shape for his consumption stream over his life; but in order to make room for some accumulated property at the end of his life to bequeath to his children, he would have had to start his life's consumption stream at a lower absolute level. He would have consumed less over his life in order to save and accumulate a property in order to leave some wealth to his son, so that his son could in turn plan his consumption on a more ample scale so that he (the son) could be consuming at the same level as the father at any given point of calendar time.

In the opposite case in which perfect selfishness would have resulted in the father's standard being at any given date lower than that of the son, perfect altruism would cause the son to aid his aged parent and at that time to reduce his own saving and his own consumption in order to make some contribution to the consumption of his parent. The father in this case would have planned his consumption stream on a more ample scale and would have needed to save less as he counted on support in his old age from his son.

We can now appreciate the importance of the discussion in the last chapter (page 208) about the conditions in which perfect selfishness was likely to make a citizen's consumption stream rise at a more rapid or at a slower rate than his earnings. In so far as there is no difference between the earning power of a young man and of an older man at the same point in calendar time the rate of rise of a man's earning power will be an index of the growth rate of income per head in a progressive steadily-growing economy. Suppose, for example, that the wage rate is growing steadily as shown by the curve $E_1E_2E_3E_4$ in Figure 25(i) or (ii). At the point of time A_1 the wage rate is A_1E_1; at the point of time A_2 it is A_2E_2; and similarly for all other points on the curve. Let us assume that a man entering on adulthood at time A_1 plans, on the principle of perfect selfishness, a consumption pattern C_1D_1 over the remaining years of his life; in the case of Figure 25(i) the CD-curve is more steeply sloped than the E-curve (as was the case with the CD-curve in Figure 20), while in the case of Figure 25(ii) the CD-curve is less steeply sloped than the E-curve (as was the case with the C'D'-curve in Figure 20).[1] We assume for the purpose of Figure 25 that a citizen's adulthood lasts for 40 years and that after 30 years of adulthood his own sons leave home to start their own 40 years of adulthood; and so on from generation to generation.

Thus at time A_2 the second generation will enter adulthood. They

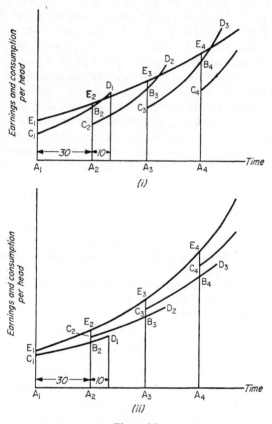

Figure 25

[1] It will be observed that in Figure 25(ii) the CD-curve lies below the E-curve for the whole of its length. But this does not mean that the citizen in question is saving throughout his adult life. The E-curve shows the wage rate ruling in the market; but the citizen will in fact be earning nothing during his retirement. The citizen entering adulthood at time A_1 will have a consumption pattern shown by the curve C_1D_1 over his adult life. His earnings pattern will start on the E-curve, but at some point (not shown in Figure 25) he will retire; and his earnings will no longer be on the E-curve but will fall abruptly to zero. Cf. the relationship between the C'D'-curve and the EF-curve in Figure 20.

will start at a higher earnings level than their fathers. If the wage rate is going up at 2 per cent per annum, then after 30 years it will be some 80 per cent higher than at the start.[1] That is to say, A_2E_2 will be 80 per cent greater than A_1E_1. If the second generation plans the same time shape for its consumption stream, A_2C_2 will be 80 per cent greater than A_1C_1, and so on. Thus if in Figure 25(i) or (ii) we drew a curve through the consumption starting points $C_1C_2C_3C_4$, this curve would grow at the same rate as the $E_1E_2E_3E_4$-curve.

It follows at once, as can be readily seen from Figure 25(i), that in the case in which the CD-curves are more steeply sloped than the E-curve, the point B_2 will be above the point C_2, the point B_3 will be above the point C_3, and so on. On the other hand, as can be seen from Figure 25(ii), where the CD-curves are less steeply sloped than the E-curve, the point B_2 will be below the point C_2, and so on. In other words, where perfect selfishness would lead a citizen to plan to increase his consumption more rapidly than his earnings, we shall have an inter-generation inequality of the kind in which the father is better off than the son during those years (i.e. from B_2 to D_1 in Figure 25(i)) in which their adulthoods overlap. Conversely where perfect selfishness leads to a less rapid rise in a man's consumption than in his earnings, sons will be better off than their fathers during the overlap of their adulthood from B_2 to D_1 in Figure 25(ii).

Suppose now that the world is converted from a state of perfect selfishness to one of perfect altruism. In the case of Figure 25(i) the fathers will plan to save more in order to leave some wealth to their sons. The proportion of the national income saved will rise. If and when a new state of steady growth is reached, it will be one in which (cf. page 104 above) the ratio of capital to other resources is higher because the propensity to save is higher. For this reason the rate of return on capital will be lower. With a lower rate of interest (i) and a given elasticity of substitution between present and future consumption (σ) the rate at which each citizen plans to raise his consumption over time ($\hat{c} = \sigma i$) will be reduced. The slope of the CD-curves in Figure 25(i) will be gentler. A new state of steady growth will be reached only when this process has occurred on a scale sufficient to reduce the slope of the CD-curves to that of the E-curve. The point B_2 will then coincide with the point C_2, B_3 with C_3, and so on. Inter-generation inequality will have been removed by perfect altruism which will have caused fathers to save to bequeath to their sons on a sufficient scale so to reduce the rate of interest that each citizen's consumption rises over time at the same rate as his earnings.

In the case of Figure 25(ii) the converse process would take place.

[1] $(1 \cdot 02)^{30} = 1 \cdot 811.$

Fathers would now save less as they relied on help in their old age from their children. The reduction in the propensity to save would raise the rate of interest. The rate at which each citizen would plan his consumption to rise over life would rise. At some rate of interest the CD-curves would become as steeply sloped as the E-curve. The point B_2 would coincide with C_2, B_3 with C_3, and so on. Perfect altruism would call forth just that amount of help from son to father which would cause just that reduction in the propensity to save which would cause just that rise in the rate of interest which would cause the planned rate of growth in consumption over a citizen's life to coincide with the rate of growth in his earnings.

It is interesting to note that with our present simplifying assumptions (including, in particular, the assumptions that a citizen's needs are constant over his life and that the elasticity of substitution between present and future consumption is constant) perfect altruism would in a steadily growing economy in which there was no period of retirement always lead to fathers helping their sons and never to sons helping their fathers. This follows from the fact which we expounded in the last chapter (pp. 211–212) that perfect selfishness would in these conditions always cause a citizen's consumption to rise more rapidly than his earnings. As is the case in Figure 25(i), the points B would be above the points C. Perfect altruism would then always lead to fathers helping their sons by accumulating something to bequeath to them.

It is also of interest to note the fact that perfect altruism does not imply that the father is directly interested in the welfare of his grandsons or of his great-grandsons or still remoter generations. If the father treats his son's needs as his own, and if the son in turn treats the grandson's needs as his (the son's) own, then the father will indirectly treat the grandson's needs as his (the father's) own. In terms of Figure 25(i) we can express this interconnection as follows. We start with perfect selfishness and with the points B above the points C. When the world is converted to perfect altruism, the father (generation 1) saves to raise the son's (generation 2) starting point of consumption (C_2) towards the father's contemporaneous level of consumption (B_2). But the son (generation 2) will be doing the same *vis-a-vis* the grandson (generation 3) and in order to make the necessary savings for this purpose he must plan *pro tanto* a lower starting point (C_2) for his own consumption. The father must save enough to leave to his son to close the gap between C_2 and B_2 in spite of the fact that the son's conversion to perfect altruism *vis-à-vis* the grandson will be tending to reduce C_2. The father regards the needs of his son, but one of the needs of his son is to regard the needs of the grandson, and so on down the generations.

Conversely in the case of Figure 25(ii) it is only necessary for each son to be concerned with the welfare of his parent for the concern to have been passed back in history up the generations. The son helps the father to raise the father's standard to the son's, but the father's standard needs to be raised all the more because the father has used some of his earnings to help the grandfather, and so on. Thus it is only necessary to have perfect altruism on the part of each generation towards the generation next on each side to it (i.e. on the part of each individual citizen towards his father and towards his son) for the needs of any generation in history to be indirectly fully regarded by any other (past or future) generation—provided, of course, that there always has been, is, and ever will be perfect foresight.

Let us now build a precise model of the influences which we have discussed in general terms in the preceding paragraphs. For this purpose we must take a production system which is capable of leading to a state of steady growth. For this purpose we will take the system discussed on pages 99–103 above, in which there are three factors K, L, and N, in which the proportional marginal products of these factors are constant at U, Q, and Z, in which there are constant returns to scale (so that $U + Q + Z = 1$), in which the growth rate of population is constant at l, and in which the growth rate of technical progress is constant at r.[1] We know from equations (7.14) and (7.15) that in these conditions, provided the proportion of income saved is constant, a state of steady growth is possible in which the growth rate of capital is equal to the growth rate of output, and both are given by the expression

$$y = k = \frac{Ql + r}{1 - U}$$

and in which the growth rate of the wage rate is given by

$$w_l = y - l = \frac{r - Zl}{1 - U}$$

The analysis in this and the preceding chapter shows that the assumption of perfect altruism requires that in a state of steady growth the growth rate of consumption per head should be equal both to (i) the growth rate of the wage rate and also to (ii) σi (see page 205 above). It follows that

---

[1] The case in which a state of steady growth is possible because there are only two factors with labour-expanding technical progress (cf. p. 94 above) is examined in detail in the note at the end of the present chapter (pp. 243–261 below).

H

$$\sigma i = \frac{r - Zl}{1 - U}$$

$$\text{or } i = \frac{r - Zl}{\sigma(1 - U)} \tag{13.1}$$

This expression determines the rate of interest which, on the basis of the analysis on pages 223–224 above, is necessary to make the individual citizen's consumption pattern over his life correspond to the growth rate of the wage rate in the steadily progressing economy.[1]

Now we know from equation (6.1) that $k = \dfrac{SY}{K}$ and from equation (4.3) that $i = \dfrac{UY}{K}$. It follows that $S = \dfrac{U}{i} k$ or from (7.14) and (13.1) that

$$S = \sigma U \frac{r + Ql}{r - Zl} \tag{13.2}[2]$$

This gives the value which S must have in a state of steady growth under our assumption of perfect altruism.

It is to be observed from this expression that S will be greater, (i) the greater is σ, (ii) the greater is l, and (iii) the less is r. These results are to be expected. A high σ will tend to make each citizen plan to enjoy a rapidly rising level of consumption through his life, so that perfect altruism will then require him to save much to bequeath to his children until the rate of interest is sufficiently reduced to lower his planned rate of rise of consumption. A high l or a low r will mean that the growth rate of the wage rate is less than it would otherwise be, so that perfect altruism will require each citizen to save sufficiently to bequeath to his children to bring down the rate of interest to a level sufficient to lower his planned rate of rise of consumption to the low growth rate of the wage rate.[3]

---

[1] We assume $r > Zl$ so that the wage rate is rising and not falling.

[2] We assume $\sigma U \dfrac{r + Ql}{r - Zl} < 1$, i.e. $\sigma < \dfrac{r - Zl}{U(r + Ql)}$, so that we do not get the nonsense answer that more than the total national income should be saved. We will deal later (pp. 235–236 below) with the case in which $\sigma > \dfrac{r - Zl}{U(r + Ql)}$.

[3] It is less straightforward to decide what the effects of the size of U, Q, and Z are upon S. If we keep σ, r, and l constant and differentiate equation (13.2) we get $dS \dfrac{(r - Zl)^2}{\sigma} = dU(r - Zl)(r + Ql) + dQ(r - Zl)Ul + dZ(r + Ql)Ul$. But $dU + dQ + dZ = 0$. We can examine three cases.

(i) If $dU = 0$ and $dZ = -dQ$, then $dS \dfrac{(r - Zl)^2}{\sigma} = dZ(Q + Z)Ul^2$ so that S is raised by an increase in Z and a decrease in Q.

So far in this chapter we have considered only the case of an economy which is in a state of steady growth. But we can in fact extend our present model to the case of an economy which is starting out of a state of steady growth. We are considering only those cases in which there are no problems either of inter-class or of inter-generation inequality. The former we have assumed away through confining our attention to a Propdem; and the latter disappear through our assumption of perfect altruism which means that there is such a transfer of resources between generations that consumption per head at any one point of time is the same for every citizen in the economy. We are, therefore, dealing with an economy in which consumption per head is the same for every citizen and, therefore, rises at the same growth rate for every citizen.

We start at some particular point of time when the economy is not necessarily in a state of steady growth. There is at this point of time a certain capital stock, a certain labour force, and a certain state of technical knowledge which results in the production of a certain level of output. We are concerned only with the answer to the one question: What proportion of today's income should be spent and what proportion saved and invested in capital goods to increase tomorrow's output? We can rephrase this question in the following way: What is the highest possible level of consumption per head today (i.e. the lowest possible value of S today) which (i) will enable each existing citizen from now on to increase his consumption at a rate equal to σ times the rate of interest ruling at each future date and (ii) will enable each new citizen as he comes to adulthood to start his consumption at the same level as each existing citizen and then to raise his consumption every day in his life at a rate equal to σ times the rate of interest ruling each day of his life?

Only if both of these conditions are fulfilled will (i) each citizen have the best preferred time shape for his own consumption and (ii) there be no inter-generation inequality.

We are interested solely in deciding what is the proper value of S today; but in order to decide this it is necessary (as the rephrasing of the question in the previous paragraph indicates) to consider the whole course of future events into the infinite future. If today,

(ii) If $dQ = 0$ and $dZ = -dU$, then $dS\dfrac{(r - Zl)^2}{\sigma} = dZ(r + Ql)(Ul + Zl - r)$ so that S is raised by an increase in Z and a decrease in U if $r < l(U + Z)$ and *vice versa* if $r > l(U + Z)$.

(iii) If $dZ = 0$ and $dQ = -dU$, then $dS\dfrac{(r - Zl)^2}{\sigma} = dQ(r - Zl)(Ul - Ql - r)$ so that S is raised by an increase in Q and a decrease in U if $Ul > r + Ql$ and *vice versa* if $Ul < r + Ql$.

tomorrow, the next day, and thereafter for every day in the future consumption per head is to grow at a rate equal to σi, then it follows that the choice of a level for S today will once and for all determine the level of S for every day in the future. Today there is a certain income produced; it is decided what proportion S of this should be saved; this determines the amount left over for today's consumption and thus the level of consumption per head today; but given today's rate of interest (which is itself determined by the initial amounts of land, labour, and capital today) σi determines the rate at which consumption per head should grow between today and tomorrow, and this together with the growth of population between today and tomorrow determines total consumption tomorrow; but meanwhile tomorrow's total output has been determined by the growth of population, the growth of technical knowledge, and the growth of the capital stock which was itself determined by today's decision as to how much of today's output should be saved and added to the capital stock; and thus, tomorrow's total consumption and tomorrow's total output having been determined by today's decision about the division of today's output between consumption and savings, tomorrow's savings is also determined. Tomorrow's rate of interest will also be determined since tomorrow's capital stock, labour supply, and technical knowledge is determined. Then tomorrow's savings and rate of interest being determined the next day's total consumption and total income will in turn be determined, so that the next day's savings and rate of interest will be determined. Thus if consumption per head is at every future date raised at a rate equal to σi, the single decision about today's level of S will determine the future course of S and i for the rest of time.

If the level of S chosen for today is low, the rise in output due to capital accumulation will be too small relatively to the rise in consumption at the rate σi, and tomorrow's S will fall. If today's level of S is sufficiently low, this process will become cumulative through time. Tomorrow's S will be much lower than today's simply because today's S was so low that capital accumulation made little contribution to tomorrow's output; but then tomorrow's savings can make still less contribution to the next day's output, so that the next day's S will again be abruptly reduced. If today's S is sufficiently low, this process will eventually cause consumption to have grown to a higher level than output. S will have become negative and the community will be living on its capital. This process cannot go on indefinitely; at some point a finite stock of capital would be completely consumed. The consumption pattern rising always at a growth rate equal to σi cannot be maintained. Today's initial level of consumption was set too high.

If, on the other hand, today's S is set too high, the consumption pattern will not break down; but on the other hand, the consumption pattern could have been maintained even if a higher initial level of consumption had been chosen. If a very high level of S is chosen today, then there will be a large addition to the amount of capital available to produce output tomorrow, so that tomorrow's output will be much increased and tomorrow's S will thus be raised. This process also can be cumulative in the sense that S may go on throughout time rising and rising towards unity when practically all output will be pointlessly saved simply in order to increase output so that still more may be saved.

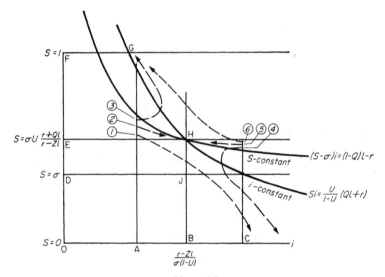

Figure 26

In between these low and high values of S there is some inter-mediate value of today's S which will enable consumption per head always to be increased at a growth rate equal to σi and yet will not cause S to become negative or to approach unity in the future. We shall now proceed by means of Figure 26 to show that in the case of our simple model in which σ, l, r, Q, U, and Z are all constant,[1] there exists a value of today's S which will cause S to move to its steady-state value of $\sigma U \dfrac{r + Ql}{r - Zl}$ at which it can continue indefinitely. Any value of today's S greater than this would be unnecessarily high since

[1] And in which $\sigma < \dfrac{r - Zl}{U(r + Ql)}$. See footnote 2 on p. 226.

it would cause S to rise indefinitely towards unity, and any value of today's S less than this would be too low since it would cause S in the future to fall below zero.

In Figure 26 we measure S up the vertical axis and i along the horizontal axis. At the point of time with which we are concerned there exists a certain stock of capital and a certain labour force which together with the existing amount of land and the existing state of technical knowledge will determine the marginal product of capital and so the current rate of interest. Let us suppose that this rate of interest is equal to OA in Figure 26. Then the single decision which we now have to make is at what level to fix today's value of S. Three such starting points are shown at points (1) (2) and (3) on Figure 26. We shall now show that if we start at too low a value of S, as at point (1), the value of S will move along a path which ultimately reduces it to zero; that if we start at too high a value of S, as at the point (3), the value of S will move along a path which will ultimately make it approach nearer and nearer to the point G at which $S = 1$; and that there is an intermediate starting point, as at the point (2), from which S will move to the point H at which it has its continuing steady-state value of $S = U \dfrac{r + Ql}{r - Zl}$. The proof of these propositions is as follows.

Whether we are in a state of steady growth or not, we have from (4.3) and (6.1)

$$k = \frac{Si}{U} \tag{13.3}$$

Moreover, from equation (4.4) $y = Uk + Ql + r$ or from (13.3)

$$y = Si + Ql + r \tag{13.4}$$

Finally if $\hat{c}$ stands for the growth rate of consumption per head then $\hat{c} + l$ is the rate of growth of total consumption (c). For example, if consumption per head is rising at 2 per cent per annum and the total number of heads is rising at 3 per cent per annum, total consumption will be rising at 5 per cent per annum. If $\hat{c}$ is always kept equal to σi, we have

$$c = \sigma i + l \tag{13.5}$$

We can now divide the area of Figure 26(i) as between those parts in which i is rising and those parts in which i is falling and (ii) as between those parts in which S is rising and those parts in which S is falling.

Since $i = \dfrac{UY}{K}$ and U is constant, i will be rising or falling according as $\dfrac{Y}{K}$ is rising or falling, i.e. according as $y \gtrless k$. From (13.3) and

(13.4) it can then be seen that i will be rising or falling according as

$Si \lessgtr \dfrac{U}{1-U}(Ql + r)$. If on Figure 26 we draw a curve (the i-constant

curve) such that the rectangle under it (e.g. the rectangle OEHB) is

constant and equal to $\dfrac{U}{1-U}(Ql + r)$, then if S and i are such that the

point S, i on Figure 26 lies to the North East of the i-constant curve

we shall have $Si > \dfrac{U}{1-U}(Ql + r)$ and i will be falling. But if S and i

are such that the point S, i lies to the South West of the i-constant
curve, then i will be rising.

S will be rising or falling according as total consumption is rising
at a smaller or greater growth rate than total income, i.e. according as
$c \lessgtr y$. From (13.4) and (13.5) we can then see that S will be rising or
falling according as $(S - \sigma)i \gtrless (1 - Q)l - r$. In Figure 26 measure
$OD = \sigma$ up the vertical axis and with the axes DF and DJ (i.e. from
an origin at D) draw the curve such that the rectangle under it (e.g.
DJHE) is constant and equal to $(1 - Q)l - r$. Call this the S-constant
curve. Then if we have any values of S and i such that the point S, i
lies to the North East of this S-constant curve we shall have $(S - \sigma)i$
$> (1 - Q)l - r$ and S will be rising. If, however, the point S, i
lies to the South West of the S-constant curve, then $(S - \sigma)i$
$< (1 - Q)l - r$ and S will be falling.[1]

On the i-constant curve i will be neither falling nor rising and on
the S-constant curve S will be neither falling nor rising. Where these
two curves intersect, we are at the steady-state values of S and i,

which will both be constant. When $Si = \dfrac{U}{1-U}(Ql + r)$ and

$(S - \sigma)i = (1 - Q)l - r$ we have $S = \sigma U \dfrac{r + Ql}{r - Zl}$ and $i = \dfrac{r - Zl}{\sigma(1 - U)}$

and these are the steady-state values of S and i which we have already
derived in equations (13.1) and (13.2).

[1] In Figure 26 we have drawn $\sigma < \sigma U \dfrac{r + Ql}{r - Zl}$. It follows that $r - (1 - U - Q)l$
$< Ur + UQl$, so that $r(1 - U) < (1 - U)(1 - Q)l$ or $(1 - Q)l - r > 0$. In
this case the area under the S-constant curve is positive. In Figure 27 we redraw
the situation with $\sigma > \sigma U \dfrac{r + Ql}{r - Zl}$ and therefore $(1 - Q)l < r$, in which case the
area under the S-constant curve will be negative.

We can now return to our consideration of the future paths of S and i which are implied in the choice of starting points for S at points (1), (2), or (3), when the starting amounts of K, L, and N are such as to make the initial value of i equal to OA. All three of these starting points lie to the South-West of both the i-constant and the S-constant curves so that at these points S will be falling and i will be rising. Each path will start in a South-Easterly direction.

From any starting point so low that, as at (1), the South-Easterly path of S and i cuts the line HB below B, the value of S will ultimately fall below zero.[1] Such a path cannot therefore be maintained indefinitely.

If we start at too high a point as at (3), then the point S, i will move East fairly quickly (it is far to the South-West of the i-constant curve) but only slowly Southwards (it is very near the S-constant curve). It will cross the S-constant curve; and it will do so when it is moving in a directly Eastward direction, since at its crossing S will be neither rising nor falling. It will then still be South-West of the i-constant curve, but North-East of the S-constant curve, so that its movement will now be in a North-Easterly direction. This means that it will cross the i-constant curve, and this it will do in a directly Northerly direction, since at its crossing i will be neither rising nor falling. It will then be North-East of both the i-constant and the S-constant curves and it will now move in a North-Westerly direction. This it will continue to do indefinitely. It could only cross the i-constant curve vertically, because at any such crossing, i would be neither rising nor falling. But this would involve its moving down on to the i-constant curve; but it cannot move downwards because it is North-West of the S-constant curve. Therefore, it continues indefinitely in a North-Westerly direction. It will in fact move more and more slowly towards the point G on Figure 26 at which S is constant

---

[1] This can be proved as follows. Immediately to the East of HB the point S, i will be to the South-West of both the i-constant and the S-constant curves. It will be moving South-East. Its path could, however, cut the i-constant curve only if the path changed direction and moved vertically upwards, because if ever it did cut the i-constant curve i would no longer be rising. But it cannot move upwards, because it is below the S-constant curve. Therefore, it cannot cut the i-constant curve. Therefore S falls towards zero as i increases. Now $1 - S = \dfrac{C}{Y}$ so that from (13.4) and (13.5) $\dfrac{1}{1-S} \dfrac{d(1-S)}{dt} = c - y = (\sigma - S)i + (1 - Q)l - r$. This expression is positive since S is falling, and, as soon as S is below σ, this expression increases as S decreases and i increases. This means that for all values of S less than σ the proportion of income spent on consumption $(1 - S)$ has an increasing growth rate over time. At some point $(1 - S)$ must come to exceed unity; or, in other words, at some point S must become negative.

at 1 and i is constant at $\frac{U}{1-U}(Ql + r)$.[1] To move towards a point at which S approaches ever more nearly to unity is, as we have seen, wasteful and uneconomic.

In between points (1) and (3) there will be some point (2) such that the South-Easterly movement from (2) will bring the point S, i to the steady-state point H at which $i = \frac{r - Zl}{\sigma(1 - U)}$ and $S = \sigma U \frac{r + Ql}{r - Zl}$. This can be maintained indefinitely and it does not involve the uneconomic waste of S rising indefinitely towards unity. Point (2) is the correct level for the initial value of S.

We can analyse the situation in an exactly similar manner if initially the amount of capital is so scarce relatively to the size of the working population and the amount of land that the rate of interest is above its steady-state level. Suppose it is equal to OC in Figure 26. Then we have to choose between starting points for S such as (4) (5) and (6). By a process of reasoning exactly similar to that adopted for the points (1) (2) and (3) we can argue as follows. If we start at too high a level as at (6) the path will move consistently in a North-Westerly direction until it approaches ever more slowly the point G at which $S = 1$. This is too high a starting point because a higher initial level of consumption could have been chosen without leading to a negative value of S. If we start with too low a level of S, as at point (4), the path will start in a North-Westerly direction, but will soon cut the S-constant curve in a directly Westerly direction. It will then bend in a South-Westerly direction, and then cut the i-constant curve in a Southerly direction. It will then proceed in a South-Easterly direction until S becomes negative. The path cannot be maintained indefinitely. In between there is a starting point such as (5) from which the path will be in a North-Westerly direction to the steady-

---

[1] This can be proved as follows. $\frac{1}{S}\frac{dS}{dt} = -\frac{1-S}{S}\frac{1}{1-S}\frac{d(1-S)}{dt}$ which, from the previous footnote, $= \frac{1-S}{S}((S - \sigma)i + r - (1 - Q)l)$. S is continuously rising, but as $S \rightarrow 1$ so $\frac{1}{S}\frac{dS}{dt} \rightarrow 0$. At the same time, since U is constant and $i = \frac{UY}{K}$, we have $\frac{1}{i}\frac{di}{dt} = y - k = -\frac{1-U}{U}\left(Si - \frac{U}{1-U}(r + Ql)\right)$. Therefore, as $S \rightarrow 1$, $\frac{1}{i}\frac{di}{dt} \rightarrow -\frac{1-U}{U}\left(i - \frac{U}{1-U}(r + Ql)\right)$. i is continuously falling, so that as $i \rightarrow \frac{U}{1-U}(r + Ql)$ so $\frac{1}{i}\frac{di}{dt} \rightarrow 0$. In other words S rises more and more slowly towards 1 and i falls more and more slowly towards $\frac{U}{1-U}(Ql + r)$.

state point H. S can then be indefinitely maintained at this level. The starting point (5) therefore indicates a path which can be indefinitely maintained without involving the waste of an indefinite rise of S towards unity.

As we explained in the footnote on page 231, in Figure 26 we drew $\sigma < \sigma U \dfrac{r + Ql}{r - Zl}$ which implies that $(1 - Q)l > r$. An exactly similar analysis can, however, be employed when $r > (1 - Q)l$ which implies $\sigma > \sigma U \dfrac{r + Ql}{r - Zl}$. This situation is depicted in Figure 27. The axes, the i-constant curve, and the steady-state values of S and i (i.e. the point H) are exactly the same in Figures 26 and 27. But in Figure 27 there is a new S-constant curve which is drawn in the following

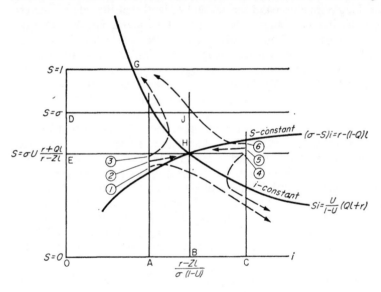

Figure 27

way. S is constant if $c = y$, i.e. if $(\sigma - S)i$ is now positive at the value $r - (1 - Q)l$. To draw the S-constant curve we must, therefore, in Figure 27 take D as the origin and measure $(\sigma - S)$ downwards from D on the axis DEO and i to the left from D along the axis DJ. The S-constant curve is now so drawn that the rectangle above it (e.g. EDJH) is constant in respect to the origin at D. To the North-West of the S-constant curve we will have $(\sigma - S)i < r - (1 - Q)l$ so that S will be rising; and conversely, to the South-East of the S-constant curve S will be falling. We can then consider three starting points such as (1) (2) and (3) in the case in which the initial value of i is less than its steady-state value and three starting points such as (4) (5) and (6) in the case in which the initial value of i is greater than its steady-state value. By a process of reasoning exactly analogous to that used in the case of Figure 26, it can be shown that if we start at any point which is too high, such as point (3) or (6), the value of S will rise indefinitely towards unity. If we start at any point which is too low, such as point (1) or (4), the value of S will become negative. But there exist intermediate starting points, such as (2) or (5), which lead to the steady-state solution at H. These are paths which can be maintained indefinitely without the waste involved in raising S towards unity.

We have so far avoided an obvious difficulty in this analysis. We have (see footnotes on pages 226 and 229) simply assumed for the purposes of Figures 26 and 27 that the steady-state value of S—namely $S = \sigma U \dfrac{r + Ql}{r - Zl}$—was less than one. But there is no apparent reason why this should be so. Indeed, if $\sigma > \dfrac{1}{U} \dfrac{r - Zl}{r + Ql}$ the steady-state value of S will be greater than one.[1] What is the meaning of this?

We can best reach an answer to this question by considering the steady-state value of the rate of interest. Since in a state of steady growth the equilibrium rate of interest must equal the rate of profit, we have from (7.16)

$$i = \frac{U}{S} \frac{Ql + r}{1 - U} \tag{13.6}$$

Given U, Q, l, and r the steady-state value of i is, therefore, lower the higher is S. This is as one might expect. The higher is S, the more abundant is capital relative to other factors in the steady-state and the lower, therefore, is the rate of interest. But with the productive system which we are considering (i.e. U, Q, Z, and r all constant) there is a lower limit to the steady-state value of i which is set by raising S to the limit of one in (13.6). i cannot fall below $\dfrac{U}{1 - U}(Ql + r)$. Even though citizens ploughed back always the whole of their income into capital investment, there would result a steady-state in which capital kept in balance with labour growth and

---

[1] In terms of Figures 26 and 27 the intersection of the i-constant and the S-constant curves at H will lie above the upper horizontal line marking $S = 1$. In the case of Figure 27 this can happen only if $\sigma > 1$, so that the point D which marks the origin of the S-constant curve is above the upper horizontal line. But in Figure 26 it can happen even though $\sigma < 1$.

technical progress in such a way that the marginal product of capital remained constant at $\dfrac{U}{1-U}(Ql + r)$.

But if the elasticity of substitution between this year's and next year's consumption is constant at σ, then the growth rate (σi) which an individual citizen will plan for his consumption path cannot fall below $\sigma\dfrac{U}{1-U}(Ql + r)$. But in the steady-state the growth rate of the wage rate is $\dfrac{r - Zl}{1 - U}$. If, therefore, $\sigma\dfrac{U}{1-U}(Qi + r) > \dfrac{r - Zl}{1 - U}$ (i.e. if $\sigma > \dfrac{1}{U}\dfrac{r - Zl}{r + Ql}$) the individual citizen, however low he may make the starting point of his consumption, will always plan to raise his consumption at a growth rate higher than the growth rate of the wage rate, so that he will always end his career at a higher standard of living than the standard at which his children are starting their careers. Perfect altruism would, therefore, lead him to reduce still further the starting point of his own consumption.

Since the citizen's son would be behaving in the same sort of way *vis-à-vis* his son—and so on down the generations—the result would be that everyone was always saving the whole of his income in order to leave property to children to enable them to leave property to grandchildren—and so on down the generations—in order that some day (which would never arrive) some generation (which would never be born) should have a tremendous blow-out of consumption (which would never occur).

This excess of present austerity in aid of a future blow-out which never arrives can occur in a less dramatic form. We have already shown (Chapter VIII above) that if in a state of steady growth a savings proportion (S) is maintained which is greater than the proportional marginal product of capital (U), then there is a less dramatic waste of the same kind as that discussed in the preceding paragraphs. For if $S > U$, then in the steady-state the level of consumption will be lower at every moment of time than it might otherwise be. If, in fact, S were reduced towards U, then consumption would, of course, be immediately raised, and also we would move to a new steady state in which consumption was at all times at a higher level than it would have been if S had not been reduced towards U. The maintenance of S above U means that the community is saving and accumulating capital continuously for a blow-out which never comes.

It is clear that this situation may well occur as a result of the assumption of perfect altruism which we are examining in the present chapter. The steady-state value of S (at the point H in Figures 26 and 27) may well be greater than U. This will be so if $\sigma U \dfrac{r + Ql}{r - Zl} > U$,

i.e. if $\sigma > \dfrac{r - Zl}{r + Ql}$. This is clearly much more likely to occur than

$\sigma > \dfrac{1}{U} \dfrac{r - Zl}{r + Ql}$ which leads to the absurdity that the whole of income should always be saved. Perfect altruism can in these less extreme conditions also lead to excessive savings.

There are, however, four factors which we have not considered in the analysis in this chapter, all of which are likely to make savings less than would otherwise be the case, and thus to reduce the danger of an excessive savings proportion.

(1) So far we have argued only on the extreme assumptions of perfect selfishness (Chapter XII) or of perfect altruism (Chapter XIII). But in fact there may well, of course, be an intermediate state of affairs. A father is prepared to see his son's starting standard somewhat lower, but not lower to a limitless degree, than his own (the father's) contemporaneous standard. A son is prepared to see his father's ending standard somewhat lower, but not lower to a limitless degree, than his own (the son's) contemporaneous standard. Fathers will save to bequeath to their children, or sons will reduce their savings to help their fathers, to reduce partially but not wholly the gap between their standards. (Cf. the note at the end of this chapter, pp. 249–252 below.) Excessive savings are likely to be a danger in circumstances in which perfect altruism would lead to much capital accumulation for the purpose of making bequests to children. If altruism is not perfect, such accumulation will be reduced.

2. We have so far been tacitly assuming that the world will go on for ever without end. But suppose that it was known that the world would come to a sudden end at a given future time. The result would be to reduce the proportion of income which it would be appropriate to save today. If the end of the world is very far ahead, this effect may well be negligible. But if it is at all near at hand, the effect will be very appreciable.

The point can readily be understood in the following way. Suppose we have a case of a world which is expected to go on for ever and, as a result, we get into a steady-state of the kind depicted by the point H on Figure 26 or 27. Suppose, however, that in the year AD 3000 the world is in fact blown to pieces by a gigantic nuclear explosion. Then all the capital stock which exists in AD 3000 will be wasted. Since the last generation will have no surviving children, it could have lived well during the years 2970 to 3000. It need not have saved to leave to its children but could have consumed the whole of its capital stock. Indeed, its prospective standard would for this reason have been so high that it could have helped its parents to bring their standard up to its own. Thus the generation from 2940 to 2970 could also have lived better and could have helped its parents to live better from 2910 to 2940. And so on, backwards down the generations. Thus the generation from 1950 to 1980 need have accumulated less to help the generation from 1980 to 2010. Somewhere in between there would have been a generation in which no help was needed either from father to son or from son to father. If the disaster in 3000 had thus been accurately foreseen, the proportion of income saved in 1950 would properly have been somewhat reduced.

3. We have already seen (pages 206–207 above) that σ may depend upon the level of consumption and, in particular, that it may become very small as consumption reaches some upper limit beyond which a still further rise is not desired (i.e. $PQ_5 = RQ_5$ in Figure 19). The fact that σ may become very small in the future when consumption per head has grown very high will also provide a very good reason for reducing today's savings proportion. The generation of 2970 to 3000, having a very high standard will have a low σ and will, therefore, plan to have only a slowly rising standard over the years 2970 to 3000. This means that they will have a relatively high starting point in 2970. The parents of the generation 2940 to 2970 will also have planned a rather slowly rising pattern of consumption over the years 2940 to 2970. The ending point of the 2940 to 2970 generation might well threaten to be lower than the starting point of the 2970 to 3000 generation. Perfect altruism would call on the later generation to reduce its savings in order to help its parents; and so on down the line of generations. Thus the generation of 1950 to 1980 need save less because the starting point of the generation 1980 to 2010 would be higher because the starting point of the generation of 2010 to 2040 would be higher because . . . because . . . because the starting point of the generation 2970 to 3000 was raised because its σ was very low.

4. We have also seen that because of the existence of a minimum subsistence level (cf. the low level of consumption $LQ_1 = KQ_1$ in Figure 19) the value of σ is also likely to be very low for very low levels of consumption. This fact will certainly remove the extreme form of the wasteful absurdity of excessive savings. S will never in fact rise to 1, because if it did do so consumption would fall to zero. But before consumption had fallen to zero, the minimum subsistence level would have been reached. If σ at this level were zero, then consumption per head would be planned to be constant over time and it would, therefore, necessarily rise at a growth rate less than the growth rate of the wage rate. Perfect altruism would now lead sons to

dissave to help their fathers, and each generation would tend to anticipate the consumption of its own future higher earnings. S would fall towards zero.

Thus a low level of σ when consumption per head is low will always tend to avoid very high values of S. For if S is very high, consumption per head is very low; and if consumption per head is very low, then σ is very low; and if σ is very low, σi is very low so that the growth rate of consumption over a citizen's life is very low; but if this is so, it will be less than the growth rate of wages so that sons will dissave to help their fathers; and in consequence S will not be so excessively high.

In the real world, of course, it is not only σ which may change. The rate of technical progress (r) may vary from year to year. The proportional marginal products of the factors U, Q, Z) may not remain constant either because the elasticities of substitution between the factors are not equal to unity or else because technical progress is biassed. The rate of growth of the population (l) may also change either for extraneous non-economic reasons or else, as we saw in Chapter XI, because of changes in the standard of consumption itself. The choice of the most economic level for today's saving proportion is, therefore, even more complicated than we have indicated in the very simple model presented in this chapter. In principle, if the course of future events could be correctly foreseen, there is a solution. Each citizen should discount to the present at the relevant rates of interest his future earnings (recognizing, of course, the facts that both his future earnings and the relevant future interest rates will be affected by all the possible changes which we have just enumerated); he must plan a time shape for his own consumption which will make the growth rate of his consumption equal to σi at every future date (recognizing, of course, the facts that the relevant rates of interest are dependent on future changes in all the relevant factors and also that his own σ will depend upon the starting level of his own consumption); if he is perfectly altruistic, he must plan bequests to his children which will make their starting levels equal to his ending level of consumption (recognizing that this will involve all the decisions which his son will have to make about his starting level which will depend upon the future interest rates, earnings, etc., during the son's life and upon what he must in turn plan to leave to the third generation); and then he must fix on a starting point for his own consumption which will enable him to carry out this plan without any spare resources left over at his death.[1]

---

[1] It is worth noting that the simple rules, such that S should not exceed U or that with perfect altruism the rate of interest should be such as to equate the

Clearly no one can in fact act just like this. Does this mean that the whole analysis carried out in this and the previous chapter is worthless?

The analysis has at least one important, even though negative, usefulness. It makes it clear that a rational economic calculus of today's level of savings must consider the possible course of events as far into the future as is feasible. It is unfortunately an inescapable fact that a fully rational decision solely for today's savings does theoretically involve a plan to cover the whole future course of events. It is worth noting that this is true even if there were perfect selfishness. It might at first sight appear as if this were not so because in this case the individual citizen need not concern himself with anything which will happen after his own death. He must know the future course of his own savings and the rates of interest which will rule over his own life, but need not be concerned with their subsequent course. This is, of course, true. But his own future earnings and the future rate of interest ruling towards the end of his life will depend upon what the younger generation are saving out of their incomes; and what they are then saving will depend *inter alia* upon what they expect the rates of interest and earnings to be at the end of their lives, which will depend upon what the third generation will then be saving—and so on *ad infinitum*. A rational decision for today's savings even with perfect selfishness will in fact be affected by what is going to be done some generations ahead.

In addition to this most important negative conclusion there may be some important positive insights gained from this analysis, particularly for those cases in which an economy seems to have settled down to a more or less steady growth rate and in which there is no reason to expect any change one way or another from this state of steady growth. Citizens will, of course, be influenced largely by habit and customs in their savings arrangement and in the help which they extend to their parents or to their children. But these habits may gradually change and they may well change in part under the influences which we have discussed in this and the preceding chapter High interest rates may well make them plan for a higher growth rule of consumption over their lives; the observation that young persons' starting levels are much below old persons' ending levels (or *vice versa*) may well influence young people in deciding to save more to help *their* children (or to save less to help their parents); and so on.

Moreover, one possible misapprehension of the meaning of our

growth rate of consumption over an individual's life with the growth rate of the wage rate, depend upon the economy being in a state of steady growth. Where conditions do not approximate to these of steady growth, even these few simple guide lines are lost.

analysis must be avoided. Throughout the analysis we have been concerned only with the single decision how much to save today. When, for example, in Figures 26 and 27, we have considered what this implies for future time paths of S, there has been no implication whatsoever that that time path must be followed. For example, if the initial starting point for consumption has been fixed too low (today's S too high) then a rigid subsequent adherence to a growth rate of consumption equal to σi will involve a wasteful uneconomic accumulation of capital (cf. paths (3) and (6) in Figures 26 and 27). Of course, in fact, as soon as these implications were realized, the plan would be revised. Today our citizen realizes that his resources are going to go further than he had expected yesterday; he revises his plan and starts again today with a lower S than he had planned yesterday. As a result of the revision of his ideas his consumption between yesterday and today has risen at a growth rate higher than σi. But this should, of course, in no way inhibit him from indulging in the higher level of consumption today. Yesterday's consumption is a byegone which he cannot now affect. The fact that his growth rate of consumption between yesterday and today is greater than σi is merely a recognition of the fact that yesterday's consumption was too low, a fact which he cannot change, though he may now regret it. He would have been somewhat better off if he had consumed yesterday rather more at the expense of today, tomorrow, and the next day. Each day then a citizen can renew his plan and fix his savings for that day. Given his capital resources today and his revised ideas about the future course of his earnings, of the yields which he will get on his capital, and of his children's needs, how much should he consume and how much save today? Each day's decision involves a renewed examination of future prospects on which one's views may change in the light of further knowledge and further experience.

Decisions about savings, which are essentially decisions about the choice between different available future time shapes of consumption, are thus among the most difficult to base on a rational economic calculus. There are a number of reasons why the individual may make incorrect decisions and it is possible that these decisions might be improved (though it should never be forgotten that they may also be worsened) by state intervention. For the government can always increase the level of the community's savings by levying taxes on individuals' income, the revenue from which is saved by the State and directly or indirectly used to finance additions to the community's capital stock. Alternatively, the government could borrow some of the individual's savings (thus short circuiting them from investment in addition to the community's capital stock) and use the revenue from these loans to pay out social dividends to citizens to

242 The Growing Economy

supplement their other resources and thus to encourage them to raise their consumption levels.

In the first place, the State may wish to encourage savings, if the State decides that inter-generation altruism is the correct policy and if individual selfishness is causing the end points of one generation's consumption to be above the starting points of the next generation's consumption.[1] In this case, State savings through a budget surplus financed by tax revenue and used to finance investment in real capital will lower the rate of interest, will thus cause individual citizens to plan a less rapidly rising growth rate for their individual consumption paths and will thus close the gap between one generation's end consumption level and the next's starting point.

In the second place, the State may wish to discourage savings if, in conditions approximating to those of a state of steady growth which it has no reason to believe will not continue indefinitely, it finds that the savings proportion (S) exceeds the proportional marginal product of capital (U) which in conditions of perfect competition can be measured by the proportion of the national income being paid out in profits on capital. For in this case, as we have seen, it can be assumed that individual savings decisions are leading to an excessively and wastefully high level of savings.

In the third place, as we have seen, a rational decision about present savings levels depends upon a correct anticipation of future developments. In some cases the State may be able to make better forecasts than the generality of individual citizens. Suppose, for example, that the State can foresee that the present abnormal age structure of the population (e.g. one in which there is an abnormally small number of women of child-bearing age) will probably lead to a much higher rate of growth of population in the future. This could be expected to cause the wage rate to rise much less rapidly in the future than in the past. A correct forecast of this would cause the present generations of an altruistic community to save more to meet the greater needs of the future generations whose earnings would not have risen as might be expected from current growth rates of earnings. In such a condition State savings to supplement private savings might help to forestall the evil days ahead.

Finally (cf. the analysis in the next chapter), action may be taken by the State in the interests of greater inter-class equality to limit or restrict the accumulation of wealth by rich parents for the purpose of richly endowing their own children. If this is so, citizens will be

---

[1] Alternatively the State might take action to discourage savings if the selfishness of children towards their parents was causing the end levels of one generation's consumption to be below the starting levels of the next's generation's consumption.

impeded from exercising freely their own individual inter-generation altruism. The State may need to save in order to compensate for the reduced accumulation of capital by private individuals.

We will return to these problems in the final chapter of this volume (Chapter XXIII, pages 489–499).

Note to Chapter XIII

LIFE-CYCLE SAVINGS, INHERITANCE, AND ECONOMIC GROWTH

I. *The Assumptions*

The object of this note is to present a mathematical model of the interrelationships between (i) certain macro-economic variables in a state of steady growth (in particular, S, the proportion of total national income saved) and (ii) the main forces determining personal motives for savings (in particular, saving for old-age and saving to leave property to one's children). We shall be concerned only with the situation in conditions of steady growth. Moreover, while we shall be concerned with inequalities in the standard of living between citizens of one generation and those of another, we shall assume that all citizens of the same age at any one time are exactly equal in earning power and in the ownership of property.

The model is built on the following very strict assumptions:

(1) We assume a constant-returns-to-scale production function with labour-expanding technical progress with only two factors, labour and capital, and only one output which can be used for consumption or for addition to the capital stock. There are diminishing returns to each factor taken separately and there is perfect competition, so that each factor receives its marginal product. We shall make frequent use of the well-known propositions that with such a productive system in a state of steady growth (i) the rate of growth of total output, of total consumption, of total savings, etc., will be equal to the sum of the rate of growth of the working population and of the rate of technical progress and (ii) the rate of growth of output per head, of consumption per head, of the wage rate, etc., will be equal to the rate of technical progress. We assume that the working population is growing at a constant proportional rate, l, and that the rate of labour-expanding technical progress is a constant, l', so that the rate of growth of total output is $l + l'$.

(2) We make the following demographic and biological assumptions. (i) Citizens are born as fully trained adults ready to start earning. (ii) Each citizen then works for F years and then retires. (iii) Each citizen dies at the age G (i.e. he enjoys $G - F$ years of retirement).

(iv) At the age of H years each citizen produces e^{lH} children (e^{lH} not necessarily being a whole number), so that the number of births can rise at the constant rate of l. (v) There is no distinction between men and women. These assumptions enable one to consider both savings for old age and savings for one's heirs with the minimum of complication. It is not difficult to see how the following analysis could in principle (but at the expense of clumsy elaboration) be extended to cover more realistic biological and demographic assumptions.[1]

(3) Each individual has certain and correct expectations. He knows that the rate of interest (i) will remain constant at its existing steady-state level, that he will have e^{lH} children at the age H, that he will retire at the age F, that he will die at the age G, and that his wage rate will rise at the rate l'. There is a perfect capital market on which he can lend his savings, or can borrow to finance his consumption, at the rate of interest, i. He can mortgage the future, but he cannot plan to leave an outstanding debt at his death. He may, however, plan to make a gift to his children; or his children may intend to make a gift to him, in which case he can foretell it exactly. Such transfers between generations are all made when the parent is aged H, i.e. children inherit at birth a gift from their parents or at birth children borrow and mortgage their own future earnings to help out their ageing parents. It is, in fact, quite immaterial at what stage any intergenerational transfer is made; this particular stage is assumed solely for convenience of exposition.

(4) With this background each citizen plans the pattern of his life's consumption. We shall assume that he always chooses to increase his consumption at a rate σi, where σ is a constant and i is the rate of interest. His problem will always be to choose between (i) a high starting level of consumption which does not grow rapidly or (ii) a low starting level of consumption which grows rapidly over the years. If the rate of interest is high, he is more likely to choose (ii), since the higher the rate of interest the more future consumption he can gain at the expense of a unit of consumption today. We assume that he plans to raise his consumption at the steady rate σi, i.e. at a constant multiple of the rate of interest. (See pp. 202–205 above.)

We now have three influences on a citizen's savings. (i) He may save to raise the rate at which his consumption rises over his life

---

[1] It would, of course, be particularly easy to modify assumptions (iv) and (v) and to replace them with the assumptions that an equal number of boy and girl babies are born, that every man and woman marries a spouse of the same age as him- or herself, and that each set of parents have $2e^{lH}$ children when the parents are aged H years. But it is so much simpler to speak of each parent having e^{lH} children, of each child having one parent, and of each separate parent (or child) deciding whether he should support his children (or parent) that I have maintained the peculiar biological assumption (v).

span. (ii) He may save in order to make a given time pattern of steadily rising consumption compatible with a time pattern of earned income which will rise with the wage rate so long as he works but will fall to zero on his retirement. (iii) He may save to give property to his children.

II. *The Structure of the Model*

Our first task will be to determine the total value of capital (K) which will be owned by individual citizens at any one time, namely at $t = o$. Consider first the amount of capital ($\hat{K}_\theta$) which is owned by any one individual born at $t = -\theta$ and therefore aged θ at $t = o$. If he has planned his consumption correctly, the amount of his capital at any one time must be sufficient to finance the excess of his future consumption and of what he will hand over in the future to his children over his future earnings. Or, in other words, $\hat{K}_\theta$ must be equal to the discounted value at time $t = o$ of the future consumption plus the future bequests to his children minus the future earnings of a man aged θ at $t = o$.

Let us start with the present value of the future bequests which he will make to his children. Let $\hat{I}$ represent the amount of property which a citizen born at time $t = o$ will receive at $t = o$ from his parent.[1] In a state of steady growth the amount of property received by a citizen at his birth must grow (like the wage rate, output per head, and similar *per caput* values) at the rate l'. The citizen aged θ at $t = o$ will, therefore, have received $\hat{I}e^{-l'\theta}$ at his birth, and at $t = H - \theta$ will have to give to each of his children $\hat{I}e^{l'(H-\theta)}$. He will have e^{lH} children at time $t = H - \theta$ and will, therefore, at that time have to give a total of $\hat{I}e^{lH + l'(H-\theta)}$. The present value at $t = o$ of this sum at $t = H - \theta$, discounted at the steady-state rate of interest i, we can express by

$$\hat{I}_\theta = \hat{I}e^{lH + (l'-i)(H-\theta)}. \tag{13.7}$$

This formula rules only for citizens who have not yet reached the age H; after that age they have no future bequests to make. Thus (13.7) is operative for $o < \theta < H$; and the corresponding quantity is zero for $H < \theta < G$.

Next let us consider the value at time $t = o$ of the future consumption of our citizen aged θ at time $t = o$. Let $\hat{C}$ represent the starting level of consumption of a citizen born and starting to consume at $t = o$. This starting level of consumption must in a steady state, like all similar *per caput* terms, be rising at the late l'. Thus our citizen born at $t = -\theta$ will have had a starting level of consumption

---

[1] $\hat{I}$ will have a negative value if it turns out that, instead of parents endowing their children, children help to support their parents.

equal to $\hat{C}e^{-l'\theta}$. This level he will have raised at the rate σi throughout his life and at time T in the future, when he is aged $T + \theta$, his consumption level will be $\hat{C}e^{-l'\theta + \sigma i(T+\theta)}$. The present value at $t = o$ of his consumption at $t = T$ is, therefore, $\hat{C}e^{(\sigma i - l')\theta + (\sigma - 1)iT}$, so that the value at $t = o$ of all his coming consumption we can express

$$\hat{C}_\theta = \hat{C}e^{(\sigma i - l')\theta} \int_o^{G-\theta} e^{(\sigma - 1)iT} dT \tag{13.8}$$

Finally let us consider the value at $t = o$ of the future earnings of our citizen aged θ. Let W represent the wage rate ruling at $t = o$. The wage rate at any future date T will be $We^{l'T}$. The value at $t = o$ of the wage to be earned at $t = T$ will, therefore, be $We^{(l'-i)T}$, so that the value to our citizen aged θ at $t = o$ of all his earnings still to come will be

$$W_\theta = W \int_o^{F-\theta} e^{(l'-i)T} dT \tag{13.9}$$

There is a prospect of future earnings only for persons under the age of F so that (13.9) is operative only for $o < \theta < F$. For $F < \theta < G$ the corresponding figure becomes zero.

We have then

$$\hat{K}_\theta = \hat{I}_\theta + \hat{C}_\theta - W_\theta$$

where $\hat{I}_\theta$, $\hat{C}_\theta$, and W_θ have the values given in (13.7), (13.8), and (13.9).

Let B be the number of births in the year $t = o$. Then the number of births θ years before and so the number of persons aged θ at $t = o$ will be $Be^{-l\theta}$. The total property owned at $t = o$ by all persons aged θ will be $Be^{-l\theta}\hat{K}_\theta$, so that the total property owned by persons of all ages at $t = o$ will be

$$K = \int_o^H Be^{-l\theta}\hat{I}_\theta d\theta + \int_o^G Be^{-l\theta}\hat{C}_\theta d\theta - \int_o^F Be^{-l\theta}W_\theta d\theta$$

$$= B\hat{I}e^{(l+l'-i)H} \int_o^H e^{(i-l-l')\theta} d\theta$$

$$+ B\hat{C} \int_o^G e^{(\sigma i - l - l')\theta} \int_o^{G-\theta} e^{(\sigma i - i)T} dT d\theta$$

$$- BW \int_o^F e^{-l\theta} \int_o^{F-\theta} e^{(l'-i)T} dT d\theta.$$

If one performs these integrations[1] and writes $\phi_T(u)$ for $\dfrac{e^{uT}-1}{u}$, then (a) when $i \neq l + l'$,

$$K = B\hat{I}\phi_H(l + l' - i)$$

$$+ \frac{B\hat{C}}{i - l - l'}\{\phi_G(\sigma i - l - l') - \phi_G(\sigma i - i)\}$$

$$+ \frac{BW}{i - l - l'}\{\phi_F(l' - i) - \phi_F(-l)\} \qquad (13.10a)$$

or (b) when $i = l + l'$,

$$K = B\hat{I}H + \frac{B\hat{C}}{\sigma i - i}\{Ge^{(\sigma i - i)G} - \phi_G(\sigma i - i)\}$$

$$+ \frac{BW}{l}\{Fe^{-lF} - \phi_F(-l)\} \qquad (13.10b)$$

We next proceed to determine the values of total wages, total profits, and total consumption at $t = o$.

We have already seen that the number born at time $t = \theta$ and, therefore, aged θ years at time $t = o$ is $Be^{-l\theta}$. Therefore, the number of workers alive at time $t = o$ is $\int_o^F Be^{-l\theta}d\theta = B\phi_F(-l)$. The total wage bill at time $t = o$ is, therefore, $WB\phi_F(-l)$.

The total profits at $t = o$ must equal iK. If we write U for the proportion of the national income going to profits and, therefore, $1 - U$ for the proportion paid in wages, we have

$$\frac{iK}{BW\phi_F(-l)} = \frac{U}{1 - U} \qquad (13.11)$$

[1]
$$\int_o^F e^{a\theta} \int_o^{F-\theta} e^{bT}\, dT d\theta$$

$$= \int_o^F e^{a\theta}\frac{e^{b(F-\theta)} - 1}{b}\, d\theta$$

$$= \frac{1}{b}\left\{e^{bF}\frac{e^{(a-b)F} - 1}{a - b} - \frac{e^{aF} - 1}{a}\right\}$$

so that, if $a = b$, the above expression becomes

$$\frac{1}{b}\{Fe^{bF} - \phi_F(b)\},$$

but, if $a \neq b$, then the expression becomes

$$\frac{b(e^{aF} - 1) - a(e^{bF} - 1)}{ab(a - b)} = \frac{1}{a - b}\{\phi_F(a) - \phi_F(b)\}$$

We have also seen that the starting level at time $t = -\theta$ of consumption of a person born at time $t = -\theta$ (and therefore aged θ years at time $t = o$) will have been $\hat{C}e^{-l'\theta}$. But such a citizen will have planned his consumption to rise at the rate σi so that the consumption level at time $t = o$ of a citizen aged θ years at time $t = o$ is $\hat{C}e^{(\sigma i - l')\theta}$. As we have just seen, there are at time $t = o$ $Be^{-l\theta}$ citizens born θ years ago. Therefore, the total consumption at time $t = o$ of all citizens aged θ years at time $t = o$ is $B\hat{C}e^{(\sigma i - l - l')\theta}$. It follows that total consumption by all citizens at time $t = o$ is

$$\int_{o}^{G} B\hat{C}e^{(\sigma i - l - l')\theta}d\theta = B\hat{C}\phi_G(\sigma i - l - l').$$

Let S be the proportion of total national income saved, so that $1 - S$ is the proportion of total income spent on consumption. Then, since $1 - U$ is the proportion of the national income which goes to wages, $\dfrac{1 - S}{1 - U}$ is the ratio of consumption to wages, so that

$$\frac{\hat{C}\phi_G(\sigma i - l - l')}{W\phi_F(-l)} = \frac{1 - S}{1 - U} \tag{13.12}$$

With a constant-returns-to-scale production function with only two factors of production, labour and capital, the capital–labour ratio chosen for production at time $t = o$ can be expressed as a function of the rate of interest. The higher the rate of interest, the more labour-intensive the technique of production. But the marginal product of labour and so the real wage rate can be expressed at any one time as a function of the capital–labour ratio. Thus the wage rate at time $t = o$ can be expressed as a function of the rate of interest. Moreover, if to each level of the rate of interest at time $t = o$ there corresponds a given ratio of capital to labour and a given wage rate, then we can also express the ratio of profits (i.e. capital times the rate of interest) to wages as a function of the rate of interest. It follows that we can write

$$W = W(i) \tag{13.13}$$

and $$U = U(i) \tag{13.14}$$

the nature of the functions $U(\ )$ and $W(\ )$ depending upon the nature of the production function.

If Y is the total national income and K the total national stock of capital, we can write $U = \dfrac{iK}{Y}$. Moreover, we can write $\dfrac{SY}{K}$ for the proportional rate of growth of the capital stock; but in a state of steady growth the proportional rate of growth of the capital stock must equal the proportional rate of growth of total output, namely $l + l'$, so that $\dfrac{SY}{K} = l + l'$. It follows that in a state of steady growth

$$S = \frac{l + l'}{i} U \qquad (13.15)$$

We have now a system involving the determination of seven variables ($\hat{I}$, $\hat{C}$, W, S, U, K, and i) in terms of seven parameters (B, l, l', σ, F, G, and H) and of the form of the production function. We already have six independent equations between these variables, namely equations (13.10) to (13.15). A final equation can be devised to express how much property a parent will plan to accumulate to bequeath to his children (or alternatively how much a child will mortgage his future in order to make a gift to his parent). We will devote a separate section to this relationship, since it is the central purpose of this note to build inheritance into the theory of personal savings.

III. *The Factors Determining Inheritance*

The first possible assumption which can be made about inheritance is simply that of 'perfect selfishness', i.e. that a parent thinks only of himself and a child only of himself and there is no positive or negative inheritance, so that

$$\hat{I} = o \qquad (13.16)$$

Equations (13.10) to (13.16) will then determine the variables in our system, including the variable i.

Consider in these circumstances a citizen born at time $t = o$, now aged H years and producing e^{lH} children at time $t = H$. This citizen's consumption will be $\hat{C}e^{\sigma iH}$, since he will have planned his initial consumption $\hat{C}$ to rise at the rate σi over the first H years of his life. But in a state of steady growth the initial starting level for consumption must rise at the rate l', so that our citizen's children in the year H will each of them start his consumption at a level equal to $\hat{C}e^{l'H}$. From then on the parent and each child will raise their consumption levels at the same rate σi, so that from age H to age G (when he dies) the ratio of the son's to the parent's standard of living can be expressed by the equation

$$\gamma = \frac{e^{l'H}}{e^{\sigma iH}} \qquad (13.17)$$

If i as determined by equations (13.10) to (13.16) is $> \dfrac{l'}{\sigma}$, then $\gamma < 1$ and the parent enjoys a higher standard than the son; and *vice versa*. The standard of living will progress in a zig-zag manner as depicted in Figure 28. The starting levels of consumption for each generation will lie on a curve (the broken line in Figure 28) which grows exponentially at the rate l'. But each individual's consumption through his life rises exponentially at the rate σi, i.e. along lines such

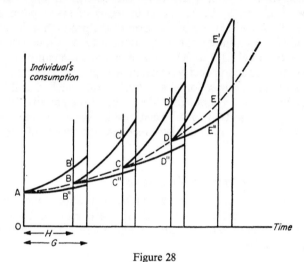

Figure 28

as AB′, BC′, CD′, DE′ if $i > \dfrac{l'}{\sigma}$ or lines such as AB″, BC″, CD″, DE″ if $i < \dfrac{l'}{\sigma}$. The ratio γ is shown by the ratio of the height of B′ (or B″) to the height of B above the horizontal axis.

We are now in a position to introduce an alternative assumption about the factors influencing inheritance. Suppose that there is a given degree of altruism of parents towards their children and of children towards their parent. If a child's standard of living is at any given time much below the parent's, then the parent will aid the child by reducing his own consumption to provide for his child an inheritance sufficient to bring the child's standard up to what he regards as a tolerable fraction of his own. Let this fraction be γ'. Then if γ as determined by equations (13.10) to (13.17) is $< \gamma'$, the parent will give to his child a sufficient inheritance to make $\gamma = \gamma'$. Thus as far as the parent's plans are concerned we have the condition $\gamma \geqslant \gamma'$.

The parent will thus plan the starting level of his own consumption on the basis that he must transfer sufficient to each of his children to prevent the child's starting level of consumption falling below the fraction γ' of the parent's level of consumption at the time of the birth of his children. The parent has this degree of concern with his children's welfare, though he cares nothing for the welfare of his grandchildren. Nevertheless through his children's action the parent is indirectly affected by considerations for the welfare of the grandchildren. For the child will plan his own initial consumption level at a sufficiently low level to leave a suitable inheritance for the grandchildren. Thus when the parent passes to his child sufficient to raise that child's starting level to an adequate level, he is indirectly through the child helping to raise the standards of the grandchildren; and so on through the generations.

One can deal in an exactly similar manner with the case in which equations (13.10) to (13.17) would lead to a value of $\gamma > 1$. Suppose that children are not prepared to see their own standard of living rise above γ'' times that of their parents, where γ'' is a parameter greater than unity. Then if y as determined by equations (13.10) to (13.17) were $> \gamma''$, children would cut down their consumption as a result of mortgaging their future to help their parents.

If parents are accumulating to bequeath property to their children, savings will be *pro tanto* increased, the capital–labour ratio in the state of steady growth will be higher, and the rate of interest will be lower. Thus γ as given in equation (13.17) will be higher. We will be in a steady state when inheritance ($\hat{I}$) is positive and at such a level that the rate of interest has reached a level at which

$$\left.\begin{array}{c} \gamma' = \dfrac{e^{l'H}}{e^{\sigma_i H}} \\[2ex] \text{or} \qquad i = \dfrac{l'H + \log\left(\dfrac{1}{\gamma'}\right)}{\sigma H} \end{array}\right\} \qquad (13.18)$$

If children are mortgaging their future to finance the current consumption of the parents, national savings will be so much the lower, the capital–labour ratio will be lower, and the rate of interest higher. γ will be lower. We will be in a steady state with $\hat{I} < o$ and

$$\left.\begin{array}{c} \gamma'' = \dfrac{e^{l'H}}{e^{\sigma_i H}} \\[2ex] \text{or} \qquad i = \dfrac{l'H - \log \gamma''}{\sigma H} \end{array}\right\} \qquad (13.19)$$

With our assumption of partial altruism we reach the following conclusions. If equations (13.10) to (13.16) result in a value of i such that $\gamma' < \dfrac{e^{l'H}}{e^{\sigma_i H}} < \gamma''$, then there can be a steady state with no inherit-ance. 'Transport costs' between generations (as represented by the degree of selfishness which still remain) are so great that no 'trade' (as represented by inter-generational transfers) takes place. But if the value of i resulting from equations (13.10) to (13.16) causes $\dfrac{e^{l\,H}}{e^{\sigma_i H}}$ to be either $< \gamma'$ or $> \gamma''$, then we can have a steady state with *either*

$$\hat{I} > o \text{ and } i = \frac{l'H + \log\left(\frac{1}{\gamma'}\right)}{\sigma H}$$

or
$$\hat{I} < o \text{ and } i = \frac{l' - \log \gamma''}{\sigma H}$$

If we assume that there is perfect altruism then $\gamma' = \gamma'' = 1$ and from equations (13.18) or (13.19) we obtain

$$i = \frac{l'}{\sigma} \qquad\qquad (13.20)$$

Parents and children transfer property in the one direction or the other to the extent necessary to ensure that at any one time everyone enjoys the same standard of living. The value of i obtained from (13.20) can then be used in equations (13.10) to (13.15) to determine $\hat{I}$, $\hat{C}$, W, S, U, and K. If as a result $\hat{I} > o$, then perfect altruism requires that parents help their children; and *vice versa*

In this case of perfect altruism i is determined solely by the two parameters l' and σ. The values of the parameters B, l, H, F, and G do not affect the value of i. Now given the value of i and given the production function we will know the real wage rate (equation 13.13) and the distribution of income between the factors (equation 13.14). If we also know the value of l, we shall know the proportion of total income saved (equation 13.15). Knowing the movements in the labour force, the rate of technical progress, the proportion of total national income saved, and the ratio of capital to labour ($K/B\phi_F(-l)$ in equation 13.11), we shall then know all the macro-economic variables, and so the time paths in the state of steady growth of total capital, total income, total consumption, total investment, and the wage rate. All this we know independently of the values of H, F, and G. The individual life-cycle problems do not affect the macro-economic outcome. They do, of course, affect the individual's life story—the starting level of consumption for each individual (equation 13.12) and the amount which each individual must leave to his children (or will receive from his children) (equation 13.10). If the parents refuse to die (G is great) that will no doubt burden the population of working age, keep their consumption low, and make them support their parents (or receive less inheritance from them). But it will not affect the total level of consumption or the total stock of capital in the community at any one time.

Of special interest in the case of perfect altruism is the proportion of the national income which will be saved. From equations (13.15) and (13.20) this is seen to be

$$S = U\sigma\left(1 + \frac{l}{l'}\right) \qquad (13.21)$$

Now we have seen in Chapter VIII that the highest possible level of consumption at each point of time in a state of steady growth is obtained if $S = U$. If $S > U$, then total national consumption is held permanently below the level which it could at any one time have attained with a lower value of S. This will be so if $\sigma > \dfrac{l'}{l + l'}$. Thus altruism by leading to parents saving to leave property to their children could possibly raise S above the critical level, U. If $S = U$, then from equation (13.15) we have

$$i = l + l' \qquad (13.22)$$

We will call the value of i given in equation (13.22) the 'golden-rule' value of i; and we will call the value of i given in equation (13.20) the 'perfect-altruism' value of i. This value of i optimizes the time path of each individual's consumption over his life-span and equalizes the standards of living of all individuals at any one moment of time. But if $\sigma > \dfrac{l'}{l + l'}$, this value of i will not give an optimum solution; consumption will be kept permanently lower than it need be.[1] We shall call the 'perfect-altruism' value of i the 'optimum' value of i, only if $\sigma \leqslant \dfrac{l'}{l + l'}$.

[1] J. A. Mirrlees in an unpublished paper has shown that savings according to a "Ramsey" principle by immortal citizens in conditions otherwise similar to those assumed in this paper will always lead (whatever the starting point) to a state of steady growth in which S has the value given in equation (13.21) above, provided that $\sigma \leqslant \dfrac{l'}{l + l'}$. If this condition is not fulfilled, no "Ramsey" optimum path exists.

IV. *The Solution of the System*

We will now confine ourselves to the two extreme assumptions of perfect selfishness $(\hat{l} = o)$ or perfect altruism $\left(i = \dfrac{l'}{\sigma}\right)$. We are concerned then with a system expressed in equations (13.10) to (13.15) together with either equation (13.16) or equation (13.20). In particular we want to know in the case of perfect selfishness what will be the value of i and in the case of perfect altruism what will be the value—or at least the sign—of $\hat{l}$. From equations (13.10) to (13.15) we can obtain the following relationship between $\hat{l}$ and i:

(a) When $i \neq l + l'$ we use equation (13.10a) with equations (13.11) to (13.15) and obtain

$$\hat{l} = W(i)\phi_F(-l)\frac{\phi_G(\sigma i - i)}{\phi_G(\sigma i - l - l')}\frac{a - b}{c}$$

where

$$a = \frac{1 - \dfrac{l + l'}{i}\,U(i)}{1 - U(i)}$$

$$b = \frac{\phi_F(l' - i)}{\phi_F(-l)}\frac{\phi_G(\sigma i - l - l')}{\phi_G(\sigma i - i)}$$

and

$$c = 1 - e^{(l + l' - i)H}$$

(13.23a)

(b) When $i = l + l'$ and, therefore, $S = U$, we use equation (13.10b) with equations (13.11) to (13.15) and obtain:

$$\hat{l} = \frac{W(i)\phi_F(-l)}{H}\left\{\frac{1}{i}\frac{U}{1 - U} + \frac{1}{i} - \frac{F}{e^{lF} - 1}\right.$$

$$\left. - \frac{1}{(1 - \sigma)i} + \frac{G}{e^{(1 - \sigma)iG} - 1)}\right\}$$

But by differentiation of a and b in equation (13.23a) we have, when $i = l + l'$,

$$\frac{da}{di} = \frac{1}{i}\frac{U}{1 - U}$$

(13.23b)

and

$$\frac{db}{di} = -\frac{1}{l} + \frac{F}{e^{lF} - 1} + \frac{1}{(1 - \sigma)i} - \frac{G}{e^{(1 - \sigma)iG} - 1}$$

so that in this case

$$\hat{l} = \frac{W(i)\phi_F(-l)}{H}\left\{\frac{da}{di} - \frac{db}{di}\right\}$$

We can observe the following characteristics of the expression for $\hat{I}$ in (13.23a) and (13.23b):

(1) Since $W(i)$, $\phi_F(-l)$, $\phi_G(\sigma i - i)$, $\phi_G(\sigma i - l - l')$, and H are all > 0, the sign of $\hat{I}$ will be the same as the sign of $\dfrac{a-b}{c}$ if $i \neq l + l'$ or the same as the sign of $\dfrac{d(a-b)}{di}$ if $i = l + l'$.

(2) The term c in (13.23a) is $\gtrless o$ as $i \gtrless l + l'$. It follows that if $i > l + l'$, then $\hat{I} \gtrless o$ as $a \gtrless b$. But if $i < l + l'$, then $\hat{I} \gtrless o$ as $a \lessgtr b$.

(3) If, however, $i = l + l'$, then $\hat{I} \gtrless o$ as $\dfrac{d(a-b)}{di} \gtrless o$.

(4) If we have perfect selfishness and $\hat{I} = o$, then we can have steady states either with $\dfrac{a-b}{c} = o$ and $i \neq l + l'$ or with $\dfrac{da}{di} - \dfrac{db}{di} = o$ and $i = l + l'$.

(5) Suppose that we have perfect altruism so that in the steady state $i = \dfrac{l'}{\sigma}$. Then if $F = G$ so that there is no period of retirement in old age, we have from (13.23a)

$$\hat{I} = W\phi_F\!\left(l' - \frac{l'}{\sigma}\right)\frac{U}{U-1}\,\frac{1 - \sigma\dfrac{l+l'}{l'}}{1 - e^{\left(l+l'-\frac{l'}{\sigma}\right)H}}$$

From this it can be seen that if $l + l' \neq i = \dfrac{l'}{\sigma}$, $\hat{I}$ must be $> o$, whether $\dfrac{l'}{\sigma}$ is $\gtrless l + l'$, i.e. whether the perfect-altruism value of i is or is not also the 'optimum' value. Moreover, if $\dfrac{l'}{\sigma} = l + l' = i$ and $F = G$, then from (13.23b) we see that

$$\hat{I} = \frac{W\phi_F(-l)}{H}\,\frac{l}{l+l'}\,\frac{U}{1-U}$$

so that $\hat{I}$ is also $> o$ in this case. In other words, if parents have no period of retirement during which they need to live on their capital, perfect unselfishness implies that they will always accumulate something to bequeath to their children. (Cf. page 224 above.)

Let us next consider the form which a and b in equations (13.23) may take as functions of i.

One can say of b, (i) that b is always $> o$ whatever the value of i, (ii) that for each value of i there is only one value of b, (iii) that when $i = o$ b has a finite positive value, (iv) that when $i = l + l'$, $b = 1$, and (v) that as $i \to \infty$ so b also $\to \infty$. This does not, however, imply that b rises monotonically, as i increases. From the expression for $\dfrac{db}{di}$ when $i = l + l'$, given in equation (13.23b), one can see that it may be $>$ or $< o$. For example with $F = 40$, $G = 50$, $l = 0 \cdot 01$ and $l' = 0 \cdot 04$, $\dfrac{db}{di} = +4 \cdot 4$ if $\sigma = 0 \cdot 8$ and $\dfrac{db}{di} = -2 \cdot 24$ if $\sigma = 0 \cdot 1$.[1] Thus the function b has the general shape shown in Figure 29. At the point $i = l + l'$, $b = 1$, but at this point $\dfrac{db}{di}$ may be $< o$ as in the case of the continuous line in Figure 29; or we may have $\dfrac{db}{di} > o$ as in the case of the broken line in the figure.

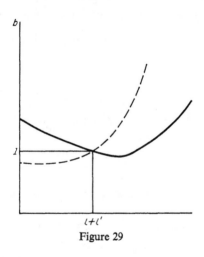

Figure 29

Two general statements can be made about the expression $a = \dfrac{1 - S}{1 - U} = \dfrac{1 - \dfrac{l + l'}{i} U}{1 - U}$ in equation (13.23a). First, $a = 1$ when

[1] As an interesting limiting case, if $F = G$ (i.e. there were no period of retirement) and if $i = l + l' = \dfrac{l'}{\sigma}$ (i.e. the 'golden-rule' level happened to coincide with the 'perfect-altruism' level of i), then $\dfrac{db}{di} = 0$.

$i = l + l'$. Second, as long as we confine our attention to those cases (which are the only ones in which a steady-state equilibrium is economically possible) in which $1 > U > o$ and $1 > S > o$, then $a < 1$ when $i < l + l'$ and $a > 1$ when $i > l + l'$. This implies that in these cases (as can be verified from the expression for $\frac{da}{di}$ in equation (13.23b), $\frac{da}{di} > o$ at $i = l + l'$.

For the rest we will confine our attention to the particular case of a production function with a constant elasticity of substitution between the two factors, labour and capital. Such a function is given by $Y = R\{\bar{U}K^{(\mu-1)/\mu} + (1 - \bar{U})L^{(\mu-1)/\mu}\}^{\mu/(\mu-1)}$ where Y is total output, K capital, L Labour (in efficiency units which may be increased either by population growth or by labour-expanding technical progress), μ is the numerical value of the constant elasticity of substitution between K and L, and R and $\bar{U}$ are constants.[1] By differentiation of this function we obtain

$$U = \frac{K}{Y}\frac{\partial Y}{\partial K} = Ai^{1-\mu}$$

where A is a constant with the value $\bar{U}^{\mu}R^{\mu-1}$. In this case the value of a in equation (13.23a) can be expressed as

$$a = \frac{1 - S}{1 - U} = \frac{1 - \dfrac{l + l'}{i}U}{1 - U} = \frac{1 - (l + l')Ai^{-\mu}}{1 - Ai^{1-}}$$

Differentiation of this expression gives

$$\frac{da}{di} = \frac{Ai^{-\mu}}{(1 - U)^2}\left\{(1 - S)(1 - \mu) + \frac{l + l'}{i}\mu(1 - U)\right\}$$

$$= \frac{Ai^{-\mu}}{(1 - U)^2}\left\{1 - S + \mu\frac{l + l' - i}{i}\right\}$$

from which it can be seen that $\frac{da}{di}$ is $> o$ if either $\mu < 1$ or $i < l + l'$.

We must now distinguish two cases: (i) where $\mu < 1$ and (ii) where $\mu > 1$.

(i) With $\mu < 1$, the steady-state equilibrium value of $S = (l + l')Ai^{-\mu}$ increases as i decreases. In order that the steady-state

---

[1] Mr D. G. Champernowne devised this production function in a comment which he wrote on an unpublished paper of mine in 1944; but his note remained unpublished.

I

value of S should not exceed unity, i has a minimum value of $\{(l + l')A\}^{1/\mu}$. But the value of $U = Ai^{1-\mu}$ increases as i increases and in order that U should not exceed unity we have a maximum value of i of $A^{-1/(1-\mu)}$. A steady state is, therefore, possible only if this i_{max} is greater than this i_{min}, i.e. if $l + l' < A^{-1/(1-\mu)}$, i.e. if $l + l'$ is less than the i_{max}. In this case we have a curve of the kind shown in Figure 30.

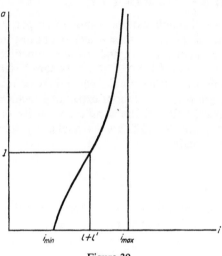

Figure 30

When $i = i_{min}$, $S = 1$ and $a = o$. Since $\mu < 1$, $\dfrac{da}{di}$ is throughout $> o$.

At $i = l + l'$, $a = 1$; and as $i \to i_{max}$, $U \to 1$, and $a \to \infty$.

(ii) With $\mu > 1$, both the steady-state value of S and the value of U decrease and tend towards zero as $i \to \infty$. It follows that $a \to 1$ as $i \to \infty$. Moreover, both S and U rise without limit as $i \to o$. From this we have two minimum values of i, one set by the requirement that $S = \dfrac{l + l'}{i}$ $U < 1$ and one by the requirement that $U < 1$. We must now subdivide into two sub-cases: (iia) where i_{min} is set by the requirement $S < 1$ and (iib) where i_{min} is set by the requirement $U < 1$.

(iia) In this case as i decreases we reach $S = \dfrac{l + l'}{i}$ $U = 1$ with $U < 1$. Therefore, $i_{min} < l + l'$. At i_{min} $a = o$. $\dfrac{da}{di} > o$ so long as $i < l + l'$. At $i = l + l'$, $a = 1$. With $i > l + l'$, $a > 1$. But as $i \to \infty$ $a \to 1$. The curve is of the kind shown in Figure 31.

(iib) In this case as i decreases we reach $U = 1$ with $S =$

$\dfrac{l + l'}{i} U < 1$. Therefore $i_{min} > l + l'$. As i falls towards i_{min}, $U \to 1$ so that $a \to \infty$. With $i > l + l'$, $a > o$. But as $i \to \infty$, $a \to 1$, so that we have a curve of the kind shown in Figure 32.

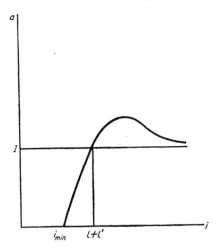

Figure 31

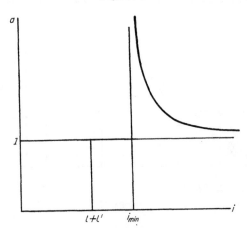

Figure 32

If we put the curves a and b together, it is clear that the four types of case shown as cases I, II, III, and IV on Figure 33 are all possible, though it is not claimed that these are the only possible cases. In each case we have used propositions (2) and (3) on page 255 above to indicate the sign of $\dot{I}$ for the different ranges of possible values of i.

In case I with perfect selfishness and $\hat{I} = o$, no steady-state position is possible. We could, however, have a steady-state position with perfect altruism and $i = \dfrac{l'}{\sigma}$, provided that $i_{\min} < \dfrac{l'}{\sigma} < i_{\max}$. But in this case we must have $\hat{I} > o$, so that in these conditions with perfect altruism parents would necessarily be accumulating to endow their children, whether $\dfrac{l'}{\sigma}$ were greater or less than $l + l'$.[1]

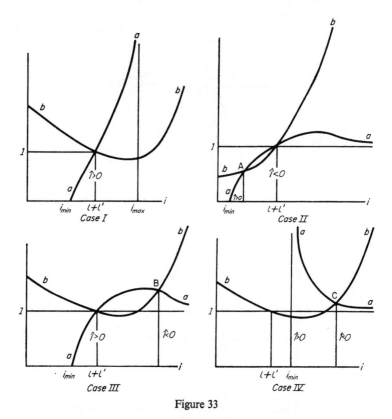

Figure 33

[1] In all four cases I to IV it should be borne in mind that the perfect altruism value of $_i\left(\text{namely, } \dfrac{l'}{\sigma}\right)$ is the optimum value only if it is not less than the golden-rule value of i (namely, $l + l'$). If $\dfrac{l'}{\sigma} < l + l'$, then $S > U$ and too much is saved. Also as noted in proposition (5) on p. 255 above, if $F = G$ then the value $i = \dfrac{l'}{\sigma}$ can occur only within ranges with $\hat{I} > 0$. The reader is left to apply these points himself to the discussion of cases I to IV.

In case II there is a perfect-selfishness steady-state position at the intersection A. This is at a value of $i < l + l'$ so that $S > U$ and perfect selfishness leads to more than golden-rule savings. Case III is similar to case II except that the perfect-selfishness steady-state position at the intersection B is at a value of $i > l + l'$, so that the level of perfect-selfishness savings is now less than the golden-rule level. Inspection of cases II and III shows that there could be an intermediate case at which the curves a and b happened to be tangential at the point $i = l + l'$ and $a = b = 1$. This is the fluke case where golden-rule savings and perfect-selfishness savings happen to coincide.

In cases II and III and in this intermediate fluke case, a perfect-altruism steady-state is possible provided that $i_{min} < \dfrac{l'}{\sigma}$. According as $\dfrac{l'}{\sigma}$ corresponded to a value of i above (or below) the perfect selfishness value of i (at the intersection A or B), so perfect altruism would involve $\hat{l} < o$ and children helping their parents (or $\hat{l} > o$ and parents helping their children).

Case IV illustrates the possibility that no golden-rule steady-state is possible since $i_{min} > l + l'$. In this case there is a possible perfect-selfishness steady-state at the intersection C. Moreover, a perfect-altruism steady-state with $i = \dfrac{l'}{\sigma}$ is also possible, provided that $\dfrac{l'}{\sigma} > i_{min}$. In this case parents will help their children if $i = \dfrac{l'}{\sigma}$ lies to the left of C and children will help their parents if $i = \dfrac{l'}{\sigma}$ lies to the right of C.

The above perfect-selfishness steady-state points at the inter-sections A, B, and C conform with common sense. Suppose that one starts in a perfect-selfishness steady-state at one of these points, and that mankind is then converted to perfect altruism. Then on the lines of the argument in Section III above, according as $\dfrac{l'}{\sigma}$ is greater (or less) than the initial perfect-selfishness value of i, this conversion will make children wish to help their parents (or parents wish to help their children). In the former case there is less net saving as children mortgage their future to help their parents; but in the latter there will be more saving as parents accumulate to bequeath to their children. In the former case i rises towards $\dfrac{l'}{\sigma}$ and in the latter it falls towards $\dfrac{l'}{\sigma}$.

Thus the movement is in the correct direction to attain the new perfect-altruism steady-state position.

CHAPTER XIV

FROM PROPDEM OR PLANTCAP
TO PROPCAP

In the two preceding chapters we assumed that we were dealing with a Propdem, that is to say with an economy in which there was no interclass inequality because all citizens of the same age at the same time possessed the same earning capacity and owned the same amount of property. We did this because we wanted in those chapters to isolate the problems of intergenerational inequality so as to concentrate on the motives on the part of one generation to save or to dissave to help another generation. In other chapters we have from time to time made an assumption at the other extreme, namely that we are in a Plantcap where some persons own all the property but do no work while others do all the work but own no property.

In reality, of course, the situation is somewhere between these two extremes. In the more realistic intermediate type of society, which we have called a Propcap (see page 46 above), there are inequalities in the ownership of earning capacity, some individuals being endowed (whether by inborn ability or by the luck of social circumstances) with a greater ability to earn by their work than others. There are also inequalities in the ownership of property, some individuals at any one time possessing more wealth than others. These inequalities are in fact very closely interconnected in a double way.

In the first place, the ownership of a large amount of property will convey on the possessor a number of advantages in training and social opportunities which will help him and his children to obtain well-paid positions. In the very simple one-product economy with which we are at present dealing it is difficult to find a place for this important phenomenon; in our present model we must think in terms of some persons simply being able to do a greater amount of effective work per hour than others and passing this extra ability on to their children.

But in the second place a high earning capacity will help to raise a citizen's income; and a high income will in turn make it possible for him to save more and will thus tend to raise the property owned by any citizen who possesses a high earning capacity; for property is simply the sum of past savings and past inheritance. Now we have already considered (pp. 206–207 above) reasons why the very poor and the very rich may plan the pattern of their consumption levels over time to rise at a lower rate than the moderately rich (the elasticity of substitution between today's and tomorrow's consumption may be numerically smaller at very low and very high incomes than at intermediate incomes). Let us assume that we are dealing with a community in which the rich have not yet reached the extreme degrees of wealth at which the elasticity of substitution between one day's consumption and another's becomes very small. In such a community the poor will probably save a lower proportion of their incomes than the rich. If this is so, it follows that those with high earned incomes are likely, through a relatively high ratio of savings to income, to accumulate properties which stand in a higher ratio to their earnings than is the case with persons with a low earning capacity.

In this chapter we intend to construct a simple model to illustrate the way in which these interconnections between high and low earning capacities and between high and low savings ratios may end in the formation of a society which is intermediate between a Propdem and a Plantcap—that is to say, in a Propcap in which there are different classes of citizen, the richest class owning a high proportion of property and doing some, but a relatively small, amount of the work and the poorest class doing the greatest share of the work and owning some, but a relatively small, amount of the economy's property.

Let us then consider a society in which there is a limited number of distinct social classes. There is no class distinction between the life-cycle patterns of childhood, working life, and retirement; and all citizens have the same fertility and mortality rates, so that there is also no class distinction in the size of families and the rate of population growth. The members of the different classes do not, however, intermarry. They are distinct from each other in their earning capacities, each member of class 1 having the same earning capacity as each other member of class 1 but each member of class 1 having a lower earning capacity than each member of class 2; and so on up the class scale. Without begging the question whether it be for genetic or social reasons, we assume that these earning capacities are inherited within each class from father to son. This does not imply that earning capacities necessarily remain unchanged over time; technical progress and/or capital accumulation may be raising everyone's earning capacity; but if this is so, it is raising each class's earning capacity at the same growth rate and the earning capacity of a member of class 1 remains the same fraction of the earning capacity of a member of class 2 as time goes on. Finally, citizens help only their own parents or their own children; there are no interclass transfers of property and no death duties or other taxes.

Our problem is to see what would happen to the distribution of property and so to the distribution of income from property and so to the distribution of total income between the members of these different social classes as these different classes earn, save, and accumulate property, passing this property on to their children or back to their parents. Earned income will be unequally distributed simply because citizens in class 1 have a lower earning capacity than citizens in class 2, and so on. But if citizens in class 1 save a lower proportion of income than citizens in class 2, property will tend to be even more unequally concentrated than earning capacity simply because those with a high earning capacity will save much, and thus accumulate much property, relatively to their incomes. We will construct a very simple model, in which we shall neglect land and assume all property to take the form of the ownership of a stock of our single product, in order to show how the economy may come to rest with a stable, but unequal distribution of income and wealth.

Now if we compare any two classes, say class 1 and class 2, the distribution of property between the classes will be constant only if the citizens in class 1 are accumulating capital at the same growth rate as the citizens in class 2. If the citizens in class 1 have a level of savings which bears a lower proportion to their stock of property than does the savings of class 2 to the existing stock of property owned by class 2, the capital stock of class 1 will be growing at a lower rate than the capital stock of class 2 and the share of the community's capital owned by class 1 will be falling relatively to the share owned by class 2. Let us use k_1 to denote the growth rate of the capital owned by class 1. Then we have

$$k_1 = \frac{S_1(W_{l1}L_1 + iK_1)}{K_1} \tag{14.1}$$

where W_{l1} is the wage rate earned by a worker in class 1, i is the rate of interest, S_1 is the proportion of income saved in class 1, L_1 is the number of workers in class 1, and K_1 is the total property owned by class 1.

The validity of (14.1) can readily be seen. $W_{l1}L_1$ is the wage income of class 1 and iK_1 is the property income of class 1. $W_{l1}L_1 + iK_1 = Y_1$ is therefore the total income of class 1. Thus (14.1) can be expressed as $k_1 = \dfrac{S_1 Y_1}{K_1}$ which states that the growth rate of the stock of property of class 1 is the current addition to that stock ($S_1 Y_1$) as a proportion of the existing stock (K_1).

Let us write η_1 for the proportion of the total stock of capital which belongs to class 1 $\left(\text{i.e. } \eta_1 = \dfrac{K_1}{K}\right)$ and let us write λ_1' for the proportion of total earning capacity (i.e. the proportion of the total wage bill) which accrues to class 1.[1] Since Q is the proportion of the total national income which goes to wages, $\lambda_1' Q Y$ is the total wages earned in class 1. Similarly, $iK = (1 - Q)Y$ is the total of property incomes in the community so that $\eta_1 iK$ or $\eta_1(1 - Q)Y$ is the total of property incomes accruing to class 1. Thus from (14.1) we have

$$k_1 = \frac{S_1\{\lambda_1' Q Y + \eta_1(1 - Q)Y\}}{\eta_1 K}$$

$$= \frac{S_1 i\{\lambda_1' Q + \eta_1(1 - Q)\}Y}{\eta_1(1 - Q)Y},$$

so that
$$k_1 = S_1 i\left(1 + \frac{\lambda_1'}{\eta_1}\frac{Q}{1 - Q}\right)$$

and similarly
$$k_2 = S_2 i\left(1 + \frac{\lambda_2'}{\eta_2}\frac{Q}{1 - Q}\right) \qquad (14.2)$$

$$k_3 = S_3 i\left(1 + \frac{\lambda_3'}{\eta_3}\frac{Q}{1 - Q}\right)$$

and so on for all the other distinct classes.

Let us for the moment speak as if there were only two classes, class 1 and class 2. We do this only for convenience. We shall shortly extend the analysis to more classes. In the two-class case we have $\lambda_1' + \lambda_2' = 1$ and $\eta_1 + \eta_2 = 1$. Both earning capacity and property must be shared between the two classes; and the share which does not go to class 1 must go to class 2, and *vice versa*. Since we are assuming that the population of each class is growing at the same rate and that the effectiveness per worker (though it differs absolutely from class to class) is growing at the same rate in each class, λ_1' and λ_2' are constant. We are asking what determines η_1 and η_2. Let us assume for the present that S_1, S_2, and Q, as well as λ_1' and λ_2', remain constant. Suppose that we started with $\eta_1 = \lambda_1'$, and, therefore, also with $\eta_2 = \lambda_2'$. From (14.2) we should have

$$k_1 = \frac{S_1 i}{1 - Q} \quad \text{and} \quad k_2 = \frac{S_2 i}{1 - Q}$$

---

[1] The wage rates payable to different classes will be in proportion to the worker's efficiency, so that λ_1' represents the proportion of the total labour force *measured in efficiency units* (cf. p. 57 above) to be found in class 1. We keep λ_1 to represent the proportion of the total labour force *measured in natural units* (i.e. the proportion of the total number of workers) to be found in class 1.

Thus k_1 would be $< k_2$, if $S_1 < S_2$. But if $k_1 < k_2$, the proportion of total property owned by class 1 will be falling so that η_1 will be falling and, therefore, η_2 rising.

But this fall in the share of property going to class 1 will not go beyond a certain point. From (14.2) it can be seen that

$$\frac{k_1}{i} = S_1\left(1 + \frac{\lambda_1'}{\eta_1}\frac{Q}{1-Q}\right)$$

and

$$\frac{k_2}{i} = S_2\left(1 + \frac{\lambda_2'}{\eta_2}\frac{Q}{1-Q}\right)$$

Thus as η_1 falls and η_2 rises, $\frac{k_1}{i}$ will rise and $\frac{k_2}{i}$ will fall; and $\frac{k_1}{i}$ would rise towards infinity as η_1 fell towards zero. At some point in the fall of η_1 and the rise of η_2, $\frac{k_1}{i}$ would become equal to $\frac{k_2}{i}$; and then with $k_1 = k_2$ there would be no further change in η_1 and η_2.

The common sense of all this is clear. If the distribution of property were the same as the distribution of earning capacity ($\eta_1 = \lambda_1'$), then both classes would have the same ratio of total income to property. As a consequence the class which saved a higher proportion of its income would have a higher ratio of savings to existing property and its property would, therefore, be rising at a higher rate than the property of the other class. But as this process developed, the thrifty class would come to have a lower ratio of earned income to property income than would the other class; and so it would come to have a lower ratio of total income to property than would the other class. At some point the fact that it was saving a higher proportion of its total income would be just offset by the fact that it had a lower ratio of total income to property, so that the ratio of savings to property of the thrifty class would have become equal to the ratio of savings to property of the other class which had a relatively high ratio of total income to property but saved a relatively low proportion of its income. At this point both properties would grow at the same growth rate and there would be no further change in the distribution of property.

All this can be illustrated geometrically. Consider the relationship between the growth rate of the capital stock (k_1) and the proportion of the community's total property owned (η_1) by a single class, say class 1. From (14.2) we can write

$$\left(\frac{k_1}{i} - S_1\right)\eta_1 = S_1\lambda_1'\frac{Q}{1-Q} \tag{14.3}$$

which gives a relationship between $\frac{k_1}{i}$ and η_1 on our present assumption that S_1, λ_1', and Q are constant. This relationship is illustrated in Figure 34. Measure η_1 horizontally along the axis O_1Y_1 from O_1 and measure $\frac{k_1}{i}$ vertically up the axis O_1X_1 from O_1. Measure O_1O_1' equal to the savings ratio S_1. Then in respect of the vertical axis $O_1'X_1$ and the horizontal axis $O_1'Y_1'$ draw the curve FAG such that

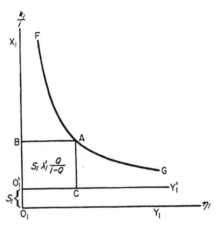

Figure 34

any rectangle under this curve (e.g. the rectangle $O_1'BAC$) has a constant area equal to $S_1\lambda_1' \frac{Q}{1-Q}$. The curve FAG then shows the required relationship between $\frac{k_1}{i}$ measured vertically from O_1 and η_1 measured horizontally from O_1. This can be seen in the following way. Consider the value of $\frac{k_1}{i}$ equal to O_1B. We wish to show that BA will be the value of η_1 which satisfies (14.3) for this value of $\frac{k_1}{i}$. It can be seen that

$$(O_1B - S_1) \times BA = S_1\lambda_1' \frac{Q}{1-Q}$$

It follows that BA is the value of η_1 which satisfies $\left(\frac{k_1}{i} - S_1\right)\eta_1 = S_1\lambda_1' \frac{Q}{1-Q}$ when $\frac{k_1}{i} = O_1B$.

We can use this construction to show the interplay between the earning capacities, savings proportions, and property ownerships of any number of classes. This we do on Figure 35 for three classes; but the principle of that figure could evidently be readily extended to cover a greater number of classes. Suppose we start in a position in which the proportions of total property owned by classes 1, 2, and 3 (i.e. $\eta_1 + \eta_2 + \eta_3 = 1$) are given. Draw a line O_1Y_3 of unit length and divide this into three parts, $O_1O_2 = \eta_1$, $O_2O_3 = \eta_2$, and $O_3Y_3 = \eta_3$. Draw a curve F_1G_1 which shows the relationship between η_1 and $\dfrac{k_1}{i}$ measured from the origin O_1. This is done in

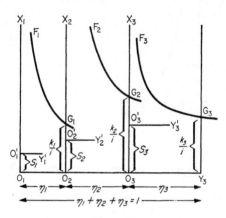

Figure 35

exactly the same way as Figure 34 was constructed: that is to say, measure O_1O_1 equal to S_1 up the vertical axis O_1X_1; draw the horizontal axis $O_1'Y_1'$; and then draw the curve F_1G_1 such that the rectangle under this curve in respect of the axes $O_1'Y_1'$ and $O_1'X_1$ is constant at $S_1\lambda_1' \dfrac{Q}{1-Q}$. It follows that since $O_1O_2 = \eta_1$, $O_2G_1 = \dfrac{k_1}{i}$. We can then similarly use the point O_2 as the origin for a curve F_2G_2 which shows the relationship between η_2 and $\dfrac{k_2}{i}$; and since $O_2O_3 = \eta_2$, $O_3G_2 = \dfrac{k_2}{i}$. And similarly for η_3 and $\dfrac{k_3}{i}$, with the result that $Y_3G_3 = \dfrac{k_3}{i}$.

Now in Figure 35 as we have drawn it we have $\dfrac{k_2}{i} > \dfrac{k_3}{i} > \dfrac{k_1}{i}$, or $k_2 > k_3 > k_1$. Since the property of class 2 is growing at a higher growth rate than that of both the other classes, η_2 will be rising. Since the property of class 1 is growing at a lower rate than that of either of the other two classes, η_1 will be falling. On the other hand η_3 may be rising or falling; but since k_3 lies in between k_1 and k_2, if η_3 is rising it will be rising less rapidly than η_2 and if it is falling it will be falling less rapidly than η_1. In this way the values of η_1, η_2, and η_3 in Figure 35 will be adjusting themselves until $O_2G_1 = O_3G_2 = Y_3G_3$. At this point $k_1 = k_2 = k_3$. All three properties will be growing at the same rate so that η_1, η_2, and η_3 will no longer be changing. And so long as S_1, S_2, S_3, λ_1', λ_2', λ_3', and Q remain constant, this distribution of property ownership among the three classes will remain unchanged.

It may be of interest to consider one or two special cases. This is most easily done with a two-class model which is illustrated in Figure 36. We draw the line O_1O_2 of unit length, measuring η_1 to the right from O_1 and η_2 to the left from O_2. Measure O_1O_1' equal to S_1 and draw the axis $O_1'L$. Then draw the curve FABG so that the rectangle under it in respect of the axes $O_1'L$ and $O_1'X_1$ is constant at $S_1\lambda_1' \dfrac{Q}{1-Q}$. Then the curve FABG gives the relationship between η_1 measured to the right along O_1O_2 and $\dfrac{k_1}{i}$ measured vertically up O_1X_1. We do exactly the same thing for η_2 and $\dfrac{k_2}{i}$, measuring $\dfrac{k_2}{i}$ up the axis O_2X_2 and η_2 to the left along the axis O_2O_1. In other words, we measure O_2O_2' equal to S_2 and draw the axis $O_2'E$. We then draw the curve JAK such that the rectangle under this curve in respect of the axes $O_2'X_2$ and $O_2'E$ is equal to $S_2\lambda_2' \dfrac{Q}{1-Q}$. If we start at any point to the left of the point A, so that $k_1 > k_2$, then η_1 will be growing and η_2 will be falling. Conversely, if we start at any point to the right of A, η_1 will be falling and η_2 growing. Only if we are at the point A will the distribution of property between the two classes be constant.

We can now examine some special cases.

We have a true Plantcap when class 1, the workers, do not save ($S_1 = 0$) and when class 2, the capitalists, do no work ($\lambda_2' = 0$). With $S_1 = 0$, O_1' coincides with O_1 in Figure 36 and the area of the rectangle under the curve FABG becomes zero $\left(S_1\lambda_1'\dfrac{Q}{1-Q} = 0\right)$. In other words, the curve FABG coincides with the axes $X_1O_1O_2$. With $\lambda_2' = 0$ the area under the curve JAK becomes zero $\left(S_2\lambda_2'\dfrac{Q}{1-Q} = 0\right)$, so that the curve JAK coincides with the axes $X_2O_2'E$. Thus in this special case the two 'curves' intersect at the point E. We have then $\eta_2 = 1$ and $\eta_1 = 0$; since the workers do no saving, the proportion of property owned by the capitalists becomes unity. At this point we have also $\dfrac{k_2}{i} = S_2$. Since all property is owned by this class, $k_2 = k$. We know also that $i = \dfrac{UY}{K}$ (i.e. total profits as a ratio of total capital). Moreover, $S_2 = S_p$, the proportion of profits saved, since

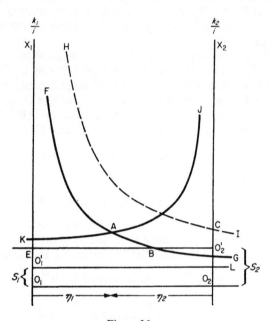

Figure 36

the incomes of class 2 coincide with total profits. Thus we have $k = \dfrac{S_p UY}{K}$, which with $U + Q = 1$ is our familiar formula for the rate of capital accumulation in a Plantcap (cf. p. 76 above).

Suppose that class 1 did no saving, but that class 2 did do some work as well as saving. We would once more have the curve FABG coincide with the axes $X_1 O_1 O_2$ since with $S_1 = 0$ we have $S_1 \lambda_1' \dfrac{Q}{1 - Q} = 0$. But now the curve JAK would not coincide with the axes $X_2 O_2' E$. The two curves would intersect at the point K instead of the point E. Once more $\eta_2 = 1$ and $k_2 = k$, since class 1 does no saving and owns no capital. But now $\dfrac{k_2}{i} > S_2$. Capital accumulation financed by savings from capitalists' property incomes is supplemented by that financed by savings from capitalists' earned incomes. In fact we have $k = k_2 = S_2 i\left(1 + \lambda_2' \dfrac{Q}{1-Q}\right)$.

Suppose now we have the case in which capitalists do no work (i.e. $\lambda_2' = 0$) but workers do some saving ($S_1 > 0$) as well as working ($\lambda_1' = 1$). We assume, however, that the proportion of income saved by workers is less than the proportion of income saved by capitalists ($S_1 < S_2$). Since $\lambda_2' = 0$, the curve JAK coincides with the axes $X_2 O_2' E$. Since neither λ_1' nor $S_1 = 0$, the curve FABG does not coincide with the axes $X_1 O_1 O_2$. As drawn in Figure 36 the two curves now cut at the point B, in which case $\eta_1 = EB$ and $\eta_2 = BO_2'$. In this case $\dfrac{k_1}{i} = \dfrac{k_2}{i} = O_2 O_2' = S_2$. In other words $k = k_1 = k_2 = \dfrac{S_2 UY}{K}$. We have exactly the same formula for the rate of capital accumulation as in the case of the pure Plantcap—namely $k = \dfrac{S_p UY}{K}$

where S_p is the proportion of income saved by the capitalist class which does no work. The distribution of property between workers and capitalists adjusts itself until this result occurs—that is to say, until the savings by workers from their earnings and their property incomes bears the same proportion to workers' property as does the savings by capitalists solely from their property incomes to capitalists' property. It is just as if the proportion S_p of all property incomes and nothing of wages was saved. The fact that workers have earned income as well as property income from which to save just makes up for the fact that they save a smaller proportion of their incomes.

But this is not the only possible outcome. If Q were sufficiently large the rectangle under the curve FABG $\left(S_1 \lambda_1' \dfrac{Q}{1-Q} = S_1 \dfrac{Q}{1-Q}\right)$ would be increased and the curve FABG might be raised to HCI. This curve cuts $X_2 O_2' E$ (which with $\lambda_2' = 0$ represents JAK) at the point C. We now have $k_1 > k_2$ so long as $\eta_1 < 1$. In other words workers' property grows continuously more rapidly than the capitalists' property and in the end capitalists' property becomes a negligible proportion of the total. Moreover, in the end we have $\dfrac{k}{i} = \dfrac{k_1}{i} = O_2 C$ which is greater than S_2. The workers' savings out of their earnings (which is now a high proportion of total income) more than compensates for the fact that they save a smaller proportion of their income than do capitalists who, however, have no earned income; and so workers' property continuously rises more rapidly than does capitalists' property. From (14.2) we can see that with $\lambda_2' = 0$ and $\lambda_1' = 1$, as η_1 approaches 1 $\dfrac{k_1}{i}$ approaches $S_1\Big(1 + \dfrac{Q}{1-Q}\Big) = \dfrac{S_1}{1-Q}$; and with $\lambda_2' = 0$, we have $\dfrac{k_2}{i} = S_2$. The curve HCI will pass above the point O_2' (i.e. the two curves will intersect at the point C on the axis $O_2'X_2$) if at these values $\dfrac{k_1}{i} > \dfrac{k_2}{i}$, i.e. if $\dfrac{S_1}{1-Q} > S_2$. If, for example, $Q = \frac{3}{4}$, then the equilibrium will be at a point like B if $S_1 < \frac{1}{4} S_2$ but at a point like C if $S_1 > \frac{1}{4} S_2$. In the former case the non-working capitalists will dominate the economy from the point of view of the rate of capital accumulation; in the latter case the property-owning workers will come to dominate the situation and the economy will come to approximate to a Propdem made up of these property-owning workers.

Another special case is where $S_1 = S_2$ and the axes $O'L$ and $O_2'E$ coincide. In this case when η_1 and η_2 have so adjusted themselves that $\dfrac{k_1}{i} = \dfrac{k_2}{i}$ we shall from (14.2) have

$$S_1\Big(1 + \frac{\lambda_1'}{\eta_1}\frac{Q}{1-Q}\Big) = S_2\Big(1 + \frac{\lambda_2'}{\eta_2}\frac{Q}{1-Q}\Big)$$

or since $S_1 = S_2$, $\lambda_2' = 1 - \lambda_1'$, and $\eta_2 = 1 - \eta_1$,

$$\frac{\lambda_1'}{\eta_1} = \frac{1 - \lambda_1'}{1 - \eta_1} \text{ so that } \eta_1 = \lambda_1' \text{ and } \eta_2 = \lambda_2'.$$

In other words in this case we would end up with the distribution of the ownership of property between the two classes equal to the distribution of earning capacity between the two classes. If in addition there were equality of earning capacity by the members of the two classes, this would constitute a true and complete Propdem; there would be an equal distribution of property and of earning capacity.

In the general case we shall have an equilibrium at a point such as A in Figure 36. It is clear from the figure that if both classes save and both classes work, the two curves must intersect at some point at which η_1 is a fraction lying between 0 and 1. Each class will come to own some definite finite proportion of the total property. It may be of interest to take a numerical example of the outcome. Suppose

$\lambda_1' = \frac{3}{4}$, $\lambda_2' = \frac{1}{4}$, $S_1 = \frac{1}{10}$, $S_2 = \frac{1}{5}$, and $Q = \frac{1}{2}$.[1] Then we would have $\eta_1 = 41$ per cent and $\eta_2 = 59$ per cent as the equilibrium distribution of property between the two classes.

In order to be able to discuss the consequential distribution of income and of property between persons we must now make some assumption about the values of λ_1 and λ_2 (the proportion of the number of workers in each class) relatively to the values of λ_1' and λ_2' (the proportion of the total wage bill earned by each class). Suppose that, while $\lambda_1' = \frac{3}{4}$ and $\lambda_2' = \frac{1}{4}$ (as assumed in the preceding paragraph), $\lambda_1 = \frac{6}{7}$ and $\lambda_2 = \frac{1}{7}$. In other words effective work per head is much lower in class 1 than in class 2. Class 1 has $\frac{6}{7}$ of the total working population, but only $\frac{3}{4}$ of the total earning capacity.[2]

We can now compare the resulting distribution of income and property between the members of the two classes. First, we have $\frac{K_1}{K_2} = \frac{\eta_1}{\eta_2} = \frac{0\cdot41}{0\cdot59} = 0\cdot695$, which shows that the total property owned by class 1 will be $69\frac{1}{2}$ per cent of that owned by class 2. Second, $\frac{K_1}{L_1} \div \frac{K_2}{L_2} = \frac{K_1}{K_2} \frac{\lambda_2}{\lambda_1} = \frac{0\cdot695}{6\cdot0} = 0\cdot116$, which shows that the amount of property owned by a single member of class 1 will be only $11\cdot6$ per cent of the property owned by a member of class 2. Third, since $Y_1 = \{\lambda_1'Q + \eta_1(1 - Q)\}Y$ and $Y_2 = \{\lambda_2'Q + \eta_2(1 - Q)Y\}$ we have

$$\frac{Y_1}{Y_2} = \frac{\lambda_1'Q + \eta_1(1 - Q)}{\lambda_2'Q + \eta_2(1 - Q)} = \frac{0\cdot75 \times 0\cdot5 + 0\cdot41 \times 0\cdot5}{0\cdot25 \times 0\cdot5 + 0\cdot59 \times 0\cdot5} = 1\cdot38,$$

which shows that the total income of class 1 will be 138 per cent as great as the total income of class 2, the total earnings of class 1 being 300 per cent as great as the total earnings of class 2 $\left(\frac{\lambda_1'}{\lambda_2'} = 3\right)$ and the total property incomes of class 1 being only $69\frac{1}{2}$ per cent as great as

[1] The curves FAGB and JAK in Figure 36 are in fact drawn on this numerical basis.

[2] We have $\lambda_1 = \dfrac{L_1}{L_1 + L_2} = \dfrac{\dfrac{W_{l1}L_1}{QY}}{\dfrac{W_{l1}L_1}{QY} + \dfrac{W_{l1}}{W_{l2}}\cdot\dfrac{W_{l2}L_2}{QY}} = \dfrac{\lambda_1'}{\lambda_1' + \dfrac{W_{l1}}{W_{l2}}\lambda_2'}$ where W_{l1} and W_{l2} measure the wage rates paid to workers in class 1 and class 2 respectively. It follows that $\dfrac{W_{l1}}{W_{l2}} = \dfrac{\lambda_1'(1 - \lambda_1)}{\lambda_1\lambda_2'} = \dfrac{\lambda_1'\lambda_2}{\lambda_1\lambda_2'}$. In our numerical example, therefore, $\dfrac{W_{l1}}{W_{l2}} = \frac{1}{2}$. Each member of class 1 has only one half of the earning capacity of a member of class 2.

those of class $2\left(\dfrac{\eta_1}{\eta_2} = 0\cdot695\right)$. Fourth, $\dfrac{Y_1}{L_1} \div \dfrac{Y_2}{L_2} = \dfrac{Y_1\,\lambda_2}{Y_2\,\lambda_1} = \dfrac{1\cdot38}{6\cdot0} =$
$0\cdot23$, which shows that income per head for a member of class 1 will be only 23 per cent as high as that for a member of class 2. Finally if we write Q_1 and Q_2 for the proportions of income in classes 1 and 2 which are earned incomes we have

$$Q_1 = \frac{\lambda_1' Q Y}{\{\lambda_1' Q + \eta_1(1 - Q)\}Y}$$

and similarly

$$Q_2 = \frac{\lambda' Q}{\{\lambda_2' Q + \eta_2(1 - Q)\}}.$$

From this we obtain $Q_1 = 0\cdot646$ and $Q_2 = 0\cdot298$. About 65 per cent of income in class 1 and 30 per cent of income in class 2 will be earned income.

The proportion of the national income saved will settle down at a constant level between S_1 and S_2. We have $SY = S_1Y_1 + S_2Y_2 = S_1\{\lambda_1'Q + \eta_1(1 - Q)\}Y + S_2\{\lambda_2'Q + \eta_2(1 - Q)\}Y$, so that $S = S_1\{\lambda_1'Q + \eta_1(1 - Q)\} + S_2\{\lambda_2'Q + \eta_2(1 - Q)\}$. Thus with S_1, S_2, λ_1', λ_2', and Q constant, S will be given and constant as soon as η_1 and η_2 have found their equilibrium levels. In this model we shall always end up with a constant proportion of income saved.[1]

Thus in this model (i.e. with Q constant and $U + Q = 1$) assuming that the other conditions for a state of steady growth are fulfilled—namely, that the rate of population growth (l) and the rate of technical progress (r) are constant—the economy will in fact always move into a state of steady growth. We have from (4.4) a growth rate of total output expressed by

$$y = (1 - Q)k + Ql + r$$

where Q, l, and r are constant, and we have from (6.1) a rate of capital accumulation expressed by

$$k = \frac{SY}{K}$$

where sooner or later S will be constant at the value given in the preceding paragraph. Thus on the principles discussed in Chapter

---

[1] With our numerical example $S = 0\cdot1 \times 0\cdot5\,(0\cdot75 + 0\cdot41) + 0\cdot2 \times 0\cdot5$ $(0\cdot25 + 0\cdot59) = 0\cdot142$. In other words, when the distribution of property has reached its equilibrium level with $\eta_1 = 0\cdot41$ and $\eta_2 = 0\cdot59$, a constant proportion, namely $14\cdot2$ per cent, of the national income will be being saved, while class 1 saves 10 per cent and class 2 20 per cent of their incomes.

VII, pages 99–103, above the economy will move into a state of steady growth in which from (7.14) the growth rate of output and rate of capital accumulation will be

$$y = k = l + \frac{r}{Q}$$

Moreover, we shall have also $k_1 = k_2 = k = l + \dfrac{r}{Q}$, since on the basis of the preceding analysis of this chapter the distribution of property between the two classes will have become such that the growth rate of the properties of both classes in the community will be equal.

The model which we have so far developed in this chapter is a very mechanistic one, in that we have simply assumed that each class of citizen has a fixed savings proportion, though for each class it is fixed at a different level. But in Chapters XII and XIII we tried to go behind the savings proportion by examining the substitutability between present and future consumption on which the motive to save depends. If we try to explain in these terms why the savings proportion in class 1 may be less than the savings proportion in class 2, although both classes are faced with the same rate of interest, with the same growth rate in their earning capacity, with the same demographic conditions (length of life, age at retirement, number of children, etc.), and with the same degree of intergenerational selfishness or altruism, we can do so only by assuming that $\sigma_1 < \sigma_2$. That is to say, we must assume that faced with a common rate of interest, members of class 1 plan to have a slower growth rate of consumption than do members of class 2. This implies that $c_1 = \sigma_1 i < c_2 = \sigma_2 i$.

Let us first consider the case in which there is perfect selfishness in both classes and in which the elasticities of substitution between present and future consumption are fixed in both classes but at a lower level in class 1 than in class 2 ($\sigma_1 < \sigma_2$). In this case the life-cycle pattern of consumption will imply a less rapid growth rate of consumption over his life for each member of class 1 than for each member of class 2 ($c_1 < c_2$) and, with other conditions the same, the smaller incentive to postpone consumption in class 1 than in class 2 will imply a lower savings ratio in class 1 than in class 2 ($S_1 < S_2$). But the growth rate of the wage rate (w_l) will be the same for both classes, even though at any given time the wage rate for a worker in class 1 is absolutely lower than for a worker in class 2 ($W_{l1} < W_{l2}$). This means that the ratio of the son's to the father's standard of living during their overlapping years of adulthood would be higher in class 1 than in class 2; for the starting point in the life cycle of consumption will go up in both classes at the same growth rate (namely, w_l) whereas the growth rate of consumption during the life cycle will be lower in class 1 than in class 2 ($c_1 < c_2$). In terms of Figure 25 the E-curve will have the same growth rate for both classes, but the CD-curve will rise less quickly for class 1 than for class 2, so that $\frac{CA}{BA}$ will be higher for class 1 than for class 2.

Such a situation would be compatible with a state of steady growth. With an appropriate distribution of property between the two classes, reached on the lines discussed at length in the present chapter, we could reach a state of affairs in which (i) S_1 and S_2 were constant with $S_1 < S_2$ and (ii) the property of both classes grew at the same steady-state growth rate, namely $k_1 = k_2 = l + \frac{r}{Q}$.

But the existence of two unequal, but constant values for σ (namely, σ_1 and σ_2) would not be compatible with a state of steady growth if there were perfect altruism. In the case of perfect selfishness, depending upon the absolute levels of σ_1 and σ_2, we might end up with a state of steady growth (i) in which $w_l < c_1 < c_2$—the case in which in both classes fathers would be better off than their sons during the overlapping years of their adulthoods—or (ii) in which $c_1 < c_2 < w_l$—the case in which in both classes sons would have a higher standard of living than their fathers—or (iii) in which $c_1 < w_l < c_2$—the case in which fathers would be worse off than their sons in class 1 but better off than their sons in class 2. Suppose that, in a steady-state with perfect selfishness, there should be an outbreak of perfect altruism. What would happen?

In case (i) above in both classes savings would increase as fathers accumulate property to leave to their sons; the rate of interest would fall; c_1 and c_2 would fall; and this would go on as long as both c_1 and c_2 were greater than w_l. In case (ii) both classes would save less as sons mortgaged the future to help their parents; the rate of interest would rise; c_1 and c_2 would both rise; and this would go on so long as c_1 and c_2 were both less than w_l.

We are left, therefore, only with case (iii) in which c_1 and c_2 have so adjusted themselves to w_l that $c_1 < w_l < c_2$. But this situation is clearly incompatible with a state of steady growth and perfect altruism. For in such conditions sons would always want to reduce their standards still further in order to help their fathers in class 1 while fathers would wish always to reduce their standards to help their sons in class 2. There would be no end to this process; for with a common rate of interest, i, and with fixed and constant but different σ's ($\sigma_1 < \sigma_2$), we would necessarily have $c_1 < c_2$; and with a common rate of rise of earnings, w_l, it would, therefore, be impossible for fathers' and sons' standards to be the same in both classes simultaneously.

There are, in fact, two ways out of this absurdity.

(1) The limitless desire in class 2 to save from present income to help the next generation might so reduce the standard of present consumption in class 2 that it would be unreasonable to assume that σ_2 remained constant at a high level. As present consumption fell to a subsistence level σ_2 might fall to zero. (Cf. pp. 206–207 above.) Conversely in class 1 as each generation lived more and more luxuriously on the basis of mortgaging the future, σ_1 might rise from its initial low level. At some point we might have $\sigma_1 = \sigma_2$, so that $c_1 = c_2$, in which case fathers' and sons' standards could be equal to each other in both classes simultaneously. It should, however, be noted that while there may be a tendency of this kind at work in the real world, the situation would not be compatible with the states of steady growth which we have examined in this volume. For this solution depends upon σ rising (or falling) with a rise (or fall) in the standard of living. In a growing economy standards may well be rising in all classes. If σ is rising for this reason in all classes, then the savings proportion will not be constant. But a constant savings proportion has been a necessary feature of all the steady-state models in this volume.

(2) In the second place, altruism may well be imperfect; and the degree of imperfection of altruism may well depend upon the standard of living. Thus even though σ_2 may not fall, so that the life-cycle growth rate of consumption in class 2 (c_2) remains higher than the growth rate of earnings (w_l), yet the efforts of fathers to help their sons in class 2 may not be limitless. After stinting themselves to a certain extent each generation in class 2 may cease to make still further attempts to close the intergenerational gap in class 2. Fathers' standards may remain above sons' standards; altruism may wither away because standards are low.

Our model is, of course, in fact too simple to portray all the influences at work. Nevertheless some of the forces which we have examined may well be at work in modified forms in the real world. Thus the poor may well plan a life-cycle growth rate of consumption less than that of the rich; and this may well mean that in the poorer classes there is rather a tendency for children to be called upon to help their parents, whereas in the richer classes parents may well be expected rather to help their children. The additional savings of the rich (in order to leave money to their children) and the additional dissavings or diminished savings of the poor (to raise funds to help their parents) may mean that at any one time motives of intergenerational altruism in fact serve also somewhat to mitigate the severities of interclass inequalities, some of the savings of the rich indirectly, as it were, sustaining the current standards of the poor. Or, in other words, the heavy savings of the rich will tend to keep up the supply of capital and thus to keep down the rate of interest, thereby making it less expensive for the poor to mortgage the future in aid of the older generation. But the consequential high saving proportion of the rich and low saving proportion of the poor will tend meanwhile to accentuate inequalities by raising the ratio of property to earnings among the rich and lowering it among the poor. The precise models of the present chapter should not be pressed too far; but they may give hints of important forces at work in the real world.

In this chapter we have argued as if there were only two or three distinct classes of earners and property owners in the economy. This also is somewhat unreal. In fact in a modern economy based on private enterprise and private property there is often a whole range of individual variation from the very rich to the very poor. But the analysis in this chapter can readily be extended to meet this situation. Indeed each separate family could be treated as a separate class for the purpose of the analysis conducted in this chapter. What we have tried to do in this chapter is to illustrate by means of a precise model the interaction of two basic factors—namely, inequalities in earning capacity and inequalities in savings ratios—which will cause inequalities in income and property.

For a complete account these factors would need to be supplemented by many other considerations. In the real world pure environmental luck will play an important role in determining both a man's earning capacity (has he been lucky in his choice of training and occupation?) and also the value of his property (has he been lucky in his choice of investments?). Marriage and inheritance will also play an important modifying role. If marriage were entirely random, it would play an important equalizing role. For the richest citizens would then be likely to marry partners less rich than themselves and the poorest citizens to marry partners richer than themselves. Similarly the ablest citizens would be likely to marry partners less able than themselves and the least able citizens to marry partners abler than themselves. Thus the properties and the abilities inherited by the offspring would tend to be more nearly of an average, neither concentrated at the extreme top nor at the extreme bottom of the scale. This equalizing force is much modified by the tendency for the rich to marry the rich, the able to marry the able, the poor to marry the poor, and so on. But even so marriage must introduce some equalizing tendency; for the richest citizen must marry someone less rich than himself, the poorest citizen someone less poor than himself, the ablest citizen someone less able than himself, and the feeblest citizen someone less feeble than himself.

A further factor which may tend to increase or to decrease inequalities is differential fertility. If the wealthy have smaller families than the poor, then the large properties will be split up among few heirs while the small properties are more widely dispersed among many heirs. Low fertility at the upper end of the scale and high fertility at the lower end of the scale will thus tend to increase inequalities in the distribution of properties; and *vice versa*. Thus in so far as large properties and incomes are, in the way examined earlier in this chapter, associated with high earning capacity and in so far as high earning capacity is genetically influenced, a somewhat greater fertility at the top than at the bottom end of the scale would have a double advantage; it would improve the genetic make-up of the population and it would diminish inequalities in the ownership of property.

Inequalities are continuously being renewed by environmental and genetic luck; a man who by the luck of the genetic draw is endowed with great ability and who by the luck of the environmental draw happens to take up the right activity at the right time in the right place, will probably make a fortune and pass on to his children some at least of both the environmental and genetic advantages. Others whose genetic and environmental luck is less will probably move down the scale. In the manner discussed earlier in this chapter the resulting differences in earning capacity and in savings ratios will determine the limits of the resulting inequalities of income and wealth. Such inequalities in their turn may be modified by differential fertility of the rich and the poor, by intermarriage between different classes of persons, and in the modern community by various forms of tax. Our purpose in this chapter, however, has not been to give a general account of all these factors, but rather to give a much simplified but precise model of the interaction between two of them, namely inequalities of earning capacity and of savings ratios.[1]

[1] For a fuller discussion of the more general issues the reader is referred to J. E. Meade, *Efficiency, Equality, and the Ownership of Property*, Chapter V.

THE MANY-PRODUCT MODEL

CHAPTER XV

CAPITALISTIC PRODUCTION WITH MANY PRODUCTS

Up to this point in this volume we have considered the productive system in the case in which there was only one product which constituted both the consumption good and also the man-made instrument of production, the capital good. An example of this is the corn economy in which cereal farming is the only process of production, and in which inputs of land, labour, and seed corn produce only one output, namely corn which in turn can be used either for consumption or as an input of seed corn for next year's productive process. We intend now to take one further substantial step towards reality by allowing for the fact that there are many different products in the economy.

These products can be either goods for final consumption or else man-made instruments of production which together with inputs of original factors like labour and land, are used as inputs in some processes of production to produce other products which in their turn may be either goods for final consumption or else man-made instruments of production to be used in further processes of production. In this chapter we will describe some features of such a productive system as it operates on any one day, leaving till later chapters an examination of the way in which such productive system will develop through time from day to day.

The schema shown in Table VI can be used to describe such a system of production on any one day, say day 0. At any time, e.g. on day 0, given the state of technical knowledge on that day, there are a number of possible productive processes open to entrepreneurs to operate. We call these processes a, b, c, d, etc. On the lines already discussed at length in Chapters XI and XIV of *The Stationary Economy* we will assume that in each of these productive processes the technical co-efficients of production are rigidly fixed. Thus, as shown in Table VI, process a is a process of production open for use on day 0 in which inputs of L_a units of labour (L), N_a units of land (N), J_a units of some man-made instrument of production, i.e. of some intermediate product or capital good (J), and K_a units of some other intermediate product (K) can be taken on at the beginning of day 0 to produce by the end of day 0 an output of land equal to $\bar{N}_a$, outputs of the intermediate products J and K equal to J_a and $\bar{K}_a$, and outputs of products for final consumption X and Y equal to X_a and Y_a. And similarly for the other processes b, c, d, etc.

Table VI

	Processes a b c etc.	Total Inputs and Outputs
Outputs at 4 p.m. on day 0	$Y_a\ Y_b\ Y_c$. $X_a\ X_b\ X_c$. $\bar{K}_a\ \bar{K}_b\ \bar{K}_c$. $J_a\ J_b\ J_c$. $\bar{N}_a\ \bar{N}_b\ \bar{N}_c$.	$Y_0 = S_{a0}Y_a + S_{b0}Y_b + S_{c0}Y_c + .$. $X_0 = S_{a0}X_a + S_{b0}X_b + S_{c0}X_c + .$. $\bar{K} = S_{a0}\bar{K}_a + S_{b0}\bar{K}_b + S_{c0}\bar{K}_c + .$. $J_0 = S_{a0}J_a + S_{b0}J_b + S_{c0}J_c + .$. $\bar{N}_0 = S_{a0}\bar{N}_a + S_{b0}\bar{N}_b + S_{c0}\bar{N}_c + .$.
Inputs at 8 a.m. on day 0	$K_a\ K_b\ K_c$. $J_a\ J_b\ J_c$. $N_a\ N_b\ N_c$. $L_a\ L_b\ L_c$.	$K_0 = S_{a0}K_a + S_{b0}K_b + S_{c0}K_c$ . . $J_0 = S_{a0}J_a + S_{b0}J_b + S_{c0}J_c$ . . $N_0 = S_{a0}N_a + S_{b0}N_b + S_{c0}N_c$ . . $L_0 = S_{a0}L_a + S_{b0}L_b + S_{c0}L_c$ . .
Scale of Operations	$S_{a0}\ S_{b0}\ S_{c0}$	

Since we are assuming constant returns to scale, each of these processes can be operated on any given scale. If one uses $2L_a$, $2N_a$, $2J_a$, and $2K_a$ in process a one will produce $2\bar{N}_a$, $2\bar{J}_a$, $2\bar{K}_a$, $2X_a$, and $2Y_a$ units of output at the end of the day. Thus if S_{a0} measures the scale on which process a is operated on day 0, $S_{a0}L_a$ is the amount of labour employed in process a on day 0, $S_{a0}X_a$ is the output of X from process a at the end of day 0, and so on for the other inputs and outputs. Similarly, the inputs and outputs of the other processes on day 0 depend upon the scales on which these processes are operated, namely S_{b0}, S_{c0}, etc. . . .

The total inputs and outputs of the economy on day 0 (which we will call L_0, N_0, K_0, J_0, and $\bar{N}_0$, $\bar{K}_0$, J_0, X_0, Y_0 respectively) are thus shown in the right-hand column of Table VI as the sum of the inputs and outputs of the various processes.

It will be seen from Table VI that we now have four broad types of variable in our productive activities.

(i) We have the inputs of labour into the various processes L_a, L_b, etc. There may, of course, be different forms of labour with different capacities so that although in Table VI we allow only for one type of labour, L, we do not need to assume that there is only one input in this category.

(ii) We have the inputs of natural resources such as the inputs of N into the various processes, i.e. inputs of those factors of production which are neither man-made nor direct human effort. Such resources, however, we shall no longer assume to be necessarily indestructible nor incapable of improvement by human agency. Minerals are provided by nature; but once they are mined and used up in production, they are no longer available. Land, which can be initially of varying qualities, can be made more fertile by good husbandry or less fertile if its qualities are 'mined'. We cannot, therefore, assume that the amount of any natural resource which is used as an input into any process on day 0 will necessarily appear again as an output at the end of day 0. It may be used up or altered into some slightly different (improved or worsened) resource. In Table VI we have allowed only for one natural resource (N). But there are, of course, a very large number if, as we must, we include all the various qualities of a resource (improved land is a different resource from unimproved land). Thus the output of a particular resource at the end of a day's operation may differ from the input of that resource at the beginning of the day's operations ($\bar{N}_a$ is not necessarily equal in amount to N_a.)

(iii) We have the whole vast range of man-made products which are themselves used as instruments of production. There is, of course. a vast range of these, which in Table VI we have represented only by the two products J and K. These products, of which we shall have much to say in the sequel, are in the nature of things both inputs (J_a, K_a, etc.) and outputs ($\bar{J}_a$, $\bar{K}_a$, etc.) though they may well, of course, be inputs of one process and outputs of another.

(iv) Finally we have the goods and services (e.g. X and Y) which are outputs but not inputs of the productive processes. These are the goods and services which are ready for final consumption by the citizens in the economy.

Many of the firms or farms operating the processes shown in Table VI will be close competitors with each other, there being a large number of similar competing dairy farms or of similar competing steel mills. But, of course, many firms or farms will be very different from each other. The balance of inputs and output in a dairy farm will be very different from that in a steel mill. A large number of the items of input or of output in any particular process are likely to be zero. Thus a dairy farm is unlikely to produce steel as an output, while a steel mill is unlikely to use animal feeding stuffs as an input or to produce butter as an output. Moreover, many of the processes which are technically available for operation on day 0 will not in fact be operated because they are technically dominated by other processes or because in the given conditions the desired outputs can be more economically produced by other processes which are more intensive in the most valuable outputs and in the cheapest inputs. Thus many of the scales shown at the bottom of Table VI may be zero. But we have already made these points in discussing productive processes in Chapter IX of *The Stationary Economy*. The one essential difference between the many productive processes discussed there and the firms or farms of Table VI is the existence in our present system of the man-made instruments of production J and K which can be the inputs of some processes and the outputs of others. If the four rows marked J, $\bar{K}$, J, and K were eliminated from Table VI we should be essentially back in Chapter IX of *The Stationary Economy*.

There is, however, one formal difference which should be explained, namely in the treatment of the natural instruments of production. Both in *The Stationary Economy* and throughout this volume we treat the services of labour (L and M) as inputs to which there is no corresponding output. If we were in a Slave economy it would be quite reasonable to do otherwise. L could stand for the 'input' of slaves who go into the farm in the morning and $\bar{L}$ for the 'output' of slaves left over from the farm's operations in the evening. But we choose to treat this matter differently and to think of the input of labour not as the input of so many men, but as the input of so many hours of work by a given number of men. It is the hours of work and not the men which the entrepreneur purchases at the beginning of the day, and the entrepreneur has no labour to sell as an output at the end of the day's operation.

As far as land or natural resources are concerned, so long as they are unalterable in amount or quality, we can adopt either way of looking at the situation. *Either* we can suppose that the entrepreneur hires the services of an acre of land for so many hours, just as he hires the services of a worker for so many hours *or else* we can suppose that he purchases an acre of land as his input in which case he has at the end of the day the same acre of land left over from his operations as an output which he can sell. In *The Stationary Economy* and up to the present point in this volume also we have treated land in the former way, just as we have treated labour. But from now on we shall find it more convenient to treat it in the latter way, as we have done in Table VI.

A basic reason for this is that many natural resources are not in fact indestructible or unalterable in quality. The natural resource, like the man-made instrument of production, may go into the firm or farm in the morning in one quantity or quality and come out of the firm or farm in the evening in a different amount or quality. In these cases, since $\bar{N}_a$ may differ from N_a and indeed $\bar{N}$ may differ from N, just as $\bar{J}_a$ may differ from J_a and $\bar{J}$ from J, it is more convenient to construct our model in terms of the actual gross inputs and outputs of the instruments themselves rather than in terms of the hire of their net services. The reasons for doing this and its implications will be discussed in more detail later (cf. pp. 295–298 below).

In considering the instruments of production such as J and K it is of great importance to appreciate the many varied forms that they may take. It is sometimes helpful to divide them into two main categories: raw materials and components on the one hand and plant and machinery on the other hand. A raw material or component, such as crude leather or a screw, is embodied once and for all in some final product, such as a shoe or a piece of furniture, which is sold to the consumer. A plant or a machine, such as a textile factory or a baker's oven, is used over a period of time to produce a continuous output of goods for final consumption, so many shirts or so many loaves of bread a year.

A raw material which is being worked up into a final consumption good may go through a series of stages, and at each stage it must be regarded as a different product. Thus at 8 a.m. on day 0 there may be an input of some labour (L_0) and of some crude leather (J_0) which has become partially treated leather (J_0') by the end of day 0. On day 1 there is an input of some more labour (L_1) and of this partially treated leather (J_1') which by the end of the day has become an output of a slightly more fully treated product (J_1''); and so on. J is a different product from J' which in turn is a different product from J'', and so on. Each day the product changes until at last at 4 p.m. on day 100 it emerges as a finished shoe (X_{100}). Each day the output becomes more valuable; but the important thing to realize is that it is not the same product.

In the case of a machine there is a similar point. A new loom is used as an input on day 0 (K_0) together with some labour (L_0) to produce by the end of the day some shirts (X_0); and it is itself available at the end of the day ($\bar{K}_0'$). But the loom at the end of the day ($\bar{K}_0'$) is not the same product as it was at the beginning of the day (K_0). It is more used and it is older (i.e. has a day's less useful life in front of it). A new loom (K) will be worth more than an older and more used loom (K'). On day 1 the day-old loom (K_1') is used with some labour (L_1) to produce some shirts (X_1) and a two-day old loom ($\bar{K}_2''$); and so on. A raw material at different stages of being worked up into a finished product or a machine at different stages of its useful life must be treated as a different product. There is thus a vast variety of intermediate products.

While the distinction between raw materials or components on the one hand and plant or machinery on the other may be a useful one for some purposes, it is not in fact an absolute one. Thus an intermediate product may partake of both qualities; a sheep may be being reared both for its wool and its mutton, but it is a machine in so far as it is being used to produce so much wool per annum and a raw material in so far as it is being worked up into mutton. Moreover, a raw material may be being worked up into a machine; steel may be being embodied once for all into a loom. Or a machine may be being used to produce an annual output of components; a lathe may be turning a series of axles for embodiment in bicycles. And there are many much more complicated chains of relationship: some of a raw material (steel) may be used to produce a machine (a coal cutter) which is used to produce a raw material (coal) which is used to produce a still larger supply of the first raw material (steel) which is used to produce a machine (a loom) which is used to produce a consumption good (a shirt). Instruments of production display an almost infinite variety and have a myriad interconnections.

With these considerations in mind we shall think of the productive system in the following way. We shall continue to treat the day as our atom of time for thinking about the firm or farm. At 8 a.m. on day 0 the entrepreneur who is running any firm or farm hires a certain number of hours of work from each of a number of workers, these services to be provided during day 0 and to be paid after they have been provided, i.e. at 8 a.m. on day 1. In this respect our model is exactly the same as it has been throughout the earlier chapters of this volume (cf. Chapter II, pp. 33–34 above). But at 8 a.m. on day 0 our entrepreneur does not (as we have hitherto assumed) hire the services of a unit of land or of a unit of a stock of a capital good; instead of this we now assume that he purchases the natural resource or instrument of production outright. We have already alluded to the reason for making this change in our model. So long as land (N) was assumed to be constant in amount and quality it was easy to assume that its services were hired for a day and that at the end of the day the same amount of land of the same quality must be returned to the owner (just as the worker whose services were hired for a day went home the same free man at the end of the day's work). But if the natural resource is used up or altered in quality in the course of the day's operation, it is no longer possible to analyse the situation in terms simply of hiring its services for a day. And similarly with the capital good. So long as there was only one man-made product (a stock of corn) it was simple to say what was meant by hiring the services of that capital good for one day; the same amount of the same product must be returned to the owner at the end of the day. But where the capital good may itself be used up or altered in quality in the course of the day's operations one cannot readily build a model simply in terms of hiring its use for a day.

Thus all the instruments of production, whether natural resources or man-made, are in our new model owned by the entrepreneurs running the actual firms and farms which are using them. But the entrepreneur who thus owns the instruments may have borrowed the money for their purchase directly or indirectly from other citizens so that it is not only entrepreneurs who are property owners; the entrepreneurs' ownership of the land may be offset by Mr A's ownership of securities of one kind or another which represent the indebtedness of the entrepreneur and his firm or farm to Mr A.

At 8 a.m. on day 0 then the entrepreneur hires the services of labour and also purchases the instruments of production of all kinds which he is going to use in the firm during day 0. These are the inputs of day 0 into the firm. Production goes on during the day; at 4 p.m. operations cease and there is a certain output ready for sale. This output consists both of finished consumption goods now ready for sale to Mrs A, Mrs B, Mrs C, etc., and also of all the instruments of production which are left over from the operations of day 0 or have been produced during the operations of day 0. At 8 a.m. on day 1 this output of the previous day is all sold by the entrepreneur. Mrs A B C, etc., all purchase their consumption goods for the families' needs at 8 a.m. each day, purchasing on day 1 the output of day 0. The instruments of production produced during or left over from the operations of day 0 are also all 'sold' at 8 a.m. on day 1 for use by entrepreneurs during the operations of day 1. Some will actually be sold by one entrepreneur to another (e.g. by one firm producing raw materials, component parts, tools, or machines for use by other firms) but a very large amount of any one firm's output in this sense will, of course, be 'sold' back by the entrepreneur to himself for use during the coming days. A farm's land and tractors or a firm's plant and machinery which appears as its output at 4 p.m. on day 0 will be sold back to the same firm or farm at 8 a.m. on day 1 for use as part of its instruments of production during day 1.

This may seem a very unnatural way of representing things; but it must be remembered that we are assuming perfect competition in all markets, including the market for every instrument of production. A firm's plant and machinery or a farm's land and tractors could thus be sold at the ruling market price if the entrepreneur wished to do so or they could be supplemented by purchase of additional amounts at these ruling prices. What we are representing is the fact that in this system the firm's gross output at the end of the day's operations will next morning have a definite value set by the competitive market prices ruling at 8 a.m. that morning. The value of this gross output is

K

the amount of money for which it could be sold. In fact part is sold to final consumers or to other entrepreneurs and part is retained in the firm; but to make clear the fact that in our competitive markets the whole has a definite market value we simply speak as if the whole output were sold in the market and the entrepreneur bought from the market what he planned to use during the coming day.

We shall explain at length in the next chapter the modifications which we shall make in our assumptions about the monetary and financial institutions in order to make them relevant to the problems of a many-product economy. But we shall still be assuming (i) that there is a currency unit which we will continue to call the \$1 note and (ii) that there is a Central Bank which sets at 8 a.m. each day a rate of interest at which money can be lent or borrowed for the day. Thus i_0 will represent the rate of interest at which the Central Bank will lend or borrow money at 8 a.m. on day 0, the principal and interest being repayable at 8 a.m. on day 1.

We can now illustrate our model by considering the profit and loss account in respect of, say, process a operated on a unitary scale ($S_{a0} = 1$) on day 0. The outputs produced on day 0 (X_a, Y_a, $\bar{J}_a$, $\bar{K}_a$, and $\bar{N}_a$) are sold at 8 a.m. on day 1 at the prices then ruling (P_{x1}, P_{y1}, P_{j1}, P_{k1}, and P_{n1}). The costs incurred at the same time (i.e. at 8 a.m. on day 1) are the wages of the labour employed during day 0 ($W_{l0}L_a$) and the cost with interest of the other inputs purchased at 8 a.m. on day 0 at the prices then ruling i.e. $(1 + i_0)\,(P_{j0}J_a + P_{k0}K_a + P_{n0}N_a)$.[1]

Thus the excess of receipts over outgoings at 8 a.m. on day 1 in respect of the operation of process a on a unit scale during day 0 is

$$P_{x1}X_a + P_{y1}Y_a + P_{j1}\bar{J}_a + P_{k1}\bar{K}_a + P_{n1}\bar{N}_a$$
$$-W_{l0}L_a - (1 + i_0)(P_{j0}J_a + P_{k0}\bar{K}_a + P_{n0}N_a).$$

This can be expressed as

$$\left.\begin{aligned}
&P_{x1}X_a + P_{y1}Y_a \\
&+ P_{j1}(\bar{J}_a - J_a) + P_{k1}(\bar{K}_a - K_a) + P_{n1}(\bar{N}_a - N_a) \\
&+ (P_{j1} - P_{j0})J_a + (P_{k1} - P_{k0})K_a + (P_{n1} - P_{n0})N_a \\
&- W_{l0}L_a \\
&- i_0(P_{j0}J_a + P_{k0}K_a + P_{n0}N_a)
\end{aligned}\right\} \qquad (15.1)$$

[1] It is to be remembered that all the prices (i.e. all the P's) are those ruling at the beginning of the day to which the subscript refers. Thus P_{x1} is the price of X ruling at 8 a.m. on day 1. But in the cases of the wage rate payable for the hire of a unit of labour (W_l) and of the rate of interest payable for a loan of money (i) the subscript refers to the day for which the labour was hired and the money

In this last expression the terms in the first row are simply the receipts at 8 a.m. on day 1 for the sale of the output of consumption goods. The terms in the second row are the values (at the prices ruling at 8 a.m. on day 1) of the net outputs (if $\bar{J}_a > J_a$, etc.) or the cost (also at the prices ruling at 8 a.m. on day 1) of the net inputs (if $J_a < J_a$, etc.) of the intermediate products with which process a is concerned either as net outputs or net inputs. The terms in the third row make up the capital gains or losses made on the capital goods bought at the prices ruling at 8 a.m. on day 0 and sold or accounted for at the prices ruling at 8 a.m. on day 1. Thus if P_j has risen $(P_{j1} > P_{j0})$, there is an appreciation in the course of day 1 in the value of the capital $(P_{j0}J_a)$ invested in J, this capital gain being equal to $(P_{j1} - P_{j0})J_a$. The term in the fourth row is simply the wages payable at 8 a.m. on day 1 in respect of the labour employed in process a during day 0. The term in the last row is the interest payable at 8 a.m. on day 1 on the capital invested at 8 a.m. on day 0 in the purchase of the capital goods at that time $(P_{j0}J_a + P_{k0}K_a + P_{n0}N_a)$. Thus the expression states that the net profit or loss actually made on the operations of day 0 and realized at 8 a.m. on day 1 is the receipts from the sale of consumption goods *plus* the receipts from selling the net outputs of any capital goods *plus* the capital gains on any capital goods which have appreciated in value *less* the costs of buying the net inputs of any capital goods *less* the capital losses on any capital goods which have depreciated in value *less* the wage costs *less* the interest payable on the capital invested in the process at the beginning of day 1.

So much for the net profit or loss actually realized on process a if it is operated during day 0. Let us now consider how it is that the prices fixed at 8 a.m. on day 0 are determined in our model. At 8 a.m. on day 0 any entrepreneur has a given set of expectations about the prices which will rule at 8 a.m. on day 1; in accordance with the notation described on page 38 above, we will call these prices which at the beginning of day 0 are expected to rule at the beginning of day 1 ${}_0P_{x1}$, ${}_0P_{y1}$, ${}_0P_{j1}$, ${}_0P_{k1}$, and ${}_0P_{n1}$. If the prices, wage rate, and rate of interest actually ruling at 8 a.m. on day 0 are P_{x0}, P_{y0}, P_{j0}, P_{k0}, P_{n0}, W_{l0}, and i_0, the net profit or loss expected by this entrepreneur at 8 a.m. on day 0 to be gained on operating process a will be exactly as given in (15.1) with the substitution of ${}_0P_{x1}$, ${}_0P_{y1}$, ${}_0P_{j1}$, ${}_0P_{k1}$, and ${}_0P_{n1}$ for P_{x1}, P_{y1}, P_{j1}, P_{k1}, and P_{n1}. And similarly for the net profits or losses to be expected on the other processes.

Now at 8 a.m. on day 0 (i) i_0 is fixed by the Central Bank, (ii) each entrepreneur will have certain price expectations (${}_0P_{x1}$, ${}_0P_{y1}$, etc.),

borrowed. Thus W_{l0} and i_0 refer to the wage rate and interest fixed at 8 a.m. on day 0 but payable at 8 a.m. on day 1.

(iii) the input and output co-efficients of each process are determined technically (L_a, X_a, Y_a, $\bar{J}_a$, J_a, etc.), (iv) there will be certain total quantities of labour (L_0) and of land (N_0), seeking employment; and (v) yesterday's (i.e. day -1's) outputs of the various intermediate products will have determined the quantities of the intermediate products available to be bought for inputs at 8 a.m. on day 0 ($\bar{J}_{-1} \geqslant J_0$, etc.). Given these known elements in the market situation competition between the entrepreneurs at 8 a.m. on day 0 will determine the prices $P_{j0}\, P_{k0}\, P_{n0}$ and the wage rate W_{l0}.

If these input prices were very low very many entrepreneurs would expect very many processes to be very profitable. Competition among the entrepreneurs would bid up the prices and would bid up especially the prices of those inputs which were important in the processes which were expected to be most profitable by most entrepreneurs. As these prices rose, certain entrepreneurs would drop out of the bidding for inputs for certain processes which at lower input prices they expected to be profitable but which they now expect to show a loss. Thus as the input prices are bid up there will be a smaller and smaller excess demand for inputs.

If expectations were held with absolute certainty (which, be it noted, does not necessarily imply that the expectations turn out in fact to be correct) and if each entrepreneur could borrow without limit at the given rate of interest i_0, a market equilibrium of input prices at 8 a.m. on day 0 could not exist so long as any single entrepreneur expected a profit on any single process. For so long as this were so it would pay that entrepreneur to expand the scale of that operation still further. This could mean that if one particular entrepreneur were more optimistic about all future prices than any of his competitors the whole of the economic activity of the community would be concentrated in his hands. He would outbid his competitors on all processes. Our model can be saved from this absurd result in either of two ways.

In the first place, we may assume that expectations are not held with absolute certainty. If an entrepreneur does not hold his expectations with complete certainty about the selling prices which will rule for his outputs at 8 a.m. on day 1, he will not expand the scale of any process indefinitely even though he expects on balance to make a profit on it. For if he invests a very great deal of capital in any one process, he stands to make an intolerable loss if his expectation should in fact turn out to be badly wrong. For this sort of reason entrepreneurs will drop out of the bidding for inputs when they have acquired certain amounts of inputs even though they may still expect to make a net profit; and so the market for the inputs at 8 a.m. on day 0 will be cleared even though many entrepreneurs, some more and some less optimistic about prices, are taking on quantities of inputs in many processes. We will examine these effects of uncertainty in Chapters XXI and XXII below.

In the second place, we could assume that while expectations were held with certainty there were always a large number of entrepreneurs who held any one set of expectations, so that these could continue to be competition between them. Thus entrepreneurs A_1 A_2, A_3, etc., might be specially optimistic about the future price of X, while entrepreneurs B_1, B_2, B_3, etc., were specially optimistic about the price of Y, and so on. In this case the entrepreneurs in group A would undertake the processes which were intensive in the output of X, while entrepreneurs in group B undertook the processes which were intensive in the output of Y, and so on. In this case while many different processes might be undertaken (i) no process would be being undertaken on which the entrepreneur concerned expected to make a loss and (ii) all processes which were undertaken would be on terms on which the entrepreneur in question would expect just to cover his costs and to make neither profit nor loss. Proposition (i) is obvious. Proposition (ii) is true for the following reason. Suppose that a profit were still expected on any one process by any one entrepreneur. Since *ex hypothesi* there is a large number of competing entrepreneurs with this same set of expectations, they would all in competition with one another try to expand this process and in consequence they would bid up the prices of the relevant inputs until no net profit was expected by them.

It is obvious that if group A's expectations differ from group B's, and so on, then it is highly probable that a large number of different processes will in fact be operated, group A being specially optimistic about the future price of X and therefore operating a process which was particularly intensive in the output of X, and so on. But even if all entrepreneurs held exactly the same set of expectations, so that no individual entrepreneur was specially attracted to any one process, it would not follow that only one process would be chosen for operation. Consider two situations on day 0. In situation I the expected price of X $({}_0P_{x1})$ is rather high while the expected price of Y $({}_0P_{y1})$ is rather low, and in situation II these expectations are reversed $({}_0P_{x1}$ being relatively low and ${}_0P_{y1}$ relatively high). In all other respects the two situations are the same; the total supplies of the available inputs (L_0, J_0, K_0, N_0, etc.) are the same; technical knowledge (the range of processes a, b, etc., available for operation) is the same; and all other price expectations $({}_0P_{j1}, {}_0P_{k1}$, etc.) are the same.

To take an example, comparing situation I with situation II the price which is expected to rule at 8 a.m. on day 1 for butter (X) is higher, and that for shirts (Y) is lower. Thus a change of expectations from those of situation II to those of situation I will make butter-intensive processes show a net profit and shirt-intensive processes a net loss. Entrepreneurs will, therefore, plan at 8 a.m. on day 0 to expand the former and to contract the latter processes. But as this happens the demand for inputs (cows and churns) in which the butter-intensive processes are intensive will go up, while the demand for inputs (looms and raw cotton) in which the latter processes are intensive will go down. The prices at 8 a.m. on day 0 of the former inputs will rise and of the latter inputs will fall. There will also be a reshuffling of inputs among the processes. Some labour may be attracted by an improved wage offer to transfer to processes in which more butter can be produced by using more labour with given amounts of cows and churns away from processes in which less shirts will be produced because less labour is employed with a given amount of looms and raw cotton. Thus an equilibrium suitable to situation I expectations can be found such that (i) no processes are worked which are expected to be unprofitable and (ii) all processes which are worked are expected just to cover their costs. This equilibrium is achieved by a rise in the price of inputs in which butter-production is intensive and a fall in the price of inputs in which shirt-production is intensive; and in the process of readjustment there will be some expansion of butter production and some contraction of shirt production to meet the higher expected demand price for butter and the lower expected demand price for shirts.

The situation is in fact exactly comparable to that discussed in Chapters IX, XI, and XIV of *The Stationary Economy*. Producers expect certain selling prices for outputs $(_0P_{x1}, {}_0P_{y1}, {}_0P_{j1}, {}_0P_{k1}, {}_0P_{n1})$. There are certain total supplies of inputs or factors of production (L_0, J_0, K_0, N_0) available. They compete for these inputs to produce the outputs by means of processes of production which are determined by the given state of technical knowledge and which vary in their input-intensities and their output-intensities. As a result the prices offered for the inputs are determined; these resulting input prices are W_{l0} in the case of L_0, and $(1 + i_0)P_{j0}$, $(1 + i_0)P_{k0}$, and $(1 + i_0)P_{n0}$ in the cases of J_0, K_0, and N_0; for in the case of these inputs of capital goods the cost of each input which must be compared with the selling price of the output is the price of that capital good plus a day's interest on that capital cost.

These input prices will then measure the (expected) value of the marginal product of each input. As explained in Chapters XI and XIV of *The Stationary Economy*, in these conditions the price paid for any one input in a competitive condition will measure the value of its marginal product. Suppose, for example, that at 8 a.m. on day 0 there had been one more unit of J_0 for sale in the market for capital goods. The price of this input (P_{j0}) would tend to fall so that its cost to users $(1 + i_0)P_{j0}$ would fall. Processes which were input-intensive in J_0 would tend to expand. The prices of other inputs which were also intensive in these processes would be driven up. There would be a general reshuffling of the inputs among the processes until one more unit of J_0 were employed with the same amount of the other inputs (L_0, K_0, N_0). As a result there would be increases in certain outputs and, perhaps, decreases in certain other outputs. The value of the marginal product of J_0 would be the selling price of those outputs which had gone up less the selling price of those outputs which had gone down, and this would be equal to $(1 + i_0)P_{j0}$.[1]

So far throughout this chapter we have treated the productive system as if at any one time it were composed of a finite (even though very large) number of separate processes a, b, c, etc., each of which had a set of fixed co-efficients of inputs and outputs. An alternative model would be to assume that co-efficients were not fixed but that there was a continuous possibility of substitution between one input and another, and between one output and another and a continuous possibility of transformation of one input into any one output. In *The Stationary Economy* we have already argued[2] that if there are very large number of different processes with very fine gradations in the differences between their fixed technical co-efficients, then we can treat a model based on fixed co-efficients as if there were in fact continuous substitutability and transformability between inputs and outputs. To substitute a little labour for a little land in dairy farming one moves from a process which produces a unit of butter with a certain amount of land and a certain amount of labour to one which is otherwise exactly the same but employs a little more land and a little less labour. We shall for the rest of this volume assume that there is a very large range of fixed-co-efficient processes with very fine gradations in the co-efficients so that, while we can use the fixed co-efficient type of model for our analysis, we can also talk of the system, when we wish to do so, as if there were continuous substitutability and transformability between inputs and outputs.

It is, however, to be noted that whereas in *The Stationary Economy* and in the preceding chapters of the present volume we have been conducting the analysis in terms of the net marginal products of the inputs (including the net marginal product of the single capital good K in the preceding chapters of this volume) we shall for the rest of this volume be speaking in terms of the net marginal product of the input labour (L) but of the gross marginal products of the inputs of the capital goods (J, K, N). As far as labour is concerned, there is

[1] Cf. *The Stationary Economy*, p. 183.
[2] Cf. *The Stationary Economy*, pp. 159-60.

little that need be said. Our present treatment differs in no respect
from the previous treatment in *The Stationary Economy* and in the
earlier chapters of this volume.

But as far as capital instruments of production are concerned,
there is an important difference. Consider the marginal product of J_0.
Suppose that one more unit of input J_0, the other inputs remaining
constant, would, after the appropriate reshuffling of the inputs
among the various processes, lead to changes in outputs in the
economy as a whole of ΔX_0, ΔY_0, ΔJ_0, $\Delta \bar{K}_0$, and $\Delta \bar{N}_0$, some of
which terms might be negative. Then the value of the *gross* marginal
product of J_0 is

$$P_{x1}\Delta X_0 + P_{y1}\Delta Y_0 + P_{j1}\Delta J_0 + P_{k1}\Delta \bar{K}_0 + P_{n1}\Delta \bar{N}_0 \quad (15.2)$$

The *gross* cost of one more unit of J_0 is $(1 + i_0)P_{j0}$ and, as we have
seen, in equilibrium these two expressions would be equal. Now the
value of the *net* marginal product of J_0 can be considered as the value
of the gross marginal product less the cost of replacing the unit of J_0
itself; and the net cost of using one more unit of J_0, i.e. the cost of
hiring the services of one unit of J_0 for one day, can be considered as
the gross cost of J_0 less the cost of replacing that unit. Thus we could
express the equality between the *net* cost of hiring for one day the
services of a unit of J_0 and the value of the *net* marginal product of
J_0 by the equation

$$(1 + i_0)P_{j0} - P_{j1} = P_{x1}\Delta X_0 + P_{y1}\Delta Y_0$$
$$+ P_{j1}\Delta J_0 + P_{k1}\Delta \bar{K}_0 + P_{n1}\Delta \bar{N}_0 - P_{j1}$$

If, as we assumed in the earlier chapters of this volume, there were
only one product, namely J_0 in our example, we would have
$\Delta X_0 = \Delta Y_0 = \Delta \bar{K}_0 = \Delta \bar{N}_0 =$ zero. If, as we were also assuming in
the earlier chapters of this volume, the money price of this product
were kept constant, we would have $P_{j0} = P_{j1}$. In this case the above
equation reduces to

$$i_0 P_{j0} = (\Delta J_0 - 1)P_{j0}$$
$$\text{or } i_0 = \Delta J_0 - 1$$

In this case $\Delta J_0 - 1$ is the net marginal product of an input of one
unit of the capital good J_0, since it is the gross increment of output
(ΔJ_0) less the replacement of that one unit of input; and this is in this
case equal to the rate of interest i_0. This is the simple formula
which we were able to use in Part 1 of this volume. We can no longer
do so. We shall have to argue in terms of the *gross* cost of purchasing
one more unit of any capital good being in competitive conditions
equal to the expected value of its *gross* marginal product.

There are essentially two reasons for this.

In the first place, the quality of an instrument may change from one day to the next. A 51-day-old loom is not the same thing as a 50-day-old loom. The measurement of a net product, however, involves the measurement of the output that remains after the replacement of the original input in precisely the same form.

In the second place, the prices of various instruments may vary from day to day. Even if a 51-day-old loom were exactly the same instrument as a 50-day-old loom, the entrepreneur purchasing the 50-day-old loom would consider as part of his expected profit not merely the value of the net output of the loom but any expected appreciation in the value of the loom itself.

This second point can be put in the following way. From (15.2) we know (assuming the amount of N to remain constant) that the value of the gross addition to the product due to the input on day 0 of one more unit of J is

$$P_{x1}\Delta X_0 + P_{y1}\Delta Y_0 + P_{j1}\Delta J_0 + P_{k1}\Delta K_0$$

The rate of profit on the additional unit of J_0 (i'_{j0}) is then given by the formula

$$i'_{j0} = \frac{P_{x1}\Delta X_0 + P_{y1}\Delta Y_0 + P_{j1}\Delta J_0 + P_{k1}\Delta K_0 - P_{j0}}{P_{j0}}$$

since this is equal to the addition to tomorrow's gross receipts less today's additional cost (P_{j0}) expressed as a ratio to the cost of today's investment (P_{j0}); or, in other words, the rate of profit on the additional investment is the additional profit made expressed as a ratio to the cost of the additional investment.

It follows that

$$i'_{j0} = \frac{P_{x1}\Delta X_0 + P_{y1}\Delta Y_0 + P_{k1}\Delta K_0 + P_{j1}(\Delta J_0 - 1)}{P_{j0}} + \frac{P_{j1} - P_{j0}}{P_{j0}}$$

But $P_{x1}\Delta X_0 + P_{y1}\Delta Y_0 + P_{k1}\Delta K_0 + P_{j1}(\Delta J_0 - 1)$ is the value of the *net* marginal product of J, since $\Delta J_0 - 1$ is the *net* addition to J produced through an input of 1 unit of J_0 leading to an output of ΔJ_0 units. But in a competitive system the value of the marginal net product of J is equal to the rental which would be paid for the hire of the services of a unit of J for one day, i.e. it is equal to W_{j0}. Moreover, $\dfrac{P_{j1} - P_{j0}}{P_{j0}}$ is the proportional rise in the price of J between 8 a.m. on day 0 and day 1. We can, therefore, say that in our competitive economy in equilibrium with perfect foresight

$$i'_0 = \frac{W_{j0}}{P_{j0}} + p_{j0}$$

or, in words, that the rate of profit on J equals the current rate of return on J plus the rate of capital gain on J. And similarly for the other instruments of production:

$$i'_{k0} = \frac{W_{k0}}{P_{k0}} + p_{k0} \quad \text{etc.}$$

If the economic system is to be in equilibrium as it moves through time, the rate of profit on each instrument must be the same (or else some entrepreneur would wish that he had invested more capital in the high yielder and less in the low yielder) and it must also be equal to the rate of interest at which money can be borrowed (or else entrepreneurs would wish that they had increased or decreased the total amount of money borrowed for investment in the instrument). We can conclude then that in competitive equilibrium growth we must have each day

$$i = \frac{W_j}{P_j} + p_j = \frac{W_k}{P_k} + p_k = \quad \text{etc.}$$

This, alas, is a much more complicated state of affairs than the simple condition

$$i = \frac{W_k}{P_k} = W_k$$

which has been all that we have required in Part 1 of this volume (cf. equation (4.3)).

If, however, we allow for the great variety of instruments of production and for the expression of their marginal products in gross rather than in net terms, the principles upon which entrepreneurs will act in attempts to maximize their incomes are basically the same as those which we have discussed at great length in *The Stationary Economy*. They will make adjustments to their input programmes, their output programmes, and their production programmes so long as such adjustments are likely to increase profits. As we have seen in *The Stationary Economy* the profitability of such adjustments rests upon two sets of considerations. First, one must know what are the technical possibilities of substituting one input for another, of substituting one output for another, or transforming one input into another output.[1] Second, one must know what are the market prices at which the inputs can be purchased and the outputs sold.

---

[1] There exist, of course, as before possibilities of complementarities between inputs or between outputs in input and output programmes and possibilities of antipathies between an input and an output in production programmes. See *The Stationary Economy*, pp. 136–46.

In *The Stationary Economy* there were no man-made instruments of production among the inputs or the outputs; now there are. Otherwise the principles of profit maximization are the same: industries which are showing a profit will be expanded and those which are showing a loss will be contracted; within any industry one input (whether it be of an original factor or of a man-made instrument of production) should be substituted for another or one output (whether it be of a consumption good or of an instrument of production) for another if the ratio between their prices differs from the technically possible marginal rate of substitution between them; and within any industry the amount of any one input (of any kind) which is transferred into a given output (of any kind) should be changed if the marginal product of the input in terms of the output differs from the ratio between their market prices.

In *The Stationary Economy* we spoke of input programmes, output programmes, and production programmes being flexible or rigid according to the ease or difficulty of substituting one input for another, substituting one output for another, or transforming one input into another output. We will now give a few examples of the flexibilities and rigidities which may be introduced into such programmes by the existence of man-made instruments of production.

In input programmes very considerable flexibility may exist in the choice between certain raw materials. Aluminium or copper may be used according to their relative prices for the production of certain products. There may in some cases be some possibilities of substitutability between labour and raw materials. One method of production, requiring much labour, may cut timber very carefully so as to economize its use, while an alternative method may economize labour by cutting the timber in an easier but more lavish way. There may, of course, be great rigidities in the use of machines which are already built and designed in a particular way. Thus a very specialized machine may require a fixed amount of labour to operate it and may consume a fixed amount of raw material per day. Here there is no possibility of substitution between labour and machine or raw material and machine. But it may be possible, when the time comes, to replace the machine with a different machine which is itself more expensive, but which uses less labour and/or less raw material input to achieve the same output.[1]

In the output programmes there is now one special possibility of high substitutability which it is important to note. In the model

---

[1] Apart, of course, from the output of the used machine itself. In the one case the process will produce, in addition to the finished product, a day-old machine of the first variety and in the second case it will produce the finished product plus a day-old machine of the second and more expensive variety.

which we have constructed in the present chapter we assume that consumption goods (X, Y) cannot be used as instruments of production (J, K) nor instruments of production as consumption goods. But there are certain products of which this seems untrue. Thus coal can be bought by final consumers for use in the domestic grate or by an entrepreneur to raise steam in a factory's boilers. Corn can be eaten as food or put back as seed or as feeding stuffs for animals into the productive system of the farm. Normally, however, if not universally, there are at least some slight differences in the product as sold for the two purposes. Domestic coal is likely to differ in size or quality or method of delivery from industrial coal. Corn is consumed by the final consumer only after processing or packaging into bread or other forms of foodstuff. But where the product used by the final consumer is practically the same as that used by industry there is a high degree of substitutability between the two products in the output programme. Thus domestic coal (X) and industrial coal (J) may be very easy substitutes for each other in the coal mine's output programme.

The existence of instruments of production will, however, in certain cases introduce a special form of rigidity into an output programme. We are treating as a firm's output at 4 p.m. on any day not only that amount of finished goods which it has produced during the day, but also that amount of instruments of production (including machines) which are left over from the day's operations for use in the productive process on the following day. Thus if shirts require looms for their production, the output of shirts of a textile factory on day 0 must be accompanied by an 'output' by the same factory on the same day of the looms used in their production and left over for use on day 1. There is thus a degree of rigidity in the output of finished products and the output of the machines actually used in their production.

The existence of instruments of production may involve special links between certain inputs and certain outputs. Thus if a particular product is necessarily made out of a given amount of a given raw material, there will be a fixed ratio between the output of that product and the input of that material. Often there is a choice between materials or even a choice between material and, say, labour (see p. 299 above) in the production of a product; but in some cases the linkage between an output and a raw material input may be a relatively fixed one. Another very strong linkage will exist between the input and output of machines. Thus if in a textile factory on any day there is an input of a loom of a certain age, there will that same evening necessarily be an output of a one-day-older loom, unless the loom has been scrapped in the course of the day.

Subject to these limitations it will be the entrepreneur's object to make such adjustments as are possible to his input, output, and production programmes until the rates of substitution between inputs and between outputs and the rates of transformation between any input and any output (whether the inputs be of hours of work or of instruments of production and whether the outputs be of final consumption goods or of instruments of production) correspond to the ratios between the market prices of the inputs and outputs concerned.

Note to Chapter XV

THE DEFINITION OF INCOME, SAVINGS, AND INVESTMENT IN A MANY-PRODUCT GROWING ECONOMY

The expression in (15.1) on page 290 gives the net entrepreneurial profit made in respect of the operation of process a on a unitary scale during day 0. The total entrepreneurial profits made in respect of the operation of all processes at the actual scales adopted on day 0 can, therefore, be expressed as

$$
\left.
\begin{aligned}
& P_{x1}X_0 + P_{y1}Y_0 \\
& + P_{j1}(\bar{J}_0 - J_0) + P_{k1}(\bar{K}_0 - K_0) + P_{n1}(\bar{N}_0 - N_0) \\
& + (P_{j1} - P_{j0})J_0 + (P_{k1} - P_{k0})K_0 + (P_{n1} - P_{n0})N_0 \\
& - W_{l0}L_0 \\
& - i_0(P_{j0}J_0 + P_{k0}K_0 + P_{n0}N_0) \\
& \text{where } X_0 = S_{a0}X_a + S_{b0}X_b + S_{c0}X_c + \ldots \text{ etc.}
\end{aligned}
\right\}
\tag{15.3}
$$

and similarly for Y_0, $\bar{J}_0$, J_0, $\bar{K}_0$, K_0, $\bar{N}_0$, N_0, and L_0.

But $W_{l0}L_0$ is the total wage bill paid in respect of the operations of day 0 and $i_0(P_{j0}J_0 + P_{k0}K_0 + P_{n0}N_0)$ is the total interest earned on capital in respect of its use during day 0. If we define the total national income as total entrepreneurial profit plus total wages plus total interest, then the sum of the first three lines in (15.3) above gives an expression for the national income of day 0.

The first of these three lines represents consumption. If we define investment as equal to savings and as income minus consumption, then the sum of the second and third lines of the expression in (15.3) measures savings and investment.

The second line in (15.3) measures the current value of net additions to the physical stock and the third line measures the increase in price of the initial physical capital stock. We have, therefore, defined income as including capital gains and investment as the increase in the value of the real capital stock (whether it be due to price or quantity increase) and not as the value of the net addition to the physical stock. Savings are accordingly defined as that part of income (inclusive of capital gains) which is not spent on consumption.

CHAPTER XVI

MONEY, PRICES, AND INTEREST IN A MANY-PRODUCT ECONOMY

We have shown in the last chapter that the decisions of the entrepreneurs in our many-product economy on any one day as to what to produce and what prices to offer for their inputs are essentially the same as those discussed at length for a many-product economy in *The Stationary Economy*, provided that we know at 8 a.m. on day 0—when the production decisions are made—what selling prices are expected to rule at 8 a.m. on day 1 for the outputs of the productive processes of day 0. We must accordingly turn our attention to the factors which determine the selling prices which, at 8 a.m. on any one day, are expected to rule at 8 a.m. on the following day.

This question can be broken down into two separate groups of questions. (1) What determines the general level of expected prices? Will there be a general inflation or deflation of prices? (2) What determines the expected relative prices? Will the price of one consumption good go up or down relatively to that of another consumption good? Will the price of one instrument of production go up or down relatively to that of another instrument of production? Will the prices of instruments of production be high or low relatively to those of consumption goods? In Part 1 of this volume in which we were assuming that there was only one product the second group of questions—about movements in relative prices—could not arise. The first group of questions—about movements in the general level of prices, i.e. about movements in the money price of our single product —was answered by making an assumption about monetary policy whereby the general level of money demand was so regulated that the money demand price offered for the single product was assumed to be kept stable and thus, through experience, was assumed to be expected to remain stable.

We can make a similar sort of assumption about financial policy in our present more complicated model, namely that the total money demand for products is so controlled that a general index of the money prices at which products can be sold is kept constant. We have then to decide what price index we shall assume to be stabilized and by what devices of financial policy this stabilization shall be achieved. We could in fact choose any price index we liked for our stabilization policy. At the present stage of our analysis it is little more than a device for providing a *numeraire* in terms of which we can measure and discuss relative prices. We choose then rather arbitrarily to assume that the financial authorities decide to stabilize a cost of living index, namely in an economy with only two consumption goods, X and Y, some index of the prices P_x and P_y. We shall not construct any elaborate price index for this purpose. Let us suppose simply that the authorities decide to stabilize the cost of 1 unit of X plus 1 unit of Y, or in other words to keep stable the sum of $P_x + P_y$.[1] Suppose $P_x + P_y$ is to be stabilized at \$2. Then if P_x rises to three times P_y we shall have $P_x = \$1 \cdot 50$ and $P_y = \$0 \cdot 50$, whereas if P_x falls to only half P_y we shall have $P_x = \$0 \cdot \dot{6}$ and $P_y = \$1 \cdot \dot{3}$; and so on. In each case $P_x + P_y = \$2 \cdot 0$.

But by what instruments of financial policy are we to assume that this stabilization of the money cost of living is achieved? On any day—e.g. at 8 a.m. on day 0—there will be certain supplies of X and Y for sale in the market, namely the outputs X_{-1} and Y_{-1} of day -1. The purchasers of these goods at 8 a.m. on day 0—Mrs A, Mrs B, Mrs C, etc.—will come into the market with certain sums to spend. Their husbands will have received certain incomes in wages and interest on their capital over the previous days and at 8 a.m. on day 0 will receive the wages and interest in respect of the productive activities of day -1. They will also at 8 a.m. on day 0 own certain accumulated properties. In view of these incomes and properties, and in view of the prospective rates of interest, their prospective earnings, their prospects of retirement, and their prospects of aid in their old age from their children or their intentions to accumulate property to bequeath to their children—in fact, in view of all the considerations which we have discussed in Chapters XII and XIII above—they will decide how much to spend on consumption goods on day 0 and how much to save. If the amount which they so determine to spend on consumption is low relatively to the supplies X_{-1} and Y_{-1}, then the price index $P_{x0} + P_{y0}$ will threaten to fall below its stabilized target, if on the other hand the amount to be spent on consumption is high and/or the supplies available are low, the price index will threaten to be driven up above the stabilized target.

The authorities can, however, influence the amount of income available for expenditure by consumers on day 0 by means of the budgetary policy already described in Chapter II (page 40 above).

---

[1] Our price index is a simple weighted average of the prices of X and Y, the weights given to the two prices being the same. We can regard this as the result of choosing units for the measurement of X and Y (and so of P_x and P_y) such that the number of units of X and the number of units of Y which enter into the 'basketful' of X and Y whose cost we wish to stabilize are the same.

We assume now that the authorities have a system of income taxes and of income subsidies which can be varied very rapidly, indeed in our model daily, so that the net income available to consumers can be so reduced or so supplemented as to induce them to cut down or to raise their total expenditure on consumption to the extent necessary to maintain the demand for consumption goods on any one day in such a relationship with the supplies of consumption goods coming on to the market that day that the price index $P_x + P_y$ is kept at its stabilized target. We assume that the authorities are so successful in this fiscal policy of control over consumers' demands that the price index is in fact successfully held on target each day and that, in consequence, all citizens expect—and correctly expect—that this cost-of-living index will remain stable in the future.

By an assumption about budgetary policy of this kind we can assume that a general index of prices of consumption goods is in fact stabilized so that producers come to expect such stability. But this does not, of course, mean that the future price of any one individual consumption good is known. Whether P_x will be high or low is still a matter on which the individual entrepreneur must form his own expectation in the light of the relevant probable market developments. This involves the whole range of considerations which we examined in Chapters II and III of *The Stationary Economy*. What are likely to be the supplies of X and of all other consumers' products and, in particular, of products which are close substitutes for, or complements of, X in consumers' demands, which will come on to the market tomorrow? What is likely to have occurred to consumers' preferences as between these products as their tastes are changing or as the distribution of income between rich and poor is changing or as the average standard of living is rising or falling? Each entrepreneur, as he makes up his mind at 8 a.m. today about what his production plans should be, will have to make his own assessment as to whether the price obtainable tomorrow for X is likely to be appreciably different from the price of X which ruled yesterday in the market.[1]

So much for the prices which may be expected at 8 a.m. on day 0 to rule for consumption goods at 8 a.m. on day 1 ($_0P_{x1}$, $_0P_{y1}$). We turn

[1] If it were only a question of forecasting one day ahead what changes are likely to have taken place in the markets for particular consumption goods, the problem would not be at all intractable. But as we shall see below (pp. 246–257) in order to forecast what the value of an instrument of production will be in the immediate future it will often be necessary to consider the probable developments in the much more distant future of the markets for the consumption goods which that instrument will produce. Market forecasts of consumption goods are above all needed for the determination of the value of capital goods, including, of course, all consumption goods which are still in the process of production.

now to the determination of the prices which may be expected to rule for instruments of production $({_0}P_{j1}, {_0}P_{k1})$. In order to discuss this we must return once more to the financial policies by means of which we are assuming that the cost of living is stabilized. We have assumed a policy of budgetary taxation or subsidization of incomes of a kind which so adjusts each day the amount of net spendable incomes to the available supplies of consumption goods that the price index, $P_x + P_y$, is stabilized. But this policy, it would seem, might involve a permanent budget deficit if it was continuously necessary for the government, in order to prevent a fall in the price index, $P_x + P_y$, to supplement private incomes by payment of income subsidies out of the budget; or in the reverse situation the policy might involve a continuous budget surplus. What does this imply? And how might it be possible, if so desired, to get rid of the continuing lack of balance in the budget without abandoning the policy of price stabilization? Let us consider the case in which a continuous supplementation of private incomes through a budget deficit becomes necessary for the stabilization of the price index, $P_x + P_y$.

The budget deficit in this case represents a way by which private savings are accompanied by public dissavings, so that total savings are reduced (cf. Chapter I, pp. 24–25 above). The government is borrowing part of the savings of the private citizens by means of the government debt which it is issuing so as to obtain the money to pay in income subsidies to the private citizens, so as to raise their demand for consumption goods above the level which it would otherwise attain. Such action would not have been necessary if either (1) private consumers had themselves decided to save a smaller proportion of their incomes or (2) if private producers had decided to devote more of their resources to the production of instruments of production and less to the production of consumption goods. In this latter case the supply of consumption goods on the market would be diminished so that the income subsidies would no longer be needed to maintain the demand prices for them and, at the same time, the savings of the private citizens could be being used to purchase the greater quantity of instruments of production which were being made available and which would need borrowed funds for their purchase.

If the monetary authorities reduce the rate of interest and in particular, as we shall show later in this chapter, if they persuade entrepreneurs to believe that this lowered rate of interest will last into the future, there will be an incentive on the part of the entrepreneurs to increase their demand for instruments of production and thus to offer higher prices for instruments of production relatively to the prices of consumption goods. And if as a result higher prices of instruments of production relatively to prices of consumption goods are expected to rule in the future, inputs will be devoted to the production of instruments of production rather than of consumption goods. The output of instruments of production will rise relatively to the output of consumption goods and income subsidies will no longer be required to maintain the demand price of consumption goods.

Thus the authorities can stabilize the prices of consumption goods *either* by (1) income subsidization with a high rate of interest, in which case the price offered for instruments of production will be relatively low, the output of instruments will be low and of consumption goods high, and the budget deficit will be a means of reducing total savings below private savings, *or else* at the other extreme by (2) income taxation and a very low rate of interest, in which case the price offered for instruments of production will be very high, their output will be high and the output of consumption goods will be low, and the taxation of personal incomes with the resulting budget surplus will be a means of supplementing private savings with public savings and of reducing total demand for consumption goods in line with their supply. Or, of course, an intermediate policy could be found whereby the rate of interest was set at a level which caused such a demand for instruments of production and thus such a pattern of output of instruments of production and of consumption goods that the balance of supply and demand for consumption goods was maintained without any continuing need for taxation or subsidization of private incomes. The choice between these combinations of budgetary policy (determining the level of income taxation or subsidization) and of monetary policy (determining the rate of interest) as instruments for the permanent stabilization of the price level $P_x + P_y$ will depend upon whether, on the grounds discussed above in Chapter VIII (pp. 106–110) and Chapter XIII (pp. 241–243) it is desired to raise or to reduce total savings above or below the level which private savings would find in the absence of income taxation or subsidization. We shall return to this question in our final chapter (cf. Chapter XXIII, pp. 489–499).

It remains, therefore, for us to explain how a change in the expected rate of interest will affect the expected price of instruments of production. We can best discuss this in the framework of the question what determines the expected price of any given instrument of production. If an entrepreneur at 8 a.m. on day 0 plans to produce an output of an instrument, namely J_0, what price will he expect to get for it when he sells it at 8 a.m. on day 1? On what, in other words, does $_0P_{j1}$ depend? This depends upon what value an entrepreneur at 8 a.m. on day 1 is likely to place on the use of such an instrument (J_1) as an input into his production system.

Let us approach the matter from the point of view of the purchaser of the instrument at 8 a.m. on day 1. Consider then entrepreneur A who at 8 a.m. on day 1 is making up his mind what price to offer for the instrument *J*. Suppose that the future course of the rate of interest and of all other prices, other than the price of the instrument itself, were precisely known. Suppose further that the instrument *J* has only one possible future use. If it is used at all, then all the various inputs (of labour and of other instruments) and outputs (of consumption goods and of other instruments) which will be associated with it on day 1 and on every future day are fixed and determined.

Let O_2, O_3, O_4, etc., be the amounts received at 8 a.m. on days 2, 3, 4, etc., for the sale of the outputs (other than the instrument itself) which will be produced by means of this instrument in the course of days 1, 2, 3, etc. Let I_1, I_2, I_3, etc., be the cost as at 8 a.m. on days 1, 2, 3, etc., of any inputs of other instruments which will be necessary to operate or develop the instrument in question on days 1, 2, 3, etc. Let W_2, W_3, W_4, etc., be the payments which will be made at 8 a.m. on days 2, 3, 4, etc., to labour for the development or operation of the instrument in the course of days 1, 2, 3, etc. Let i_1, i_2, i_3, etc., be the daily rates at which interest will be charged for loans used during days 1, 2, 3, etc. Let P_1 be the price which entrepreneur A will offer for *J* at 8 a.m. on day 1, and let $_1P_2''$, $_1P_3''$, etc., be the value which the instrument itself is expected at 8 a.m. on day 1 by entrepreneur A to have at 8 a.m. on days 2, 3, etc.[1] We assume further that entrepreneur A not only expects the instrument to be worth $_1P_3'''$ at 8 a.m. on day 3, but also expects that entrepreneur B at 8 a.m. on day 2 will expect the instrument to have this value at 8 a.m. on day 3 (i.e. $_2P_3''' = {}_1P_3'''$); and so on.

Now if entrepreneur A who purchases the instrument at 8 a.m. on day 1 in competition with others bids up the price of the instrument to its full value to him we shall have

$$(P_1 + I_1)(1 + i_1) = O_2 - W_2 + {}_1P_2''$$

so that $P_1 = -I_1 + \dfrac{O_2 - W_2 + {}_1P_2''}{1 + i_1}$. $P_1 + I_1$ is the outlay of money which entrepreneur A will make on day 1 for the purchase of the instrument in question and of any other instruments which must go with it. On this he pays interest at i_1, so that his total cost by the end of the day is $(P_1 + I_1)(1 + i_1)$. At 8 a.m. on day 2 he will receive O_2 for the sale of the output produced by the instrument during day 1 and $_1P_2''$ for the sale to entrepreneur B (who may be himself or some

---

[1] The physical instrument with which we are concerned (*J*) will be a different product (*J''*) on day 2 (after one day's use); it will be yet another product on day 3 (*J'''*) after two days' use; and so on (cf. page 287 above). *P* is the price of *J*, *P''* the price of *J'''*, and so on.

other entrepreneur) of the instrument itself. But entrepreneur A will be W_2 out of pocket on the payment for the labour services which operated or developed the machine on day 1. Thus if entrepreneur A bids the price of the machine on day 1 up to $P_1 = -I_1 + \dfrac{O_2 - W_2 + {}_1P_2'}{1 + i_1}$ he will make no profit or loss on the day's operations.

But what price can the instrument be expected to have on day 2? This will be given by a similar formula for day 2, so that

$$ {}_1P_2'' = -I_2 + \frac{O_3 - W_3 + {}_1P_3'''}{1 + i_2} $$

since entrepreneur B who takes on the machine on day 2 will be faced with the same market situation advanced by one day. If we use this value of ${}_1P_2''$ in the formula for P_1, we get

$$ P_1 = -I_1 $$
$$ + \frac{O_2 - W_2 - I_2}{1 + i_1} $$
$$ + \frac{O_3 - W_3 + {}_1P_3'''}{(1 + i_1)(1 + i_2)} $$

But ${}_1P_3'''$ can be obtained by a similar formula for day 3; and so on indefinitely for ${}_1P_4''''$, etc. We end up with the following value of P_1:

$$ P_1 = -I_1 $$
$$ + \frac{O_2 - W_2 - I_2}{1 + i_1} $$
$$ + \frac{O_3 - W_3 - I_3}{(1 + i_1)(1 + i_2)} $$
$$ + \dots\dots\dots\dots $$
$$ + \frac{O_T - W_T + {}_1P_T}{(1 + i_1)(1 + i_2) \dots (1 + i_{T-1})} $$

This expression has as many terms as there will be days $(T - 1)$ in the useful life of the instrument, ${}_1P_T$ being the expected scrap value of the machine at 8 a.m. on day T. Thus the value on day 1 of the instrument itself and of any other inputs that must necessarily go with it $(P_1 + I_1)$ will be the sum of a series of terms each relating to a subsequent day in the history of the instrument. Each term consists of the excess of the value of outputs over inputs $(O - W - I)$ which

will be payable at 8 a.m. on that day in connection with the processing
or the operation of the raw material or machine; but each of these
terms is discounted by a factor $\dfrac{1}{(1 + i_1)(1 + i_2) \ldots}$ which depends
upon the rates of interest which will rule on every day between 8 a.m.
on day 1 and 8 a.m. on the relevant future day. Let us call
$\dfrac{1}{(1 + i_1)(1 + i_2)(1 + i_3)}$ the 'discount factor for day 4' and denote it
by D_4, and similar for D_2, D_3, etc. Then we have

$$P_1 + I_1 = D_2(O_2 - W_2 - I_2) + D_3(O_3 - W_3 - I_3) + \text{etc.} \ldots$$

D_2, D_3, D_4, etc., will be progressively smaller fractions. The power of
compound interest is very great; and unless the rate of interest itself
is expected to fall progressively to zero, the discount factors which
refer to distant future dates will become very small indeed.

Suppose by way of illustration that the rate of interest is expected
to be the same for every future day and is expected to be either at a
daily rate of (i) 20 per cent or (ii) 10 per cent or (iii) 5 per cent per
annum ($i_1 = i_2 = i_3$, etc., = (i) 0·002, (ii) 0·001, and (iii) 0·0005).
Then Table VII gives the values which the discount factor D will have
for different periods ahead.[1]

Table VII

Value of Discount Factor

		Number of Years Ahead						
		1	2	5	10	25	50	100
Rate	(p.a.) 20%	0·82	0·67	0·37	0·14	0·0061	0·000096	0·0000000021
of	10%	0·90	0·82	0·61	0·37	0·082	0·0068	0·000045
Interest	5%	0·95	0·90	0·78	0·61	0·29	0·082	0·0067

Thus, for example, if the daily rate of interest is at a rate of 10 per
cent per annum, today's value of an instrument of production will be
enhanced by only just over 8 per cent (0·082) of the value of the
excess of output over input which the instrument of production will
make possible 25 years (i.e. 2500 days) hence. It is to be observed how
rapidly the discount factors drop towards zero for periods which are
a considerable number of years ahead.

[1] In the Table VII D is given for a number of years ahead. We are assuming
100 days in a year so that D for five years ahead is D_{500} in our notation. Similarly i
is the rate of interest per day, so that an $i = 0·002$ is a daily rate of interest of
$100 \times 0·002 = 20$ per cent per annum.

There is one other effect of compound interest which is brought out very well in Table VII. A change in the rate of interest which is expected to be permanent will have a much greater relative effect on those elements in the present value of an instrument of production which depend upon its earning power in the distant future than upon those which depend upon its earning power in the near future. As the table shows a rise in the rate of interest from 5 per cent to 10 per cent per annum will lower the discount factors for all elements in the present value of the instrument; since it costs more to borrow money, it will be less worth while to offer a high price now for an instrument whose earnings will come later. But because the interest charge is compounded (the cost of waiting for 3 days includes the interest payable at the beginning of day 4 which includes the interest payable on the interest payable at the beginning of day 3 which includes the interest payable on the interest payable at the beginning of day 2 on the money borrowed at the beginning of day 1) the rise in the rate of interest has a much more serious effect in reducing the present value of earnings in the distant future than of earnings in the near future. Thus from Table VII it can be seen that a rise in the rate of interest from 5 per cent to 10 per cent per annum will reduce the element of the present value which depends upon earnings 5 years hence in the ratio of $0 \cdot 78$ to $0 \cdot 61$ (i.e. a fall of 22 per cent) whereas in the case of earnings 25 years hence the reduction will be in the ratio of $0 \cdot 29$ to $0 \cdot 082$ (i.e. a fall of no less than 72 per cent).

Different types of instrument of production will have different patterns of expected yields over subsequent days. Let us take a few examples.

First, suppose someone is considering purchasing at 8 a.m. on day 1 some immature wine which he will simply keep for 5 years (500 days), without any cost of storage, until it is mature. Then all inputs and outputs are zero except O_{501} which is the final value of the wine. We then have from the formula on page 310:

$$P_1 = D_{501}O_{501}$$

Consider next an existing house which without any current repairs will last for ever bringing in a constant rent each day equal to O. Then all the I's and W's in the formula on page 310 are zero and $O_2 = O_3 = O_3 =$ etc. $= O$. We then have

$$P_1 = (D_2 + D_3 + D_4 + D_5 + \ldots)O.$$

If the rate of interest is expected to be constant at i, then we have

$$P_1 = \left\{ \frac{1}{1+i} + \frac{1}{(1+i)^2} + \frac{1}{(1+i)^3} + \text{etc.} \ldots \right\} O = \frac{O}{i}.$$

In other words if the rent received from the house is at a rate of $1 a day ($100 per annum) and the rate of interest is 10 per cent per annum, the value of the house is $1000. Whereas if the rate of interest were only 5 per cent per annum, the value of the house would be $2000. $100 a year represents a return of 10 per cent per annum on $1000 and of 5 per cent per annum on $2000.

Suppose next that the instrument of production were a half-finished machine on which I must be spent per day for the next year (i.e. days 1 to 100 inclusive) for its completion and which would then give a net yield of O per day for the next 10 years (i.e. from day 101 to 1100 inclusive). Then the formula would become

$$P_1 = -(1 + D_2 + D_3 + \ldots + D_{100})I$$
$$+(D_{101} + D_{102} + \ldots + D_{1100})O.$$

In this case the early elements in the series would be negative; the value on day 1 of the half-finished machine will be depressed by the out-of-pocket expenses which will still be necessary for its completion. These negative values must be more than offset by the discounted values of later earnings for it to have a positive net value on day 1.

We can now return to the question what determines the prices which entrepreneurs can expect to realize one day for any instrument of production which they produce during day 0. An entrepreneur who at 8 a.m. on day 0 is considering the production of an instrument for sale at 8 a.m. on day 1 must consider the factors (which we have just outlined) which will determine the price (P_1) which the purchaser of his product (who may, of course, well be himself) will offer for it. This price will depend upon (i) the time shape of the final outputs, (ii) the level of the final outputs, (iii) the prices of the final outputs, (iv) the time shape of the inputs, (v) the level of the inputs, (vi) the prices of the inputs, and (vii) the rates of interest that are expected to go with the use of the instrument in future periods. The expectation of increased earnings or decreased expenditures connected with the instrument at any time in the future will, of course, enhance its present value. But, particularly with high rates of interest, increases in earnings or decreases in expenditures which are expected in early periods will be much more influential than those which are expected for distant periods ahead.

In particular we can now justify our previous assertion (see p. 306 above) that a fall in the rate of interest is likely to raise the value (i.e. the expected selling price) of instruments of production.

If we write $O_2 - W_2 - I_2 = G_2$, $O_3 - W_3 - I_3 = G_3$, and so on, the formula on page 310 becomes

$$P_1 + I_1 = D_2G_2 + D_3G_3 + \ldots D_TG_T$$

where G_2 may be called the 'cash flow' of day 2—i.e., the excess of receipts (O_2) over expenditures ($W_2 + I_2$) expected to result on day 2 from the investment—and where T measures the useful life of the investment. We can say then that the value of the machine on day 1 (P_1) together with any other expenditure necessarily incurred with it (I_1) will be equal to the 'discounted cash flow' expected from it. With given expected cash flows (G_2, G_3, . . . G_T) the present value of the investment will be greater the higher are the discount factors (D_2, D_3, . . . D_T), i.e. the lower are the relevant rates of interest.

But while a reduction in the rate of interest which is expected to be permanent will tend to raise the expected prices of instruments of production, it will not raise them all by the same amount. It will affect the prices of instruments relatively to each other as well as raising the general level of prices of instruments relatively to the general level of the prices of consumption goods. A permanent fall in interest rates will, as we have seen from Table VII, have a much greater effect in raising the discount factors which apply to earnings and expenses in the distant future than to those which apply to earnings and expenses in the near future. Thus those instruments whose earnings will accrue in the distant future and whose expenses will accrue in the near future will be the most enhanced in present value by an expected fall in future interest rates. Those whose earnings are in the near future and whose expenses are relatively postponed will rise little in value.

In the preceding paragraphs we have tried to show the effect which changes in the rate of interest at which money can be lent and borrowed will have upon the selling price of an instrument of production. We have seen how a fall in the rate of interest will tend to raise the selling prices of instruments of production. But it is very clear from an examination of the discount factors on pages 310–312 above that the leverage effect of a fall in the rate of interest in raising the selling prices of instruments of production will be very much greater if the fall in the interest rate is expected to be permanent or at least long lasting. Suppose that initially the rate of interest is at a daily rate of 10 per cent per annum and is expected to remain at 10 per cent per annum indefinitely. Suppose then that on day 0 the day's rate of interest is reduced to 5 per cent per annum. Compare then two situations: in Situation I the rate is expected to remain at 5 per cent per annum for only one year but then to return to 10 per cent per annum for subsequent days, while in Situation II the rate is expected to remain permanently at the lower level of 5 per cent per annum. Then (see Table VII on page 310 above) before the change the discount factor for returns on an instrument 10 years ahead would be 0.37; in Situation I this would rise only to 0.39^{1} but in Situation II it would go up to 0.61. The permanent fall in the rate of interest would have a very much greater effect in raising the present value of distant future yields on any capital instrument.

But so far in this volume we have assumed that the Central Bank controls and fixes each day's interest solely by offering to borrow, or lend for the current day at a given daily rate of interest (i_0 at 8 a.m. on day 0, i_1 at 8 a.m. on day 1, and so on). If the Central Bank fixes only the rate of interest for each day, how can it influence the expectations of the citizens about the future rates of interest? If in fact it could reduce only the rate of interest for one day (without any effect on expected future rates of interest), the effect of interest-rate policy upon the present value of instruments of production would be negligible. The Central Bank could conceivably overcome this difficulty on one single occasion by undertaking a solemn pledge to keep its daily rate in the future at a given level, fixed now once and for all in advance. This would enable citizens to realize that a current reduction in the rate of interest would be permanent. But this, of course, would imply that the rate of interest could never again be changed, so that, whatever might happen in the economy, interest-rate policy could never be used again.

There is, however, an intermediate course for the Central Bank if it is willing to offer to borrow or lend on stated terms for periods longer than a single day. Let us take as the most simple example the man who is considering the purchase of an instrument of the kind considered on page 311 above. He is considering the price (P_1) to be offered at 8 a.m. on day 1 for a stock of wine which will cost nothing to hold but will be worth $100 ($O_{1001}$ = 100) in 10 years' time, i.e. at 8 a.m. on day 1001. If he can borrow $60 now from the Central Bank in return for a promise to repay $100 in 10 years' time, he will know that he can make a sure profit on the investment in the wine provided that he can purchase it now at a price less than $60 ($P_1 <$ 60). Now the values of the discount factors in Table VII (page 310) can be used to indicate what are the rates of interest implied in long-term loans of this kind on the assumption that the relevant daily rates of interest remain constant over the period of the loan. Thus the fact that the discount factor for two years at a daily rate of 10 per cent per annum is 0.82 means that $100 payable two years hence is worth $82 now if the daily rate of interest is constant at 10 per cent per annum over the two-year period. To receive now

---

[1] Column 1 of Table VII shows that a reduction of daily interest rates for one year from 10 to 5 per cent per annum raises present values in the ratio of 0.95 to 0.90; and $0.37 \times \dfrac{0.95}{0.90} = 0.39$.

$82 for a promise to pay $100 in two years' time implies a 10 per cen per annum rate of interest on two-year loans.

Accordingly we shall now assume that our Central Bank at 8 a.m. on day 0 offers to borrow or lend on stated terms not only money for one day, but money for two days, money for three days, money for four days, and so on *ad infinitum*. Let us consider in rather more detail what this implies. Suppose that the Central Bank at 8 a.m. on day 0 offers to borrow or lend A_0

  (I) in return for payment of A_1 at 8 a.m. on day 1
or (II) in return for payment of A_2 at 8 a.m. on day 2
or (III) in return for payment of A_3 at 8 a.m. on day 3
or (IV) in return for payment of A_4 at 8 a.m. on day 4

and so on.

We can see at once from offer I that $A_0(1 + i_0) = A_1$. Indeed this formula merely gives the definition of the rate of interest for day 0. $A_0(1 + i_0)$ is the principal *plus* interest payable in a day's time and this is equal to A_1. Thus given A_0 and A_1 we have $i_0 = \dfrac{A_1 - A_0}{A_0}$.

Now consider a citizen who at 8 a.m. on day 0 lends A_0 to the Central Bank on offer I and simultaneously borrows A_0 for the Central Bank on offer II. At 8 a.m. on day 0 he has in effect neither lent nor borrowed net. But at 8 a.m. on day 1 he will receive A_1 from the Central Bank and at 8 a.m. on day 2 he will have to pay A_2 to the Central Bank. In effect he has at 8 a.m. on day 0 made a 'forward' deal with the Central Bank whereby the Central Bank promises to lend him A_1 at 8 a.m. on day 1 in return for a repayment of A_2 at 8 a.m. on day 2. We can write then $A_1(1 + {}_0i_1^*) = A_2$ where we call ${}_0i_1^*$ the 'forward' rate of interest fixed at 8 a.m. on day 0 to operate for day 1. Similarly, we can use the expression $A_2(1 + {}_0i_2^*) = A_3$, to define ${}_0i_2^*$ as the 'forward' rate of interest fixed at 8 a.m. on day 0 to operate for day 2. And so on for ${}_0i_3^*$, ${}_0i_4^*$, etc.

If the Central Bank has a simple schedule of offers of this kind for loans of various lengths, then the value of bonds of more complicated characters will by a process of 'interest arbitrage' be determined in the market. Consider for example the value at 8 a.m. on day 0 of a bond which is simply a promise on the part of the debtor to pay

B_1 at the beginning of day 1 plus
B_2 at the beginning of day 2 plus
B_3 at the beginning of day 3. Then the value of this bond at 8 a.m. on day 0 will be

$$P_{b0} = \frac{B_1}{1 + i_0} + \frac{B_2}{(1 + i_0)(1 + {}_0i_1{}^*)} + \frac{B_3}{(1 + i_0)(1 + {}_0i_1{}^*)(1 + {}_0i_2{}^*)}$$

For suppose that P_{b0} were less than this. Then an investor could borrow $\dfrac{B_1}{1 + i_0}$ on offer I, $\dfrac{B_2}{(1 + i_0)(1 + {}_0i_1{}^*)}$ on offer II, and $\dfrac{B_3}{(1 + i_0)(1 + {}_0i_1{}^*)(1 + {}_0i_2{}^*)}$ on offer III from the Central Bank and use part of this to purchase, at a P_{b0} less than this, the bond in question. The difference between these two sums he could retain as an immediate and costless profit. When 8 a.m. on day 1 came he would receive B_1 on the bond; and this would be just enough to repay the interest on his offer-I borrowing from the Central Bank; since he has to pay A_1 for each A_0 borrowed, he would have to pay $\dfrac{A_1}{A_0} \times \dfrac{B_1}{1 + i_0} = B_1$ on his offer-I borrowing. When 8 a.m. on day 2 came, he would receive B_2 from the bond which would just suffice to repay his offer-II borrowing from the Central Bank; since on A_0 he has to pay A_2, on $\dfrac{B_2}{(1 + i_0)(1 + {}_0i_1{}^*)}$ he would have to pay $\dfrac{B_2}{(1 + i_0)(1 + {}_0i_1{}^*)} \dfrac{A_2}{A_1} \dfrac{A_1}{A_0} = B_2$. And similarly, on day 3 his receipt of B_3 from the bond would just suffice to repay his offer-III borrowing from the Central Bank.

We have now to distinguish clearly between

(i) a 'spot' rate of interest, e.g. i_3
(ii) a 'forward' rate of interest, e.g. ${}_0i_3^*$
(iii) a long-term rate of interest, e.g. $i_{(0-2)}$

and (iv) an expected rate of interest, e.g. ${}_0i_3$.

Let us consider each of these in turn.

(i) By the 'spot' rate of interest we mean the rate of interest actually ruling on any one day for that day. Thus if at 8 a.m. on day 3 the Central Bank does actually borrow and lend at a rate of interest i_3 for the day, repayment being made at 8 a.m. on day 4, then i_3 is the actual 'spot' rate of interest on day 3.

(ii) If at 8 a.m. on day 0 the Central Bank will enter into a contract with any citizen that at 8 a.m. on day 3 it (the Central Bank) will borrow from (or lend to) that citizen a stated sum of money at a rate of interest ${}_0i_3^*$ which will be payable on the loan at 8 a.m. on day 4, then ${}_0i_3^*$ is the 'forward' rate of interest fixed on day 0 to operate on day 3. This type of contract, as we have seen, can be organized by the bank making offers on day 0 of different lengths of loans on different terms. (In our notation on page 315 we would have ${}_0i_3^*$ given by the relationship between A_3 and A_3, since $A_3\{1 + {}_0i_3^*\} = A_4$.)

(iii) An offer-IV loan in terms of our notation on page 315 means the payment of A_4 at 8 a.m. on day 4 in return for A_0 at 8 a.m. on day 0. If the daily rate of interest were constant on days 0, 1, 2, and 3 at $i_{(0-3)}$ we would have $A_0\{1 + i_{(0-3)}\}^4 = A_4$. We may call this the long-term rate of interest ruling at 8 a.m on day 0 for a four-day loan. It is the constant rate of interest at which the sum borrowed (A_0) must be compounded over four days to give the principal and interest which are then repayable (A_4). Since

$$\frac{A_4}{A_0} = \frac{A_1}{A_0}\frac{A_2}{A_1}\frac{A_3}{A_2}\frac{A_4}{A_3} = (1 + i_0)(1 + {}_0i_1^*)(1 + {}_0i_2^*)(1 + {}_0i_3^*)$$

we have $\{1 + i_{(0-3)}\}^4 = (1 + i_0)(1 + {}_0i_1^*)(1 + {}_0i_2^*)(1 + {}_0i_3^*)$. The long-term rate is an average of the 'forward' short-term rates which rule over the length of life of the long loan.

(iv) Finally ${}_0i_3$ is the rate of interest which a citizen at 8 a.m. on day 0 expects to rule during day 3. It is to be noted that ${}_0i_3$ is not necessarily equal to ${}_0i_3^*$. Citizen A may think that when day 3 arrives monetary policy will make the Central Bank then set a spot rate of interest (i_3) which is considerably lower than ${}_0i_3^*$ $\left\{ = \dfrac{A_4 - A_3}{A_3} \right\}$, i.e. lower than the rate at which at 8 a.m. on day 0 it is possible to make a contract with the Central Bank for loans or borrowings which will take place on day 3. Citizen A could on day 0 borrow on offer III from the Central Bank and lend on offer IV to the Central Bank. By so doing he is contracting to pay A_3 at 8 a.m. on day 3 and to receive A_4 at 8 a.m. on day 4, with an interest yield of ${}_0i_3^*$. To finance this transaction when the time comes he expects to be able to borrow 'spot' from the Central Bank at 8 a.m. on day 3 the sum A_3 at a rate of interest of only ${}_0i_3$. He expects, therefore, to make a profit of $A_3({}_0i_3^* - {}_0i_3)$ in the course of day 3. Thus a citizen who thinks that the actual 'spot' rates in the future will be lower than the corresponding 'forward' rates which are implied in the current long-term rates of interest for loans of various lengths will be tempted to lend long (e.g. on offer IV) and borrow short (e.g. on offer III). He will thereby expect to earn a higher interest rate on his long-term loans than he will eventually have to pay on the money which will be needed to renew his short-term borrowing. On the other hand, a citizen who expects that the actual 'spot' rates in the future will be higher than the 'forward' rates implied in the current structure of long-term rates of interest will be tempted to borrow long and to lend short.

Thus we shall assume from now on that the Central Bank will lend (or borrow) at any one time on stated terms for loans of different durations (which, as we have seen, is the same thing as assuming that at any one time it will deal in a 'forward' market for future loans of a day's duration). This, as we have seen, will enable it not only to lower (or raise) the spot rate of interest on day 0 (i.e. i_0) but also the whole structure of rates for long-, middle-, and short-term loans. This in turn will enable entrepreneurs who are considering what price to pay for an instrument on which the net returns will be earned only in the long-, middle-, or short-distance future to be able to lay their plans without any uncertainty about future interest rates. Since each can borrow in a future market at a rate fixed now for the future period over which the borrowing must extend, there is a set of discount factors (see pages 310–313 above) based on 'forward' interest rates on which a firm calculation of profit and loss can be based.

Thus the Central Bank can raise or lower the whole structure of long-term and short-term interest rates at any time without prejudice to its interest-rate policy on future days. It may set now a 'forward' rate (e.g. $_0i_3^*$) which differs from what when the time comes, turns out to be the most appropriate 'spot' rate (e.g. i_3). We shall argue later that it should as far as possible find a set of rates such that the 'forward' rate is equal to the 'spot' rate for each period (e.g. $_0i_3^* = i_3$). But the assumptions which we are making do not prevent the Central Bank from setting a 'spot' rate, when the time comes, which differs from the 'forward' rate previously set for that period, if it finds that it has misjudged the course of events. Nor do the assumptions which we are making prevent any citizen who judges that the Central Bank has made such a misjudgement from speculating on his own private judgement and borrowing long and lending short (or *vice versa*) if he thinks that spot rates will in the future turn out to be higher (or lower) than the Central Bank expects.

We may now summarize the assumptions which we have outlined in this and the preceding chapters for the market institutions in our multi-product growing economy. This we do by means of Figure 37 which may be compared with Figure 1 on page 13 to see the complications which we introduce as we turn from a one-product to a many-product economy.

As far as the movements of real goods and services are concerned, we assume (i) that (solid line 1) there is a daily movement of the services of different types of labour L and M, from the homes into the firms and farms; (ii) that (solid line 2) there is a daily flow of instruments of production which are both the outputs of certain firms and farms ($J \bar{K} \bar{N}$) and also the inputs into the same or other firms and farms ($J K N$); and (iii) that (solid line 3) there is a daily flow of consumption goods ($X \ Y Z$) from the firms and farms through the shops into the homes.

As far as monetary flows are concerned we assume (i) that (broken line 1) the only direct payment from the firms and farms to the homes is for the wages of the labour services; (ii) that (broken line 2) there are daily transfers of money from one firm to another in payment of the instruments of production transferred from one firm to another, (iii) that (broken line 3) there is a daily payment from the firms and farms to the money and capital market of interest, profits, dividends, repayment of capital, etc., upon the money capital raised to finance the enterprises; (iv) that (broken line 4) there is a daily payment from the money and capital market to the entrepreneurs in the firms and farms of new capital funds raised by the firms and farms for their capital developments; (v) that (broken line 5) there is a daily flow from the homes through the shops into the firms and farms of money spent on the purchases of goods ($X\ Y Z$) for personal

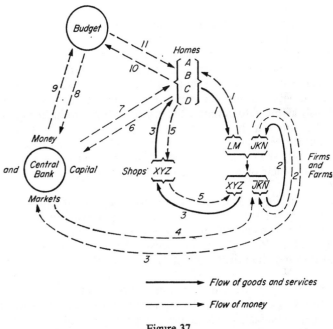

Figure 37

consumption; (vi) that (broken line 6) there is a daily flow of money from the homes onto the money and capital market in the investment of new personal savings in loans to the Central Bank, to the government, or to firms and farms or in other forms of security issued by the firms and farms; (vii) that (broken line 7) there is a daily flow of funds from the money and capital market to the homes in the form of interest, dividends, profits, repayments of principal, etc., to the private citizens on investments previously made by them; (viii) that there is either (broken line 8) a net flow of funds from the government's budget onto the money and capital market in payment of interest or repayment of principal on an existing national debt or in the addition to an existing governmental investment in private industry (a national asset) or (broken line 9) a net flow of funds to the government through increased government borrowing or through the payment of interest, dividends, capital sums, etc., by the private sector of the economy on any assets in private industry already owned by the government; and (ix) that there is either (broken line 10) a net payment of taxes by the private citizens to the government or (broken line 11) a net payment of subsidies by the government to the private citizens to control the expenditure of the citizens on goods for private consumption ($X\ Y\ Z$).

The main differences between Figures 1 and 37 can be summarized under three heads.

First, in Figure 37 there are the movements of instruments of production and the payments for them between the firms. Such transactions did not exist in Figure 1 because the private citizens (as contrasted with the entrepreneurs running the firms and farms) were previously assumed to purchase the instruments of production (K and N) and to hire out their services to the firms and farms just as they hired out the services of their own labour. Now the private citizens hire out only their labour services. The firms and farms purchase outright for their own ownership the instruments of production (J, K, N).

Second, in Figure 37 the firms and farms pay the ordinary citizens directly only for their labour services. All payments in respect of property (instruments of production) go indirectly through the money and capital market. Previously the firms and farms were assumed to pay the private citizens directly for the services of K and N.

Third, in Figure 37 there are two control centres—the Central Bank and the government's budget, whereas in Figure 1 there was no governmental budget. The existence of the budget involves both taxes and subsidies in the government's direct dealings with citizens and also payments of interest and of principal as between the government and the money and capital market.

CHAPTER XVII

THE STATIONARY STATE

In the last chapter we attempted to show how through its fiscal policy the government might set out to stabilize the general level of the prices of consumption goods and how, given any set of expectations about other relevant prices, through its monetary policy it might set out to influence the current selling prices of instruments of production. A reduction of interest rates, we argued, would in general tend to raise the selling prices of instruments of production relatively to those of consumption goods. But we have not yet tackled the problem to what extent citizens can accurately forecast the future course of prices. As we shall argue in the next chapter accurate forecasting of future prices is a necessary condition for the maintenance of equilibrium through time; and we shall have much to say on this matter in subsequent chapters.

Meanwhile in the present chapter we will deal with one very special set of circumstances in which, although there are a number of different products, there is conceptually no great difficulty in assuming that citizens have perfect foresight about the future course of prices. This would be the case if, although there were many products and many instruments of production, yet we were in a stationary state.

Let us consider first of all how a growing economy with only one product of the kind discussed in Part 1 of this volume might reach not merely a state of steady growth, but actually a stationary state. One possible way in which this might happen is as follows. Suppose that our economic system is one in which there is no technical progress but in which land is an important factor of production but is limited in amount. Population has been growing and capital has been being accumulated. But the pressure of labour and capital on the fixed and limited amount of land has caused a continuous decline in the marginal and the average products of labour and of capital.

The consequential fall in output per head and so in the standard of living continues so long as population pressure on the land increases. At some point the fall in standards has caused such a rise in specific mortality rates that, given the level of specific fertility rates, population growth ceases and the population ultimately becomes one which is constant in size and in its age and sex composition (cf. Chapter XI).

L

322   *The Growing Economy*

Meanwhile the rate of interest continues to fall so long as capital is being accumulated and is pressing on the land. So long as this continues, the rate at which each citizen plans to raise his consumption over his life-time ($\hat{c} = \sigma i$) falls because the marginal product of capital (i) is falling and perhaps also because the elasticity of substitution between today's and tomorrow's consumption (σ) falls as the standard of living is seriously lowered (cf. pp. 206–207 above).

After a point no net savings will take place. For suppose, in the first case, that there were perfect selfishness in the sense of Chapter XII above. As i and therefore $\hat{c} = \sigma i$ falls, the curve of consumption over the life cycle will become flatter and flatter. There will ultimately be less savings during youth to finance heavy consumption during retirement. At some point the savings of the young at any one time will be offset by the dissaving of the elderly in retirement.

If, on the other hand, there were perfect altruism in the sense of Chapter XIII the process of capital accumulation would go on until the marginal product of capital and the rate of interest were reduced to zero. For as long as c were positive (which, with $c = \sigma i$, would be the case so long as i were positive) the elderly in retirement would have a higher standard of living than they had at the outset of their careers. But if the wage rate were stagnant, this would mean that elderly parents would have a higher standard of living than their children during the period of overlap of their adulthoods. But in this case perfect altruism would require the parents to save still more to help their children. Capital accumulation would thus continue until the rate of interest were zero, so that the level of consumption over the life cycle were also stagnant ($\hat{c} = 0$).

Thus whether there were perfect selfishness or perfect altruism net savings would ultimately fall to zero, though the rate of interest would be positive in the former case and zero in the latter case. Everything will now repeat itself. The wage rate, the rate of interest, the rent of land, the total output of the economy, the size and composition of the population, and the size of the real capital stock— everything is stable and constant at this stagnation level.

Now there is no reason why essentially the same process should not occur in an economy in which there were many products, if at the same time there were no technical progress but a fixed amount of natural resources which constitute very important elements of input into the productive process. The standard of living could fall until the population was constant. The rate of interest could fall until, with perfect selfishness among savers, there was no net addition to the community's stocks of instruments of production.

In such a stationary stagnation economy everything could repeat itself. There would be no elements of change which would call for changes in relative prices. In this case, if by financial policy a general index of prices were stabilized, every individual price would be stable. And if every individual price had been stable for a long time, every citizen might well expect that every individual price would be stable in the future; and if he did so expect, his expectations would turn out to be correct. We would have perfect foresight of completely stable prices. The formulae on page 298 for equilibrium in the various markets for instruments of production would now be simplified to

$$i = \frac{W_k}{P_k} = \frac{W_j}{P_j} = \quad \text{etc.}$$

For this stationary state to be reached in an economy with many kinds of instruments of production in it, there is one special condition which must be fulfilled. In order to understand this, let us examine more closely the nature of the stationary state with man-made instruments of production. Consider any one process of production in it—the textile industry for example. Because of the nature of perfect potential competition with constant returns to scale which we have discussed in *The Stationary Economy* (Chapter I, p. 31), it makes no essential difference to our analysis whether there are a large number of small competing firms each carrying out this process on a small scale or a single monopoly firm (subject to perfect potential competition) accounting for the whole of the process; and it makes no difference to the analysis whether we consider one firm or the whole corpus of firms operating this process. It will be convenient for the present analysis to consider the whole industry as if it were a single firm subject to perfect potential competition.

Every morning at 8 a.m. there enter as inputs into our textile firm a certain number of man-hours of work, a certain quantity of raw cotton, a certain quantity of demi-semi-processed cotton (yarn), a certain quantity of semi-processed cotton (cloth), a certain quantity of brand-new machines (new spindles, looms, etc.), a certain quantity of middle-aged machines, a certain quantity of senile machines, and so on. At 4 p.m. there emerges from the factory an output which, on the one hand, includes no man-hours of work, no completely raw cotton, and no brand-new machines, but, on the other hand, does contain some finished shirts ready for the consumer. At the same time many elements of output will correspond to elements of input; semi-processed cotton, for example, which is today's output will constitute part of tomorrow's input. It follows that there cannot be a true stationary state with man-made instruments of production unless one has what may be called a balanced stock of instruments.

The point can be illustrated by taking an example of a particular machine. Suppose that a loom has a useful life of 10 years or 1,000 days in the conditions of the stationary equilibrium which we are considering. Then our industry must start with a stock of looms of which $\frac{1}{1,000}$th part are brand new, $\frac{1}{1,000}$th part are 1 day old, $\frac{1}{1,000}$th part 2 days old, and so on. In this case the inputs and outputs of our textile industry can continue day in day out at the same level. Each day $\frac{1}{1,000}$th part of the stock of machines will enter as an input of brand-new machines and will appear as an output of 1-day-old machines. Each day this same number of 1-day-old machines will enter as an input and will appear as an output of 2-day-old machines; and so on. But if all the machines had been installed on the same day, then the smooth flow of inputs and outputs could not be maintained. On day 1 all the stock of machines would enter as an input of new machines and appear as an output of 1-day-old machines. On day 2 all machines would enter as an output of 1-day-old machines and appear as an output of 2-day-old machines. And so on. No input of brand-new machines would be needed at all until day 1,001 when the whole of the old stock would be simultaneously scrapped and need replacement by brand-new machines. For the industry which produced brand-new machines it is obvious that a steady flow of inputs and outputs could not in these circumstances be maintained. In order, therefore, to have a stationary state with man-made instruments of production we need now to be in a situation in which there is in this sense a balanced stock of instruments.

This does not, however, imply that even if the other conditions necessary for a stationary state of the economy are fulfilled, this state will never be reached if we start with an unbalanced stock of looms. Take the extreme example given in the last paragraph. Suppose all the looms have been installed on the same day and that normally looms last 1,000 days. This will give rise to what may be called a severe 'echo' effect. Every 1,000th day there will tend to be a very heavy demand for new looms with no demand for new looms in the interim. But this would mean that there was a huge excess demand for new looms (and, therefore, a very high price for new looms) at certain peak periods of the cycle, followed by a greatly deficient demand (and, therefore, extremely low prices for new looms) at other periods of the cycle.

For this reason, however marked the first echoes were, they would in the long run be likely to die out. As long as they persist there will be periods when the price of new looms is particularly high (because the demand for new looms is abnormally high) and periods when for the opposite reason their price is particularly low. As long as this goes on entrepreneurs will have some incentive to replace their looms at periods other than that of the peak prices, either by replacing them rather sooner or by replacing them rather later than they would otherwise have done. By this means the age distribution of the stock of looms is likely to become more and more evenly balanced. The echoes will in all probability ultimately become negligible.

Many of the conditions for this full stationary equilibrium are exactly the same as those discussed in Chapter IX of *The Stationary Economy*. We will not repeat them here. But there are three additional sets of condition.

(1) First, the total population must have so grown (given the limited stock of natural resources and the total of man-made instruments of production that has been accumulated) that the standard of living is such that mortality matches fertility and there is a constant population of a constant age and sex distribution.

(2) Second, the total of man-made instruments of production must have been so accumulated (given the limited stock of natural resources and the size to which the working population has grown) that the rate of interest has so fallen that with perfect selfishness among savers the savings of the young equals the dissavings of the old.

(3) Third, the market for each instrument of production must be in continual balance. This involves three important sub-conditions.

(*a*) It is no longer sufficient that the owner of each instrument should be paid a reward for it equal to the value of its marginal product in every line of use. This is still necessary. An instrument J must be shifted from use in process a to use in process b if the value of its marginal product is higher in b than in a. But it is also necessary that the rate of current return on J should be the same as on K, i.e. that $\dfrac{W_j}{P_j} = \dfrac{W_k}{P_k}$. Otherwise it would be profitable not so much to make a different use of J or of K, but to produce more J and less K. If $\dfrac{W_j}{P_j} > \dfrac{W_k}{P_k}$, then profit can be increased by substituting J for K in productive processes until the value of the marginal net product of J had so fallen and of K had so risen that $\dfrac{W_j}{P_j} = \dfrac{W_k}{P_k}$.

(*b*) It is necessary, in order to preserve a constant money demand for all instruments of production, that the money rate of interest should be set by the Central Bank at this level $i = \dfrac{W_j}{P_j} = \dfrac{W_k}{P_k}$.

(*c*) It is necessary that time should be allowed to pass until all 'echo' effects in the markets for man-made instruments of production had died out.

Note to Chapter XVII

INPUT–OUTPUT IN THE STATIONARY STATE

The Stationary State which we have examined in the present chapter of this volume has many characteristics in common with the *Stationary Economy* examined at length in Volume I of this work. In both there is no technical progress and no growth in the inputs of the original factors land and labour, the constancy of the labour supplied being simply assumed in the *Stationary Economy* but being the result of the adjustment of mortality to the standard of living in the Stationary State. There remains, however, one absolutely outstanding difference, namely the existence of capital and of man-made instruments of production in the Stationary State which simply did not exist in the *Stationary Economy*.

In the *Stationary Economy* since all outputs were consumption goods and all inputs were original factors (land or labour) it was quite straightforward to assess what original factors were needed to produce what final goods for consumption. But the existence of intermediate capital goods (the outputs of some processes and the inputs of other processes) makes it difficult in the Stationary State to make such an assessment. A demand for a final consumption good (e.g. a shirt) is a demand for the original factors (e.g. labour) used in the textile industry and also for the intermediate products (e.g. raw cotton and looms) which are used in this industry but produced in some other industry. In turn the demand for raw cotton and looms is a demand not only for the original factors employed in the processes producing raw cotton and looms, but also for other instruments of production (e.g. tractors and fertilizers used to produce raw cotton and steel and machine tools used to produce looms). And so on in an infinite regress.

Moreover, there may be many circular chains in these series of demands. Thus labour may be used to produce coal which is used to produce steel which is used to produce machine tools which are used to produce motor vehicles which are used to carry coal which is used to produce steel which is used to produce machine tools which are used to produce looms which are used to produce shirts. There is an almost infinitely complex intertwining of such productive relationships in a modern economy through the use of intermediate products. When one has taken all these into account, what in the end are the ultimate scarce resources which the production of an extra shirt requires? This is the set of problems which we shall discuss in this note.

For this purpose we shall make use of the very simple numerical example shown in Table VIII. This table (which is constructed on the same principles as the right-hand half of Table VI) illustrates a stationary economy which is making use of six productive processes, labelled *a* to *f*. In this economy as a whole (right-hand column of Table VIII) 1000 units of labour (*L*) together with 100,000 units each of four instruments of production (*N*, *H*, *J*, and *K*) enter the firms and farms each morning and, since we are in a stationary state, produce by the evening the same number, i.e. 100,000 units, of each of the four instruments of production ($\bar{N}$, $\bar{H}$, $\bar{J}$, and $\bar{K}$) and a certain amount of each of three consumption goods (300 units of *Z*, 200 units of *Y*, and 100 units of *X*).

Table VIII

		a (Z)	*b* (Y)	*c* (X)	*d* (K)	*e* (J)	*f* (H)	Total *a* to *f*
Outputs	Z	300	—	—	—	—	—	300
	Y	—	200	—	—	—	—	200
	X	—	—	100	—	—	—	100
	$\bar{K}$	—	—	—	98,000	1,000	1,000	100,000
	$\bar{J}$	—	—	—	68,000	21,000	11,000	100,000
	$\bar{H}$	—	—	—	78,000	11,000	11,000	100,000
	$\bar{N}$	—	—	—	10,000	80,000	10,000	100,000
Inputs	K	300	—	—	97,400	1,100	1,200	100,000
	J	—	200	—	68,200	20,200	11,400	100,000
	H	—	—	100	78,100	11,100	10,700	100,000
	N	—	—	—	10,000	80,000	10,000	100,000
	L	—	—	—	100	100	800	1,000

In our example the final product *Z* (e.g. coal for the domestic hearth) is practically identical with the instrument of production *K* (e.g. coal for the industrial boiler). Process *a* states simply that 300 units of *K* are converted into 300 units of *Z* without any noticeable application of other inputs. One can imagine *Z* and *K* as being identical products with the intermediate product (*K*) simply waiting in a shop (process *a*) for a single day before being sold. Similarly *Y* is more or less identical with *J* (process *b*) and *X* with *H* (process *c*).

The three remaining processes need more consideration. The 1000 units of *L* are distributed each morning among these three processes

—100 in process d, 100 in process e, and 800 in process f. Similarly, the 100,000 units of N are distributed each morning among these three processes—10,000 in process d, 80,000 in process e, and 10,000 in process f. But N is a natural and indestructible instrument of production, and the output $\bar{N}$ at the end of each day is in each of the three processes necessarily exactly equal to its input at the beginning of that day. As far as the man-made instruments of production are concerned, process d is one which uses an excess of inputs over outputs of H and J (e.g. an input of 78,100 units of H with an output of only 78,000 units of $\bar{H}$) in order to produce an excess of output over input of K (e.g. an output of 98,000 units of $\bar{K}$ with an input of only 97,400 units of K). Similarly, process e produces a net output of J with net inputs of H and K, while process f produces a net output of $\bar{H}$ with net inputs of J and K.

Thus in any process the excess (or deficiency) of the output over the input of any instrument of production measures the net daily production (or absorption) of that instrument by that process. Thus $\bar{K} - K$ in process d is 600 units and in process e is -100 units, which means that process d contributes a net daily output of 600 units of K, whereas process e absorbs a net daily input of 100 units of K. While the difference $\bar{K} - K$ thus measures the daily current net input or output, the absolute figure K represents the total capital stock. Process d thus produces a net daily output of 600 units of K, but to do so uses up net daily inputs of 200 units of J and 100 units of H and employs a total capital equipment of 97,400 units of K, 68,200 units of J, and 78,100 units of H.

The economy is in a stationary equilibrium, so that the total output of each instrument from all the processes combined is equal to the total input of that instrument into all the processes combined. This is illustrated by the fact that the total for $\bar{K}$ is equal to the total for K in the right-hand column of Table VIII.

In the case of each instrument we have assumed that this total, which represents the constant stock of the instrument in the economy, is 100,000 units. These total figures can be arbitrarily chosen in the sense that we can define a unit of K in such a way that there are in fact 100,000 units in the total capital stock. Similarly, we can choose units of H and J which represent $\dfrac{1}{100,000}$th part of the total stock of each; and we can choose units for L such that there is a daily input of 1000 units of it into the economy as a whole. But having chosen arbitrarily our units for L, N, H, J, and K for arithmetical convenience, it is no longer possible to choose arbitrarily out units for Z, Y, and X. Since we assume that Z is the same product as K, a daily output of 300 units of Z with a stock of

100,000 units of K expresses the significant fact that the daily net output of this product for final consumption is $\frac{3}{1000}$ of the capital stock of it; and that in the cases of Y and X these ratios of output to capital in the economy as a whole are significantly different at $\frac{2}{1000}$ and $\frac{1}{1000}$.

In addition to the very restricted number of products there is another important respect in which the economy illustrated in Table VIII represents only a very simplified model of reality. As far as *net* outputs are concerned, each process is a single-product process. Thus process a produces a net output only of Z, process b only of Y, process c only of X, process d only of K, process e only of J, and process f only of H. This has one extremely important implication: it makes it impossible to deal with ageing machines. As we have already explained (cf. page 300 above), the only way to deal with, say, an ageing loom is to have one process which has inputs of labour and a brand-new loom and outputs of shirts and a one-day-old loom, a second process which has inputs of labour and a one-day-old loom and outputs of shirts and a two-day-old loom, and so on. But processes of that kind involve net outputs of more than one product, e.g. of shirts and of a two-day-old loom.

The model of the economy described in Table VIII thus implies a simple form of capital equipment. Machines, for example, must not deteriorate with age, in the sense that they become an inferior product with age, although they may diminish in quantity as time passes. Thus an input of looms (K) in a process leads to an output of looms $(\bar{K})$ at the end of the day. $\bar{K}$ may be less in quantity than K, if the process is one which uses up looms to produce shirts. But the looms which do survive the day's operations must be as good as new; $\bar{K}$, though less than K in amount, must be the same in quality as K. This is an unnatural simplification of reality.[1] It allows us to consider certain important aspects of reality—namely, the relationship between stocks and flows of capital goods and the relationships between inputs and outputs in different processes; but it excludes from consideration all those problems of capital goods which are especially related to the ageing of machines.

Table VIII represents a stationary economy with man-made instruments of production. It simply describes the inputs and outputs

---

[1] In my *A Neo-Classical Theory of Economic Growth* I have called this the assumption of 'depreciation by evaporation'. It is as if capital goods took the form of, say, a stock of steel which evaporated at a certain rate, each remaining ton of steel being equivalent to every other ton of steel regardless of its age.

which are in fact occurring in this economy. The economy is producing for final consumption 300 units of Z, 200 units of Y, and 100 units of X. Is there any way in which we can say how many of the 1000 units of L are in fact, directly and indirectly, being used to produce Z, how many to produce Y, and how many to produce X? Similarly, is there any way of saying how many of the total 100,000 units of N are used for each final consumption good and how many of the 100,000 units of the stocks of each of H, J, and K are engaged in the production of each consumption good?

There is no way of answering these questions by immediate examination of the table. Z is made out of K; but K is produced not only to make Z but also to make J, which in turn is used to produce not only Y but also K and H, the latter of which is used to produce not only X but also K and J. Although Z is made only from K, we cannot allocate all the factors employed in process d to the production of Z because K is used also for other purposes; and we must allocate to the production of Z some of the factors employed in processes e and f because some J and H are used to produce K which is used to produce Z.

Nevertheless, on our assumption that there are constant returns to scale in all processes we can in a very meaningful way allocate the use of the factors of production to the direct or indirect production of each of the final consumption goods. We can in fact break Table VIII down into three sub-systems. The first of these (which will be derived in Table IX below) would show the inputs and outputs required to produce final consumption only of the 300 units of Z without any production of Y or X on the assumptions (i) that only the six processes shown in Table VIII are available for use, (ii) that there are constant returns to scale so that in each of the six processes shown in Table VIII every input and output may be varied in the same proportion, and (iii) that the sub-system is a stationary system in the sense that for each instrument of production separately the total input into the sub-system is equal to the total output from the sub-system. Similar sub-systems can be derived to isolate the inputs needed to produce the 200 units of Y without any Z or X or the 100 units of X without any Z or Y. How does one derive these sub-systems?

Our task is to determine on what scale should each of the various processes a to f of Table VIII be operated (assuming always that, because of constant returns to scale, every input and every output in each process can be varied in the same proportion) so that (i) the economy will produce 300 units of Z and no output of Y or X and (ii), since we are in a stationary economy, the total output of each instrument is equal to the total input of each instrument (i.e. $H = \bar{H}$,

$J = \bar{J}$, and $K = \bar{K}$). It is clear that process a must be operated on the scale shown in Table VIII, since we require the output of 300 units of Z to continue, while processes b and c can be totally discontinued, since we need no outputs of Y or X. Processes d, e, and f can all be reduced in scale (since we need only the instruments for the production of Z and not for Y or X); but no one of them can be wholly closed down (since we need some J and some H to produce the K which must be produced to make Z).

Let S_d represent the scale on which process d must be operated, in the sense that S_d is the fraction which must be applied to very input and output in column d of Table VIII when we wish to produce 300 units of Z and no units of Y or X. Similarly, let S_e and S_f represent the scales on which processes e and f must be operated to produce 300 units of Z and no output of Y or X. If now we look along the row marked $\bar{K}$ in Table VIII, we see that in the Z-sub-system the total output of $\bar{K}$ will be

$$98,000S_d + 1000S_e + 1000S_f$$

instead of 100,000 (as in the right-hand column of Table VIII). If we look along the row marked K in Table VIII, we see that in the Z-sub-system the total input K will now be

$$300 + 97,400S_d + 1100S_e + 1200S_f$$

instead of the 100,000 units for the whole system. But the total output must be equal to the total input for each instrument, so that

$$(98,000 - 97,400)S_d + (1000 - 1100)S_e + (1000 - 1200)S_f = 300$$

or
$$6S_d - S_e - 2S_f = 3 \qquad (17.1)$$

Similarly, the total output of J must equal the input of $J(\bar{J} = J)$. Since no J is needed for process b, we have

$$68,000S_d + 21,000S_e + 11,000S_f$$
$$= 68,200S_d + 20,200S_e + 11,400S_f$$

or
$$-S_d + 4S_e - 2S_f = 0 \qquad (17.2)$$

Similarly, since $\bar{H} = H$ and since no H is needed for process c, we have

$$78,000S_d + 11,000S_e + 11,000S_f$$
$$= 78,100S_d + 11,100S_e + 10,700S_f$$

or
$$-S_d - S_e + 3S_f = 0 \qquad (17.3)$$

Equations (17.1), (17.2), and (17.3) give us three equations for our three unknown fractions S_d, S_e, and S_f. By solving these simultaneous equations we find that $S_d = \frac{2}{3}$, $S_e = \frac{1}{3}$, and $S_f = \frac{1}{3}$. Table IX simply reproduces Table VIII with process a unchanged, processes b and c scaled down to zero, process d scaled down to $\frac{2}{3}$ of its level in Table VIII, and processes e and f scaled down to $\frac{1}{3}$ of their levels in Table VIII. We can then see from the right-hand column of Table IX the total inputs and outputs which would be needed to produce Z, but not Y or X, with the processes of Table VIII. The 300 units of Z would require $366\frac{2}{3}$ units of L (of which $66\frac{2}{3}$ would be employed in process d, $33\frac{1}{3}$ in process e, and $266\frac{2}{3}$ in process f), $36{,}666\frac{2}{3}$ units of N

Table IX

		a (Z)	b (Y)	c (X)	d (K)	e (J)	f (H)	Total a to f
Outputs	Z	300	—	—	—	—	—	300
	Y	—	0	—	—	—	—	0
	X	—	—	0	—	—	—	0
	$\bar{K}$	—	—	—	$65{,}333\frac{1}{3}$	$333\frac{1}{3}$	$333\frac{1}{3}$	66,000
	J	—	—	—	$45{,}333\frac{1}{3}$	7,000	$3{,}666\frac{2}{3}$	56,000
	$\bar{H}$	—	—	—	52,000	$3{,}666\frac{2}{3}$	$3{,}666\frac{2}{3}$	$59{,}333\frac{1}{3}$
	$\bar{N}$	—	—	—	$6{,}666\frac{2}{3}$	$26{,}666\frac{2}{3}$	$3{,}333\frac{1}{3}$	$36{,}666\frac{2}{3}$
Inputs	K	300	—	—	$64{,}933\frac{1}{3}$	$366\frac{2}{3}$	400	66,000
	J	—	0	—	$45{,}466\frac{2}{3}$	$6{,}733\frac{1}{3}$	3,800	56,000
	H	—	—	0	$52{,}066\frac{2}{3}$	3,700	$3{,}566\frac{2}{3}$	$59{,}333\frac{1}{3}$
	N	—	—	—	$6{,}666\frac{2}{3}$	$26{,}666\frac{2}{3}$	$3{,}333\frac{1}{3}$	$36{,}666\frac{2}{3}$
	L	—	—	—	$66\frac{2}{3}$	$33\frac{1}{3}$	$266\frac{2}{3}$	$366\frac{2}{3}$

($666\frac{2}{3}$ in process d, $26{,}666\frac{2}{3}$ in process e, and $3333\frac{1}{3}$ in process f), a capital stock of $59{,}333\frac{1}{3}$ units of H (of which each morning $52{,}066\frac{2}{3}$ would be invested in process d, 3700 in process e, and $3566\frac{2}{3}$ in process f), and similarly for the capital stocks of J and K.

We can proceed in an exactly similar way to obtain sub-systems for Y and X which isolate the total inputs and outputs needed to produce either 200 units of Y without any Z or X or 100 units of X without any Z or Y. We would find that the following scales of operation of the various processes were required for these sub-systems:

	Scale of operation needed for process					
	I	II	III	IV	V	V
Z sub-system	1	0	0	$0\cdot\dot{6}$	$0\cdot\dot{3}$	$0\cdot\dot{3}$
Y sub-system	0	1	0	$0\cdot\dot{1}$	$0\cdot3\dot{5}$	$0\cdot1\dot{5}$
X sub-system	0	0	1	$0\cdot\dot{2}$	$0\cdot\dot{3}\dot{1}$	$0\cdot\dot{5}\dot{1}$
Total	1	1	1	1	1	1

We could draw up tables for the Y- and X-sub-systems which correspond to Table IX which we have already drawn up for the Z-sub-system. We would then have in the right-hand columns of these tables the total inputs of each instrument of production and of labour services required to produce 300 units of Z, 200 units of Y, or 100 units of X in isolation. This information is summarized in Table X. We now know, for example, that of the 1000 units of L in the economy as a whole 367 units are needed directly or indirectly for the production of the 300 units of Z, 171 for the production of the 200 units of Y, and 462 for the production of the 100 units of X. Similarly, we know that of the 100,000 units of H in the capital stock of the community, 59,333 units are directly or indirectly used to produce Z. 14,285 to produce Y, and 26,382 to produce X.

Table X

		Sub-Systems			Total System
		Z	Y	X	
Outputs of	Z	300	—	—	300
Consumption	Y	—	200	—	200
Goods	X	—	—	100	100
Stocks of	$K = \bar{K}$	66,000	11,400	22,600	100,000
Instruments	$J = \bar{J}$	56,000	16,725	27,275	100,000
of	$H = \bar{H}$	59,333	14,285	26,382	100,000
Production	$N = \bar{N}$	36,667	31,111	32,222	100,000
Input of Labour Services	L	367	171	462	1,000

So far in this chapter we have analysed only the quantitive relationships between physical inputs and outputs in the economy. We have observed only how many hours of work, acres of land, tons of coal, etc., are required to produce a given number of shirts, loaves of bread, and so on. We started (Table VIII) with a description of the total amounts of physical inputs and outputs in each separate productive process in the economy. We have now (Table X) reached the point at which we have decomposed this total picture to show the physical quantities of the various inputs which are needed directly or indirectly to produce the given quantities of each final consumption good.

We have up to this point said nothing about the prices and costs of the various inputs and outputs. What will be the market price of Z relatively to that of Y or of X? What will be the market prices of the man-made instruments, H, J, and K? What will be the market wage of labour, rent of land, rate of interest? We need this information, in addition to the decomposition of the physical productive relationships which we have already undertaken, before we can answer any questions about the ultimate break-down of the costs of X, Y, and Z in our economy. Ultimately the costs of production of these final outputs in our stationary state can be broken down into wages of labour, rent of land, and interest on capital. But, as a glance at Table X will show, this question cannot be answered without knowing the prices of the instruments of production. The stock of capital goods invested directly or indirectly in the production of Z includes an above-average ratio of K to J. If the price of K is very high relatively to that of J, the production of Z will account for a much higher proportion of the total capital invested in the economy than it will do if the price of K is very low relatively to that of J. In order to consider the relative factor-intensities of the three final products Z, Y, and X we need to know not only the physical decomposition of the productive system (which we have now achieved in Table X) and the rates of wages, rents, and interest, but also the market prices of the man-made instruments of production. We must turn to the price–cost relationships that exist in the economy illustrated in Tables VIII to X.

The description of the physical productive system given in Table VIII itself sets certain limitations to the cost–price relationships in the economy. For the economy to be in equilibrium it is a necessary condition that total costs should be just covered by total receipts in each of the six processes.[1] Otherwise entrepreneurs would have an incentive to close down or to expand one or more of the processes. We can, therefore, write down from Table VIII the following six equations, each expressing for one of the processes the fact that total receipts from the sale of outputs are equal to the total cost of the inputs:

Process a

$$300 P_z = 300(1 + i)P_k, \text{ i.e. } P_z = (1 + i)P_k$$

---

[1] This condition, while a necessary one, is not a sufficient one for equilibrium. For it might still be possible by using a process of production which is not included among the six shown in Table VIII for an entrepreneur at current prices to make a net profit, in the sense of obtaining receipts from the sale of his output, which exceeded the cost of his inputs. This possibility, as we shall see below, plays a vital role in the ultimate analysis.

Process b

$$P_y = (1 + i)P_j$$

Process c

$$P_x = (1 + i)P_h$$

Process d

$$98{,}000P_k + 68{,}000P_j + 78{,}000P_h + 10{,}000P_n$$
$$= (1 + i)(97{,}400P_k + 68{,}200P_j + 78{,}100P_h + 10{,}000P_n) + 100W_l$$

i.e. $P_k(6 - 974i) + P_j(-2 - 682i) + P_h(-1 - 781i) - 100iP_n$
$- W_l = 0.$

Process e

$$P_k(-1 - 11i) + P_j(8 - 202i) + P_h(-1 - 111i) - 800iP_n - W_l = 0.$$

Process f

$$P_k(-2 - 12i) + P_j(-4 - 114i) + P_h(3 - 197i) - 100iP_n - 8W_l = 0.$$

where P_z, P_y, P_x, P_k, P_j, P_h, and P_n are the market money prices of Z, Y, X, K, J, H, and N respectively, W_l is the wage rate and i is the daily rate of interest (expressed as a rate *per diem* so that $100i$ expresses the rate *per annum*). In each of the above equations between total receipts and total costs in each process, the cost of the instruments is, as we have already explained (p. 295 above), represented by the price of the instrument plus the interest for one day payable on the loan with which the purchase of the instrument has been financed.

Now it can be seen that in the above price equations the price of land (P_n) appears only in the form iP_n, which is, of course, the daily rent (W_n) payable to hire the services of a unit of land. Let us then continue our analysis of costs in terms of the rent for hiring the services for a day of a unit of land ($W_n = iP_n$) instead of in terms of the outright purchase of a unit of land (P_n). (See Chapter II, p. 32 above.)

We have in the above relationships six equations connecting the nine unknowns, P_z, P_y, P_x, P_k, P_j, P_h, W_n, W_l, and i. We can interpret this result in the following way. Suppose that the three basic input prices W_n, W_l, and i were given. Then each of the product prices P_z, P_y, P_x, P_k, P_j, and P_h would be determined. Given the money wage rate, the money rent for a unit of land, and the rate of interest, we can build up the money cost of each product. It is true that the money cost of each product will depend not only upon the cost of labour and land and the rate of interest, but also upon the cost of the intermediate products with which it is itself made. But this difficulty is looked after by the set of six simultaneous price equations given above. If the three basic input costs are known, there is only one set of product prices which will make total receipts equal to total costs in each process.

If now we add an assumption about monetary policy we can reduce the degrees of freedom in our price relationships from three to two. Suppose that the financial authorities keep a price index of the three consumption goods, X, Y, and Z, constant. We will weight each consumption good by the quantities shown as consumed in Table VIII. Suppose then that the authorities keep the money cost of 300 units of Z plus 200 units of Y plus 100 units of X constant at $100. Then we would have a seventh price relationship, namely

$$300P_z + 200P_y + 100P_x = \$100$$

We can now say that given any two of the three basic input prices—W_l, W_n, and i—the third basic input price must be set at that level which is necessary to make the total cost of 300 Z *plus* 200 Y *plus* 100 X add up to the given $100; and the three basic input prices will then determine, in the way which we have just examined, the cost price of each of the six products.

These seven price equations thus set certain limitations within which prices may vary. But there are still two degrees of freedom and we must go on to consider what the actual price relationships will be within these limitations.

The possibilities are illustrated numerically in Table XI. In Case I we simply assume that $W_n = 0$ and $i = 0$. With these values of W_n and i in our seven price equations on pages 334 to 336 we obtain the

Table XI

	I	Cases II	III
P_z	$0·12\dot{2}$	$0·12\dot{2}$	$0·1681$
P_y	$0·08\dot{5}$	$0·120\dot{5}$	$0·0911$
P_x	$0·46\dot{2}$	$0·39\dot{2}$	$0·3140$
P_k	$0·12\dot{2}$	$0·12\dot{2}$	$0·1679$
P_j	$0·08\dot{5}$	$0·120\dot{5}$	$0·0910$
P_h	$0·46\dot{2}$	$0·39\dot{2}$	$0·3135$
W_n	0	$0·0005$	$0·000214$
W_l	$0·1$	$0·05$	$0·0214$
i	0	0	$0·001$

Notes:

Case I	$W_n = 0$	$i = 0$
Case II	$W_l = 100 W_n$	$i = 0$
Case III	$W_l = 100 W_n$	$i = 0·001$

solutions for the product prices and the price of labour shown in column I of Table XI. In Case II we assume again that $i = 0$; but we now assume that the wage rate and the rent of land are such that the total wage bill (1000 W_l) is the same as the total of rents for land (100,000 W_n), i.e. that $W_l = 100 \ W_n$; and we obtain the prices listed in column II of Table XI. In Case III we assume as in Case II that $W_l = 100 \ W_n$, but we now assume that $i = 0 \cdot 001$ (i.e. that interest is at a daily rate of $\dfrac{1}{100}$ of 10 per cent a day, the equivalent of 10 per cent per annum); and we obtain the prices shown in column III of the table.

Before we comment on these price relationships we will express the information contained in Table XI in a somewhat different manner. Since we now know for each of the three cases I, II, and III the prices of all products and of all original factors, we can now calculate from these prices (Table XI) and from the quantities of physical inputs and outputs (right-hand column of Table VIII) the money values (i) of total expenditure on the three consumption goods, Z, Y, and X, (ii) of the capital stocks of the three intermediate products K, J, and H, and (iii) of the incomes going in interest, rents, and wages. These are shown in Table XII.

Table XII

	I	II	III
		Cases	
	\$	\$	\$
$P_z Z$	36·6	36·6	50·4
$P_y Y$	17·1	24·1	18·2
$P_x X$	46·2	39·2	31·4
Total Expenditure on Consumption: $P_z Z + P_y Y + P_x X$	100·0	100·0	100·0
$P_k K$	12,222·2	12,222·2	16,790·0
$P_j J$	8,555·5	12,055·5	9,100·0
$P_h H$	46,222·2	39,222·2	31,350·0
Total Value of Capital Stock: $P_k K + P_j J + P_h H$	67,000·0	63,500·0	57,240·0
Interest: $i(P_k K + P_j J + P_h H)$	0	0	57·2
Rent: $W_n N$	0	50	21·4
Wages: $W_l L$	100·0	50	21·4
Total income: $i(P_k K + P_j J + P_h H) + W_n N + W_l L$	100·0	100·0	100·0

Thus we know that the daily output of Z is 300 (Table VIII) and that P_z is \$0·1$\overset{.}{2}$, \$0·1$\overset{.}{2}$, and \$0·1681 in Cases I, II, and III respectively (Table XI). It follows that ZP_z or the total amount spent on Z must be \$36·$\overset{.}{6}$, \$136·$\overset{.}{6}$, and \$50·4 in Cases I, II, and III respectively; and these figures are accordingly shown in the first row of Table XII. The other figures in Table XII are similarly obtained from the quantity figures in the right-hand column of Table VIII and the price figures in Table XI.

Cases I, II, and III describe only three out of the infinite number of possible combinations of factor prices (W_l, W_n, and i) and the consequential product prices (P_z, P_y, P_x, P_k, P_j, and P_h) which would be compatible with the absence of net profits or losses in the economic system described in Table VIII. If that system were a completely rigid one, that would be all that could be said. Which of the price combinations in fact ruled could not be determined by any competitive economic forces. But for the system to be completely rigid in this sense two sets of extreme conditions must be fulfilled. First, consumers must spend on consumption the whole of their incomes, and they must demand the final products Z, Y, and X in the proportion of 300 units of Z and 200 units of Y to every 100 units of X, whatever may be the distibution of money incomes, the rate of interest, or the prices of the final products. They must do this whether (as in Cases I and II where the rate of interest is zero) the price of the capital-intensive product Z is low relatively to the prices of Y and X or whether (as in Case III where the rate of interest is higher) the price of Z is high relatively to those of Y and X. Second, there must be no possibility of entrepreneurs using processes other than the six processes described in Table VIII or of substituting one input for another or one output for another or of transforming one input into one output within any one of the six processes. They must, for example, have no greater incentive to use less labour and more land for any purpose when the rent of land is zero (Case I) than when the rent of land is equal to the wage of labour (Cases II and III).

When, however, there are flexibilities in consumers' expenditure and/or in entrepreneurs' production programmes, it no longer remains arbitrary which of the possible combinations of money prices and costs will produce an equilibrium. Table VIII would now represent only one of the many physical combinations of inputs and outputs which were possible in the current state of technical knowledge in the economy; and it is not certain that it represents an equilibrium situation even though it represents a technically possible situation. To take a very simple possibility, there might be no set of prices and incomes which would ever induce consumers to purchase as much as 300 units of Z for every 200 units of Y and 100 units of X

consumed. In such a case the allocation of resources described in Table VIII, though it might be technically feasible, would in fact never occur in reality. But let us see what is involved in the situations in which the physical quantities described in Table VIII and the price relationships described either in Case I or Case II or Case III of Tables XI and XII do in fact describe a full equilibrium situation in our economy.

In Case I the rate of interest is zero. It could represent an equilibrium situation, therefore, only if the economy had reached a perfect-altruism stagnant state of the kind described on page 322 above. At the same time technical conditions must be such that there were no known unused processes at which, at a zero rate of interest and with the other prices shown for Case I on Table XI, a net profit will be made. This implies that if one more unit of any instrument of production (say, one more unit of J) were to drop from heaven there would be no possible reshuffling of the inputs among the various known processes which would enable the sum of the net increments of outputs valued at their existing prices to exceed the price of the additional unit of J. In this sense a zero rate of interest implies that technical conditions are such that the value of the net marginal product of the capital good, J, is zero. And similarly for the other capital goods, H and K.

In Case I the rent of land (N) is also zero. For this to be so, technical conditions must be such that there are no known unused processes in which (defined in a similar way as for the instrument J in the preceding paragraph) the value of the net marginal product of N is positive.

If such alternative processes were known, in which a unit of J, H, K, or N could earn a net reward, then the price situation in Case I of Table XI could not persist. There would be a tendency for the rate of interest and/or the rent of land to be driven up by the pull of these other unused processes.

Since in Case I the rate of interest and the rent of land are both zero, the whole of the national income goes in wages of labour and the cost-prices of products correspond solely to the amounts of labour directly or indirectly used for the production of each of them. For Case I to represent an equilibrium, demand conditions must be such that when the whole national income is paid out in wages and the prices of Z, Y, and X are determined in this way by their labour costs, consumers will in fact choose to purchase the 300 units of Z, the 200 units of Y, and the 100 units of X which will be supplied.

In Case II the rate of interest is again zero. Once more the economy must have reached a perfect-altruism stagnation situation. But the nature of the technical conditions and of the demand conditions which are necessary to make Case II an equilibrium situation are not the same as for Case I. Consumers must be prepared to consume in Case II the same quantities of Z, Y, and X as in Case I, although the prices of these goods are different; and this may well be due to the fact that consumers' tastes are different in Case II than Case I. Moreover, processes which may have been known in Case I but which it was not profitable to use in Case-I conditions (with, for example, labour costing $0 \cdot 1$) might be profitable in the conditions of Case II (with labour costing only $0 \cdot 05$); and, *vice versa*, many processes which might be known but unprofitable in Case-II conditions might be profitable in Case-I conditions. For Case II rather than Case I to represent an equilibrium situation may, therefore, imply different conditions of consumers' tastes and of technical possibilities of production; and it will certainly do so if the substitutability and the transformability between consumer goods in consumers' tastes and between outputs and inputs in output, input, and production programmes are at all large. For in Case I and Case II consumers choose the same consumption patterns and producers the same output, input, and production programmes, although there are great differences in the relative prices of all inputs and outputs. If substitutabilities and transformabilities are at all appreciable, this could only be so if consumers' tastes and technical possibilities differed between the two cases.

It is interesting to note that if Case II rather than Case I represented the equilibrium situation, the ratio of the value of the capital stock in the community to the total national income would be lower, even though all physical quantities of inputs and outputs were the same. Thus in Case I the total value of the capital stock is $67,000 and the *annual* national income is $100 \times \$100$ or $10,000, so that the ratio of capital value to annual income is $6 \cdot 7$. In Case II this ratio is only $6 \cdot 35$. This is so because Y is more important relatively to X as an element in the daily output than is J relatively to H in the capital stock. The result is that a rise in the price of Y and J relatively to that of X and H raises the value of output more than it raises the value of the capital stock.[1]

---

[1] We must note the awkward fact that the price of land (P_n) would in Case II rise towards infinity. An acre of land would be an asset which would earn $0 \cdot 0005$ a day or $0 \cdot 05$ a year. The capitalization of this fixed income at a zero rate of interest gives an infinitely high price for the asset, land. The other instruments K, J, and H have finite values because their net marginal products, as well as the rate of interest at which these are capitalized, are zero. Their market values depend upon the cost-price of their replacement in the various processes. The existence of assets like land which, however high may be the price offered for them, cannot be increased in supply to bring their marginal products down to zero is likely in fact to prevent the rate of interest from falling to zero. As real

Case III represents a situation in which, as in Case II, the rent of land and the rate of wages which entrepreneurs are prepared to pay to obtain inputs of land and labour turn out to be such that total income from rents equals total income from wages. But in Case III a perfect-selfishness stationary state has been reached (cf. p. 322 above) in which the rate of interest is still positive, i.e. when it is at a daily rate of 10 per cent per annum. Now Z and K are the capital-intensive products; and P_z and P_k are much higher, and P_y, P_j, P_x, and P_h considerably lower, in Case III than in Case II.[1] Since K is un-important relatively to J and H in the capital stock, the ratio of capital to annual income falls to $5 \cdot 7$. Interest accounts for $57 \cdot 2$ per cent and rents and wages each for $21 \cdot 4$ per cent of the national income. Once again, unless substitutabilities and transformabilities are minimal, for Case III to represent an equilibrium both con-sumers' tastes and technical conditions must be different from those necessary to let either Case I or Case II represent an equilibrium situation. At the cost-prices which will result from the factor prices of Case III consumers must be content with the supplies of Z, Y, and X and entrepreneurs with the processes of production shown in Table VIII.

Let us suppose that the quantities described in Table VIII and the prices and costs given in Case III of Tables XI and XII do in fact represent a stationary-state equilibrium. In Table X we have already derived from Table VIII the answer to the question how much of the various physical inputs are directly or indirectly needed to produce each of the outputs of final consumption goods, Z, Y, and X. We can now deal with the relative factor-intensities of the three final goods, Z, Y, and X, by applying the prices of Case III of Tables XI and XII to the three quantitative sub-systems of Table X. This is done in Table XIII.

The figures in this table are obtained simply by multiplying the equilibrium quantities of Table X by the equilibrium prices of Table XI. The right-hand column of Table XIII turns out, of course, to be the same as the figures in Case III of Table XII, which represents the values of inputs and outputs for this case for the whole economy. But the first three columns of Table XIII now show the values of output, of stocks of various instruments, and of the factor incomes accounted

capital is accumulated and the rate of interest falls towards zero, the value of land and so of total property rises towards infinity; and citizens are likely to stop saving before they are infinitely wealthy.

[1] It is to be observed that in Cases I and II $P_z = P_k$, $P_y = P_j$, and $P_x = P_h$ because Z is made solely from K, Y solely from J, and X solely from H, and the interest cost on investment in K, J, and H is zero. But in Case III P_z is slightly greater than P_k, P_y than P_j, and P_x than P_h because of the interest cost on the day's delay which it takes to convert K into Z, J into Y, and H into X.

for in the whole system by the production of Z, Y, and X separately. We can see now that, with our equilibrium set of quantities and of prices, of the total cost of production of Z 69 per cent represents interest, $15\frac{1}{2}$ per cent rent of land, and $15\frac{1}{2}$ per cent of wages, while in the case of Y these percentages are $43\frac{1}{2}$ per cent, 37 per cent, and $19\frac{1}{2}$ per cent respectively.

Table XIII

	Z	Sub-Systems Y	X	Total System
	$	$	$	$
$P_z Z$	50·4	—	—	50·4
$P_y Y$	—	18·2	—	18·2
$P_x X$	—	—	31·4	31·4
Total Consumption	50·4	18·2	31·4	100·0
$P_k K$	11,080	1,915	3,795	16,790·0
$P_j J$	5,095	1,525	2,480	9,100·0
$P_h H$	18,610	4,480	8,260	31,350·0
Total Value of Capital Stock	34,785	7,920	14,535	57,240·0
	$ %	$ %	$ %	
Interest:				
$i(P_k K + P_j J + P_h H)$	34·8 69·0	7·9 43·5	14·5 46·0	57·2
Rent: $W_n N$	7·8 15·5	6·7 37·0	6·9 22·0	21·4
Wages: $W_l L$	7·8 15·5	3·6 19·5	10·0 32·0	21·4
Total Income	50·4 100	18·2 100	31·4 100	100·0

Suppose then that we started in the equilibrium depicted in Table XIII and that there were a shift of demand (at the ruling prices and incomes) of $1 from Y to Z. This would represent indirectly a decrease of $0·04 in the demand for the services of labour (in the sense that at current wage rates and other costs $0·195 less would be spent on wages for labour to produce Y and $0·155 more to produce Z), a similar decrease of $0·215 in the demand for the services of land, and an increase of $0·255 in the demand for the services of capital, in the sense of a net increase in the amount of interest that would be paid on capital stock if all capital goods continued to be available at current prices.

But current prices would, of course, change. The fall in the rates of rent and of wages which would be caused by the indirect fall in demand for N and L would cause rent- and wage-intensive products like Y and X (and J and H) to fall relatively to interest-intensive products like Z (and K). Not only would the rate of interest have to be raised by the Central Bank to prevent the expanded demand for all capital goods in the capital-intensive Z-sub-system from causing an inflation of all prices and incomes; but the cost of interest-intensive instruments like K would rise relatively to rent- and wage-intensive instruments like J and H. There would be an incentive for producers not only to substitute the now relatively cheap labour and land for capital stocks of instruments of production in their production programmes, but also to alter the form of their capital investment and to use more of the now relatively cheaper rent- and wage-intensive instruments like J and H instead of the now relatively expensive interest-intensive instruments like K in their capital stocks.

But at this point we must stop this analysis. For we cannot indulge further, even for stationary systems, in comparative statics based upon the assumption of constant supplies of the basic factors of production, if these systems include man-made instruments of production. The process of change started off by the shift of demand from Y to Z will be similar to a process of economic growth in that as it takes place over time the stocks of the various man-made instruments of production, H, J, and K, will be altered. In *The Stationary Economy* we could indulge in comparative statics to our hearts' content because a precise meaning could be attached to an assumption that the inputs of the original factors, L and N, were the same (or differed by precisely stated amounts) in the two static situations which were compared. But, alas, there is no easy way of defining a constant stock of total capital when it is made up of a miscellaneous collection of different physical instruments, the quantities and the prices of which have altered between the two situations which are being compared. We must return from the description in this note of factor intensities in a many-product stationary state to the more difficult, but more realistic problems of the process of the development of such an economy through time.

CHAPTER XVIII

EQUILIBRIUM GROWTH IN A COMPETITIVE ECONOMY

In the last chapter we considered the conditions in which a many-product economy with man-made instruments of production might be in equilibrium in a stationary state. We must now turn to the basically different and, alas, much more difficult problems connected with the notion of equilibrium in a many-product economy with man-made investments of production, which is growing through time. For it is our intention in this volume as far as possible to analyse the movement through time of an economy which, while it is growing, nevertheless remains in equilibrium. Equilibrium movement through time essentially means that the citizens who take decisions about economic matters on any one day should not later, when they look back, regret what they have decided. In our perfectly competitive economy, in so far as the productive decisions of the entrepreneurs are concerned, this will certainly be true if (i) they know at 8 a.m. on any day what the technical possibilities of production are during that day and (ii) they have correctly foreseen the selling prices at which they can sell their output at 8 a.m. on the next day. In Part 1 of this volume we avoided this difficulty by assuming that there was only one product and that its money price was successfully stabilized by monetary action. Entrepreneurs had no difficulty in forecasting the future course of prices.

But this easy way out of the difficulty is no longer open to us. There are now a large number of different products, both consumption goods and instruments of production. Although we can, as we have already explained (see pp. 304–307 above), assume a successful financial policy which stabilizes some general index of selling prices, this does not get over our difficulty. For in a growing economy relative prices will certainly be changing, so that the expectation that the general level of money prices will be unchanged is not the same thing as the expectation that the price of a particular product which is of especial interest to a particular entrepreneur will remain unchanged.

We can still assume full employment to be maintained in our competitive system in the way in which we have assumed it to occur throughout the earlier chapters of the present volume. Given the prices at which the different entrepreneurs expect to be able to sell their products tomorrow morning and given the technical possibilities of production today, competition at 8 a.m. this morning among the entrepreneurs who hire the labour and the workers who sell their hours of labour can take place in such a way that the wage rate rises (or falls) until there is no excess demand for (or supply of) labour.

But even though we assume such conditions of perfect competition that there is always continuous full employment, this does not mean that the economic system will be in equilibrium. Disequilibrium will show itself through incorrect anticipations of price changes. Entrepreneurs at 8 a.m. on day 0 will determine their output programmes for day 0 knowing the cost of inputs at the beginning of day 0 but anticipating the prices at which the outputs of day 0's productive operations will be sold at 8 a.m. on day 1. In fact the prices of day 1 may turn out to be other than those which were anticipated and the entrepreneurs may wish that they had adopted some other output programme for day 0. While all resources will be employed on day 0, a 'wrong' set of outputs may be produced for use on day 1. Equilibrium movement through time can thus be defined as the state of affairs which would rule if all price changes were correctly anticipated.

One must distinguish between inconsistent and incorrect anticipations. Anticipations may be inconsistent. For example, on day 0 the sellers of an instrument may expect a higher price to rule on day 1 than do the buyers of the instrument so that either the sellers or the buyers (or both) must be disappointed. If the actual price on day 1 does not disappoint the sellers, then the buyers will in fact have to pay a higher price than they had anticipated and may wish that they had conducted their operations on day 0 in such a way as to need less of this instrument on day 1. If the actual price on day 1 does not disappoint the buyers, then the sellers may wish that they had produced less of it on day 0. But consistency of anticipations does not guarantee their correctness. Thus sellers and buyers may both anticipate the same price; but at this price sellers may decide to produce 100 units during day 0 while buyers may conduct their operations on day 0 so as to need 50 units of the product at the anticipated price on day 1. On day 1 at the anticipated price supply will exceed demand and the actual price on day 1 that will clear the market will be lower than anyone had anticipated.

With our present model then equilibrium through time is to be interpreted in terms of every potential buyer and seller correctly anticipating the movement of prices through time. This implies (i) that they all anticipate the same price and (ii) that at this anticipated price the total quantities which sellers plan to sell are equal to the total quantities which buyers plan to buy.

In some sense this implies perfect foresight. But can one attach any real meaning to an assumption of perfect foresight in this context? Citizen A would have to know what the totality of other citizens were going to do on the market in order to know what was going to happen to prices; and in this knowledge he would decide what he was going to do. But citizen B, included in the totality which citizen A was considering, would have to know what the totality of citizens excluding B and including A was going to do before deciding what he was going to do; and similarly for citizens C, D, E, etc. How can each continuously maintain a correct forecast of what the others are going to do except by the merest fluke?

Difficult as it may be to forecast correctly the selling price of something which he is planning to produce, entrepreneur A may try to comfort himself with the thought that, in our present perfectly competitive economy, he has at least only to consider at 8 a.m. on day 0 the prices of 8 a.m. on day 1 when he can sell all his produce in a perfect market and that he need not bother his head about days 2, 3, 4, etc. If so, he will be deluding himself. Suppose that entrepreneur A at 8 a.m. on day 0 is considering the production of an instrument (J_0) for sale to entrepreneur B as an input (J_1) at 8 a.m. on day 1. Theoretically, it can be shown, the price which A will receive from B (if B and everyone else has perfect foresight) may well depend upon the whole future history of the economy until kingdom come.

We can illustrate this by considering only one particular element, namely the future wage rate, which will affect the costs of operating, and so the value of, the machine (J). The price which it will be worth while offering for this machine will depend upon many things; but among these considerations is the future cost of the labour force needed to operate the machine. Now it is clear that the wage which will rule in the future will depend upon the whole supply-demand position in the labour market. In order, therefore, to know accurately the wage cost which will be incurred in the operation of the machine, say two years from now, entrepreneur B must know not only what will have happened to the supply of labour two years ahead but also what will have happened to influence the competing demands for labour in all other uses two years ahead; and this in turn will depend upon what will have happened to the supplies of the other inputs (the stocks of various instruments of production) with which the labour must co-operate, what will have happened to technical progress (the productivity of labour is alternative uses), what will have happened to the demand prices for various products (will the demand for other labour-intensive products have risen or fallen?), and so on.

It might at first sight appear that, difficult as this all is, at least there is a limit to the future time over which these relationships must be examined. In considering the current value to him of a machine which will only last for 10 years it might at first sight appear that entrepreneur B need not concern himself with anything which will happen in the economy more than 10 years hence. After all the machine will be dead by then and its present value cannot, therefore, be affected by any such distant dates. But, alas, even this comfort must be abandoned. The present value of the machine will depend *inter alia* upon the profit which can be expected to be made on it 9 years hence, and that will depend *inter alia* upon the wage rate ruling 9 years hence, and that will depend *inter alia* upon the demand for labour 9 years hence to make some other machine for some totally different industry which will last for, say, another 10 years, and that will depend *inter alia* upon the profit which can be expected on that second machine in that second industry 19 years hence, and that will depend *inter alia* upon the wage rate ruling 19 years hence—and so on either literally *ad infinitum* or until such time as a result of a nuclear explosion or other dramatic event the whole community shall cease to exist.[1]

What then can our entrepreneur A do in his attempt to foresee what the selling price of his product will be tomorrow morning (P_{j1})? Let us suppose that in despair he sets up a high-powered market-research unit in his business, staffed with fully trained economic theorists and econometricians, and hands the question over to them. How will they set about the task? Let us suppose that they start by asking their employer, entrepreneur A, whether they are to allow for the fact that entrepreneur B may make a mistake in his forecasts of what he can earn on the machine, J, when he has bought it. Let us suppose further that entrepreneur A answers this question by pointing out that all other entrepreneurs—including entrepreneur B—are now so enlightened that they in their turn have set up equally efficient market-research units which will prevent them from making mistakes. In other words, entrepreneur A instructs his market-research unit to forecast the price P_{j1} on the assumption that that price and all other future prices are equilibrium prices in the sense that no buyer or seller in the future will ever regret any transaction in which he takes part.

[1] Throughout the rest of this volume we shall assume that the world will come to an end at some future finite date, which may, of course, be very distant. This assumption greatly simplifies the exposition and in particular avoids a basic difficulty in defining an efficient time path (see pp. 483–484 below). The astronomers do in fact tell us that this world will not last for ever. It is a red-letter day in the life of an economist when he can simplify his analysis by the choice of a realistic assumption.

Entrepreneur A's market-research unit would next need to approach a consultant firm of eschatologists, cosmologists, and nuclear strategists in order to discover at what precise date in the future human society on this earth was going to end. Let us suppose that the answer is midday on day $T + 1$ (where $T = 10,000,000$).

Next they would have to commission some University department of applied economics to work out on the basis of past data and in consultation with a consultant firm of sociologists, social psychologists, and fashion experts what the future demand and savings functions of the population were going to be. That is to say they would need to know how much of each consumption good, X and Y, would be purchased at any point of time (and how much income would in consequence be saved) by any citizen with a given income, a given rate of interest, and given prices of the consumption goods, P_x and P_y.

Next, they would need to find out from a consultant firm of demographers what was going to happen to the population between day 0 and day T.

Finally, they would need to find out from a consultant firm of technologists what were going to be all the technical possibilities of production on every day from day 0 to day T. Such forecasts of technical possibilities could be laid out in the form shown in Table XIV.

This table illustrates the possibilities only for today, tomorrow, and the next day (days 0, 1, and 2); but the ideas can readily in principle be extended for any number of further periods into the future. We assume that in the whole economy there are only three inputs, labour (L) and two intermediate products (J and K), and two consumption goods (X and Y). The schema could readily be extended to cover more than one type of labour and many more intermediate products and consumption goods.[1] On day 0 there are a certain number of processes available for the production of these outputs by means of these inputs. We have in Table XIV illustrated the position with the assumption that there are only two processes available, a and b; but once more the ideas can readily in principle be extended to cover a large number of processes.

Technical progress can only mean that new processes are discovered. Accordingly in Table XIV we assume that the technologists report that on day 1 a further process c and on day 2 a further process d will be discovered and will become available for use. When a new process is discovered and becomes available for use, this does not

---

[1] We have for simplification omitted land (N) on the grounds given above (pp. 286–287) that it is difficult to treat land and man-made intermediate products differently.

mean that an existing process is forgotten. Thus technical progress enlarges the range of available processes. On day 0 processes a and b are available; on day 1 processes a, b, and c will be available; and on day 2 processes a, b, c, and d. But a newly discovered process may dominate technically an old process. Suppose that in process c no

Table XIV

		Processes			
		a	b	c	d
Day 2	Outputs	Y_a X_a $\bar{K}_a$ J_a	Y_b X_b $\bar{K}_b$ J_b	Y_c X_c $\bar{K}_c$ J_c	Y_d X_d $\bar{K}_d$ J_d
	Inputs	K_a J_a L_a	K_b J_b L_b	K_c J_c L_c	K_d J_d L_d
	Scale	0	0	S_{c2}	S_{d2}
Day 1	Outputs	Y_a X_a $\bar{K}_a$ J_a	Y_b X_b $\bar{K}_b$ J_b	Y_c X_c $\bar{K}_c$ J_c	
	Inputs	K_a J_a L_a	K_b J_b L_b	K_c J_c L_c	
	Scale	0	S_{b1}	S_{c1}	
Day 0	Outputs	Y_a X_a $\bar{K}_a$ J_a	Y_b X_b $\bar{K}_b$ J_b		
	Inputs	K_a J_a L_a	K_b J_b L_b		
	Scale	S_{a0}	S_{b0}		

input co-efficient will be higher and no output co-efficient will be lower than in process a, but at least one input co-efficient will be lower or one output co-efficient higher than in process a, then process a is technically inferior to process c. After day 0 process a will never be used because the use of process c would always enable more of something to be produced or less of some cost to be incurred without any short-fall in other outputs or any excess of other costs.[1] Of course, a new process c may be invented which does not dominate process a. Suppose, for example, that the two processes were exactly the same in all respects except that $J_a > J_c$ and $K_a < K_c$. Then the invention is one which enables a producer to produce the same output with the same inputs except that less J and more K is employed. It is an invention for substituting K for J. It will be profitable to use it if the price of K is low relatively to the price of J, but not if the price of K is high relatively to the price of J. In the example given in Table XIV we have assumed, simply in order to simplify our future use of the table, that process c will dominate process a technically and process d will dominate process b technically, so that with the introduction of process c on day 1 we have eliminated further consideration of process a and with the introduction of process d on day 2 we have eliminated further consideration of process b. We have shown this in the table by marking as zero the scales on which process a will be used on days 1 and 2 and on which process b will be used on day 2.

With all this information (enumerated on page 348) entrepreneur A's market-research unit can now set to work to forecast the price P_{j1}. The research unit has been told by the demographers that each day there will be certain total supplies of labour coming forward on to the labour market—namely L_0, L_1, L_2, etc. But each day the total use of labour must not exceed the available labour supply, so that the research unit will know that the following constraints will have to be observed:

$$\left.\begin{array}{l} S_{a0}L_a + S_{b0}L_b \leqslant L_0 \\ S_{b1}L_b + S_{c1}L_c \leqslant L_1 \\ S_{c2}L_c + S_{d2}L_d \leqslant L_2 \end{array}\right\} \qquad (18.1)$$

The above expressions state that the demand for labour in the various processes must be equal to, or less than, the total available supply of labour. Normally the demand will be equal to the supply. We are assuming a flexible labour market so that the wage rate ruling at 8 a.m. on day 0 is reduced until entrepreneurs expand their operations so that all labour is employed. In this model the only possibility that the demand for labour should remain less than the supply of labour would be in the case in which the supply of labour was so great relatively to the supply of the instruments of production with which it had to work (J_0, K_0) that the physical marginal product of labour was literally zero. In this case even though the wage rate was zero, the demand for labour would remain less than the supply.[2]

---

[1] See *The Stationary Economy*, pp. 127–8.
[2] Cf. *The Stationary Economy*, p. 190.

In the normal case the wage rate will be positive and the demand for labour will equal the supply.

The link between the productive system on day 0 and day 1 is provided by the existence of intermediate products. Each day the use of any one instrument of production must not exceed the quantity of that instrument actually available for use. Thus the research unit will know that:

$$\left.\begin{array}{l} S_{a0}J_a + S_{b0}J_b \leqslant J_{-1} \\ S_{b1}J_b + S_{c1}J_c \leqslant S_{a0}J_a + S_{b0}J_b \\ S_{c2}J_c + S_{d2}J_d \leqslant S_{b1}J_b + S_{a1}J_c \end{array}\right\} \quad (18.2)$$

At 8 a.m. on day 0 there is a given supply of the instrument of production J equal to the output of that instrument on day -1, namely J_{-1}. The use of that instrument on day 0 in process a ($S_{a0}J_a$) and in process b ($S_{b0}J_b$) must be equal to or less than that available supply. If the demand is less than the supply, then the price of the instrument will be zero ($P_{j0} = 0$); if, however, the price is positive, then the instrument must be scarce and the whole available supply will be used. Now the scales on which processes a and b are in fact used on day 0 will determine the output of J of day 0, available for use on day 1, namely $S_{a0}J_a + S_{b0}J_b$. The amount of J used as an input on day 1 ($S_{b1}J_b + S_{c1}J_c$) must be equal to or less than this available supply. And similarly the output of J on day 1 provides a link with the scale of operations on day 2, since the output on day 1 sets an upper limit to the input on day 2.

There will be a similar set of conditions for the other instrument of production, namely

$$\left.\begin{array}{l} S_{a0}K_a + S_{b0}K_b \leqslant \bar{K}_{-1} \\ S_{b1}K_b + S_{c1}K_c \leqslant S_{a0}\bar{K}_a + S_{b0}\bar{K}_b \\ S_{c2}K_c + S_{d2}K_d \leqslant S_{b1}\bar{K}_b + S_{c1}\bar{K}_c \end{array}\right\} \quad (18.3)[1]$$

The research unit must find out what the existing supplies of instruments of production are. In our model this means that it must discover what yesterday's output of instruments of production were (namely, J_{-1} and $\bar{K}_{-1}$), since these are the inputs of instruments

---

[1] A growth in the supplies of the instruments of production—J_{-1}, J_0, J_1, and $\bar{K}_{-1}, \bar{K}_0, \bar{K}_1$—represents capital accumulation, a greater and greater supply of real instruments of production being available for use. This implies that each day a combination of processes is chosen which are not too intensive in the outputs X and Y but are intensive in the outputs $\bar{J}$ and $\bar{K}$, so that there is a net output $(\bar{J} - J)$ and $(\bar{K} - K)$ of the instruments of production. People are saving sufficient and the rate of interest is low enough (cf. p. 307) to raise the selling prices of instruments relatively to the selling prices of consumption goods to induce entrepreneurs to expand the productive processes which are intensive in $\bar{J}$ and $\bar{K}$ relatively to those which are intensive in X and Y.

which are available to the economy at 8 a.m. on day 0 (namely, J_0 and K_0). Together with the information given to it by the demographers it will now know

$$\left. \begin{array}{l} J_0 \; K_0 \\ L_0 \, L_1 \, L_k \dots \dots L_T \end{array} \right\} \qquad (18.4)$$

The knowledge of these inputs given in (18.4) together with the knowledge of the technical constraints on the future development of the economy given in (18.1), (18.2), and (18.3) will now give the research unit a complete description of the limits set to the future flows of outputs in the economy. But there are, of course, within these limits innumerable possible patterns of output flows over the days 0 to T. On day 0 within the limits set by the initial inputs L_0, J_0, and K_0 and by the technological possibilities of (18.1), (18.2), and (18.3) there is a large number of possible patterns of outputs for the day $(X_0, \; Y_0, \; \bar{J}_0, \; \bar{K}_0)$ according to the scales chosen for the various processes available on day 0. Each of these patterns will present a different set of inputs available at 8 a.m. on day 1 (L_1, J_1, K_1) and each one of these sets of inputs can in its turn lead to a large number of patterns of outputs for day 1. Thus as the research unit peers into the future, the more distant the date the greater the number of possible patterns of productive activity in the community.

We have already indicated (pp. 346–347 above) that, in order to forecast the price P_{j1}, entrepreneur A's research unit would have to consider the whole future course of the economy. Since, through the interplay of the prices of supply and demand in each market at each point of time, the quantities available on the market will affect the prices offered for the various products and the prices offered will in turn affect the quantities produced, it is necessary for the research unit to determine the whole future course of quantities and prices in the economy.

The future quantities[1] which have to be determined are

$$\left. \begin{array}{l} X_0, \; X_1, \; X_2 \dots \dots X_T \\ Y_0, \; Y_1, \; Y_2 \dots \dots Y_T \\ J_0, \; J_1, \; J_2 \;\;\; \dots \dots J_T \\ \bar{K}_0, \; \bar{K}_1, \; \bar{K}_2 \dots \dots \bar{K}_T \end{array} \right\} \qquad (18.5)$$

The above represent all the future outputs of consumption goods and instruments of production. Up till 8 a.m. on day 0 the outputs of

---

[1] We assume that the research unit is burning the midnight oil. It is making its calculations between 4 p.m. on day -1 (when the outputs $\bar{J}_{-1}$ and $\bar{K}_{-1}$ are known) and 8 a.m. on day 0 (when the decisions about X_0, Y_0, $\bar{J}_0$, and $\bar{K}_0$ are still to be taken).

day 0 (X_0, Y_0, etc.) are still unknown. On day $T + 1$ the world is going to end at midday so that there will be no output after day T.
The future prices which have to be determined are

$$\left. \begin{array}{l} W_{l0}, W_{l1}, W_{l2} \ldots \ldots W_{lT} \ W_{l,T+1} \\ i_0, i_1, i_2 \qquad \ldots \ldots i_T \ i_{T+1} \\ P_{x0}, P_{x1}, P_{x2} \ \ldots \ldots P_{xT} \ P_{x,T+1} \\ P_{y0}, P_{y1}, P_{y2} \ \ldots \ldots P_{yT} \ P_{y,T+1} \\ P_{j0}, P_{j1}, P_{j2} \ \ldots \ldots P_{jT} \ P_{j,T+1} \\ P_{k0}, P_{k1}, P_{k2} \ \ldots \ldots P_{kT} \ P_{k,T+1} \end{array} \right\} \qquad (18.6)$$

All the prices at 8 a.m. on day 0 are still to be determined. After midday on day $T + 1$ the economy will no longer exist so that no market prices can exist after those set at 8 a.m. on day $T + 1$.

The research unit has now to find a set of output flows for (18.5) and a set of price movements for (18.6) which satisfy all the requirements of the competitive economic system moving in an equilibrium manner, i.e. in such a way that no buyer or seller, producer or consumer ever regrets his actions. The requirements which must be satisfied can be enumerated as follows.

(1) The output flows must be within the technical limits set by (18.1), (18.2), (18.3), and (18.4).

(2) $P_{x0} + P_{y0} = P_{x1} + P_{y1} = \ldots = P_{x,T+1} + P_{y,T+1} = \$2$, on the assumption that it is the declared policy of the authorities so to control total money demand as to stabilize the price index $P_x + P_y$ at \$2 (see page 304 above).

(3) $W_{l\,T+1} = i_{T+1} = P_{j,T+1} = P_{k,T+1} = 0$. Since the world is to end at midday on day $T + 1$, no one at 8 a.m. on that day will make any bid for factors of production to produce during day $T + 1$. The end of the world will come before the day's output can appear. The prices of all inputs at 8 a.m. on day $T + 1$ will, therefore, be zero. This is not true of the prices of consumption goods. (Indeed, we have already stated that $P_{x,T+1} + P_{y,T+1} = \$2$.) Consumers on day $T + 1$ will have between 8 a.m. and midday on that day to consume, as they wait quietly for the end, the supplies of X and Y which they can purchase that morning.

(4) On any one day the relationships between the input prices and the output prices of that day (e.g. for day 3 between W_{l3}, i_3, P_{j3}, P_{k3} and P_{x4}, P_{y4}, P_{j4}, P_{k4}) must be such that (i) no process which is being used is making a net profit or loss, since otherwise entrepreneurs would regret not having contracted or expanded that process and (ii) no process which is not being used could make a net profit, since otherwise entrepreneurs would regret not having introduced that process.

M

(5) The scales chosen for the various processes and so the outputs produced on any one day must be such that, at the prices ruling for the sale of the outputs of that day, the value of the day's output is maximized. For if this were not so, it would have been possible for some entrepreneur to have increased his profit by using some of the available inputs to produce a more valuable output than they were in fact producing. Looking back he would regret not having made a profit in this way.

(6) The prices and the quantities of the consumption goods at 8 a.m. on each day must be compatible with the consumers' demand functions. The development of the wage rate and the rate of interest together with the accumulation of property by the various classes of citizen will determine the level and distribution of personal incomes. The quantities of X and Y on the market at any one time must be equal to the amounts which, at the ruling prices of X and Y and with the given level and distribution of personal incomes, the consumers would wish to purchase at that time.

(7) Let us assume that it is the government's declared policy to see that interest rates are set in such a manner that there is no need to pay out any subsidies to consumers, or to impose any taxes on them, for the purpose of maintaining the stability of the cost of living, $P_x + P_y$. In the absence of such consumer subsidies or taxes there will be certain limited supplies of X and Y which consumers will purchase at any one time at this stabilized level for the prices at which such goods are available in the shops. It must be assumed, therefore, that the Central Bank succeeds at each point of time in setting rates of interest such that entrepreneurs' demands for instruments of production take up just so much of the community's resources as are not needed to fulfil the untaxed-unsubsidized consumers' demands, so that full employment of resources is maintained.

On the basis of the information which we are assuming it to have collected from various sources it would be theoretically possible for entrepreneur A's research unit, on the conditions (1) to (7) enumerated above, to calculate a set of all the future outputs of (18.5) and of all the future prices of (18.6) which would represent an equilibrium path through time. Among these prices is P_{j1}, which the research unit is now in a position to report to its employer.[1]

---

[1] We shall not at this point go any more deeply into the methods involved in finding an equilibrium set of future quantities and prices which satisfies the conditions (1) to (7) stated above. As will shortly become clear this question is very closely analogous to the questions which a planning authority in a socialist economy would have to answer; and we shall be returning to the problem in the next chapter when we discuss the formation of a plan for a socialist economy.

But one difficulty still remains. It is not at all certain that there will be only one set of future outputs and of future prices which will constitute an equilibrium path through time. Let us take a simple example of the possibility of two equilibrium growth paths. Suppose that we are in a Plantcap, that owners consume mainly goods which we will call 'luxuries', that workers consume mainly goods which we will call 'necessities', that luxuries are directly and indirectly very capital-intensive in their production, and that necessities are directly and indirectly very labour-intensive in their production. Suppose that the economy starts off now on a path which concentrates on building up a productive apparatus to produce many luxuries and few necessities, because the future selling price of luxuries is expected to be high and that of necessities is expected to be low. The production of luxuries and of instruments to produce luxuries is capital-intensive, so that this growth path increases the demand for the use of instruments of production rather than for labour and thus enriches the owners of property rather than the workers; and just because the owners (who are thus enriched) spend their money mainly on luxuries the demand for, and so the selling prices of, luxuries does turn out to be high as was expected. Nobody's expectations are disappointed and so this growth path turns out to be an equilibrium path.

But this might also have been the case if the expectation had been that the price of luxuries would be low and that of necessities high. The production of necessities is assumed to be labour-intensive so that its expansion would have enriched the workers rather than the owners, and the workers do demand necessities rather than luxuries. Once again the growth path might be an equilibrium one.[1]

To return to the problem of our entrepreneur A who is interested in forecasting the price P_{j1}, his research unit may have to report that there are two or more possible equilibrium paths for the future economy, and that the price P_{j1} will be different according to which path is chosen. And which path is chosen will, of course, depend upon which path every other entrepreneur assumes will be chosen. Only if they all assume that the same path will be chosen will they in fact act with a consistent set of expectations so that they could all take decisions which none would regret in the future. Clearly such consistency of expectations would be a mere fluke unless it were achieved by some outside—presumably governmental—guidance. The possibility of there being more than one equilibrium path is, therefore, a reason for governmental action in the sphere of planning

[1] Figure 20 on page 73 of *The Stationary Economy* illustrates a static position in which there are two equilibrium situations. For a further analysis of this static possibility see the note at the end of this chapter (pp. 357–359 below).

which we will consider later in our discussion of 'indicative planning' in Chapter XXII. For the moment we will assume (what may well be the case) that there is only one unique equilibrium growth path and that entrepreneur A's research unit reports to entrepreneur A the resulting value of P_{j1}.

It may, however, already have occurred to the attentive reader that even in this case the research unit would find insuperable difficulties in carrying out its elaborate task, that the cost of doing so might well impose on entrepreneur A an expenditure which was much greater than any loss which he might occur from guessing the future price P_{j1}, and that in any case it would be a rather wasteful duplication of effort that every individual entrepreneur should be employing an equally elaborate research unit to do exactly the same calculations which would be necessary for the forecasting of each particular price in which each particular entrepreneur was interested. These thoughts are all justified. The calculations could not be carried out with the precision outlined above; it would not pay individual entrepreneurs to commission them; and the task, in so far as it or something like it can be done, is clearly one which it would be economical to carry out jointly for the use of many or all entrepreneurs simultaneously.

Nevertheless the fairy story related in this chapter may have its utility. It has been designed primarily to illustrate the very important, even if awkward, fact that in any economy growing through time a general equilibrium set of outputs and prices involves interrelationships between all prices and all quantities of all goods and services *at all points of time*. Just as in *The Stationary Economy*, in a general many-product equilibrium every price and output is related to every other price and output; the difference is that in *The Growing Economy* we can no longer assume that the price and the output of each product is constant over time.

There is, however, a second important use for our fairy story. We shall argue later (Chapter XXIII, pp. 479–483 below), that *equilibrium* growth, as we have defined it in the present chapter, is the same as *efficient* growth in a way in which we will define it in Chapter XXIII. Each individual entrepreneur may not find it worth while to indulge in the extensive researches outlined in the present chapter. It may pay him to use much cheaper, if less accurate ways, of 'guessing' what P_{j1} will be. Yet it may pay the community as a whole through its government or some other communal institution to carry out the sort of general forecasting of an equilibrium set of prices and quantities which we have described in the present chapter. We will show in Chapter XXII how this activity relates to what we shall call 'indicative planning'. Indeed, if equilibrium growth is efficient growth, there is an obvious relationship between the activities of entrepreneur A's research unit (described in this chapter) and the functions of a governmental planning unit.

For this reason it is worth while pursuing a bit further and with rather more rigorous analysis the problems theoretically involved in making a precise estimate of the future course of events, taking all the relevant factors into account. It is clear from the general nature of the problem as we have already outlined it in the present chapter that one of the basic problems facing an entrepreneur in any major decision about investment in an instrument of production at the present moment is the interconnection between many various parts of the economy over considerable future periods of time. It is in connection with the working out of the implications for present actions of these future interconnections between various sectors of the economy that national economic plans are devised. Accordingly we will illustrate the problems in their starkest form in the next chapter by considering the basic problems involved in forming a total economic plan in a fully planned economy, the object of the plan being that the present actions of those in charge of the economy will have the most desirable effects in view of all their future implications through the nexus of economic interrelationships in the whole economy.

Note to Chapter XVIII

MULTIPLE EQUILIBRIA

The purpose of this note is to show that the two equilibrium points Q_1 and Q_3 shown in Figure 20 on page 73 of *The Stationary Economy* are a simple static analogy of the dynamic possibility of two equilibrium growth paths discussed on page 355 above. Figure 38 reproduces Figure 20 of *The Stationary Economy*, showing, however, not the offer curves of the two groups A and B (i.e. the curves $O-O_a$ and $O-O_b$ of Figure 20 of *The Stationary Economy*) but the pattern of indifference curves of the two groups which must lie behind these offer curves.

In Figure 38 we suppose[1] that group A produces a fixed output of X, namely OA units of X, and that group B produces a fixed output of Y, namely OB units of Y. The two groups then exchange some X for some Y in a perfectly competitive market. We measure B's consumption of Y vertically downward from the point B and B's consumption of X horizontally to the right from the point B. We can then draw a set of indifference curves for the group B, namely I_b', I_b'',

---

[1] The reader is referred to Chapter IV of *The Stationary Economy* for a full discussion of the figure.

I_b''', etc. Similarly we measure A's consumption of Y (and X) vertically up (and horizontally to the left from) the point A; and we can then draw A's indifference curves I_a', I_a'', I_a''', etc.

The points Q_1 and Q_3 in Figure 38 correspond to the points Q_1 and Q_3 in Figure 20 of *The Stationary Economy*. We have chosen to draw a set of indifference curves which would mean that there were these two possible equilibrium points of exchange. If the terms of trade were very favourable to group A (as with the slope of the line marked α which shows that much Y can be obtained for each unit of X)

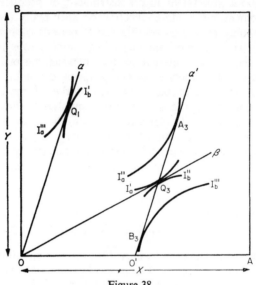

Figure 38

then both groups A and B would be content with the trading point Q_1. If, however, the terms of trade were very favourable to group B (as with the line marked β) both groups would be content with the point Q_3.

We can now see what lies behind this possibility of a double equilibrium. Draw through the point Q_3 the line marked α', parallel to the line marked α; and let the line α' cut OA at the point O'. Since Q_3 is an equilibrium point there must be an A-indifference curve (I_a') and a B-indifference curve (I_b') both tangential to the terms of trade line β at this point, and therefore tangential to each other. Inspection of the figure then shows that there must be an A-indifference curve (I_a'') tangential to the line α' at some point (A_3) north-east of Q_3, and that there must be a B-indifference curve (I_b''') tangential to the line α' at some point (B_3) south-west of Q_3.

Suppose now that we start at the equilibrium point Q_1 with terms of trade given by the line α. Suppose then that group A is forced to pay a tribute of OO' units of X to group B. The group A now starts with only AO' units of X to trade; and group B starts with OB units of Y plus OO' units of X to trade. Trade starts from the point O' instead of from the point O. If the terms of trade were unchanged (α' parallel to α), group A would wish to trade to the point A_3, but group B would wish to trade to the point B_3. There would be a large excess demand for Y and a large excess supply of X; this occurs because group A when its real income has fallen has reduced mainly its demand for X (A_3 is far to the right of, but only a little below, Q_1) whereas group B when its real income has risen has increased its demand mainly for Y (B_3 is much below and only moderately to the right of Q_1). In other words both group A and group B concentrate changes in their incomes mainly on changes in demand for their own products.

It is this which gives the possibility of a double equilibrium. When the terms of trade move against group A (from line α to line β), this transfers real income from group B to group A. But a transfer of real income from group B to group A in the absence of a change in the terms of trade would cause an excess demand for B's product Y and an excess supply of A's product X. The shift of real income would therefore necessitate a change in the terms of trade against A's product X. Multiple equilibria may, therefore, occur where a transfer of income and wealth from group A to group B would itself cause a shift of demand from the products which group A was specially concerned in producing to the products which group B was specially concerned in producing. A deterioration in the terms of trade against A 'causes' a reduction in the real income of A and a rise in the real income of B; this transfer of real income 'causes' a shift of demand from A's product to B's product; and this shift of demand 'causes' a deterioration in the terms of trade against A. The cycle is closed. Either the initial (Q_1) or the new (Q_3) position is one in which supply equals demand for both products.

CHAPTER XIX

PLANNED GROWTH IN A SOCIALIST ECONOMY

Let us then consider how the Central Authority in a Plansoc might cope with these problems. Let us put the problems in terms of the simple example given on pp. 347–356 above and illustrated in Table XIV. At 8 a.m. on day 0 the Central Authority has at its disposal certain resources for employment, namely L_0 units of labour, $\bar{J}_{-1}$ units of the intermediate product J, and $\bar{K}_{-1}$ units of the intermediate product K, $\bar{J}_{-1}$ and $\bar{K}_{-1}$ being the outputs of J and K respectively of the previous day, namely day -1. The sole problem with which the Central Authority is concerned is to decide how best to use L_0, $\bar{J}_{-1}$, and $\bar{K}_{-1}$ during day 0. But in order to do this it will have to look beyond day 0 to see what intermediate products are required on day 1, since the use of the available resources during day 0 will determine what man-made instruments of production are available for use on day 1; and so on. For this purpose the Central Authority at 8 a.m. on day 0 must make a plan which involves forecasting what it considers are likely to be the needs of days 1, 2, 3, etc., but which does not involve hard and fast decisions about how resources will in fact be used on days 1, 2, 3, etc. The best possible forecasts of how resources will be used on days 1, 2, 3, etc., are needed to form hard and fast decisions about how to allocate resources at 8 a.m. on day 0 for use during day 0. But it is not until 8 a.m. on day 1 that hard and fast decisions need to be taken about how resources are used during day 1; and when the morning of day 1 comes the plan can be revised in the light of new knowledge, new experience, and new guesses about days 2, 3, etc.

Let us suppose that for this purpose of deciding how resources should be allocated at 8 a.m. on day 0 the Central Authority in our Plansoc is making a 3-day plan, i.e. a plan for the use of resources over the three days 0, 1, and 2. In order to formulate such a plan the Central Authority must (1) have certain knowledge or make certain guesses about the supplies of certain inputs, (2) have certain knowledge or make certain guesses about technical production possibilities, and (3) make certain judgements about how it will value certain outputs relatively to each other. Let us consider each of these in turn.

(1) The Central Authority must be informed how much labour and how much intermediate products it has initially at 8 a.m. on day 0 at its disposal. It must know L_0, J_{-1}, and $\bar{K}_{-1}$. It must also make some independent forecasts of what, over the period of the plan, is going to happen to those resources which are given independently of the plan and which are not themselves the products of industry. In the present model this means simply that it must make, on demographic principles, forecasts of L_1 and L_2, since in our present simple model we are treating land in the same way as a man-made instrument of production and are considering only labour as an original factor whose supply is not itself an outcome of the productive process.

(2) The Central Authority must have knowledge of, or make the best guesses it can about, the technical possibilities of production that rule during day 0 and that will rule during the future days—day 1 and day 2—of the plan. It must, that is to say, make estimates of all the technical co-efficients (Y_a, Y_b, Y_c, Y_d, K_a, K_b, K_c, K_d, etc., etc.) which are displayed in Table XIV. This implies that it must not only know the technical possibilities which exist on day 0 (i.e. the technical co-efficients for processes a and b) but must also make estimates of what new technical possibilities will arise in the future days of the plan (i.e. the technical co-efficients in process c which is going to be invented on day 1 and the technical co-efficients in process d which is going to be invented on day 2). It is, for example, impossible to make a correct estimate about how many of today's resources should be devoted to the production of a raw material until some estimate is made of how tomorrow's technical inventions may affect the needs for that material. There may at first sight appear to be an inconsistency in this assumption that tomorrow's new technical co-efficients are known, or at least reasonably guessed, today. Can one know what the effects of an invention will be without having made the invention? And if the invention were already made, would not the process of production itself be already available for use today? Invention does, of course, introduce necessarily a large measure of uncertainty into plans. But to make a plan one must make assumptions about what inputs will be needed to produce what outputs in future periods of the plan; and one can to some extent make reasonably well informed guesses about the sort of technical progress which is likely to occur in the near future without having actually made that technical progress.[1]

---

[1] The unavoidable uncertainty about future technical progress well illustrates the limited purpose of the plan, to which we drew attention above (p. 360). The purpose of the plan made at 8 a.m. on day 0 is solely to improve the hard and fast decision which must then inevitably be taken about the use of resources on day 0. But to do this one must plan ahead the activities of days 1 and 2, in order to know what instruments of production shonld be made on day 0 for future use. But in

(3) The final purpose of all production is to produce various goods and services for final consumption at various points in time. In the 3-day plan, X_0, X_1, X_2, Y_0, Y_1, Y_2 will be the six relevant outputs of consumption goods. Different plans which could be formed at 8 a.m. on day 0 for the use of resources would have different effects upon these six outputs. One plan would use resources which produced much Y relatively to X so that $\dfrac{Y_0}{X_0}$, $\dfrac{Y_1}{X_1}$ and $\dfrac{Y_2}{X_2}$ would all be high; another plan would produce always little Y and much X. One plan would produce few consumption goods in the present and many in the future, so that $\dfrac{X_1}{X_0}$, $\dfrac{X_2}{X_1}$, $\dfrac{Y_1}{Y_0}$, and $\dfrac{Y_2}{Y_1}$ would all be high whereas another plan would produce much for consumption now and little for the future. In order to choose between these plans the Central Authority must decide how to value the outputs of the different consumption goods at different points of time relatively to each other. This it can do by setting a present valuation, V, on each such output, which we will call V_{x1}, V_{x2}, V_{x3}, V_{y1}, V_{y2}, and V_{y3} respectively.[1] We will have much to say in the sequel about the principles upon which these V's might best be determined. For the moment we will concentrate only on their meaning and implications when they have been determined. Thus suppose that $\dfrac{V_{x2}}{V_{y3}} = 3$. This implies that the Central Authority has decided to plan the use of resources at 8 a.m. on day 0 on the assumption that a unit of output of X ready for consumption at 8 a.m. on day 2 is worth three times as much as a unit of output of Y ready for consumption at 8 a.m. on day 3. If, therefore, it were possible to revise the plan in such a way that, by altering somewhat the use of L_0, J_{-1}, and $\bar{K}_{-1}$ at 8 a.m. on day 0 and by subsequent modifications of planned uses of resources during days 1 and 2, it were possible to obtain 1 more unit of X_1 at the expense of losing $2\frac{1}{2}$ units of Y_2 without any change in any other final outputs, then the revised plan would be adopted. It would obtain 1 more unit of X for consumption on day 2 at the cost of $2\frac{1}{2}$ units of Y for consumption on day 3, whereas the Central Authority values 1 more unit of X for

order to know the best activities for days 1 and 2 one must forecast what will be the technical possibilities of production on those future days. When the morning of day 1 comes there is no need to allocate the resources then available on the basis of the plan made on day 0. A new and revised plan can be made on the basis of, *inter alia*, improved information about present and future technical possibilities.

[1] V_{x1} is the valuation set on a unit of X coming forward to be consumed at the beginning of *day 1* and, therefore, produced as a result of the operations of *day 0*. Thus V_{x1} refers to X_0, V_{x2} to X_1, and so on, just as P_{x1} refers to X_0, P_{x2} to X_1 and so on. (See p. 301.)

consumption on day 2 as being worth 3 units of Y for consumption on day 3.

It will be observed that in the above we have said nothing about the valuation to be set by the Central Authority on the inputs or outputs of the intermediate products. In so far as the inputs and outputs of days 0 and 1 and the inputs of day 2 are concerned, nothing need be said. The Central Authority is interested as final objectives of policy only in feeding, clothing, housing, and supplying with other consumption goods the citizens of the community. These outputs must have relative social valuations put upon them to determine in advance their importance as conflicting final objectives of the plan. But the output of steel on day 1 (J_1) which will be used as an input into the productive process of day 2 (J_2) has no value as an ultimate objective of policy. Its size will be determined by the requirements of the plan to produce X_0, X_1, X_2, Y_0, Y_1, Y_2; but given these final outputs it is a matter of complete indifference in itself whether J_1 or J_2 is large or small in quantity.

The situation is, however, quite different in the 3-day plan in the case of the outputs of the intermediate products which will be produced at the end of the 3-day plan (namely $\bar{J}_2$ and $\bar{K}_2$) and which will be available for use at the beginning of the period (day 3) which lies beyond and outside the plan. The size of these outputs—i.e. the quantity of capital goods accumulated by the end of the plan period—is not a matter of indifference to the Central Authority. How much should the plan be devised to keep down consumption levels during the plan in order to accumulate larger amounts of capital goods to put into the production process after the plan period? Somehow or other the outputs $\bar{J}_2$ and $\bar{K}_2$ must be valued relatively to the outputs X_0, X_1, X_2, Y_0, Y_1, Y_2. Here there are three possibilities.

(i) Suppose that the end of the world were confidently expected to occur at midday on day 3. Then we could set the valuations of $\bar{J}_2$ and $\bar{K}_2$ at zero (i.e. $V_{j3} = V_{k3} = 0$).[1] Any productive activity on day 3 would be useless because, in our model, the fruits of day 3's productive activities would not appear until after midday on day 3, by which time all consumers will be dead. But since it is useless to try to produce anything on day 3, inputs of J_3 and K_3 would be useless. This is the same as saying that outputs of $\bar{J}_2$ and $\bar{K}_2$ are valueless, though outputs of X_2 and Y_2 (which can be consumed during the morning of day 3) still have a value.

(ii) If we cannot make the convenient assumption that the end of

[1] Just as V_{x3} is the valuation set in the plan on a unit of X produced on day 2 but ready for consumption on day 3, so V_{j3} is the valuation set on a unit of J produced on day 2 but ready for use in the productive system on day 3. Thus V_{j3} refers to $\bar{J}_2$ or to J_3.

the world is in sight, then by some means or another some value must be imputed in the plan to the supplies of capital goods which will be left over as a result of the plan to carry on productive operations after the end of the plan. One way of doing this would be for the authorities to fix the social valuations V_{j3} and V_{k3} at certain positive values, which would imply how many units of X_0, X_1, X_2, Y_0, Y_1, or Y_2 they would be willing to give up in order to increase $\bar{J}_2$ or $\bar{K}_2$ by one unit. An alternative method is to fix in advance of the plan certain minimum quantities of J and K which must be provided by the plan for the initiation of production after the end of the planning period (i.e. minimum values for the quantities $\bar{J}_2$ and $\bar{K}_2$) and then to plan the use of resources over the 3-day period, days 0, 1, and 2 subject to this requirement. We will return to the question how the valuations V_{j3} and V_{k3} or, alternatively, the minimum quantities for $\bar{J}_2$ and $\bar{K}_2$ might be settled when we come to discuss the principles upon which the other valuations (V_{x1}, V_{x2}, etc.) might be determined.

(iii) A third possibility is, of course, to avoid the need to settle in advance any valuation of $\bar{J}_2$ and $\bar{K}_2$ by extending the period of the plan. The true values of $\bar{J}_2$ and $\bar{K}_2$ will, of course, depend upon how they in turn can best be used on day 3. If, therefore, the Central Authority devises a 4-day plan to cover day 3 as well as days 0, 1, and 2, $\bar{J}_k$ and $\bar{K}_k$ become intermediate products within the period of the plan and, therefore, as we have already argued, do not need to be valued in advance of the plan. But this third procedure only shifts the problem one day further forward. For the purposes of a 4-day plan the Central Authority would need to know how to value the output of intermediate products which will be left over at the end of the fourth day (end of day 3). Theoretically, the Central Authority could go on extending the period of the plan indefinitely into the future; indeed, in theory it could plan to cover an endless stretch of future time. If, however, consultation with the eschatologists, cosmologists, or nuclear strategists informed it that the world will indeed come to an end 3,000,000,000 days ahead, it could make a plan to cover that period giving zero valuations to all outputs beyond that period.

Theoretically this would be by far the best solution of the problem if it were not for the fact that uncertainty and ignorance about, for example, technical possibilities or population supplies 10 million years ahead is so extreme that it would be absurd for the Central Authority to go through the motions of planning over that whole period in order to make the best possible guess as to what will be the value of a particular piece of capital equipment 10 years ahead. In fact some procedure akin to the second possibility discussed above is inevitable—namely, to fix a terminal date for the plan and in a somewhat arbitrary manner to fix social valuations or minimum quantities to the various capital goods that will be left over at the end of the period covered by the plan. We will return later to a further discussion of the setting of these rather arbitrary valuations or minimum quantities.

The Central Authority in the Plansoc is now confronted with a problem in Linear Programming of a kind discussed at some length in Chapter XIV of *The Stationary Economy*; and in the following discussion we shall assume that the reader is familiar with the ground covered in that chapter. The present problem of the Central Authority is to find what are the scales on which the various productive processes should be operated on each day of the plan so as to maximize the social valuations of the outputs of consumption goods and of the capital goods which will be left over at the end of the plan, everything being subject to the constraints which are set by the scarcity of labour at any date in the plan and by the fact that it cannot in any day covered by the plan use more intermediate products than have been produced on the preceding day. The possible processes available for use during the period of the plan and the technical possibilities of production within each process have been shown in Table XIV; and the planning problem itself is set out as a Primal in a Linear Programming operation in Table XV.

Table XV

Primal Problem: to find values of S_{a0}, S_{b0}, S_{b1}, S_{c1}, S_{c2}, and S_{d2} such that

$$
\begin{aligned}
& S_{a0}(V_{x1}X_a + V_{y1}Y_a) + S_{b0}(V_{x1}X_b + V_{y1}Y_b) \\
& + S_{b1}(V_{x2}X_b + V_{y2}Y_b) + S_{c1}(V_{x2}X_c + V_{y2}Y_c) \\
& + S_{c2}(V_{x3}X_c + V_{y3}Y_c + V_{j3}\bar{J}_c + V_{k3}\bar{K}_c) \\
& + S_{d2}(V_{x3}X_d + V_{y3}Y_d + V_{j3}\bar{J}_d + V_{k3}\bar{K}_d)
\end{aligned}
$$

is maximized, subject to the constraints:

(i)	$L_a S_{a0} + L_b S_{b0}$	$\leqslant L_0$
(ii)	$L_b S_{b1} + L_c S_{c1}$	$\leqslant L_1$
(iii)	$L_c S_{c2} + L_d S_{d2}$	$\leqslant L_2$
(iv)	$J_a S_{a0} + J_b S_{b0}$	$\leqslant J_{-1}$
(v)	$K_a S_{a0} + K_a S_{b0}$	$\leqslant \bar{K}_{-1}$
(vi)	$-J_a S_{a0} - J_b S_{b0} + J_b S_{b1} + J_c S_{c1}$	$\leqslant 0$
(vii)	$-\bar{K}_a S_{a0} - \bar{K}_b S_{b0} + K_b S_{b1} + K_c S_{c1}$	$\leqslant 0$
(viii)	$- \bar{J}_b S_{b1} - \bar{J}_c S_{c1} + J_c S_{c2} + J_d S_{d2}$	$\leqslant 0$
(ix)	$- \bar{K}_b S_{b1} - \bar{K}_c S_{c1} + K_c S_{c2} + K_d S_{d2}$	$\leqslant 0$
(x)	All the S's $\geqslant 0$.	

It may be useful to comment on the plan in terms of Table XV. The sole object of the Central Authority at 8 a.m. on day 0 is to decide on values for S_{a0} and S_{b0}. The action which it has to take is to decide on what scale the various operations shall be conducted on day 0. But, as we have seen, in order to do this in a way which will maximize the social value of output over time it must form a plan which determines not only S_{a0} and S_{b0} but also the scales on which the various processes should be operated in the future days of the planning period (S_{b1}, S_{c1}, S_{c2}, S_{d2}).[1] The object of the plan then is to find values of these six S's which will maximize the social value of the resulting outputs.

Operating S_{a0} will produce an output of X_0 equal to $S_{a0}X_a$, since X_a is the output of X obtained by operating this process on a unitary scale. The social value of this output is $S_{a0}V_{x1}X_a$. Similarly this activity will produce an output of Y_0 with a social value of $S_{a0}V_{y1}Y_a$. The outputs of the intermediate products, J and K, which will be produced through S_{a0} and S_{b0} do not, as we have seen, need to be given any direct social valuation. We are not interested directly in the scale on which J_0 and K_0 are produced. These intermediate products will be required to produce outputs on day 1, and they will receive indirectly their proper social valuations through the value put upon the final products whose production they make possible. Thus the social value of the output of process a on day 0 is $S_{a0}(V_{x1} + V_{y1}Y_a)$. And similarly for the social values of the outputs of process b on day 0 and of processes b and c on day 1.

But when it comes to the valuation of the output of the processes c and d on day 2 the Central Authority must, as we have already seen, include a social valuation of the outputs of the intermediate products which will be left over for the community to use after the end of the plan, since the production of final goods which they make possible will not be covered by the plan and their social value will not therefore be indirectly covered by a valuation of the future outputs which they make possible. The Central Authority must include, therefore, in the value of the product whose social value is to be maximized an output of $\bar{J}_2$ equal to $S_{c2}\bar{J}_c + S_{d2}\bar{J}_d$ and an output of $\bar{K}_2$ equal to $S_{c2}\bar{K}_c + S_{d2}\bar{K}_d$, and these must be given a social valuation (V_{j3} and V_{k3} respectively).[2] Thus in assessing the social value of the outputs of day 2 not only the outputs of consumption goods but also the terms $S_{c2}(V_{j3}\bar{J}_c + V_{k3}\bar{K}_c)$ and $S_{d2}(V_{j3}\bar{J}_d + V_{k3}\bar{K}_d)$ must be included.

So much for the social valuation of the output which it is desired

---

[1] It is assumed that $S_{a1} = S_{a2} = S_{b2} = 0$ because process a is dominated by process c and process b by process d. See p. 350 above.

[2] If the world were known to be coming to an end at midday on day 3, we could put $V_{j3} = V_{k3} = 0$ (see p. 363 above).

to maximize. Let us now turn to the 10 constraints shown on Table XV. The operation of S_{a0} and S_{b0} on day 0 will require $S_{a0}L_a + S_{b0}L_b$ units of labour; and constraint (i) simply states that the activities on day 0 must not be on such scales as to cause a demand for labour which exceeds the available supply, L_0. Constraints (ii) and (iii) similarly state that the scales of the various processes planned for days 1 and 2 must not be so great as to give rise to a demand for labour which will exceed the supplies which will then be available.

At 8 a.m. on day 0 there will be certain supplies of the intermediate products available for use during that day. These supplies are the outputs of these products on the previous day (day -1) and are, therefore, equal to $\bar{J}_{-1}$ and $\bar{K}_{-1}$. The demand for J for use in S_{a0} is J_aS_{a0} and in S_{b0} is J_bS_{b0}. Constraint (iv) thus states that the scale of the activities on day 0 must not be so great as to cause a demand for J_0 which exceeds the available supply $\bar{J}_{-1}$. Constraint (v) expresses a similar limitation on the demand for K on day 0.

Constraints (vi), (vii), (viii), and (ix) express the fact that throughout the period of the plan the demand for any one intermediate product on any one day must not exceed the supply of that product produced on the previous day. It is these constraints which link the processes of different days together and are the distinguishing feature on the production side of a plan of successive processes over time (discussed in this chapter) as contrasted with a plan for production in which one period's potential output is not affected by the output of any other period (discussed in Chapter XIV of *The Stationary Economy*). Consider constraint (vi). The output of J on day 0 is $\bar{J}_aS_{a0} + \bar{J}_bS_{b0}$. The demand for inputs of J on day 1 is $J_bS_{b1} + J_cS_{c1}$. Constraint (vi) states that the latter processes must be on a sufficiently restricted scale relatively to the former processes for the demand for J at 8 a.m. on day 1 not to exceed the supply then available. Constraints (vii), (viii), and (ix) impose similar limitations on the demands for K on day 1 and for J and K on day 2.

The constraints under (x) merely tell the computer not to suggest to the planners that their problems may be eased by running some processes in reverse, turning output into inputs instead of inputs into outputs. Sausage machines can turn pigs into sausages; but one cannot turn the handle the other way round and turn sausages into pigs. If at any time in the plan there is a shortage of certain inputs and an excess of certain outputs, the computer—unless otherwise instructed—might advise the planners to use some process in reverse and to turn relatively plentiful outputs into relatively scarce inputs.

Now the computer can be asked to solve the problem set out in Table XV. It will then report to the Central Authority the values of the S's which will maximize the social value of the total planned output over the period of the plan. Incidentally this will, of course, determine what the physical outputs and inputs of the various goods and factors will be over the period of the plan. For example, the output of X of day 1, available for consumption on day 2, (X_1) will be equal to $S_{b1}X_b + S_{c1}X_c$. The output of the intermediate product J on day 1 will be $S_{b1}J_b + S_{c1}J_c$ and the input of this product on day 2 will be $S_{c2}J_c + S_{d2}J_d$. And so on for all the physical quantities of inputs and outputs over the period of the plan.

But as has been explained at length in Chapter XIV of *The Stationary Economy*, pp. 213–16 and 224–30 to every Primal problem in Linear Programming (the solution of which determines the physical quantities of inputs and outputs) there corresponds a Dual problem (the solution of which determines the 'shadow prices' or implied marginal social values of those inputs or outputs which have not already had valuations put upon them by the Central Authority for the definition of the Primal problem). Table XVI shows the Dual problem which corresponds to the Primal problem of Table XV. To each of the first nine constraints in the Primal there corresponds a 'shadow price' to be found by the solution of the Dual. Thus constraint (i) in the Primal concerns the supply–demand balance for L_0 and to this there corresponds an implied 'shadow valuation' of L_0, namely V_{l0}, which is one of the unknowns to be found by the solution of the Dual. Similarly constraints (ii) and (iii) of the Primal concern the supply–demand balance for L_1 and L_2, to which there correspond implied 'shadow valuations' of L_1 and L_2, namely V_{l1} and V_{l2}. Constraints (iv) and (v) of the Primal concern the supply–demand balance for the original given supplies at the beginning of the plan period (8 a.m. on day 0) of the capital goods $\bar{J}_{-1}$ and $\bar{K}_{-1}$, to which there correspond implied 'shadow valuations' V_{j0} and V_{k0}. Constraints (vi), (vii), (viii), and (ix) of the Primal concern the supply–demand balance for intermediate products during the course of the plan. Thus constraint (vi) concerns the balance between the output of J of day 0 $(\bar{J}_0)$ and the demand for inputs of J for the productive system on day 1 (J_1). To this there corresponds an implied 'shadow valuation', V_{j1}, which measures the value to the plan as a whole of having one additional unit of J_1. This explains the list of 'shadow valuations' which are stated at the top of Table XVI as the unknowns to be determined by the solution of the Dual.

As has been explained in Chapter XIV of *The Stationary Economy* the method of procedure (the reasons for which we have tried to make intuitively clear in the example given on pp. 224–30 of *The Stationary Economy*) for the solution of the Dual is as follows. Just as the solution of the Primal involves finding (subject to certain

Table XVI

Dual Problem: to find values of $V_{l0}, V_{l1}, V_{l2}, V_{j0}, V_{k0}, V_{j1}, V_{k1}, V_{j2},$ and V_{k2} such that

$$V_{l0}L_0 + V_{l1}L_1 + V_{l2}L_2 + V_{j0}J_{-1} + V_{k0}K_{-1} + V_{j1}\times 0 + V_{k1}\times 0 + V_{j2}\times 0 + V_{k2}\times 0$$

is minimized subject to the constraints:

(i) $\quad L_a V_{l0} \qquad + J_a V_{j0} + K_a V_{k0} - J_a V_{j1} - \bar{K}_a V_{k1} \qquad\qquad\qquad \geqslant V_{x1}X_a + V_{y1}Y_a$

(ii) $\quad L_b V_{l0} \qquad + J_b V_{j0} + K_b V_{k0} - J_b V_{j1} - \bar{K}_b V_{k1} \qquad\qquad\qquad \geqslant V_{x1}X_b + V_{y1}Y_b$

(iii) $\quad L_b V_{l1} \qquad + J_b V_{j1} + K_b V_{k1} - J_b V_{j2} - \bar{K}_b V_{k2} \qquad\qquad\qquad \geqslant V_{x2}X_b + V_{y2}Y_b$

(iv) $\quad L_c V_{l1} \qquad + J_c V_{j1} + K_c V_{k1} - J_c V_{j2} - \bar{K}_c V_{k2} \qquad\qquad\qquad \geqslant V_{x2}X_c + V_{y2}Y_c$

(v) $\quad L_c V_{l2} \qquad + J_c V_{j2} + K_c V_{k2} \qquad\qquad\qquad\qquad \geqslant V_{x3}X_c + V_{y3}Y_c + V_{j3}J_c + V_{k3}\bar{K}_c$

(vi) $\quad L_d V_{l2} \qquad + J_d V_{j2} + K_d V_{k2} \qquad\qquad\qquad\qquad \geqslant V_{x3}X_d + V_{y3}Y_d + V_{j3}J_d + V_{k3}\bar{K}_d$

(vii) All the V's $\geqslant 0.$

constraints) the quantities of the various final outputs of the plan which, at the given social valuations of each output, maximize the total value of these outputs, so the solution of the Dual involves finding (subject to certain constraints) the 'shadow valuations' of the various original inputs into the plan which, at the given quantities available of such inputs, minimizes the total cost of such inputs. Thus in Table XVI it is stated that $V_{l0}L_0 + V_{l1}L_1 + V_{l2}L_2 + V_{j0}J_{-1} + V_{k0}\bar{K}_{-1}$ is to be minimized subject to certain constraints. Since there is no 'original' supply of the intermediate products J_1, J_2, K_1, K_2 to be put into the planned production system from outside, the 'shadow valuations' of these inputs are given zero weights in the calculation of the total cost of original outside inputs which is to be minimized.

The first six constraints which are relevant to the solution of the Dual problem are that no individual production process (the six unknowns of the Primal—namely S_{a0}, S_{b0}, S_{b1}, S_{c1}, S_{c2}, S_{d2}) should be run at a net profit. The shadow valuations of the various original outside inputs must not be set so low for this to be possible. Thus constraint (i) in Table XVI states that S_{a0} should not make a net profit; that is to say that the costs of the inputs needed to operate S_{a0} on a unitary scale multiplied by their shadow prices ($L_aV_{l0} + J_aV_{j0} + K_aV_{k0}$) should not be less than the outputs of the intermediate products multiplied by their shadow valuations ($\bar{J}_aV_{j1} + \bar{K}_aV_{k1}$) *plus* the outputs of the final products multiplied by the social valuations actually put upon them by the Central Authority ($V_{x1}X_a + V_{y1}Y_a$). Constraints (ii), (iii), and (iv) state exactly similar conditions for the scales of processes S_{b0}, S_{b1}, and S_{c1}. Constraints (v) and (vi) state the same conditions for the scales of processes S_{c2} and S_{d2}, the only difference being that in these cases the valuations (V_{j3}, V_{k3}) set on the outputs of the intermediate products ($\bar{J}_c$, $\bar{K}_c$, $\bar{J}_d$, $\bar{K}_d$) are in this case not 'shadow valuations' whose values are to be determined but are the actual known valuations already set by the Central Authority on the capital goods which will be accumulated by the end of the planning period.

Finally constraint (vii) simply tells the computer that in its anxiety to get the total costs of the inputs down it must not arrange for any input to be used on such a scale that it simply gets in the way and reduces the total value of the planned output. Better to leave part of the available supply of an input unemployed if no further positive use for it can be found. The marginal values of the inputs must either be positive or zero; they must not be negative.

As has been explained in Chapter XIV of *The Stationary Economy* there are certain relationships between the solutions of the Primal and of the Dual.

(1) The maximum value of the outputs of final products of the

plan as calculated for the Primal will in fact be found by the computer to be equal to the minimum cost of the original inputs into the plan as calculated for the Dual. There will be no net profit or loss in the plan as a whole.

(2) If in the Primal the computer says that some particular process should be used (e.g. $S_{c1} > 0$), then in the Dual it will say that 'shadow valuations' will be such that that process will exactly cover its costs ($L_c V_{l1} + J_c V_{j1} + K_c V_{k1} - J_c V_{j2} - \bar{K}_c V_{k2} = V_{x2} X_c + V_{y2} Y_c$). There will be no net profit or loss made on any process which is used.

(3) If in the Dual the computer says that some particular process would make a loss (e.g. values for V_{l1}, V_{j1}, V_{k1}, V_{j2}, and V_{k2} are determined to be such that
$$L_b V_{b1} + K_b V_{j1} + K_b V_{k1} - J_b V_{j2} - \bar{K}_b V_{k2} > V_{x2} X_b + V_{y2} Y_b,$$
then in the Primal it will say that the corresponding process should not be used ($S_{b1} = 0$). No process should be included in the plan on which a net loss will be made.

(4) If in the Dual the computer says that any particular 'shadow valuation' is positive (e.g. $V_{j1} > 0$), then in the Primal it will say that the corresponding resource should be fully employed ($\bar{J}_a S_{a0} + J_b S_{b0} = J_b S_{b1} + J_c S_{c1}$). A resource at any point in the plan, whether it be an original factor or an intermediate product, will only have a positive social value if the demand for it at that point in the plan is sufficient to absorb the whole supply available.

(5) If in the Primal the computer says that for any resource at any point in the plan the available supply will exceed the demand (e.g. S_{a0}, S_{b0}, S_{b1}, S_{c1} found to be such that $\bar{K}_a S_{a0} + \bar{K}_b S_{b0} > K_b S_{b1} + K_c S_{c1}$), then in the Dual it will say that the corresponding 'shadow valuation' is zero ($V_{k1} = 0$). If, for example, the plan involves at any point of time producing a by-product in excess of the demand for it, the implied social valuation of that resource at that point in the plan is zero.

With the solutions of the Primal and of the Dual we have a set of inputs and outputs planned over the period of the plan and a set of social valuations, allotted from the outside by the Central Authority in the case of the outputs of consumption goods and of capital goods left over at the end of the plan and indirectly calculated for the other inputs and outputs as being implied by the given social valuations of the various final outputs, by the scarcities of the original inputs, and by the technical possibilities of transforming inputs into outputs. These shadow valuations measure the marginal products of the various inputs as valued by the social valuations allotted to final products by the Central Authority.[1] Thus if V_{j1} is calculated as equal to $3, this means that, if there were dropped from heaven one more

[1] See Chapter XIV of *The Stationary Economy*, pp. 215–16.

unit of J available for use in the productive system at 8 a.m. on day 1, the plan could be so reorganized that the total value at 8 a.m. on day 0 of all the outputs of the plan over the period of the plan could be increased by \$3.

There remains one outstanding problem for the Central Authority. How should it decide upon the valuations V_{x1}, V_{x2}, V_{x3}, V_{y1}, V_{y2}, V_{y3}, V_{j3}, and V_{k3} which it itself places upon the final outputs of the plan? A similar question arose in connection with the planning problem discussed in *The Stationary Economy* in the case of the static planning problem of determining the best use of resources in a stationary economy in which there was no change through time in population, capital equipment, or technical knowledge. We had then to discuss the principles upon which the values of P_z, P_y, P_x were to be fixed under the central plan discussed in Chapter XIV, pp. 208–11 of *The Stationary Economy*. In that connection we argued as follows. Given the values allotted by the Central Authority to the outputs and given the various relevant constraints, the computer reports on what scale the various outputs should be produced to maximize the value of total output. But if the value allotted to one particular output is very high, the computer may report a plan which produces an extremely large output of that product and an extremely low output of other products on which only a low value has been set by the Central Authority. But if the output of the former is going to be so large and of the latter so small, then the value to be attached to marginal increments of the former should be much lower and that attached to marginal increments of the latter should be much higher. In Chapter XIV, pp. 208–11 of *The Stationary Economy* we discussed how the Central Authority could fix on a set of valuations of outputs; could see what outputs resulted; could lower somewhat the valuations set on those products whose planned outputs were excessively high and raise somewhat the valuations for those products whose planned outputs were excessively low; could recalculate the planned outputs on the basis of the revised values allotted to the outputs; could reconsider the relations between the resulting outputs and these new values; and could continue this process of successive adjustment until a planned programme was reached in which the patterns of the outputs and of the values attached to each output were in the opinion of the Central Authority suited to each other, that is to say, until the social valuations allotted to each product corresponded to the marginal rates at which the Central Authority considered that one product could be substituted for another without loss of social welfare when the supplies of the products were equal to the outputs resulting from a plan based on these valuations.[1]

[1] See the note at the end of this chapter (pp. 387–389) for the discussion of a

Exactly the same problem arises in a somewhat more complicated form in our present problem of planning over time. The Central Authority now has three (instead of one) types of comparisons between output patterns and valuation patterns to make in order to see whether the valuations set by them and the resulting outputs are compatible with each other.

(1) First, as in the case of the type of planning problem discussed in Chapter XIV of *The Stationary Economy* the Central Authority must consider whether the ratio in which the various consumption goods are planned to be produced at any one time is compatible with the relative valuations set on those products at that same time, i.e. whether $\frac{X_0}{Y_0}$ is compatible with $\frac{V_{x1}}{V_{y1}}$, $\frac{X_1}{Y_1}$ with $\frac{V_{x2}}{V_{y2}}$, and $\frac{X_2}{Y_2}$ with $\frac{V_{x3}}{V_{y3}}$.

(2) Second—a question which did not arise in the problem considered in Chapter XIV of *The Stationary Economy*—the Central Authority must consider whether the time pattern of the planned outputs is compatible with the time pattern of the valuations of the same products, i.e. whether $\frac{X_1}{X_0}$ is compatible with $\frac{V_{x2}}{V_{x1}}$, $\frac{X_2}{X_1}$ with $\frac{V_{x3}}{V_{x2}}$, $\frac{Y_1}{Y_0}$ with $\frac{V_{y2}}{V_{y1}}$, and $\frac{Y_2}{Y_1}$ with $\frac{V_{y3}}{V_{y2}}$.

(3) Third—another question which did not arise in the problem considered in Chapter XIV of *The Stationary Economy*—the Central Authority must consider whether the valuations set on the intermediate products which will be left over at the end of the period of the plan and the outputs of these products resulting from the plan are appropriate. This will involve considering both whether there is a 'correct' make-up of the stock of capital goods which will be left over at the end of the plan $\left(\text{i.e. whether} \frac{J_2}{K_2} \text{is compatible with} \frac{V_{j3}}{V_{k3}}\right)$ and also whether there is a 'correct' balance between consumption during the plan period and the stocks of capital goods accumulated by the end of the period (i.e. whether $\frac{J_2}{X_2}$ is compatible with $\frac{V_{j3}}{V_{x3}}$, $\frac{J_2}{X_1}$ with $\frac{V_{j3}}{V_{x2}}$, and so on).

We will deal with each of these aspects of valuation in turn.

(1) We need not say a great deal about the first of these three valuation problems because it is essentially the same as that discussed in Chapter XIV of *The Stationary Economy*. There is, however, one basic difference which makes the present problem less easy to handle

difficulty which may be encountered in reaching a determinate solution of the plan by the process described in the text.

than the former static problem. In the static case the problem could be solved by a process of trial and error in the market itself: certain supplies of X and Y are put on the market by the Central Authority; the consumers offer prices P_x and P_y for these supplies; if these market P's differ from the P's used in the plan to value the outputs X and Y, then the P's used in the plan can be adjusted in the direction of the actual market P's and new outputs calculated with these new valuations; then new supplies of X and Y can then be put on the market and the new resulting market P's observed; the valuations used for the plan can then be adjusted again in the direction of these new market P's; and so on until the market P's actually coincide with the valuations used for the plan.

This process in its straightforward, simple form is suitable only for a stationary economy. In a plan drawn up to cover a number of future days in which, owing to population growth, capital accumulation, and technical progress, supplies of various consumption goods per consumer should properly be planned to change over time, it is impossible to decide by a direct market-trial-and-error procedure whether the relative valuations set for future days upon the various consumption goods are compatible with the future planned supplies of those same goods. For example, it is impossible for the Central Authority at 8 a.m. on day 0 to find out by a market trial-and-error procedure whether if the planned supplies X_2 and Y_2 were put on the market at 8 a.m. on day 3 the ratio of prices $\dfrac{P_{x3}}{P_{y3}}$ which the consumers would offer in a free market for these consumption goods would correspond to the ratio of the valuations $\dfrac{V_{x3}}{V_{y3}}$ which the Central Authority has set in the plan on these outputs. *A fortiori* it is impossible for the Central Authority on day 0 to go on making a succession of actual market trials in the conditions which will rule on day 3 in order to see whether the day-3 valuations set in the plan made on day 0 are correct.

But this does not, of course, mean that no information can be obtained from the market for consumption goods to help with the fixation of correct valuations of future supplies of consumption goods. Each day the Central Authority can distribute money incomes to the citizens and allow them to compete freely in the shops for whatever supplies of consumption goods are put on the market that day. There will result each day certain prices P_x, P_y, etc., which will show how consumers value marginal increments of each product.[1] This means that on day 0 the Central Authority will have evidence

---

[1] See *The Stationary Economy*, pp. 201–3.

showing for every day up to day 0 the relative valuations which consumers did in fact put on the commodities when they were supplied in various quantities to citizens at various standards of living. From this evidence the Central Authority can make its own estimate of what the relative prices would be that citizens in a free market would pay for various total quantities of X and Y supplied to consuming populations of various sizes with money incomes distributed among the citizens on whatever principle the Central Authority considered to be equitable. Having formed this estimate of a demand function it can then carry out a simulated market-trial-and-error process for the future days covered by its plan. At 8 a.m. on day 0 it sets certain valuations for X_2 and Y_2—namely V_{x3} and V_{y3}; it calculates what planned supplies of X and Y (X_2 and Y_2) would be forthcoming for consumption on day 3 at the valuations set in its plan; it forecasts on the basis of L_3 the number of consumers who will need X and Y on day 3; it determines on what basis it will distribute money incomes between these consumers; and then from its estimated demand function based on past market experience it estimates what the price ratio $\dfrac{P_{x3}}{P_{y3}}$ would be in these conditions. If $\dfrac{P_{x3}}{P_{y3}}$ is $> \dfrac{V_{x3}}{V_{y3}}$, then $\dfrac{V_{x3}}{V_{y3}}$ is raised somewhat, and the plan is recalculated. This process of recalculation with adjusted valuations can go on until the $\dfrac{P_{x3}}{P_{y3}}$ which the estimated demand schedule says will arise from the sale of the resulting planned supplies in the other conditions envisaged for day 3, coincides with the $\dfrac{V_{x3}}{V_{y3}}$ used for the valuation of X_2 and Y_2 in the plan.

(2) The relative valuation at 8 a.m. on day 0 of supplies of any given consumption good planned for different future days raises a set of problems which had no place in the static planning problem discussed in Chapter XIV of *The Stationary Economy*. It will be helpful to consider this set of problems in a way which enables us most readily to consider the form which the similar problems take in a competitive private enterprise economy. In order to make this comparison as straightforward a matter as possible we will make the assumption that the Central Authority in our Plansoc does in fact organize a free market for consumption goods. It distributes certain money incomes among the consumers and allows these to spend them freely in the shops on the available supplies of X and Y in the shops at 8 a.m. each morning. We assume further that the Central Authority in the Plansoc issues each day just that amount of money income to consumers which is sufficient to stabilize the money price index $P_x + P_y$ for the

goods X and Y at \$2. Thus both in the Plansoc and also in the Propcap which we examined in the last chapter there is a free market for the determination of the relative prices of consumption goods each day, and, in addition, the general cost of living index is stabilized at $P_x + P_y = \$2$.

The best way to proceed is to consider the relationships between the P's (the money price of any consumption that will in fact rule for that product at whatever date it in fact comes into the market for consumption goods) and the V's (the valuations expressed in terms of money which the planners will set at 8 a.m. on day 0 when the plan is made on the various outputs of consumption goods which will appear at future dates in the plan). Now we can assume that the planners aim at making the ratio between the valuations which they set upon any two products which will appear at the same date in the plan equal to the ratio of the prices which the consumers at that day will in fact set upon them in the market. To take an example, we may assume that the planners aim at setting $\dfrac{V_{x2}}{V_{y2}}$ at the level $\dfrac{P_{x2}}{P_{y2}}$. $\dfrac{P_{x2}}{P_{y2}}$ (where P_{x2} and P_{y2} are the actual prices which the consumers are forecast as actually going to pay for X_1 and Y_1 at 8 a.m. on day 2) measures the marginal rate of substitution between X and Y in the consumers' budget at 8 a.m. on day 2. This is the way to 'optimize production'.[1] Suppose, for example, $\dfrac{P_{x2}}{P_{y2}} = 4$ but $\dfrac{V_{x2}}{V_{y2}} = 3$. $\dfrac{P_{x2}}{P_{y2}} = 4$ would mean that consumers at 8 a.m. on day 2 would be better off if they could have 1 more unit of X, at the cost of anything less than 4 units of Y_1. But $\dfrac{V_{x2}}{V_{y2}} = 3$ would imply that the computer had jiggled about with the planned production until at the margin one could produce 1 more unit of X_1 at the cost of only 3 units of Y_1, such being the valuations which the planners had told the computer to put upon outputs of X_1 and Y_1.

But all this does not imply that the ratio between the marginal valuations for the planners of the same combination of consumption goods appearing at two different future dates should be the same as the ratio between the prices which consumers will in fact pay for this same combination of goods at the two different dates. For example, because of the policies which we are assuming for the stabilization of the price level we know that $P_x + P_y$ will be constant at \$2 and that, therefore, $\dfrac{P_{x2} + P_{y2}}{P_{x1} + P_{y1}} = 1$. We can examine our present problem by

---

[1] Cf. *The Stationary Economy*, pp. 187–8, 197–8, and 207.

asking whether this implies that $\dfrac{V_{x2} + V_{y2}}{V_{x1} + V_{y1}}$ should also be set equal
to 1. But we can show that this will not necessarily be the correct valuation policy for the Central Authority to adopt by considering what its consequence might be upon the planned outputs. If the Central Authority set the same valuation upon 1 unit of X plus 1 unit of Y (what we will call a unit of XY) produced for consumption on day 2 as it did for a unit of XY for consumption on day 1, then the computer would plan for producing less units of $X_0 Y_0$ and more units of $X_1 Y_1$ so long as it was possible to produce more than 1 unit of $X_1 Y_1$ for each unit reduction in the production of $X_0 Y_0$. The outcome would depend upon the technical possibilities of the production process. But by using resources today in processes designed not to produce consumption goods for today but to produce capital goods today to be used to produce consumption goods tomorrow, one may well be able to obtain more consumption goods tomorrow than one gave up today. If the possibilities of this productive substitution of consumption goods tomorrow for consumption goods today continued more or less without limit, then to set $V_{x2} + V_{y2} = V_{x1} + V_{y1}$ would mean that no XY at all was produced for consumption at 8 a.m. on day 1, so that a still larger output of XY could be produced for consumption at 8 a.m. on day 2. But clearly the Central Authority would be dissatisfied with a set of valuations which resulted in a dearth of consumption goods for day 1 followed by a plethora on day 2. This could be avoided by lowering $\dfrac{V_{x2} + V_{y2}}{V_{x1} + V_{y1}}$ and so making the computer give a higher relative value to the production of XY in the earlier period. At some level of $\dfrac{V_{x2} + V_{y2}}{V_{x1} + V_{y1}}$ the plan would indicate that some $X_0 Y_0$ as well as some $X_1 Y_1$ should be produced; and, other things being equal, the lower the level at which the Central Authority set $\dfrac{V_{x2} + V_{y2}}{V_{x1} + V_{y1}}$, the greater the output of $X_0 Y_0$ could be expected to be relatively to that of $X_1 Y_1$, since the earlier output would be valued more highly relatively to the latter. Now we could call $\dfrac{V_{x2} + V_{y2}}{V_{x1} + V_{y1}}$ the rate at which money prices should be discounted between 8 a.m. on day 2 and 8 a.m. on day 1. The analogy with the rate of interest in a market system is now clear.

Let us write

$$V_{x0} + V_{y0} = P_x + P_y = \$2$$

$$V_{x1} + V_{y1} = \frac{\$2}{1 + i_0}$$

$$V_{x2} + V_{y2} = \frac{\$2}{(1 + i_0)(1 + i_1)}$$

$$V_{x3} + V_{y3} = \frac{\$2}{(1 + i_0)(1 + i_1)(1 + i_2)} \text{ etc.}$$

These expressions enable us to see clearly the analogy between the choice of the valuation ratios such as $\frac{V_{x2} + V_{y2}}{V_{x1} + V_{y1}}$ and $\frac{V_{x3} + V_{y3}}{V_{x2} + V_{y2}}$ and the rate of interest at which in a market the prices of future goods are discounted. We have from the above expressions $\frac{V_{x2} + V_{y2}}{V_{x1} + V_{y1}} = \frac{1}{1 + i_1}$, and $\frac{V_{x3} + V_{y3}}{V_{x2} + V_{y2}} = \frac{1}{1 + i_2}$ and so on. We can, therefore, treat the social valuations, the V's, as being the equivalent of the present discounted values of the market prices of the commodities appearing at the relevant date. For the products appearing on the market at 8 a.m. on day 0 we use the actual market prices of the products as the base for our whole system of social valuations in the plan ($V_{x0} + V_{y0} = P_x + P_y$); for the products which will appear on the market at 8 a.m. on day 1 we discount the market prices ($P_x + P_y$) by a factor $\left(\frac{1}{1 + i_0}\right)$; for the products which will appear on the market at 8 a.m. on day 2 we discount the market prices ($P_x + P_y$) by a factor $\left(\frac{1}{1 + i_0} \cdot \frac{1}{1 + i_1}\right)$; and so on for the products appearing on the market on each subsequent day of the plan. The levels of the rates of interest i_0, i_1, i_2, etc., in these expressions are simply the levels implied by the valuation ratios which are used in the plan to get the desired time pattern of output of consumption goods. Thus as we have seen $\frac{V_{x2} + V_{y2}}{V_{x1} + V_{y1}} = \frac{1}{1 + i_1}$ or $i_1 = \frac{V_{x1} + V_{y1}}{V_{x2} + V_{y2}} - 1$, which expresses the rate of interest on day 1 (i_1) which is implied in the choice of a valuation ratio over time of $\frac{V_{x2} + V_{y2}}{V_{x1} + V_{y1}}$.

These i's which are thus implied in the choice by the Central Authority of the social valuations V_{x1}, V_{y1}, V_{x2}, V_{y2}, etc., can be regarded from two points of view: first, as measuring what may perhaps be called 'the marginal product of waiting' in the *production plan*, and, second, as indicating the proper marginal choice between immediate and postponed consumption in the *consumption plan*.

To illustrate the former point, if i_1 were set at 2 per cent per day,

then we have $\dfrac{V_{x1} + V_{y1}}{V_{x2} + V_{y2}} = 1 \cdot 02$. This simply means that the Central

Authority sets a valuation on a unit of $X_0 Y_0$ which is 2 per cent higher than the valuation which it sets on a unit of $X_1 Y_1$. The obedient computer will jiggle around with the plan until it is possible at the margin to produce $1 \cdot 02$ more units of $X_1 Y_1$ for every unit reduction of the output $X_0 Y_0$. In this sense resources will be used in the plan in such a way that on day 1 the marginal product of waiting is 2 per cent per day—$1 \cdot 02$ units of XY could be obtained tomorrow for every unit of XY by which today's consumption is cut.

Such are the production implications of choosing given levels for the i's. But on what criteria can the Central Authority decide whether the correct i's have been chosen? The answer to this question clearly depends upon a judgement whether the resulting time pattern for the *production* of XY corresponds to the time pattern for the *consumption* of XY which would be considered socially desirable.

Let us consider this problem from the analogy with a purely competitive market economy. Consider first the case where there is only one consumption good, X, so that the whole production-planning problem boils down to a choice of various processes over time in order to select those processes which at any given time either (i) produce X itself most economically given the resources and technical knowledge then available or (ii) produce J, K, etc., most economically in the proportions which are most suitable to enable X to be produced most economically in larger amounts in the future. Given the i's—i_0, i_1, i_2, etc.—chosen by the Central Authority for the social valuations of the X's—V_{x1}, V_{x2}, V_{x3}, etc.—there will result from the plan a given time pattern of production of X—X_0, X_1, X_2, etc. Let us write $\dfrac{X_1 - X_0}{X_0} = x_1$ and $\dfrac{L_2 - L_1}{L_1} = l_1$. In this case x_1 represents the growth rate in the supply of X available for consumers between 8 a.m. on day 1 and 8 a.m. on day 2[1] and l_1 represents the growth rate in the working population (which we take as representing the body of consumers) between 8 a.m. on day 1 and 8 a.m. on day 2. Thus $x_1 - l_1$ represents the growth rate in consumption per head from 8 a.m. on day 1 to 8 a.m. on day 2.

In Chapter XII (pp. 202–205 above) we have shown how, if σ represents the elasticity of substitution in the consumers' choice between consumption on day 2 and consumption on day 1 and if i_1 represents the rate of interest which rules between day 1 and day 2,

---

[1] X_0 is the output of X of day 0 available for consumption at the beginning of day 1.

then the consumer will choose to increase his consumption at a growth rate between day 1 and day 2 equal to σi_1. It is this sort of assessment which the Central Authority must now make on behalf of the consumers. Having chosen an i_1 there will result, from the implied social valuations of X_0 and X_1 and from the growth rate of the population, a growth rate of supplies available for consumption per head of $x_1 - l_1$. This must be compared with the growth rate of consumption per head which would be best for consumers when by giving up one more unit of X_0 they can obtain $(1 + i_1)$ additional units of X_1. This 'desired' growth rate of consumption per head corresponds to the σi_1 of the market in which consumers' choice was free.

We will express this assessment of desirability of the growth rate for consumption in terms of the Central Authority determining what it considers to be a desirable value for σ. If it chooses a low value for σ, it is in effect saying that the level of consumption today should be depressed below the level of consumption tomorrow by a given amount only if there was much to be gained thereby, i.e. only if the 'marginal product of waiting' is very high. On the basis of some initially given series of i's for the period of the plan, the computer will inform the Central Authority as to what time pattern of consumption —X_0, X_1, X_2, etc.—maximizes the value of the plan at the social valuations implied by the i's. If then it is found that the resulting $x_1 - l_1 > \sigma i_1$, this means that the supply X_0 is too low relatively to the supply X_1 in view of the most desirable time pattern of consumption corresponding to a 'marginal product of waiting' as low as i_1. The Central Authority could then recalculate the plan on the basis of a higher i_1. This would raise σi_1 (the desired rate of growth of consumption per head) and, by lowering the social valuation of X_1 relative to that of X_0,[1] would tend to lower the planned supplies of X_1 relatively to those of X_0, so that $x_1 - l_1$ would be reduced; with σi_1 raised and $x_1 - l_1$ lowered the equality $x_1 - l_1 = \sigma i_1$ might be attained. By such a process of trial and error a series of i's might be found such that $x_0 - l_0 = \sigma i_0$, $x_1 - l_1 = \sigma i_1$, and so on.

The preceding explanation has been made solely in terms of a single consumption good, X. In fact, of course, there are many different consumption goods. In this case, as we have seen, the Central Authority must decide upon what it considers will be the appropriate price relationships to express consumers' choices over the period of the plan as between the supplies of different consumption goods at any one time, and this—given also a decision

---

[1] $\dfrac{V_{x2}}{V_{x1}} = \dfrac{1}{1 + i_1}$ when there is only one consumption good X and when P_x therefore is stabilized in money terms. See p. 378 above.

about what general index of prices should be stabilized—will give an array of consumers' prices over the plan. In terms of our simple model with only two consumption goods this array of prices will be of the following kind:

Table XVII

		Commodity	
		X	Y
	day 1	$P_{x1} + P_{y1}$	$= \$2$
Prices at 8 a.m. on	day 2	$P_{x2} + P_{y2}$	$= \$2$
	day 3	$P_{x3} + P_{y3}$	$= \$2$

These prices must be changed into social valuations for the formation of the plan at 8 a.m. on day 0 by the choice of interest rates, i_0, i_1, i_2, and this will give the following array of valuations:[1]

Table XVIII

		Commodity	
		X	Y
Valuations for supplies available at 8 a.m. on	day 1	$V_{x1} = \dfrac{P_{x1}}{1+i_0}$	$V_{y1} = \dfrac{P_{y1}}{1+i_0}$
	day 2	$V_{x2} = \dfrac{P_{x2}}{(1+i_0)(1+i_1)}$	$V_{y2} = \dfrac{P_{y2}}{(1+i_0)(1+i_1)}$
	day 3	$V_{x3} = \dfrac{P_{x3}}{(1+i_0)(1+i_1)(1+i_2)}$	$V_{y3} = \dfrac{P_{y3}}{(1+i_0)(1+i_1)(1+i_2)}$

These valuations being given to the computer the plan will then produce an array of consumption good supplies per head of the population:

Table XIX

		Commodity	
		X	Y
Supplies available per head of population for consumption at 8 a.m. on	day 1	$\dfrac{X_0}{L_1}$	$\dfrac{Y_0}{L_1}$
	day 2	$\dfrac{X_1}{L_2}$	$\dfrac{Y_1}{L_2}$
	day 3	$\dfrac{X_2}{L_3}$	$\dfrac{Y_2}{L_3}$

[1] Since $P_{x2} + P_{y2} = \$2$, this array implies $V_{x1} + V_{y1} = \dfrac{\$2}{(1+i_0)}$, $V_{x2} + V_{y2} = \dfrac{\$2}{(1+i_0)(1+i_1)}$, and so on.

In order to decide whether the plan should be adopted in this form or not the Central Authority then has two basic sets of comparisons to make:

(i) It must examine from Table XIX at any one time (say at 8 a.m. on day 2) the supplies per head $\left(\dfrac{X_1}{L_2} \text{ and } \dfrac{Y_1}{L_2}\right)$ of the various consumption goods and must decide whether these are what is wanted, taking into account both the income effects and the substitution effects on consumers' choice.[1] For this purpose it must estimate whether with standards of living indicated by the $\dfrac{X_1}{L_2}$ and $\dfrac{Y_1}{L_2}$ of Table XIX and the relative prices P_{x1} and P_{y1} indicated in Table XVII, X_1 and Y_1 do represent suitable supplies of X and Y to meet demands on day 1. If not, then the P's of Table XVII and so the V's of Table XVIII must be adjusted relatively to each other.

(ii) It must examine from Table XIX the change in the standard of living over time $\left(\text{e.g. compare } \dfrac{X_1}{L_2}, \dfrac{Y_1}{L_2} \text{ with } \dfrac{X_0}{L_1}, \dfrac{Y_0}{L_1}\right)$ and must decide whether this represents the most desirable time pattern of consumption given the fact that i_1 (in Table XVIII) represents the 'marginal product' of postponing the consumption of 1 unit of $X + 1$ unit of Y from 8 a.m. on day 1 to 8 a.m. on day 2. If not, the i's and thus the V's of Table XVIII must be revised.

(3) There remains the third problem of valuation mentioned above (p. 373), namely how to value the capital goods which will be left over at the end of the plan period both relatively to each other and relatively to the consumption goods produced during the period of the plan. As we have already really suggested (p. 364 above) this is almost bound to be a very arbitrary matter, since the only really satisfactory way of coping with the problem is to assess the value of the capital good existing at any future point of time by extending the period of the plan into a more distant future so that the value of the capital goods can be based upon their future usefulness. This procedure is, however, ruled out because beyond a certain point of time uncertainty becomes so great that it would be pure folly to construct a plan to cover such remote contingencies.

The sort of procedure—arbitrary though it is—which must be adopted is of the following kind. The Central Authority could fix provisionally some quite arbitrary valuations upon the various capital goods which will be left over at the end of the period of the

---

[1] Cf. *The Stationary Economy*, Chapters II and III.

plan—in our simple 3-day plan model it would fix quite arbitrary provisional values for V_{j3} and V_{k3}.[1] On the basis of these valuations the computer would be asked to solve the Primal problem of Table XV. This would give certain values of the outputs of $\bar{J}_2$ and $\bar{K}_2$ (namely $\bar{J}_c S_{c2} + \bar{J}_d S_{d2}$ and $\bar{K}_c S_{c2} + \bar{K}_d S_{d2}$). These quantities $\bar{J}_2$ and $\bar{K}_k$ could be compared relatively to each other on 'commonsense' lines. An obvious starting point is to compare $\dfrac{\bar{J}_2}{\bar{K}_2}$ with $\dfrac{J_{-1}}{\bar{K}_{-1}}$ (i.e. with the relative quantities of J and K existing at 8 a.m. on day 0 when the plan is being prepared). If, for example, $\dfrac{\bar{J}_2}{\bar{K}_2}$ were much greater than $\dfrac{J_{-1}}{\bar{K}_{-1}}$, it might be considered wise to lower $\dfrac{V_{j3}}{V_{k3}}$ and so to plan for a fall in $\dfrac{\bar{J}_2}{\bar{K}_2}$, unless there were obvious 'commonsensical' reasons to believe that future technical progress or future developments of consumers' tastes after the close of the planning period were likely to make supplies of J much more useful relatively to supplies of K or unless there were obvious 'commonsensical' reasons to believe that the current supplies of J were much too low relatively to the current supplies of K.[2]

But there is a second and perhaps more arbitrary type of comparison which must be made, namely whether the supplies $\bar{J}_2$ and $\bar{K}_2$ are too large or too small relatively to the supplies $X_0, X_1, X_2, Y_0, Y_1, Y_2$. Have the valuations V_{j3} and V_{k3} been set so high relatively to the valuations set on the X's and Y's that too much of the community's resources have gone into the production of capital goods for use

---

[1] These present valuations V_{j3} and V_{k3} of the J and K which will be available at 8 a.m. on day 3 imply certain monetary shadow prices which (if the valuations V_{j3} and V_{k3} turn out to be correct) will rule for J and K at the beginning of day 3—namely P_{j3} and P_{k3}. Just as $V_{x3} = \dfrac{P_{x3}}{(1 + i_0)(1 + i_1)(1 + i_2)}$ (see p. 381) so $V_{j3} = \dfrac{P_{j3}}{(1 + i_0)(1 + i_1)(1 + i_2)}$. In this case $\dfrac{P_{j3}}{P_{x3}}$ equals $\dfrac{V_{j3}}{V_{x3}}$, a ratio which measures the marginal rate at which J_2 can be substituted for X_2 in the plan.

[2] This 'commonsense' judgment can be given some quantitative precision. On the basis of the provisionally fixed valuations for the X's and Y's during the period of the plan and for the J and K left over at the end of the plan, the solution of the Dual of Table XVI will give shadow valuations for the initial supplies of J and K (namely V_{j0} and V_{k0}). If the resulting $\dfrac{V_{j0}}{V_{k0}}$ is much higher than the relative valuations of J and K in previous plans (from which the current supplies of J and K have emerged), there is some indication that $\dfrac{J_{-1}}{\bar{K}_{-1}}$ is 'too low'.

after the end of the period of the plan relatively to the production of consumption goods for enjoyment during the period of the plan? Pointers which might be used in such an assessment might be comparisons of $\dfrac{J_2}{J_{-1}}$ and $\dfrac{\bar{K}_2}{\bar{K}_{-2}}$ with $\dfrac{X_2}{X_{-1}}$ and $\dfrac{Y_2}{Y_{-1}}$. If the former were much greater than the latter, this would indicate that the plan was one which gave a much greater rate of growth to the supply of capital goods than to the supply of consumption goods. This would be an appropriate state of affairs if the Central Authority consciously desired to keep the rate of growth of consumption over the period of the plan very low in order to have the capital equipment to make possible a much more rapid rate of growth of consumption at some period after the planning period. But to maintain indefinitely a steady rate of growth of output of consumption goods it would probably be appropriate to adjust V_{j3} and V_{k3} until $\dfrac{J_2}{J_{-1}}$ and $\dfrac{\bar{K}_2}{\bar{K}_{-1}}$ were more or less in line with $\dfrac{X_2}{X_{-1}}$ and $\dfrac{Y_2}{Y_{-1}}$.

The method which we have so far outlined consists in the Central Authority fixing certain provisional valuations (V_{j3} and V_{k3}) for the capital goods to be supplied at the end of the period of the plan, and observing the resulting quantities of these supplies ($\bar{J}_2$ and $\bar{K}_2$), and then readjusting the valuations if these supplies seem inappropriate to these valuations. An alternative method could be employed which could be so operated as in the end to achieve the same result. The Central Authority could as before fix valuations on the X's and the Y's, but instead of fixing valuations on $\bar{J}_2$ and $\bar{K}_2$ it could fix minimum quantities for these variables (say, J^* and K^*). It would in this case be asking the computer to decide upon the scales of the various processes (S_{a0}, S_{b0}, S_{b1}, S_{c1}, S_{c2}, S_{d2}) which would maximize the value of the outputs of X and Y over the period of the plan subject to the additional constraints that the supplies of J and K at the end of the plan should not fall short of certain minimum levels.

In this case in the Primal of Table XV in the value of the plan which was to be maximized the elements $S_{c2}(V_{j3}\bar{J}_c + V_{k3}\bar{K}_c)$ and $S_{d2}(V_{j3}\bar{J}_d + V_{k3}\bar{K}_d)$ would be omitted, but there would be two added constraints, namely

$$S_{c2}\bar{J}_c + S_{d2}\bar{J}_d \geqslant J^*$$

and $$S_{c2}\bar{K}_c + S_{d2}\bar{K}_d \geqslant K^*$$

In the Dual of Table XVI two corresponding shadow prices (V_{j3} and V_{k3}) would have to be added to the list of the unknown V's to be determined and from the total cost of the inputs which was to be minimized would have to be *subtracted* the two terms $V_{j3}J^*$ and $V_{k3}K^*$, since the shadow values of these two final *outputs* would reduce the net cost of the shadow values of the original inputs.

These revised Primal and Dual problems could be solved. In the previous case the Central Authority had to decide whether the final supplies of J and K (namely, $\bar{J}_2$ and $\bar{K}_2$) which resulted from the plan were appropriate in view of all the relevant quantities of other outputs and valuations, including the valuations which were provisionally allotted to $\bar{J}_2$ and $\bar{K}_2$ (namely, V_{j3} and V_{k3}). In this revised form of the problem, the Central Authority would have to decide whether the provisionally fixed final minimum supplies of J and K (namely J^* and K^*) were appropriate in view of all the relevant quantities and valuations in the plan, including the shadow valuations of J^* and K^* which resulted from the plan (namely, V_{j3} and V_{k3}). If in the former case $\bar{J}_2$ and $\bar{K}_2$ were considered to be too high, then the plan would have to be reworked on the basis of lowered valuations, V_{j3} and V_{k3}. If in the latter case J^* and K^* were considered to be too high, then the plan would have to be reworked on lower values for J^* and K^*. But in the end the two methods should result in the same identical plan.

We can perhaps summarize in the following way. Through a solution of the Primal and Dual problems for a Plan covering a longish period of future time, in conditions in which reasonable guesses can be made about the future growth of population and the future course of technical progress, the Central Authority can hope to find a system of 'planned' valuations and quantities which match each other in an efficient production of an array of consumption goods which has both a desirable time pattern and a desirable product mix. The resulting valuations will then represent the marginal rates at which the various inputs and/or outputs could be substituted for each other in the plan. Thus $\dfrac{V_{l0}}{V_{y3}} = 6$, would imply that 1 more unit of L available at 8 a.m. on day 0 would enable the plan to be so modified that 6 more units of Y could be made available for consumption at 8 a.m. on day 3. For $V_{l0} = 6V_{y3}$ would mean that the computer had jiggled about with the plan on the assumption, as it were, that saving one unit of labour on day 0 had the same social value as producing 6 units of Y for consumption on day 3. In other words the marginal product of L_0 would be six units of Y_2. And similarly for all other valuation ratios.

From such ratios it would be possible to calculate elasticities of substitution or of transformation between different inputs and/or outputs. Consider a plan which has determined, for example, $\dfrac{X_2}{Y_2}$

N

given $\dfrac{V_{x3}}{V_{y3}}$.[1] Suppose that the plan is then reworked with a change in the V's such that all the other original inputs and final outputs remain unchanged but that $\dfrac{X_2}{Y_2}$ is up by 2 per cent while $\dfrac{V_{x3}}{V_{y3}}$ is up by 1 per cent. Then we may say that the elasticity of substitution between X_2 and Y_2 in the plan has a numerical value equal to 2, because (keeping all other relevant inputs and outputs constant) a 1 per cent rise in the ratio of the valuation of X_2 to that of Y_2 is sufficient to lead to a 2 per cent increase in the quantity of X_2 to that of Y_2. Similarly if, keeping all other original inputs and final outputs constant, a *rise* of 1 per cent in $\dfrac{V_{l1}}{V_{l2}}$ would be needed to match a *fall* of $\frac{1}{2}$ per cent in $\dfrac{L_1}{L_2}$, we could say that the elasticity of substitution between L_1 and L_2 in the plan had a numerical value equal to $\frac{1}{2}$. A 1 per cent fall in the shadow wage of labour on day 1 discounted to its present value relatively to the shadow wage of labour on day 2 discounted to its present value would be necessary to make economic a $\frac{1}{2}$ of 1 per cent rise in the ratio of labour employed on day 1 to labour employed on day 2 without any other change in original inputs or final outputs. Similarly if a 1 per cent rise in $\dfrac{V_{x3}}{V_{l0}}$ were needed to match a 4 per cent increase in $\dfrac{X_2}{L_0}$, we could say that the elasticity of transformation of L_0 into X_2 was numerically equal to 4.

These elasticities of substitution and of transformation will be numerically greater, the more distant dated are the terms which are involved. Thus the elasticity of substitution between X_{200} and Y_{200} is likely to be much greater than the elasticity of substitution between X_1 and Y_1. The amounts of X_1 (bread) and Y_1 (clothes) which can be produced will be fairly rigidly fixed by the amount of J_{-1} (ploughs) and $\bar{K}_{-1}$ (looms) already produced. But the amounts of these final goods which can be produced in the distant future are much more flexible, since the intervening period can be used to produce more of one sort of intermediate product than of another (e.g. more J to produce X and less K to produce Y). Thus any many-product production system of the kind we are now considering is much more flexible if one is considering present decisions to effect future changes in final outputs than if one is considering present decisions to make immediate changes in final outputs. This is a feature of reality and will show itself in the Plansoc which we have been

---

[1] It is to be remembered that X_2 is the output of day 2 available for consumption on day 3, so that V_{x3} is the valuation of X_2 in the plan.

considering in this chapter. It would also show itself in the private-enterprise Propcap which we examined in the last chapter.

Note to Chapter XIX

THE DETERMINATENESS OF THE PLAN

As we have argued on pages 374–375 above the planning authority could seek a solution of the plan by an iterative process in which initial arbitrary social valuations were set for final outputs, the resulting optimum outputs were calculated, the social valuations were then revised in the light of these outputs, the outputs were then recalculated, and so on. When the possibilities of production are represented by a limited number of discrete processes in each of which the inputs and outputs are rigidly fixed, this iterative process may not by itself lead to any determinate solution.

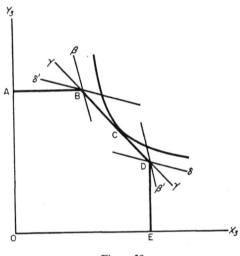

Figure 39

For the sort of reasons discussed at length in Chapter XI of *The Stationary Economy* with processes of this kind with fixed technical coefficients the production possibilities must be represented not by a continuous curve but by a kinked line made up of a series of straight-line segments such as those shown on Figure 46 on page 175 of *The Stationary Economy*. This very simple possibility is reproduced in Figure 39. We assume that, given all the other outputs and inputs in the plan, the production possibilities would give the choice between

Y_3 and X_3 shown by the kinked line ABDE in Figure 39.[1] The social indifference curves between X_3 and Y_3 (as determined by the planning authority) are such that the combination at C is the most desirable one. At this point the social valuation of X_3 in terms of Y_3 $\left(\text{i.e. } \dfrac{V_{x4}}{V_{y4}}\right)$ should be given by the slope of the line γ which is tangential to the social indifference curve at the point C. But if the computer is told to work out the best plan on the social valuations represented by the slope of γ, it will probably tell the planners to plan for the output at B or the output at D. If in its search for the most valuable set of outputs it moves along the kinked line ABDE from a starting point near A, it will come to a halt at B. Conversely if it starts its search near E, it will come to a halt at D.

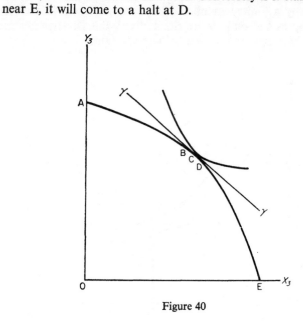

Figure 40

Suppose that it reports B as being the best plan at social valuations represented by γ. The planning authority considers that with the small output of X_3 and the large output of Y_3 represented by the point B, the social valuation of X_3 should be raised relatively to that

---

[1] We can use exactly the same illustrative story as was used for Figure 46 of *The Stationary Economy*. By day 3 the plan can have produced 1000 sheep; if these are planned to be exclusively of the wool-bearing variety they will produce at the point B; if they are planned to be exclusively of the mutton-bearing variety they will produce at the point D; and if a mixed flock is planned, one can plan for any combination of Y and X on the line BD.

of Y_3. It tells the computer to do its sums once more on the basis of a valuation such as that given by the line β, which represents a higher $\dfrac{V_{x4}}{V_{y4}}$. The computer will now state that D is the best output combination. If at D the planning authority were to consider that, with the large supply of X_3 and shortage of Y_3, a lower valuation of X_3—such as that depicted by the line δ—were appropriate, then the computer would report the combination B once more as being that which would maximize the value of the plan. For no valuations would the computer report the output combination C, however long or delicately the iterative procedure was conducted.

We shall, however, ignore this problem. We are assuming (see page 295 above) that there is such a large range of processes with such fine gradations in the differences between the coefficients that the system for all practical purposes can be treated as if there were continuous substitutability and transformability between the inputs and outputs. This means that our kinked lines (such as ABDE in Figure 39) are made up of a very large number of very short straight-line segments with very little difference in the slopes between the neighbouring segments, as in Figure 40. In this case it would make no appreciable difference if the computer insisted on the planned output being at B or D instead of at C.

CHAPTER XX

A FOUR-PRODUCT MODEL

In the preceding two chapters we have treated growth in a many-product economy in very general terms. In this chapter we will construct a more limited model, but one which is designed to bring out some particular features of the real world which have been somewhat obscured in the more general model. We have already (page 287 above) drawn attention to the fact that in the cases of raw materials which are being worked up into a finished product and of fixed capital goods which are being used over a long period of time there is a technically fixed relationship between certain inputs and outputs of the productive processes on any one day. Thus the yarn and the 100-day-old loom which go into the weaving process this morning come out as cloth and as a 101-day-old loom this evening. Cloth is not the same product as yarn and a 101-day-old loom is not the same product as a 100-day-old loom, although there are fixed technical relationships between the inputs of yarn and of 100-day-old looms and the outputs of cloth and of 101-day-old looms.

In particular in the case of fixed machinery such as a loom the product may be continually changing its character. A loom constructed in 1900—which we will call a loom of the 1900 vintage—will not be exactly the same as a loom constructed in 1901 for two reasons: first, because technical progress may make it possible to construct a technically better loom in 1901 than in 1900, and, second, because a change in factor prices may—even in the absence of any new technical knowledge—make it profitable to produce automatic looms in 1901 instead of the handlooms of 1900. Thus it is not only true that any given loom (say, a loom of the 1900 vintage) will become a different product as time passes, since when it is 50 years old (in 1950) it will be much more nearly worn out than when it is new (in 1900); it is also true that a 50-year-old loom is not the same product in any two years, since the 50-year-old loom of 1950 is a hand loom of the 1900 vintage while the 50-year-old loom of 1951 is an automatic loom of the 1901 vintage.

To make full allowance for this phenomenon we would have to put certain rather far-reaching restrictions on the model of the last two chapters. In so far as fixed capital goods were of this nature, the intermediate products would never repeat themselves from day to day; and, therefore, the processes which were actually used on any one day would none of them be used on any other day. Thus consider processes a, b, c, and d of Table XIV (page 349 above). Suppose process a is one which uses an input (J) of a 100-day-old loom made on day-100 (i.e. of the -100 vintage); then process a can in fact be used only on day 0. On no other day does the product J exist. Moreover, process a cannot now give rise to a product $\bar{J}$, since the loom which will be left over at the end of day 0 is not a 100-day-old loom of vintage -100 (namely J) but a 101-day-old loom of vintage -100 which is quite another product (say J'). Thus Table XIV would have to be reconstructed on the lines of Table XX. In Table XX

Table XX

		a	b	Processes c	d	e	f
Day 2	Outputs					X_e Y_e $\bar{K}_e'''$ J_e'''	X_f Y_f $\bar{K}_f'''$ J_f'''
	Inputs					K_e'' J_e'' L_e	K_f'' J_f'' L_f
Day 1	Outputs			X_c Y_c $\bar{K}_c''$ J_c''	X_d Y_d $\bar{K}_d''$ J_d''		
	Inputs			K_c' J_c' L_c	K_d' J_d' L_d		
Day 0	Outputs	X_a Y_a $\bar{K}_a'$ J_a'	X_b Y_b $\bar{K}_b'$ J_b'				
	Inputs	K_a J_a L_a	K_b J_b L_b				

processes *a* and *b* are used on day 0 when the fixed capital goods of the particular vintages and ages *J* and *K* are available. But these fixed capital goods produce somewhat different fixed capital goods (namely *J'* and *K'*) which are the inputs on day 1 of the somewhat different processes *c* and *d* and which in turn produce yet a new set of fixed capital goods (*J''* and *K''*) which are the inputs of yet another set of processes (*e* and *f*) on day 2, and so on. Thus the processes actually used on day 1 will necessarily differ from those used on day 0 not only because technical progress and innovation may make new methods available (a phenomenon covered in our previous Table XIV) but also because the inputs available on day 1 will be somewhat different in quality from those available on day 0. The set of intermediate products available for use on day 1 (*J'* and *K'*) will differ from those available on day 0 because the set of fixed capital goods available for use will differ from day to day for the reasons just given.[1]

This phenomenon of a change in the sets of intermediate products available for use from one day to the next does not invalidate the analysis of Chapters XVIII and XIX. They could have been written on the basis of a set of processes of the kind depicted in Table XX rather than on the basis of Table XIV. But it does seriously affect the outcome of the analysis, since what is done today (e.g. what type of new loom is produced today) will in a rather rigid manner limit the range of choices open for many future periods. It is the purpose of this chapter to build and discuss a highly simplified model, but one which does isolate and bring out some of the implications of this particular phenomenon.

There are two different forms in which this phenomenon may show itself, the first relating to the period during which some product is being made (the period of gestation) and the second relating to the period during which some fixed capital good is being used (the life period of the instrument). Consider, for example, the construction and use of a ship. Once the keel has been laid down the future history of this enterprise is determined within fairly strict limits. Successive stages of construction must follow each other over the coming months and, when the ship has been launched, the ship must be used over the years for a series of voyages of the kind for which it was

---

[1] It is not implied that there will be no overlap between the intermediate products available for use on one day and those available on another. Thus raw cotton of a particular grade will be the same on day 1 as on day 0. And it is possible that the looms constructed on day −50 were of precisely the same kind as those constructed on day −49 in which case a 50-day-old loom will be the same product on day 1 as on day 0. It is contended only that in very many cases the intermediate products available for use will not remain unchanged in quality between one day and the next.

designed in the first place. There may, of course, be some flexibility both during the period of construction (when minor changes of design can be made) and during the period of use (when the ship can be used for somewhat different purposes); and, of course, there always remains the ultimate possibility of scrapping the enterprise— of leaving the vessel half built or of breaking it up when it has been built. These rigidities are a major cause of uncertainty. Whether or not it will in the end turn out that it was worth while embarking on the whole enterprise will depend upon

(i) what happens to the cost of the inputs necessary to build the ship during the period of gestation—what happens to the cost of steel plates, the wages of shipwrights, the rate of interest, etc.;

(ii) what happens in the way of technical progress in methods of shipbuilding during the period of gestation;

(iii) what happens to the cost of the inputs necessary to run the ship once it has been built—to the wages of the crews, the cost of the fuel, the rate of interest, etc.

(iv) what happens in the way of technical progress in the operation of the ship during its life; and

(v) what happens to the price at which its services can be sold— whether freight rates are high or low over the period of the ship's use.

If the period of gestation of the instrument is much shorter than its life period, then uncertainties (i) and (ii) are much less important than uncertainties (iii), (iv), and (v). If the ship can be built in a day, the cost of the inputs necessary for its construction and their efficiency will be known more or less precisely; but the costs and efficiency of operation of the ship and the price at which its services can be sold may remain a matter of great uncertainty. In this chapter we shall confine our attention to the rigidity problems which arise from the life period of instruments of production and we shall ignore the similar problems that arise in the construction of instruments of production by assuming that the gestation period is extremely short.[1] This concentration on the rigidity problems due to the fact that fixed capital goods may have a long life during which their forms and uses are more or less rigidly predetermined will greatly simplify the exposition and will serve well to illustrate the sort of problems which are introduced by these rigidities. Moreover, in fact the life period of machines is normally longer than their period of gestation.[2]

[1] In fact (see p. 404 below) we shall assume a gestation period of one day.

[2] But it should not be forgotten that there are many particular problems which arise from the gestation period which implies an inevitable delay between a decision to construct a machine and the time at which it can first be used to produce its effect on final output.

Even if we confine our attention to the life period of machines and other fixed instruments of production, there are two closely related questions which remain to be answered. First, what determines the length of useful life of the instrument of production? And, second, how flexible is the use of the instrument during its life? In the model which we shall describe in this chapter we will make a very simple assumption which will provide the answers to both these questions. We shall assume that once a 'machine' has been constructed it will remain physically unchanged for an indefinite period, that it needs a daily input of labour of a fixed amount to operate it, that it requires no other inputs for its operation, and that so long as it is operated it produces a fixed daily output of a given and constant amount of one particular product. Thus a particular loom once made requires L units of labour to operate it, requires no inputs of raw materials and the like, and produces X units of cloth per day so long as it is operated.

This set of assumptions carries with it the following implications:

(i) The machine does not depreciate physically as a result either of decay through age or of wear and tear through use. Machines may go out of use because they become obsolescent. This indeed will be an important feature of our model. But they do not go out of use because of physical depreciation.

(ii) When a machine is being built there is great flexibility in its design, which may be affected both by improvements in technical knowledge and also by the choice between machines suitable for very labour-intensive techniques of operation (if labour is expected to be cheap in the future) and machines suitable for less labour-intensive techniques of operation (if labour is expected to be expensive in the future). But once the machine is built existing technical knowledge and the chosen technique of production is firmly embodied in it and from then onwards indefinitely the machine can be used only to produce a given daily output of a particular product with the employment of a fixed number of workers. This illustrates the phenomenon of rigidities in an extreme form. In the real world as technical progress takes place or as the real wage rate rises it may be possible to tinker with an existing machine so as to alter the amount of labour needed to operate it or the amount of output which it will produce. But undoubtedly in the real world the main choices must be made at the time when the machine is built. It is at that moment that, within rather narrow limits, the inputs and outputs associated with the machine are in fact determined.

The choice of type of machine at the moment of its construction is illustrated in Figure 41. Let us suppose that at current prices of various forms of machine a given sum, say $100,000, is to be invested in the purchase of looms which will employ labour (L) to produce cloth (X). Given the present state of technical knowledge the various forms of machine will give inputs and outputs represented by the crosses on Figure 41. Thus one type of loom (which we will call the Automatic loom) will mean that an investment of $100,000 will require OL_a labour to operate this set of looms and will produce AL_a units of cloth per day. But a set of handlooms also costing $100,000 would employ OL_b units of labour and produce BL_b units of cloth per day. And similarly for the other points marked with a cross on the

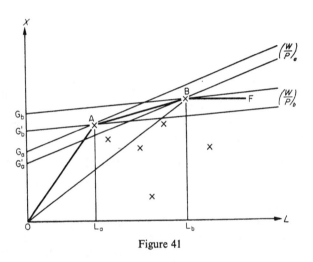

Figure 41

figure. But in the case shown in the figure only machines of type A or of type B would be chosen. There is in fact an available production function shown by the heavy kinked line OABF.[1] By using $50,000 of the $100,000 to purchase A-type looms and giving the other half of the money to charity, the entrepreneur would find himself half-way up the line OA. By spending $50,000 on A-type looms and $50,000 on the B-type looms he would find himself half-way up the line AB. By spending all the $100,000 on B-type looms and employing unnecessary labour to make unnecessary cups of tea he will find himself somewhere on the line BF. All the crosses which lie below the line OABF are thus technically dominated by the A- or B-types of loom.

Which type of loom the entrepreneur will choose will depend upon the price at which he expects to sell cloth (P) relatively to the wage which he expects to have to pay to his labour (W). If the wage rate

[1] Cf. *The Stationary Economy*, pp. 177–80.

measured in terms of cloth $\left(\dfrac{W}{P}\right)$ is expected to be high, as in the case of the lines marked $\left(\dfrac{W}{P}\right)_a$, he will invest in the A-type looms and will expect to make a gross profit on his \$100,000 investment of OG_a per day. If at this high wage rate he invested in B-type looms, he would make a daily profit of only OG'_a. If the real wage rate in terms of cloth were expected to be low, as in the case of the line marked $\left(\dfrac{W}{P}\right)_b$, he will invest in the B-type looms and will expect to make a daily gross profit of OG_b. If at this low wage rate he invested in A-type looms, he would make a profit of only OG'_b.[1]

In fact, of course, the real wage rate in terms of cloth $\left(\dfrac{W}{P}\right)$ will not remain constant for all future time after the purchase of the looms. This fact will affect two decisions to be made by the entrepreneur: first, the decision as to which type of loom to purchase in the first place; and, second, the decision when to scrap the loom once it has been installed. Let us deal first with the second of these two problems. Suppose that the real wage rate in terms of cloth starts at a low level and then gradually rises day to day, so that the $\left(\dfrac{W}{P}\right)$-lines start with a gentle slope such as the $\left(\dfrac{W}{P}\right)_b$-lines and gradually become steeper and steeper as time passes. Any loom which has been installed will be operated so long as any profit can be made on its operation, i.e. so long as the point G in Figure 41 is above the origin O. Suppose that B-type (labour-intensive) looms have been installed. Then they will be operated so long as the real wage rate in terms of cloth is less than the output per head working on B-type looms, i.e. so long as the slope of the $\left(\dfrac{W}{P}\right)$-lines is less steep than $\dfrac{BL_b}{OL_b}$, i.e. the slope of the line OB. As soon as the real wage rate rises above this, the B-type looms are obsolete because their operation would mean that the revenue from the sale of the cloth would not cover the wage cost of its production. But if A-type looms had been installed, they could still be profitably operated even when the real wage rate had risen to $\dfrac{BL_b}{OL_b}$. They would become unprofitable only when the real wage rate had risen as high as $\dfrac{AL_a}{OL_a}$, i.e. when the $\left(\dfrac{W}{P}\right)$-lines had become as steeply sloped as the line OA.

[1] Cf. *The Stationary Economy*, pp. 118–19.

One can now see the nature of the problem of choice between types of investment when future prices are likely to be changing. Suppose that at present the real wage rate is low, as depicted by the $\left(\frac{W}{P}\right)_b$ -lines. Then in the immediate future B-type looms will earn more than A-type looms (a profit of OG_b instead of a profit of OG_b'). But as soon as the real wage rate rises above the slope of the line AB, the A-type looms will earn a higher profit (a profit of OG_a instead of OG_a' as soon as the real wage rate has risen to the slope of the $\left(\frac{W}{P}\right)_a$ -lines). Thus in this case by choosing B-type looms the entrepreneur will make larger immediate profits but will make smaller profits in later years and will face earlier obsolescence of his machinery, whereas the A-type looms will give smaller immediate profits but larger and more long-lasting later profits.

Which type of loom will be preferred will depend upon (i) how soon and how quickly the wage rate is expected to rise and (ii) what is the current and what is expected to be the future levels of the rate of interest. The present value of each type of machinery can be represented by[1]

$$V_0 = \frac{G_1}{1 + i_0} + \frac{G_2}{(1 + i_0)(1 + i_1)} + \frac{G_T}{(1 + i_0)(1 + i_1) \ldots 1 + i_{T-1}}$$

where G_1, G_2, etc., represent the excess of the money receipts from sale of product over the money labour costs of production expected at 8 a.m. on days 1, 2, etc. Day T represents the day on which the machine is expected to become obsolescent because of the rise in the real wage rate. The i's represent the money rates of interest expected to rule on the successive days. It will be unprofitable to invest at all in any types of loom if V_0 for every type of loom is less than the $100,000 which is the cost of the looms whose productivity we are comparing. Any type of loom for which V_0 is greater than $100,000 will show a net profit over its life; but it will be most profitable to choose that type of loom for which V_0 is the greatest.

Comparing A-type with B-type looms, we have seen that with a rising real wage rate (i.e. with a falling price of cloth and/or a rising money wage rate) the early G's may be higher with the latter and the later G's higher with the former type of loom,and the day of obsolescence, T, is likely to be later with the former than with the latter. Given this difference in the pattern of the G's (which depends solely upon the technical differences between the looms and upon the expected movements in the money price of the

[1] Cf. p. 309 above.

product and the money wage rate), the level and future behaviour of the rate of interest will determine which type of loom has the higher present value. If future i's are expected to be high, then early profits are much more important relatively to later profits.[1] In this case the B-type loom may be preferable to the A-type loom. But if future rates of interest are expected to be low, then the A-type loom may be preferable to the B-type loom. In brief the A-type loom is the more likely to be preferable (i) the higher and more quickly rising is the money wage rate (ii) the lower and the more quickly falling is the money price of the product, and (iii) the lower and more quickly falling is the rate of interest.

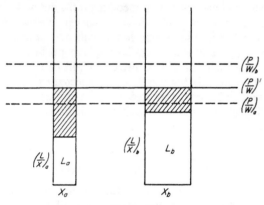

Figure 42

In Figure 41 we have shown these relationships in terms of a geometrical construction which was extensively used in *The Stationary Economy*. There is, however, an alternative geometrical representation of these relationships which is shown in Figure 42 and which, as we shall show, is a convenient method for the purpose of developing our present model. Figure 42 also represents the choice between an A-type and a B-type loom. With an A-type loom costing \$100,000 an amount of labour, L_a, must be employed; and in Figure 42 this amount of labour is represented by the *area* of the rectangle marked L_a (instead of by the *length* of the line OL_a in Figure 41). Similarly, the amount of labour, L_b, which must be used with a B-type loom costing \$100,000 is represented by the area of the rectangle marked L_b in Figure 42. The daily outputs which will be produced by each loom are represented by the widths, X_a and X_b, of the two rectangles. It follows that the height of each rectangle, namely $\dfrac{L_a}{X_a}$ and $\dfrac{L_b}{X_b}$,

[1] Cf. p. 313 above.

measures the labour cost per unit of output involved in using each of
the two looms. The B-type loom produces more output than the
A-type loom (the base of the rectangle is wider for the B-type than for
the A-type loom), so that the capital cost per unit of output is lower
for the B-type than for the A-type loom. On the other hand the height
of the B-rectangle is greater than that of the A-rectangle, so that the
labour cost per unit of output is higher for the B-type than for the
A-type loom.

Which type of loom will be preferred will, therefore, depend upon
the level of the expected real wage rate in terms of the output, cloth.
In Figure 41 we considered this by drawing lines whose slope represented the real wage for a unit of labour in terms of cloth $\left(\frac{W}{P}\right)$. In
Figure 42 we consider the same phenomenon by drawing a line whose
height represents the real value of a unit of cloth measured in terms of
labour $\left(\frac{P}{W}\right)$. Whether or not a profit can be made on the use of a
given loom will depend upon whether the value of a unit of output
measured in terms of labour, namely $\frac{P}{W}$, is greater or less than the
labour cost per unit of output, namely $\frac{L}{X}$. $\frac{P}{W} - \frac{L}{X}$ represents the
labour value per unit of output less the labour cost per unit of
output, i.e. the profit margin per unit of output measured in terms
of its purchasing power over labour.[1] Total profit (always measured
in terms of its purchasing power over labour) is thus represented by
$\left(\frac{P}{W} - \frac{L}{X}\right)X$. If the price of the product and the money wage rate
are such as to give a labour value per unit of output of $\left(\frac{P}{W}\right)'$ in
Figure 42, then the total profits (measured in terms of labour) on
the A-type and on the B-type looms would be shown by the shaded
rectangles in Figure 42. The level of $\left(\frac{P}{W}\right)'$ has been so chosen that
total profit is the same on each type of loom (the two shaded
rectangles are equal in area). If now the money price of the product
rises and/or the money wage rate falls so that $\frac{P}{W}$ rises from $\left(\frac{P}{W}\right)'$
to, say, $\left(\frac{P}{W}\right)_b$ in Figure 42, then the profit rectangle on the B-type

[1] If the price of a unit of cloth were \$10 and the wage rate were \$5, a unit of
cloth would be worth two units of labour. If the labour cost of a unit of cloth is
less than two units of labour, some net surplus is made on the production.

loom is greater than the profit rectangle on the *A*-type loom. If the money price of the product falls and/or the money wage rate rises so that $\left(\dfrac{P}{W}\right)$ falls to $\left(\dfrac{P}{W}\right)_a$, then the *A*-type loom is the more profitable. If $\dfrac{P}{W}$ falls below $\left(\dfrac{L}{X}\right)_b$ but remains above $\left(\dfrac{L}{X}\right)_a$, then the *A*-type loom will be profitable to operate but the *B*-type loom will have become obsolete—the value of its output will not even cover its labour cost.

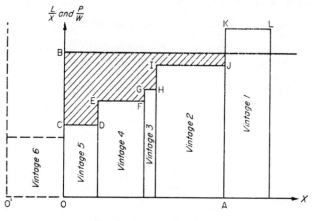

Figure 43

It is possible to use a diagram like Figure 42 to illustrate all the relationships between prices, costs, interest rates, etc., which we previously illustrated with Figure 41. We can reach the same conclusions about the choice of techniques and the length of profitable life of a given machine once it has been installed. We shall not repeat these arguments again. We can, however, now proceed to use diagrams of the type illustrated in Figure 42 to explain the output which will be produced at any given time by any given firm. This firm possesses a collection of different looms installed at different dates in the past, i.e. looms of different 'vintages'. These will differ in many respects. In some past years much more investment will have been undertaken than in other years; in later years technical knowledge will have been greater so that newer looms are technically superior to older looms; in some years, because of differences in expectations, more labour-intensive, and in other years less labour-intensive, types of loom may have been chosen. But regardless of the reason for any differences let us arrange, as in Figure 43, the equipment of looms in a series from right to left so that the labour-cost per unit of output falls as we move from right to left. Let each vintage set of looms be represented by a rectangle whose width measures the total output that can be produced by that set of looms and whose area represents the total labour needed to operate them. Once the looms have been installed it will always pay the entrepreneur to use looms with a lower labour cost per unit of input rather than looms with a higher labour cost per unit of input. Thus in Figure 43 the set of looms of vintage 5 will be used in preference to the set of looms of vintage 4, and so on down the list of vintages. Suppose now that the price of the product and the wage of labour are such that the labour value of the product[1] is equal to OB in Figure 43. Then it will be profitable to operate looms of vintages 5, 4, 3, and 2 but unprofitable to operate looms of vintage 1. Output will, therefore, be OA; employment will be equal to the sum of the four rectangles marked vintages 5, 4, 3, and 2; and total profit, measured in terms of its purchasing power over labour, will be equal to the shaded area in Figure 43.

When a new act of investment in new looms takes place, another rectangle is added to the set of rectangles in Figure 43. We have depicted this by means of the vintage-6 rectangle shown in the figure, We shall throughout the rest of this chapter always add new vintages to the left of the existing array of vintages. In other words we shall be assuming that labour cost per unit of output is always lower on new machinery than on any existing old machinery. If there is continuous technical progress, there is some reason for expecting that this will be the case. Technical progress may very probably tend to reduce both labour cost and capital cost per unit of output (i.e. to lower the height and to increase the width of the rectangles shown in Figure 42 which show the labour cost and the output relating to an investment of a given cost).[2] But technical progress does not always have this effect, since technical progress may be very biassed in favour of wages (cf. p. 74 above). This can be seen from Figure 42. Suppose

---

[1] Strictly speaking in our model, if we are considering the decision of an entrepreneur at 8 a.m. on day 0 about how much to produce and how much labour to hire during day 0, it is $\frac{{}_0 P_1}{W_0}$ with which we are concerned. It is the relationship between the price at which he expects to sell day 0's product at 8 a.m. on day 1—namely ${}_0 P_1$—and the actual wage rate which he has contracted at 8 a.m. on day 0 to pay at 8 a.m. on day 1—namely W_0—that will determine his decisions.

[2] In Figure 42 the width of the rectangles measures output per unit of capital of a given cost, because in Figure 42 the two rectangles relate to investments of a given sum, namely \$100,000. In Figure 43, however, the width of the rectangles is determined not only by the output per unit of capital invested, but also by the total amount of resources invested in each vintage set of machines.

that $\frac{P}{W}$ is expected to be at the level $\left(\frac{P}{W}\right)_b$. Suppose that in 1900 only the A-type loom is known, but that in 1901 the labour-intensive B-type loom is invented. Then it is quite possible that A-type looms will be installed in 1900 and B-type looms in 1901. In this case the new rectangle would in Figure 43 have to be inserted to the right of some of the existing rectangles.

There is another reason why this might happen. Suppose that we are dealing with an economy in which (for example because of an excessively rapid rate of population growth and the absence of technical progress) the real wage rate is continuously falling and, in particular, is continuously falling in terms of the product with whose production we are concerned. Then there will be a tendency to choose more and more labour-intensive techniques as time passes; and in the absence of technical progress the height of the rectangles relevant to this year's investment will be greater than that relevant to machines installed in earlier years.

But in an economy in which (i) technical progress is not markedly biassed in favour of wages and (ii) the real wage rate is continuously rising so that less and less labour-intensive techniques are continuously chosen out of any given set available at any one time, new machinery will always have a lower labour cost per unit of output than old machinery. The new rectangle must always be added to the left of the figure.

If investment in new machinery is going on daily, then there will be a very large number of different vintages of machinery in existence at any one time, each vintage containing only a small amount of machinery and, therefore, accounting for only a small amount of output. In this case the stepped line CDEFGHIJKL of Figure 43 can be approximately represented by a continuous curve such as BCD in Figure 44. Suppose that on day 0 our firm has a set of equipment which can be arrayed as in Figure 44, so that O_0B represents the labour cost of production on the lowest-cost machinery and X_0D the highest-cost machinery which must be brought into use if an output as great as O_0X_0 is to be produced. Suppose that at 8 a.m. on day 0 the ruling wage rate (payable at 8 a.m. on day 1) is W_0 and that the price of the produce which at 8 a.m. on day 0 is expected to be received for the sale of day 0's output at 8 a.m. on day 1 is $_0P_1$. Then with $O_0E = \frac{_0P_1}{W_0}$, the output planned for day 0 will be O_0X_0; the amount of labour employed for day 0 will be measured by the area O_0BDX_0; and the profit expected on the operations of day 0, measured in terms of its purchasing power over labour, will be represented by the area BED.

In the course of day 0 certain additional machinery will have been installed. Suppose this to be designed to produce an output equal to O_0O_1 and to employ an amount of labour equal to O_0O_1AB. Then at 8 a.m. on day 1 the entrepreneur is faced with a new supply curve, namely ABCD. If the wage rate fixed at 8 a.m. on day 1 has risen to W_1 and/or the price then anticipated to rule at the beginning of day 2 has fallen to $_1P_2$ (so that $\frac{P}{W}$ has fallen by EG) then output on day 1 will be O_1X_1; employment on day 1 will be O_1ACX_1; and profit expected on day 1's operations will be AFC. Between day 0 and day 1 output will have risen by O_1O_0 *minus* X_1X_0 (the output of the new machines less the output of the obsolete machines); employment

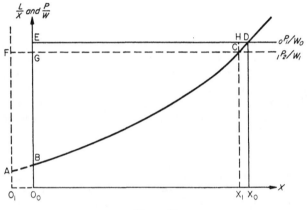

Figure 44

will have fallen by X_1CDX_0 *minus* O_1ABO_0 (the employment on the obsolete machines less the employment on the new machines); and the expected profit will have risen by AFGB *minus* CHD *minus* GEHC (the new profits on the new machines less the old profit on the obsolete machines less the fall of profit margin on the machines used on both days).

Using this simple sort of construction, let us now build a model of the economy in which there are four industries, each producing one product—namely, two consumption goods, clothes (X) and food (Y) and two capital goods, bricks (J) and steel (K). Each industry employs only labour (L) and a set of vintage machines—of looms in the case of clothes, of ploughs in the case of food, of kilns in the case of bricks, and of mills in the case of steel. Looms, ploughs, kilns, and mills are all made out of bricks and steel. Thus the output of bricks and steel of day 0 (i.e. available at 8 a.m. on day 1) are used in the course of day 1 to be put together—without any cost—in various ways decided upon at 8 a.m. on day 1 so as to produce looms, ploughs, kilns, and mills which are available for use to produce clothes, food, bricks, and steel on day 2. These we will call looms, ploughs, kilns, and mills of day-2 vintage. Thus in effect there is a negligible gestation period of only 1 day for each type of machinery.

The looms, ploughs, kilns, and mills of each vintage fully embody all technical progress and all possible substitution between labour and machinery. That is to say, once a loom has been constructed it can produce only a fixed daily output of clothes and requires a fixed amount of labour for its operation. Moreover, these instruments are subject to no physical depreciation; but they may, of course, become obsolete in the way which we have already discussed.

As far as the labour market is concerned, we assume that labour is perfectly mobile between the four industries, so that each day the same wage rate must be paid in all four industries. Moreover, we assume that each day the money wage rate is so set by a process of competitive bargaining that there is full employment of labour.

We make a very simple assumption about price expectations, namely that the price which producers expect at 8 a.m. on any day to rule for a given product at 8 a.m. on the next day is the price which was ruling at 8 a.m. on the previous day. (In our notation $_0P_1 = P_{-1}$.) The meaning of this is that a certain price of clothes, say, ruled in the market on Monday morning. On Tuesday morning, when the producers of clothes have to decide how much to produce for sale on Wednesday morning, they plan on the basis that Wednesday morning's price will not differ from the most recently experienced actual price—namely, Monday morning's price.

The financial authorities are assumed to behave in the way discussed above (Chapter XVI, pp. 303–307). That is to say, they can adjust taxes on, and subsidies to, personal incomes so finely and quickly that consumers' expenditure is so adjusted to the available supplies of clothes and food on the market on any one day that a simple price index of consumption goods—namely, $P_x + P_y$—is kept constant. The monetary authorities also fix a short-term rate of interest—i—each morning. This, as we shall see, will affect expenditure on bricks and steel and so the price level of capital goods—$P_j + P_k$. The authorities may then adjust i—upwards to discourage investment in machinery made out of bricks and steel if they wish to be able to reduce personal taxation (and thus encourage personal consumption) and downwards to encourage investment if they wish to be able to reduce subsidies to personal incomes or to raise personal taxation (and thus discourage personal consumption). We will have more to say in the sequel about the way in which these financial policies interact.

Let us now consider how this four-product model would operate. This is illustrated in Figure 45 where the solid lines represent the position at 8 a.m. on day 0 and the broken lines represent the position at 8 a.m. on day 1.[1] Let us first consider what it is which determines the outputs and employments in the four industries on day 0. The prices which are then expected to rule at 8 a.m. on day 1 are already determined because of our assumption that the prices

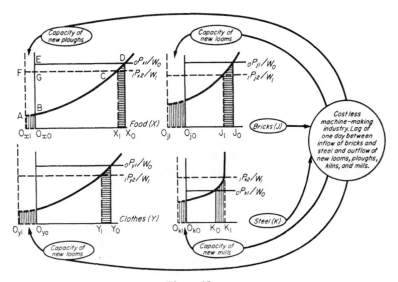

Figure 45

which actually ruled at 8 a.m. on day 1 will be expected at 8 a.m. on day 0 to rule at 8 a.m. on day 1. (Thus $_0P_{x1} = P_{x-1}$, $_0P_{y1} = P_{y-1}$, $_0P_{j1} = P_{j-1}$, and $_0P_{k1} = P_{k-1}$ where P_{x-1}, P_{y-1}, P_{j-1}, and P_{k-1} are already given historical facts.) Moreover, the array of machines available for use on day 0 in each industry will also be given historical facts, being composed of the machinery which was available for use on day 1 *plus* the new machinery constructed during day 1 from the output of bricks and steel of day 2. (Thus in the food industry there will be a supply curve such as BCD; and there will be similar supply curves as shown for the other three industries.) If the money wage rate, fixed at 8 a.m. on day 0 and payable at 8 a.m. on day 1, were

[1] The meaning of the four sections of Figure 45 can be readily understood by comparing Figure 44 which has just been described in detail, with the top left hand section of Figure 45. It will be seen that this section of Figure 45 is exactly the same as Figure 44.

known, each entrepreneur in each industry would be in a position to fix the output and employment which would maximize the profit expected by him on the operations of day 0. The lower the money wage rate, the higher the expected value of each product in terms of labour and the larger the output and employment which will be planned for day 0. We are assuming that competition will set the money wage rate at a level which causes the total demand for labour by all entrepreneurs to equal the total available supply of labour. (Thus in terms of Figure 45 the wage rate W_0 will be set at a level which causes $\frac{_0P_{x1}}{W_0}$, $\frac{_0P_{y1}}{W_0}$, $\frac{_0P_{j1}}{W_0}$, and $\frac{_0P_{k1}}{W_0}$ to be at such levels that the sum of the area $O_{x0}BDX_0$—i.e. the employment given in the food industry—and of the corresponding areas in the other three industries is equal to the total manpower available for employment on day 0. Thus the total employments and the outputs—$O_{x0}X_0$, $O_{y0}Y_0$, $O_{j0}J_0$, and $O_{k0}K_0$—of day 0 are fully determined.)

In order to build a bridge between the outputs and employments of day 0 and the outputs and employments of day 1 we must consider what it is which determines the prices of the products which actually rule at 8 a.m. on day 0, because it is these which—according to our simple assumption about price expectations—will determine the prices which entrepreneurs will expect to get at 8 a.m. on day 2 for what they produce during day 1 ($P_0 = {}_1P_2$). We will consider the determination in the market at 8 a.m. on day 0 of, first, the prices of the consumption goods (P_{x0} and P_{y0}) and, second, the prices of the capital goods (P_{j0} and P_{k0}). In both cases the supplies of the products coming on to the market for sale at 8 a.m. on day 0 are already determined by the decisions taken about production and employment at 8 a.m. on day -1. We have, therefore, to consider what it is which determines the demands at 8 a.m. on day 0, first, for clothes and food and, second, for bricks and steel.

As far as the consumption goods are concerned we are making the basic monetary assumption that by means of a flexible fiscal policy the authorities so control total personal expenditure on consumption goods that the simple price index $P_x + P_y$ is constant at a predetermined level. The relative prices of the two consumption goods will then be determined by the supplies put on the market (i.e. the outputs of day -1) together with the nature of the consumers' preferences. We shall not elaborate this analysis here.[1]

The determination of the market prices for bricks and steel involves all the problems of investment decisions which we have outlined earlier in this chapter (pp. 394–403). The outputs of bricks and of

---

[1] Cf. *The Stationary Economy*, Chapters II and III.

steel of day −1 will be being purchased at 8 a.m. on day 0 to make up into looms, ploughs, kilns, and mills to increase the capacity of the four industries for production on day 1. The outputs of bricks and of steel available for purchase at 8 a.m. on day 0 are given facts. The demand for these materials will be derived from the demand for looms, ploughs, kilns, and mills for the extension of manufacturing capacity. The demand for such instruments of production in general will be high, (i) if high profits are expected in the future—i.e. if future product prices are expected to be high relatively to the future money wage rate and if technical knowledge is such as to enable large additional outputs to be produced with given additions to capital equipment—and (ii) if the authorities have set a low rate of interest and if entrepreneurs expect future interest rates to be low, so that given profit expectations are discounted at low rates of interest and result in high present valuations of new machines.

Such will be the factors which will influence the general level of prices of capital goods, bricks and steel. The price of bricks relatively to the price of steel will depend upon the sort of machinery which is in demand. Thus mills may be made mainly of steel and kilns mainly of bricks. Moreover, the relative demand for bricks and steel may be influenced by technical progress; steel may be used in newly dis-covered ways to replace bricks as a material for the construction of certain types of machine. Finally, machines of a labour-intensive type may conceivably have a different make-up of steel and bricks from that of machines of a less labour-intensive type. There will thus result a set of prices, P_{j0} and P_{k0}, which—given the entrepreneurs' expectations about future prices, wage rates, rates of interest and given the present state of technical knowledge about the construction of machinery—will clear the market for the given supply of bricks and steel at 8 a.m. on day 0. The machines made from these bricks and steel during day 0 will add to manufacturing capacity at 8 a.m. on day 1.

According to our simple assumption about price expectations these prices which actually rule in the market at 8 a.m. on day 0 will at 8 a.m. on day 1 be expected to rule at 8 a.m. on day 2. ($_1P_{x2}$, $_1P_{y2}$, $_1P_{jk}$, and $_1P_{k2}$ are thus now given.) We can now see how outputs and employments on day 1 are determined. There will be certain exten-sions to capacity between 8 a.m. on day 0 and 8 a.m. on day 1 due to the machines made during day 0 from the bricks and steel produced during day −1. (In Figure 45 we depict the output of these new ploughs as $O_{x1}O_{x0}$ and the employment on these new ploughs as $O_{x1}ABO_{x0}$, so that the food industry has a supply curve ABCD on day 1 instead of the supply curve of BCD of day 0. And similarly for the other three industries.) With the prices of the four products which are expected at 8 a.m. on day 1 to rule at 8 a.m. on day 2 given, competition will now set the wage rate at a level which will give a total demand for labour equal to the new supply of manpower seeking employment for day 1. (With $_1P_{x2}$, $_1P_{y2}$, $_1P_{j2}$, and $_1P_{k2}$ given, W_1 will be set at a level such that the area $O_{x1}ACX_1$ *plus* the corresponding areas for the other three industries is equal to the manpower seeking employment at 8 a.m. on day 1.) Thus the outputs and employments of day 1 are determined.

The prices which actually rule for the four products in the market at 8 a.m. on day 1 will now in turn be determined by the previous day's (day 0's) output of the four products and by the conditions of demand for consumption goods and for capital goods for investment in new machinery, which rule at 8 a.m. on day 1. Once again the general level of money prices will be anchored by the fact that through fiscal policy the cost of living ($P_{x1} + P_{y1}$) is kept constant at the same predetermined level. The prices of bricks and steel (P_{j1} and P_{k1}) will have changed (J_0 and K_0 may be different from J_{-1} and K_{-1}) in so far as the supplies available have changed or in so far as entrepreneurs' expectations about future prices, wages, and interest rates have changed or in so far as technical progress between day 0 and day 1 has affected the type of machinery which is desired.

We are now in a position to determine outputs and employments on day 2. Extensions of capacity in the four industries will have been constructed during day 1 from the output of bricks and steel of day 0 to come into operation on day 2. With the prices of the four commodities ruling at 8 a.m. on day 1 determined, we have determined the prices expected at 8 a.m. on day 2 to rule at 8 a.m. on day 3. The wage rate of day 1 will then be set by competition to give full employment; and thus the outputs and employments of the four industries will be determined for day 2. And so on, from one day to the next.

In the development of the economy between day 0 and day 1 depicted in Figure 45 there are certain features which may be observed. We have shown a development which is based on the assumption that the money wage rate rises between day 0 and day 1 (i.e. $W_1 > W_0$). That this must be so can be seen from the fact that we have assumed both $\dfrac{_0P_{x1}}{W_0} > \dfrac{_1P_{x2}}{W_1}$ and $\dfrac{_0P_{y1}}{W_0} > \dfrac{_1P_{y2}}{W_1}$. The expected value of both clothes and food in terms of labour falls from one day to the next. But as we are assuming that the price level $P_x + P_y$ is stabilized, it is impossible that both P_x and P_y should have fallen between day -1 and day 0; and, therefore, with our simple assumption about price expectations it is impossible that both $_0P_{x1} > _1P_{x2}$ and $_0P_{y1} > _1P_{y2}$. It follows that W_1 must be $> W_0$.

But we have in Figure 45 assumed that as between day -1 and day 0 there has been a great increase in the demand for steel relatively to the demand for bricks (perhaps because of a technical invention). As a result the price of steel between day -1 and day 0 and so—with our assumption about price expectations—the expected price of steel between day 0 and day 1 has risen more sharply than the money wage rate. Thus while $\dfrac{_0P_{j1}}{W_0} > \dfrac{_1P_{j2}}{W_1}, \dfrac{_0P_{k1}}{W_0} < \dfrac{_1P_{k2}}{W_1}$. The expected value of steel in terms of labour has actually risen in spite of the rise in the money wage rate; and it has thus become profitable between day 0 and day 1 to bring back into operation some old steel mills which were considered obsolete on day 0. Indeed, such is the demand for steel that there are no existing steel mills left which are not brought into operation on day 1 so that the supply curve of steel has become completely inelastic. In the other three industries additional labour is employed on the new looms, ploughs, and kilns (the areas shaded vertically) but some existing labour is released from old looms ploughs, and kilns now made obsolete by the rise in the wage rate relatively to the product prices (the areas shaded horizontally). But in the steel industry additional labour is needed to man up both the newly installed mills and also the old previously obsolete mills now brought back into operation (the two vertically shaded areas). As between day 0 and day 1 the total manpower seeking employment must have changed by an amount equal to the difference between the sum of the five vertically shaded areas and the sum of the three horizontally shaded areas. If the manpower supply had risen more (or less), than this then W_1 would have been lower (or higher); in consequence $\dfrac{_1P_{x2}}{W_1}, \dfrac{_1P_{y2}}{W_1}, \dfrac{_1P_{j2}}{W_1}$, and $\dfrac{_1P_{k2}}{W_1}$ would all have been higher (or lower) and somewhat more (or less) employment would have been given on the old machinery throughout industry.

It is hoped that this model will give some idea of the mode of operation of a competitive many-product economy in which fixed capital instruments, embodying the technical knowledge and the choice of techniques ruling at the time of their construction, play a central role. But even in the very simple model which we have built the relationships between the different variables are so complicated that it is not possible in any simple manner to determine the precise way in which such an economy would grow as time passed. There are, above all, two essential parts of the economy, the workings of which depend essentially upon expectations of future developments in the economy.

First and foremost, there are the expectations about the longer-run developments of prices, wages, and interest rates which, given the technical knowledge available at the time, will determine the entrepreneurs' plans for investment in new machinery at any given time. These expectations will themselves be influenced by what has happened to prices, wages, and interest rates over a considerable period of past time as well as by any special knowledge which entrepreneurs may have about probable future developments of consumers' tastes (affecting the relative demands for food and clothing) or about probable technical developments (affecting the demands for bricks and steel) or about probable governmental policies (affecting the rate of interest) or about future demographic developments (affecting the supply of labour). It is this set of expectations which will affect the demand for bricks and steel at every point of time.

But, secondly, there are the expectations about what is going to happen a very short time ahead (in our model, what is going to happen tomorrow) to determine the demand for the outputs that can be produced in the immediate future with the existing capital equipment. These expectations are probably greatly influenced by what has happened in the immediate past. In our model we represent this by assuming that tomorrow's selling prices are expected to be the same as yesterday's, although more complicated assumptions—for example, that selling prices will rise or fall between yesterday and tomorrow at the rate experienced over the last few days—might be more realistic.

Although we must leave this model without really setting it to work properly, contenting ourselves solely with getting a vague impressionistic picture from it, there are, however, one or two general relationships on which we can comment. We will make these comments in the form of considering what it is which determines the course of the real wage rate as the economy develops. Since we are assuming that the money cost of living—namely, $P_x + P_y$ in our model—is stabilized by governmental fiscal policy (controlling the amount spent by consumers on the available supplies of consumption goods) we need not for this purpose distinguish between the real wage rate and the money wage rate. If the money wage rate goes up, so will the real wage rate.

It is interesting to observe, first of all, a close relationship between the wage rate, on the one hand, and the financial authorities' choice between monetary policy and fiscal policy, on the other hand. Consider the economy on day 0 in two otherwise exactly equivalent situations; but in Situation I the authorities set a given high rate of interest and announce that they intend to keep it at this high rate in the future, whereas in Situation II they set a low rate of interest and decide that they intend to keep it at this low level in the future. The first effect of this will be that in Situation II the demand for bricks and steel will be greater than in Situation I, since the future expected profits of industry will be discounted at a lower rate of interest and so give a higher present value for any new machinery. But with higher selling prices for bricks and steel but an unchanged stabilized set of prices for food and clothing there will at any given money wage rate be an increased demand for labour in the brick and steel industries without any decline in the demand for labour in the clothing and food industries. Given an unchanged supply of labour the money wage rate will be higher in Situation II than in Situation I so that labour is released (because it is expensive) from the food and clothing industry and absorbed (because selling prices have risen) in the bricks and steel industry. More bricks and steel but less clothing and food will be produced.

At first sight this is a paradoxical result. How can it be that while the real wage rate is higher in Situation II than in Situation I (indicating a higher standard of living), the output of clothing and food is lower in Situation II than in Situation I (indicating a lower standard of living)? The answer, of course, is that the policy of cheaper money and lower interest rates adopted by the authorities in Situation II must be accompanied by a sterner fiscal policy of higher tax rates on personal incomes if an inflation of the cost of living is to be avoided. For in Situation II less clothing and food will, as we have seen, be being put into the market. Consumers' demands must be cut back correspondingly by higher taxation on personal incomes. The greater money expenditures on investment in machinery made out of the increased production of bricks and steel will be matched by higher public savings through the increased budgetary surplus due to the increased rates of tax on personal incomes.

But given the balance between monetary and fiscal policies as determined by the financial authorities what will determine the movement of wage rates through time? This can be regarded as a race between the growth of population, on the one hand, and the opportunities for new employment offered by new investment in new productive capacity, on the other hand. Consider the area $O_{x1}ABO_{x0}$ in Figure 45. This represents the additional demand for labour to man-up the new ploughs on day 1. According as this area *plus* the corresponding areas in the three other industries is less (or greater) than the growth in the working population between day 0 and day 1, so old previously obsolete machinery must be brought back into operation to give full employment (or else some machinery which has been in use must now be rendered obsolete in order to prevent an excess demand for labour). In the former case the wage rate must fall to restore profitability to previously obsolete machinery (and in the latter case the wage rate must rise to render some more machinery obsolete so as to release labour for the new machinery).

We may conclude that there is more likely to be an upward movement in the real wage rate,

(i) The less rapid is the rate of growth of the working population,

(ii) The greater is the level of total investment, i.e. the more of their incomes persons save instead of spending on consumption and the more the authorities are prepared to set a low level of interest rates with a high level of personal taxation,

(iii) The greater the proportion of the total investment which is flowing into labour-intensive industries in which much new labour must be employed with each additional $1-worth of machinery,

(iv) The more biassed in favour of wages is technical progress, i.e. the more technical progress cuts capital costs of production and the less it cuts labour costs of production on new machinery, and

(v) The less rapid the rise in future wage rates which is expected, since this will (as we have seen above, p. 398) induce entrepreneurs to invest in labour-intensive types of capital equipment.[1]

We have in the above analysis been considering the determinants of the wage rate, i.e. of the marginal product of labour. These movements in the *marginal* product of labour may be quite different from the movements in the *average* product of labour. The real wage rate is not necessarily a good index of real output per head. This distinction can be clearly seen in our present model. The marginal product of labour in any one industry on any one day is what would be added to the output of that industry by having one more unit of labour to employ in that industry on that day. If one more unit of labour were employed, it would always be employed on the machine which had just become obsolete, i.e. on that unused machine which had the lowest labour cost per unit of output. It follows that in terms of any one given product the marginal product of labour between day 0 and day 1 rises or falls according as some more machinery becomes obsolete or some previously obsolete machinery is brought back into use between day 0 and day 1. Thus in Figure 45 between day 0 and day 1 the marginal product of labour and so the wage rate rises if measured in terms of clothes, food, or bricks, but falls if measured in terms of steel.

Consider now the case in which there is some moderate rate of growth of population, heavy savings and investment, but technical

---

[1] It is interesting to observe that point (v) introduces an element of negative feedback into the economic system. If wage rates are rising rapidly this will probably make entrepreneurs expect a rapid rise of wage rates in the future. But this expectation will make entrepreneurs avoid labour-intensive forms of investment. But this in turn will cause the demand for labour and, therefore, the money wage rate to rise less rapidly than it would otherwise have done.

progress markedly biassed against wages. Let us suppose that the additional employment given by the heavy, but biassed new investment is just equal to the increase in the manpower seeking work. Then in each industry there might be no change in the margin at which it became unprofitable to use old machinery; there would on balance be no need to absorb labour by bringing back previously obsolete machinery into use or to release labour by making obsolete some machinery which had up to now been used. The marginal product and so the wage rate of labour could remain unchanged in terms of every product.[1] But the average product of labour, real output per head, would certainly be increased. For on the new equipment employing the new labour output per head would be exceptionally high, while there would be no change in output per head in respect of the previously existing labour force working on the same machines as before.

Thus in this case there would be a rise in output per head but no rise in the real wage rate needed to give full employment. There would be a shift of income from wages to profits due to the labour-saving nature of the new machinery. If everything else had been the same except that technical progress had been still more markedly biassed against wages, previously obsolete machinery would have had to be called back into use in order to give employment to those new workers who could not find work on the new machines. In this case output per head might well still rise, but there would be a fall in the marginal product of labour and in the wage rate. Technical progress in this case would have been so biassed against wages as to cause the real wage rate to fall absolutely, while output per head was rising.[2]

[1] This could be the outcome only if there were no change in the relative prices of clothing, food, bricks, and steel. Of course, in fact some of these prices would be likely to rise and others to fall relatively to each other. There would probably therefore be a fall in the marginal product of labour measured in terms of some products (whose prices had risen relatively to the others) and a rise when measured in terms of other products (whose prices had fallen relatively to the others). But this does not alter the broad conclusion of the main text.

[2] If the relative demand prices for the various products were unchanged (see the previous footnote) then in our present model, however biassed technical progress might be, the real wage rate could not fall absolutely unless the working population were growing. For if there were a constant working population and if—as we are assuming—existing machines last for ever without any physical deterioration, a real wage rate lower than the existing wage rate would cause an excess demand for labour in every industry. Some previously obsolete machines would be recalled into employment and this would represent a demand for labour additional to the existing demand, while the supply of labour was unchanged. With physically everlasting machinery, new investment—however biassed in character—could only represent an increased demand for labour; and this, with a constant supply of labour, would necessarily cause a rise in the real wage rate.

CHAPTER XXI

RISK, UNCERTAINTY, AND ENTERPRISE

Our discussion in the preceding chapters on growth in a many-product economy has shown the great importance of knowing how to deal with the problem of uncertainty about future developments. It is, as we have seen, impossible to plan today's activities without reference to the prices at which today's output will sell tomorrow, these prices being themselves in part determined by what people tomorrow expect the next day's prices to be—and so on into the indefinite future. Thus risk and uncertainty is an essential feature of our present model of economic growth. In the next chapter we will discuss some ways in which risks and uncertainties may be reduced; but, as we shall see then, great risk and uncertainty is nevertheless bound to remain. In this chapter we intend to discuss two matters which are bound to arise from this inevitable existence of risk and uncertainyt.

First, even in our otherwise extremely simple model—with no indivisibilities and with perfect competition—the existence of risks and uncertainties will, as we shall argue, give a real function for the entrepreneur. In addition to the factors of production land, labour, and man-made instruments of production, there is now yet another basic component in the productive process, namely the estimating and bearing of risks and uncertainties. One of our tasks in this chapter is to see what is the function of this new 'factor of production'.

Second, we shall have to discuss in this chapter what individual entrepreneurs' attitudes to risks and uncertainties may be and what it is, therefore, which decides which risks and uncertainties a man will face and which he will not.

In this chapter we shall maintain all the simplifying assumptions which we have consistently maintained throughout the rest of this volume. This necessarily introduces many important unrealities in our model; and this is particularly true of our discussion of risk and uncertainty. But, as it is hoped will appear to the reader from the following discussion, there are certain very important gains to be set against the introduction of these simplifying but unrealistic assumptions. In particular, in the discussion of enterprise and of the bearing of risks and uncertainties they will enable us to isolate for discussion in a simple and intelligible form some of the basic features of bearing risks and facing uncertainties.

Let us start then by describing the way in which we shall assume that entrepreneurial decisions are made and risks and uncertainties are borne in our present model.

In the first place, the existence of a perfect market and of perfect competition means that we need only consider risks and uncertainties from one day to the next. We shall continue to make the assumptions made on page 289 above, namely that the entrepreneur in charge of a firm or farm sells the whole of the output of day 0 of that firm or farm at 8 a.m. on day 1, including all the half-used machines, etc., which are being employed in that firm. He may, of course, buy back at 8 a.m. on day 1 much of the output of day 0 of his own firm or farm in order to use this half-used machinery, etc., again on day 1 to produce output for sale at 8 a.m. on day 2. As we have pointed out, we make this assumption merely as a convenient way of emphasizing the fact that we are assuming that there is a perfectly competitive market for everything (including half-used machinery) and in consequence that everything (including half-used machinery) has a single, precise money value at 8 a.m. on each day. This means that at 8 a.m. on each day each entrepreneur takes an entirely new set of decisions as to what he will do on that day. At 8 a.m. on each day he hires labour at a certain, known wage for that day; he borrows money at a certain, known rate of interest for the day; with this money he purchases man-made instruments of production at certain, known prices; and with this labour and these instruments of production he produces certain, known outputs of various products, the technical possibilities open for use during day 0 being *ex hypothesi* already known at 8 a.m. on day 0. He then sells these outputs at 8 a.m. on day 1 at prices which are not known until 8 a.m. on day 1. It is solely the uncertainty about the prices which will rule at 8 a.m. on day 1 which introduces an element of risk and uncertainty into the entrepreneur's decisions taken at 8 a.m. on day 0. We shall define as his entrepreneurial profit or loss for day 0 the excess (or deficiency) of the actual receipts from selling his outputs of day 0 at the prices ruling at 8 a.m. on day 1 over the costs incurred at 8 a.m. on day 0 in wages and cost of instruments of production, including the day's interest on the cost of those instruments (cf. the expression (15.1) in Chapter XV, p. 290 above).

We shall assume that each firm or farm is run by only one entrepreneur. There is one man initiating and in charge of the activities of each firm or farm during day 0; it is he who at 8 a.m. on day 0 hires labour, borrows money capital, purchases machines, etc., and decides what to produce with these inputs during day 0, who sells the output at 8 a.m. on day 1, and who pays the predetermined wages and repays with predetermined interest his borrowed capital at 8 a.m. on day 1. He is the only person concerned in the operations of the firm who incurs any risk or faces any uncertainty. Entrepreneurial risk and uncertainty covers all risks and uncertainties in our model.

This assumption—that each firm is operated by only one taker of risks and uncertainties—removes from our discussion a problem of decision making which is in fact of central importance in the real world, namely how decisions are, or can best be, made by groups of persons. In a partnership or a company in which there are many persons holding equity interests (e.g. ordinary shares) and in a number of other corporate bodies, a *single* decision must often be taken in conditions of risk and uncertainty which affects the separate interests of *many individual* partners. One partner may wish to take more risks than does another. How in such circumstances is the choice made between a decision which plays safe for a certain but low yield and a decision which risks much for an uncertain but very high yield? It is hoped that in a later volume in this series, when we come to deal with group decisions—including governmental decisions which affect many individual citizens—we shall be able to return to questions of this kind. But in this volume we are attempting to confine ourselves to situations in which decisions could be relegated to individual citizens operating independently of each other in a market. By assuming that each decision-making unit (a firm or farm) is operated by only one decision-maker who runs all the risks and uncertainties connected with the decision (the single entrepreneur) we avoid problems of group decisions, important though these be in the real world where one manager decides on behalf of many share-holders.

As we are assuming in this volume that there are no indivisibilities and no economies or diseconomies of large-scale operation, firms can be as large or as small as one likes without having any effect upon their efficiency. This means that, even though each firm is run by only one entrepreneur, yet each entrepreneur can determine freely the scale on which he wishes to engage in bearing any risk or uncertainty. Moreover, while we assume that each firm is operated by only one entrepreneur, we do not assume that each entrepreneur can operate only one firm. An entrepreneur can, therefore, spread his risks and uncertainties over many operations. Thus a given entrepreneur—Mr A—can decide at 8 a.m. to organize a large firm to produce shoes plus a moderate sized firm to produce bricks plus a small farm to produce corn. By so doing he will be deciding both the scale and the diversity of his total bearing of risk and uncertainty.

We shall assume further that the entrepreneurs go on working and lending out their own property at interest in the ordinary way like other citizens. They have, therefore, incomes from wages and from interest on their property. The entrepreneurial profits (or losses) which they make on running firms and farms are thus net sums additional to (or to be subtracted from) their normal incomes from work and from the ownership of property. We have thus isolated the problems of risks and uncertainties by reducing them to one single form in which any citizen can take part—namely the purchase of inputs at known prices at 8 a.m. on any one day in order to sell outputs at unknown prices one day ahead in the future. Each citizen can decide whether he will take part in such risky and uncertain activities, on what scale he will do so, and on what pattern he will spread his total risk over many various individual risks. Moreover, each such entrepreneur takes decisions the soundness or unsoundness of which affect only his own income and wealth.

In this model the citizens who will become entrepreneurs in any industry are those who (i) are most optimistic about the future prices of the outputs of the industry and (ii) have temperaments which make them little averse to the bearing of risks and uncertainties or, indeed, which make them positively enjoy the suspense of a gambler. But those who become successful entrepreneurs will be those who make the most accurate forecasts of the course of product prices. It is here that the real social function of entrepreneurship lies in our model. It is the entrepreneurs whose business it is to judge which prices are likely to rise and which to fall and, on the basis of this, to guide today's resources of men and of instruments of production into those processes which produce the outputs which will in fact be most wanted tomorrow. The actual profit or loss which an individual entrepreneur actually makes is thus an accurate measure of the extent to which he has made a good or a bad forecast of the future needs of his fellow citizens.

In so far as the production of consumption goods is concerned, this statement needs no qualification, so long as we are working on the assumptions made in this volume. For the price at which clothes and food are sold tomorrow will accurately measure the value of clothes and food to the citizens tomorrow. But in so far as the production of instruments of production are concerned, we must qualify the statement made at the end of the preceding paragraph. The price of looms tomorrow may be high because some ill-informed entrepreneur tomorrow bids up their price because he overestimates the selling price of cloth which will rule the day after tomorrow. The entrepreneur using the looms will make a loss, but the entrepreneur making the looms will himself have made a profit. Successful entrepreneurship can take the form of successfully anticipating the future

o

unsuccessful follies of others. But if consistently unsuccessful entrepreneurs are somehow or another eliminated from the business
scene, then there will be a strong tendency for the size of today's
actual entrepreneurial profits to measure the success of entrepreneurs
in forecasting today the real needs of consumers either for tomorrow
(which will influence tomorrow's prices of consumption goods) or for
later periods (which will influence tomorrow's prices of capital
goods).

We are thus faced with the following situation. It is the optimistic
gamblers who will want to become entrepreneurs. It is those who
are skilled or lucky in forecasting future prices who will guide the
community's resources into the most useful lines of business. There
does not on the face of it seem to be any reason why those who are
temperamentally optimistic and like gambling should be especially
good at making accurate forecasts of future prices. It is only if there
is some social mechanism at work which encourages those who want
to be entrepreneurs to take business risks if they are good at forecasting the future course of prices and discourage them if they are
bad at forecasting future prices.

There is, of course, a strong force of this kind at work even in our
present simplified economic model; but in order properly to understand it we must modify a statement which we made earlier in this
chapter. If a citizen today hires labour and borrows money on a very
large scale and makes a serious mistake in his judgment of tomorrow's
selling prices for his products, he may make so large a loss that he is
unable to meet it out of his own resources. In this case he will have to
default upon his undertakings to pay predetermined wages and to
repay his borrowing with predetermined interest out of tomorrow's
receipts. In other words it is not always strictly true to say that each
citizen who goes in for a business enterprise is himself bearing all the
risks and uncertainties associated with that enterprise. This would be
strictly true only if each entrepreneur never financed any enterprise
on a larger scale than he could finance out of his own personal
resources, however low tomorrow's selling prices turned out to be.
Strictly speaking for this purpose we would have to assume that no
entrepreneur contracted at 8 a.m. on day 0 to pay at 8 a.m. on day 1
in wages and in repayment of, and interest on, money borrowed
more than the wages, capital, and interest which was due to him at
8 a.m. on day 1 from his contracts with others. He would then be
able to meet his contractual obligations at 8 a.m. on day 1 even if his
receipts from the sales of his products fell to zero. We need not
perhaps make quite such an extreme assumption as this. Virtually all
risks and uncertainties will be borne by the entrepreneur if people
refuse to contract to work for, or lend to, any entrepreneur who

cannot cover out of his own personal resources a substantial proportion of what he has contracted to pay to all the workers he has hired and to all his creditors. Without being too precise we will in fact assume that entrepreneurs cannot undertake risky and uncertain operations on a larger scale than this so that virtually no entrepreneurs actually ever fail to meet their contractual obligations and virtually all risks and uncertainties are borne by entrepreneurs.

But as soon as we make an assumption of this kind there is a very strong force at work diminishing the scale of operations of unsuccessful entrepreneurs and increasing the scale of operations of successful entrepreneurs. Those who make bad forecasts will make losses; their personal wealth will be reduced; and the scale on which they can operate as entrepreneurs in the future will be reduced. Those who make good forecasts will make profits; their personal wealth will be increased; and the scale on which they can—and, as we shall see, probably also on which they will wish to—operate as entrepreneurs will be increased. Thus there will be a strong tendency for the use of the community's resources to be guided by those who both are not too averse to facing risks and uncertainties and also are skilled at making good forecasts of future prices.

Let us now consider how one can usefully describe a citizen's— Mr A's—attitude to risk and we shall illustrate this problem by means of Figure 46. The method which we shall adopt is strictly analogous to that adopted in the Note to Chapter XII and Figure 23 (pp. 212–219 above). At that point we were concerned with describing a man's attitude to variations in his standard of living—whether or not he preferred one-quarter of a year at a level of $0 *plus* three-quarters of a year at a level of $100 to one whole year at a level of $50. We are now concerned with describing a man's attitude to risks and uncertainties regarding his income—whether or not he prefers 1 chance in 4 of a receipt of, say, $0 *plus* 3 chances in 4 of a receipt of, say, $100 to a certainty of, say, $50. The things to be described are not the same—one concerns attitudes to variations or stability in standards over time and the other attitudes to chances or certainty of a standard of living at a given point of time; but the methods of description are essentially the same.

For our present purpose we need to take two benchmarks of levels of possible entrepreneurial profit or loss in order to make comparisons with other possible levels of profit or loss. It is convenient to take two extreme figures—at the one extreme the largest conceivable loss the citizen might make and at the other extreme the largest possible gain which he might make. In our present model the largest loss which Mr A can make on any one day's entrepreneurial activities is set by the total contractual obligations which he has incurred towards his employees and his creditors. We have argued that the scale of his entrepreneurial activities will be necessarily limited, being restrained to a proper relationship with his own total personal resources. Thus we assume in Figure 46 that the largest possible loss which Mr A can incur on day 0's operations is $100. Theoretically there is no upper limit to the profit which Mr A might make on day 0's operations since there is no upper limit to the level of the money prices at 8 a.m. on day 1 at which he might sell the particular products which he has chosen to produce. But there will be some height to these prices which he considers to be beyond the range of possible imagination. There is some maximum to the profit of which he will contemplate the possibility for day 0's operations. In Figure 46 we have set this

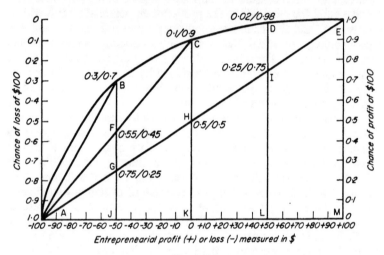

Figure 46

maximum conceivable profit also at $100, although there is no reason other than simplicity of exposition of our model why the maximum conceivable profit should be the same as the maximum conceivable loss.

We can now describe Mr A's attitude to risk and uncertainty on day 0 by drawing a curve like the curve ABCDE. Consider the point H. We ask Mr A whether he would prefer (I) the certainty of no profit or loss or (II) an entrepreneurial venture which would give him a 50 per cent chance of a loss of $100 *plus* a 50 per cent chance of a profit of $100. If he prefers (I) to (II) he has some aversion to risk and uncertainty. The mathematical expectations of (I) and (II) are the same—in both cases of a zero net profit or loss; but (I) gives a certain return of zero while (II) gives a risky and uncertain return of zero—i.e. an equal chance of loss or of profit. If Mr A prefers (II) to (I), then he must take a positive delight in running risks. If he is indifferent between (I) and (II), he is simply unaffected one way or the other by risk and uncertainty. We shall assume that all citizens have some aversion to risk and uncertainty. This aversion may be due to either of two causes. Suppose Mr A to have an income from work and property (i.e. apart from his entrepreneurial profit or loss) of $200. Then if he makes a profit of $100 he will have $300; and if he makes a loss of $100, he will have only $100 left. A reduction in his spendable income from $200 to $100 may cut into necessities of life, while a rise in his spendable income from $200 to $300 may only enable him to acquire some unimportant luxuries. For this reason—a true diminishing marginal utility of income—a certain income of $200 is worth more to him than an equal chance of $100 or of $300. But, secondly, even if in some basic psychological sense Mr A would enjoy the 'luxuries' which he could get when his income rose from $200 to $300 just as much as the 'essentials' which he could get when his income rose from $100 to $200, he might still prefer a certainty of $200 tomorrow to an equal chance of $100 or of $300. He might simply prefer to know where he stood. We shall assume that for either or both of these reasons all citizens have some aversion to risk and uncertainty.

If this is so, Mr A will prefer not to undertake any entrepreneurial venture rather than one which involves an equal chance of a profit of $100 or of a loss of $100. But suppose the enterprise promised a 60 per cent chance of a profit of $100 and only a 40 per cent chance of a loss of $100, or better still that it promised an 80 per cent chance of a profit of $100 and only a 20 per cent chance of a loss of $100. Clearly if it promised a 100 per cent chance of a profit of $100 and a 0 per cent chance of a loss of $100, he would undertake the enterprise. At some point between a 50-50 chance and a 100-0 chance he would just be willing to undertake the enterprise. Suppose that at a 90 per cent chance of a profit of $100 *plus* a 10 per cent chance of a loss of $100 he is just on the margin of indifference between undertaking the enterprise or not undertaking any risk of profit or loss, then we draw KC in Figure 46 with a height of 0·9. C is then above H and is one point on the curve showing Mr A's aversion to risk and uncertainty.

Similarly the point B will be above the point G in Figure 46 if Mr A has an aversion to risk and uncertainty. Give Mr A the choice of (I) a fixed tax of $50 or (II) getting off the tax by undertaking an enterprise with a 25 per cent chance of a profit of $100 *plus* a 75 per cent chance of a loss of $100. The mathematical expectation is the same for (I) and (II), namely a net loss of $50. But with (II) there is some risk and uncertainty—the possible outcome varying between a probable loss of $100 and an improbable gain of $100—while with (I) there is no risk or uncertainty—just a certain loss of $50. The man who is averse to risk and uncertainty will demand something better than the straight odds on a fair bet; he will require, let us say, not a 25 per cent but a 70 per cent chance of a profit of $100 combined not with a 75 per cent but with only a 30 per cent chance of a loss of $100 to make him just willing to take the bet instead of paying a fine of $50. In this case we draw JB with a height of 0·7. B is another point on the curve showing Mr A's aversion to risk and uncertainty and B is above G. And similarly for the point D which will lie above the point I.

We can then conclude that in the case of any citizen who has any aversion to risk and uncertainty the curve ABCDE will lie above the straight line AGHIE. But we can go on to make one further statement. Join the points A and C with the straight line AFC. We can assert that the point B will lie not merely above the point G, but also above the point F. We can show this in the following way.

The point J lies half way between A and K. If Mr A is averse to risk and uncertainty, then we can say that he prefers

(I) a certainty of a loss of $50
to (II) a 50 per cent chance of a loss of $100 *plus* a 50 per cent chance of no profit or loss.

But the height of KC being 0·9 or 90 per cent, we can say that no profit or loss is the equivalent of a 10 per cent chance of a loss of $100 *plus* a 90 per cent chance of a gain of $100. Thus we can say that Mr A will prefer

(I) a certainty of a loss of $50
to (II) a 50 per cent chance of a loss of $100
plus a 50 per cent chance of a 10 per cent chance of a loss of $100
plus a 50 per cent chance of a 90 per cent chance of a profit of $100.

Or in other words Mr A will prefer

(I) a certainty of a loss of $50
to (II) a 55 per cent chance of a loss of $100
plus a 45 per cent chance of a profit of $100

so that the point B will lie above the point F. The chance of the $100 loss must be reduced to, say, 30 per cent and the chance of the $100 profit raised to, say, 70 per cent before Mr A would prefer the gamble to a fixed loss of $50.

We can in this way show that if we take any two points on the curve (such as B and D) and draw a straight line between them, the point on the curve which lies half way horizontally between them (such as C) will lie above the straight line (BD). If this is universally true of the curve ABCDE, then we can now say of it

(i) that it will always lie above the straight line AGHIE (people are averters of risk and uncertainty and will require more than the fair odds on a bet to induce them to exchange a certain income for a gamble)

(ii) that its height rises as we move from left to right (the larger the certain profit, the better must be the terms of the bet with loss of $100 and gain of $100 to compensate for the certain profit), and

(iii) that it will become less and less steeply sloped as one moves from left to right (because of the diminishing marginal utility of income, the difference between a fixed income of $200 and a fixed income of $150 is less important to a man than the difference between a fixed income of $150 and one of $100, so that the odds on a bet between a given loss and a given gain need improve less to compensate for the loss of a fixed income of $200 instead of for the loss of a fixed income of $150 than they need improve to compensate for the loss of a fixed income of $150 instead of for the loss of a fixed income of $100).

We will call the height of the curve ABCDE the chance-utility index for Mr A on day 0. Given this chance-utility index we should be able to measure (in terms of a fixed certain addition to or subtraction from his income) the equivalent value to Mr A of any stated business venture. Suppose, for example, that Mr A is contemplating a business undertaking which he believes to give him

        (i) a 20 per cent chance of a gain of $100
plus (ii) a 60 per cent chance of a gain of $50
plus (iii) a 15 per cent chance of a loss of $50
plus (iv) a 5 per cent chance of a loss of $100.

Now in Figure 46 we read off from Mr A's chance-utility index that a gain of $50 is the equivalent to him of a 98 per cent chance of a gain of $100 *plus* a 2 per cent chance of a loss of $100 and that a loss of $50 is the equivalent to him of a 70 per cent chance of a gain of $100 *plus* a 30 per cent chance of a loss of $100. It follows that this business enterprise gives him the equivalent of

        (i) a 20 per cent chance of a gain of $100
plus (ii) a 60 per cent chance of a 98 per cent chance of a gain of $100
        plus a 60 per cent chance of a 2 per cent chance of a loss of $100

plus (iii) a 15 per cent chance of a 70 per cent chance of a gain of $100
     plus a 15 per cent chance of a 30 per cent chance of a loss of $100
plus (iv) a 5 per cent chance of a loss of $100.

In other words the prospect is the equivalent to him of

    (i) a 20 per cent + a 60 per cent × 98 per cent + a 15 per cent
      × 70 per cent chance of a gain of $100
plus (ii) a 60 per cent × 2 per cent + a 15 per cent × 30 per cent + a
      5 per cent chance of a loss of $100

or, in other words, of

    (i) an 89·3 per cent chance of a gain of $100
plus (ii) a 10·7 per cent chance of a loss of $100.

We can now look once more at Mr A's chance-utility index on
Figure 46 and see that a 0·107/0·893 risk as between a loss of $100
and a gain of $100 is the equivalent of a certain loss of about $3 or so.
This particular venture is not worth while his taking, given his very
marked aversion to risk and uncertainty.[1] This is so, even though the
mathematical expectation of profit or loss from this enterprise
(namely a 20 per cent chance of $100 *plus* a 60 per cent chance of $50
plus a 15 per cent chance of −$50 *plus* a 5 per cent chance of −$100)
is a positive profit of as much as $37·5.

This method of assessing the worthwhileness of undertaking a
given business enterprise can thus be reduced to finding the level of
the certain profit or loss which, given our entrepreneur's attitude to
risk and uncertainty and his estimation of the probabilities of various
possible outcomes of profit or loss from this enterprise, is the
equivalent to him of taking this particular business gamble. But from
Figure 46 it is clear that the last step in our procedure—namely the
reading from Figure 46 of the actual equivalent certain profit or loss
—can be omitted. Since the curve ABCDE in Figure 46 slopes upwards consistently, we can say that he will do the best for himself if
he gets as high as possible as he can on this curve, because that is the
same thing as saying that he gets as far as possible to the right (i.e.
the lowest possible certain loss or the highest possible certain profit).
In other words in the example given in the last paragraph we could
have stopped at the point at which we reached the conclusion that the

[1] He has obviously a great aversion to running any chance of the disastrous
catastrophe of a loss as great as $100. The point B shows that he would prefer a
certain loss of $50 to a 30 per cent chance of loss of $100 even though this chance
was combined with a 70 per cent chance of a gain of $100. Such is the increasing
utility of income to him as his income falls that, while he can contemplate a loss of
$50, only the most attractive odds will induce him to run any chance of a further
loss of $50 (i.e. of a total loss of $100).

particular venture under discussion was the equivalent to him of an 89·3 per cent chance of a profit of $100 (combined, of course, with a 10·7 per cent chance of a loss of $100). This is worse than doing nothing because, as we know from Figure 46, doing nothing is the equivalent to him of a 90 per cent chance of a profit of $100 (combined, of course, with a 10 per cent chance of a loss of $100). In other words, given the chance-utility index of Figure 46, our potential entrepreneur should choose that business enterprise whose potential outcomes, when combined in the way we have explained, give him the highest combined chance-utility index.

In the numerical example which we have just given we have considered our entrepreneur-citizen faced with a choice between doing nothing or undertaking one particular business venture. But in fact he will be faced with a choice between more than these two simple alternatives. (1) He can do nothing, (2) he can venture much in industry X, (3) or much in industry Y, (4) or little in industry X, (5) or little in industry Y, (6) or a little in both industries, and so on and so on. We can call all these the 'policies' between which he has to choose. At the same time the money loss or profit which he can expect to make if he chooses any one policy will depend upon to-morrow's state of the market. If the demand for X is very high and for Y very low, policy (1) will give no profit or loss, policy (2) will give a large profit, policy (3) a large loss, policy (4) a small profit, policy (5) a small loss, and policy (6) no profit or loss. Let us call this State A of the market. If the demand for X is very high and for Y fairly high, then policy (1) will give no profit or loss, policy (2) will give a very large profit, policy (3) a reasonably large profit, policy (4) a moderate profit, policy (5) a small profit, and policy (6) a reasonably large profit. Let us call this State B of the market. And so on for many other possible States of tomorrow's market.

We can now generalize the choice which he has to make in the way shown in Table XXI. There are a very large number of possible market States which he has to contemplate, namely A, B, C, D, E, etc. With a very large number of industries and with an almost infinite number of gradations of level of demand for the various products, he will in fact have to contemplate an almost infinite number of possible market States. In fact he must base his decisions on the contemplation of a limited number of typical or representative States. He must next make up his mind what he expects the probabilities of these different market states to be. If he expects a 1 in 10 chance of State A, a 3 in 10 chance of State B, etc., we write these probabilities as $\pi_a = 0·1$, $\pi_b = 0·3$, etc. He must then consider the money profit or loss which he expects to incur if he adopts any particular policy and is faced with any given state of the market.

Thus suppose that, if he adopts policy 3 and if in fact the state of tomorrow's market turns out to be State C, then he will make a profit of \$20; in this case we write $c_3 = \$20$ in Table XXI. And so on for all the other money outcomes of the different policies in the different States of the market. Each of these money profits or losses has

Table XXI

		States of Tomorrow's Market					
		A	B	C	D	E	etc.
		with probabilities of occurrence of					
		π_a	π_b	π_c	π_d	π_e	etc.
		where the sum of the π's $= 1$.					
Policies	1. Money Profit or Loss Total Chance Utility	a_1 $\pi_a U(a_1)+\pi_b U(b_1)+\pi_c U(c_1)+\pi_d U(d_1)+\pi_e U(e_1)+..$	b_1	c_1	d_1	$e_1 ...$	
	2. Money Profit or Loss Total Chance Utility	a_2 $\pi_a U(a_2)+\pi_b U(b_2)+\pi_c U(c_2)+\pi_d U(d_2)+\pi_e U(e_2)+..$	b_2	c_2	d_2	$e_2 ...$	
	3. Money Profit or Loss Total Chance Utility	a_3 $\pi_a U(a_3)+\pi_b U(b_3)+\pi_c U(c_3)+\pi_d U(d_3)+\pi_e U(e_3)+..$	b_3	c_3	d_3	$e_3 ...$	
	4. etc.						

from Figure 46 a given chance-utility index; thus, with our example, if c_3 is a profit of \$20, we can see from Figure 46 that the chance-utility index of c_3—which we call $U(c_3)$—is about $0 \cdot 94$. Suppose π_c—the probability of State C occurring—is assessed by our potential entrepreneur at 1 in 10. Then the adoption of policy 3 will give a $0 \cdot 1$ chance of a profit of \$20, i.e. a $0 \cdot 1$ chance of the equivalent of a $0 \cdot 94$ chance of a profit of \$100 (combined with a $0 \cdot 1$ chance of the equivalent of a $0 \cdot 06$ chance of a loss of \$100). Thus the possibility of State C occurring will contribute $0 \cdot 094$ to the final total chance-utility index derived from policy 3. The possibilities of States A, B, D, or E occurring will contribute similar additional elements to the total chance-utility index derived from policy 3. In Table XXI that policy should be chosen which gives the highest total chance-utility when all the various money outcomes from that policy have been converted into their equivalent chance-utility indices and have been weighted by the probabilities of each particular outcome.

Table XXI generalizes the problem involved in the choice between enterprises of different degrees and kinds of chance. In order to bring out and illustrate some of the possible types of chance between which the choice must be made we will now elaborate a simplified numerical example of the general schema shown in Table XXI. For this we will assume:

(1) that we are concerned with the decisions of an individual potential entrepreneur—Mr A—with the attitude to chance shown in Figure 46;

(2) that he is faced only with three outlets, namely taking no risk, or risking up to a maximum of a loss of $100 in the transport industry or in the hotel industry or in some combination of the two;

(3) that in each of the two industries there are only two possible outcomes—namely either a loss of a given amount or a gain of the same given amount, so that if—for example—Mr A risks the investment of $30 in the transport industry he is faced with only two possible outcomes in that industry, either losing his $30 or making a net profit of $30; and

(4) that the chances of profit or loss in the two industries are in part independent of each other (people may for quite disconnected reasons spend more or less on transport and more or less on hotels) and in part dependent upon each other (e.g. both industries will tend to do well if the weather turns out fine and badly if the weather turns out wet).

When we are considering the way in which Mr A would be best advised to spread his risks over a number of industries this last point—namely how far the risks in the various industries are independent of each other or how far they are interconnected—is of great importance. Consider the connections between the risks in the transport industry and in the hotel industry which are illustrated in Table XXII. There we consider the risks to be completely independent of each other except for one influence—namely that of the weather, which is assumed to affect the profitability of each industry. There is a 25 per cent chance that tomorrow's weather will be wet. Wet weather is bad for both industries and reduces the chance of profit in the transport industry from 50 per cent to 10 per cent and the chance of profit in the hotel industry from 90 per cent to 20 per cent.

There are in fact eight possible outcomes which Mr A has to face and which we can enumerate as in Table XXIII. In Table XXIII W and F stand for wet and fine weather, P_t and L_t for profit and loss in the transport industry, and P_h and L_h for profit and loss in the hotel industry. Thus, for example, outcome (3) in Table XXIII represents the case in which the weather turns out to be wet, and a loss is made in the transport industry, but a profit is made in the hotel industry. And similarly for the other outcomes in the first column of the table.

Table XXII

Wet Weather 25% Chance	Transport Industry	10% chance of Profit
		90% chance of Loss
	Hotel Industry	20% chance of Profit
		80% chance of Loss
Fine Weather 75% Chance	Transport Industry	50% chance of Profit
		50% chance of Loss
	Hotel Industry	90% chance of Profit
		10% chance of Loss

In the second column of Table XXIII we show the probabilities of each of these eight outcomes which result from the assumptions made in Table XXII. Thus consider the probability of outcome (3). We know from Table XXII that the probability of wet weather is 25 per cent so that only 25 per cent of the outcomes will be wet (W).

Table XXIII

Outcome	Probability of Outcome
(1) WP_tP_h	$0{\cdot}25 \times 0{\cdot}1 \times 0{\cdot}2 = \frac{1}{2}\%$
(2) WP_tL_h	$0{\cdot}25 \times 0{\cdot}1 \times 0{\cdot}8 = 2\%$
(3) WL_tP_h	$0{\cdot}25 \times 0{\cdot}9 \times 0{\cdot}2 = 4\frac{1}{2}\%$
(4) WL_tL_h	$0{\cdot}25 \times 0{\cdot}9 \times 0{\cdot}8 = 18\%$
(5) FP_tP_h	$0{\cdot}75 \times 0{\cdot}5 \times 0{\cdot}9 = 33\frac{3}{4}\%$
(6) FP_tL_h	$0{\cdot}75 \times 0{\cdot}5 \times 0{\cdot}1 = 3\frac{3}{4}\%$
(7) FL_tP_h	$0{\cdot}75 \times 0{\cdot}5 \times 0{\cdot}9 = 33\frac{3}{4}\%$
(8) FL_tL_h	$0{\cdot}75 \times 0{\cdot}5 \times 0{\cdot}1 = 3\frac{3}{4}\%$
	Total 100%

But of this 25 per cent of all possible cases of outcomes, we know from Table XXII that 90 per cent of those wet days will be marked by a loss in the transport industry, so that 90 per cent of 25 per cent (i.e. $22\frac{1}{2}$ per cent) of all possible outcomes will be wet days with losses in the transport industry (WL_t). But we know from Table XXII that of these $22\frac{1}{2}$ per cent wet-weather-transport-loss outcomes out of all possible outcomes 20 per cent will be causes in which profits are made in the hotel industry. Thus 20 per cent of $22\frac{1}{2}$ per cent (i.e. $4\frac{1}{2}$ per cent) of all possible outcomes will represent cases of wet weather, losses in the transport industry, and profits in the hotel industry (WL_tP_h).

Table XXIII provides the elementary bricks from which various combined probabilities can be constructed. Such combinations are illustrated in Table XXIV. Combination 1 is simply a division between the first four and the last four outcomes of Table XXIII. The first four outcomes cover all the cases of wet weather and the probabilities of these four outcomes add up to 25 per cent, while the probabilities of the last four outcomes which cover all the cases of fine weather add up to 75 per cent. Our Mr A will not in fact have any interest in Combination 1 of Table XXIV, since he is not directly concerned with the question whether the weather will be wet or fine; he is directly concerned only with the profitability of various industries. If he is considering only the possibility of investing in the transport industry and is not considering the possibility of the hotel industry at all, then he will be concerned only with the probability of profit and of loss in the transport industry. These are shown in Combination (2) of Table XXIV. Outcomes (1), (2), (5), and (6) of Table XXIII are those in which the transport industry makes a profit and the probabilities of these outcomes add up to 40 per cent, while the probabilities of the outcomes in which the transport industry makes a loss add up to 60 per cent. Similarly combination (3) of Table XXIV shows that the probabilities of the outcomes in which the hotel industry makes a profit add up to $72\frac{1}{2}$ per cent, while the probabilities of the outcomes in which it makes a loss add up to $27\frac{1}{2}$ per cent; and Mr A will be interested only in this combination if he is thinking solely of entering the hotel industry.

If, however, Mr A is considering the possibility of spreading his risks over the two industries, he will be concerned with combination (4) of Table XXIV, since he is now directly interested in all the four possibilities of combined profit or loss in the two industries. Indeed combination (4) of Table XXIV gives the basic set of probabilities with which Mr A is concerned. From this set he can see at once the probability of any one of the four possible combinations of profit and loss in the two industries. Or, if he becomes interested in only one industry, he can derive the probabilities for combinations (2) and (3)

Table XXIV

Combination 1 Wet or Fine		Combination 2 Profit or Loss in Transport Industry		Combination 3 Profit or Loss in Hotel Industry		Combination 4 Joint Profit or Loss in both Industries	
Outcome	Probability	Outcome	Probability	Outcome	Probability	Outcome	Probability
W $(1) + (2) + (3) + (4)$	25%	P_t $(1) + (2) + (5) + (6)$	40%	P_h $(1) + (3) + (5) + (7)$	$72\frac{1}{2}\%$	$P_t P_h$ $(1) + (5)$	$34\frac{1}{4}\%$
						$P_t L_h$ $(2) + (6)$	$5\frac{3}{4}\%$
F $(5) + (6) + (7) + (8)$	75%	L_t $(3) + (4) + (7) + (8)$	60%	L_h $(2) + (4) + (6) + (8)$	$27\frac{1}{2}\%$	$L_t P_h$ $(3) + (7)$	$38\frac{1}{4}\%$
						$L_t L_h$ $(4) + (8)$	$21\frac{3}{4}\%$
Total	100%		100%		100%		100%

of Table XXIV from the probabilities given for combination (4) in Table XXIV. Thus the probability of profits in the transport industry shown in combination (2) (P_t) is the sum of the probabilities from combination (4) of profits in the transport industry with profits in the hotel industry (P_tP_h) and of profits in the transport industry with losses in the hotel industry (P_tL_h), i.e. 40 per cent $= 34\frac{1}{4}$ per cent $+ 5\frac{3}{4}$ per cent. And similarly for the other probabilities shown in combinations (2) and (3) of Table XXIV.

It is interesting to observe from Table XXIV the importance of the common factor—namely, the weather—as an influence on the profitability of the two industries. Suppose that there were no such common factor, but that the risks of profit or loss in the two industries—while quite independent of each other—were as shown in combinations (2) and (3) of Table XXIV. In other words there is a 40/60 chance of profit to loss in the transport industry and a $72\cdot5/27\cdot5$ chance of profit to loss in the hotel industry. In Table XXV

Table XXV

Outcome	Probability
(1) P_tP_h	$0\cdot4 \times 0\cdot725 = 29\ \%$
(2) P_tL_h	$0\cdot4 \times 0\cdot275 = 11\ \%$
(3) L_tP_h	$0\cdot6 \times 0\cdot725 = 43\frac{1}{2}\%$
(4) L_tL_h	$0\cdot6 \times 0\cdot275 = 16\frac{1}{2}\%$
	Total 100%

we can, on the analogy of Table XXIII, work out the probabilities of joint profit or loss in the two industries on the assumption that there is no common factor affecting them. For example, consider outcome (1) of Table XXV. 40 per cent of the possible cases will be cases of profits in the transport industry; but $72\frac{1}{2}$ per cent of these cases (as of all cases taken at random so far as the hotel industry is concerned) will be cases of profit in the hotel industry. Thus $72\frac{1}{2}$ per cent of 40 per cent (i.e. 29 per cent) of all possible cases will be cases in which profits are made in both industries. It is interesting to compare the probabilities in Table XXV (where the risks in the two industries are independent) with those of combination (4) in Table XXIV (where the risks in the two industries are interdependent because of the common influence—the weather). There are greater combined risks in the latter case than in the former. The fact that wet weather affects both industries adversely means that as a result of the interdependence of the risks the probability of both industries making a loss $(L_t L_h)$ is raised from $16\frac{1}{2}$ to $21\frac{3}{4}$ per cent and the probability that both will make a profit is raised from 29 to $34\frac{1}{4}$ per cent. But the probability that losses in hotels will be offset by profits in transport is reduced from 11 to $5\frac{3}{4}$ per cent, while the probability that losses in transport will be offset by profits in hotels is reduced from $43\frac{1}{2}$ to $38\frac{1}{4}$ per cent.[1]

We are now at last in a position to apply these probabilities to our arithmetical illustration of Mr A's choice of policy. This is done in Table XXVI. Mr A at 8 a.m. on day 0 is interested in four possible outcomes affecting the prices at which he can sell the products of the transport industry and of the hotel industry at 8 a.m. on day 1. These four states of the market are those which would *either* cause him to make a profit equal to his investment in each industry $(P_t P_h)$ *or* cause him to lose what he invested in the hotel industry but to make a profit equal to his investment in the transport industry $(P_t L_h)$ *or* cause him to lose in the transport but gain in the hotel industry $(L_t P_h)$ *or* cause him to lose in both $(L_t L_h)$. The probabilities of these outcomes are shown in the first two rows of Table XXVI on two assumptions: (α) that there is no common factor affecting the risks in the two industries so that the probabilities are as shown in Table XXV and (β) that there is a common factor affecting the risks so that the probabilities are as shown in combination (4) of Table XXIV.

We now suppose that Mr A considers seven different policies as to the amount and nature of the chances which he might take at 8 a.m. on day 0. The first policy which he considers is to take no risks. In this case whatever the state of the market turns out to be, he will make no profit or loss. From Figure 46 we can see that his chance-utility index for a zero profit or loss is $0 \cdot 9$; it is the equivalent in his estimation of a 90 per cent chance of a profit of \$100 combined with a 10 per cent chance of a loss of \$100. The fact that with this policy he has an average expectation of no profit or loss, and that it has a chance-utility index of $0 \cdot 9$ are shown in the two last columns of Table XXVI.

Policy 2 is to invest as much as he can (namely \$100) in the trans-

---

[1] In the example given in the text the common factor (the weather) affects the profitability of both industries in the same direction; wet weather increases the probability of loss in both industries and fine weather increases the probability of gain in both industries. Thus it is less easy to offset risks than would be the case if there were no common factor at work. But the common factor might, of course, work in the opposite direction. Consider the cinema industry and the hotel industry. Wet weather now tends to raise the profits of cinemas and to raise the losses of hotels (since people tend to stay at home and to take indoor amusements in wet weather); and *vice versa* in fine weather. The common factor would now tend to increase the probabilities of losses in one industry being offset by profits in the other and to reduce the probabilities of both industries simultaneously making either profits or losses.

Table XXVI

Probabilities of { (α) Risks Independent { (β) Risks Interdependent	Profit in Transport, Profit in Hotel P_tP_h 0·29 / 0·3425	Profit in Transport, Loss in Hotel P_tL_h 0·11 / 0·0575	Loss in Transport, Profit in Hotel L_tP_h 0·435 / 0·3825	Loss in Transport, Loss in Hotel L_tL_h 0·165 / 0·2175	Average Expectation of Profit or Loss (−) on Assumption α	β	Total Chance-Utility Index on Assumption α	β
1. No Risks Profit or Loss (−) $	0	0	0	0	0	0		
Utility Index of Profit or Loss	0·9	0·9	0·9	0·9			0·9	0·9
2. Risk $100 in Transport Profit or Loss (−) $	100	100	−100	−100	−20	−20		
Utility Index of Profit or Loss	1	1	0	0			0·4	0·4
3. Risk $100 in Hotel Profit or Loss (−) $	100	−100	100	−100	45	45		
Utility Index of Profit or Loss	1	0	1	0			0·725	0·725
4. Risk $50 in Each Industry Profit or Loss (−) $ Transport	50	50	−50	−50	12·5	12·5		
" " Hotel	50	−50	50	−50				
" " Combined	100	0	0	−100				
Utility Index of Combined Profit or Loss	1	0·9	0·9	0			0·7805	0·7385
5. Risk $50 in Hotel Profit or Loss (−) $	50	−50	50	−50	22·5	22·5		
Utility Index of Profit or Loss	0·98	0·7	0·98	0·7			0·9030	0·9030
6. Risk $25 in Each Industry Profit or Loss (−) $ Transport	25	25	−25	−25	6·25	6·25		
" " Hotel	25	−25	25	−25				
" " Combined	50	0	0	−50				
Utility Index of Combined Profit or Loss	0·98	0·9	0·9	0·7			0·8922	0·8839
7. Risk $1 in Transport and $49 in Hotel Profit or Loss (−) $ Transport	1	1	−1	−1	21·85	21·85		
" " Hotel	49	−49	49	−49				
" " Combined	50	−48	48	−50				
Utility Index of Combined Profit or Loss	0·98	0·72	0·978	0·7			0·90633	0·903385

States of Market

Policies

port industry. In this case with outcomes P_tP_h and P_tL_h (whose combined probability is 0·4 on both assumptions α and β) he will make a profit of $100, while with outcomes L_tP_h and L_tL_h (whose combined probability is 0·6) he will make a loss of $100. This choice is clearly equivalent to a 40 per cent chance of a gain of $100 combined with a 60 per cent chance of a loss of $100 and has, therefore, a chance-utility index of 0·4 as shown in the last column of the table. It is clearly worse than taking no risks (policy 1). Indeed not only is it more risky than taking no risks, but the average expectation of profit or loss is one of a loss of $20 (i.e. a 40 per cent chance of a gain of $100 less a 60 per cent chance of a loss of $100). Policy 2 as contrasted with policy 1 would *increase* risk and uncertainty and *reduce* average yield. It is not attractive to Mr A who in any case is averse to risk and uncertainty and will only undertake risks and uncertainties in order to increase his average expectation of income.

Policy 3, to invest his maximum of $100 in the hotel industry, will give Mr A a $72\frac{1}{2}$ per cent chance of a gain of $100 ($P_tP_h$ and L_tP_h have a combined probability of $72\frac{1}{2}$ per cent on both assumptions α and β) and only a $27\frac{1}{2}$ per cent chance of a loss of $100. This, as is shown in the last column but one of Table XXVI does give an average expected yield of $45 of profit which in itself is very attractive. But the investment is after all the equivalent of only a $72\frac{1}{2}$ per cent chance of a profit of $100 combined with a $27\frac{1}{2}$ per cent chance of a loss of $100, and—as shown in the last column of Table XXVI it has, therefore, a chance-utility index of 0·725. Mr A would prefer to take no risk, which—as we are assuming in Figure 46—is the equivalent to him of a 90 per cent chance of a profit of $100 combined with a 10 per cent chance of a loss of $100.

It is thus the great risk involved (the $27\frac{1}{2}$ per cent chance of the crippling loss of $100) which puts Mr A off the acceptance of policy 3. There are two possible ways of trying to reduce the deterrent effect of this risk and uncertainty. The first which is illustrated in policy 4 is to spread the same investment over both industries in combination; in this case while a crippling loss of $100 is still possible, its probability will be reduced. The second which is illustrated in policy 5 is to continue to concentrate all investment in the hotel industry (where the expected yield is higher than in the transport industry) but to reduce the scale of the investment so that a crippling loss of $100 is no longer possible.

Suppose then, as is illustrated in policy 4, Mr A invests $50 in the transport industry and $50 in the hotel industry. As is shown in Table XXVI he will now make a profit of $100 only in the case of P_tP_h; and the other extreme he will suffer the crippling loss of $100 only in the case of L_tL_h. With the other two outcomes (P_tL_h and

$L_t P_h$) loss and gain will cancel each other and he will make no profit
or loss. The fourth row of policy 4 in Table XXVI gives the utility
indices of these profits or losses of 100, 0, 0, and -100 as 1, 0·9,
0·9, and 0. If these utility indices are weighted with the probabilities
of the four outcomes, on assumption α we get a combined utility
index of 0·7805 and on assumption β one of 0·7385. If the profits
or losses themselves are weighted by their probabilities we get an
expected yield of \$12·5 on both assumptions α and β.[1] In brief, as
compared with policy 3, policy 4 causes a large fall in average
expected yield because of the inclusion of the unprofitable transport
industry; but nevertheless its chance-utility index is higher and it is
more attractive to Mr A than policy 3 because it reduces the risk of
crippling loss.[2] The attractiveness of policy 4 is greater on assumption
α (utility index of 0·7805) when there is no common factor causing the
losses in both industries to be combined than with assumption β
(utility index of 0·7385) when there is the common factor of wet
weather to increase the risk of a loss in one industry being associated
with a loss in the other. But in both cases it is still more attractive for
Mr A to take no risk (utility index of 0·9). In spite of an average
expected profit of \$12·5 the risk is still too great. To do nothing is the
equivalent to Mr A of a 90 per cent chance of a gain of \$100 combined
with a 10 per cent chance of a loss of \$100, whereas policy 4 gives an
outcome which even on assumption α is the equivalent to him of
only a 78·05 per cent chance of a gain of \$100 combined with a
21·95 per cent chance of a loss of \$100.

With policy 5 Mr A reduces his risk of crippling loss by halving the
scale of his risk-taking, but concentrating it all in the profitable hotel
industry. The possible profits and losses and the average expected
yield are, therefore, all half as much as with policy 3. From Figure 46
we can see that the chance-utility indices of the returns 50 and -50
are 0·98 and 0·7. If we weight the utility 0·98 with the probability of
a profit of \$50 (namely, $72\frac{1}{2}$ per cent since the probability of $P_t P_h$ and
$L_t P_h$ is $72\frac{1}{2}$ per cent on both assumptions α and β) and the utility 0·7
with the probability of a loss of \$50 (namely, $27\frac{1}{2}$ per cent) we obtain

[1] It is an accident of our particular example that the average expected profit or
loss from each policy is the same for assumption α as for assumption β. This is
due to the fact that in every outcome in our example, the profit made with $P_t P_h$ is
equal to the loss made with $L_t L_h$, while the profit (or loss) made with $P_t L_h$ is
equal to the loss (or profit) made with $L_t P_h$. If this were not so, the average
expected profit or loss with policies 4, 6, and 7 where the risks are spread over the
two industries would not necessarily be the same with assumption α, when the
risks are independent, as with assumption β, when the risks are interdependent.

[2] With policy 3 a loss of \$100 is made in cases $P_t L_h$ and $L_t L_h$ with a combined
probability of $27\frac{1}{2}$ per cent. With policy 4 a loss of \$100 is made only with $L_t L_h$
with a probability of $16\frac{1}{2}$ per cent on assumption α and of $21\frac{3}{4}$ per cent on
assumption β.

a combined chance-utility index of 90·3 per cent. This is greater than the chance-utility index of taking no risk (namely, 90 per cent). Mr A has now found a business venture which is more attractive to him than taking no risk. The expected yield of $22·5 outweighs the risk and uncertainty now that, by reducing the scale of his enterprise, he has avoided the possibility of the crippling loss of $100.

But might he not do still better by keeping his total risk down in scale to $50 (as in policy 5) instead of $100 (as in policies 2, 3, and 4), but at the same time spreading this over the two industries? In policy 6 he considers the possibility of investing $25 in each industry. The combined expected profits or losses turn out to be 50, 0, 0, and −50 in the four possible states of the market and these have chance-utility indices of 0·98, 0·9, 0·9, and 0·7. On assumptions α and β about probabilities of the four possible outcomes the expected average yield turns out to be $6·25; and the total utility index turns out to be 0·8922 on assumption α and 0·8839 on assumption β. It is interesting to observe that whereas (policies 3 and 4) spreading a total risk of $100 evenly between the two industries instead of concentrating on the profitable industry increases the attractiveness of the venture, yet spreading a total risk of only $50 in the same way reduces the attractiveness of the venture (total chance-utility in policy 5 is 0·903 and in policy 6 is at the most 0·8922). Indeed, while policy 5 is more attractive than taking no risks, policy 6 is less attractive than taking no risks. As between policy 5 and 6 there has been some reduction of risk; the profits and losses are the same from $P_t P_h$ and $L_t L_h$ for both policies, but policy 5 gives the variation −50 and 50 and policy 6 gives a steady 0 and 0 for $P_t L_h$ and $L_t P_h$. But $L_t P_h$ is much more probable than $P_t L_h$, so that the greater steadiness is achieved at the expense of a large loss of yield from $22·5 with policy 5 to $6·5 with policy 4. Since both policies avoid completely the chance of the crippling loss of $100, the extra steadiness between policy 5 and policy 6 is not worth the loss of yield. And since policy 6 still includes the same chance of the very substantial loss of $50, Mr A would prefer to take no risks at all.

But this does not mean that no improvement can be made to policy 5 by spreading the total risk of $50 over the two industries. In policy 7 $1 of this risk is taken in the transport industry and $49 in the hotel industry. This gives combined profits or losses in the two industries of $50, −$48, $48, −$50. As compared with the $50, −$50, $50, −$50 of policy 5, there has been a transfer of income of $2 from $L_t P_h$ to $P_t L_h$. Since $L_t P_h$ is more probable than $P_t L_h$, this involves a loss in expected yield of $0·65 (from $22·5 to $21·85). But to lose $2 when one is rich with a gain of $50 means much less in utility than to gain $2 when one is poor with a loss of $50. Indeed we have assumed in the chance-utility indices of policy 7 that a change of income between $+\$50$ and $+\$48$ accounts for a change of the utility index of only $0 \cdot 002$ (from $0 \cdot 98$ to $0 \cdot 978$), whereas a change of income from $-\$48$ to $-\$50$ accounts for the ten times greater change of the utility index of $0 \cdot 02$ (from $0 \cdot 72$ to $0 \cdot 7$).[1] The improvement of marginal utility between $L_t P_h$ and $P_t L_h$ is now so great, that if we weight the chance-utility indices $0 \cdot 98$, $0 \cdot 72$, $0 \cdot 978$, $0 \cdot 7$ with the probabilities of the four outcomes we obtain a higher total index than with policy 5. On assumption α the improvement is from $0 \cdot 90$ to $0 \cdot 90633$ and on assumption β from $0 \cdot 903$ to $0 \cdot 903385$. It is an interesting fact that circumstances can arise in which it pays to invest something in an industry like transport (on which there is a negative expected yield as can be seen from policy 2) as a means of diversifying and so spreading the risk borne in other profitable industries. Of the seven policies examined by Mr A policy 7 is on balance the most attractive.

We have so far spoken of this process of choice by Mr A of policies in conditions of risk and uncertainty as if he had a clear idea of what was the probability which he should attach to each possible outcome which might result from each policy. In terms of Table XXI (page 426 above) we have argued as if the probabilities π_a, π_b, π_c, etc., were clear and precise entities in Mr A's mind. In some cases this is near the truth. For example, an entrepreneur in the real world may be faced with the chance of fire which will cause his output to be completely destroyed so that he will face a loss on day 1 equal to the total of his commitments for purchases of inputs on day 0. Past experience may well suggest that every day something very near, say, $\dfrac{1}{100,000}$ of all firms are destroyed in this way, while it is a matter of pure chance which particular firm is hit. This type of chance approximates to a straightforward gamble on throwing dice, tossing coins, playing roulette, and so on. Cases of this kind we may call cases of risk rather than of uncertainty. In essence they are based upon past experience of a large number of events which suggest that, unless there is some basic change in underlying conditions, there is in fact a

[1] The chance-utility indices of $0 \cdot 72$ and $0 \cdot 978$ are not shown in Figure 46. But they are compatible with the principle of diminishing marginal utility on which the figure is based. Thus between $+\$50$ and $+\$100$ the utility index rises by $0 \cdot 02$ from $0 \cdot 98$ to $1 \cdot 00$, i.e. at a rate of $0 \cdot 0004$ per \$1. Between \$0 and $+\$50$ it rises by $0 \cdot 08$ from $0 \cdot 9$ to $0 \cdot 98$, i.e. at a rate of $0 \cdot 0016$ per \$1. In the text we have assumed it to rise by $0 \cdot 002$ between $+\$48$ and $+\$50$, i.e. at a rate of $0 \cdot 001$ per \$1 which is in between the earlier rate of $0 \cdot 0016$ and the later rate of $0 \cdot 0004$. Similarly, between $-\$100$ and $-\$50$ the average rate of rise of utility per \$1 is $0 \cdot 014$ and between $-\$50$ and \$50 is $0 \cdot 004$. For the rate of rise between $-\$50$ and $-\$48$ we have assumed the intermediate rate of $0 \cdot 01$ per \$1.

straightforward, more or less precise, probability of, say, $\dfrac{1}{100,000}$ that this particular event will happen to this particular firm tomorrow.

At the other extreme is the sort of case in which there does not exist that past experience of large numbers of similar past cases on which to base an estimate of the chances. Such a case might arise with the invention of a new product for consumers' use—of television sets, for example. The producers who are producing and selling such goods for the first time may have no past experience on which to judge the probability that the enterprise will make a profit or loss. Some market research enquiries may inspire their guesses; and examination of their own probable reactions to the use of television may give them a 'hunch'. But they are in fact making a guess about the probabilities of profit and loss which is based upon no actual cases of experienced outcome in the real world. These we may call cases of uncertainty.

Most cases lie in between these two extremes of pure risk or pure uncertainty. Even the first case (risk of fire) is not really a case in which the probabilities are as certain as in the case of tossing heads-or-tails with a fair coin. For circumstances may change tomorrow. There may be an epidemic of arson among criminals or freak dry weather may significantly increase the chances of fire. The precise probability of the fire hazard is based on the 'hunch' that relevant underlying conditions will not in fact be much different tomorrow from what they have been for many days in the past. But with a growing economy in which inventions are taking place and in which, because of changes in capital–labour–land ratios, new techniques are being adopted, relevant underlying conditions are in many cases likely to be changing. Starting at the other extreme, once television sets have been put on the market underlying conditions may not change so rapidly from day to day for experience of the actual profitability of the production of television sets to be irrelevant for the useful revision of initial hunches about the probable outcome of profits. In order to decide whether or not to undertake a given business venture the entrepreneur must make some estimate of the probabilities of profits and losses of different magnitudes; and in fact these probabilities or degrees of belief in different outcomes are likely to be hunches revised in the light of relevant experience, pure uncertainties turning into risks.

But how can experience be used to revise initial hunches? Table XXVII gives an example of how this might be done. We consider Mr A confronted with only one entrepreneurial possibility—i.e. only one 'policy' in terms of Tables XXI and XXVI; we suppose that there are only two possible outcomes to this policy which we call 'profit' and 'loss'; and we ask how he can revise an initial hunch

Table XXVII

Hypotheses	Initial Probability of Each Hypothesis π_{h0} (a)	Probability on Each Hypothesis of Outcome P_1 (b)	Revised Probability of Each Hypothesis π_{h1} (c)	Probability on Each Hypothesis of Outcome P_1L_2 (d)	Revised Probability of Each Hypothesis π_{h2} (e)	Probability on Each Hypothesis of Outcome $P_1L_2L_3$ (f)	Revised Probability of Each Hypothesis π_{h3} (g)	Probability on Each Hypothesis of Outcome $P_1L_2L_3P_4L_5L_6$ (h)	Revised Probability of Each Hypothesis π_{h6} (i)
(1) 90% chance of Profit	0·1	0·9	0·184	$0·9\times0·1=0·09$	0·0475	$0·9\times0·1\times0·1=0·009$	0·009	0·000081	0·001
(2) 80%	0·1	0·8	0·163	$0·8\times0·2=0·16$	0·085	$0·8\times0·2\times0·2=0·032$	0·033	0·001024	0·009
(3) 70%	0·1	0·7	0·143	$0·7\times0·3=0·21$	0·111	$0·7\times0·3\times0·3=0·062$	0·064	0·003844	0·033
(4) 60%	0·1	0·6	0·122	$0·6\times0·4=0·24$	0·127	$0·6\times0·4\times0·4=0·096$	0·099	0·009216	0·079
(5) 50%	0·1	0·5	0·102	$0·5\times0·5=0·25$	0·132	$0·5\times0·5\times0·5=0·125$	0·129	0·015625	0·135
(6) 40%	0·1	0·4	0·082	$0·4\times0·6=0·24$	0·127	$0·4\times0·6\times0·6=0·144$	0·149	0·020736	0·180
(7) 40%	0·1	0·4	0·082	$0·4\times0·6=0·24$	0·127	$0·4\times0·6\times0·6=0·144$	0·149	0·020736	0·180
(8) 30%	0·1	0·3	0·061	$0·3\times0·7=0·21$	0·111	$0·3\times0·7\times0·7=0·147$	0·152	0·021609	0·186
(9) 20%	0·1	0·2	0·041	$0·2\times0·8=0·16$	0·085	$0·2\times0·8\times0·8=0·128$	0·132	0·016384	0·141
(10) 10%	0·1	0·1	0·020	$0·1\times0·9=0·09$	0·0475	$0·1\times0·9\times0·9=0·081$	0·084	0·006561	0·056
Average Chance of Profit	0·49		0·61		0·49		0·40		0·39

about the probability of profit in the light of actual experience of profit and loss.[1] Initially, at 8 a.m. on day 0, Mr A does not know what probability to attach to the making of a profit as opposed to a loss at 8 a.m. on day 1. He may be operating in a world in which in fact there is a 90 per cent chance of profit, or in a world in which in fact there is an 80 per cent chance of profit, and so on down the scale of probability of profit. We can express this by saying that there is one hypothesis (Hypothesis 1 in Table XXVII) that the world is of such a kind that there is a 90 per cent chance of making a profit in this enterprise, that there is a second hypothesis (Hypothesis 2) that the world is in fact of such a kind that there is an 80 per cent chance of making a profit in this enterprise, and so on down the list. Mr A might be in a frame of mind of believing that Hypothesis 1 is just as likely as Hypothesis 2 and so on down the list. But it will be seen in Table XXVII that we have assumed that there are two hypotheses (Hypotheses 6 and 7) about the nature of the real world which would both imply a 40 per cent chance of profit in this enterprise. Suppose that Mr A initially believes that each hypothesis about the nature of the world is as likely or as unlikely as each other hypothesis. This state of mind is indicated in column (*a*) of Table XXVII where it is shown that each of the ten hypotheses about the nature of the world is assessed by Mr A as having a 10 per cent probability of being the correct hypothesis. It implies that Mr A does in fact start with a hunch that a 40 per cent probability of profit (the result of the two Hypotheses 6 and 7) is twice as likely to represent the true state of affairs as a 90 per cent or an 80 per cent or a 70 per cent or a 60 per cent or a 50 per cent or a 30 per cent or a 20 per cent or a 10 per cent probability of profit. Assuming there to be two Hypotheses each of which would entail a 40 per cent probability of profit is merely a device, convenient for purposes of exposition, for assuming that Mr A starts with a hunch that a 40 per cent probability of profit is itself twice as probable as any other specific probability of profit named in Table XXVII.

If Mr A starts in this frame of mind, what is a reasonable figure for him to place on the probability of a profitable outcome from this particular entrepreneurial risk for the purpose of calculating on the principles of Table XXI and Table XXVI whether this is an enterprise that he would like to undertake? He has in fact a 10 per cent chance

---

[1] In terms of Table XXI we are considering only the two possible outcomes *A* and *B* (which bring profit and loss respectively if policy 1 is adopted). We are concerned with the determination of the probabilities of profit and loss namely the π_a and π_b of Table XXI. But since in this case $\pi_b = 1 - \pi_a$, we are concerned only with the determination of the probability π_a. The same principles as are applied in the text in Table XXVII to this simple case could be applied to the general case of Table XXI for the determination of π_a, π_b, π_c, π_d, π_e, etc.

of a 90 per cent chance of profit *plus* a 10 per cent chance of an 80 per cent chance of profit *plus* a 10 per cent chance of a 70 per cent chance of profit and so on. His chance of profit is $0 \cdot 1 \times 0 \cdot 9 + 0 \cdot 1 \times 0 \cdot 8 + 0 \cdot 1 \times 0 \cdot 7 + 0 \cdot 1 \times 0 \cdot 6 + 0 \cdot 1 \times 0 \cdot 5 + 0 \cdot 2 \times 0 \cdot 4 + 0 \cdot 1 \times 0 \cdot 3 + 0 \cdot 1 \times 0 \cdot 2 + 0 \cdot 1 \times 0 \cdot 1 = 0 \cdot 49$. In other words in his initial frame of mind it would be reasonable for him to operate on the assumption that he was faced with a 49 per cent chance of profit and this figure is accordingly shown at the bottom of column (*a*).

The principle may be illustrated from the chance of drawing a Red (Profit) or a Black (Loss) ball from an urn. If Mr A were virtually certain (as in the case of the risk of fire) that he was drawing from an urn which contained 40 Red and 60 Black balls, he would expect a 40 per cent chance of Red. But suppose that there are 10 urns one containing 90 Red and 10 Black balls, one containing 80 Red and 20 Blacks, and so on down the list (there being, however, two urns containing 40 Red and 60 Black). Suppose further that Mr A does not know from which urn he is drawing but does believe there to be an equal 10 per cent chance of his being confronted with each particular urn. Then his chances of drawing Red are 49 per cent. There is a 10 per cent chance that he is drawing from an urn with a 90 per cent chance of Red *plus* a 10 per cent chance that he is drawing from an urn with an 80 per cent chance of Red, and so on.

Suppose now that Mr A does undertake this entrepreneurial risk and that at 8 a.m. on day 1 he finds that he has in fact made a profit. He has now some—though still very limited—experience on which to base his estimations of the probabilities of the Hypotheses 1 to 10 about the nature of the world. The fact that the first outcome has been a profit and not a loss is some—though slight—indication that the Hypotheses giving a high chance of profit are more likely than those giving a low chance of profit. How can this experience be used to revise the initial equal probabilities attached to each hypothesis?

Now (cf. column (*b*) of Table XXVII) the chance of having obtained a profit on day 1 is $0 \cdot 9$ if Hypothesis 1 were in fact true but only $0 \cdot 1$ if Hypothesis 10 about the nature of the world were true. But the profit has now actually been experienced. So we may say that on the present evidence Hypothesis 1 is nine times as probable as Hypothesis 10. Similarly, the chance of having obtained a profit on day 1 is $0 \cdot 8$ if Hypothesis 2 were in fact true but only $0 \cdot 1$ if Hypothesis 10 were true; and since a profit has in fact been obtained, on current evidence we may say that Hypothesis 2 is eight times as probable as Hypothesis 10. In column (*c*) of Table XXVII we write down a series of probabilities which add up to unity (since we are acting on the assumption that one of the given ten Hypotheses must be true) but which bear the same relationships to each other as do the corresponding figures in column (*b*) to each other. Thus the revised probability of Hypothesis 1 being true (0·184) is nine times as great as the revised probability of Hypothesis 10 being true (0·020), and so on.[1]

The figures in column (*c*) are then the revised probabilities which at 8 a.m. on day 1, in view of both his initial hunches and the actual experience of day 1's profit, Mr A might reasonably attach to his belief in the 10 hypotheses about the nature of the market in which he is operating. He can now revise his probability of a profitable outcome for the coming day's operations. He now believes himself to be confronted with

a 0·184 chance of a 0·9 chance of profit
plus a 0·163 chance of a 0·8 chance of profit
plus a 0·143 chance of a 0·7 chance of profit

and so on. This chance adds up to a 61 per cent chance of profit; and, as a result of experiencing an actual profit on day 0's operations, it would be reasonable for him to raise from 49 per cent to 61 per cent his expectation of a profit on day 1's operations.

But suppose at 8 a.m. on day 2 a loss is experienced as the outcome of day 1's operations. Mr A has now had actual experience of a profit on day 1 and a loss on day 2 ($P_1 L_2$). Column (*d*) of Table XXVII shows the probabilities of this particular sequence of outcomes on each of the ten hypotheses about the actual nature of the market. If Mr A had in fact been drawing balls from an urn which always contained 90 Red and 10 Black balls, the chance of his drawing first Red and then Black would be $0·9 \times 0·1 = 0·09$ or 9 per cent.[2] If he had been drawing from an urn containing always 80 Red and 20 Black balls, the chance of his drawing first Red and then Black would be $0·8 \times 0·2 = 0·16$ or 16 per cent. And so on down the figures in column (*d*). Thus we can say that the chance of his having the experience which he has in fact had up to date—namely $P_1 L_2$—is $\frac{0·25}{0·09}$ or $2\frac{7}{9}$ times as probable on Hypothesis 5 as on Hypothesis 1.

But he has in fact experienced $P_1 L_2$; so we may say that the chance of Hypothesis 5 being correct can on the evidence now available be

---

[1] The slight numerical inaccuracies are due to rounding off the revised probabilities to the nearest third decimal place in such a way that they add up to unity.

[2] On 90 per cent of the possible first draws he would draw Red and, confining his subsequent attention only to this 90 per cent of possible first draws, he would on the second occasion draw Black on only 10 per cent of these 90 per cent of possible cases. Thus he would draw first Red and then Black from such an urn on 10 per cent of 90 per cent (or 0·09) of all the possible cases.

assessed as $2\frac{7}{9}$ times as great as the chance of Hypothesis 1 being correct. Column (e) accordingly gives revised probabilities for each Hypothesis which once more add up to unity but bear the same relationship to each other as the figures in column (d) bear to each other.

And so on for the calculations in columns (f), (g), (h), and (i) of Table XXVII. Suppose that at 8 a.m. on day 6, for example, the actual experiences of the first six day's operations have been $P_1L_2L_3P_4L_5L_6$. The chance of this particular outcome on Hypothesis 1 is $0 \cdot 9 \times 0 \cdot 1 \times 0 \cdot 1 \times 0 \cdot 9 \times 0 \cdot 1 \times 0 \cdot 1 = 0 \cdot 00081$ and on Hypothesis 2 is $0 \cdot 8 \times 0 \cdot 2 \times 0 \cdot 2 \times 0 \cdot 8 \times 0 \cdot 2 \times 0 \cdot 2 = 0 \cdot 001024$. But since this particular outcome has in fact been experienced, we may take this as evidence that Hypothesis 2 is $\frac{1024}{81}$ times as probable as Hypothesis 1. The figures in column (i) are thus probabilities which sum up to unity but (subject to errors of rounding off to three figures) bear the same ratio to each other as do the corresponding figures of column (h).

At the bottom of columns (a), (c), (e), (g), and (i) we give the average expectation of profit which can be obtained by weighting the chance of profit from each hypothesis by the relevant chance of that hypothesis being true. At 8 a.m. on day 0 this expectation is just under 50 per cent—namely 49 per cent. It would have been exactly 50 per cent if it had not been for the fact that the existence of two instead of one hypotheses that entailed a 40 per cent chance of profit brought the average down slightly. After the first experience of a profitable outcome the average chance of profit was raised from just under 50 per cent to just over 60 per cent. This was the best guess that could be made on the basis of the initial hunches combined with the very limited actual experience. After the two days' experience of one profit and one loss the average chance of profit was brought back again, as one might expect, to about 50 per cent.

After three days there was an experience of one profit and two losses and after six days of two profits and four losses, in both cases experiences of 1 profit out of 3 chances. This outcome is in between a 30 per cent and a 40 per cent chance, being nearer to a 30 per cent chance than to a 40 per cent chance. Yet at the end of the third day's experience the prospective average chance of profit is still 40 per cent. This is due to the fact that the initial hunches are still very influential after only three experiences; and in these initial hunches there are (i) two hypotheses of a 40 per cent chance as against only one hypothesis of a 30 per cent chance and (ii) six hypotheses giving chances of profit greater than 40 per cent as against only two hypotheses giving chances less than 30 per cent. After six days with once again a 1 in 3 actual outcome of profit, the average chance of profit has been reduced a bit below 40 per cent but only fractionally to 39 per cent. The two Hypotheses carrying a 40 per cent chance of profit are still very important particularly as the actual outcome of 1 in 3 (i.e. $33\frac{1}{2}$ per cent) is not greatly different from a 40 per cent chance. It is still very probable that either Hypothesis 6 or 7 is the correct one.

The procedure which we have illustrated in Table XXVII for the modification of initial hunches by experience rests on the assumption that Mr A considers the underlying conditions to remain unchanged. But, as we have already observed, in a growing economy with inventions and changes in labour–capital–land ratios, underlying market conditions do not remain unchanged. This means that Mr A may well revise the probabilities of profit (as shown at the bottom of columns (a), (c), (e), (g), and (i)) because of new hunches, and may pay little attention to recent experiences of profit or loss because he thinks that the relevant underlying conditions have changed. He may, that is to say, at any time make a new set of initial hypotheses and start again. But these new initial hypotheses will themselves be based on hunches which are affected by past experience.

It is arguable that Mr A, for the purposes of the sort of decisions shown in Tables XXI and XXVI above, should in this process of revising hunches on the basis of experience treat the figures shown at the bottom of columns (a), (c), (e), (g), and (i) of Table XXVII as the probabilities with which at that particular time profit is expected from the business enterprise under discussion. The argument on which the analysis of Tables XXI and XXVI (pages 426 and 433) was based is constructed on the basis of certain probabilities for given outcomes (the π_a, π_b, π_c, π_d, π_e, etc., of Table XXI and the probabilities of rows (α) and (β) of Table XXVI); and if the argument is examined it will be seen that no difference is made in it between a probability of 50 per cent for an outcome which is the simple, direct result—as it were—of drawing Red and Black balls from an urn containing 50 Red and 50 Black, and a probability of 50 per cent for an outcome which is the result of drawing Red or Black from an urn which has a 50 per cent chance of being an urn containing 90 Red and 10 Black balls and a 50 per cent chance of being an urn which contains 10 Red and 90 Black balls. For the latter case also gives a $0\cdot5 \times 0\cdot9 + 0\cdot5 \times 0\cdot1 = 0\cdot5$ chance of drawing Red. In other words the argument on which the analysis of Tables XXI and XXVI is based draws no distinction between the probability of an outcome which is the objective measure from past experience of a given risk and the probability of an outcome which is the subjective expression of a degree of belief in a given outcome (i.e. of a hunch) in a condition of uncertainty.

But would Mr A necessarily in fact react in the same way in the two situations? Compare columns (*a*) and (*i*) of Table XXVII. The average chance of profit in the first case is 49 per cent and in the second case is only 39 per cent. If other conditions (e.g. the possibilities of profit in other industries and the amount of Mr A's personal resources) have remained unchanged, it would be illogical for Mr A to be more reluctant to enter into this enterprise on day 0 with a 49 per cent chance of profit than to enter into it on day 6 with only a 39 per cent chance of profit. But is it not conceivable that he might be more reluctant on day 0 than on day 6 on the grounds that on day 0 he is very uncertain about the 49 per cent chance of profit, whereas on day 6 he is fairly sure where he stands as to the 39 per cent chance of profit? What was all uncertainty on day 0 is more like a known risk on day 6. On day 0 the probability that the chance of profit is 50 per cent or 40 per cent or 30 per cent or 20 per cent (i.e. that either Hypothesis (5), (6), (7), (8), or (9) is correct) is $0 \cdot 1 + 0 \cdot 1 + 0 \cdot 1 + 0 \cdot 1 + 0 \cdot 1 = 50$ per cent, whereas on day 6 it is no less than $0 \cdot 135 + 0 \cdot 180 + 0 \cdot 180 + 0 \cdot 186 + 0 \cdot 141 = 82 \cdot 2$ per cent. It may be illogical to do so; but Mr A may be more uncomfortable when acting only on an uncertain hunch than when he is acting on a fairly certain degree of risk, even though the chance of a favourable outcome may be the same in the two cases.[1] The 49 per cent chance of column (*a*) is based on pure hunch, while the 39 per cent chance of column (*i*) is based on a considerable degree of experience.

[1] Consider the following example. Mr A is promised a prize of $100 on one of the following four chances, namely

  (*a*) that the first card he draws from an ordinary pack will be a diamond, a spade, or a club
  (*b*) that the first card he draws from an ordinary pack will be a heart
  (*c*) that the price of a commodity will go up
  (*d*) that the price of a commodity will not go up.

He is asked to place the hazards on which he will obtain his prize in his order of preference. Is it possible that he will order them (*a*) (*c*) (*b*) (*d*)? If he prefers (*a*) to (*c*) he prefers staking the prize on a precise risk with a probability of $\frac{3}{4}$ rather than on the—to him—uncertain chance that a given price will go up; if he prefers (*b*) to (*d*) he prefers staking the prize on a precise chance with a probability of $\frac{1}{4}$ than on the uncertain chance that the same given price will not go up. But the price will either go up or not go up. He could not, therefore, choose the order (*a*) (*c*) (*b*) (*d*) if he acted solely on probabilities. The preference of (*a*) for (*c*) implies then that he considers that there is a less than $\frac{3}{4}$ chance that the price will go up; but if this is so, he must consider there to be a more than $\frac{1}{4}$ chance that the price will not go up. And in this case he would prefer (*d*) to (*b*). But if, in addition to the actual probabilities, he prefers gambling on known risks (the draw of a card from a pack) rather than on uncertain hunches (the price of a commodity about which he has no experience at all) he might prefer the order (*a*) (*c*) (*b*) (*d*) or even in the extreme case, the order (*a*) (*b*) (*c*) (*d*).

CHAPTER XXII

THREE METHODS OF REDUCING RISK AND UNCERTAINTY

We may summarize the previous chapter by saying: (i) that where risk and uncertainty exists there is a real social function for the successful entrepreneur who is good at forecasting in what lines of business given inputs will produce outputs of great value; (ii) that, on the assumption that citizens cannot obtain by borrowing resources to take risks which are out of all proportion to their own individual resources of property and earning power, successful entrepreneurs (who are good at forecasting) will in fact tend to drive out unsuccessful entrepreneurs (who are bad at forecasting); (iii) that all citizens are assumed to be averse to risk in the sense that they prefer a given certain yield to the same average expectation of yield subject to the risk of a greater or smaller yield; and (iv) that citizens may prefer a given degree of risk to the same degree of uncertainty. The net result of (iii) and (iv) is that lines of activity in which risk and uncertainty are great will on balance be avoided. This means that the demand will be reduced for the inputs of resources in which risky and uncertain lines of production are intensive and that the supply will be reduced of the outputs of products in which such lines are intensive. The prices of the inputs needed in risky and uncertain lines will be depressed and the prices of the outputs of these lines will be raised until there is a margin of extra profit in these lines of production such that the additional average yield expected in these lines of production outweighs the risk and uncertainty involved in them.

Thus risk and uncertainty are real social costs of production. Because citizens dislike taking risks and being uncertain of their rewards, the value of the marginal product of resources used in risky and uncertain lines of production will be higher than in other less risky and less uncertain lines of production without any tendency for the forces of competition to move more resources into the risky and uncertain lines in which marginal products are high. Clearly it would be to the advantage of economic efficiency if risks and uncertainties could be reduced, provided that this could be done in ways which involved little or no costs of any other kind. In this chapter we will briefly discuss three possible ways of reducing the burden of risk and uncertainty.

Some of the methods discussed in this chapter do actually reduce or eliminate risk and uncertainty. Many of them, however, do not reduce the actual risk of an adverse event, but do reduce the burden of such risks by spreading a number of independent risks over a number of citizens instead of concentrating each risk on one citizen. It is, therefore, important to realize what the spreading of risks involves. This is illustrated in Tables XXVIII and XXIX.

We suppose that there are four houses A, B, C, and D each of the same value and each owned by a different individual citizen, Mr A, B, C, or D. We suppose further that there is a quite independent risk attached to each house that in the course of the year it will be destroyed by fire. For the sake of numerical illustration we assume that there is a 1 in 10 chance for each house that it will be destroyed by fire and, therefore, a 9 in 10 chance that it will not be so destroyed. As Table XXVIII shows, there are sixteen possible events which may occur in the course of the year. Event 1 is that all houses are destroyed in the year. Event 2 is that only house D escapes, event 3 that only house C escapes, . . . event 6 that only houses A and B are destroyed, . . . event 12 that only house A is destroyed, . . . event 16 that no house is destroyed.

The third column of Table XXVIII then shows the probability of each event occurring in the course of the year. Consider, for example, event 9 in which houses A and D survive, but B and C are destroyed, Since there is a $\frac{9}{10}$ chance that A will survive, a $\frac{1}{10}$ chance that B will burn, a $\frac{1}{10}$ that C will burn, and a $\frac{9}{10}$ chance that D will survive, and since these chances are independent, there is a $\frac{9}{10} \times \frac{1}{10} \times \frac{1}{10} \times \frac{9}{10} = \frac{81}{10,000}$ chance that this event will occur.

The fourth column of Table XXVIII then shows the chance that an event in a given class will occur. Consider, for example, the chance that two out of the four houses will burn in the course of the year. As the table shows there are 6 possible combinations of disaster (events 6 to 11 inclusive) which result in two houses being destroyed and each of these events has 81 chances out of 10,000 of occurring. There are, therefore, 6×81 or 486 chances out of 10,000 that two of the four houses will burn.

In this way the final column of Table XXVIII shows that there are

1 chance in 10,000 that 4 houses will burn
36 chances in 10,000 that 3 houses will burn
486 chances in 10,000 that 2 houses will burn
2,916 chances in 10,000 that 1 house will burn

Table XXXVIII

Class of Event	Event Fire (F) destroys houses: A	B	C	D		Chance of Individual Event	Chance of an event in a given class
All houses burn	F	F	F	F	1	$\frac{1}{10} \times \frac{1}{10} \times \frac{1}{10} \times \frac{1}{10} = \frac{1}{10,000}$	$1 \times \frac{1}{10,000} = \frac{1}{10,000}$
Three houses burn	F	F	F	—	2	$\frac{1}{10} \times \frac{1}{10} \times \frac{1}{10} \times \frac{9}{10} = \frac{9}{10,000}$	$4 \times \frac{9}{10,000} = \frac{36}{10,000}$
	F	F	—	F	3	Ditto	
	F	—	F	F	4	Ditto	
	—	F	F	F	5	Ditto	
Two houses burn	F	F	—	—	6	$\frac{1}{10} \times \frac{1}{10} \times \frac{9}{10} \times \frac{9}{10} = \frac{81}{10,000}$	$6 \times \frac{81}{10,000} = \frac{486}{10,000}$
	F	—	F	—	7	Ditto	
	F	—	—	F	8	Ditto	
	—	F	F	—	9	Ditto	
	—	F	—	F	10	Ditto	
	—	—	F	F	11	Ditto	
One house burns	F	—	—	—	12	$\frac{1}{10} \times \frac{9}{10} \times \frac{9}{10} \times \frac{9}{10} = \frac{729}{10,000}$	$4 \times \frac{729}{10,000} = \frac{2916}{10,000}$
	—	F	—	—	13	Ditto	
	—	—	F	—	14	Ditto	
	—	—	—	F	15	Ditto	
No house burns	—	—	—	—	16	$\frac{9}{10} \times \frac{9}{10} \times \frac{9}{10} \times \frac{9}{10} = \frac{6561}{10,000}$	$1 \times \frac{6561}{10,000} = \frac{6561}{10,000}$
							Total $\frac{10,000}{10,000}$

6,561 chances in 10,000 that 0 house will burn
a total of
10,000 chances in 10,000 that 4, 3, 2, 1, or 0 houses will burn.

Suppose now that Messrs A, B, C, and D in Situation I each bear their own risk but in Situation II form a pool in which they agree to divide equally between them any loss from fire which may occur to any of them during the year. The two resulting Situations, as they affect the risk facing any one of the four citizens (e.g. Mr A) is shown in Table XXIX. If Mr A bears his own risks (Situation I), he simply

Table XXIX

Proportion of Property lost	Situation I. No pooling of risks.	Situation II. Complete pooling of risks.
Whole	$\dfrac{1000}{10,000}$	$\dfrac{1}{10,000}$
$\frac{3}{4}$	Nil	$\dfrac{36}{10,000}$
$\frac{1}{2}$	Nil	$\dfrac{486}{10,000}$
$\frac{1}{4}$	Nil	$\dfrac{2916}{10,000}$
None	$\dfrac{9000}{10,000}$	$\dfrac{6561}{10,000}$
Mathematical Expectation of loss	$\dfrac{1000}{10,000} \times 1$ $= \dfrac{1}{10}$	$\dfrac{1}{10,000} \times 1 + \dfrac{36}{10,000} \times \dfrac{3}{4}$ $+ \dfrac{486}{10,000} \times \dfrac{1}{2} + \dfrac{2916}{10,000} \times \dfrac{1}{4}$ $= \dfrac{1}{10}$

is faced with a 1 in 10 chance of losing the whole of his property. If he pools his risks with those of Messrs B, C, and D (Situation II), there is (as Table XXVIII shows) only a 1 in 10 chance that all the pool's property will be lost through the destruction of all four houses, 36 chances in 10,000 that three-quarters of the pool's property will be

P

lost through the burning of three of the four houses, and so on down the last column of Table XXIX. Mr A's mathematical expectation of loss is unchanged as is shown at the bottom of Table XXIX. In Situation I he has a simple expectation of 1 chance in 10 of losing all his property. In Situation II he has a 1 in 10,000 chance of losing all his property *plus* a 36 in 10,000 chance of losing three-quarters of his property *plus* a 486 in 10,000 chance of losing half of his property *plus* a 2,916 in 10,000 chance of losing a quarter of his property, which works out at an average expectation of losing one-tenth of his property. But the risk of the complete catastrophe of losing all his property is reduced from $\frac{1}{10}$ in Situation I to only $\frac{1}{10,000}$ in Situation II at the expense of a lower chance of getting off scot free *plus* an increased risk of losing some part ($\frac{3}{4}$, $\frac{1}{2}$, or $\frac{1}{4}$) of his property. But on the principles discussed on pages 419–425 above and illustrated in Figure 46, Mr A may greatly prefer Situation II to Situation I. His chance-utility index is likely to be raised by the pooling of risks with his fellow citizens.

With this preliminary analysis of the principle of spreading or sharing risks, we will now turn to a discussion of three different methods of reducing the burden of risks and uncertainty.

1. SPREADING AND OFFSETTING RISKS AND UNCERTAINTIES BY INSURANCE AND BETTING

A first and familiar way in which the burden of some risks can be greatly diminished is by means of insurance. The cases in which insurance can operate most successfully are where (i) the hazard is a pure objective risk unaccompanied by any element of uncertainty and (ii) there are many separate individuals subject to the same risk. Consider, for example, fire insurance. Suppose that the risk of a firm's output being destroyed by fire on any one day were 1 in 100,000. Suppose that past experience had demonstrated that the risk of any one firm being subject to this disaster could be reliably assessed at this figure, as if the risk were analogous to the drawing of the Queen of Spades from a well-shuffled pack of 100,000 different cards. Suppose further that there are a large number of individual firms and that the chances of fire for the different firms are independent of each other. Then competitive insurance companies can be set up to make a profit by inviting entrepreneurs to pay into an insurance fund a daily premium somewhat greater than $\frac{1}{100,000}$ of the value of their firms' daily output in return for which the insurance company undertakes to make good any loss from fire which any such firm may experience. If each insurance company covers a large number of these independent risks, the probability is overwhelming that the company's daily payments of claims averaged over a series of days will be very nearly exactly equal to $\frac{1}{100,000}$th part of the value of the property insured.

There will thus be an incentive for some entrepreneurs to set up insurance companies which will compete by offering to cover fire hazards in return for a premium which is slightly above the actual risk of the hazard insured. The other entrepreneurs will have exchanged the hazard of total loss by fire for a small fall in their average expected yield, i.e. for the excess of their premiums over the actuarial risk of fire. The entrepreneurs operating the insurance companies will themselves be incurring some hazards since there is always the freak possibility that an inordinately large number of firms will be destroyed by fire (will, as it were, all draw the Queen of Spades) at the same time; and there is always the uncertainty that perhaps the nature of the risk will change (the number of other cards in the pack will be altered) as, for example, an unexpected technical change increases the chances of fire. The entrepreneurs in the insurance companies will themselves need some expected return on their venture (i.e. some level of the premiums paid above the actuarial level of the fire risk) to attract them into this somewhat hazardous business. Moreover, if things should go very unluckily for an individual insurance company and if the total claims on that insurance company should exceed the total premiums by more than the personal resources of the entrepreneur running the insurance company, the insurance company might not be able to meet in full all the claims made on it. Thus risk is not eliminated. The entrepreneurs running the insurance companies run some risk of losing their own personal wealth and even the entrepreneurs whose firms are insured face some ultimate chance that they may not be fully compensated for their losses. But by spreading the risks the burden of risk has been enormously reduced by insurance. The ordinary entrepreneur at the expense of a very small fall in his expected yield has virtually eliminated a risk of total ruin; and this has been done by a specialized class of entrepreneurs in insurance who are also facing only a very small risk of making any substantial loss.

It is interesting to observe that in the very unreal model with which we are dealing in this volume, in which there are no indivisibilities and no actual costs of management (only costs of bearing risks and uncertainties), our ordinary entrepreneurs could have equally well reduced the burden of the risks from fire even in the absence of an insurance market. This they could have done by spreading their own risks over a larger number of smaller firms. Consider Mr A, an entrepreneur running a firm which produces X. If he insured against fire for a daily premium of about $\frac{1}{100,000}$ of his daily output, he would in fact have pooled the risk of fire with the other (say, 49,999) firms insuring with the same insurance company. But if there are literally no economies of scale and literally no indivisibilities and if there were literally no costs of management but only costs of facing risks and uncertainties, there would be nothing to prevent Mr A from producing his same output X in 50,000 independent firms (spread, as it were, all over the country in so far as fire hazards were concerned), each firm being only $\frac{1}{50,000}$ of the size of the single firm with which he was first concerned. In this way Mr A, by spreading his fire risk over 50,000 very small firms instead of pooling a fire risk for a large firm with 49,999 other firms, also achieves a virtual elimination of the risk of total loss from fire, though in this case he himself still carries the ultimate remaining risk and uncertainty previously carried by the entrepreneur in the insurance company. Of course, in real life where resources are not infinitely divisible and where there are real costs involved in running many independent firms simultaneously, the two possibilities—of pooling risks through insurance and of spreading risks over many enterprises—are quite different. The essential advantage of insurance is that it provides a market for the pooling of risks which cannot be easily directly spread because of indivisibilities and other obstacles to the multiplication of small separate activities.

In addition to an 'insurance' market in which independent risks can be pooled, there is another type of market, which we may call a 'betting' market in which the hazardous effects of interdependent risks or of uncertainties may be offset against each other. Let us take two examples.

(1) If it is wet tomorrow, it will be wet for everyone. There may be a more-or-less objective risk of wet weather (1 chance in 3, for example); but unlike a fire hazard, if it is wet for Mr A it will also be wet for Messrs B, C, D, E, etc., as well. It is not, therefore, like fire a hazard against which simple insurance will spread the risks. If Messrs A, B, C, D, and E all pay premiums to an insurance company of one third of the value insured against destruction by wet weather tomorrow and if tomorrow is wet, then the insurance company will have to pay total claims equal to three times the premiums received; it will make a loss equal to twice the premium income. If it is fine tomorrow, the insurance company will make a profit equal to its premium income. The risk has not been spread; it has simply been

shifted to the insurance company.[1] But something can be done to reduce the burden of risk and uncertainty if there are some persons to whom wet weather brings gain (say, the cinema industry) and others to whom it brings loss (say, the hotel industry). As we shall see shortly, a 'betting' market can be set up in which the risk of gain to the former is offset against a risk of loss to the latter.

(2) Consider a case of subjective uncertainty. Television has been invented and sets are about to be put upon the market. If television in fact turns out to appeal to the public more than do the cinemas, the producers of television sets will make large profits and the cinema industry will make losses. If television turns out not to appeal, the producers of television sets will make losses and the cinema industry will make profits. Again through a 'betting' market the hazards of producers of television sets and of cinema showings could be partially offset against each other.

The essential feature of these two examples is that, while in neither case is there an objective risk falling independently on a large number of individuals (and, therefore, capable of spreading by simple insurance), yet there are hazards of a kind in which one man's meat is another man's poison. In the first case, wet weather is meat to the cinema operators and poison to the hotel industry; in the second case, a fashion for television is poison to the cinema operators but meat to the producers of television sets.

Let us consider a case which is an amalgam of the two cases mentioned in the preceding paragraphs. Suppose that the cinema industry will profit from wet weather and that the hotel industry will profit from fine weather. But suppose also that tomorrow's weather is not simply a matter of objective risk, but has also in it an element of subjective uncertainty. Reasonable men may differ about their assessment of the probabilities of good or bad weather; cinema operators may have a higher expectation than hotel keepers of fine weather or *vice versa*. There is now the possibility of a wager between cinema operators and hotel keepers about the weather which will enable them partially to offset the weather hazards against each other. Cinema operators can lay a bet with hotel keepers that the weather will be fine and *vice versa*. If the weather turns out to be fine, the hotel keepers will owe the cinema operators money on the bet, and this will transfer some of the fine-weather profits of the hotel keepers to make up for the fine-weather losses of the cinema

[1] Simply for the purpose of illustrating a case where an objective risk cannot be the subject of simple insurance because the risk is not spread *independently* over many individuals, we neglect the possibility that the risks of wet weather can be spread over a long series of days in each of which there is an independent chance of 1 in 3 of wet weather.

operators. If the weather turns out to be wet, then some of the wet-weather profits of the cinema operators can be used to offset the wet-weather losses of the hotel keepers.

It is not necessary that the cinema operators should bet directly with the hotel keepers. A separate industry—let us for the time being call it the 'betting' industry—may grow up. Other entrepreneurs may set up betting firms in which they undertake to take bets for and against wet weather. They offer odds on bets for or against wet weather tomorrow. The cinema operators place bets with these betting firms on tomorrow's weather being fine and the hotel operators place bets with the betting firms on tomorrow's weather being wet.

This can be called a brand of insurance. The cinema operators can be said to be paying premiums to insure against fine weather and the hotel operators to be paying premiums to insure against wet weather. But let us for purposes of exposition continue to discuss this type of insurance in terms of betting. If, at any given odds which are offered by the betting firms, the amount of bets placed on fine weather by the cinema operators is equal to the amount of bets placed on wet weather by the hotel keepers, then the betting firms themselves face no hazards. If the weather is wet, the returns paid out to the hotel keepers will be equal to the amount of money wagered by the cinema operators; and *vice versa* if the weather turns out to be fine.

One can see then how a competitive betting market could develop. Entrepreneurs in the betting industry can make a profit with little risk if (i) they charge some small commission on the bets laid and (ii) the odds offered are such that the bets laid in the one direction are equal to the bets laid in the other direction. Thus the individual entrepreneur in the betting industry in order to attract custom to his firm will tend to cut the commission which he demands as low as possible and in order to reduce his own risks will adjust the odds which he offers so as to balance his books.

Suppose for example that a betting firm is offering odds of $1 to $2 for wet weather as against fine weather. Suppose that at these odds (i) cinema operators are betting $300,000 (i.e. will pay $300,000 if it is wet and will receive $150,000 if it is fine) but (ii) hotel keepers are betting $100,000 (i.e. will pay $100,000 if it is fine and will receive $200,000 if it is wet). The betting entrepreneur is now taking himself a great hazard; he will lose $50,000 if it is fine and will gain $100,000 if it is wet. Unless he wishes to lay such a bet himself, he will alter the odds which he offers from $1 to $2 to, say, $1 to $2·1. Hotel operators are now more attracted to this particular betting firm and cinema operators are encouraged to look for other firms whose odds have not moved against them.

If for the betting industry as a whole hotel operators are betting on a smaller scale than cinema operators, then competition between the betting firms will improve the odds for hotel keepers and worsen the odds for cinema operators. There are a number of ways in which this may tend to encourage bets by hotel keepers and discourage bets by cinema operators and thus bring the betting market into balance.

First, the movement of the odds in favour of hotel keepers and against cinema operators will raise the average expectation of profit in hotel keeping and reduce the average expectation of profit in the cinema industry. The costs of the hotel industry are reduced because the premium for insurance against losses due to wet weather are reduced. Similarly, costs in the cinema industry are raised. This will tend to lead to an expansion of the hotel industry relatively to the cinema industry and thus to an expansion of bets placed by the former relatively to bets placed by the latter.

Second, the improvement in the terms on which hotel keepers can place bets will induce them to bet on a larger scale in the sense that they will lay bets which get them a larger betting prize in the case of wet weather. But the fact that they can get this cover against the risk of wet weather on better terms may mean that they get the increased cover in return for wagering a smaller sum which they will have to pay if the weather is wet and they lose their bet. We will return to this point below.

Third, there may well be outside gamblers who are prepared to bet on fine or wet weather if they think that the odds offered are specially favourable. Suppose, for example, that someone considers that the probability of wet weather is in fact $\frac{3}{4}$ while the odds offered are $1 to $2 for wet weather as against fine weather. If he bets $100 on the weather being wet (i.e. will pay $100 if fine and receive $50 if wet), he has an average expectation of a profit of $25 (i.e. a 3 in 4 chance of $+$$50 plus a 1 in 4 chance of $-$$100). But he is incurring some risk. He may have a chance-utility function which makes him think that the extra risk is worth the extra average expected yield. If he enters the market, he is in fact bearing some of the risks of the cinema industry. By betting (like a hotel keeper) in favour of wet weather, he is improving the market from the point of view of the cinema operators. Through the market he is providing a net $100 for cinema operators if the weather is fine and is taking a net $50 from them if the weather is wet. An improvement in the odds to the advantage of hotel keepers may thus bring in outside risk bearers to place bets as if they were hotel keepers and thus help to balance the market.

The second of these points can be readily elaborated by means of Figure 47. We assume that a hotel keeper will make a maximum income of H_f if the weather is fine and a minimum of H_w if it is wet. We can, therefore, take incomes of H_f and H_c as the maximum and minimum benchmarks against which we can construct (in the manner described on pp. 419–420 for the construction of Figure 46) the hotel keepers' chance-utility index for all incomes between the minimum H_w and the maximum H_f. In Figure 47 we draw the curve AFHIKLNO to show this chance-utility index. Thus OE = unity; and if, for example, FB = 0·7 we mean by that that the hotel keeper would be indifferent between a sure income equal to $H_w + AB$ and a 70 per cent chance of fine-weather income of H_f combined with a 30 per cent chance of a wet-weather income of H_w.

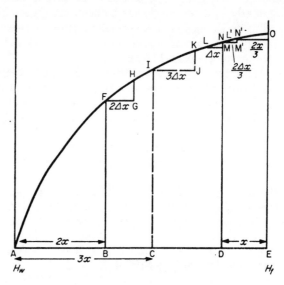

Figure 47

Now suppose that the hotel keeper is betting x at 2 to 1 odds that the weather will be Wet, i.e. is contracting to pay x if Fine and to receive $2x$ if Wet. Then if Fine his income is reduced by DE and has a chance-utility index DN instead of unity (OE = 1); and if Wet his income is increased by AB and has a chance-utility index FB instead of zero. Is x the correct sum for him to wager in view of (i) his attitude to risk (ii) his expectation of Wet and Fine, and (iii) the odds he can get on the bet?

Suppose he bets a little bit more, i.e. $x + \Delta x$ instead of x. His income and utility index if Fine will be reduced from N to L, where LM = Δx. His income and utility index if Wet will be increased from F to H where, at odds of 2 to 1, $FG = 2\Delta x$. Suppose that his own subjective probability of Wet is equal to π_h. Then he stands to lose an extra NM utility with a probability $1 - \pi_h$ and to get an extra HG utility with a probability π_h. He will be attracted to expand his bet if

$$\pi_h HG > (1 - \pi_h)NM, \text{ i.e. if } \frac{HG}{MN} > \frac{1 - \pi_h}{\pi_h}.$$

If Δx is a very small marginal increment to x, we can conclude that x is the correct amount to bet when x is such that $\frac{HG}{NM}$ is equal to $\frac{1 - \pi_h}{\pi_h}$, and that the bet should be increased or decreased according as $\frac{HG}{MN} \lessgtr \frac{1 - \pi_h}{\pi_h}$. It can readily be seen from Figure 47 that as x (and therefore $2x$ also) is increased, Δx (and therefore $2\Delta x$ also) remaining unchanged, HG falls and NM rises because of the diminishing slope of the utility index curve. With π_h given, there will be some value of x at which $\frac{HG}{NM}$ (which with a very small x would start at a very high level) falls to equality with $\frac{1 - \pi_h}{\pi_h}$.

Let us suppose that for odds of \$2 if Wet to \$1 if Fine this value of x is that shown in Figure 47, so that $\frac{HG}{NM} = \frac{1 - \pi_h}{\pi_h}$. Suppose now (i) that the odds improve from the hotel keeper's point of view from \$2 if Wet against \$1 if Fine to \$3 if Wet against \$1 if Fine and (ii) that for the time being the hotel keeper continues to contract to pay \$x if Fine. He will remain at the point N if Fine; but if Wet he will receive an addition to his income H_w of AC $(= 3x)$ instead of AB$(= 2x)$ and his income and utility point will move from F to I. Suppose now once again he considers increasing the size of his stake by Δx so that, if Fine, once again he would move from N to L. But now if Wet, he moves from I to K where $IJ = 3\Delta x$. In other words at the new odds by increasing his stake by Δx he increases his utility index if Wet by KJ. He should increase (or decrease) his stake as a result of the improved odds according as $KJ \lessgtr HG$. For, on the basis of the argument of the preceding paragraph, he should now increase or decrease his bet according as $\frac{KJ}{NM} \lessgtr \frac{1 - \pi_h}{\pi_h}$; and since we are assuming that $\frac{HG}{NM} = \frac{1 - \pi_h}{\pi_h}$, $\frac{KJ}{NM}$ is $\lessgtr \frac{1 - \pi_h}{\pi_h}$ according as $KJ \lessgtr HG$.

Now KJ will be greater (or less) than HG according as the

marginal utility of income (the slope of the utility index curve) diminishes only slowly (or rapidly). There are two influences at work. (i) The fact that IJ > FG would cause KJ > HG if the slope did not diminish in steepness. (ii) The fact that the slope diminishes in itself tends to cause KJ < HG.

But while as a result of the improvement in the odds the amount (x) which the hotel keeper will stake may fall if the marginal utility of income falls rapidly, yet it will not fall so much that the amount of the prize which the hotel keeper stands to gain if Wet is also reduced. Suppose the hotel keeper's stake were reduced from x to $\frac{2}{3}x$. Then he would move from N to N' if Fine, but stay at F if Wet, since 3 times the stake of $\frac{2}{3}x$ is equal to $2x$, i.e. to AB. Now let him consider whether he should increase his stake by a small increment equal to $\frac{2}{3}\Delta x$, so that if Fine he would move from N' to L' and if Wet from F to H (where the increase of his earnings if Wet is FG $= 3 \times \frac{2}{3}\Delta x = 2\Delta x$). Now N'M' is less than NM because (i) L'M' is only $\frac{2}{3}$ of LM and (ii) the slope $\dfrac{\text{N'M'}}{\text{L'M'}}$ is less than the slope $\dfrac{\text{NM}}{\text{LM}}$. But we are assuming that $\dfrac{\text{HG}}{\text{NM}} = \dfrac{1 - \pi_h}{\pi_h}$. It follows that $\dfrac{\text{HG}}{\text{N'M'}} > \dfrac{1 - \pi_h}{\pi_h}$. In other words when the odds improve from \$2 against \$1 to \$3 against \$1, the hotel keeper should certainly maintain his stake at a level which is sufficient to raise the prize he will win if it is Wet.

Conversely when the odds move against him the cinema operator will reduce (or increase) his stake which he pays if Wet according as the marginal utility of income to him diminishes rapidly (or slowly). But he ought in any case to increase his stake by less than is sufficient to obtain the same prize as before for himself if it is Fine.

Before we return to the main question under discussion (namely the forces which determine the odds in the market for bets), it is useful to observe that at every given odds there is a scale of betting which for each hotel keeper or cinema operator will remove all risks due to weather. Let us measure by $\dfrac{1 - \pi}{\pi}$ the odds offered in the market for bets for Wet versus Fine weather.[1]

Now at any given odds $\dfrac{1 - \pi}{\pi}$ there is always a scale of betting which will remove all risks for the hotel keeper. Call this—stake $\bar{x}_h$.

---

[1] If the odds in the market were \$2 if Wet and \$1 if Fine, $\dfrac{1 - \pi}{\pi}$ would be $\dfrac{2}{1}$ so that π would be $\frac{1}{3}$. In other words the odds would correspond to those of a 'fair bet' if there were an objective probability of Wet of $\frac{1}{3}$.

Then if Fine, the net profit of the hotel keeper will be $H_f - \bar{x}_h$ and if Wet, his net profit will be $H_w + \dfrac{1 - \pi}{\pi}\bar{x}_h$. Thus if

$$H_f - \bar{x}_h = H_w + \frac{1 - \pi}{\pi}\bar{x}_h$$

i.e. if
$$\bar{x}_h = \pi(H_f - H_w) \tag{22.1}$$

the hotel keeper will make the same net income whether Wet or Fine. This riskless net income is $H_f - \bar{x}_h$ where $\bar{x}_h$ has the value given in (22.1) above, that is to say he can ensure a riskless income of

$$H_f - \pi(H_f - H_w)$$

i.e. of
$$\pi H_w + (1 - \pi)H_f \tag{22.2}$$

If the hotel keeper expects Wet with a subjective probability equal to π_h, then if he does not place a bet his average expectation of profit will be

$$\pi_h H_w + (1 - \pi_h)H_f \tag{22.3}$$

If we subtract (22.2) from (22.3) we obtain

$$(\pi_h - \pi)(H_f - H_w) \tag{22.4}$$

which shows the change in the average expected yield due to betting on a scale which eliminates all weather hazards for him.

It is to be observed that if $\pi_h > \pi$, then the expression in (22.4) is positive. If the odds offered on Wet weather are more favourable than correspond to the hotel keeper's own subjective expectations, (i.e. if $\dfrac{1 - \pi}{\pi} > \dfrac{1 - \pi_h}{\pi_h}$ i.e. if $\pi_h > \pi$) the hotel keeper can lay a bet which simultaneously both removes all his risks and uncertainties and also raises his average expectation of profit. Indeed if $\pi_h > \pi$, the hotel keeper can always raise his average expected profit without limit by extending the scale of his bet. If he bets \$1 more, he will lose \$1 more if Fine and gain \$$\dfrac{1 - \pi}{\pi}$ more if Wet. But he expects π_h chances of Wet and $1 - \pi_h$ chances of Fine. Therefore the average expected net additional income from the additional \$1 of bet is

$$\$\left\{\pi_h \frac{1 - \pi}{\pi} - (1 - \pi_h)\right\}$$

$$= \$\frac{\pi_h - \pi}{\pi} \tag{22.5}$$

which is $\lessgtr 0$ as $\pi_h \lessgtr \pi$.

Let us now consider the hotel keeper's behaviour in three cases: (i) where the odds he is offered correspond to his own subjective assessment of the probability of the risk (i.e. $\pi_h = \pi$), (ii) where the odds offered are less favourable to him than that ($\pi_h < \pi$), and (iii) where the odds offered are more favourable ($\pi_h > \pi$).

(i) In the first case, as we have just seen in (22.5), however much or little he bets he will not affect his average expectation of profit. But there is a scale of bet, namely that shown in (22.1), which will completely eliminate risk. If he has an aversion to taking hazards, he will then bet on just this scale necessary to eliminate all risk.

(ii) In the second case, the more he bets, the lower his average expectation of profit. If he bets on a scale sufficient to eliminate all risk, he will have reduced his expected income considerably. He will presumably stop somewhere short of this, when a point has come at which his risk is so substantially reduced that it is not worth while to bet on a still larger scale because the fall in average expected income would not be worth the elimination of the small remaining risk.

(iii) In the third case, the more he bets, the higher his average expectation of profit. He will certainly bet up to the scale on which he eliminates all risk, because up to that point he will be both reducing risk and increasing his average expectation of profit by increasing the scale of his bet. If he bets on a still greater scale he will be introducing risks once again. The hotel keeper by betting on Wet weather on a sufficiently grand scale introduces the risk of making a loss if the weather is Fine, because his bet is now so large that the extra profitability of his business from Fine weather is more than offset by the size of the loss on his bet. But in spite of this fact, in this third case he is likely to bet on a scale which is somewhat bigger than that which is sufficient to eliminate all risk from his business, because by betting on a somewhat larger scale he can increase his average expectation of income at the cost of introducing only a small element of risk.

To summarize, the hotel keeper will stop at a level of bet below that which is sufficient to eliminate all risk if the market odds are below those which correspond to his subjective assessment of the probability of wet weather; he will increase the scale of his betting up to the level required to eliminate all risk if the odds rise to what he subjectively considers to be a 'fair bet'; and he will raise the scale of his betting beyond the level required to eliminate all risk if the odds still further improve.

These points are illustrated in Figure 48. If a stake of BC is chosen by the hotel keeper, such that $AC - BC = \dfrac{1 - \pi}{\pi} BC$, i.e. such that $H_f - H_w - x = \dfrac{1 - \pi}{\pi} x$, i.e. such that $x = \pi(H_f - H_w)$, then—as can be seen from the Figure 48 the hotel keeper will get the same income and the same utility index at the point N, whether wet or fine. Now as we saw in discussing Figure 47, he should increase (or decrease) his stake x by a small amount Δx according as $\dfrac{HG}{NM} \lesseqgtr \dfrac{1 - \pi_h}{\pi_h}$. Since for very small distances each side of the same point N, the slope $\dfrac{HG}{NG}$ will be approximately the same as the slope $\dfrac{NM}{LM}$, we can write $\dfrac{HG}{NM} = \dfrac{NG}{LM} = \dfrac{1 - \pi}{\pi}$. We can, therefore, conclude that the hotel keeper should increase his stake above (or reduce it below) the level needed to eliminate all his risks according as $\dfrac{HG}{NM} = \dfrac{1 - \pi}{\pi} \lesseqgtr \dfrac{1 - \pi_h}{\pi_h}$, i.e. as $\pi_h \lesseqgtr \pi$.

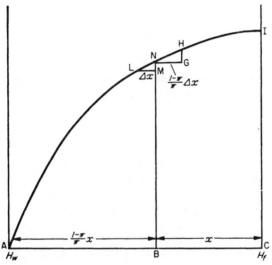

Figure 48

Thus the market for bets can be analysed in the same way as other markets. It is a market in which cinema operators (and others) wish to offer Income-If-Wet in return for Income-If-Fine, while hotel keepers and others are offering Income-If-Fine in return for Income-If-Wet. The odds are the price or terms of trade between these two goods. If cinema operators are offering too much Income-If-Wet, the odds will move against them. This as we have seen will (i) encourage the number of hotel keepers and discourage the number of cinema operators by lowering costs for the former and increasing them for the latter, thus tending to increase offers of Income-If-Fine and to decrease offers of Income-If-Wet and (ii) encourage possible outside gamblers (i.e. risk-bearers) to speculate by offering Income-If-Fine for Income-If-Wet if they think that the odds have now become very favourable indeed to a bet that the weather will be Wet. But as far as existing hotel keepers and cinema operators are concerned it is possible that the movement of the odds against the latter will induce the latter to offer more Income-If-Wet in order to purchase almost as much Income-If-Fine as before; and although the existing hotel keepers will certainly increase the amount of Income-If-Wet which they wish to buy on the improved terms, it is possible that the increased offer of Income-If-Wet by the existing cinema operators will outweigh the increased demand by the existing hotel keepers. In this sort of case a small shift of the demand curve (e.g. a small growth in the size of the cinema industry relatively to the hotel industry) could cause a very large movement in the odds against the cinema operators before balance was restored in the betting market.[1]

Of course the odds at which the market is finally balanced may not correspond to those which would represent a fair bet on the weather. Suppose for the moment that the risk of Wet weather is a purely objective risk, the probability of tomorrow being Wet being recognized by everyone—cinema operators, hotel keepers, and outside gamblers—to be a definite figure, say 1 chance in 3. It is to be observed that this does not imply that the odds in the market will necessarily settle at the 'fair bet' level of \$1 to \$2 for Fine as opposed to Wet. For suppose that the odds were at this 'fair-bet' level but that the cinema industry were much larger in scale than the hotel industry. Since, as we have seen above (case (i) on page 460), at this level of odds each entrepreneur would bet on the level that would eliminate all risk, the bets placed by the many cinema operators would outbalance the bets placed by the small number of hotel keepers. The odds would move against the cinema operators (to, say, \$1 to \$2·1 for Fine as opposed to Wet) inducing thereby (i) a contraction of the cinema industry, (ii) an expansion of the hotel industry, (iii) an entry of pure gamblers into bets in favour of Wet weather, (iv) a contraction of the prizes in case of Fine for which the existing cinema operators betted, and (v) an expansion of the prizes in case of Wet for which the existing hotel operators betted.[2] The movement in the odds

---

[1] The problem is simply that which may arise when two offer curves both show elasticities of demand numerically less than unity. Cf. *The Stationary Economy*, pp. 72–4.

[2] Influences (iv) and (v) might, as we have seen, not be sufficient to help to restore balance in the market if each side had a very low elasticity of demand for the compensation which it sought to cover its losses in case of bad weather.

against cinema operators would continue until the market were balanced.[1]

Betting markets of this kind are a method whereby there can be some spreading of risks over the cinema and the hotel industries without the individual cinema operator himself going into the hotel industries or the individual hotel keeper going into the cinema industry. We have already seen (pp. 451–452 above) that pure insurance markets are really of most importance where there are indivisibilities and costs of management as well as of risk-bearing so that it is important to be able to spread pure insurable risks without splitting enterprise up over a myriad firms. In the same way betting markets are of most importance where there are indivisibilities and costs of management as well as of risk-bearing so that it is important to find a way of offsetting the risks of cinema operations against the risks of hotel keeping without actually undertaking both businesses simultaneously.

2. FORWARD MARKETS

From the preceding discussion it can be seen that a betting market is useful in offsetting gains and losses when one man's meat is another man's poison. A particular instance of this relationship is that which exists between the buyer and the seller of a product. If tomorrow's price of a product turns out to be high, this will raise the profits of the seller (whose revenue will thereby be enhanced) and will reduce the real income of the buyer (whose cost of living will be raised if the buyer is a final consumer and whose costs of production will be raised if the product in question is an instrument of production). These hazards could be offset between buyer and seller by the betting process which we have just discussed at length, the buyer betting that the price will be high and the seller that the price will be low. Thus if the price does turn out to be low, the seller's low profit on his sales will be wholly or partially offset by what he wins on his bet, and *vice versa*.

---

[1] If the hazards in the two industries are uncertainties of which the different entrepreneurs may make different subjective assessments, the absolute scale of betting at which the betting market will be balanced will depend upon the relative subjective assessments on both sides. If cinema operators expect Wet weather with a lower probability than do hotel keepers, the odds in the market can seem favourable both to cinema operators who are betting that the weather will be Fine (an outcome which they privately expect to be very probable) and to the hotel keepers who are betting on what they consider to be a very probable outcome, namely Wet weather. In this case the scale of betting is likely to be high. In the opposite case the scale of betting will be restricted, both sides finding the odds relatively unattractive.

But there is another market device—namely that of a 'forward market'—which can in this case be used to achieve a similar result. At 8 a.m. on day 0 a buyer and a seller of X can strike a bargain about the price at which the buyer will buy and the seller will sell a given quantity of X at 8 a.m. on day 1. In this case all uncertainty about price movements between day 0 and day 1 are removed for both buyer and seller in respect of the amount of X covered by the bargain.

Just as in the cases of betting these transactions need not take place directly between an actual buyer and seller of X, but can be developed in a competitive market by specialized entrepreneurs who deal in forward transactions in X. Thus a market 'forward' price for X (i.e. the price fixed at 8 a.m. on, say, day 0 at which people contract in advance to buy or to sell certain stated quantities of X at 8 a.m. on, say, day 1) may be quoted by such dealers. Sellers of X who want to be covered against an expectedly low price of their product can then at 8 a.m. on day 0 contract to sell certain quantities in a day's time at this forward price. Buyers who want to be covered against an exceptionally high price can similarly contract to purchase certain quantities in a day's time at this forward price. Finally, outside speculators who consider that the market forward price is induly high can, if they wish, take a speculative risk and undertake to sell certain quantities at this forward price; and they will then make a profit (or loss) by purchasing the product tomorrow at a low (or high) market price in order to acquire the quantities required to fulfil their forward contract. And conversely, if they consider the forward price to be unduly low, they can enter into a forward contract to purchase the product, hoping to resell it tomorrow at a higher market price than the forward price fixed in advance. If the total amount which producers of X and speculators wish to sell forward at a given ruling forward price exceeds the total which consumers of X and speculators wish to purchase forward at this given ruling forward price, then the forward price will be lowered in the competitive forward market. Terms will move against sellers who wish to ensure against a low price and in favour of buyers who wish to ensure themselves against a high price.

Thus the mechanism is in essence the same as that of a betting market. Those who stand to lose if tomorrow's price is low (the sellers) could bet in favour of a low price and against a high price, making up by the prize from their bet if the price turns out to be low and losing the stake on their bet if the price turns out to be high. But a similar result can be achieved by their undertaking to sell a certain quantity at a fixed market price; for if tomorrow's price does turn out to be lower than this they gain from the quantity which they can sell at the higher forward price fixed today, but if tomorrow's price turns out to be very high they lose on the quantity which they have contracted to sell at the prefixed forward price. It is, however, perhaps worthwhile pointing out in a little more detail the analogy between covering the risk by betting and by operating in the forward market. Just as the odds in the case of the bet, so the actual forward price fixed in advance in this case determines how favourable are the terms on which the seller can cover himself against a low price tomorrow.

We are now concerned with three kinds of price which are relevant for the seller (Mr A) on day 0 in respect of the product (X).

(1) First, there is the 'spot' price of X. By this is meant the price paid at 8 a.m. on any day for the product bought or sold at that time in the market. This is the actual ruling market price. Thus P_{x0} is the 'spot' price of X ruling at 8 a.m. on day 0; P_{x1} is the 'spot' price of X ruling at 8 a.m. on day 1; and so on.

(2) Second, there is the 'forward' price of X. This is, for example, the price fixed at 8 a.m. on day 0 for a transaction which will take place some time in the future—let us say at 8 a.m. on day 1. We will write this as $_0P_{x1}^*$, namely the price for X fixed at 8 a.m. on day 0 for a purchase and sale of a certain quantity contracted to take place at 8 a.m. on day 1.

(3) Third, there are the prices which are expected to rule in the future. In previous chapters we have written $_0P_{x1}$ for the price expected at 8 a.m. on day 0 to rule at 8 a.m. on day 1. But for two reasons this is an oversimplified expression. For, first, different people may have different expectations about future prices; and, secondly, people may not simply expect one definite price, but may expect with one probability a high price, with another probability a medium price, with yet another probability a low price, and so on. Let us consider the prices expected by Mr A and, solely for simplification of exposition, let us suppose that it is known for certain that the ruling spot price tomorrow will either be a given high price or a given low price.[1] We will write $_{0a}P_{x1}'$ for the high price which at 8 a.m. on day 0 Mr A thinks may rule for X at 8 a.m. on day 1, and $_{0a}P_{x1}''$ for the low price which he so expects. We suppose that he expects $_{0a}P_{x1}''$ with probability π and, therefore, $_{0a}P_{x1}'$ with probability $1 - \pi$.

Solely in order to simplify the notation we will, as we are confirming our argument to Mr A selling commodity X, write

P_0 and P_1 for the 'spot' prices ruling at 8 a.m. on day 0 and day 1,

$_0P_1^*$ for the 'forward' price fixed at 8 a.m. on day 0 for a contracted quantity to be sold at 8 a.m. on day 1, and

---

[1] Just as in our betting example the weather must be either Wet or Fine with no intermediate gradations.

$_0P_1'$ and $_0P_1''$ for the high and the low spot prices for 8 a.m. on day 1 which at 8 a.m. on day 0 Mr A expects with probabilities $1 - \pi$ and π.

Suppose that the total quantity Mr A plans at 8 a.m. on day 0 to produce for sale at 8 a.m. on day 1 is X and that he contracts to sell an amount $\bar{X}$ at the forward price $_0P_1^*$. Then

(i) if in fact the spot price at 8 a.m. on day 1 turns out to be the high price P_1', he will lose $\bar{X}(P_1' - _0P_1^*)$ as a result of the forward contract; but

(ii) if the spot price on day 1 is in fact the low price P_1'' he will gain $\bar{X}(_0P_1^* - P_1'')$ as a result of the forward contract.

Given the forward market price $_0P_1^*$ and the probabilities π and $1 - \pi$ with which he expects $_0P_1'$ and $_0P_1''$, he must choose $\bar{X}$ so as to maximize his risk utility index. This is exactly the same problem as that illustrated in Figure 47 for the betting market. Instead of H_f we have XP_1'—i.e. Mr A's revenue in the absence of any forward transaction if in fact he receives the high price P_1'. Instead of H_w we have XP_1'' or Mr A's revenue if the price turns out badly in the absence of any forward contract. Instead of DE we have $\bar{X}(P_1' - _0P_1^*)$, the amount which he loses from the forward contract if day 1's spot price turns out well; and instead of AB we have $\bar{X}(_0P_1^* - P_1'')$, the amount which he gains from the forward contract if the price turns out badly. In Figure 47 $\dfrac{AB}{DE}$ measures the betting odds. In terms of a forward market $\dfrac{AB}{DE} = \dfrac{_0P_1^* - P_1''}{P_1' - _0P_1^*}$; and the forward contract terms $_0P_1^* - P_1''$ and $P_1' - _0P_1^*$ correspond to the betting odds. Given these forward contract terms Mr A must choose $\bar{X}$ so that in Figure 47 the risk-utility index DN weighted by the probability $1 - \pi$ plus the risk-utility index BF weighted by the probability π is maximized. The whole argument is exactly the same as with the betting market; indeed, a forward market is simply another way of organizing exactly the same outcome, and we will not discuss it further.[1]

There is thus no essential difference between the institutions of a market for bets and a market for forward contracts. But there is an

---

[1] The reader may as an exercise go through the whole argument on pp. 452–463 in terms of a forward market. It is to be observed that if $\bar{X} = X$ (i.e. if Mr A sells the whole of his putput forward) then $\bar{X}\,(P_1' - _0P_1^*) + \bar{X}\,(_0P_1^* - P_1'') = X(P_1' - P_1'')$ so that we are in the position illustrated on Figure 48 where Mr A has eliminated all risk. Of course, we might have $\bar{X} > X$, in which case Mr A, having sold forward more than his total output, stands to lose by a high price and to gain by a low price.

essential difference between the offsetting of risks which (like Wet or Fine weather) cannot themselves be affected by the process of offsetting and the offsetting of risks which (like a high or low price tomorrow) can themselves be much affected by the process of offsetting. Suppose that the forward price of X ($_0P_1^*$) is very high. This will improve the producer's (Mr A's) position and may induce him to produce more because he can cover his risks on better terms. But the fact that he produces more will in itself increase tomorrow's supply and will thus tend to depress tomorrow's spot price. This is unlike the weather. The fact that the cinema operator may increase today's output if the odds move in favour of bets on Fine weather will not cause tomorrow's weather to be Finer than it would otherwise have been.

Thus competitive forward markets for the prices of goods and services can act not merely as a means whereby buyers and sellers offset risks against each other but also as very important guides as to what should be planned to be produced and consumed in the future. They may thus not only offset risks, but in fact remove risks and uncertainties. If the forward price is high, this is some indication that as at present planned tomorrow's supplies are low and tomorrow's purchases high. If this leads to an increase in the planned supply and a decrease in the planned demand, tomorrow's price will thereby have been prevented from being as high as it would otherwise have been.

It is possible to imagine a case in which by this means the organization of a complete set of forward markets would remove completely all uncertainties and give all operators in all markets perfect foresight of future developments. In this case the problems of foreseeing the future which we have discussed at length in Chapters XVIII and XIX would be completely solved. Suppose then (1) that there was no technical progress, (2) that there was no change in the size or individual composition of the population, there being no future births or deaths until the end of the world, and (3) that it was known that the world was going to come to a sudden end on a given future day. We have not in this simple model ruled out capital accumulation. People may be saving or dissaving in order to affect the time pattern of their consumption on the principles discussed above (Chapter XII). Such savings or dissavings will be causing the supplies and demands, and so the prices, of various products to be changing. Thus as total consumption per head rises, the demand for some consumption goods for which the income elasticity of demand is high will rise relatively to the demand for other consumption goods. As instruments of production are accumulated, the marginal product and so the wage of labour will rise; and labour-intensive products will rise in cost relatively to other products. There will indeed remain a thousand and one reasons why the outputs and prices of the different products will change in the future relatively to each other.

But suppose now that there is a fully organized forward market for every single good and service to be exchanged at every single day in the future, including a forward market for the hire of labour and land and for borrowing and lending money. If every individual consumer at 8 a.m. on day 0 covers the whole of every transaction in every good and service for every day in the future of the world, then each individual will eliminate all risk and uncertainty. He will know at 8 a.m. on day 0 what wage income he has contracted to receive on day 1, day 2, day 3, etc., what rent from land he has contracted to receive on day 1, day 2, day 3, etc. He will know also what amounts and at what prices he has contracted to purchase each consumption good on day 1, day 2, day 3, etc. He will, therefore, know what his income from interest will be on each future day because knowing each future rate of interest and each future balance between his other income and his consumption, he will know what his savings or dissavings will be each day in the future.

Similarly, if each entrepreneur covers the whole of his business transactions in a forward market for every future day, he will know exactly where he will stand on each future day—exactly in what quantity and at what price he will purchase every input and sell every output.

One must imagine then one superb higgle-haggle at 8 a.m. on day 0. Given at 8 a.m. on day 0 a complete set of market future prices for every good and service, every consumer and producer can go into the forward markets with his forward purchases and sales. If for any good or service for any future day forward sales exceed forward purchases, the set of forward market prices ruling at 8 a.m. on day 0 is lowered by the forces of competition. And so the grand market higgle-haggle at 8 a.m. on day 0 goes on until a complete set of forward prices is found at which forward sales equal forward purchases for each good and service for each day in the future when each individual consumer and each individual producer is content with his future plan at those prices. In this case spot prices in the future will turn out to be the same as today's forward prices (e.g. $_0P^*_{x3}$ will equal P_{x3}). When the time comes (8 a.m. on day 3), since all purchases and sales have been planned at the same forward price $(_0P^*_{x3})$ and since this is a price which satisfies all buyers and sellers for all their purchases and sales, there will be no attempt to purchase (or to sell) more than the amounts prefixed in the forward contracts at 8 a.m. on day 0 and, therefore, no tendency for the spot price (P_{x3}) to be driven above (or below) the prefixed forward price $(_0P^*_{x3})$. The forward prices will give perfect foresight of the actual price development that will in fact take place.[1]

It can now be seen why, in order to achieve perfect foresight through forward markets, we had to make such strict assumptions as those made above (p. 467). If new members of the population were to appear at future dates as consumers or producers, the future transactions as contracted at 8 a.m. on day 0 could not have covered all future transactions, since new-born consumers and producers were destined to appear. If any technical progress occurred unexpectedly, then once again when the time came consumers and producers might not be content with the forward contracts prefixed some time ago for that date. We cannot, therefore, expect forward contracts to give perfect foresight. But it is possible that they can in suitable cases help not only to *offset* risks as being buyers and sellers, but also to *reduce* the risk itself by guiding present production and consumption plans into patterns which are in fact more appropriate for future conditions. Forward markets by bringing together sellers (who know more than buyers about future conditions of supply) and buyers (who know more than sellers about future conditions of demand) may in fact cause producers and consumers to make plans which are more appropriate than they would otherwise have been for actual future developments.

3. INDICATIVE PLANNING AND CENTRALIZED MARKET RESEARCH

A fully developed system of forward markets, operating in those special conditions in which they could be completely effective, is a method of co-ordinating the future plans of the individual members of the community. Mr A plans to do such and such today because he expects his situation to be such and such tomorrow; but what his situation will be tomorrow will depend *inter alia* upon what Mr B does today which will depend upon what Mr B expects his situation

---

[1] For this to happen we must in our model imagine the Government taking part in the glorious higgle-haggle at 8 a.m. on day 0 setting in advance (i) the rate of interest at which the Central Bank will lend or borrow money on each future day and (ii) the amount of income tax or subsidy which each individual must pay or will receive on each future day. If as a result of the higgle-haggle the forward price index of consumption goods $(_0 P_x^* + _0 P_y^*)$ for any future day rises above or falls below the level at which it is to be stabilized, the Government must at 8 a.m. on day 0 raise or lower the rate of income taxation fixed for that future day in order to restrain demand on that future day. And if the higgle-haggle at 8 a.m. on day 0 results for any future day in an undesired budget surplus or deficit, then the Government must at 8 a.m. on day 0 set a lower or high forward rate of interest for that day in order to encourage or discourage private borrowing for private investment (cf. pp. 303–307). By these means we can envisage equilibrium in all forward markets with both a stable price index of consumption goods from day to day and also a desired balance in the Governmental budget on each future day.

will be tomorrow which will depend *inter alia* upon what Mr A does today. The forward purchases and sales of Messrs A and B at common competitive-market forward prices will indicate to them whether their expectations of each other's behaviour are compatible.

We have seen that the circumstances in which this device can be fully used are very limited. To be complete the forward markets would have to stretch out into the future over a more-or-less endless stretch of future time for all goods and services. To result in accurate forecasts of market conditions over this immense range of products and of time there would have to be no underlying, unforeseeable changes of conditions of human preferences or of technological skill. The community would have to consist over the whole of future time of the same individuals (capable, therefore, of covering today all future sales and purchases) with the same unchanging schedule of preferences and with the same unchanging technical knowledge and ability.

Clearly there cannot in any real situation be any perfect forecasting of future conditions through the means of forward markets. While forward markets can play a limited role in helping to see whether future plans by different individuals are compatible with each other, they may usefully be supplemented by a rather cruder device for this purpose. This may be called the method of Centralized Market Research or of Indicative Planning. It can be used in a crude limited manner or can be developed to high degrees of sophistication and refinement.

To start with a simple example, the producers of one product steel are making individual independent plans about current investment in steel mills which will increase the capacity of output of the industry over future periods. Each producer must have some idea of the price which he expects to get in the future. To form this idea he must have some idea about how much steel his competitors will be producing and about how much steel each of the innumerable users of steel will be demanding in the future for various purposes. Many of these future demands for steel will themselves depend upon present investment plans in other industries; for steel is a raw material input into many processes (e.g. a component of car bodies), and the future demand for that input will depend *inter alia* upon the present construction of the machines which use that input (e.g. of presses suitable for converting steel into car bodies). Each producer and user of steel must, therefore, take present action the fitness of which depends upon what each expects all the others to be doing. Each will make some assessment of the future market (i.e. of the total supplies and demands of others) based upon market-research techniques to find out what the trends of supply and demand are likely to be. But with each producer and consumer making an independent estimate of what every other producer and consumer will do, the total planned outputs and inputs may be very inappropriate. Individual producers may on balance seriously underestimate (or overestimate) either the amount which their competitors are planning to produce or else the total amount which all the users together were planning to use.

Suppose now that some way were found whereby each individual producer's or user's market estimate and own plans for the future of the steel market could be made available to every other individual producer or user of steel. Each could then see whether his own individual plan for output or use of the product and his own individual expectation of future prices fitted in with those of the others engaged in the market. The effect would be in many ways comparable to the organization of a forward market. Consider an individual producer who had constructed his plans on the basis of small outputs by his competitors and high demands by the users and was, therefore, expecting a high future price to rule, on the basis of which he himself planned to be ready to produce a large additional amount. He might discover that, in fact, on the present plans of the others concerned the future supply in the industry was likely to be much less scarce relatively to the demand than he had expected. He might revise his plans; and other individual producers and users might do likewise. A comparison of the new revised plans might reveal diminished, but nevertheless some remaining and perhaps even some new, incompatibilities in the individual plans. Continuous revisions and comparisons of plans could take place so that individual plans were always being adjusted in the light of the intentions of others in the industry.[1]

But there is no reason why this process should be confined to one market such as the market for steel. Indeed, there is very good logical reason why it should be extended. The production of steel needs coal. Plans for the output of steel, therefore, imply plans for the future demand for coal. But whether or not that demand will be met in the future at prices which the steel producers have envisaged for their cost of production of steel will depend upon present plans to expand the capacity of coal production and on present plans in many other industries for the future use of coal and for the future production of other substitute sources of heat and power. Centralized Market

---

[1] There is a serious dynamic problem involved in such a process of mutual examination and revision of plans. If the revisions made are too sharp, then the inconsistencies of plans may be increased. For example, if all producers cut their planned outputs too severely when a future glut was foreseen, the result might be to cause a still greater future scarcity. The problem is analogous to that discussed on pages 240–4 of *The Stationary Economy*.

Research for Steel may help. Centralized Market Research for Coal
may help. But it may then become apparent that these two elements
are not compatible, the amount of coal which the coal industry
plans to sell to the steel industry being unequal to the amount of
coal which the steel industry plans to purchase from the coal
industry. But a Centralized Coal–Steel Market Research may in turn
prove inadequate because of the implications for future plans of
other products which are being sold to (or by) the coal–steel complex
by (or to) other industries not covered by the joint Market Research
exercise.

Indeed, there are some products or services which it is not possible
to start to consider properly without considering everything at once.
Consider, for example, the market for labour in an economy in
which labour can move readily from one occupation to another.
Plans for the production of steel will depend *inter alia* upon
assumptions about how costly relatively to the selling price of steel
labour will be in the future to operate new steel mills. But the level
of the future real wage rate will depend upon the supply–demand
balance for labour throughout the economy in all its industries and
activities. Theoretically the Centralized Market Research cannot deal
with a problem of this kind until it has embraced simultaneously all
industries and activities.

But at this point it is perhaps appropriate that it should change its
name to Indicative Planning; for the emphasis changes from individual producers and consumers engaging in market research on a
wider and wider cooperative basis to one in which a central authority
is helping with a central plan constructed out of the myriad plans of
the independent individual producers and consumers. One way in
which this duet between the central authority and the individual
buyers and sellers in the community might be conducted would be
for the central authority to plan in terms of prices and the individual
buyers and sellers in terms of quantities.[1] The central authority
would issue a plan of the future course of all prices of all goods and
services. On the basis of these future prices every individual buyer and
seller would prepare a plan of the quantities of each good or service
which he would wish to buy or sell in the future. These individual
plans would be reported to the central authority which would estimate
the net excess demands or supplies of the various goods and services

[1] This method is particularly appropriate where, as we are assuming in the
present volume, there is perfect competition. It would be less appropriate in the
real world where there is not perfect competition, and where, therefore, individual buyers and sellers do not take market prices as given and altogether out of
their own control. Nevertheless we use this method in the present context because
it is the most direct way of bringing out the basic interaction between the central
authority and the community individual citizens who compose the community.

at various future dates on the basis of the totality of the individual planned demands and supplies. The central authority could then revise its plan for future price movements, raising those future prices where excess demand was threatened and *vice versa*. The individual buyers and sellers in every market would then be asked to revise their plans for the quantities which they would plan to buy and sell in the future on the revised price plan; these planned quantities would then in turn be centrally examined; the price plan would once more be revised; and so on until quantities and prices were compatible with each other. The whole process could then be continuously reviewed and revised as new technical knowledge, changes in tastes, and changes in population caused individual buyers and sellers to change their quantitative plans.[1]

The analogy between this procedure and a complete set of forward markets is apparent. In the present case while there are no actual market commitments for individual buyers and sellers for future transactions, nevertheless the central authority does provide through its price plan a guide similar to that of a set of forward-market prices and one which is continuously adjusted by a comparison between the quantities which are planned by the individuals to come on to the market. But the method of Indicative Planning is, of course, subject to the same basic deficiencies of knowledge about future events— about future changes in technical knowledge, about future changes in consumers' tastes, and about future changes in the total and in the age and sex composition of the population.

It is here, however, that Indicative Planning may be able to achieve more than a system of forward markets. When the central authority receives the individual quantitative plans of the individual buyers and sellers, it will not in fact revise its future price plan in a purely automatic manner, automatically raising any future price where there is an excess of the individually reported quantities demanded over the individually reported quantities supplied, and *vice versa*. Indeed, in many cases it will not be able to operate in this manner at all. It will certainly, for example, not be possible for the central authority to obtain individual reports from every consumer of private consumption goods as to the quantities which each consumer plans to purchase of each product in the future. Such inevitable gaps in the quantitative

---

[1] The price plan would, of course, have to include the rate of interest and the rates of income taxation and subsidization which the central authority planned for the stabilization of the cost-of-living price index and for the preservation of the desired budget balance (see footnote, page 469).These elements would have to be revised as the price plan was revised, raising income taxation if an excess demand for consumption goods threatened to drive up the money cost of living, raising the rate of interest if an undesired budget surplus threatened to appear, and so on.

reports which it receives will have to be supplemented by the central authority itself. On the basis of past experience of consumers' demands at various prices of consumption goods and at various levels and distributions of consumers' incomes and on the basis of the indications from the rest of the plan about future movements of real income and of prices, the central authority will have to formulate its own quantitative estimates of future demands by private consumers. Moreover, both for individuals' personal consumption and for individuals' productive activities in the future the central authority will have to take into account the quantities likely to be purchased and sold at various prices of various products by citizens as yet unborn or still in the nursery who cannot, therefore, be expected to put in future plans. In particular for its judgment about the future course of the supply–demand balance in the labour market the central authority will have to rely on its own centrally constructed forecasts of the future number of workers likely to be available.

Thus the Indicative Price Plan can be constructed partly upon the basis of putting together all possible existing individual plans about purchases and sales and partly upon the central construction of future supply–demand relationships from other evidence in those sections of the economy where individual quantitative plans do not exist or are inadequate. In this respect an Indicative Price Plan may have an advantage over a System of Forward Markets in that the former can, whereas the latter cannot, supplement the putting together into a coherent whole of distinct individual plans with the sort of guessing about the future which is best done—indeed in some cases solely feasible—as a central operation.[1]

It must be stressed that, just as in the case of a Plansoc (cf. pp. 360–361 above), the only purpose of the Indicative Plan formed today is to determine today's decisions about today's outputs and inputs, even though the formation of the plan necessarily involves forecasts of prices and quantities for many future periods. The sole purpose of the quantities and prices of goods and services set for tomorrow and

---

[1] If two forecasts for the future are incompatible, one at least of them must be wrong. But it does not follow that if the two forecasts are made compatible, then both are correct. It may be that, instead of only one being wrong, both have now become wrong. In Indicative Planning the emphasis must be not on making plans compatible but on making them right. Thus suppose producers of steel plan a future output of 10, while present users forecast a demand of 8. Suppose that in fact a technical innovation in some totally different industry is in fact going to expand the uses of steel to 12. It is more important for the Planners to raise the steel producers' target of output to 12 than, fussing about the incompatibility between the present plans of existing producers and users, to bring it down to 8; and it is possible that a well-constructed central body is better informed about future developments outside the industry in question, but relevant to the industry in question, than are this particular group of industrialists themselves.

the next day in today's plan is to help to decide what it is sensible to do today in preparation for tomorrow and the next day. For this purpose, as we have explained, the formation of very extensive, sophisticated, and elaborate plans for the future may be well worthwhile. But such future quantities are not themselves in the nature of targets which it should be the central authority's purpose to take effective steps to hit. On the contrary, they are merely pieces of information which are useful in reaching a sensible set of decisions about today's use of resources. Every day a new plan can be made giving, on the basis of the most recent available information, revised forecasts of future quantities and prices on which the current day's set of decisions can be based afresh. Of course, if there has been no improvement of information between yesterday and today, then the future quantities and prices in today's plan will be unchanged from yesterday's plan, and today's actual decisions about quantities and prices will coincide with those which were forecast in yesterday's plan. But this does not mean that it would have been right yesterday to treat yesterday's forecasts of today's quantities and prices as rigid targets which it would necessarily be correct to implement today.

It should also be remembered that in such an Indicative Plan no individual producer or consumer, seller or buyer is required by the central authority to conform to the plan in any particular. The whole purpose of such an Indicative Plan is to improve information in such a way that individual citizens in their transactions can base their decisions on a better set of guesses as to what tomorrow's prices will be. It should, in the ways which we have explained, mean that less mistakes are made in present economic decisions due to faulty expectations about future price movements. That is its sole purpose.

There remain, however, some basic difficulties in organizing the construction of such an Indicative Plan which we have not yet mentioned. These difficulties are due principally to certain features in a private-enterprise economic system which arise when competition is not perfect. In a strict sense, therefore, their discussion should be postponed until a later volume when we come to modify our present assumption of perfect competition. But this would be too pedantic a procedure; and we will, therefore, refer to them briefly at this point. In the real world secrecy about present intentions is an important element in the strategy of a firm which is not subject to perfect competition, but is in rivalry with a limited number of other firms which produce products similar to, but not necessarily identical with, its own products. If it has a new idea, it will wish to keep it secret until it can spring its surprise in the market and achieve a flying start over its rivals. It follows that if Indicative Planning of the kind discussed in this chapter is to be a success in market conditions of this kind, a delicate institutional set-up must be achieved. The individual firm must reveal its detailed plans to the central authority; but the central authority, although it openly publishes the central Indicative Plan which it has formed on the basis of these detailed plans of individual firms, must reveal nothing of any one individual firm's plan to any other individual firm. For if such revelations of individual plans were to take place, either the individual firms in the interests of trade secrecy would falsify the plans which they reported to the central authority or else the individual firms would get together and in a monopolized, cartellized manner share out the various trade advantages among themselves on a prearranged basis so that secrecy was no longer a matter of importance to any of them. But this does take us into problems of market structure whose discussion must be postponed to a later volume.

CHAPTER XXIII

EFFICIENCY AND DISTRIBUTION
REVISITED—CONCLUSION

We will conclude this volume by a re-consideration of the possible clash between economic efficiency and the desired distribution of welfare which we examined at length in Volume I in the case of a Stationary Economy (cf. *The Stationary Economy*, Chapter XII). We there stressed the double function of the price mechanism in a perfectly competitive private-enterprise economy. We showed how, with factors being paid rewards equal to the values of their marginal products and with factors moving freely into those uses in which their rewards were highest, one would achieve a state of economic efficiency in which it was impossible to make any one citizen better off without making at least one other citizen worse off. But we stressed the fact that the price mechanism, in addition to fulfilling this signalling role of beckoning resources from less to more productive uses, would also determine the distribution of the national income among the individual owners of the factors of production, each citizen receiving an income equal to the market rewards of the factors which he happened to own. Thus the resulting system, while it would be economically efficient, might result in an undesirable distribution of income. Governmental action might be desired in order to affect the distribution of income without impairing the efficiency of the system—that is to say in order to give more to Mrs A at the minimum reduction of income for Mrs B.

This set of problems remains essentially the same when we move from *The Stationary Economy* to *The Growing Economy*; but both the ideas of economic efficiency and of distributional justice need to be expanded and reformulated in certain ways.

Let us start then with a reconsideration of the idea of economic efficiency. Consider the system of production on day 0. Certain inputs of labour and of various instruments of production are available at 8 a.m. on day 0; these are used in various processes during day 0; at the end of day 0 there emerge certain outputs of consumption goods and certain outputs of various instruments of production which are used at 8 a.m. on day 1 either for the personal consumption needs of Mrs A, B, C, D, etc., or else to provide inputs for the productive operations of day 1. The question is whether this productive process on day 0 has been an efficient one or whether it would have been more efficient to have used the same inputs, available at 8 a.m. on day 0, in a different set of processes during day 0 to produce a different set of consumption goods for consumption by Mrs A, B, C, D, etc., at 8 a.m. on day 1 and/or a different set of instruments of production to feed back into the productive process at 8 a.m. on day 1.

Suppose that for some reason or another we could assume that there was a predetermined set of outputs of instruments of production which the productive system had to produce during day 0 and that the only question at issue was whether a better pattern of output and use could be found for the consumption goods produced during day 0. Then the whole matter could be discussed in the terms set out in Chapter XII of *The Stationary Economy*. If there were perfect competition and if all inputs at 8 a.m. on day 0 could be moved freely to those uses in which the values of their marginal products were highest, then (i) trade would be optimized, (ii) production would be maximized, and (iii) production would be optimized in so far as day 0's output of consumption goods was concerned. It should not be necessary to argue this at length here. On the lines of the analysis in *The Stationary Economy* (pp. 184–98) it can be seen (i) that if Mrs A and Mrs B can both purchase X and Y at 8 a.m. on day 1 at the same prices, P_x and P_y, the market for consumption goods at 8 a.m. on day 1 will necessarily settle down in a position in which it is impossible for Mrs A to be better off without making Mrs B worse off by an exchange of X for Y between them, (ii) that if all inputs at 8 a.m. on day 0 are offered rewards in every process which equal the value at 8 a.m. on day 1 of their marginal products in those processes, then it will be impossible so to shift factors that more X is produced without producing less of some other product (and, therefore, less of some other consumption good, since we are assuming *ex hypothesi* that the outputs of instruments of production are fixed), and (iii) that in this case it will also be impossible to reshuffle the use of inputs at 8 a.m. on day 0 in such a way that, without any change in any other output, more X and less Y are produced in such quantities that Mrs A would value the increased output of X more than she valued the decreased output of Y.

Any new problems concerning the idea of economic efficiency must, therefore, arise in connection with one or other of the following two questions:

(1) Would it in any sense be more efficient to produce during day 0 for use in the productive processes of day 1 more of one instrument

of production and less of another, e.g. more bricks and less steel or more looms and less ploughs?

(2) Would it in any sense be more efficient to provide for any one citizen, say Mrs A, more (or less) consumption goods today at the expense of providing for her less (or in order to provide for her more) consumption goods at some future date?

We need to reformulate the idea of economic efficiency in terms of an economically efficient pattern of production and consumption over a period of time. We shall refer to this idea as an 'economically efficient time-path'. We will define an economically efficient time-path in two ways: first, in a narrow way, for which only question (1) of the two above questions is relevant; and, second, in a broader way, for which question (2) above also becomes relevant.

First, then, for the narrow definition we shall say that the economic system is moving on an efficient time-path if the pattern of consumption at each point of time is such that it is impossible to make citizen A better off on any one day without making some other citizen worse off on that same day or without making A or some other citizen worse off on some other day. The system is efficient, in other words, if it is impossible to reshuffle the uses of resources at various points of time in any way which would make someone better off at some point of time without making anyone worse off at that or any other point of time. It is clear that with this definition of an efficient time-path question (2) above must be answered in the negative and only question (1) remains relevant. Question (2) implies that Mrs A will be worse off either today or on some future day; and it follows immediately that the change envisaged cannot increase efficiency on the present narrow definition.

Now it can be shown that if there were (i) perfect competition and (ii) perfect foresight about the future course of all prices, the economy would always settle down at each point of time in a situation in which not only the pattern of output of consumption goods would satisfy the efficiency conditions (as we have just explained) but also the pattern of output of instruments of production would be efficient. In other words the pattern of the output of instruments of production on day 0, ready for use at 8 a.m. on day 1, would be such that it would not be possible by producing more of one instrument and less of another to increase the welfare of any one citizen on any future day without reducing anyone's welfare at any future point of time. The economy will be on an efficient path as we have for the present narrowly defined it.

In order to prove this we must first show that in a perfect competitive system with perfect foresight of future prices it is always possible to measure the value of the marginal product of a given instrument of production at a given point of time (the marginal product of, say, J_0) as the present discounted value of the net additional future output of *consumption goods* which would be made possible directly or indirectly by having one more unit of J to use at 8 a.m. on day 0. We will consider this matter first in terms of a Plansoc and then by analogy in terms of a perfectly competitive economic system.

Now the productive system over time can be regarded as one into which each day certain inputs from outside (i.e. inputs of labour) are introduced and out of which certain final goods (i.e. consumption goods such as food and clothing) are extracted. The man-made instruments of production which are produced one day and used the next inside the productive system are of no direct interest to us; in themselves they feel no pleasures or sorrows (as working men and women do) and they satisfy no human needs (as food and clothing do). They are important only in so far as they enable a given flow of inputs of labour to produce larger subsequent outputs of food and clothing. Nevertheless if one more unit of an instrument of production were to drop like manna from heaven at some point of time it could, of course, be introduced like labour from outside into the productive system and it would enable net additions to some outputs of some consumption goods to be produced at some future dates without any additional inputs of labour into the system and without any reductions of other outputs of consumption goods.

Suppose then that we are operating a Plansoc[1] and that at 8 a.m. on day 0 one additional unit of J falls from heaven into the lap of the Central Authority. The computer is quickly set to work to do its sums afresh with one additional unit of J_0. In the Primal (cf. pp. 365–368 above) the computer tells the Central Authority so to rearrange the plan as to add the following outputs of final goods:

$$\Delta X_0 \quad \Delta X_1 \quad \Delta X_2$$
$$\Delta Y_0 \quad \Delta Y_1 \quad \Delta Y_2.$$

These, it says, are the possible changes in outputs which will now maximize the present value of the output of the Plan (namely, $V_{x1}X_0 + V_{x2}X_1 + V_{x3}X_2 + V_{y1}Y_0 + X_{y2}Y_1 + V_{y3}Y_2$) without breaking any of the constraints of the system. Thus the present value of the marginal product of J_0 is

$$V_{x1}\Delta X_0 + V_{x2}\Delta X_1 + V_{x3}\Delta X_2$$
$$+ V_{y1}\Delta Y_0 + V_{y2}\Delta Y_1 + V_{y3}\Delta Y_2 \qquad (23.1)$$

---

[1] The Plan is assumed to cover the whole of future time so that no stocks of instruments have to be left over at the end of the Plan period. In terms of Table XV $V_{j3} = V_{k3} = 0$.

The computer in the Dual (cf. pp. 368–371 above) will tell the Central Authority that the shadow price of J_0 (V_{j0}) is equal to the expression given in (23.1).

Let us now consider the analogy with a perfectly competitive system. We know (cf. page 381 above) that the social valuation in a Plansoc at 8 a.m. on day of a unit of X which will be consumed at 8 a.m. on day 1, namely V_{x1}, corresponds in a perfectly competitive system to the present discounted value of a unit of X to be obtained at 8 a.m. on day 1, namely $\dfrac{P_{x1}}{1 + i_0}$; that V_{x2} corresponds to $\dfrac{P_{x2}}{(1 + i_0)(1 + i_1)}$; and so on. We can, therefore, in terms of a perfectly competitive economy write the expression in (23.1) for the value of the marginal product of J_0 as

$$
\begin{aligned}
P_{j0} = {} & \frac{P_{x1}\Delta X_0 + P_{y1}\Delta Y_0}{1 + i_0} \\
& + \frac{P_{x2}\Delta X_1 + P_{y2}\Delta Y_1}{(1 + i_0)(1 + i_1)} \\
& + \frac{P_{x3}\Delta X_2 + P_{y3}\Delta Y_2}{(1 + i_0)(1 + i_1)(1 + i_2)}
\end{aligned}
\tag{23.2}
$$

In other words, the value of the marginal product of any instrument at any point of time can be measured by the present discounted value of the future net increments to the outputs of *consumption goods* (X and Y) which it makes it possible for the community to produce, given its other resources.

We can in fact in a perfectly competitive system with perfect foresight of future values always express the present selling value of an instrument of production in terms of the values of the future net increments of consumption goods which it will produce, as is done in the expression at (23.2). It is perhaps worthwhile giving a very clumsy, commonsensical description of the reasons why this is so. Consider the present value at 8 a.m. on day 0 of a unit of J (i.e. the value P_{j0} of J_0). Suppose this instrument is going to be used so as to

(1) produce a certain stream of outputs of X—namely, X_0, X_1, X_2,
(2) use a certain stream of inputs of L—namely L_0, L_1, L_2,
(3) use a certain stream of inputs of some other instrument of production—namely, K_0, K_1, K_2, and
(4) produce a stream of outputs of some other instrument of production—namely, $\bar{K}'_0$, $\bar{K}'_1$, $\bar{K}'_2$.

As far as the effect of (1) on the present valuation (P_{j0}) of J_0 is

Q

concerned, we can clearly discount to 8 a.m. on day 0 the future values of the relevant outputs of X.

The effect of (2) will be to reduce the valuation P_{j0} by an amount equal to the discounted value of the future wages of the L's. But these L's must be withdrawn from other possible employments. If they are withdrawn, for example, from the production of Y, the relevant wage cost at each future date will be the then current marginal products of the L's in terms of Y. Thus the discounted value of the wage bills will be equal to the discounted value of the outputs of Y lost as a result of manning up the additional unit of J_0.

As far as (3) and (4) are concerned, the operation of the additional unit of J_0 which we are trying to value will have absorbed the future use of other instruments (K_0, K_1, K_2) or will have produced additional instruments for future use $(\bar{K}_0', \bar{K}_1', \bar{K}_2')$. The valuation P_{j0} of J_0 must, therefore, be reduced by the present discounted values of the K's and increased by the present discounted values of the $\bar{K}$'s. But the future values of the K's and of the $\bar{K}''$s will themselves be equal to the discounted values of the consumption goods which they in turn could directly produce in the still more distant future less the consumption goods which could have been produced otherwise by the labour needed to man them up plus the value of any net additional instruments of production which these instruments of production might produce. And so on in an infinite regression, until ultimately the whole valuation P_{j0} can be reduced to the discounted value at 8 a.m. on day 0 of all the future net increments to the outputs of *consumption goods* which the additional unit of J_0 makes it possible to produce, given the other resources of the economy.

Having shown that the market valuation of an instrument of production in a perfectly competitive system with perfect foresight can be expressed in terms of the values of the future net increments of consumption goods that can be ascribed to it, we can now return to the question with which we are concerned. We are in the process of showing why in a perfectly competitive system with perfect foresight the economy at any one time (say, on day 0) will only settle down to an equilibrium in which it would be impossible by producing a little more of one instrument of production and a little less of some other instrument of production on day 0 to make any consumer better off at some future date without making anyone worse off at any time.

To show this consider two instruments of production, J and K. Measure units of J and K in such a way that the marginal cost on day 0 of producing 1 more unit of J is the same as the marginal cost of producing 1 more unit of K. In other words it would be possible for the economy to produce on day 0 1 more unit of J and 1 less unit of K or 1 more unit of K and 1 less unit of J. On what conditions would it be possible by altering the pattern of output of *JK* on day 0 to increase someone's welfare at some point in the future without reducing anyone's welfare at any future time? Now the economy will reach a perfectly competitive equilibrium on day 0 with the marginal cost of *J* equal to the marginal cost of *K* only if the selling price offered for *K* equals the selling price offered for *J* at 8 a.m. on day 1 (i.e. $P_{j1} = P_{k1}$). But these selling prices will as we have just shown, be equal to the present discounted value of the direct or indirect marginal products of these instruments in terms of all consumption goods over all future time.

For example, we can write

$$P_{j1} = \frac{C_{j1}}{1 + i_1} + \frac{C_{j2}}{(1 + i_1)(1 + i_2)} + \ldots$$

where C_{j1} is the value to consumers at 8 a.m. on day 2 of the additional consumption goods produced during day 1 as a result of the existence at 8 a.m. on day 1 of one more unit of the instrument *J*, C_{j2} is similarly the value of the additional consumption goods so produced during day 2, and so on. Similarly, we shall have

$$P_{k1} = \frac{C_{k1}}{1 + i_1} + \frac{C_{k2}}{(1 + i_1)(1 + i_2)} + \ldots$$

Now we can increase economic efficiency in the narrow sense in which we are using the term by producing one more unit of *J* and one less unit of *K* during day 0 only if it enables some consumer at some future day (say, at 8 .m. on day 5) to be better off without any other consumer being worse off at any time. But this would be possible only if, for example, $C_{j4} > C_{k4}$ (so that some consumer could be better off at 8 a.m. on day 5 when the outputs of day 4 are consumed), while $C_{j1} \not< C_{k1}$, $C_{j2} \not< C_{k2}$, etc. But if this were so we would have $P_{j1} > P_{k1}$ so that more *J* and less *K* would in fact have been produced during day 0. In other words if it were possible to increase the value of someone's consumption at one point of time without reducing the value of anyone's consumption at any point of time by producing one more unit of *J* and one less unit of *K*, during day 0 perfect competition would bring this about provided that the future values of $C_{j1}, C_{j2}, \ldots C_{k1}, C_{k2} \ldots$ and of i_1, i_2, etc., were correctly foreseen. Perfect competition plus perfect foresight would lead to an economically efficient time-path in the narrow sense in which we have so far considered the problem.[1] [2]

[1] In Chapter XVIII we defined an equilibrium growth path as that which would occur if there were perfect competition and perfect foresight, so that no one ever regretted their decisions. In this sense then equilibrium growth is efficient growth.

[2] Our assumption (see p. 347 above) that the world will come to an end at some finite—even though remotely distant—date is crucial for the above conclusion.

But it is now time to reconsider our present rather narrow definition of an efficient time-path. Suppose that for some reason the economic system were so ordered that it produced a surfeit of food and clothing today but an acute scarcity of all consumption goods tomorrow. In some basic sense this might properly be considered to be an inefficient arrangement. Mrs A, Mrs B, Mrs C, etc., might each individually be better off if they had less consumption goods today and more tomorrow; and as far as the productive resources of the community were concerned, it might be quite possible to make this change in the time pattern of total output of consumption goods. And yet on our present narrow definition of an efficient time-path, the existing arrangement could already be defined as an efficient one. It might be impossible to make any one consumer better off tomorrow without making that consumer or some other consumer worse off today, so that on our narrow definition the system is already an efficient one even though the time pattern of consumption is so obviously a wasteful one.

One can get round this anomaly by adopting a broader definition of an efficient time-path on the following lines. We say now that the time-path of the economic system is an efficient one if it is impossible to make one citizen better off over his or her life as a whole without making some other citizen worse off over his or her life as a whole. Thus the economic system would be an inefficient one if it were possible to produce less food today and in consequence more food tomorrow and if Mrs A would be better off over her life as a whole if she had that much less to eat today and that much more to eat tomorrow. Or, to take another possibility, the economic system would be an inefficient one if, without any change in the output of any consumption good at any point of time, Mrs A would be better off over her life as a whole without Mrs B being worse off over her life as a whole as a result of Mrs A having less to eat today and more to eat tomorrow while Mrs B had just so much more to eat today and just so much less to eat tomorrow.

Food-today and food-tomorrow are, in the case of this broader definition of economic efficiency, treated as two different consumption goods which are available to the same consumer—either Mrs A or Mrs B. One form of the optimization of production (cf. *The Station-*

Our present argument rests on the possibility of expressing the value of the marginal product of an instrument of production at any point of time solely in terms of the future *consumption* goods which it would directly or indirectly produce (see p. 480 above); and this possibility itself depends upon the assumption that a time will come, when any *capital* goods which it may directly or indirectly produce have no social value at all (see footnote on p. 480). This time necessarily comes if we assume that at some point the world will come to an end so that any instruments of production left over at that date are worthless.

ary Economy, pp. 187–8) now is the production of less food-today and more food-tomorrow in quantities which would enable Mrs A to be better off without any one else's consumption of any commodity being affected. One form of the optimization of trade (cf. *The Stationary Economy*, p. 185) now is the exchange of food-today with food-tomorrow between Mrs A and Mrs B so that Mrs A is better off without Mrs B being worse off and without anyone else's consumption or production of any consumption good being affected. It is clear that if we extend the definition of economic efficiency in this way question (2) on page 479 above now becomes relevant.

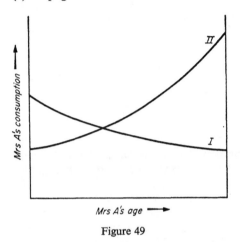

Figure 49

But this extension of the definition of economic efficiency is meaningful only if it is possible to say unambiguously whether one time pattern of consumption over her life span is preferred by Mrs A to another time pattern of consumption. Consider the two time patterns for consumption over Mrs A's life which are illustrated in Figure 49. With pattern I Mrs A lives very well when young, saves little, and has little capital to support her in her old age. With pattern II she is frugal when young but is able to live at a high standard when old. Suppose that these are no problems of uncertainty. Mrs A knows for certain from the outset what the length of her life will be, what earned income and what rate of interest on accumulated property she will command, and what the price of consumption goods at every point of time will be. Now it is possible that when young Mrs A would say that she prefers pattern I to pattern II, but that when old she would say that she preferred pattern II to pattern I. In this case she is short-sighted. In youth she discounts the pleasure of old age and/or in old age she discounts the pleasure of youth; her foresight and/or her memory is in this sense deficient. If Mrs A is in this frame of mind, then there is no un-ambiguous answer to the question whether pattern I or pattern II is preferable. There is then no meaning to our broader definition of an economically efficient time-path. It makes no sense to ask whether a change in the economy which put Mrs A on pattern II instead of pattern I would increase her welfare over her life as a whole. In this case then we would be forced to restrict our analysis to the narrower definition of economic efficiency. In effect this is saying that Mrs A is a different person when young and when old, so that the question of the distribution of her standard of living over her life time (reducing her standard when young and raising it when old) must be treated in the same way as a question not of economic efficiency but of distri-butional justice between one generation and another. We will return to this point later when we come to consider distributional justice in a Growing Economy.

Let us suppose for the time being that all citizens have perfect memories and perfect foresight in the sense that there is an unambiguous answer to the question whether one life pattern of consumption or another is preferred. We can then consider our broader definition of an economically efficient time-path, namely one in which it is impossible to make one citizen better off over his or her life as a whole without making any other worse off over his or her life as a whole. It is our purpose now to show that, as in the previous case, perfect competition combined with perfect foresight of future prices will ensure that the economic system moves on an efficient time-path as defined in this broader way.

We will set about this task in the same manner as before. We will first examine the relevant aspects of a Plansoc and we will then by analogy apply the analysis to the position in a perfectly competitive economy. Suppose then, for example, in a full Plansoc we had $\frac{V_{x1}}{V_{x5}} = 1 \cdot 2$, or in other words that the social valuation put on a unit of X available for consumption at 8 a.m. on day 1 was 20 per cent higher than the social valuation put upon a unit of X available for consumption four days later at 8 a.m. on day 5. This would mean (see page 385 above) that the productive system was so arranged that it would be possible to produce $1 \cdot 2$ more units of X_5 by sacri-ficing 1 unit of X_1 or *vice versa*.

Consider now exactly the same economic system in a perfectly competitive system. We know (see page 381 above) that $\frac{V_{x1}}{V_{x5}}$ corresponds to $P_{x1} \div \dfrac{P_{x5}}{(1 + i_1)(1 + i_2)(1 + i_3)(1 + i_4)}$. In other words we would have

$$\frac{P_{x1}(1 + i_1)(1 + i_2)(1 + i_3)(1 + i_4)}{P_{x5}} = 1 \cdot 2$$

as a measure of the number of units of X_4 (i.e. of X produced during day 4) which in this perfectly competitive system it would be possible to produce at the expense of giving up one unit of X_0. This is the marginal rate of substitution between producing X_0 and producing X_4 which is possible in the economic system as at present arranged.

That the above expression will measure the rate at which X_0 can be transformed into X_4 can be seen in the following way. Suppose that during day 0 at the margin one can produce $J_0 = J_1$ units of J instead of X_0 units of X. Suppose that the gross marginal product (see pp. 295–296 above) of the instrument J_1 would be $J_1' \equiv J_2'$ units of J' during 1, that the gross marginal product of the instrument J_2' would be $J_2'' \equiv J_3''$ units of J during day 2, that the gross marginal product of the instrument J_3'' would be $J_3''' \equiv J_4'''$ units of J''' during day 3, and that the gross marginal product of J_4''' would be X_4 units of X during day 4. Then by giving up X_0 one can at the margin obtain X_4 by the chain

$$\begin{array}{c} X_0 \\ \downarrow \\ J_1 \to J_2' \to J_3'' \to J_4''' \to X_4 \end{array}$$

Let the prices of these products be $P_{x1}, P_{j1}, P_{j2}', P_{j3}'', P_{j4}''', P_{x5}$. Then in competitive equilibrium at the margin one will have

$X_0 P_{x1} = J_1 P_{j1}$ since *ex hypothesi* the marginal cost of X_0 equals the marginal cost of J_1,

$J_1 P_{j1}(1 + i_1) = J_2' P_{j2}'$ since capital will be invested in J_1 up to the point at which the value of the gross marginal product of J in terms of J' (i.e. $J_2' P_{j2}'$) is equal to the cost with interest of J (i.e. $J_1 P_{j1}[1 + i_1]$), and similarly

$$J_2' P_{j2}'(1 + i_2) = J_3'' P_{j3}'', J_3'' P_{j3}''(1 + i_3) = J_4''' P_{j4}''',$$

$$\text{and } J_4''' P_{j4}'''(1 + i_4) = X_4 P_{x5}.$$

From this it follows that

$$X_4 P_{x5} = (1 + i_1)(1 + i_2)(1 + i_3)(1 + i_4)X_0 P_{x1}$$

or $$\frac{X_4}{X_0} = \frac{P_{x1}(1 + i_1)(1 + i_2)(1 + i_3)(1 + i_4)}{P_{x5}} = 1 \cdot 2$$

which measures the rate at which in the productive system at the margin X_0 can be transformed into X_4.

But consider now Mrs A's choice between X_0 and X_4. If she purchases 1 less unit of X_0 she saves P_{x1} in money. If she accumulates this at compound interest by 8 a.m. on day 5 she will have amassed $P_{x1}(1 + i_1)(1 + i_2)(1 + i_3)(1 + i_4)$. If the price of X at 8 a.m. on day 5 is P_{x5}, then she will be able to purchase with this

$$\frac{P_{x1}(1 + i_1)(1 + i_2)(1 + i_3)(1 + i_4)}{P_{x5}} = 1\cdot2$$

units of X_4.

Let us treat X-today and X-four-days-hence as two products. We have just seen that the ratio between the prices at which these two products are made available to Mrs A and, similarly, to Mrs B, Mrs C, Mrs D, etc., as well, is the same as the marginal rate of substitution between them in the productive system. By means of the analysis developed in Chapter XII of *The Stationary Economy* it is now possible to see how as a result of competition trade in these two products, and the production of these two products, will be optimized in the sense (i) that it will be impossible for Mrs A to be better off without Mrs B being worse off by an exchange of X-today and X-four-days-hence between them and (iii) that it will be impossible to make Mrs A better off by producing less X-today and more X-four-days-hence (or *vice versa*) and altering Mrs A's consumption pattern by these same amounts.

So much for our reformulation of the meaning of, and the conditions necessary for, a state of economic efficiency. We will turn now to the modifications which must be made to the treatment of the distribution of welfare as a result of turning from the consideration of a Stationary Economy to that of a Growing Economy. We have now three aspects instead of only one aspect of the problem of distribution:

(1) In the first place, we have as before what we may call the problem of the *interclass distribution* of welfare. By this we mean simply that at any one time one Mr A may be rich because he owns much property and/or much earning capacity, while Mr B who is of the same age as Mr A, may be poor because he owns little property and/or little earning capacity. This is the straightforward distinction between the rich and the poor classes of citizen.

(2) In the second place, we now have what we may call the problem of the *intergenerational distribution* of wealth. The young members of any given economic class may at any one time have a lower standard of living than do the older members of the same economic class. This does not imply that the member of the new generation will, taking his life as a whole, be worse off than the member of the older generation.

On the contrary in an economy in which standards are continuously improving, the member of the younger generation will at each age of his life be better off than the member of the older generation was in the past at each corresponding age of his life; but it is perfectly compatible with this that at any given date when the member of the younger generation is starting his life and the member of the older generation is ending his life, the standard of the former is lower than the standard of the latter. Conversely, the younger members of any given class may at any one given time be better off than are the older members of that same class at that same time. It is this type of inequality which we consider under the heading of intergenerational distribution.

(3) There is yet a third problem of distribution which we may call the problem of *intertemporal distribution*. By this we intend to consider those questions which depend upon the comparison of any one citizen's standard of living at different ages of his life. Mr A may have a low standard of living when young and a high standard of living when old, or *vice versa*.

The question which we have now to consider is whether, and if so in what form, the Government can intervene in the economy in order to improve the distribution of welfare in any or all of these three forms. Let us first consider intervention to affect the *intertemporal distribution* of welfare. In this case there are two possible quite distinct reasons for intervention.

(i) It is possible that citizens lack foresight and memory in the sense discussed on pages 485—486 above. In this case people when young will consume too much and will save too little and will regret when they are old that they were not more provident when young. The Government may take action to induce them to save more when young to meet their needs when old.[1] One form of such inducement would be a tax on consumption, the rate of tax being reduced according to the age of the taxpayer; the tax might turn into a subsidy to consumption when the consumer had reached a certain age, the rate of subsidy then being raised as the taxpayer's age advanced.

People who are shortsighted in this basic sense may be regarded as

[1] It is hoped that in a later volume we may be able to discuss in more detail the political basis of economic action. At this stage we say no more than that it appears quite possible for individuals to be quite happy that they should, for example, be taxed when young to provide pensions in their old age even when this does not imply any interclass redistribution from the rich to the poor classes of citizen.

discounting future utilities, simply because they are to be enjoyed in what is still the future. This is something quite different from (i) preferring $100 of income now rather than in the future because present income can be accumulated at a positive rate of interest to build up a larger income in the future or (ii) preferring an additional $100 of consumption now rather than in the future because one's present consumption level is lower than one's expected future consumption level so that the marginal utility of $100 now is greater than the marginal utility of $100 of extra consumption later. Pure time discount is something different. It means that even though the consumption level now were the same as next year's expected consumption level so that in a basic sense the real marginal utility of consumption were the same in both years, yet consumption now would be preferred to consumption next year simply because it was nearer. If in these circumstances a citizen would equate $100 this year with $105 next year, we may say that he has a rate of pure time discount of 5 per cent per annum. We will call this rate of pure time discount ρ.[1]

In these conditions our shortsighted citizen will behave in his choice of consumption patterns as if the market rate of interest were lower by ρ than it actually is. Suppose the rate of interest (i) were 8 per cent per annum and that the citizen's rate of pure time discount (ρ) were 5 per cent per annum. If he now cut down his consumption this year by $100, he would have an additional $108 to spend on consumption next year. In the absence of pure time discount ($\rho = 0$), this would have a certain effect on his choice between consumption this year and next year. In these circumstances, but with a rate of pure time discount of 5 per cent per annum ($\rho = 5$ per cent p.a.) it will need a 5 per cent gain on his consumption between this year and next year (i.e. $105 next year instead of this year) simply to offset his pure impatience. When by giving up $100 this year he can get $108 next year, the pulling power on him to postpone consumption will be as if, having no pure time preference, he could get $103 next year for each $100 given up. He will behave in other words as a man without pure time preference, but one faced with a yield on his savings of only $i - \rho$ instead of i. He will raise his consumption at a rate equal to

$$\hat{c} = \sigma(i - \rho) \tag{23.3}$$

---

[1] The basic point can be seen this way. Mr A has the same level of consumption in year 0 and in year 1. In year 0 he would be prepared to give up $105 of year 1's consumption to obtain an extra $100 of year 0's consumption because year 0 is now one year nearer to him than year 1. But in year 1 he would wish that he had given up $105 of year 0's consumption to obtain an extra $100 of year 1's consumption because year 1 is now one year nearer to him than year 0.

instead of, as on page 205 above, at a rate equal to

$$\hat{c} = \sigma i \tag{23.4}$$

where $\hat{c}$ is the growth rate in the individual's consumption level and σ expresses the underlying relationship, apart from pure nearness of time, between the utility of different levels of consumption.

What is needed to correct this situation is for the State to introduce a tax-subsidy system which has the effect of raising the yield on postponed consumption by an amount equal to ρ so that the impatient citizen arranges his consumption as if he were not in fact impatient. This inducement to save more can be introduced by taxing today's consumption more heavily (or subsidizing it less heavily) than tomorrow's consumption.

If there were no tax or subsidy a citizen by giving up $\Delta \hat{C}_1$ of consumption at the beginning of year 1 could accumulate $\Delta \hat{C}_1(1 + i_1)$ in purchasing power by the beginning of year 2. He could, therefore, thereby finance an increase in consumption at the beginning of year 2 of

$$\Delta \hat{C}_2 = \Delta \hat{C}_1(1 + i_1)$$

so that
$$\frac{\Delta \hat{C}_2}{\Delta \hat{C}_1} = 1 + i_1 \tag{23.5}$$

measures the rate at which he can obtain extra units of consumption in year 2 for each unit of consumption given up in year 1.

Suppose now that there are taxes at *ad valorem* rates of t_1 and t_2 on consumption goods bought in years 1 and 2 respectively. Then our citizen by giving up $\Delta \hat{C}_1$ of consumption releases purchasing power of this *plus* tax no longer payable, i.e. of $\Delta \hat{C}_1(1 + t_1)$. This sum can be accumulated to $\Delta \hat{C}_1(1 + t_1)(1 + i_1)$ by the beginning of year 2; and this total sum is available then to be spent on consumption including the tax on consumption in year 2, which is equal to $\Delta \hat{C}_2(1 + t_2)$. Thus we now have

$$\Delta \hat{C}_2(1 + t_2) = \Delta \hat{C}_1(1 + t_1)(1 + i_1)$$

or
$$\frac{\Delta \hat{C}_2}{\Delta \hat{C}_1} = \frac{1 + t_1}{1 + t_2}(1 + i) \tag{23.6}$$

which measures the new rate at which our citizen can acquire units of $\hat{C}_2$ for every unit of $\hat{C}_1$ given up.

Now the difference between (23.6) and (23.5) is the rise in the rate of yield on postponed consumption (let us call it ϵ) which is due to this tax system, so that we have

$$\epsilon = \frac{t_1 - t_2}{1 + t_2}(1 + i_1) \tag{23.7}$$

The Government needs to impose a falling rate of tax (i.e. $t_1 > t_2$)

which makes the value of ϵ in (23.7) equal to ρ, the rate of pure time discount which it is attempting to offset.

(ii) There is, however, a second and quite different reason why the State may wish to intervene to affect what we have called the *intertemporal distribution* of welfare. Let us suppose that citizens have no pure time discount and that they are perfectly altruistic in their intergenerational attitudes. We have explained in Chapter VIII and in Chapter XIII (pp. 235–236 above) how in these conditions if σ is constant at a high figure and if the universe is expected to exist for ever, the economy may get into a state of steady growth in which the proportion of income saved is so high that the level of consumption is kept permanently lower than it need be. People would be saving for a blow-out which was indefinitely postponed. In this case the State might wish to induce people to postpone less of their consumption from one year to the next. This could be done by a tax-subsidy system on individual consumption in which the rate of tax rose or the rate of subsidy fell as the age of the individual increased. In (23.7) ϵ would have a negative value; and the individual would receive on his postponed consumption a rate of yield which was lower than the market rate of interest. With a given σ the planned growth rate of the individual's consumption would be $\sigma(i + \epsilon)$ instead of σi, where ϵ was a negative quantity, so that $i + \epsilon < i$.

We have argued (pp. 109 and 236 above) that this anomaly arises if the proportion of income saved (S) settles down at a higher figure than the proportional marginal product of capital (U). If this threatens to happen the Government needs to impose a tax-subsidy system which gives a value of ϵ such as to reduce S to U. In the particular example which we have investigated above (pp. 235–237) we can see what this value of ϵ must be in the following way.

If $S = U$, then $i = k$, since $i = \dfrac{UY}{K}$ and $k = \dfrac{SY}{K}$ (cf. equations (4.3) and (6.1) above). But in the state of steady growth $k = \dfrac{Ql + r}{1 - U}$ (cf. equation (7.14) above). But in the state of steady growth with perfect altruism the growth rate of an individual's consumption per head—$\sigma[i + \epsilon]$—must equal the growth rate of the wage rate—$\dfrac{r - Zl}{1 - U}$ (cf. equation (7.15) above) so that $\sigma(i + \epsilon) = \dfrac{r - Zl}{1 - U}$. We have then

$$\left.\begin{array}{l} i = k = \dfrac{Ql + r}{1 - U} \\[2ex] \sigma(i + \epsilon) = \dfrac{r - Zl}{1 - U} \end{array}\right\} \qquad (23.8)$$

The three equations in (23.8) tell us what the value of ϵ must be in order to make $S = U$. Eliminating i and k between these three equations we get

$$\epsilon = -\frac{r + Ql}{1 - U}\left\{1 - \frac{r - Zl}{\sigma(r + Ql)}\right\} \tag{23.9}$$

We know from (13.2) on page 226 above that the problem of a constant $S > U$ arises only if $1 > \dfrac{1}{\sigma}\dfrac{r - Zl}{r + Ql}$. The expression in (23.9), therefore, gives one the negative value of ϵ which is necessary to remove this anomaly if it should arise.

The Government must for this purpose find a rate of rise in consumption tax (or a rate of fall in consumption subsidy) which makes the expression in (23.7) equal to the expression in (23.9) with $i = \dfrac{r + Ql}{1 - U}$. This gives

$$\frac{t_2 - t_1}{1 + t_2} = \frac{r + Ql}{1 - U + r + Ql}\left\{1 - \frac{r - Zl}{\sigma(r + Ql)}\right\}$$

as the formula for the rate at which the tax rate should rise ($t_2 > t_1$) as age increases.

We will concern ourselves no further with this last problem. The facts that the world is not expected to last for ever and, above all, that σ is not constant but becomes very low for very high levels of consumption makes the problem an unreal one. The problem of pure time discount (ρ) is, however, by no means an unreal one. Let us assume then that the State imposes a system of taxes and subsidies on consumption, the rate of tax falling or of subsidy rising with the age of the consumer, in such a way as to impose a positive ϵ equal to ρ. It is to be observed that an ϵ of the correct size could be imposed (i) with a system of taxes throughout a citizen's life span but with the tax rate falling with age, in which case the State would be faced with a budget surplus, or (ii) a subsidy system throughout a citizen's life span but with the subsidy rate rising with age, in which case the State would be faced with a budget deficit, or (iii) with a tax-subsidy system, starting with a tax falling with age and changing in mid-life span into a subsidy rising with age, in which case the State could achieve a balanced budget. For our future discussion it is important to remember that the necessary correction to make $\epsilon = \rho$ can be made at any level of general tax burden or of general subsidy benefit for any citizen. The correction to make $\epsilon = \rho$ depends not at all upon the general height of the tax burden or subsidy benefit, but only upon the rate at which the burden or benefit per unit of consumption varies with the age of the consumer. We assume now that this correction to make $\epsilon = \rho$ is made and turn to Government intervention to affect the *interclass* and *intergenerational distribution* of welfare.

If it were desired to redistribute welfare between two citizens of the same age (from one with a large property and/or high earning capacity to one with a low property and/or low capacity) without any adverse effect upon the balance between work and leisure or upon the time pattern of consumption, this would have to be done by means of a system of lump-sum taxes and subsidies. It would be necessary to take a certain amount of money away from the rich man and give it to the poor man, having judged what was the proper sum and without making the tax or the subsidy dependent upon how much either of them earned or consumed.

The reason for this is as follows. We have argued in *The Stationary Economy* (pp. 188–9) that effort will be optimized if each citizen earns a wage equal to the value of his marginal product. For when each citizen would himself acquire for his own disposal the additional wealth which he would produce by working one more hour, then he can freely balance his day between work and leisure in such a way that the additional wealth exactly compensates for the loss of leisure at the margin; and at the margin no one else is adversely affected by his decision. But suppose that of any additional income he earns some part must be paid away in tax, then the citizen will cease work at a point at which the last hour of leisure is worth only his marginal product less the tax paid. He could be better off without anyone else being worse off if he worked a little longer and obtained the whole of his marginal product. He will not be induced to do so because he will earn less than this (after payment of tax) in return for the sacrifice of his last unit of leisure.

Any tax which rises with the total income received will have this effect of upsetting the optimum balance between work and leisure. It will also have the effect of upsetting the optimum time pattern for consumption. Suppose that a citizen saves $100 more this year and receives $105 as a result next year. $5 will be added to next year's income from interest. If additional income is taxed at 20 per cent, then he receives only $4 in net addition to his income. Although the marginal product of waiting in the economy (cf. page 380 above) is 5 per cent per annum, he is offered only 4 per cent per annum net on his waiting. The rate at which he will plan to raise his consumption will be less than the optimum. The rate at which he can exchange consumption next year for consumption this year will differ from the rate at which the community can transform consumption this year into consumption next year for him (cf. pp. 486–488 above).

A general flat rate of tax on consumption in whatever year it takes place will (in the absence of any pure time discount, ρ) not disturb the optimum balance between consumption next year and consumption this year. This can be seen from equation (23.7) on page 491, from which it can be seen that if $t_1 = t_2$, then $\epsilon = 0$. Or in other words if consumption as contrasted with income is taxed at the same rate in every year of a man's life the market rate of interest i still determines the rate at which he personally can transform consumption this year into consumption next year. But this conclusion does not hold good if the rate of tax on consumption is a progressive one in the sense that a higher rate of tax per unit of consumption is paid when a man's standard of consumption is high than when it is low. For consider a man whose consumption level was rising over his life. He pays a higher rate next year than this year not simply because he is older, but because his standard of living is higher. But this makes no difference to the fact that in (23.7) we have $t_2 > t_1$ so that ϵ is a negative quantity. The progressive consumption tax has twisted the yield on savings to the individual to make it lower than the market rate for those whose level of consumption is rising.

And even a constant proportional rate of tax on consumption ($t_1 = t_2 = t_3$, etc.), while it will not distort the choice between this year's and next year's consumption will nevertheless distort the choice between work and effort. For if of any money which a man spends at any time on consumption, 10 per cent is taken in tax, then sooner or later of any income which he may earn 10 per cent will go to the Government instead of to the enjoyment of himself or of his heirs. Once again the reward of effort to the individual is less than the value of the individual's marginal product.[1]

It is for these reasons that theoretically to cope with interclass redistribution without distorting the balance between work and leisure or the balance between consumption one year and consumption the next a system of lump-sum taxes and subsidies is needed. In fact no perfect system of this kind would be practicable; but it is worthwhile examining the implications of a perfect system as a means of understanding the points at issue. For a perfect system it would be necessary to assess each citizen at birth as someone who in the absence of any equalizing tax or subsidy would achieve a given level of welfare over his life as a whole and to impose at birth on him a given lump-sum tax (or to pay over at birth to him a given lump-

[1] The above discussion has been conducted entirely in terms of taxes on income or on consumption. The reader is left to apply the same analysis in terms of subsidies per unit of income or per unit of consumption, where the distortions will exist but in the opposite direction—namely, offering a man for his marginal leisure more than he produces by his extra effort or offering him for the postponement of this year's consumption more than the marginal product of his waiting.

sum gratuity) as he was assessed to be a potentially exceptionally wealthy (or exceptionally poor) citizen. It would make no difference in our present simple model of the world when this lump-sum tax was levied or this lump-sum gratuity paid. Given the rate of interest at which money could be borrowed or savings could be invested, a given lump-sum tax at birth or a small given lump-sum tax repeated each year of his life or a much larger single lump-sum tax at his death would all impose the same burden to the taxpayer if the discounted value of each had the same value at the time of the taxpayer's birth. (Cf. page 244 above.) What is essential is that the size of the tax payment, at whatever stage of life the actual payment is made, should not vary with the income which the taxpayer chooses to earn from his work or savings or with the amount which he decides at any time to consume. Only in this case will there be no distortion in the marginal balances between work and leisure and between this year's and next year's consumption.

Let us summarize the ideal tax system up to this point at which we are dealing with *intertemporal* and *interclass*, but not with *intergenerational*, redistribution. There should be a system of a tax on consumption at a rate falling with age turning into a subsidy on consumption rising with age, the change in the rate of tax and in the rate of subsidy being such as to make $\epsilon = \rho$ in (23.7). Such a tax-subsidy system should be imposed at an average level over life which will not interfere with the balance between work and leisure. If it took the form merely of a tax on consumption starting with youth at a very high rate and falling till at old age it was at a low rate, then it would be imposing a net tax on income earned from work. For a decision to work and earn more in order to consume more at any time of life would involve some additional tax payment. Conversely, if the system were a subsidy on consumption, starting at a low rate with youth but rising to a high rate at old age, it would represent some net subsidy on work. The starting rate of tax would have to be chosen so that, at the rate of reducing tax or rising subsidy which was appropriate to make $\epsilon = \rho$, the system would end up with subsidies in old age, in such a way that over life as a whole there was no net tax or subsidy on consumption.

With this system would be combined lump-sum taxes or gratuities assessed at birth on the potential riches or poverty of the individual citizens. Any desired redistribution between rich and poor could be obtained either by high lump-sum taxes on the rich with small lump-sum gifts to the poor or else by low lump-sum taxes on the rich with high lump-sum gifts to the poor. In the former case there would be a net budget surplus and in the latter case a net budget deficit. The general level should be chosen so that the interclass redistribution by lump-sum taxes and subsidies combined with the consumption tax-subsidies designed so as to make $\epsilon = \rho$ without disturbing the balance between work and leisure, left the Government's budget in balance. In that case we would have (i) a correct intertemporal choice by every individual between consumption now and consumption tomorrow, (ii) an efficient choice by every individual between work and leisure, and (iii) no undesired distinction between rich and poor classes of citizens. If there were also perfect altruism so that parents gave to children or children to parents on a scale which removed intergenerational inequalities, we would have attained Utopia.

But what if the generations were not perfectly altruistic vis-a-vis each other? This, as we have seen (pp. 220–224 above), would mean that in the years when in their old age parents were alive at the same time as their children either the standard of living of the parents was higher than that of the children or that of the children was higher than that of the parents. In the former case if there had been perfect altruism, parents would have saved to give to their children; the increased savings would have brought down the rate of interest; with $\hat{c} = \sigma i$ the fall in the rate of interest would have induced people to plan a less rapid rise in their consumption between the years of youth and the years of age; and in consequence the gap in standards between aged parents and their young children would be closed. And in a converse manner if the absence of altruism had caused children's standards to be higher than that of their aged parents, then with the onset of altruism dissaving by the children to help their parents would have raised interest rates, have raised the rate at which people planned consumption to rise over their lives, and have narrowed the gap between the simultaneous standards of children and of their aged parents.

Let us consider what action the State might have taken, in the absence of perfect altruism, in the former case with parents' standards otherwise above those of their children.[1] The obvious remedy for the State to adopt would be to impose lump-sum taxes on the aged parents and use the revenue so raised to pay lump-sum gifts at the same time to the young children. These lump-sum taxes and gifts would be devised on a scale which (i) caused the budget to be balanced and (ii) equalized the standard of living of aged parents with those of the young children at the same point of time. These payments would in fact be fixed compulsory gifts from parents to children; and this perfect, but compulsory altruism would have all the same effects as the alternative perfect, but voluntary altruism.

---

[1] The reader is left to consider for himself the converse action which would be necessary in the opposite case.

Thus (compulsory) savings would be increased, in order that parents might make these (compulsory) gifts to their children. Increased savings would bring the rate of interest down until, in a steady state, $\hat{c} = \sigma i$ was reduced into equality with the steady-state rise in the wage rate.

Thus our ideal fiscal system for intertemporal, interclass, and intergenerational redistribution should accord with the following three Rules:

(i) a system of taxation on consumption at a rate falling with age and turning by old age into a subsidy on consumption, the rate at which the tax rate falls and the subsidy rate rises being so adjusted as to make $\epsilon = \rho$ and the general height of the initial tax rate being so set that over the individual's life time there is no net marginal tax or subsidy on the finance of additional consumption by means of additional earnings;

(ii) a system of lump-sum taxes on the richer classes and of lump-sum subsidies to the poorer classes of citizen, the height of these lump-sum taxes and subsidies being set so as to equalize standards of living between classes and, together with (i), so as to cause no budget surplus or deficit; and

(iii) a system of lump-sum taxes on the old with lump-sum payments to the young (or *vice versa*), these taxes and payments being set at rates which equalized standards of living between young and old at any one point of time without resulting in any budget deficit or surplus.

The attentive reader will have observed an unnecessary complication in these rules. Rule (iii) lays down that an individual should receive a lump-sum gift when young and pay a lump-sum tax when old (or *vice versa*) just as if he were receiving an inheritance when young and making bequests when old (or *vice versa*). Yet in discussing Rule (ii) (pp. 495–496 above) we argued that in our simple model with a perfect capital market it made no difference at what period of his life a lump-sum tax was paid—either a certain sum at death or the smaller discounted value of that sum at his birth. For exactly similar reasons the lump-sum gift to, and the lump-sum tax on, the same individual under Rule (iii) could be amalgamated into a single net lump-sum tax or payment. For example, where a gift at birth and tax at death was appropriate a single net gift or tax at birth might be paid equal to the gift at birth less the discounted value at birth of the tax payable at death. But if this was done, yet one further step could be taken by amalgamating this already amalgamated net gift or tax under Rule (iii) with the lump sum taxes and gifts designed under Rule (ii) for interclass redistribution.

If this is done our utopian system of fiscal policy for intertemporal, interclass, and intergenerational redistribution boils down to two rules: first, the tax-subsidy system on consumption according to the age of the consumer, designed as under Rule (i) above to offset for basic shortsightedness without interfering with the balance between work and leisure; and, second, a system of lump-sum taxes or gifts payable or receivable by each individual at, say, his birth. These individual lump-sum taxes and gifts would be levied or paid at rates relatively to each other which were appropriate for the removal of interclass inequalities and at a general height (i.e. high taxes with low subsidies or low taxes with high subsidies) which was appropriate for the removal of intergenerational inequalities.[1]

It is not to be thought that a tax-subsidy system of the kind just outlined is a practical possibility. In actual life, owing to various administrative difficulties many of which will already be apparent, tax-subsidy systems must be adopted which are seriously imperfect from the theoretical point of view just examined. This analysis is designed solely to bring out the main *desiderata*, namely to correct for human shortsightedness, for interclass inequalities, and for intergenerational inequalities with the minimum disturbance to the balance between work and leisure.

At the close of this volume we are still a very long way from reality. But we are in a position to emphasize two most important functions of the State.

First, in the interests of economic efficiency in a Growing Economy it is of central importance to do everything possible to improve economic forecasting. As we have seen efficient decisions about today's uses of resources depend crucially upon correct forecasts of tomorrow's prices which in turn depend upon what will happen the next day—and so on into the future. Private enterprise can develop many aids to improved forecasting without any State intervention. Forward markets, for example, are institutions of private enterprise which need no special State intervention. But part of the problem is the central co-ordination of information about many individual, independent plans; and this, which we may call Central Indicative Planning, is a function which requires the intervention of a Central Authority.

Second, a completely *laissez-faire* economy may, as we have already emphasized in *The Stationary Economy*, lead to a very undesirable distribution of welfare. State action is needed to correct this. In a Growing Economy *laissez-faire* may lead not only to an undesirable

---

[1] The implications of this for the choice of the general height of such lump-sum taxes or subsidies is discussed in the note appended at the end of this chapter (pp. 501–507 below).

interclass distributional of welfare, but also to undesirable inter-temporal and intergenerational distributions. The necessary redistributions can be achieved only through suitable State intervention.

This still leaves many issues of State intervention *versus laissez-faire* undiscussed and unresolved. In particular there are three main groups of problem still to be considered.

First, we have the problem of dynamic fluctuations and instabilities in the economy. In this volume, as in *The Stationary Economy*, we have said little or nothing of the process by which either a stationary or a growing economy is kept in equilibrium. We have, it is true, made a very simple assumption about the Central Financial Authorities through monetary and fiscal policies keeping some price index, namely $P_x + P_y$ stable. We have used this as a basis for the assumption that, by means of a flexible money wage rate combined with this stable level of selling prices for the products of labour, full employment of labour is constantly maintained. Even more basically we have often argued as if citizens had perfect foresight of future prices rather than making rather crude guesses about the future on the basis of recent past experience. All this is very unreal; and it would be the subject-matter of a volume on *The Fluctuating Economy* to fill this gap in the analysis.

Second, there is the problem of indivisibilities which we have wholly disregarded in *The Stationary Economy* and *The Growing Economy*. Yet the fact that certain economic activities must be carried out on a certain minimum absolute scale to be efficient introduces a whole range of considerations of the utmost importance in the real world; and in particular it may make it impossible to preserve perfect atomistic competition as contrasted with large units with monopolistic power. It is because of the importance of indivisibilities that we have said nothing in this volume about State intervention in demographic matters. We have pointed out how greatly population growth may affect the rate of rise or fall in the standard of living. But when it comes to discuss what is the most desirable size and growth rate for the population possible advantages of absolute size due to indivisibilities in economic activities cannot be left out of account. For this reason we postpone any discussion of State intervention in demographic affairs (which is certainly of the greatest importance) until we have discussed the theory of indivisibilities.

Third, there is the problem of externalities which also we have wholly neglected in *The Stationary Economy* and *The Growing Economy*. This is a subject matter of immense importance; and clearly where action by private individuals affects the welfare of other citizens by means other than the prices charged in the market, there is an essential case for State intervention. One such case we have briefly noted in this volume, namely the case where invention and technical improvement brought about by the costly effort of the innovator can nevertheless be used without cost by other beneficiaries (cf. pp. 113–115 above). For this reason, although technical progress is as we have shown an essential ingredient in economic growth and although there is much to be said on the actions which the State might take to promote technical progress, yet we must postpone this discussion until we discuss the theory of economic externalities. Such an analysis would have to range from the general theory of political decision making for economic matters which cannot be left to the market mechanism at all to the application of minor governmental interventions in market operations, where remedial divergences between private and social benefits exist.

In *The Stationary Economy* and *The Growing Economy* we have tried to make certain necessary preliminary exercises in economic analysis. But we are, alas, still a long way removed from any rounded judgements about the desirable nature of State activities in the economic field.

Note to Chapter XXIII

THE EFFECTS OF COMPULSORY ALTRUISM[1]

Consider a Propdem (in which, therefore, there are no interclass inequalities) in which all citizens are farsighted (so that there is no need for any tax-subsidy system on consumption according to age). We are concerned only with the setting of a single net lump-sum tax (or subsidy) to be imposed at birth at any given time on every citizen and designed to remove intergenerational inequalities. Suppose that we start in a state of steady growth with perfect selfishness in which it so happens that parents' standards of consumption are higher than their children's standards at the same point of time. At first we impose perfect, but compulsory altruism by the two-stage method of lump-sum levies on parents in old age, the proceeds being distributed simultaneously without budget surplus or deficit in lump-sum gifts to their children, the operation being on a scale sufficient to produce intergenerational equality. We assume (i) that this brings us eventually to a new state of steady growth in which the rate of interest has so fallen that the growth rate of an individual's consumption ($\hat{c} = \sigma i$) has fallen and is equal to the growth rate of real income per head (l') so that intergenerational inequality is removed and (ii) that at this point

[1] This note is best read as an addendum to the Note to Chapter XIII on 'Life-Cycle Savings, Inheritance, and Economic Growth'.

at which $i = \dfrac{l'}{\sigma}$ the proportion of the national income saved (S) happens not to be in excess of the proportional marginal product of capital (U)—i.e. that $\dfrac{l'}{\sigma} > l + l'$—so that we do not have savings in excess of the level that will maximize consumption (cf. Chapter VIII above).

In terms of Figure 33 on page 260 above we start at the point B in case III or at the point C in case IV of that figure; we assume $\dfrac{l'}{\sigma}$ to be $> l + l'$ and $\dfrac{l'}{\sigma}$ to be $> i_{min}$; and by means of a positive compulsory $\hat{I}$ we move from point B or C to the left to the value of i at which $i = \dfrac{l'}{\sigma}$.

Since, however, a positive compulsory $\hat{I}$ involves (i) a compulsory lump-sum tax (equivalent to bequests to heirs) in old age combined with (ii) a compulsory lump-sum receipt (equivalent to an inheritance) when young, we are considering the implications of operating this system of compulsory altruism by the one-stage method of a single compulsory lump-sum tax or gift for each individual at birth.

We cannot observe in detail the process of transition from the initial perfect-selfishness state of steady growth to the ultimate perfect-though-compulsory-altruism state of steady growth. But it is clear that the first stages of this transition will involve the imposition of net lump-sum taxes at birth. The early generations must be taxed in order to raise the funds which are equivalent to the extra savings required from the parents' generations in the early stages of the change in order to accumulate the funds necessary to aid the coming younger generations. In the first period of the transition, therefore, the system will involve the State accumulating capital through an excess revenue from lump-sum taxes imposed to reduce the consumption and increase the compulsory savings of the existing generations.

But when the new compulsory-perfect-altruism state of steady growth has been reached, it can be shown that, on our assumptions, each citizen at birth will no longer be subject to a net lump-sum tax but to a net lump-sum gift from the State. Suppose for the moment that the system were operated in the form of a lump-sum gift at birth (equivalent to a compulsory inheritance) *plus* a separate lump-sum tax in old age (equivalent to a compulsory bequest to children). Let $\hat{I}$ be the inheritance received by any one individual at his birth. He will have to make bequests at age H equal to $\hat{I}e^{(l + l')H}$. In the state of steady growth the per-caput inheritance, like all per-caput variables, will be rising at a growth rate l' and the number of his children will be e^{lH}, if the population (of which his family is a microcosm) is growing at a growth rate l. But with the rate of interest $i = \dfrac{l'}{\sigma}$, the value of these compulsory bequests which he has to make at age H discounted back to the date of his birth is $\hat{l}e^{(l+l'-l'/\sigma)H}$. But we are assuming that $\dfrac{l'}{\sigma} > l + l'$, so that the value of his lump-sum taxes discounted back to his birth is less than the value of his gift from the State at birth. With the amalgamated system of a single payment, he will receive a net payment at birth equal to $\hat{l}[1 - e^{(l+l'-l'/\sigma)H}]$. This net payment will itself like all per-caput payments be growing at a rate equal to l' so that at any time t in the new state of steady growth each baby at birth will receive from the State an endowment equal to $\hat{l}_0[1 - e^{(l+l'-l'/\sigma)H}]e^{l't}$, where $\hat{l}_0$ is the inheritance which a baby would have received at $t = 0$ if there had always been voluntary perfect altruism.

But where does the money come from? As we have argued, in the early stages of the transition from a perfect-selfishness steady state to a compulsory-perfect-altruism state of steady growth the State would have accumulated a capital fund through the net lump-sum taxes which it was levying on early generations. In the new state of steady growth it will own a capital fund on which it will earn interest at the rate $\dfrac{l'}{\sigma}$. But in the state of steady growth the State's total capital fund, like all other total variables, must grow not at the rate of interest $\dfrac{l'}{\sigma}$ but at the lesser growth rate $l + l'$. The State will, therefore, each year be accumulating capital through a budget surplus of an amount equal to $(l + l')$ of its capital fund and will be distributing in largesse to babies from its budget revenue an amount equal to $\left(\dfrac{l'}{\sigma} - l - l'\right)$ of its capital fund.

Thus the State is saving. This corresponds to the additional savings which must be done to bring the rate of interest down from its perfect-selfishness higher level to the lower level of $\dfrac{l'}{\sigma}$; at this point the individual's growth rate of consumption ($\hat{c} = \sigma i$) is equal to the growth rate of earnings per head (l') so that intergenerational inequality is removed.

At the same time this compulsory saving has permanently raised the standard of consumption for every individual above what it would otherwise have been, a change which is measured by the net bounty received by each baby at birth. This bounty is, of course, dissipated on extra consumption during his life by the citizen who in his private capacity remains perfectly selfish and passes nothing on to his children. Our assumption that $\dfrac{l'}{\sigma} > l + l'$ is at this point crucial. For it is only in this case (which corresponds to the condition that $S < U$) that we do not have excess savings and that an increase in S (brought about in this case by a budget surplus) permanently raises the level of consumption above what it would otherwise have been (cf. Chapter VIII, pp. 106–110 above).

It is of interest to observe that in the particular conditions examined in this note the attainment of an optimum level of savings through compulsory altruism in the way explained above involves the State owning a growing fund of real assets (i.e. owning a National Asset instead of owing a National Debt). If, however, the initial conditions with perfect selfishness and no compulsory altruism had resulted in a state of steady growth in which parents' standards were lower, instead of being higher, than their children's, then compulsory altruism would have involved the State in subsidizing the consumption of the older generations at the expense of the younger. Optimum savings would require a fall in savings and a rise in the rate of interest. As a result of the initial process of subsidizing the consumption of the elderly a National Debt would be contracted during the transition from a state of steady growth with perfect selfishness to a state of steady growth with compulsory altruism. In the latter state the National Debt (like all total quantities) would be growing at a growth rate $l + l'$; in order to prevent it growing at the higher rate, $\dfrac{l'}{\sigma}$, at which money would otherwise have to be borrowed to pay the interest on the National Debt, a tax would have to be levied on citizens equal to $\left\{ \dfrac{l'}{\sigma} - (l + l') \right\}$ times the Debt; the net budget deficit equal to $(l + l')$ times the Debt would mop up some of the private savings and thus cause the necessary reduction in savings; and the tax on the citizens would reduce their consumption by the inevitable amount which would result from the appropriate boost which had previously been given to the consumption of elderly people in earlier generations.

In the conditions examined in this note it is considerations such as these which will determine the optimum size for the National Debt or the National Asset.

On the assumption that private citizens are perfectly selfish, we can derive an expression for the size of the National Asset or of the

National Debt, which must exist in a state of steady growth if the government through its budgetary policy has instituted and is maintaining a state of compulsory intergenerational altruism.

In a state of steady growth we know that

$$\frac{SY}{K} \equiv k = l + l' \qquad (23.10)$$

where S is the proportion of income not spent on consumption, i.e. the proportion of the national income saved either by individuals or through a budget surplus. But

$$Y = WL + iK \qquad (23.11)$$

where Y is the national income, W the wage rate, L the labour supply, and K the total capital stock, all at time $t = 0$.

From (23.10) and (23.11) we have

$$S(WL + iK) = (l + l')K$$

i.e. $$K = \frac{SWL}{l + l' - iS} \qquad (23.12)$$

As we have argued earlier in this note, any citizen born at time $t = 0$ receives a net gift from the State if there is a National Asset (or must pay a net levy to the State if there is a National Debt). Let $\hat{X}$ stand for this net receipt by each citizen born at time $t = 0$. In conditions of perfect private selfishness each citizen born at time $t = 0$ will plan his future consumption over the G years of his life (i) at a steady growth rate equal to σi and (ii) at an absolute level so as to absorb over his life of G years the whole of his earnings over the F years of his working life plus the whole of his receipt, $\hat{X}$, from the State. This means that the present value at time $t = 0$ of his future consumption must equal $\hat{X}$ *plus* the present value at time $t = 0$ of his future earnings. If $\hat{C}$ is the starting level of consumption of a man born at time $t = 0$, his consumption will be $\hat{C}e^{\sigma iT}$ at time $t = T$. This will have a value of $\dfrac{\hat{C}e^{\sigma iT}}{e^{iT}}$ at time $t = 0$. Thus the value at time $t = 0$ of his future consumption over the next G years will be $\displaystyle\int_o^G \hat{C}e^{(\sigma i - i)T}dT$. This is equal to $\hat{C}\phi_G(\sigma i - i)$ where, as in the note to Chapter XIII, $\phi_T(u) = \dfrac{e^{uT}-1}{u}$. Similarly, if W is the starting level of his wage rate, he will be earning $We^{l'T}$ at time $t = T$. This will have a value of $\dfrac{We^{l'T}}{e^{iT}}$ at time $t = 0$, so that the present value at time $t = 0$ of all his earnings over the next F year is $\displaystyle\int_o^F Wl^{(l' - i)T}dT = W\phi_F(l' - i)$.

We can thus deduce that in a state of private perfect selfishness

$$\hat{C}\phi_G(\sigma i - i) = \hat{X} + W\phi_F(l' - i) \tag{23.13}$$

If K_g represents the amount of capital owned by the State at time $t = 0$, iK_g is the State's revenue from interest. Of this revenue $(l + l')K_g$ is needed as a budget surplus so that the National Asset, K_g, can grow at the same rate as total capital—namely, $l + l'$—which must be the case in a state of steady growth. $(i - l - l')K_g$ is, therefore, the State's revenue which is available to pay out to citizens on their birth. If B is the number of births at time $t = 0$, we have

$$(i - l - l')K_g = B\hat{X} \tag{23.14}$$

so that from (23.13) and (23.14)

$$K_g = \frac{\hat{C}B\phi_G(\sigma i - i) - WB\phi_F(l' - i)}{i - l - l'} \tag{23.15}$$

From (23.12) and (23.15) we have

$$\frac{K_g}{K} = \frac{l + l' - iS}{S(i - l - l')}\left\{\frac{\hat{C}B}{WL}\phi_G(\sigma i - i) - \frac{B}{L}\phi_F(l' - i)\right\} \tag{23.16}$$

From (13.12) on page 248 we have

$$\frac{\hat{C}}{W} = \frac{1 - S}{1 - U}\frac{\phi_F(-l)}{\phi_G(\sigma i - l - l')},$$

and from the paragraph before (13.1) on page 247 we have $\frac{B}{L} = \frac{1}{\phi_F(-l)}$. Compulsory altruism also means that γ in (13.17) is equal to unity, i.e. that $i = \frac{l'}{\sigma}$. Moreover, from (13.14) we know that U itself is a function of the rate of interest i and from (13.15) we know that $S = \frac{l + l'}{i}U$. If we use these expressions to simplify (23.16) we obtain

$$\frac{K_g}{K} = \frac{(1 - S)\dfrac{\phi_G(l' - i)}{\phi_G(-l)} - (1 - U)\dfrac{\phi_F(l' - i)}{\phi_F(-l)}}{U - S} \tag{23.17}$$

where

$$i = \frac{l'}{\sigma}$$

$$U = U(i) = U\left(\frac{l'}{\sigma}\right)$$

and

$$S = \frac{l + l'}{i}U = \frac{\sigma(l + l')}{l'}U\left(\frac{l'}{\sigma}\right)$$

Let us assume that $\sigma < \dfrac{l'}{l+l'}$, so that $S < U$ (i.e. $l+l' < i$) and savings do not exceed the 'golden rule' level (cf. page 253 above). Then from (23.17) we can see that K_g is $\gtrless 0$ according as

$$\frac{1-S}{1-U} \gtrless \frac{\phi_F(l'-i)}{\phi_F(-l)} \frac{\phi_G(-l)}{\phi_G(l'-i)}$$

It will be seen that, with $i > l + l'$, this is the same condition which determines whether $\hat{I}$ in (13.23a) is $\gtrless 0$. In other words, in those circumstances in which perfect private altruism would have needed some net positive inheritance of children from their parents, K_g will be positive; or, in other words, compulsory altruism will require positive capital accumulation by the State which will allow the State (instead of the parents) to endow each child at his birth. In the opposite conditions in which private perfect selfishness would require children to help their parents, the State will need to incur a National Debt, the finance of which will require some levy on children at their birth. In either case the expression in (23.17) will show the 'optimum' size of the National Asset or National Debt relatively to the total real capital wealth of the community which, in conditions of perfect private selfishness, will be needed to maintain a state of perfect compulsory altruism.

INDEX

earnings, 45 f., 120 f., 189 f., 193 ff., 208 f., 211 f., 222 ff., 239 ff., 242, 244 ff., 264, 266, 271 ff., 276, 278, 304, 311 ff., 485, 503, 505; *see also,* wages.

efficiency, 44, 58, 114 f., 117, 356, 416, 446, 477 ff., 483 ff., 488

efficiency units, 61 f., 64 ff., 94, 257, 265

employment (of labour), 33, 44, 87 ff., 104, 152, 159, 171, 173 ff., 181 f., 292, 344 f., 360, 401 ff., 408 f., 411, 413, 482

entrepreneurs, 24, 27 f., 30–4, 36, 41, 43, 54, 88, 283, 286, 288 ff., 297 f., 300, 303, 305 ff., 312, 318 ff., 325, 334, 338, 341, 345 ff., 395 ff., 401, 403, 406 ff., 412, 414–45, 446, 450 ff. 464

equilibrium growth, 7, 344–59, 483

expenditure, 24 f., 42, 76, 114, 304 f., 312 f., 320, 337 f., 356, 404

factors of production, 26, 30 ff., 42, 47 ff., 54 f., 59 ff., 64 ff., 72 ff., 85, 91–105, 112 f., 115–6, 151, 159, 164, 168, 170, 176, 178, 181, 225, 235, 243, 248, 252, 283, 285, 294, 321, 326, 341, 343, 353, 371, 390, 414, 477 f., marginal product of, 28, 33, 50 f.; 55, 62, 67 f., 152, 159, 225, 234, 239, 295 ff., 325, 339 f., 371, 446, 478, 480 f., 487; supply of, 33, 51 ff., 235, 330

family allowances, 25

fertility, 75, 118 f., 121–46, 147 f., 153 f., 157, 175, 263, 279, 321, 325

financial policy, 48, 303 f., 306, 323, 344, 406, 408, 410 f., 491 ff.

forward markets, 464–9, 471, 474, 499

government, 7 f., 24 f., 35, 40, 46, 117, 189, 241, 306, 319 ff., 354 ff., 410 f., 416, 469, 477, 489, 491–507.

government expenditure, 24–5

incentives, 69

income, distribution of, *see,* income, national.

income, national, 18, 23, 30, 44, 47, 52, 54 f., 61–2, 66 f., 72, 75 f., 78, 82, 84, 90, 94, 96, 99 ff., 103 ff., 110, 152, 167, 178, 181, 183, 188, 209 f., 223, 226 f., 231 f., 238, 242 f., 247 f., 252 f., 265, 274 301, 339 ff., 477, 502, 505; distribution of, 24, 44 ff., 61 ff., 66 f., 70 ff., 82 ff., 96, 99, 101, 178, 181, 183, 186, 220, 227, 247–8, 252 f., 264, 273 f., 338, 354, 477, 502, 505

income, personal, 18, 24 f., 34, 40 ff., 48, 63 f., 70 ff., 75, 78 f., 81 f., 88, 94 ff., 99, 101, 105, 118 ff., 146, 149, 153 ff., 157 ff., 167 ff., 172, 178, 186, 189 f., 193 ff., 208 ff., 221 ff., 235 ff., 242, 244 ff., 262 ff., 266, 271 ff., 276 ff., 304, 311 ff., 337 f., 341, 343, 348, 354, 359, 382, 404, 412, 417, 419 ff., 423 ff., 434, 436 f., 445, 451, 455 ff., 463 f., 468, 474 485, 490, 494 ff., 501, 403, 505.

income tax, 24, 40, 47, 241, 305 ff., 469, 473, 495

Indicative Planning, 356, 470, 472–6, 499

indifference, 202 f., 206, 357–8, 388, 421, 456

indivisibilities, 7, 84, 87, 111 ff., 115, 414, 451 f.

inequality, inter-class, 220, 227, 242, 262, 278, 488 f., 494 ff., 498 ff.

inequality, intergeneration, 220 f., 223, 227, 262, 486, 488–9, 494, 496–7, 498 ff., 505

inflation, 36, 39, 303, 343

inheritance, 189 f., 193., 220 f., 244, 249–53, 262, 278, 498, 502, 507

inputs, 27–8, 50 ff., 56, 61, 111, 283 ff., 303, 307 ff., 318, 322 ff., 326 ff., 343, 346, 348 ff., 360 ff., 367 f., 370 f., 384 ff., 390 ff., 401, 415, 417, 437, 446, 468, 470 f., 474, 477 f.

instruments of production, 23, 26 f., 38, 47, 49, 55, 283, 285 ff., 296 ff., 303, 305 ff., 318 ff., 333 ff., 339 ff., 343 ff., 350 ff., 357, 360 f., 394, 407, 409, 414, 417, 467, 477 ff.

insurance, 450-5, 463

interest, 24, 35 ff., 42, 44, 54, 68, 189, 319, 194 f., 209, 291 f., 301, 304, 316, 319 f., 335, 337, 341 f., 416 ff., 468, 506; compound, 15, 310 f., 488; rate of, 15, 36, 38 f., 42, 45, 51, 54, 189 ff., 194 ff., 204 ff., 216, 223 f., 226 ff., 230, 233, 235, 239 f., 242, 244, 248, 251, 275 f., 278, 290, 296, 298, 304, 306 ff., 321 f., 325, 334 f., 338 ff., 351, 354, 377 ff., 393 397 f., 400, 404, 407 ff., 415, 468 f., 473, 485, 490, 495 ff., 501 ff.

intermediate product, 283, 288, 360, 366 ff., 371, 373, 386, 391 f.

inventions, technical, 41, 56, 61, 73 f., 113, 118, 361, 409, 438, 444, 453, 501

investment, 24, 34 ff., 49, 105, 112 ff., 146, 189, 191 f., 194, 210, 227, 235, 241 f., 252, 278, 297, 301 f., 313, 319 f., 332, 334, 341, 344, 357, 395 ff., 400, 402, 404, 406, 408, 410, 412 f., 427, 429, 432, 434, 436 f., 469 f., 496

time, 20, 26–7, 28, 45, 49 f., 75, 188, 192 ff., 201, 205, 208, 221, 228, 241, 252, 344 f., 347, 356, 364, 372 ff., 379, 382, 385, 390, 410 f., 419, 470, 479 f., 484–6, 489 ff., 496 ff.
trade, optimization, of, 478, 485, 488
Trade Union Community (*Tradcom*), 48, 117
transfer payments', 25, 40

unemployment, 27, 30, 48, 81 ff., 87 ff., 152, 170 f., 174 f., 186,
utility index, 213–9

valuation, social, 363–87, 486
value, 406, 408, 411, 415, 446, 480 ff.

wage-incomes, 44 ff., 120 f., 158, 245, 264, 266, 271 f., 341, 417, 421, 468
wage-rate, 16 f., 32, 34, 41, 43 f., 47 f., 58, 64 ff., 72, 74 f., 80 ff., 89, 94 f., 99, 101, 116 ff., 120, 122, 159, 164 f., 167 ff., 179 ff., 183 ff., 190, 207 ff.,

221 ff., 225 f., 236, 238 ff., 244 ff., 252, 264, 275, 290 ff., 322, 335, 337, 342, 346 f., 350–1, 354, 394–413, 472, 492, 498, 500, 505
wages, 19, 32 f., 42, 44 ff., 53, 55, 61, 63 ff., 68, 70 ff., 82, 84, 90, 94, 96, 99, 101, 116, 118, 121, 152, 159, 177 f., 186, 191, 247 f., 265, 273, 290 f., 294, 301, 304, 319, 334, 337 f., 341 ff., 346, 386, 393, 395, 401, 408, 412 f., 416, 418, 467, 482, 494; *see also* earnings
waiting, marginal product of, 378–82
wealth, personal, 24, 48, 150, 220, 223, 262f., 279, 359, 417, 419, 451, 494; national, 507
welfare, 477, 479, 483, 488–507
Welfare State (*Welstat*), 47 f.
workers, 13 ff., 23, 44, 46 f., 50, 57, 64, 71, 79 ff., 84, 87, 117 ff., 126 ff., 151 f., 154, 158 ff., 164, 166 ff., 171 ff., 176 ff., 180 ff., 189, 233, 243, 253, 262, 264 f., 269 ff., 275, 288, 345, 355, 379, 394, 412 f., 418, 474

For Product Safety Concerns and Information please contact our EU representative GPSR@taylorandfrancis.com Taylor & Francis Verlag GmbH, Kaufingerstraße 24, 80331 München, Germany